The Encyclopedia of

and Financial Spreads

Founded in 1807, John Wiley & Sons is the oldest independent publishing company in the United States. With offices in North America, Europe, Australia and Asia, Wiley is globally committed to developing and marketing print and electronic products and services for our customers' professional and personal knowledge and understanding.

The Wiley Trading series features books by traders who have survived the market's ever changing temperament and have prospered — some by reinventing systems, others by getting back to basics. Whether a novice trader, professional or somewhere in-between, these books will provide the advice and strategies needed to prosper today and well into the future.

For a list of available titles, please visit our Web site at www.WileyFinance.com.

The Encyclopedia of Commodity and Financial Spreads

Steve Moore
Jerry Toepke
Nick Colley

WILEY
John Wiley & Sons, Inc.

Published by John Wiley & Sons, Inc., Hoboken, New Jersey
Published simultaneously in Canada

For general information on our other products and services or for technical support, please contact our Customer Care Department within the United States at (800) 762-2974, outside the United States at (317) 572-3993 or fax (317) 572-4002.

Wiley also publishes its books in a variety of electronic formats. Some content that appears in print may not be available in electronic books. For more information about Wiley products, visit our Web site at www.wiley.com.

ISBN-13: 978-0-471-71600-6
ISBN-10: 0-471-71600-6

Printed in the United States of America

10 9 8 7 6 5 4 3 2 1

Contents

Chapter 1: Introduction

A thoughtful reader may be excused for thinking the term *encyclopedia* in the title of this book exaggerates its contents. In fact, the word *snapshot* is more appropriate, and the phrase *snapshot of a cross section* even more so. Encyclopedia implies, if not wholly complete, comprehensive material either across all branches of knowledge or, at the least, in all aspects of one subject. In contrast, snapshot connotes a moment in time.

For sheer numbers, first think only of all the different markets traded on US futures exchanges. Then think of how many delivery months in each. Now think of all the possible spread combinations just between the five tradable delivery months within a single marketing year for a simple market such as corn. But then think about how many there could be for a market with serial delivery months, such as crude oil. Then think about all the possible spread combinations and permutations in Eurodollars, which trade only four delivery months per year — but always 10 years out. And then there are the *butterflies*, the *condors*, the *double butterflies*, the *double condors* — and all their *skips*!

What about trading corn against wheat? Each has only five delivery months, but there is no law requiring spreads between the two markets to be of the same delivery. What about wheat on one exchange against wheat on another? What about one currency against another? CME reduces margin for various relationships in certain ratios, such as the British pound against the Canadian dollar in a ratio of 3:4. But it also offers fractional credits for other ratios. And then there are esoteric currency relationships such as AD/BP/CD/DR/EC/JY/SE/SF in a ratio of +1:+1:+2:+10:+3:+1:+2:+1.

That, however, is for a very few specialists. But oil companies may want to protect their profit margins in the refining process with *crack* spreads, in which they buy futures in crude oil and sell futures in both gasoline and heating oil — in ratios of 5:3:2, 3:2:1, or 2:1:1. They might normally use the same delivery month in each market, but sometimes they might sell the products one month deferred. Soybean processors protect themselves with *crush* spreads, simultaneously buying 10 contracts of soybeans and selling 11 soymeal and 9 soyoil.

As you can see, simply to list all the possible spread combinations could require reams of paper. But the effort herein is to present spread relationships which have moved in the same direction during the same period of time with a tradable degree of reliability over the last 15 and 20 years. To do so requires, for each possible spread combination, comparing prices on a proposed entry date with prices on each succeeding possible exit date, for example, from 7 calendar days out through 100. In that instance, there would be 94 possible exit dates for each proposed entry date. And how many possible entry dates might there be?

But each combination must be analyzed anew each year. Each time a delivery month expires, a new 15-year study, for example, replaces price data from now 16 years ago with that from last year.

Perhaps one can appreciate the difficulty in trying to be encyclopedic. The effort herein is to provide a snapshot — a cross section of the best and most reliable seasonal spread strategies drawn from the spectrum of about 40 of the major US futures with the price data fresh at one moment in time. This work does not contain all the possible spread combinations, nor all the spread strategies of 80%-or-greater reliability, nor is it for all time. The method of research requires that it be dynamic, that it continue to refresh itself with a constant stream of new price data. The result cannot be encyclopedic, but it can reveal what the market itself has most often tended to do during a specific period of time — and offer the reader the opportunity to anticipate its recurrence in the future.

Why Spreads?

Why trade spreads? First, one must ask why trade futures at all. An investor who buys stocks pays 100% of their value. A speculator in stocks might trade on margin, putting up only 50% of underlying value. A futures trader, however, can sometimes buy or sell a futures contract for as little as 3% of its value. That's a good thing when the market moves the right way at the right time. A trader can double his margin money with a favorable price move of only 3%. But leverage is the two-edged sword of many a tragic tale.

Because a spread is most commonly a simultaneous long and short position between two related markets, a spread position usually (but not always!) entails reduced risk — of overnight, abrupt, unexpected events that might otherwise put an outright position to the two-edged sword. The experienced cynic might also note that the "floor can't run stops" for spreads. This normally reduced level of risk allows the exchanges to reduce margins for spread positions. A spread may reduce risk but also limit opportunity. That reduction in margin, however, allows not only for multiple positions but also greater opportunity to diversify.

Another reason to trade spreads is that relationships can change even when underlying markets essentially do not. Suppose corn is stuck in a range between $2.00 and $2.20 and wheat between $3.00 and $3.25. If within those ranges corn declines while wheat rises, a spread between them can move $0.45 — and most likely with little more and maybe even less margin required than for an outright position in either grain.

Thus, while a trader holding an outright long or short position can make money only if the market moves in one direction, a spread can move favorably in several different ways:

(1) long side rises faster than short side rises;
(2) long side rises, short side remains unchanged;
(3) long side remains unchanged, short side falls;
(4) long side falls more slowly than short side falls; and everybody's favorite,
(5) long side rises, short side falls.

Of course, a spread is vulnerable to the opposite of each of the above possibilities. So, even with normally reduced risk, a spread trader cannot afford complacency at the expense of responsibility.

A Series of Strategies; NOT a System

In each section within are listed several seasonal trading strategies. Each is statistically factual on its own; but, as a group, they are not meant to be part of a trading system. And they are most emphatically not recommendations.

Each is the result of seasonal research, such that the group is meant only as a series of potential trading ideas to anticipate in the future. Trading each and every one as published could often result in unintended net positions.

The Tiger Pit of Spread Trading

Trading spreads can involve certain difficulties. Not all seasonal spreads published by MRCI are recognized and granted reduced margins by the relevant exchange(s). Even spreads recognized by the exchange may not be by all brokerage or clearing firms or by floor brokers. Few, if any, brokerage firms or floor brokers will accept and execute a single order for an equity spread. Market liquidity or conditions may also limit the types of spread orders accepted by floor brokers.

Be aware of other possible anomalies. Spreads not recognized by the exchange, and even some that are, may require legging in (placing a separate order to enter or exit each side of the spread position).

Margins (Performance Bond)

Reduced margin is a major factor in the effectiveness of spread trading. Traders need to be cognizant of whether a particular spread is recognized. Current exchange minimum spread margins are normally available via the Web sites of each exchange. Some examples of locations (as of August 2005) are:

http://www.cme.com/html.wrap/wrappedpages/clearing/pbrates/PBISHomePage.htm
http://www.cbot.com/cbot/pub/page/0,3181,1041,00.html
http://www.nybot.com/margins/index.htm
http://www.nymex.com/ewd_margins.aspx
http://www.mgex.com/margin_requirements.html
http://www.kcbt.com/margins.html

It is important to note that most brokerage firms have higher margin requirements than the exchange minimums. Additionally, margin requirements tend to be volatility related and may thus increase during periods of expanded volatility, potentially resulting in an unexpected margin call.

Liquidity

Liquidity is a factor that must be addressed regardless of the market traded but is of extreme significance when trading intra-market spreads in markets such as Unleaded Gasoline at NYMEX. Attempting to enter a position in a delivery month more than three back can be difficult when trading outright futures, but it can be even more so when trying to enter a spread position.

Quotes

Few spreads are quoted over data feeds intraday. Traders can get intraday charts or quotes of contract price relationships, but this should not be misconstrued as actual spread quotes. Two futures contracts trading at given prices does not necessarily mean the spread itself traded at that price; likewise, a spread fill at a given price difference may not correspond exactly with simultaneous quotes for the individual contracts.

While you can leg into a spread, placing a spread order for the same net value may not get filled at all. Legging in has the potential shortcoming of having only one side filled. This could result in increased margin requirements. Worse yet, if the wrong leg is filled, bad things can happen quickly. If a trader finds that he must leg into or out of spread, it may be best to enter/exit the least liquid contract first.

Stops

A major factor in managing spreads is the fact that there is not likely to be a mechanism for placing a protective stop. Limit orders and market orders are accepted but rarely, if ever, can a stop order be placed. Brokers can discuss possible exceptions.

MRCI Seasonal Methodology

Seasonal analysis provides the user with a historical reference to time periods when markets have performed with a consistent end result during the same time of year. MRCI has been publishing seasonal research since 1989 for the futures market and 1990 for spreads. Two major decisions needed to be made when initially proposing to perform seasonal analysis of markets. The first was "How many years to include?" The second was "How to align the data?"

Steve Moore's history of exposure to and analysis of seasonals began in the 1970s. While working in the timber industry, he began trading and providing computer hedging analysis. He then built several computerized trading systems. He has actively traded futures markets from the early 1970s. In 1986, Steve set up a computer research facility for Stotler and Co., one of the largest futures retail brokerage firms at the time. In 1987, Stotler introduced Steve to Wayne Esserman, who had been working with seasonal spreads for years. Steve managed to program some of Wayne's concepts which were later rewritten on PCs by Nick Colley.

When MRCI first began publishing seasonal analysis, one of the primary considerations that went into the decision of how many years to use was simply how much data was available. Many contracts began trading only in the early to mid 1970s, with still others in the early 1980s. A compromise between how much data was available and how much could realistically be used for statistical reliability was made, with 15 years the result. In the interests of maintaining consistency, it has remained that way. The accompanying table shows (as far as our historical database is concerned) the starting year for most of the markets followed. For the purposes of this book, certain slight modifications have been made, which will be discussed more fully later.

Figure 1-1: List of Markets

Energy		Grains		Soy Complex		Meats	
Crude Oil(NYMEX)	1983	Corn(CBOT)	1959	Soybean(CBOT)	1959	Live Cattle(CME)	1965
Heating Oil(NYMEX)	1980	Oats(CBOT)	1974	Soybean Meal(CBOT)	1960	Feeder Cattle(CME)	1972
Unleaded Gas(NYMEX)	1985	Wheat(CBOT)	1959	Soybean Oil(CBOT)	1960	Lean Hogs(CME)	1969
Natural Gas(NYMEX)	1990	KC Wheat(CBOT)	1976	**Softs**		Pork Bellies(CME)	1963
Metals		Minn. Wheat(CBOT)	1980	Sugar(NYBOT)	1961	**Stock Indexes**	
Gold(COMEX)	1975	**Fiber**		Cocoa(NYBOT)	1960	S&P 500(CME)	1982
Silver(COMEX)	1964	Cotton(NYBOT)	1960	Coffee(NYBOT)	1974	Nasdaq 100(CME)	1996
Platinum(COMEX)	1968	Lumber(CME)	1973	Orange Juice(NYBOT)	1968	Russell 2000(CME)	1993
Copper(COMEX)	1960	**Currencies**		Rough Rice(CBOT)	1987	DJIA (CBOT)	1998
Interest Rates		US Dollar Index(NYBOT)	1986	**Miscellaneous Commodities**		**Miscellaneous Financial**	
30-Yr T-Bonds(CBOT)	1978	Australian Dollar(CME)	1987	Class III Milk(CME)	1996	S&P Midcap 400(CME)	1992
10-Yr T-Notes(CBOT)	1982	British Pound(CME)	1975	Propane(NYMEX)	1987	GSCI(CME)	1992
5-Yr T-Notes(CBOT)	1988	Canadian Dollar(CME)	1977	Palladium(NYMEX)	1977	RJ/CRB Index(NYBOT)	1986
2-Yr T-Notes(CBOT)	1990	EuroFX(CME)	1999	Aluminum(NYMEX)	1984	Mexican Peso(CME)	1995
Municipal Bonds(CBOT)	1985	Japanese Yen(CME)	1977			N. Zealand Dollar(CME)	1998
3-Mth Eurodollars(CME)	1982	Swiss Franc(CME)	1975				

After the initial hack at how many years to include, the next question was how to align the price data. The ways to do the date alignment are varied. Dates can be aligned by Julian date, calendar date, trading day from beginning of the year, or trading days from expiration. Each method has its own justification. For ease of understanding, the choice was made to align price data by calendar date. It can be a little tricky handling leap year, but utilizing this technique allows May 1st to align with May 1st every year. Julian date is almost as intuitive with leap year providing the most difficult hurdle, but trading days from beginning of the year is problematic — especially in spreads, because exchanges and even markets have different holiday schedules. Trading days from expiration is also difficult to deal with due to moving expiration dates for contracts.

Using a seven-day calendar allows for fixing the calendar and just plugging prices into the matrix. Although the fact that any given date can occur on a weekend in roughly two of every seven years can cause some issues with computing a pattern, it does not affect strategy evaluation.

Figure 1-2: Calendar Alignment

Year	3/1	3/2	3/3	3/4	3/5	3/6	3/7	3/8	3/9	3/10	3/11	3/12	3/13	3/14	3/15
2005	52.53	53.74	54.06	54.18			54.54	55.30	55.45	54.49	55.35			55.95	56.00
2004	35.35	35.23	34.32	34.98	35.52			34.94	34.60	34.53	35.28	34.79			35.84
2003	`		32.85	33.29	33.36	33.76	34.43			34.32	34.06	34.67	33.17	31.96	
2002	22.71			22.75	23.49	23.51	24.04	24.22			24.73	24.63	24.62	24.93	24.92
2001	27.55	27.74		28.34	28.22	29.03	28.54	28.30				28.29	27.88	26.77	26.97
2000	28.69	28.71	28.68		29.16	30.66	28.09	28.65	28.39				28.45	28.32	27.78
1999	12.52	12.75	13.13	13.50	13.47			13.76	13.90	14.63	14.22	14.40			14.44
1998		16.06	15.99	16.03	16.04	15.71			15.15	15.05	14.98	14.98	14.83		
1997			19.88	20.31	20.22	20.56	21.06			20.55	20.30	20.68	20.73	21.09	
1996	18.13			17.90	18.07	18.42	18.30	18.26			18.50	18.79	18.95	19.05	19.13
1995	18.06	18.05	18.26			18.26	18.29	18.13	17.98	17.90		18.09		17.94	18.08
1994	15.03	15.03	14.99	14.86			14.46	14.41	14.39	14.33	14.58			14.63	14.91
1993		20.59	20.62	21.14	20.97			20.83	20.80	20.51	20.30	20.47			20.37
1992		18.65	18.88	18.90	18.84	18.78			18.97	19.02	18.85	19.14	19.45		
1991	18.84			19.54	19.67	19.24	18.85	18.80			18.40	19.04	19.64	19.40	19.00
1990	21.24	21.34			21.70	21.52	21.29	21.11	20.81			20.49	20.51	20.45	20.80
1989	17.46	17.74	17.52			17.72	17.44	17.80	17.77	17.76			18.20	18.36	18.72
1988	15.63	15.54	15.38	15.49			15.31	15.38	15.42	15.93	16.15			15.46	15.55
1987		16.31	17.22	17.39	17.61	17.85			17.78	17.85	17.92	17.99	17.94		
1986			12.96	12.50	12.47	13.39	12.57			13.30	13.64	14.54	13.54	13.21	

After decisions on how many years to use and how to align data were made, the next issue was to decide upon a consistent method for entering and exiting a strategy. (Remember the problems with a seven-day calendar and any given date possibly falling on a weekend in a past year.) The decision was made that entry and exit for any strategy would always be made inside the seasonal window. Therefore, if historically a strategy entered on a non-trading day (weekend or holiday), entry would be considered as made on the following trading day. Conversely, if the strategy exited on a non-trading day, exit was considered to be made on the previous trading day.

Finally a decision was made that all analysis would be based on settlement prices, with entries, exits, and stops all executed on close only. It can be difficult sometimes to determine a market's actual opening price for the day. Different quote vendors process the opening range differently: It can be the first price quoted, it can be the average of the opening range. Some vendors quote only the opening range. The one universal constant across history is the daily settlement price (essentially derived from the closing range anyway).

MRCI's procedure for locating seasonal spread strategies begins by having computer software analyze each spread's possible combinations of dates from 7-90 days. Depending on the spread being analyzed, this could be as many as 25,000 possible entry and exit combinations. The most time-consuming aspect of this initial process is in isolating specific seasonal windows. Probability dictates that, if there is a valid seasonal window from, for example, March 1st to April 15th for a given spread, then there is probably a valid window from March 2nd to April 15th as well. If not, then it may well be a spurious data anomaly. The results from this initial pass can run into the thousands of strategies.

For each seasonal strategy discovered, the software evaluates each of the 100 possible strategies occurring 5 days before and 5 after the entry and exit dates looking for the "best" possible combination for that particular strategy. During this analysis, length of trade, average return, average daily return, and percentage of reliability are all pushed into a formula and considered. Computerized analysis at this stage usually reduces the number of potential strategies for evaluation to the mere hundreds for some markets.

Issues for a trader to consider at this stage include:

(1) a trade (of similar profitability) of less time exposure is usually "better" than of more;
(2) a 100% trade is theoretically "better" than an 80% trade;
(3) a trade averaging $1000 is usually "better" than a trade averaging $500.

Unfortunately, the computer cannot make all the decisions. Ultimately, the human eye and brain must make a final decision. Only trading experience can take into account the possible effects of certain nebulous aspects that are difficult to quantify — frequency and severity of historical drawdowns, First Notice Days, Last Trading Days, liquidity — but crucial in making the final selection of strategies for publication.

This book took an additional look backward at both the last 20 years (if available) and the last 15 years to ensure that strategies had been successful through both time periods.

How to Read a Strategy Table

Unique MRCI strategy sheets present each historically reliable seasonal trade with a table of its relevant detail. Charts below the table illustrate seasonal patterns and also the current market from both a daily and monthly perspective.

To detect a trade, MRCI's computer system scrutinized the last 20 years (when available) of historical price data for those trends recurrent with a minimum reliability of 80% during similar time windows. Those strategies are then subjected to further criteria established for average profit, duration of time window, duplication/overlap, and contract delivery/expiration. Once discovered and initially evaluated, a trading strategy is outlined and its crucial data tabulated and presented in the following format for closer analysis.

Strategy Detail

For each contract year included in the study, the table lists entry date and price, exit date and price, and the ultimate profit or loss (both in terms of contract price and dollar equity). *All* prices and values are definitively based on the ***settlement price*** of the dates listed. Per MRCI's analytical methodology, if an optimized trade date fell on a weekend or holiday, entry was assumed on the *following trading day* while exit was on the *prior*. The table is provided to encourage further evaluation by providing peak equity and worst drawdown dates and amounts.

(Note: In order to better represent historical fact, strategy sheets do not utilize equity protection but rather illustrate worst drawdown and ultimate results.)

The bottom section of the table calculates the strategy's historic reliability and overall average results. Prospective stop-loss amounts are not published, as those are best left to each trader and each situation. In real-time trading, MRCI urges all traders to employ at all times proper money-management techniques, one of which may be deciding upon and constantly refining risk-assessment, based on both the individual's perspective and resources and also market behavior.

Figure 1-3: Sample Strategy Detail

Buy Nov Crude Oil(NYM) / Sell Apr Crude Oil(NYM)

Moore Research Center, Inc.

Enter on approximately 07/08 - Exit on approximately 10/14

CONT YEAR	ENTRY DATE	ENTRY PRICE	EXIT DATE	EXIT PRICE	PROFIT	PROFIT AMOUNT	BEST EQUITY DATE	BEST EQUITY AMOUNT	WORST EQUITY DATE	WORST EQUITY AMOUNT
2004	07/08/04	2.10	10/14/04	3.41	1.31	1310.00	10/14/04	1310.00	08/31/04	-420.00
2003	07/08/03	1.95	10/14/03	1.96	0.01	10.00	08/07/03	990.00	09/19/03	-1130.00
2002	07/08/02	0.94	10/14/02	2.24	1.30	1300.00	09/24/02	2190.00	08/05/02	-80.00
2001	07/09/01	1.05	10/12/01	-0.51	-1.56	-1560.00	09/14/01	890.00	10/03/01	-1860.00
2000	07/10/00	1.83	10/13/00	3.00	1.17	1170.00	09/20/00	1840.00	10/05/00	-1420.00
1999	07/08/99	0.71	10/14/99	1.21	0.51	510.00	09/23/99	2140.00		
1998	07/08/98	-1.07	10/14/98	-0.94	0.12	120.00	09/30/98	690.00	08/11/98	-290.00
1997	07/08/97	-0.10	10/14/97	0.12	0.24	240.00	10/03/97	1240.00	08/25/97	-120.00
1996	07/08/96	1.14	10/14/96	2.74	1.60	1600.00	09/13/96	1940.00	07/31/96	-110.00
1995	07/10/95	-0.11	10/13/95	0.39	0.51	510.00	09/15/95	930.00	07/24/95	-100.00
1994	07/08/94	0.31	10/14/94	-0.30	-0.61	-610.00	08/01/94	460.00	09/15/94	-950.00
1993	07/08/93	-0.69	10/14/93	-0.44	0.25	250.00	09/30/93	350.00	09/15/93	-510.00
1992	07/08/92	0.38	10/14/92	0.56	0.18	180.00	09/16/92	320.00	07/09/92	-40.00
1991	07/08/91	0.57	10/14/91	1.25	0.67	670.00	10/14/91	670.00	09/09/91	-150.00
1990	07/09/90	-0.78	10/12/90	7.14	7.94	7940.00	09/24/90	8500.00		
1989	07/10/89	0.73	10/13/89	1.28	0.54	540.00	10/13/89	540.00	07/27/89	-700.00
1988	07/08/88	-0.42	10/14/88	0.73	1.15	1150.00	10/14/88	1150.00	07/14/88	-120.00
1987	07/08/87	0.13	10/14/87	0.44	0.30	300.00	08/04/87	530.00	08/24/87	-260.00
1986	07/08/86	-0.42	10/14/86	-0.17	0.25	250.00	09/02/86	1110.00	07/09/86	-110.00
1985	07/08/85	1.25	10/14/85	2.48	1.24	1240.00	10/08/85	1460.00	07/29/85	-370.00

Percentage Correct		87								
Average Profit on Winning Trades					1.22	1216.15		Winners		13
Average Loss on Trades					-1.09	-1085.00		Losers		2
Average Net Profit Per Trade					0.91	909.33		Total trades		15
Percentage Correct		90								
Average Profit on Winning Trades					1.07	1071.67		Winners		18
Average Loss on Trades					-1.09	-1085.00		Losers		2
Average Net Profit Per Trade					0.86	856.00		Total trades		20

*(NOTE: Where contract sizes have changed, all values presented have been adjusted to reflect amounts that would have resulted had current contract specifications been in effect. Also, because all entry/exit prices are based on closing settlement prices, **results are not adjusted for commissions or slippage**.)*

The table nearby briefly describes the information contained in each column of a strategy table. This data is provided both as historical detail in support of the pertinent strategy and to offer a more "third-dimensional" view.

Seasonal Pattern Charts

Most charts in this volume depict the market's seasonal pattern for 15 recent and

Figure 1-4

COL #	EXPLANATION
1	**Cont Year:** year of expiry for long-side futures contract
2	**Entry Date:** actual entry date for that year
3	**Entry Price:** actual entry price for that year
4	**Exit Date:** actual exit date for that year
5	**Exit Price:** actual exit price for that year
6	**Profit:** amount of contract price profit for that year
7	**Profit Amount:** amount of dollar equity profit returned
8	**Best Equity Date:** date of greatest open profit on close since entry (blank if never profitable)
9	**Best Equity Amount:** dollar amount of greatest open profit on close since entry (blank if never profitable)
10	**Worst Equity Date:** date of greatest open loss on close since entry (blank if never at loss)
11	**Worst Equity Amount:** amount of greatest open loss on close since entry (blank if never at loss)

consecutive years. From these visual representations may be perceived seasonal highs, seasonal lows, and seasonal trends between. The numerical index to the right of the chart measures the greatest historical tendency for the market to make a seasonal high (100) (when prices tend most consistently to be high) or a seasonal low (0) at a given time.

Figure 1-5: Sample Seasonal Pattern

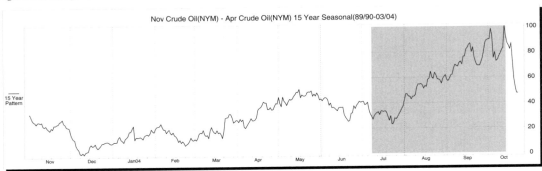

Besides illustrating the more obvious seasonal tops, seasonal bottoms, and seasonal trends, these patterns can suggest certain cause/effect phenomena which may present secondary opportunities. For instance, do smaller but well-defined movements typically precede certain events, such as a holiday or the expiry of or even first deliveries against a lead contract? If so, does there exist an implied opportunity?

Equity Spreads

When tax codes were revised in the early 1980s to change regulations governing capital gains and losses, volume and open interest in deferred futures contracts were considerably deflated as interest in spreads declined sharply. In addition, few commodity funds and pools trade spreads because trading systems are designed most typically for outright positions. Newer traders have little background or source of reference for spreads. Thus, except for commercials and some professional traders, spreads have been relegated more to the backwaters of the industry. However much ignored, they can be both a lower-risk trading vehicle and a great source of analytical information — all the while retaining a certain elegance amidst the cacophony of the marketplace.

Some Basics

Spreads are harder to track. Some of their concepts can be hard to grasp initially.

For instance, a spread being long March and short May Wheat may seem viable. If the May contract is at a higher price than the March, the spread is trading at a negative number (subtracting the price of the sell side from the price of the buy side). However, does one want the spread then to "widen" or "narrow"? Because a spreader wants the long side to increase in value relative to the short side, he wants spread values constantly to move toward a more positive value. In this case, he wants the spread first to narrow toward "0" and then widen to more positive values.

How are spreads quoted? One of two ways is easiest. Assume March Wheat is priced at $4.50 and May Wheat at $4.60. One may quote the March/May Wheat spread as trading at "minus 10 cents" (always subtracting the sell side from the buy side); or one may refer to it as trading at "10 cents premium to the May," or even as "10 cents premium to the sell side."

Although most spreads are quoted as buying one contract and selling another, there are some exceptions. In the financial area, certain spreads between various interest rate instruments are so standard as to be referred to in shorthand, as if the spread were a single entity. For instance, in decades past, one would "buy the TED spread" (*T*-Bills/*E*uro*D*ollars) or "sell the TED spread" — but not buy Euros and sell T-Bills. The same is true of the "MOB" and the "NOB."

Computing Differences

Another problem is computing the relationship of two futures contracts which have differing values per price tick. If the relationship is calculated as merely the difference of the prices, then the answer can be misleading. At minimum, it requires more calculation before a trader can assess profit or loss.

This problem can be illustrated with the following example. Assume a Heating Oil/Crude Oil spread, entered when the price of Heating Oil is 0.5600 and the price of Crude Oil is 21.00. If the price of each contract rises 100 ticks, although the *price difference* between them remains the same, the spread actually *loses* $580 in equity. However, if the price of each declines 100 ticks, again maintaining the same difference in price, the spread actually *gains* $580 in equity. In each case the original price differential remained unchanged but the *relative equity* of the contracts changed dramatically.

This situation does not exist if the dollar per tick value for the two contracts is the same. For example, assume a T-bond/T-note spread is entered with the price of bonds at 98-00 and the price of notes at 95-00. If the price of each goes up 16 ticks, the relative equity of the spread remains even (16 x $31.25 = 16 x $31.25).

Figure 1-6

To alleviate the problem in spreads wherein tick values are *not* equal, one can convert the price of each contract into an equity value for each contract. Therefore, in the Heating Oil/Crude Oil example (in which a dollar move in Heating Oil is worth $420 and one in Crude Oil is $1000), the entry price of the spread may be computed as follows:	56.00 x 420 = 23,520 21.00 x 1000 = 21,000 equals 2,520
If the price of both were to rise 100 ticks, the equity value of the spread would be: Thus, the equity of the spread declined from $2520 to $1940 with a resultant loss of $580.	57.00 x 420 = 23,940 22.00 x 1000 = 22,000 equals 1,940
Conversely, if the price of both declined 100 ticks, the equity becomes: In this instance, the spread rose in value by $580, from $2520 to $3100.	55.00 x 420 = 23,100 20.00 x 1000 = 20,000 equals 3,100

In both cases a chart of nominal price difference would display a constant value, inaccurately implying no loss or gain in trade equity. Therefore, to track the progress of an equity spread one must constantly compute the relative equity value. After all, knowing whether a trade is making or losing money is the cornerstone of good money management.

Contracts and Exchanges

Figures 1-7 and 1-8 contain keys to abbreviations included in this book. They are not only for general information but also to help readers easily decipher symbols and codes used to summarize specific historical strategies. Figure 1-7 provides keys to exchange abbreviations and month codes, while Figure 1-8 provides convenient reference to contracts, exchanges, and months listed for trading in each contract. Most information is self-explanatory, and the symbols and codes contained in these tables are generally per industry standard.

Figure 1-7

Exchange Information

Abbr	Exchange
CBOT	Chicago Board of Trade
CME	Chicago Mercantile Exchange
CMX	COMEX Division New York Mercantile Exchange
NYBOT	New York Board of Trade
IMM	International Monetary Market (CME)
MGE	Minneapolis Grain Exchange
NYM	NYMEX Division New York Mercantile Exchange

Month Codes

F	January
G	February
H	March
J	April
K	May
M	June
N	July
Q	August
U	September
V	October
X	November
Z	December

Why Seasonals Work

*The following is a revised and updated version of an article written in 1998 and included in Dr. Van K. Tharp's book, **Trade Your Way to Financial Freedom**, published by McGraw-Hill. It is as true now as it was then and may help to explain the concept behind seasonal research and how it is derived, some of its strengths and weaknesses, and some ideas on how it can be used and/or incorporated into various styles of trading.*

The seasonal approach to markets is designed to anticipate future price movement rather than constantly react to an endless stream of often contradictory news. Although numerous factors affect the markets, certain conditions and events recur at annual intervals. Perhaps the most obvious is the annual cycle of weather from warm to cold and back to warm.

Figure 1-8

Commodity Information

Futures Contract	Exch	Delivery Months
Energies		
Crude Oil	NYM	FGHJKMNQUVXZ
Heating Oil	NYM	FGHJKMNQUVXZ
Unleaded Gas	NYM	FGHJKMNQUVXZ
Natural Gas	NYM	FGHJKMNQUVXZ
Grains		
Corn	CBOT	FHKNUXZ
Kansas City Wheat	KCBT	HKNUZ
Minneapolis Wheat	MGE	HKNUZ
Oats	CBOT	HKNUZ
Wheat	CBOT	HKNUZ
Soy Complex		
Soybeans	CBOT	FHKNQUX
Soybean Meal	CBOT	FHKNQUVZ
Soybean Oil	CBOT	FHKNQUVZ
Meats		
Feeder Cattle	CME	FHJKQUVX
Live Cattle	CME	GJMQVZ
Lean Hogs	CME	GJKMNQVZ
Pork Bellies	CME	GHKNQ
Metals		
Copper	CMX	HKNUZ
Gold	CMX	GJMQVZ
Platinum	NYM	FJNV
Silver	CMX	HKNUZ
Softs & Fibers		
Cocoa	NYBOT	HKNUZ
Coffee	NYBOT	HKNUZ
Cotton	NYBOT	HKNVZ
Lumber	CME	FHKNUX
Orange Juice	NYBOT	FHKNUX
Rough Rice	CBOT	FHKNUX
Sugar #11	NYBOT	HKNV
Currencies		
Australian Dollar	CME	HMUZ
British Pound	CME	HMUZ
Canadian Dollar	CME	HMUZ
US Dollar Index	NYBOT	HMUZ
EuroFX	CME	HMUZ
Japanese Yen	CME	HMUZ
Swiss Franc	CME	HMUZ
Interest Rates		
Eurodollars	CME	HMUZ
2-Yr T-Notes	CBOT	HMUZ
5-Yr T-Notes	CBOT	HMUZ
10-Yr T-Notes	CBOT	HMUZ
30-Yr T-Bonds	CBOT	HMUZ

However, the calendar also marks the annual passing of important events, such as the due date for U.S. income taxes every April 15th. Such annual events create yearly cycles in supply and demand. Enormous supplies of grain at harvest dwindle throughout the year. Demand for heating oil typically rises as cold weather approaches but subsides as inventory is filled. Monetary liquidity may decline as taxes are paid but rise as the Federal Reserve recirculates funds.

Natural Market Rhythms

These annual cycles in supply and demand give rise to seasonal price phenomena — to greater or lesser degree and in more or less timely manner. An annual pattern of changing conditions, then, may cause a more or less well-defined annual pattern of price responses. Thus, seasonality may be defined as a market's natural rhythm, an established tendency for prices to move in the same direction at a similar time every year. As such, it becomes a valid principle subject to objective analysis in any market.

In a market strongly influenced by annual cycles, seasonal price movement may become more than just an effect of seasonal cause. It can become so ingrained as to become nearly a fundamental condition in its own right — almost as if the market had a memory of its own. Why? Once consumers and producers fall into a pattern, they tend to rely on it, almost to the point of becoming dependent on it. Vested interests then maintain it.

Figure 1-9

Annual Price Cycles		
Cycle Component	**Seasonal Pattern Characteristic**	**Fundamental Condition**
Bottom	Seasonal Low	Greatest Supply/ Least Demand
Ascent	Seasonal Rally	Increasing Demand/ Decreasing Supply
Peak	Seasonal High	Greatest Demand/ Least Supply
Descent	Seasonal Decline	Decreasing Demand/ Inreasing Supply

"Pattern" implies a degree of predictability. Futures prices move when anticipating change and adjust when that change is realized. When those changes are annual in nature, a recurring cycle of anticipation/realization evolves. This recurring phenomenon is intrinsic to the seasonal approach in trading, for it is designed to anticipate, enter, and capture recurrent trends as they emerge and exit as they are realized.

The first step, of course, is to find a market's seasonal price pattern. In the past, weekly or monthly high and low prices were used to construct relatively crude studies. Such analysis might suggest, for instance, that cattle prices in April were higher than in March 67% of the time and higher than in May 80% of the time. Computers, however, can derive a daily seasonal pattern of price behavior from a composite of daily price activity over several years. Properly constructed, such a pattern provides historical perspective on the market's annual price cycle.

Figure 1-10

Jan Heating Oil(NYM) 15 Year Seasonal(91-05)

Figure 1-11

Aug Unleaded Gas(NYM) 15 Year Seasonal(91-05)

Basic Pattern Dynamics

Consider the seasonal pattern that has evolved for January Heating Oil. Demand is least and therefore price typically low during

July — often the hottest month of the year. As the industry begins anticipating cooler weather, the market finds increasing demand for future inventory — exerting upward pressure on prices. Finally, the rally in prices tends to climax even before the onset of the coldest weather as anticipated demand is realized, refineries have geared up to meet that demand, inventories are at least adequate if not topped off, and the market begins to focus on distribution (liquidation!) into the retail market.

The other primary petroleum product encounters a different, albeit still weather-driven, cycle of demand as exhibited in the seasonal pattern for August Gasoline. Prices tend to be lower during the poorer driving conditions of winter. However, as both weather and driving conditions improve, daily consumption rises and the industry begins to anticipate the summer driving season by accumulating inventory — thereby accelerating demand and exerting upward pressure on prices. By the official opening of the driving season (Memorial Day) refineries then have enough incentive to meet that demand.

Seasonal "Pegs"

Seasonal patterns derived from daily prices rarely appear as perfect cycles. Even in patterns with distinct seasonal highs and lows, seasonal trends in between are sometimes subject to various, even conflicting forces before they are fully realized. A seasonal decline may typically be punctuated by brief rallies. For example, even though cattle prices have usually declined from March/April into June/July, they have exhibited a strong tendency to rally in early May as retail grocery outlets accumulate beef for Memorial Day barbecues. Soybean prices tend to decline

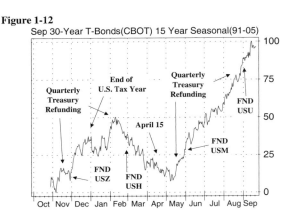

Figure 1-12

from June/July into October's harvest, but by Labor Day soybean processors return from performing pre-harvest maintenance and need soybeans to crush, creating a temporary surge in demand.

Conversely, a seasonal rally may typically be punctuated by brief dips. For example, uptrends are regularly interrupted by bouts of artificial, temporary selling pressure associated with First Notice Day for nearby contracts. Such liquidation to avoid delivery can offer opportunities to take profits and/or to enter or reinstate positions.

Therefore, a seasonal pattern constructed from daily prices can depict not only the four major components of seasonal price movement but also especially reliable segments of larger seasonal trends. Recognizing fundamental events that coincide with these punctuations can provide even greater confidence in the pattern.

Consider the seasonal price pattern that has evolved for September 30-Year

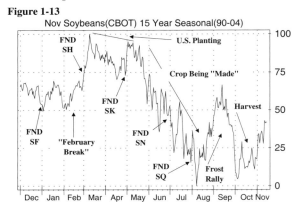

Figure 1-13

Treasury Bonds. The U.S. Federal government's fiscal year begins October 1, perhaps increasing liquidity and easing borrowing demands somewhat (even if only for accounting purposes). Is it merely coincidental that the tendency for bond prices to rise from then tends to culminate with the beginning of personal income tax payments in the new calendar year?

Does the seasonal decline into April/May reflect tighter monetary liquidity as income taxes are paid, causing a massive transfer of financial assets from out of the private and into the public sector? Notice the final decline beginning about April 15th, the due date for payment of US income taxes. Does liquidity tend to increase sharply after June 1 because funds begin to be recirculated?

Take a close look at the typical market activity surrounding December 1, March 1, June 1, and September 1 — dates of first delivery against Chicago Board of Trade quarterly futures contracts on debt instruments. Finally, notice the distinct dips during the first and second week of the second month in each quarter — November, February, May, and August. Bond traders know that prices tend to decline into the second day of a quarterly Treasury refunding — at which time the market gets a better sense of the auction's coverage.

Consider the pattern for November Soybeans as it has evolved in the 20 years since Brazil became a major producer with a crop cycle exactly opposite that in the Northern Hemisphere. Notice the tendency for prices to work sideways to lower into the "February Break" as US producers market their recent harvest and Brazil's crop develops rapidly. By the time initial notices of delivery against March contracts are posted, the fundamental dynamics for a spring rally are in place — the Brazilian crop is made (realized), the pressure of US producer selling has climaxed, the market anticipates the return of demand as cheaper river transportation becomes more available, and the market begins focusing attention on providing both an incentive for US acreage and a premium for weather risks.

By mid May, however, the amount of prime US acreage available in the Midwest for soybeans is mostly determined and planting gets underway. At the same time, Brazil begins marketing its recent harvest. The availability of these supplies and the potential of the new US crop typically combine to exert downward pressure on market prices. The minor peaks in late June and mid July identify tendencies for crop scares to occur.

By mid August, the new US crop is mostly made (realized), and futures can sometimes establish an early seasonal low. However, prices more often decline further into October's harvest low — but only after rallying into September, perhaps on commercial demand for the first new-crop soybeans and/or concerns over an early crop-damaging frost. Notice also the minor punctuations (declines and rallies) associated with First Notice Day for July, August, September, and November contracts.

Inherent Strengths/Weaknesses

Such trading patterns do not repeat without fail, of course. The seasonal methodology, as does any other, has its own inherent limitations. Of immediate practical concern to traders may be issues of timing and contraseasonal price movement. Fundamentals, both daily and longer term, inevitably ebb and flow. For instance, some summers are hotter and dryer — and at more critical times — than others. Even trends of exceptional seasonal consistency are best traded with common sense, a simple technical indicator, and/or a basic familiarity with current fundamentals to enhance selectivity and timing of entry/exit.

This raises the question of what is meant by "optimized" entry and exit dates. Think of a bell curve as used in statistical analysis of distribution. An optimized date lies at the peak of such a curve — perhaps not the ideal in any one year but the best if used for all. In real-time trading, one must also think of a seasonal pattern as an annual cycle. A pure cycle fluctuates up and down in a rhythm, a sine wave. Cycle theory recognizes real-world influences, such as the effect of larger cycles on smaller. Thus, for example, a bullish macroeconomic cycle can make a seasonal pattern "translate right" — driving seasonal uptrends longer than normal, pushing seasonal highs farther out, making seasonal downtrends appear as abrupt but brief, shallow corrections, and pulling seasonal lows to occur earlier. Conversely, a bearish macroeconomic environment could make a seasonal pattern "translate left," in cycle parlance.

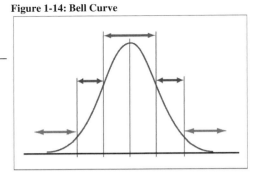

Figure 1-14: Bell Curve

How large must a valid statistical sample be? Generally, more is better. For some uses, however, "modern" history may be more practical. For example, Brazil's ascent as a major soybean producer in 1980 was a major factor in the nearly 180-degree reversal in that market's trading pattern from the 1970s. Conversely, relying solely on patterns prevalent during the disinflation of 1981-1999 could be detrimental in any new inflationary environment.

During such historic transitions in underlying fundamentals, trading patterns will evolve. Analyzing cash markets can perhaps help neutralize such effects, but certain patterns specific to futures (such as those that are delivery- or expiration-driven) can get lost in translation. Thus, both sample size and the sample itself must be appropriate for its intended use. These may be determined arbitrarily — but best so by a user fully cognizant of the consequences of that choice.

Related issues involve projecting into the future with statistics, which confirm the past but do not predict the future. The Super Bowl winner/stock market direction "phenomenon" was an example of statistical coincidence: no cause-and-effect relationship existed. However, it does raise a valid issue. When computers mechanically sift only raw data, what discoveries are truly relevant? Does the simple, isolated fact that a pattern has repeated in 14 out of the last 15 years necessarily make it valid?

Nevertheless ...

Certainly, patterns driven by known fundamentals inspire more confidence; but to know all relevant fundamentals in every market is impossible. Properly constructed seasonal patterns may typically help one find trends that have recurred in the same direction during the same period of time with a high degree of past reliability. Finding a "cluster" of such historically reliable trends of similar entry/exit dates not only reduces the odds of statistical aberration but also implies recurring fundamental conditions that presumably will exist again in the future and affect the market to one degree or another in a more or less timely manner.

A seasonal pattern merely depicts the well-worn path a market itself has tended to follow. Of course, statistics can confirm the past but cannot predict the future. But if "past is prologue," it is a market's own consistency which provides the foundation for why the seasonal approach works.

Chapter 2: Energy

Economies require energy not only to grow but simply to function. Civilization has progressed from primitive human and animal labor, taken advantage of wind, solar, and hydropower, and in recent decades harnessed nuclear energy; but the early twenty-first century still relies primarily on fossil fuels. The sheer physical volume of global trade, the financial impact in global markets, and modern practices of inventory management create an environment in which futures trading in several members of this complex thrive. For example, London's International Petroleum Exchange trades Brent crude oil, gasoil, and natural gas. Japan has two commodity exchanges, the Tokyo and the Central Japan, that trade energy markets, including gasoline, kerosene, gasoil, and crude oil. The Kansas City Board of Trade recently inaugurated a contract for natural gas. But the undisputed center of energy trading remains the New York Mercantile Exchange (NYMEX). Although the exchange also lists coal, propane, and electricity-based contracts, by far its most actively traded are crude oil, heating oil, gasoline, and natural gas.

This chapter focuses on those primary four markets. The first section discusses intramarket spreads, those between delivery months which can reflect the internal dynamics of a market. The second section examines intermarket spreads, those which portray how the different markets react with one another.

Intra-market Spreads

Spreads between delivery months of the same futures market reflect disparate pressures of supply and demand over time. Each member of the complex is briefly introduced with some basic contract specifications, a seasonal pattern illustrating its normal price tendencies, and comments helping to interpret the seasonal dynamics underlying those seasonal price movements. Thereafter follow historical price details, seasonal patterns, and comments for several of that member's intramarket seasonal spreads.

Crude Oil

According to the NYMEX Web site (http://www.nymex.com), "crude oil is the world's most actively traded commodity." The NYMEX contract trades in units of 1,000 barrels of light, sweet crude oil deliverable in Cushing, Oklahoma, which is "accessible to the international spot market via pipelines." Refiners prefer light, sweet crude oils for "their low sulfur content and relatively high yields of high-value products such as gasoline, diesel fuel, heating oil, and jet fuel." Contract specifications also allow for delivery of several grades of domestic and foreign crudes at various premiums and discounts. Thus, this futures contract has evolved into the world's largest by volume trading a physical commodity, ensuring its stature as an international pricing benchmark.

Seasonal price movement in crude oil is balanced on the twin pillars of seasonal demand for its primary products, gasoline and heating oil. During April/May, refiners consume increasing amounts of crude oil as they ramp up production to meet growing demand for gasoline going into the US driving and vacation season. From late July into October, they require increasing amounts as they ramp up production to meet growing demand for heating oil going into cold weather.

The other prominent, perhaps surprising, feature is the decline from mid October into December. Refiners in certain large-producing states are subject to tax on their year-end inventories of both crude oil and products. The industry response to such financial incentive is to accumulate inventories of crude oil going into October, maintain their runs with those inventories, and to postpone new purchases until the new year.

Figure 2-1: Cash Crude Oil Seasonal Pattern

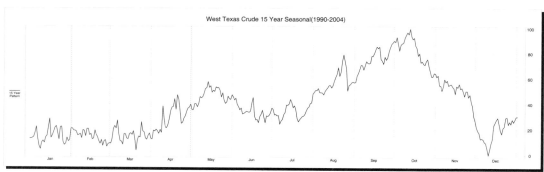

Because the fourth quarter is the season of maximum refinery production, the industry's accumulation of crude oil inventories from July through October tends to generate the heaviest and most consistent demand. Going into winter, the focus is heating oil, the world's largest regional consumer of which is the populous US Northeast. To make the transition from maximizing gasoline output, refiners may slow production late in the driving season in order to retool, reformulate, and perform maintenance on their facilities. They may take advantage of that slowdown to begin accumulating inventories of crude oil, knowing they will soon need to ramp production back toward capacity and maintain it for months.

Figure 2-2: Crude Oil Strategies

Moore Research Center, Inc.	Crude Oil Spread Strategies							
Seasonal Strategy	Entry Date	Exit Date	Win Pct	Win Yrs	Loss Years	Total Years	Average Profit	Ave Pft Per Day
Buy Nov Crude Oil(NYM) Sell Apr Crude Oil(NYM)	7/08	10/14	87 90	13 18	2 2	15 20	909 856	9 9
Buy Oct Crude Oil(NYM) Sell Apr Crude Oil(NYM)	7/14	9/17	80 85	12 17	3 3	15 20	739 704	11 11
Buy Dec Crude Oil(NYM) Sell Jun Crude Oil(NYM)	8/05	10/12	87 90	13 18	2 2	15 20	904 837	13 12
Buy Mar Crude Oil(NYM) Sell Sep Crude Oil(NYM)	12/11	1/16	80 85	12 17	3 3	15 20	859 872	23 24

Inventory accumulation precedes peak consumption. As refineries ramp up production, their consumption of crude oil increases. When consumption increasingly competes for supply with inventory accumulation, demand accelerates. Because the market wants crude oil sooner rather than later, demand accelerating from July into October tends to drive bull spreads.

The seasonal pattern for a bull spread such as November/April Crude Oil suggests the dynamic nature of this acceleration and illustrates its effect on spread movement. Statistics in the table above confirm its consistency, which holds for not only the last 15 but also the last 20 years. Notice how this spread tends to be weak during June and July, with distinct bouts of seasonal weakness providing opportunities for entry before the industry begins to accumulate in earnest.

Figure 2-3

Buy Nov Crude Oil(NYM) / Sell Apr Crude Oil(NYM)

Enter on approximately 07/08 - Exit on approximately 10/14

CONT YEAR	ENTRY DATE	ENTRY PRICE	EXIT DATE	EXIT PRICE	PROFIT	PROFIT AMOUNT	BEST EQUITY DATE	BEST EQUITY AMOUNT	WORST EQUITY DATE	WORST EQUITY AMOUNT
2004	07/08/04	2.10	10/14/04	3.41	1.31	1310.00	10/14/04	1310.00	08/31/04	-420.00
2003	07/08/03	1.95	10/14/03	1.96	0.01	10.00	08/07/03	990.00	09/19/03	-1130.00
2002	07/08/02	0.94	10/14/02	2.24	1.30	1300.00	09/24/02	2190.00	08/05/02	-80.00
2001	07/09/01	1.05	10/12/01	-0.51	-1.56	-1560.00	09/14/01	890.00	10/03/01	-1860.00
2000	07/10/00	1.83	10/13/00	3.00	1.17	1170.00	09/20/00	1840.00	10/05/00	-1420.00
1999	07/08/99	0.71	10/14/99	1.21	0.51	510.00	09/23/99	2140.00		
1998	07/08/98	-1.07	10/14/98	-0.94	0.12	120.00	09/30/98	690.00	08/11/98	-290.00
1997	07/08/97	-0.10	10/14/97	0.12	0.24	240.00	10/03/97	1240.00	08/25/97	-120.00
1996	07/08/96	1.14	10/14/96	2.74	1.60	1600.00	09/13/96	1940.00	07/31/96	-110.00
1995	07/10/95	-0.11	10/13/95	0.39	0.51	510.00	09/15/95	930.00	07/24/95	-100.00
1994	07/08/94	0.31	10/14/94	-0.30	-0.61	-610.00	08/01/94	460.00	09/15/94	-950.00
1993	07/08/93	-0.69	10/14/93	-0.44	0.25	250.00	09/30/93	350.00	09/15/93	-510.00
1992	07/08/92	0.38	10/14/92	0.56	0.18	180.00	09/16/92	320.00	07/09/92	-40.00
1991	07/08/91	0.57	10/14/91	1.25	0.67	670.00	10/14/91	670.00	09/09/91	-150.00
1990	07/09/90	-0.78	10/12/90	7.14	7.94	7940.00	09/24/90	8500.00		
1989	07/10/89	0.73	10/13/89	1.28	0.54	540.00	10/13/89	540.00	07/27/89	-700.00
1988	07/08/88	-0.42	10/14/88	0.73	1.15	1150.00	10/14/88	1150.00	07/14/88	-120.00
1987	07/08/87	0.13	10/14/87	0.44	0.30	300.00	08/04/87	530.00	08/24/87	-260.00
1986	07/08/86	-0.42	10/14/86	-0.17	0.25	250.00	09/02/86	1110.00	07/09/86	-110.00
1985	07/08/85	1.25	10/14/85	2.48	1.24	1240.00	10/08/85	1460.00	07/29/85	-370.00

Percentage Correct		87								
Average Profit on Winning Trades					1.22	1216.15		Winners		13
Average Loss on Trades					-1.09	-1085.00		Losers		2
Average Net Profit Per Trade					0.91	909.33		Total trades		15
Percentage Correct		90								
Average Profit on Winning Trades					1.07	1071.67		Winners		18
Average Loss on Trades					-1.09	-1085.00		Losers		2
Average Net Profit Per Trade					0.86	856.00		Total trades		20

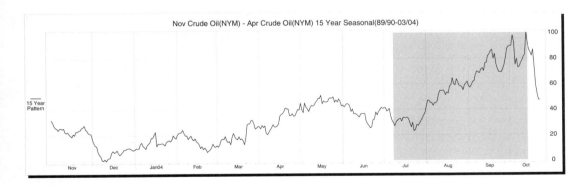

Nov Crude Oil(NYM) - Apr Crude Oil(NYM) 15 Year Seasonal(89/90-03/04)

The summary table lists one strategy for the overall seasonal trend and two for certain of its more reliable segments. The larger seasonal trend is well represented by a bull spread with the November contract on its long side because it will be the nearby, most active delivery month when the trend surges to its climax. The latter two strategies demonstrate how these dynamics permeate the market, with various bull spreads and with other entry and exit dates.

Figure 2-4

Moore Research Center, Inc.

Buy Oct Crude Oil(NYM) / Sell Apr Crude Oil(NYM)

Enter on approximately 07/14 - Exit on approximately 09/17

CONT YEAR	ENTRY DATE	ENTRY PRICE	EXIT DATE	EXIT PRICE	PROFIT	PROFIT AMOUNT	BEST EQUITY DATE	BEST EQUITY AMOUNT	WORST EQUITY DATE	WORST EQUITY AMOUNT
2004	07/14/04	2.60	09/17/04	2.79	0.18	180.00	08/19/04	660.00	09/08/04	-930.00
2003	07/14/03	2.87	09/17/03	0.71	-2.17	-2170.00	08/07/03	610.00	09/17/03	-2170.00
2002	07/15/02	1.43	09/17/02	1.84	0.41	410.00	08/21/02	1270.00	08/05/02	-360.00
2001	07/16/01	0.55	09/17/01	1.34	0.80	800.00	09/14/01	1180.00	07/18/01	-150.00
2000	07/14/00	2.42	09/15/00	4.19	1.76	1760.00	09/07/00	1830.00	07/31/00	-1220.00
1999	07/14/99	0.91	09/17/99	3.17	2.27	2270.00	09/17/99	2270.00	07/21/99	-40.00
1998	07/14/98	-1.19	09/17/98	-0.79	0.41	410.00	09/17/98	410.00	08/12/98	-550.00
1997	07/14/97	-0.28	09/17/97	-0.26	0.01	10.00	08/05/97	510.00	08/26/97	-80.00
1996	07/15/96	1.86	09/17/96	2.85	0.99	990.00	09/12/96	1870.00	07/31/96	-450.00
1995	07/14/95	-0.10	09/15/95	1.31	1.42	1420.00	09/15/95	1420.00	07/24/95	-140.00
1994	07/14/94	0.67	09/16/94	-0.72	-1.39	-1390.00	08/01/94	430.00	09/15/94	-1460.00
1993	07/14/93	-0.95	09/17/93	-1.44	-0.49	-490.00	07/27/93	410.00	09/15/93	-630.00
1992	07/14/92	0.46	09/17/92	1.00	0.54	540.00	09/17/92	540.00	08/21/92	-10.00
1991	07/15/91	0.75	09/17/91	0.76	0.01	10.00	08/19/91	420.00	09/09/91	-290.00
1990	07/16/90	-0.57	09/17/90	5.77	6.34	6340.00	09/17/90	6340.00	07/30/90	-220.00
1989	07/14/89	0.80	09/15/89	1.19	0.40	400.00	09/15/89	400.00	07/27/89	-740.00
1988	07/14/88	-0.68	09/16/88	0.20	0.89	890.00	09/14/88	940.00		
1987	07/14/87	0.28	09/17/87	0.66	0.37	370.00	08/04/87	700.00	08/24/87	-340.00
1986	07/14/86	-0.33	09/17/86	0.09	0.44	440.00	09/02/86	1030.00	07/23/86	-340.00
1985	07/15/85	1.73	09/17/85	2.62	0.89	890.00	09/16/85	930.00	07/29/85	-500.00

Percentage Correct	80									
Average Profit on Winning Trades					1.26	1261.67		Winners		12
Average Loss on Trades					-1.35	-1350.00		Losers		3
Average Net Profit Per Trade					0.74	739.33		Total trades		15
Percentage Correct	85									
Average Profit on Winning Trades					1.07	1066.47		Winners		17
Average Loss on Trades					-1.35	-1350.00		Losers		3
Average Net Profit Per Trade					0.70	704.00		Total trades		20

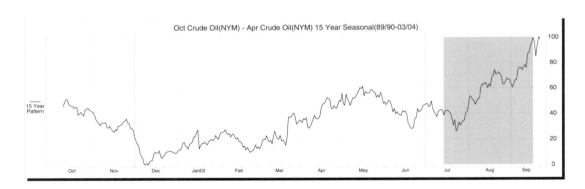

Oct Crude Oil(NYM) - Apr Crude Oil(NYM) 15 Year Seasonal(89/90-03/04)

Thus, the November/April spread has closed more favorably toward November on about October 14 than on about July 8 in 18 of the last 20 years. But July 14 has been another optimal entry, either alternative or additional, as has August 5 — each with its own characteristic. For example, while the July entries may tend to be made into weakness, the August entry (Figure 2-5) may more often be made into an emerging trend.

Figure 2-5

Moore Research Center, Inc.

Buy Dec Crude Oil(NYM) / Sell Jun Crude Oil(NYM)

Enter on approximately 08/05 - Exit on approximately 10/12

CONT YEAR	ENTRY DATE	ENTRY PRICE	EXIT DATE	EXIT PRICE	PROFIT	PROFIT AMOUNT	BEST EQUITY DATE	BEST EQUITY AMOUNT	WORST EQUITY DATE	WORST EQUITY AMOUNT
2004	08/05/04	2.61	10/12/04	3.75	1.13	1130.00	10/07/04	1580.00	08/31/04	-540.00
2003	08/05/03	3.05	10/10/03	3.05	0.01	10.00	08/26/03	130.00	09/19/03	-2220.00
2002	08/05/02	1.06	10/11/02	2.92	1.87	1870.00	09/24/02	3100.00		
2001	08/06/01	1.40	10/12/01	-0.03	-1.43	-1430.00	09/14/01	1340.00	10/03/01	-1800.00
2000	08/07/00	1.79	10/12/00	3.25	1.47	1470.00	09/20/00	2100.00	10/05/00	-980.00
1999	08/05/99	1.25	10/12/99	1.55	0.30	300.00	09/23/99	2060.00		
1998	08/05/98	-1.18	10/12/98	-1.01	0.17	170.00	09/30/98	640.00	08/11/98	-170.00
1997	08/05/97	0.25	10/10/97	0.99	0.74	740.00	10/03/97	1030.00	09/10/97	-340.00
1996	08/05/96	1.25	10/11/96	2.83	1.58	1580.00	10/08/96	2100.00	08/06/96	-20.00
1995	08/07/95	-0.05	10/12/95	0.22	0.27	270.00	09/15/95	680.00		
1994	08/05/94	0.46	10/12/94	-0.20	-0.67	-670.00			09/15/94	-950.00
1993	08/05/93	-0.52	10/12/93	-0.44	0.08	80.00	09/30/93	220.00	09/15/93	-650.00
1992	08/05/92	0.62	10/12/92	0.77	0.15	150.00	09/16/92	200.00	08/20/92	-110.00
1991	08/05/91	0.67	10/11/91	1.30	0.62	620.00	10/09/91	700.00	09/09/91	-120.00
1990	08/06/90	0.50	10/12/90	7.78	7.27	7270.00	10/11/90	7600.00		
1989	08/07/89	0.19	10/12/89	1.10	0.91	910.00	10/12/89	910.00		
1988	08/05/88	-0.30	10/12/88	0.07	0.38	380.00	10/12/88	380.00	09/07/88	-120.00
1987	08/05/87	0.35	10/12/87	0.47	0.11	110.00	10/09/87	130.00	08/20/87	-520.00
1986	08/05/86	-0.48	10/10/86	-0.13	0.34	340.00	09/02/86	1180.00		
1985	08/05/85	1.11	10/11/85	2.55	1.43	1430.00	10/08/85	1690.00		

Percentage Correct	87									
Average Profit on Winning Trades					1.20	1204.62		Winners		13
Average Loss on Trades					-1.05	-1050.00		Losers		2
Average Net Profit Per Trade					0.90	904.00		Total trades		15
Percentage Correct	90									
Average Profit on Winning Trades					1.05	1046.11		Winners		18
Average Loss on Trades					-1.05	-1050.00		Losers		2
Average Net Profit Per Trade					0.84	836.50		Total trades		20

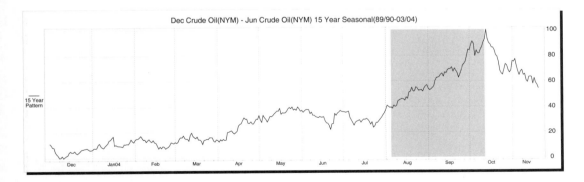

Dec Crude Oil(NYM) - Jun Crude Oil(NYM) 15 Year Seasonal(89/90-03/04)

When inventory accumulation climaxes, usually in mid October, bull spreads are exhausted. Demand decelerates as refiners subject to tax on year-end inventories postpone new purchases into the new year, maintaining their runs by drawing down their inventories. Perhaps the difficulty refiners can have in managing such cutbacks while maintaining production near capacity has made this seasonal movement more erratic.

Figure 2-6

Buy Mar Crude Oil(NYM) / Sell Sep Crude Oil(NYM)

Enter on approximately 12/11 - Exit on approximately 01/16

CONT YEAR	ENTRY DATE	ENTRY PRICE	EXIT DATE	EXIT PRICE	PROFIT	PROFIT AMOUNT	BEST EQUITY DATE	BEST EQUITY AMOUNT	WORST EQUITY DATE	WORST EQUITY AMOUNT
2005	12/13/04	0.85	01/14/05	2.39	1.54	1540.00	01/13/05	1600.00		
2004	12/11/03	2.48	01/16/04	2.89	0.40	400.00	12/18/03	850.00		
2003	12/11/02	2.11	01/16/03	5.45	3.33	3330.00	01/03/03	3880.00		
2002	12/11/01	-0.88	01/16/02	-0.82	0.06	60.00	01/07/02	960.00		
2001	12/11/00	1.96	01/16/01	3.00	1.03	1030.00	01/16/01	1030.00	12/21/00	-780.00
2000	12/13/99	2.94	01/14/00	3.92	0.98	980.00	01/14/00	980.00	01/07/00	-230.00
1999	12/11/98	-1.58	01/15/99	-0.86	0.73	730.00	01/11/99	1060.00		
1998	12/11/97	-0.44	01/16/98	-1.12	-0.69	-690.00	12/18/97	80.00	01/13/98	-690.00
1997	12/11/96	2.55	01/16/97	2.98	0.43	430.00	01/06/97	1040.00	12/12/96	-100.00
1996	12/11/95	0.66	01/16/96	0.85	0.18	180.00	01/05/96	930.00		
1995	12/12/94	-0.32	01/16/95	0.12	0.45	450.00	01/16/95	450.00	12/15/94	-180.00
1994	12/13/93	-1.39	01/14/94	-1.00	0.38	380.00	01/14/94	380.00	12/28/93	-190.00
1993	12/11/92	-0.14	01/15/93	-0.53	-0.39	-390.00	12/23/92	110.00	01/13/93	-510.00
1992	12/11/91	-0.01	01/16/92	-0.16	-0.15	-150.00	12/13/91	280.00	01/09/92	-530.00
1991	12/11/90	2.67	01/16/91	7.28	4.61	4610.00	01/16/91	4610.00	12/12/90	-40.00
1990	12/11/89	0.94	01/16/90	2.44	1.50	1500.00	01/12/90	1610.00		
1989	12/12/88	0.23	01/16/89	1.59	1.36	1360.00	01/16/89	1360.00		
1988	12/11/87	0.35	01/15/88	0.50	0.14	140.00	01/05/88	240.00	12/18/87	-310.00
1987	12/11/86	0.00	01/16/87	1.33	1.33	1330.00	01/14/87	1730.00	12/17/86	-130.00
1986	12/11/85	1.35	01/16/86	1.55	0.21	210.00	01/07/86	1630.00		

Percentage Correct	80									
Average Profit on Winning Trades					1.18	1176.67		Winners		12
Average Loss on Trades					-0.41	-410.00		Losers		3
Average Net Profit Per Trade					0.86	859.33		Total trades		15
Percentage Correct	85									
Average Profit on Winning Trades					1.10	1097.65		Winners		17
Average Loss on Trades					-0.41	-410.00		Losers		3
Average Net Profit Per Trade					0.87	871.50		Total trades		20

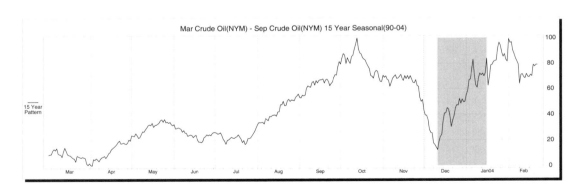

Mar Crude Oil(NYM) - Sep Crude Oil(NYM) 15 Year Seasonal(90-04)

But after a certain interval, supplies tighten. The market knows that refiners will soon return to make those delayed purchases. Usually by the second week of December, there is growing anticipation of a renewed surge in demand. With consumption still high, efforts to replenish supplies can only reaccelerate demand and reinvigorate bull spreads such as March/September. Note how moderate most drawdowns have been.

Heating Oil

Crude oil is refined into several basic product groups — kerosene, jet fuel, diesel fuel, gasoline, residuals, and distillate fuels. Chief among the distillate fuels is heating oil, which, according to NYMEX, is "also known as No. 2 fuel oil (and) accounts for about 25% of the yield of a barrel of crude, the second largest 'cut' after gasoline." The "futures contract trades in units of 42,000 gallons (1,000 barrels) and is based on delivery in New York harbor, the principal cash market trading center." Although heating oil is used to heat homes, its futures contract is far more viable and liquid because it "is also used to hedge diesel fuel and jet fuel, both of which trade in the cash market at an often stable premium to NYMEX … heating oil futures."

Figure 2-7: Cash Heating Oil Seasonal Pattern

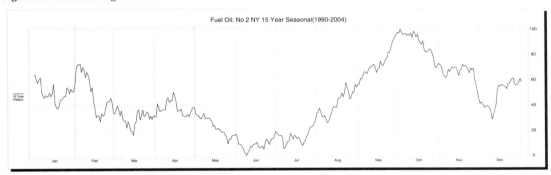

US heating oil consumption, about 80% of which is in the cold Northeast, is greatest during winter. But this market's seasonal pattern is another reminder that price precedes consumption. Logically, price tends to be low during the warm, mid-year weather when consumption is least. In August/September, production can slow as refiners retool, reformulate, and perform maintenance on their facilities before ramping up production again to focus on heating oil. But the market's function is to anticipate the onset of cooler temperatures and increasing daily consumption. As it does so, the industry begins to accumulate inventory, thereby accelerating demand. By October, with refineries again producing at capacity and inventories more sufficient, demand decelerates. Further, those refiners subject to tax on year-end inventories not only of crude oil but also of products have financial incentive to pump as much product as possible into the pipeline by the end of December. Upon the climax of this product flush, the market tends to recover into mid-winter before new demand, and therefore price, and then finally consumption decline through spring.

Figure 2-8: Heating Oil Strategies

Moore Research Center, Inc.	*Heating Oil #2(NYM) Spread Strategies*							
Seasonal Strategy	Entry Date	Exit Date	Win Pct	Win Yrs	Loss Years	Total Years	Average Profit	Ave Pft Per Day
Buy Dec Heating Oil #2(NYM)	7/31	10/12	80	12	3	15	1109	15
Sell May Heating Oil #2(NYM)			80	16	4	20	997	13
Buy Nov Heating Oil #2(NYM)	8/08	9/16	80	12	3	15	558	14
Sell Apr Heating Oil #2(NYM)			80	16	4	20	506	13
Buy Jul Heating Oil #2(NYM)	1/15	2/20	87	13	2	15	454	12
Sell Mar Heating Oil #2(NYM)			85	17	3	20	610	16

Figure 2-9

Buy Dec Heating Oil #2(NYM) / Sell May Heating Oil #2(NYM)

Enter on approximately 07/31 - Exit on approximately 10/12

CONT YEAR	ENTRY DATE	ENTRY PRICE	EXIT DATE	EXIT PRICE	PROFIT	PROFIT AMOUNT	BEST EQUITY DATE	BEST EQUITY AMOUNT	WORST EQUITY DATE	WORST EQUITY AMOUNT
2004	08/02/04	12.95	10/12/04	17.25	4.30	1806.00	09/23/04	1953.00	08/31/04	-1239.00
2003	07/31/03	8.85	10/10/03	10.85	2.00	840.00	08/07/03	1071.00	09/19/03	-2310.00
2002	07/31/02	4.85	10/11/02	9.29	4.45	1869.00	09/24/02	2835.00	08/05/02	-441.00
2001	07/31/01	5.75	10/12/01	3.30	-2.45	-1029.00	09/10/01	1806.00	10/02/01	-1302.00
2000	07/31/00	9.09	10/12/00	19.04	9.95	4179.00	09/11/00	4683.00		
1999	08/02/99	3.39	10/12/99	3.90	0.50	210.00	09/10/99	2058.00	10/11/99	-168.00
1998	07/31/98	-2.64	10/12/98	-2.54	0.10	42.00	09/18/98	588.00	08/28/98	-336.00
1997	07/31/97	3.44	10/10/97	3.64	0.20	84.00	10/03/97	588.00	09/10/97	-1050.00
1996	07/31/96	6.89	10/11/96	12.70	5.80	2436.00	10/07/96	3927.00		
1995	07/31/95	2.95	10/12/95	2.89	-0.05	-21.00	09/05/95	693.00	10/10/95	-105.00
1994	08/01/94	2.85	10/12/94	-0.78	-3.64	-1528.80			10/12/94	-1528.80
1993	08/02/93	1.70	10/12/93	2.89	1.20	504.00	09/30/93	861.00	08/09/93	-441.00
1992	07/31/92	6.99	10/12/92	7.11	0.12	50.40	10/09/92	260.40	08/25/92	-882.00
1991	07/31/91	7.69	10/11/91	8.97	1.28	537.60	10/09/91	575.40	09/17/91	-205.80
1990	07/31/90	5.32	10/12/90	21.17	15.84	6652.80	10/12/90	6652.80		
1989	07/31/89	5.25	10/12/89	8.67	3.42	1436.40	10/12/89	1436.40	08/08/89	-168.00
1988	08/01/88	3.43	10/12/88	3.82	0.39	163.80	10/12/88	163.80	09/30/88	-348.60
1987	07/31/87	2.73	10/12/87	5.56	2.83	1188.60	10/09/87	1302.00	08/25/87	-525.00
1986	07/31/86	3.95	10/10/86	0.60	-3.34	-1402.80	08/26/86	562.80	10/10/86	-1402.80
1985	07/31/85	5.79	10/11/85	10.39	4.59	1927.80	10/07/85	2276.40	08/06/85	-63.00

Percentage Correct	80								
Average Profit on Winning Trades				3.81	1600.90		Winners	12	
Average Loss on Trades				-2.05	-859.60		Losers	3	
Average Net Profit Per Trade				2.64	1108.80		Total trades	15	
Percentage Correct	80								
Average Profit on Winning Trades				3.56	1495.46		Winners	16	
Average Loss on Trades				-2.37	-995.40		Losers	4	
Average Net Profit Per Trade				2.37	997.29		Total trades	20	

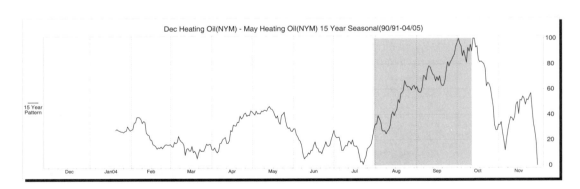

Dec Heating Oil(NYM) - May Heating Oil(NYM) 15 Year Seasonal(90/91-04/05)

The industry's anticipation of the seasonal bulge in consumption and its demand for accumulation of inventory beforehand creates the primary feature of heating oil's seasonal pattern, its vigorous seasonal trend upward from July into October. That increasing demand for the physical product pervades the price structure of heating oil futures. The sense of urgency tends to be reflected not only in the outright price but also in bull spreads as more nearby contracts outperform those deferred. Furthermore, heating oil is not a carrying charge

Figure 2-10

Moore Research Center, Inc. — *Buy Nov Heating Oil #2(NYM) / Sell Apr Heating Oil #2(NYM)*

Enter on approximately 08/08 - Exit on approximately 09/16

CONT YEAR	ENTRY DATE	ENTRY PRICE	EXIT DATE	EXIT PRICE	PROFIT	PROFIT AMOUNT	BEST EQUITY DATE	BEST EQUITY AMOUNT	WORST EQUITY DATE	WORST EQUITY AMOUNT
2004	08/09/04	8.70	09/16/04	8.90	0.20	84.00	09/14/04	147.00	08/31/04	-1407.00
2003	08/08/03	7.40	09/16/03	2.14	-5.25	-2205.00			09/16/03	-2205.00
2002	08/08/02	1.70	09/16/02	5.85	4.15	1743.00	09/10/02	1785.00		
2001	08/08/01	3.85	09/14/01	7.59	3.75	1575.00	09/14/01	1575.00	08/20/01	-231.00
2000	08/08/00	8.60	09/15/00	16.50	7.90	3318.00	09/11/00	4095.00		
1999	08/09/99	2.89	09/16/99	5.25	2.35	987.00	09/10/99	1281.00		
1998	08/10/98	-4.50	09/16/98	-3.04	1.45	609.00	09/11/98	798.00	08/11/98	-105.00
1997	08/08/97	0.75	09/16/97	-0.32	-1.08	-453.60	08/14/97	231.00	09/10/97	-861.00
1996	08/08/96	5.70	09/16/96	9.33	3.63	1524.60	09/13/96	2053.80	08/09/96	-21.00
1995	08/08/95	1.64	09/15/95	2.64	0.99	415.80	09/05/95	642.60	08/14/95	-63.00
1994	08/08/94	0.25	09/16/94	-2.10	-2.35	-987.00			09/15/94	-1113.00
1993	08/09/93	-1.20	09/16/93	-0.67	0.52	218.40	08/30/93	798.00		
1992	08/10/92	2.94	09/16/92	4.47	1.53	642.60	09/14/92	743.40	08/21/92	-184.80
1991	08/08/91	4.89	09/16/91	4.99	0.10	42.00	08/20/91	625.80	09/12/91	-163.80
1990	08/08/90	5.75	09/14/90	7.78	2.03	852.60	08/24/90	2759.40	08/09/90	-63.00
1989	08/08/89	3.14	09/15/89	5.00	1.85	777.00	09/08/89	911.40		
1988	08/08/88	1.68	09/16/88	1.96	0.28	117.60	09/01/88	210.00	09/13/88	-16.80
1987	08/10/87	0.96	09/16/87	1.28	0.31	130.20	09/14/87	315.00	08/25/87	-537.60
1986	08/08/86	2.32	09/16/86	1.32	-1.00	-420.00	08/22/86	247.80	09/15/86	-621.60
1985	08/08/85	4.76	09/16/85	7.51	2.75	1155.00	09/10/85	1978.20	08/12/85	-63.00

Percentage Correct	80								
Average Profit on Winning Trades				2.38	1001.00		Winners		12
Average Loss on Trades				-2.89	-1215.20		Losers		3
Average Net Profit Per Trade				1.33	557.76		Total trades		15
Percentage Correct	80								
Average Profit on Winning Trades				2.11	886.99		Winners		16
Average Loss on Trades				-2.42	-1016.40		Losers		4
Average Net Profit Per Trade				1.21	506.31		Total trades		20

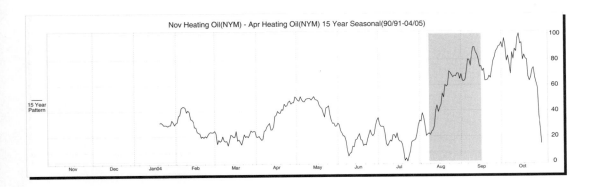

Nov Heating Oil(NYM) - Apr Heating Oil(NYM) 15 Year Seasonal(90/91-04/05)

market, such as grains and metals, in which the physical commodity is stored for long periods at a cost (of carry). Instead, the market tends to build seasonal disparities in consumption into its price structure.

Thus, during the transition from least to peak consumption, the December/May spread (Figure 2-9) benefits from the market's growing desire for product sooner rather than later. At the same time, it increasingly places more value on heating oil deliverable during the peak. Note how similar in appearance are seasonal patterns for this and for the November/April Crude Oil (Figure 2-3) spread and how similar in timing are their peaks and valleys. Also note how this optimized entry coincides with expiry of the August contract (deliverable in the last full month of summer), and how the exit coincides with the cluster of exits for crude oil strategies. The strategy for November/April Heating Oil, with its window during the heat of summer and the peak of driving season, reveals the counterintuitive nature of such spreads.

Bear spreads such as July/March reflect the exhaustion, or liquidation, after the climax of accumulation. If bull spreads ride the back of steady accumulation into the October peak, bear spreads portray the typically treacherous tumble thereafter. Seasonal patterns for bear spreads are simply inverted to those for bull spreads, with seasonal lows for bear spreads coinciding with seasonal highs for bull spreads. Unlike trends of accumulation, those of exhaustion tend to be more erratic and less reliable. The pattern for this bear spread, for example, illustrates the seasonal trend from October through February. It has a more ragged appearance, as if unstable. In technical terms, think of a liquidating market subject to bouts of panicky short-covering. In fundamental terms, think of unexpected cold snaps.

Nonetheless, from mid January, normally the coldest month of the year, the spread tends to assume a higher degree of reliability. Consumption peaks, anxiety eases, and the market aggressively removes premium from March — as if in a final liquidation sale.

Of note in the strategy table for this spread (Figure 2-12) is the severity of drawdown and loss in 2003. The probable cause? The runup to the Iraq incursion in March 2003 increased the value of all energy products — a perfect example of abnormal fundamentals superseding normal market forces to generate a true contraseasonal move.

Figure 2-11: Jul/Mar Heating Oil Monthly

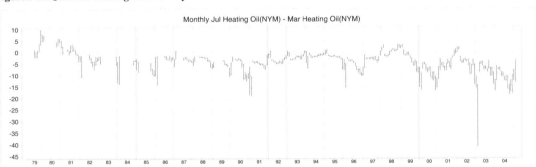

Figure 2-12

Buy Jul Heating Oil #2(NYM) / Sell Mar Heating Oil #2(NYM)

Enter on approximately 01/15 - Exit on approximately 02/20

CONT YEAR	ENTRY DATE	ENTRY PRICE	EXIT DATE	EXIT PRICE	PROFIT	PROFIT AMOUNT	BEST EQUITY DATE	BEST EQUITY AMOUNT	WORST EQUITY DATE	WORST EQUITY AMOUNT
2005	01/18/05	-11.75	02/18/05	-7.79	3.96	1663.20	02/07/05	3418.80	01/25/05	-378.00
2004	01/15/04	-12.40	02/20/04	-6.09	6.30	2646.00	02/20/04	2646.00	01/23/04	-1953.00
2003	01/15/03	-14.45	02/20/03	-25.07	-10.62	-4460.40	01/21/03	630.00	02/07/03	-5720.40
2002	01/15/02	1.35	02/20/02	1.50	0.16	67.20	01/30/02	294.00	01/24/02	-168.00
2001	01/16/01	-10.04	02/20/01	-3.50	6.55	2751.00	02/20/01	2751.00	01/22/01	-651.00
2000	01/18/00	-10.54	02/18/00	-9.98	0.57	239.40	02/15/00	743.40	01/21/00	-2079.00
1999	01/15/99	2.50	02/19/99	2.56	0.07	29.40	02/09/99	298.20		
1998	01/15/98	1.42	02/20/98	2.45	1.02	428.40	02/17/98	651.00	01/29/98	-96.60
1997	01/15/97	-9.00	02/20/97	-2.69	6.30	2646.00	02/20/97	2646.00		
1996	01/15/96	-4.60	02/20/96	-7.74	-3.14	-1318.80	01/25/96	592.20	02/14/96	-2272.20
1995	01/16/95	0.39	02/17/95	0.50	0.10	42.00	02/16/95	168.00	02/07/95	-474.60
1994	01/17/94	-3.14	02/18/94	-2.03	1.11	466.20	01/20/94	697.20	02/02/94	-1692.60
1993	01/15/93	-0.55	02/19/93	-0.09	0.47	197.40	01/22/93	466.20	02/08/93	-306.60
1992	01/15/92	-2.42	02/20/92	-0.66	1.77	743.40	02/18/92	886.20	01/16/92	-151.20
1991	01/15/91	-16.70	02/20/91	-15.10	1.59	667.80	01/18/91	4372.20	02/11/91	-1092.00
1990	01/15/90	-8.18	02/20/90	-2.71	5.48	2301.60	02/09/90	2650.20		
1989	01/16/89	-6.37	02/17/89	-4.97	1.39	583.80	02/14/89	840.00	02/06/89	-121.80
1988	01/15/88	-4.44	02/19/88	-2.18	2.26	949.20	02/17/88	1117.20		
1987	01/15/87	-6.27	02/20/87	-1.00	5.26	2209.20	02/11/87	2284.80		
1986	01/15/86	-5.95	02/20/86	-7.51	-1.56	-655.20	02/04/86	1864.80	02/19/86	-722.40

Percentage Correct	87									
Average Profit on Winning Trades					2.31	968.26		Winners		13
Average Loss on Trades					-6.88	-2889.60		Losers		2
Average Net Profit Per Trade					1.08	453.88		Total trades		15
Percentage Correct	85									
Average Profit on Winning Trades					2.61	1095.95		Winners		17
Average Loss on Trades					-5.11	-2144.80		Losers		3
Average Net Profit Per Trade					1.45	609.84		Total trades		20

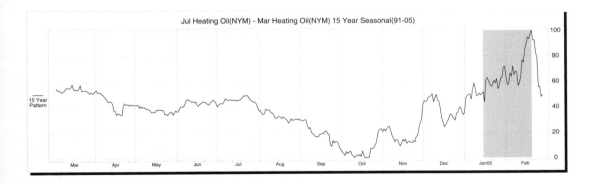

Jul Heating Oil(NYM) - Mar Heating Oil(NYM) 15 Year Seasonal(91-05)

Gasoline

Gasoline, according to NYMEX, "is the largest single volume refined product sold in the United States and accounts for almost half of national oil consumption." Distillate fuels are refined from the heavier molecules of crude oil, gasoline from the lighter. Because refiners can transform heavier molecules into lighter in the cracking process, they can adjust the proportion of gasoline produced. This futures contract also "trades in units of 42,000 gallons … (and) … is based on delivery at petroleum products terminals in the harbor, the major East Coast trading center for imports and domestic shipments from refineries in the New York harbor area or from the Gulf Coast. … Contract specifications conform to those for reformulated gasoline, required in many areas for controlling emissions." More populous regions of the country require gasoline formulated to stricter emission standards during the driving season, the months of transition being April and September.

Figure 2-13: Cash Gasoline Seasonal Pattern

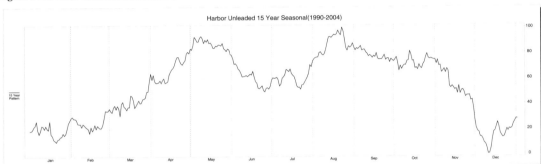

Because individuals consume most gasoline, the US summer vacation and driving season creates a seasonal bulge in consumption. The seasonal pattern illustrates twin price peaks that encompass the driving season, which traditionally opens Memorial Day (last Monday in May) and ends Labor Day (first Monday in September). During March/April, better weather improves driving conditions which increases daily consumption. That higher rate of usage competes for supply even as the industry accumulates inventory of summer blends, and demand accelerates. But as the driving season begins in late May, refiners are running at capacity, inventories are being topped off, and demand decelerates. By late August, when refiners begin to retool and to reformulate for winter blends, remaining supplies of summer blends can be squeezed. The end of driving season triggers a decline in consumption reinforced by driving conditions that deteriorate into winter.

Figure 2-14: Unleaded Gasoline Strategies

Moore Research Center, Inc.	Unleaded Gasoline Spread Strategies							
Seasonal Strategy	Entry Date	Exit Date	Win Pct	Win Yrs	Loss Years	Total Years	Average Profit	Ave Pft Per Day
Buy Jul Unleaded Reg.(NYM)	2/28	5/09	80	12	3	15	735	10
Sell Nov Unleaded Reg.(NYM)			84	16	3	19	736	10
Buy Jun Unleaded Reg.(NYM)	3/12	5/09	80	12	3	15	542	9
Sell Oct Unleaded Reg.(NYM)			80	16	4	20	765	13
Buy May Unleaded Reg.(NYM)	4/12	4/27	93	14	1	15	652	41
Sell Sep Unleaded Reg.(NYM)			90	18	2	20	818	51

Figure 2-14: Unleaded Gasoline Spread Strats continued

Moore Research Center, Inc.	**Unleaded Gasoline Spread Strategies**							
Seasonal Strategy	Entry Date	Exit Date	Win Pct	Win Yrs	Loss Years	Total Years	Average Profit	Ave Pft Per Day
Buy Dec Unleaded Reg.(NYM)	5/24	6/28	93	14	1	15	974	27
Sell Aug Unleaded Reg.(NYM)			89	17	2	19	856	24
Buy Nov Unleaded Reg.(NYM)	7/23	9/11	80	12	3	15	541	11
Sell Feb Unleaded Reg.(NYM)			80	16	4	20	558	11
Buy Dec Unleaded Reg.(NYM)	7/23	10/28	80	12	3	15	405	4
Sell Feb Unleaded Reg.(NYM)			80	16	4	20	468	5
Buy Oct Unleaded Reg.(NYM)	7/24	8/21	93	14	1	15	885	31
Sell Feb Unleaded Reg.(NYM)			95	19	1	20	734	25
Buy Jan Unleaded Reg.(NYM)	12/10	12/16	93	14	1	15	565	81
Sell May Unleaded Reg.(NYM)			90	18	2	20	475	68
Buy Jan Unleaded Reg.(NYM)	12/10	12/28	87	13	2	15	679	36
Sell May Unleaded Reg.(NYM)			85	17	3	20	646	34
Buy Feb Unleaded Reg.(NYM)	12/11	1/06	93	14	1	15	760	28
Sell Jun Unleaded Reg.(NYM)			95	19	1	20	721	27

Reliable seasonal spreads tend to appear more for gasoline than for heating oil — perhaps because gasoline consumption is more universal and greater by volume, perhaps because there are two distinct blends. In fact, some commercial traders prefer not to spread across April and September because they consider winter and summer blends to be apples and oranges. The summary table above, however, suggests potent trading opportunities.

During the transition from heating season to driving season, demand for gasoline accelerates as consumption increases while the industry accumulates inventories. The effect appears in the seasonal pattern for the June/October spread (Figure 2-16). Throughout March, April, and into May — or until supply anxieties are relieved, the market places an increasing premium on gasoline deliverable during the driving season. This tendency also holds well for the 19 years in which gasoline futures have traded.

Embedded in the strategy table for the July/March Heating Oil spread (Figure 2-12) discussed earlier were details of contraseasonal bull spreading going into the Iraq incursion in March 2003. This strategy discloses details of the contraseasonal bear spreading thereafter. The obvious implication is that the extraordinary event, the invasion itself, was the pivot around which normal dynamics and price movement was inverted. Anxious accumulation climaxed, the market exhaled, and began liquidating in relief.

The May/September (Figure 2-17) spread suggests how eager the market is for its first deliveries of gasoline blended for summer driving. This early in the season, limited supply heightens market anxiety as time runs out on supply deliverable in May.

The bear spread December/August (Figure 2-18) illustrates the aftereffects of a much anticipated event. After intense preparation for the traditional opening of the driving and vacation season on Memorial Day (last Monday in May), the event itself becomes the climax and the market slumps in exhaustion. Inventories have been accumulated, refiners run at capacity, and, after a burst of holiday driving, demand decelerates as consumption eases into July.

Figure 2-15

Buy Jul Unleaded Reg.(NYM) / Sell Nov Unleaded Reg.(NYM)

Moore Research Center, Inc.

Enter on approximately 02/28 - Exit on approximately 05/09

CONT YEAR	ENTRY DATE	ENTRY PRICE	EXIT DATE	EXIT PRICE	PROFIT	PROFIT AMOUNT	BEST EQUITY DATE	BEST EQUITY AMOUNT	WORST EQUITY DATE	WORST EQUITY AMOUNT
2005	02/28/05	11.34	05/09/05	7.65	-3.70	-1554.00	03/08/05	756.00	05/04/05	-2016.00
2004	03/01/04	14.75	05/07/04	21.89	7.15	3003.00	05/07/04	3003.00	03/09/04	-840.00
2003	02/28/03	18.30	05/09/03	9.15	-9.15	-3843.00	03/10/03	756.00	05/07/03	-4935.00
2002	02/28/02	6.64	05/09/02	6.92	0.27	113.40	04/09/02	1932.00		
2001	02/28/01	11.00	05/09/01	21.39	10.40	4368.00	05/04/01	4683.00	03/19/01	-142.80
2000	02/28/00	12.15	05/09/00	17.65	5.50	2310.00	05/09/00	2310.00	04/05/00	-2268.00
1999	03/01/99	0.35	05/07/99	3.28	2.94	1234.80	05/04/99	1785.00		
1998	03/02/98	1.60	05/08/98	1.64	0.05	21.00	04/17/98	567.00	03/09/98	-567.00
1997	02/28/97	5.54	05/09/97	5.25	-0.30	-126.00	03/20/97	231.00	04/16/97	-483.00
1996	02/28/96	6.55	05/09/96	10.45	3.91	1642.20	04/29/96	2688.00	03/04/96	-63.00
1995	02/28/95	2.95	05/09/95	5.70	2.75	1155.00	05/05/95	1318.80	03/03/95	-117.60
1994	02/28/94	2.44	05/09/94	3.10	0.65	273.00	04/25/94	567.00	03/10/94	-147.00
1993	03/02/93	3.57	05/07/93	4.29	0.72	302.40	05/06/93	323.40	04/26/93	-54.60
1992	02/28/92	5.95	05/08/92	7.21	1.26	529.20	05/05/92	798.00	04/14/92	-327.60
1991	02/28/91	7.25	05/09/91	11.06	3.81	1600.20	05/09/91	1600.20		
1990	02/28/90	6.03	05/09/90	6.49	0.45	189.00	04/03/90	436.80	04/30/90	-680.40
1989	02/28/89	6.42	05/09/89	12.35	5.92	2486.40	05/01/89	3859.80	03/03/89	-205.80
1988	03/01/88	3.00	05/09/88	3.23	0.24	100.80	04/28/88	180.60	03/08/88	-457.80
1987	03/02/87	1.83	05/08/87	2.25	0.42	176.40	03/17/87	932.40		

Percentage Correct	80				
Average Profit on Winning Trades		3.28	1379.35	Winners	12
Average Loss on Trades		-4.38	-1841.00	Losers	3
Average Net Profit Per Trade		1.75	735.28	Total trades	15

Percentage Correct	84				
Average Profit on Winning Trades		2.90	1219.05	Winners	16
Average Loss on Trades		-4.38	-1841.00	Losers	3
Average Net Profit Per Trade		1.75	735.88	Total trades	19

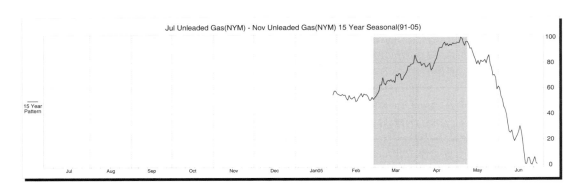

Jul Unleaded Gas(NYM) - Nov Unleaded Gas(NYM) 15 Year Seasonal(91-05)

15 Year Pattern

The seasonal pattern in Figure 2-19 illustrates the reversal in market desire toward winter blends of gasoline during the transition from driving season into winter. Despite heavy consumption, the spread tends to be soft during July because gasoline production is high, distributors are liquidating inventories of summer blends, and winter blends are not yet permissible in many regions. But late in the driving season the market must begin to prepare

Figure 2-16

Buy Jun Unleaded Reg.(NYM) / Sell Oct Unleaded Reg.(NYM)

Enter on approximately 03/12 - Exit on approximately 05/09

CONT YEAR	ENTRY DATE	ENTRY PRICE	EXIT DATE	EXIT PRICE	PROFIT	PROFIT AMOUNT	BEST EQUITY DATE	BEST EQUITY AMOUNT	WORST EQUITY DATE	WORST EQUITY AMOUNT
2005	03/14/05	9.00	05/09/05	3.61	-5.38	-2259.60	04/25/05	462.00	05/04/05	-2641.80
2004	03/12/04	13.70	05/07/04	23.30	9.60	4032.00	05/07/04	4032.00	04/05/04	-546.00
2003	03/12/03	21.59	05/09/03	9.07	-12.53	-5262.60			05/07/03	-6573.00
2002	03/12/02	9.71	05/09/02	4.69	-5.02	-2108.40	03/18/02	777.00	05/09/02	-2108.40
2001	03/12/01	10.35	05/09/01	24.93	14.58	6123.60	05/09/01	6123.60	03/19/01	-100.80
2000	03/13/00	15.20	05/09/00	18.60	3.40	1428.00	05/09/00	1428.00	04/05/00	-3465.00
1999	03/12/99	1.53	05/07/99	2.35	0.83	348.60	03/31/99	1197.00	03/16/99	-84.00
1998	03/12/98	-0.39	05/08/98	-0.30	0.09	37.80	03/26/98	936.60	04/06/98	-42.00
1997	03/12/97	5.47	05/09/97	5.68	0.21	88.20	03/20/97	449.40	04/03/97	-474.60
1996	03/12/96	6.78	05/09/96	11.48	4.69	1969.80	04/29/96	3704.40		
1995	03/13/95	2.05	05/09/95	6.62	4.57	1919.40	05/02/95	2347.80	03/14/95	-84.00
1994	03/14/94	1.48	05/09/94	1.89	0.42	176.40	04/15/94	663.60	05/06/94	-109.20
1993	03/12/93	2.80	05/07/93	3.93	1.14	478.80	05/06/93	550.20	03/22/93	-205.80
1992	03/12/92	5.50	05/08/92	5.74	0.24	100.80	05/04/92	588.00	04/14/92	-823.20
1991	03/12/91	9.24	05/09/91	11.76	2.52	1058.40	05/09/91	1058.40	04/03/91	-571.20
1990	03/12/90	5.15	05/09/90	8.07	2.91	1222.20	05/09/90	1222.20	04/12/90	-466.20
1989	03/13/89	7.13	05/09/89	12.18	5.06	2125.20	04/27/89	4267.20		
1988	03/14/88	1.75	05/09/88	3.44	1.69	709.80	05/06/88	722.40		
1987	03/12/87	3.35	05/08/87	1.15	-2.19	-919.80	03/13/87	155.40	04/20/87	-1075.20
1986	03/12/86	-0.60	05/09/86	9.00	9.60	4032.00	04/30/86	4733.40		

Percentage Correct		80								
Average Profit on Winning Trades					3.52	1480.15		Winners		12
Average Loss on Trades					-7.64	-3210.20		Losers		3
Average Net Profit Per Trade					1.29	542.08		Total trades		15
Percentage Correct		80								
Average Profit on Winning Trades					3.85	1615.69		Winners		16
Average Loss on Trades					-6.28	-2637.60		Losers		4
Average Net Profit Per Trade					1.82	765.03		Total trades		20

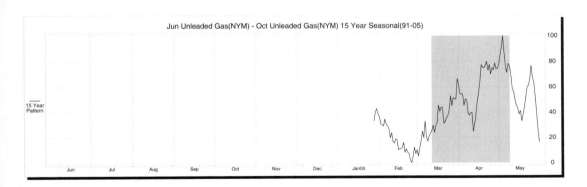

Jun Unleaded Gas(NYM) - Oct Unleaded Gas(NYM) 15 Year Seasonal(91-05)

for the September switchover to winter blends, inventories of which are low. Gasoline consumption begins to decline in mid September, but refiners are focused on producing heating oil at the expense of gasoline. Thus, gasoline deliverable in October or thereafter tends to lead bull spreads into early November until those supply anxieties are alleviated. Notice that drawdowns for the three-month December/February spread strategy (Figure 2-20) were mostly modest.

Figure 2-17

Buy May Unleaded Reg.(NYM) / Sell Sep Unleaded Reg.(NYM)

Enter on approximately 04/12 - Exit on approximately 04/27

CONT YEAR	ENTRY DATE	ENTRY PRICE	EXIT DATE	EXIT PRICE	PROFIT	PROFIT AMOUNT	BEST EQUITY DATE	BEST EQUITY AMOUNT	WORST EQUITY DATE	WORST EQUITY AMOUNT
2005	04/12/05	-1.52	04/27/05	0.49	2.01	844.20	04/25/05	2721.60	04/13/05	-630.00
2004	04/12/04	11.07	04/27/04	10.79	-0.27	-113.40			04/21/04	-806.40
2003	04/14/03	9.18	04/25/03	13.18	4.00	1680.00	04/25/03	1680.00	04/15/03	-71.40
2002	04/12/02	3.68	04/26/02	4.18	0.49	205.80	04/18/02	1075.20	04/25/02	-37.80
2001	04/12/01	15.82	04/27/01	23.65	7.82	3284.40	04/27/01	3284.40		
2000	04/12/00	7.59	04/27/00	7.85	0.27	113.40	04/20/00	1566.60		
1999	04/12/99	0.69	04/27/99	1.03	0.34	142.80	04/22/99	310.80	04/21/99	-21.00
1998	04/13/98	-2.45	04/27/98	-1.35	1.10	462.00	04/17/98	789.60		
1997	04/14/97	3.88	04/25/97	4.17	0.30	126.00	04/21/97	277.20	04/16/97	-260.40
1996	04/12/96	13.21	04/26/96	16.92	3.70	1554.00	04/26/96	1554.00	04/18/96	-1751.40
1995	04/12/95	4.91	04/27/95	6.29	1.38	579.60	04/27/95	579.60	04/24/95	-117.60
1994	04/12/94	0.53	04/26/94	0.75	0.21	88.20	04/15/94	226.80	04/21/94	-126.00
1993	04/12/93	0.57	04/27/93	0.58	0.02	8.40	04/19/93	390.60	04/13/93	-21.00
1992	04/13/92	0.05	04/27/92	1.85	1.80	756.00	04/21/92	911.40	04/14/92	-159.60
1991	04/12/91	9.51	04/26/91	9.61	0.11	46.20	04/18/91	743.40	04/25/91	-121.80
1990	04/12/90	2.54	04/27/90	4.25	1.70	714.00	04/24/90	1297.80		
1989	04/12/89	12.75	04/27/89	18.59	5.83	2448.60	04/27/89	2448.60	04/13/89	-256.20
1988	04/12/88	3.07	04/27/88	2.13	-0.94	-394.80			04/25/88	-655.20
1987	04/13/87	-0.22	04/27/87	0.78	1.02	428.40	04/27/87	428.40	04/20/87	-121.80
1986	04/14/86	5.04	04/25/86	13.10	8.05	3381.00	04/25/86	3381.00	04/17/86	-235.20

Percentage Correct	93									
Average Profit on Winning Trades					1.68	706.50		Winners		14
Average Loss on Trades					-0.27	-113.40		Losers		1
Average Net Profit Per Trade					1.55	651.84		Total trades		15
Percentage Correct	90									
Average Profit on Winning Trades					2.23	936.83		Winners		18
Average Loss on Trades					-0.61	-254.10		Losers		2
Average Net Profit Per Trade					1.95	817.74		Total trades		20

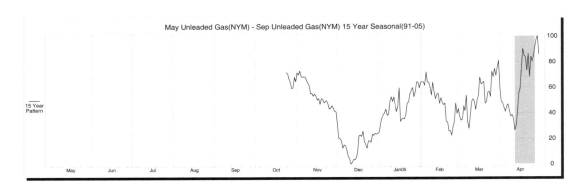

May Unleaded Gas(NYM) - Sep Unleaded Gas(NYM) 15 Year Seasonal(91-05)

15 Year Pattern

    The strategies with October and November on the long side portray the initial surge in bull spreads during the overall seasonal trend. Notice how tight the cluster of entry dates is for all three strategies. Because school begins in earnest in September, the last chance families have to vacation is in August — helping make it the climax to consumption. Both the November/February (Figure 2-19) and October/February (Figure 2-21) strategies also

Figure 2-18

Buy Dec Unleaded Reg.(NYM) / Sell Aug Unleaded Reg.(NYM)

Enter on approximately 05/24 - Exit on approximately 06/28

CONT YEAR	ENTRY DATE	ENTRY PRICE	EXIT DATE	EXIT PRICE	PROFIT	PROFIT AMOUNT	BEST EQUITY DATE	BEST EQUITY AMOUNT	WORST EQUITY DATE	WORST EQUITY AMOUNT
2004	05/24/04	-22.05	06/28/04	-12.79	9.25	3885.00	06/16/04	4418.40		
2003	05/27/03	-10.20	06/27/03	-9.84	0.35	147.00	06/24/03	777.00	06/11/03	-1428.00
2002	05/24/02	-8.70	06/28/02	-7.62	1.07	449.40	06/11/02	982.80		
2001	05/24/01	-16.09	06/28/01	-2.07	14.03	5892.60	06/28/01	5892.60		
2000	05/24/00	-15.92	06/28/00	-20.39	-4.48	-1881.60			06/15/00	-3351.60
1999	05/24/99	-1.72	06/28/99	-1.68	0.04	16.80	06/22/99	180.60	06/08/99	-298.20
1998	05/26/98	-1.17	06/26/98	1.01	2.20	924.00	06/15/98	1029.00	05/28/98	-113.40
1997	05/27/97	-4.45	06/27/97	-2.59	1.86	781.20	06/24/97	1226.40		
1996	05/24/96	-8.30	06/28/96	-5.14	3.15	1323.00	06/26/96	1692.60		
1995	05/24/95	-5.20	06/28/95	-4.98	0.22	92.40	06/26/95	558.60	06/20/95	-273.00
1994	05/24/94	0.79	06/28/94	1.43	0.64	268.80	06/22/94	483.00	06/01/94	-239.40
1993	05/24/93	-3.98	06/28/93	-2.20	1.78	747.60	06/10/93	1062.60		
1992	05/26/92	-7.10	06/26/92	-3.75	3.35	1407.00	06/26/92	1407.00		
1991	05/24/91	-7.42	06/28/91	-6.12	1.30	546.00	06/20/91	911.40	05/30/91	-46.20
1990	05/24/90	-5.42	06/28/90	-5.38	0.04	16.80	06/11/90	1037.40	06/25/90	-487.20
1989	05/24/89	-11.67	06/28/89	-9.86	1.81	760.20	06/21/89	1281.00	06/02/89	-168.00
1988	05/24/88	-2.85	06/28/88	-5.76	-2.91	-1222.20			06/28/88	-1222.20
1987	05/26/87	-3.20	06/26/87	-2.28	0.92	386.40	06/22/87	415.80		
1986	05/27/86	-7.89	06/27/86	-3.78	4.11	1726.20	06/06/86	1869.00		

Percentage Correct	93								
Average Profit on Winning Trades				2.81	1178.40		Winners	14	
Average Loss on Trades				-4.48	-1881.60		Losers	1	
Average Net Profit Per Trade				2.32	974.40		Total trades	15	
Percentage Correct	89								
Average Profit on Winning Trades				2.71	1139.44		Winners	17	
Average Loss on Trades				-3.69	-1551.90		Losers	2	
Average Net Profit Per Trade				2.04	856.14		Total trades	19	

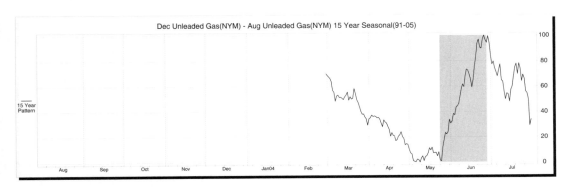

Dec Unleaded Gas(NYM) - Aug Unleaded Gas(NYM) 15 Year Seasonal(91-05)

capture the market's rising anxiety about ever tighter immediate supplies. The February contract, though far deferred and thus less liquid, represents gasoline deliverable late in the season for winter blends.

The last three strategies in the table depict the whiplash-like effect on demand after the December tax flush. Refiners in certain large-producing states are subject to tax on year-end

Figure 2-19

Moore Research Center, Inc.	Buy Nov Unleaded Reg.(NYM) / Sell Feb Unleaded Reg.(NYM)

Enter on approximately 07/23 - Exit on approximately 09/11

CONT YEAR	ENTRY DATE	ENTRY PRICE	EXIT DATE	EXIT PRICE	PROFIT	PROFIT AMOUNT	BEST EQUITY DATE	BEST EQUITY AMOUNT	WORST EQUITY DATE	WORST EQUITY AMOUNT
2004	07/23/04	3.45	09/10/04	1.29	-2.15	-903.00	08/13/04	483.00	08/31/04	-1407.00
2003	07/23/03	2.50	09/11/03	3.03	0.54	226.80	08/22/03	1323.00	09/03/03	-210.00
2002	07/23/02	1.14	09/11/02	1.25	0.10	42.00	08/21/02	189.00	09/03/02	-411.60
2001	07/23/01	-0.79	09/10/01	2.12	2.92	1226.40	09/07/01	1247.40		
2000	07/24/00	1.65	09/11/00	6.04	4.40	1848.00	09/07/00	1953.00	07/27/00	-126.00
1999	07/23/99	1.37	09/10/99	3.69	2.32	974.40	09/10/99	974.40	07/27/99	-75.60
1998	07/23/98	-3.09	09/11/98	-2.39	0.70	294.00	08/17/98	415.80		
1997	07/23/97	-0.08	09/11/97	0.35	0.43	180.60	09/03/97	424.20		
1996	07/23/96	2.10	09/11/96	2.97	0.88	369.60	09/05/96	462.00	07/29/96	-168.00
1995	07/25/95	-0.15	09/11/95	0.78	0.94	394.80	09/05/95	583.80	07/26/95	-37.80
1994	07/25/94	-4.13	09/09/94	-5.46	-1.33	-558.60	08/09/94	499.80	09/07/94	-701.40
1993	07/23/93	-0.69	09/10/93	-0.95	-0.25	-105.00	08/17/93	294.00	09/10/93	-105.00
1992	07/23/92	0.04	09/11/92	0.15	0.10	42.00	09/03/92	399.00	08/05/92	-239.40
1991	07/23/91	1.78	09/11/91	1.90	0.12	50.40	08/12/91	462.00	09/10/91	-96.60
1990	07/23/90	0.46	09/11/90	10.07	9.61	4036.20	09/10/90	4376.40	07/25/90	-134.40
1989	07/24/89	1.14	09/11/89	3.55	2.40	1008.00	09/11/89	1008.00	08/04/89	-268.80
1988	07/25/88	0.26	09/09/88	1.39	1.13	474.60	09/01/88	495.60	07/26/88	-67.20
1987	07/23/87	-0.52	09/11/87	-0.54	-0.02	-8.40	08/04/87	126.00	08/25/87	-168.00
1986	07/23/86	-0.30	09/11/86	1.31	1.61	676.20	08/20/86	840.00	07/31/86	-336.00
1985	07/23/85	2.29	09/11/85	4.40	2.11	886.20	09/11/85	886.20	08/15/85	-575.40

Percentage Correct	80			
Average Profit on Winning Trades		1.92	807.10	Winners	12
Average Loss on Trades		-1.24	-522.20	Losers	3
Average Net Profit Per Trade		1.29	541.24	Total trades	15
Percentage Correct	80			
Average Profit on Winning Trades		1.89	795.64	Winners	16
Average Loss on Trades		-0.94	-393.75	Losers	4
Average Net Profit Per Trade		1.33	557.76	Total trades	20

HYPOTHETICAL PERFORMANCE RESULTS HAVE MANY INHERENT LIMITATIONS, SOME OF WHICH ARE DESCRIBED BELOW. NO REPRESENTATION IS BEING MADE THAT ANY ACCOUNT WILL OR IS LIKELY TO ACHIEVE PROFITS OR LOSSES SIMILAR TO THOSE SHOWN. IN FACT, THERE ARE FREQUENTLY SHARP DIFFERENCES BETWEEN HYPOTHETICAL PERFORMANCE RESULTS AND THE ACTUAL RESULTS SUBSEQUENTLY ACHIEVED BY ANY PARTICULAR TRADING PROGRAM. ONE OF THE LIMITATIONS OF HYPOTHETICAL PERFORMANCE RESULTS IS THAT THEY ARE GENERALLY PREPARED WITH THE BENEFIT OF HINDSIGHT. IN ADDITION, HYPOTHETICAL TRADING DOES NOT INVOLVE FINANCIAL RISK, AND NO HYPOTHETICAL TRADING RECORD CAN COMPLETELY ACCOUNT FOR THE IMPACT OF FINANCIAL RISK IN ACTUAL TRADING. FOR EXAMPLE, THE ABILITY TO WITHSTAND LOSSES OR ADHERE TO A PARTICULAR TRADING PROGRAM IN SPITE OF TRADING LOSSES ARE MATERIAL POINTS WHICH CAN ALSO ADVERSELY AFFECT ACTUAL TRADING RESULTS. THERE ARE NUMEROUS OTHER FACTORS RELATED TO THE MARKETS IN GENERAL OR TO THE IMPLEMENTATION OF ANY SPECIFIC TRADING PROGRAM WHICH CANNOT BE FULLY ACCOUNTED FOR IN THE PREPARATION OF HYPOTHETICAL PERFORMANCE RESULTS AND ALL OF WHICH CAN ADVERSELY AFFECT ACTUAL TRADING RESULTS. RESULTS NOT ADJUSTED FOR COMMISSION AND SLIPPAGE.

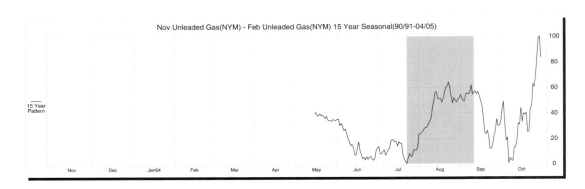

Nov Unleaded Gas(NYM) - Feb Unleaded Gas(NYM) 15 Year Seasonal(90/91-04/05)

inventories of petroleum products. Thus, they have financial incentive to pump as much product into both literal and figurative pipelines as possible before the calendar changes. By mid December, the market anticipates not only the climax to that flush but also an urgent surge in demand for suddenly much tighter supplies. Much like the summer entry dates that cluster tightly around July 23-24, those strategies in Figures 2-22, 2-23, and 2-24 do so

Figure 2-20

Moore Research Center, Inc.

Buy Dec Unleaded Reg.(NYM) / Sell Feb Unleaded Reg.(NYM)

Enter on approximately 07/23 - Exit on approximately 10/28

CONT YEAR	ENTRY DATE	ENTRY PRICE	EXIT DATE	EXIT PRICE	PROFIT	PROFIT AMOUNT	BEST EQUITY DATE	BEST EQUITY AMOUNT	WORST EQUITY DATE	WORST EQUITY AMOUNT
2004	07/23/04	0.50	10/28/04	-2.09	-2.60	-1092.00	09/23/04	189.00	10/28/04	-1092.00
2003	07/23/03	0.54	10/28/03	0.75	0.20	84.00	08/21/03	546.00	09/22/03	-504.00
2002	07/23/02	0.11	10/28/02	2.70	2.58	1083.60	10/28/02	1083.60	09/03/02	-105.00
2001	07/23/01	-0.75	10/26/01	-1.75	-1.00	-420.00	09/14/01	588.00	10/18/01	-567.00
2000	07/24/00	0.35	10/27/00	2.75	2.40	1008.00	10/24/00	1533.00	10/05/00	-273.00
1999	07/23/99	0.67	10/28/99	0.69	0.02	8.40	09/29/99	911.40	10/14/99	-84.00
1998	07/23/98	-2.37	10/28/98	-0.52	1.85	777.00	10/02/98	785.40		
1997	07/23/97	-0.50	10/28/97	-0.41	0.09	37.80	10/03/97	218.40	09/18/97	-21.00
1996	07/23/96	1.00	10/28/96	2.23	1.24	520.80	10/28/96	520.80	09/23/96	-315.00
1995	07/25/95	-0.35	10/27/95	-0.60	-0.24	-100.80	09/19/95	340.20	10/19/95	-205.80
1994	07/25/94	0.86	10/28/94	4.10	3.24	1360.80	10/20/94	1465.80	09/21/94	-571.20
1993	07/23/93	-0.89	10/28/93	-0.64	0.25	105.00	10/14/93	315.00	10/25/93	-100.80
1992	07/23/92	-0.45	10/28/92	0.25	0.70	294.00	10/28/92	294.00	09/30/92	-168.00
1991	07/23/91	0.53	10/28/91	1.44	0.91	382.20	10/28/91	382.20	09/24/91	-172.20
1990	07/23/90	-0.29	10/26/90	4.53	4.83	2028.60	08/22/90	2301.60	07/25/90	-67.20
1989	07/24/89	0.20	10/27/89	0.46	0.27	113.40	09/21/89	1146.60	10/24/89	-155.40
1988	07/25/88	-0.20	10/28/88	4.36	4.57	1919.40	10/25/88	2192.40	07/26/88	-113.40
1987	07/23/87	-0.69	10/28/87	0.40	1.10	462.00	10/28/87	462.00	08/25/87	-142.80
1986	07/23/86	-0.60	10/28/86	-1.08	-0.49	-205.80	08/07/86	802.20	10/22/86	-214.20
1985	07/23/85	1.65	10/28/85	4.00	2.35	987.00	10/23/85	1423.80	08/29/85	-672.00

Percentage Correct	80									
Average Profit on Winning Trades					1.53	640.85		Winners		12
Average Loss on Trades					-1.28	-537.60		Losers		3
Average Net Profit Per Trade					0.96	405.16		Total trades		15
Percentage Correct	80									
Average Profit on Winning Trades					1.66	698.25		Winners		16
Average Loss on Trades					-1.08	-454.65		Losers		4
Average Net Profit Per Trade					1.11	467.67		Total trades		20

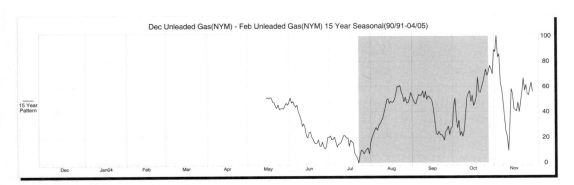

Dec Unleaded Gas(NYM) - Feb Unleaded Gas(NYM) 15 Year Seasonal(90/91-04/05)

around December 10-11. The nearly immaculate reliability of the shorter strategies shows how timely the reversal and robust the recovery.

Figure 2-21

Buy Oct Unleaded Reg.(NYM) / Sell Feb Unleaded Reg.(NYM)

Enter on approximately 07/24 - Exit on approximately 08/21

CONT YEAR	ENTRY DATE	ENTRY PRICE	EXIT DATE	EXIT PRICE	PROFIT	PROFIT AMOUNT	BEST EQUITY DATE	BEST EQUITY AMOUNT	WORST EQUITY DATE	WORST EQUITY AMOUNT
2004	07/26/04	6.63	08/20/04	4.25	-2.38	-999.60	08/13/04	575.40	08/04/04	-1545.60
2003	07/24/03	5.60	08/21/03	13.04	7.45	3129.00	08/21/03	3129.00	07/29/03	-168.00
2002	07/24/02	2.89	08/21/02	3.09	0.20	84.00	07/30/02	92.40	08/07/02	-327.60
2001	07/24/01	-0.10	08/21/01	2.00	2.10	882.00	08/14/01	1327.20		
2000	07/24/00	4.35	08/21/00	6.69	2.35	987.00	08/17/00	991.20	08/07/00	-260.40
1999	07/26/99	1.97	08/20/99	4.00	2.02	848.40	08/09/99	1230.60		
1998	07/24/98	-3.15	08/21/98	-3.01	0.14	58.80	08/17/98	306.60	08/10/98	-151.20
1997	07/24/97	0.88	08/21/97	3.19	2.32	974.40	08/20/97	1205.40		
1996	07/24/96	3.79	08/21/96	4.18	0.39	163.80	08/19/96	415.80	07/29/96	-231.00
1995	07/25/95	0.44	08/21/95	0.75	0.31	130.20	08/11/95	487.20	07/26/95	-121.80
1994	07/25/94	-2.23	08/19/94	-2.10	0.14	58.80	08/04/94	852.60	08/16/94	-33.60
1993	07/26/93	-0.19	08/20/93	0.39	0.60	252.00	08/17/93	562.80	07/30/93	-63.00
1992	07/24/92	1.29	08/21/92	1.60	0.31	130.20	08/18/92	357.00	08/05/92	-407.40
1991	07/24/91	3.39	08/21/91	5.21	1.83	768.60	08/12/91	1171.80	07/29/91	-84.00
1990	07/24/90	1.09	08/21/90	14.92	13.83	5808.60	08/21/90	5808.60	07/25/90	-63.00
1989	07/24/89	2.14	08/21/89	2.33	0.18	75.60	08/18/89	226.80	08/04/89	-495.60
1988	07/25/88	1.96	08/19/88	2.24	0.27	113.40	08/02/88	285.60	08/10/88	-462.00
1987	07/24/87	-0.21	08/21/87	-0.01	0.20	84.00	07/29/87	147.00	08/18/87	-121.80
1986	07/24/86	-0.05	08/21/86	2.49	2.54	1066.80	08/20/86	1129.80	07/31/86	-390.60
1985	07/24/85	3.87	08/21/85	4.04	0.17	71.40	07/29/85	323.40	08/13/85	-655.20

Percentage Correct		93								
Average Profit on Winning Trades					2.43	1019.70		Winners		14
Average Loss on Trades					-2.38	-999.60		Losers		1
Average Net Profit Per Trade					2.11	885.08		Total trades		15
Percentage Correct		95								
Average Profit on Winning Trades					1.97	825.63		Winners		19
Average Loss on Trades					-2.38	-999.60		Losers		1
Average Net Profit Per Trade					1.75	734.37		Total trades		20

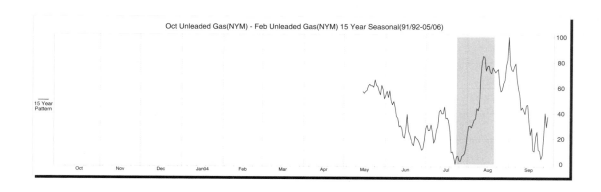

Oct Unleaded Gas(NYM) - Feb Unleaded Gas(NYM) 15 Year Seasonal(91/92-05/06)

Chapter 2: Energy

Figure 2-22

Moore Research Center, Inc. — Buy Jan Unleaded Reg.(NYM) / Sell May Unleaded Reg.(NYM)

Enter on approximately 12/10 - Exit on approximately 12/16

CONT YEAR	ENTRY DATE	ENTRY PRICE	EXIT DATE	EXIT PRICE	PROFIT	PROFIT AMOUNT	BEST EQUITY DATE	BEST EQUITY AMOUNT	WORST EQUITY DATE	WORST EQUITY AMOUNT
2005	12/10/04	-13.65	12/16/04	-14.06	-0.42	-176.40	12/13/04	394.80	12/16/04	-176.40
2004	12/10/03	-7.86	12/16/03	-6.98	0.89	373.80	12/12/03	382.20		
2003	12/10/02	-4.81	12/16/02	-0.34	4.48	1881.60	12/16/02	1881.60	12/11/02	-210.00
2002	12/10/01	-10.15	12/14/01	-8.60	1.55	651.00	12/14/01	651.00	12/11/01	-42.00
2001	12/11/00	-6.55	12/15/00	-5.53	1.03	432.60	12/15/00	432.60		
2000	12/10/99	-0.06	12/16/99	1.36	1.44	604.80	12/16/99	604.80	12/14/99	-235.20
1999	12/10/98	-7.11	12/16/98	-6.28	0.84	352.80	12/16/98	352.80		
1998	12/10/97	-3.96	12/16/97	-3.20	0.76	319.20	12/16/97	319.20	12/11/97	-37.80
1997	12/10/96	-0.37	12/16/96	0.09	0.48	201.60	12/16/96	201.60	12/11/96	-424.20
1996	12/11/95	-0.98	12/15/95	3.04	4.02	1688.40	12/15/95	1688.40		
1995	12/12/94	-2.91	12/16/94	-1.80	1.12	470.40	12/14/94	491.40		
1994	12/10/93	-7.96	12/16/93	-7.57	0.38	159.60	12/16/93	159.60	12/13/93	-256.20
1993	12/10/92	-7.15	12/16/92	-5.75	1.40	588.00	12/16/92	588.00		
1992	12/10/91	-7.78	12/16/91	-6.86	0.92	386.40	12/16/91	386.40	12/11/91	-75.60
1991	12/10/90	-5.17	12/14/90	-3.86	1.30	546.00	12/14/90	546.00		
1990	12/11/89	-6.53	12/15/89	-6.35	0.18	75.60	12/15/89	75.60		
1989	12/12/88	-1.23	12/16/88	-0.92	0.31	130.20	12/16/88	130.20	12/14/88	-256.20
1988	12/10/87	-2.64	12/16/87	-2.54	0.09	37.80	12/15/87	42.00	12/11/87	-29.40
1987	12/10/86	-2.14	12/16/86	-3.46	-1.33	-558.60			12/16/86	-558.60
1986	12/10/85	-1.90	12/16/85	1.25	3.16	1327.20	12/13/85	1331.40		

Percentage Correct	93							
Average Profit on Winning Trades					1.47	618.30	Winners	14
Average Loss on Trades					-0.42	-176.40	Losers	1
Average Net Profit Per Trade					1.35	565.32	Total trades	15
Percentage Correct	90							
Average Profit on Winning Trades					1.35	568.17	Winners	18
Average Loss on Trades					-0.87	-367.50	Losers	2
Average Net Profit Per Trade					1.13	474.60	Total trades	20

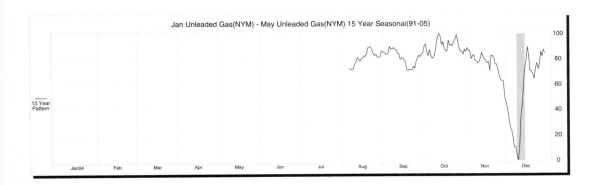

Jan Unleaded Gas(NYM) - May Unleaded Gas(NYM) 15 Year Seasonal(91-05)

15 Year Pattern

Chapter 2: Energy

Figure 2-23

Buy Jan Unleaded Reg.(NYM) / Sell May Unleaded Reg.(NYM)

Enter on approximately 12/10 - Exit on approximately 12/28

CONT YEAR	ENTRY DATE	ENTRY PRICE	EXIT DATE	EXIT PRICE	PROFIT	PROFIT AMOUNT	BEST EQUITY DATE	BEST EQUITY AMOUNT	WORST EQUITY DATE	WORST EQUITY AMOUNT
2005	12/10/04	-13.65	12/28/04	-14.61	-0.96	-403.20	12/22/04	684.60	12/28/04	-403.20
2004	12/10/03	-7.86	12/24/03	-6.30	1.56	655.20	12/24/03	655.20		
2003	12/10/02	-4.81	12/27/02	1.59	6.42	2696.40	12/26/02	2717.40	12/11/02	-210.00
2002	12/10/01	-10.15	12/28/01	-7.71	2.44	1024.80	12/21/01	1079.40	12/11/01	-42.00
2001	12/11/00	-6.55	12/28/00	-0.96	5.59	2347.80	12/28/00	2347.80		
2000	12/10/99	-0.06	12/28/99	-0.10	-0.03	-12.60	12/20/99	651.00	12/14/99	-235.20
1999	12/10/98	-7.11	12/28/98	-6.67	0.45	189.00	12/16/98	352.80	12/22/98	-184.80
1998	12/10/97	-3.96	12/26/97	-2.77	1.19	499.80	12/18/97	613.20	12/11/97	-37.80
1997	12/10/96	-0.37	12/27/96	0.19	0.58	243.60	12/19/96	659.40	12/11/96	-424.20
1996	12/11/95	-0.98	12/28/95	1.78	2.76	1159.20	12/18/95	1747.20		
1995	12/12/94	-2.91	12/28/94	-1.72	1.19	499.80	12/28/94	499.80		
1994	12/10/93	-7.96	12/28/93	-7.50	0.45	189.00	12/21/93	394.80	12/13/93	-256.20
1993	12/10/92	-7.15	12/28/92	-6.09	1.07	449.40	12/18/92	865.20		
1992	12/10/91	-7.78	12/27/91	-6.43	1.35	567.00	12/17/91	583.80	12/11/91	-75.60
1991	12/10/90	-5.17	12/28/90	-4.98	0.18	75.60	12/14/90	546.00	12/20/90	-63.00
1990	12/11/89	-6.53	12/28/89	-2.64	3.90	1638.00	12/26/89	2007.60		
1989	12/12/88	-1.23	12/28/88	-0.66	0.58	243.60	12/21/88	394.80	12/14/88	-256.20
1988	12/10/87	-2.64	12/28/87	-2.30	0.34	142.80	12/22/87	735.00	12/11/87	-29.40
1987	12/10/86	-2.14	12/24/86	-4.03	-1.90	-798.00			12/24/86	-798.00
1986	12/10/85	-1.90	12/27/85	1.70	3.61	1516.20	12/27/85	1516.20		

Percentage Correct		87								
Average Profit on Winning Trades					1.94	815.12		Winners		13
Average Loss on Trades					-0.50	-207.90		Losers		2
Average Net Profit Per Trade					1.62	678.72		Total trades		15
Percentage Correct		85								
Average Profit on Winning Trades					1.98	831.60		Winners		17
Average Loss on Trades					-0.96	-404.60		Losers		3
Average Net Profit Per Trade					1.54	646.17		Total trades		20

Jan Unleaded Gas(NYM) - May Unleaded Gas(NYM) 15 Year Seasonal(91-05)

Chapter 2: Energy

Figure 2-24

Moore Research Center, Inc.
Buy Feb Unleaded Reg.(NYM) / Sell Jun Unleaded Reg.(NYM)

Enter on approximately 12/11 - Exit on approximately 01/06

CONT YEAR	ENTRY DATE	ENTRY PRICE	EXIT DATE	EXIT PRICE	PROFIT	PROFIT AMOUNT	BEST EQUITY DATE	BEST EQUITY AMOUNT	WORST EQUITY DATE	WORST EQUITY AMOUNT
2005	12/13/04	-9.00	01/06/05	-7.48	1.52	638.40	01/06/05	638.40	12/28/04	-1050.00
2004	12/11/03	-5.35	01/06/04	-2.59	2.77	1163.40	01/05/04	1596.00		
2003	12/11/02	-4.60	01/06/03	0.13	4.73	1986.60	12/26/02	3364.20		
2002	12/11/01	-8.89	01/04/02	-6.42	2.47	1037.40	01/03/02	1062.60		
2001	12/11/00	-4.94	01/05/01	-0.90	4.04	1696.80	01/05/01	1696.80		
2000	12/13/99	-0.55	01/06/00	-0.76	-0.21	-88.20	12/16/99	705.60	01/05/00	-260.40
1999	12/11/98	-6.00	01/06/99	-5.20	0.80	336.00	01/06/99	336.00	12/22/98	-298.20
1998	12/11/97	-2.91	01/06/98	-2.87	0.04	16.80	12/18/97	470.40	01/05/98	-218.40
1997	12/11/96	-0.30	01/06/97	1.89	2.19	919.80	01/06/97	919.80		
1996	12/11/95	-0.75	01/05/96	2.60	3.36	1411.20	01/05/96	1411.20		
1995	12/12/94	-2.95	01/06/95	-1.12	1.82	764.40	01/05/95	907.20	12/27/94	-109.20
1994	12/13/93	-6.96	01/06/94	-5.77	1.20	504.00	01/05/94	651.00	12/27/93	-88.20
1993	12/11/92	-6.40	01/06/93	-5.50	0.90	378.00	12/23/92	441.00		
1992	12/11/91	-6.56	01/06/92	-5.07	1.49	625.80	01/06/92	625.80	12/23/91	-197.40
1991	12/11/90	-2.29	01/04/91	-2.28	0.01	4.20	12/14/90	138.60	01/02/91	-193.20
1990	12/11/89	-4.65	01/05/90	-1.17	3.47	1457.40	01/03/90	2217.60		
1989	12/12/88	-1.25	01/06/89	-0.78	0.47	197.40	01/06/89	197.40	12/14/88	-310.80
1988	12/11/87	-3.02	01/06/88	-2.70	0.33	138.60	12/18/87	378.00		
1987	12/11/86	-2.76	01/06/87	-2.61	0.14	58.80	01/06/87	58.80	12/18/86	-361.20
1986	12/11/85	0.00	01/06/86	2.81	2.81	1180.20	01/06/86	1180.20		

Percentage Correct	93									
Average Profit on Winning Trades					1.95	820.20		Winners		14
Average Loss on Trades					-0.21	-88.20		Losers		1
Average Net Profit Per Trade					1.81	759.64		Total trades		15
Percentage Correct	95									
Average Profit on Winning Trades					1.82	763.96		Winners		19
Average Loss on Trades					-0.21	-88.20		Losers		1
Average Net Profit Per Trade					1.72	721.35		Total trades		20

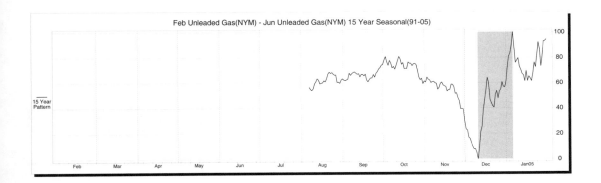

Feb Unleaded Gas(NYM) - Jun Unleaded Gas(NYM) 15 Year Seasonal(91-05)

15 Year Pattern

Natural Gas

"Natural gas accounts for almost a quarter of United States energy consumption," according to NYMEX, heating perhaps half of US homes. It is also a major fuel used in manufacturing, to heat office buildings, and, since the early 1990s, for most new electricity generation. "The futures contract trades in units of 10,000 million British thermal units (mmBtu). The price is based on delivery at the Henry Hub in Louisiana, the nexus of 16 intra- and interstate natural gas pipeline systems that draw supplies from the region's prolific gas deposits. The pipelines serve markets throughout the US East Coast, the Gulf Coast, the Midwest, and up to the Canadian border."

Figure 2-25: Jan Natural Gas Seasonal Pattern

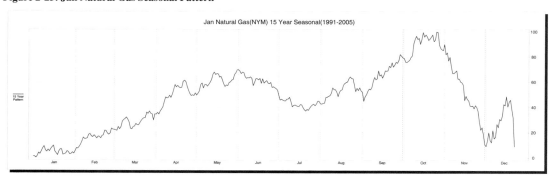

Seasonal bulges in consumption are driven by demand not only for heat in cold-weather regions but also for generating electricity to run air conditioners in hot-weather regions. Again, price precedes consumption. Barring price spikes, price tends normally to be low during January and again in July, the coldest and hottest months of the year, respectively. Price normally peaks during seasonal transitions, most often April-June and again in October. By March, when supplies are depleted, temperatures moderate in cold-weather regions but rise in hot-weather regions. During the injection season, the peak of which is May-September, cold-weather utilities typically buy excess gas and inject it into storage for high-demand winter months. That inventory accumulation competes with consumption in hot-weather regions. During July, consumption in cold-weather regions is least; but by August the market begins to grow anxious about how adequate winter supplies will be by the end of the injection season on November 1.

Figure 2-26: Natural Gas Spread Strategies

Moore Research Center, Inc.	Natural Gas Spread Strategies							
Seasonal Strategy	Entry Date	Exit Date	Win Pct	Win Yrs	Loss Years	Total Years	Average Profit	Ave Pft Per Day
Buy Jul Natural Gas(NYM) Sell Dec Natural Gas(NYM)	3/03	4/12	81	13	3	16	547	13
Buy Jan Natural Gas(NYM) Sell Sep Natural Gas(NYM)	5/23	7/21	93	14	1	15	1299	22
Buy Sep Natural Gas(NYM) Sell Jun Natural Gas(NYM)	4/18	4/30	94	15	1	16	306	24
Buy Dec Natural Gas(NYM) Sell Jun Natural Gas(NYM)	4/22	5/22	81	13	3	16	809	26

Figure 2-26: Natural Gas Strategies continued

Moore Research Center, Inc.		*Natural Gas Spread Strategies*							
Seasonal Strategy	Entry Date	Exit Date	Win Pct	Win Yrs	Loss Years	Total Years	Average Profit	Ave Pft Per Day
Buy Dec Natural Gas(NYM) Sell Jul Natural Gas(NYM)	5/14	6/28	93	14	1	15	1190	26
Buy Feb Natural Gas(NYM) Sell Nov Natural Gas(NYM)	6/06	7/22	100	15	0	15	823	18
Buy Dec Natural Gas(NYM) Sell Sep Natural Gas(NYM)	6/19	7/22	93	14	1	15	949	28
Buy Nov Natural Gas(NYM) Sell Oct Natural Gas(NYM)	8/29	9/14	100	15	0	15	549	32
Buy Nov Natural Gas(NYM) Sell Dec Natural Gas(NYM)	10/11	10/26	93	14	1	15	788	49
Buy Mar Natural Gas(NYM) Sell Jan Natural Gas(NYM)	11/22	11/30	93	14	1	15	628	70
Buy Apr Natural Gas(NYM) Sell May Natural Gas(NYM)	11/29	12/15	87	13	2	15	493	29
Buy Jun Natural Gas(NYM) Sell Mar Natural Gas(NYM)	12/20	2/16	93	14	1	15	4095	69
Buy Jun Natural Gas(NYM) Sell Feb Natural Gas(NYM)	12/21	1/23	93	14	1	15	3933	116
Buy May Natural Gas(NYM) Sell Apr Natural Gas(NYM)	12/21	3/12	93	14	1	15	1185	14

Natural gas spreads seem to differ from those for crude oil and its products. In those markets, periods of accumulation are associated with conventional bull spreads in which nearby contracts outperform deferred. Conversely, periods of exhaustion and liquidation are marked by conventional bear spreads in which nearby contracts underperform deferred. Of all the natural gas strategies listed (Figure 2-26), only a few, such as the first, assume the cast of a conventional bull spread, long nearby/short deferred. The second is more typical.

After heavy winter consumption, inventories tend to be at their lowest levels of the year. This spread suggests the initial surge in demand from utilities in warm-weather regions that will soon need gas to generate electricity to run air conditioners. Thus, demand for gas deliverable during the heat of summer grows; but, while heating season is still winding down, demand for gas deliverable next December is at best subdued.

The new injection season, during which utilities replenish depleted supplies, begins in earnest during April/May. The series of strategies beginning mid April show how market concerns over price and supply tend continually to roll forward. Prior to mid April, as suggested by the July/December spread, the market seems anxious about the immediate need to begin replenishing depleted supply. As physical supplies are injected and storage builds, the focus seems to shift away from ensuring immediate needs to eventual needs.

In other words, deferred concerns progressively outweigh those immediate. This market seems to be one which builds seasonal disparities in consumption into its price structure. With the exception of the first, spreads listed for entry beginning mid April and exited by August portray how well gas deliverable during the coldest winter months (December-February) outperforms other months. For example, because more gas will be consumed

Figure 2-27

Buy Jul Natural Gas(NYM) / Sell Dec Natural Gas(NYM)

Enter on approximately 03/03 - Exit on approximately 04/12

CONT YEAR	ENTRY DATE	ENTRY PRICE	EXIT DATE	EXIT PRICE	PROFIT	PROFIT AMOUNT	BEST EQUITY DATE	BEST EQUITY AMOUNT	WORST EQUITY DATE	WORST EQUITY AMOUNT
2005	03/03/05	-0.810	04/12/05	-0.890	-0.077	-770.00	03/15/05	1790.00	04/12/05	-770.00
2004	03/03/04	-0.350	04/12/04	-0.320	0.033	330.00	03/17/04	570.00	03/25/04	-240.00
2003	03/03/03	-0.190	04/11/03	-0.060	0.127	1270.00	03/07/03	1550.00	04/03/03	-150.00
2002	03/04/02	-0.620	04/12/02	-0.510	0.116	1160.00	04/02/02	2300.00	03/05/02	-70.00
2001	03/05/01	-0.180	04/12/01	-0.280	-0.102	-1020.00	03/27/01	100.00	04/12/01	-1020.00
2000	03/03/00	-0.260	04/12/00	-0.190	0.075	750.00	03/28/00	760.00	03/08/00	-250.00
1999	03/03/99	-0.490	04/12/99	-0.330	0.159	1590.00	04/12/99	1590.00	03/18/99	-150.00
1998	03/03/98	-0.280	04/09/98	-0.190	0.086	860.00	04/08/98	920.00	03/10/98	-370.00
1997	03/03/97	-0.340	04/11/97	-0.300	0.045	450.00	03/07/97	1180.00	04/02/97	-30.00
1996	03/04/96	-0.160	04/12/96	-0.040	0.123	1230.00	04/09/96	1230.00	03/05/96	-70.00
1995	03/03/95	-0.290	04/12/95	-0.210	0.084	840.00	04/04/95	1080.00	03/06/95	-80.00
1994	03/03/94	-0.260	04/12/94	-0.240	0.016	160.00	04/04/94	300.00	03/25/94	-300.00
1993	03/03/93	-0.480	04/12/93	-0.280	0.193	1930.00	04/12/93	1930.00		
1992	03/03/92	-0.600	04/10/92	-0.590	0.016	160.00	03/30/92	640.00	04/07/92	-70.00
1991	03/04/91	-0.680	04/12/91	-0.670	0.011	110.00	03/28/91	300.00	03/08/91	-250.00
1990	04/03/90	-0.470	04/12/90	-0.500	-0.030	-300.00			04/04/90	-1150.00

Percentage Correct	81								
Average Profit on Winning Trades				0.083	833.85		Winners		13
Average Loss on Trades				-0.070	-696.67		Losers		3
Average Net Profit Per Trade				0.055	546.87		Total trades		16

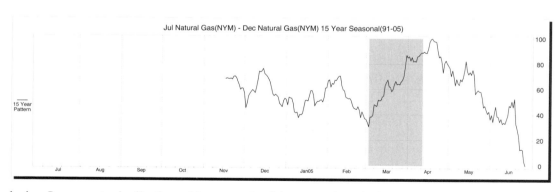

Jul Natural Gas(NYM) - Dec Natural Gas(NYM) 15 Year Seasonal(91-05)

during January, typically the coldest month of the year, than during September, a so-called shoulder month when temperatures are neither hot nor cold, gas deliverable for the former becomes increasingly more valuable than for the latter. Notice in this summary table another cluster of dates, this time for exit around July 21-22.

Figure 2-28

Buy Jan Natural Gas(NYM) / Sell Sep Natural Gas(NYM)

Enter on approximately 05/23 - Exit on approximately 07/21

CONT YEAR	ENTRY DATE	ENTRY PRICE	EXIT DATE	EXIT PRICE	PROFIT	PROFIT AMOUNT	BEST EQUITY DATE	BEST EQUITY AMOUNT	WORST EQUITY DATE	WORST EQUITY AMOUNT
2005	05/24/04	0.460	07/21/04	0.850	0.392	3920.00	07/20/04	4170.00		
2004	05/23/03	0.290	07/21/03	0.550	0.257	2570.00	07/18/03	2690.00	06/02/03	-60.00
2003	05/23/02	0.600	07/19/02	0.780	0.179	1790.00	07/12/02	2730.00	05/29/02	-50.00
2002	05/23/01	0.460	07/20/01	0.710	0.245	2450.00	07/06/01	3620.00	05/31/01	-490.00
2001	05/23/00	0.220	07/21/00	0.140	-0.088	-880.00	05/30/00	150.00	06/27/00	-1700.00
2000	05/24/99	0.420	07/21/99	0.480	0.062	620.00	07/20/99	790.00	06/09/99	-880.00
1999	05/26/98	0.410	07/21/98	0.630	0.214	2140.00	07/21/98	2140.00	06/30/98	-860.00
1998	05/23/97	0.250	07/21/97	0.340	0.084	840.00	06/11/97	840.00	05/27/97	-170.00
1997	05/23/96	0.060	07/19/96	0.060	0.007	70.00	05/30/96	270.00	07/15/96	-1400.00
1996	05/23/95	0.170	07/21/95	0.370	0.200	2000.00	07/21/95	2000.00	05/24/95	-70.00
1995	05/23/94	0.260	07/21/94	0.310	0.049	490.00	07/21/94	490.00	07/01/94	-1150.00
1994	05/24/93	0.380	07/21/93	0.450	0.064	640.00	07/20/93	700.00	06/18/93	-830.00
1993	05/26/92	0.450	07/21/92	0.460	0.002	20.00	06/29/92	1240.00		
1992	05/23/91	0.680	07/19/91	0.830	0.146	1460.00	07/16/91	1600.00	06/10/91	-20.00
1991	05/23/90	0.620	07/20/90	0.760	0.136	1360.00	07/20/90	1360.00		

Percentage Correct		93								
Average Profit on Winning Trades					0.146	1455.00		Winners		14
Average Loss on Trades					-0.088	-880.00		Losers		1
Average Net Profit Per Trade					0.130	1299.33		Total trades		15

HYPOTHETICAL PERFORMANCE RESULTS HAVE MANY INHERENT LIMITATIONS, SOME OF WHICH ARE DESCRIBED BELOW. NO REPRESENTATION IS BEING MADE THAT ANY ACCOUNT WILL OR IS LIKELY TO ACHIEVE PROFITS OR LOSSES SIMILAR TO THOSE SHOWN. IN FACT, THERE ARE FREQUENTLY SHARP DIFFERENCES BETWEEN HYPOTHETICAL PERFORMANCE RESULTS AND THE ACTUAL RESULTS SUBSEQUENTLY ACHIEVED BY ANY PARTICULAR TRADING PROGRAM. ONE OF THE LIMITATIONS OF HYPOTHETICAL PERFORMANCE RESULTS IS THAT THEY ARE GENERALLY PREPARED WITH THE BENEFIT OF HINDSIGHT. IN ADDITION, HYPOTHETICAL TRADING DOES NOT INVOLVE FINANCIAL RISK, AND NO HYPOTHETICAL TRADING RECORD CAN COMPLETELY ACCOUNT FOR THE IMPACT OF FINANCIAL RISK IN ACTUAL TRADING. FOR EXAMPLE, THE ABILITY TO WITHSTAND LOSSES OR ADHERE TO A PARTICULAR TRADING PROGRAM IN SPITE OF TRADING LOSSES ARE MATERIAL POINTS WHICH CAN ALSO ADVERSELY AFFECT ACTUAL TRADING RESULTS. THERE ARE NUMEROUS OTHER FACTORS RELATED TO THE MARKETS IN GENERAL OR TO THE IMPLEMENTATION OF ANY SPECIFIC TRADING PROGRAM WHICH CANNOT BE FULLY ACCOUNTED FOR IN THE PREPARATION OF HYPOTHETICAL PERFORMANCE RESULTS AND ALL OF WHICH CAN ADVERSELY AFFECT ACTUAL TRADING RESULTS. RESULTS NOT ADJUSTED FOR COMMISSION AND SLIPPAGE.

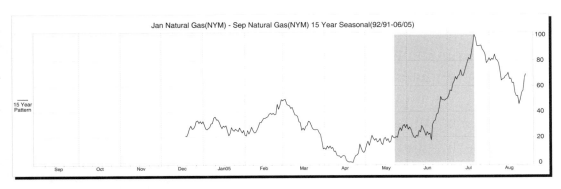

Jan Natural Gas(NYM) - Sep Natural Gas(NYM) 15 Year Seasonal(92/91-06/05)

   The November/October (Figure 2-34) and the November/December (Figure 2-35) spreads suggest how pivotal to this market is the date November 1, the end of the injection season and the beginning of the heating season. The former spread places increasingly more value on gas deliverable during the first month of heavy withdrawals while the latter suggests a last-minute, whiplash-like surge in demand to ensure adequate inventories.

Figure 2-29

							BEST	**BEST**	**WORST**	**WORST**
CONT YEAR	**ENTRY DATE**	**ENTRY PRICE**	**EXIT DATE**	**EXIT PRICE**	**PROFIT**	**PROFIT AMOUNT**	**EQUITY DATE**	**EQUITY AMOUNT**	**EQUITY DATE**	**EQUITY AMOUNT**

Moore Research Center, Inc.

Buy Sep Natural Gas(NYM) / Sell Jun Natural Gas(NYM)

Enter on approximately 04/18 - Exit on approximately 04/30

CONT YEAR	ENTRY DATE	ENTRY PRICE	EXIT DATE	EXIT PRICE	PROFIT	PROFIT AMOUNT	BEST EQUITY DATE	BEST EQUITY AMOUNT	WORST EQUITY DATE	WORST EQUITY AMOUNT
2005	04/18/05	0.190	04/29/05	0.220	0.024	240.00	04/29/05	240.00	04/26/05	-320.00
2004	04/19/04	0.090	04/30/04	0.110	0.022	220.00	04/30/04	220.00	04/26/04	-160.00
2003	04/21/03	-0.010	04/30/03	0.100	0.117	1170.00	04/30/03	1170.00		
2002	04/18/02	0.040	04/30/02	0.050	0.005	50.00	04/26/02	270.00	04/22/02	-60.00
2001	04/18/01	0.090	04/30/01	0.160	0.068	680.00	04/30/01	680.00		
2000	04/18/00	0.010	04/28/00	0.010	0.009	90.00	04/27/00	200.00	04/24/00	-10.00
1999	04/19/99	0.030	04/30/99	0.040	0.016	160.00	04/30/99	160.00	04/26/99	-100.00
1998	04/20/98	0.020	04/30/98	0.100	0.079	790.00	04/30/98	790.00	04/21/98	-160.00
1997	04/18/97	0.020	04/30/97	0.020	0.006	60.00	04/28/97	380.00	04/24/97	-40.00
1996	04/18/96	-0.070	04/30/96	-0.050	0.024	240.00	04/24/96	520.00	04/19/96	-110.00
1995	04/18/95	0.030	04/28/95	0.060	0.025	250.00	04/27/95	280.00	04/19/95	-360.00
1994	04/18/94	-0.010	04/29/94	0.080	0.099	990.00	04/29/94	990.00		
1993	04/19/93	-0.050	04/30/93	-0.050	0.006	60.00	04/26/93	750.00	04/22/93	-380.00
1992	04/20/92	0.000	04/30/92	0.000	0.001	10.00	04/24/92	140.00	04/22/92	-310.00
1991	04/18/91	0.050	04/30/91	0.020	-0.034	-340.00	04/22/91	100.00	04/30/91	-340.00
1990	04/18/90	0.090	04/30/90	0.110	0.023	230.00	04/20/90	350.00		

Percentage Correct		94						
Average Profit on Winning Trades					0.035	349.33	Winners	15
Average Loss on Trades					-0.034	-340.00	Losers	1
Average Net Profit Per Trade					0.031	306.25	Total trades	16

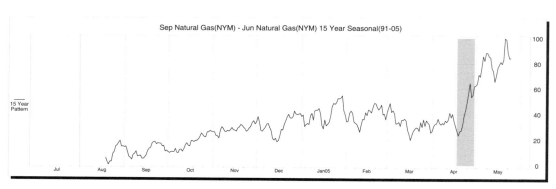

Sep Natural Gas(NYM) - Jun Natural Gas(NYM) 15 Year Seasonal(91-05)

After the heating season begins, spreads begin to perform more conventionally like bear spreads. Inventory accumulation has peaked, and premiums have already been placed on gas deliverable during months of peak usage. As the heating season progresses, utilities aggressively sell power by drawing on their inventories. In other words, the heating season generates liquidation. Thus, deferred contracts begin to outperform those more nearby as the market begins to deflate premiums on those nearby contracts.

Figure 2-30

Buy Dec Natural Gas(NYM) / Sell Jun Natural Gas(NYM)

Enter on approximately 04/22 - Exit on approximately 05/22

CONT YEAR	ENTRY DATE	ENTRY PRICE	EXIT DATE	EXIT PRICE	PROFIT	PROFIT AMOUNT	BEST EQUITY DATE	BEST EQUITY AMOUNT	WORST EQUITY DATE	WORST EQUITY AMOUNT
2005	04/22/05	1.070	05/20/05	1.240	0.167	1670.00	05/20/05	1670.00	04/26/05	-90.00
2004	04/22/04	0.450	05/21/04	0.430	-0.024	-240.00	05/18/04	320.00	05/13/04	-600.00
2003	04/22/03	0.170	05/22/03	0.340	0.163	1630.00	04/28/03	2150.00		
2002	04/22/02	0.450	05/22/02	0.670	0.223	2230.00	05/20/02	2310.00		
2001	04/23/01	0.440	05/22/01	0.560	0.119	1190.00	05/07/01	1530.00		
2000	04/24/00	0.190	05/22/00	0.240	0.051	510.00	05/16/00	880.00		
1999	04/22/99	0.330	05/21/99	0.420	0.085	850.00	05/12/99	910.00	04/26/99	-180.00
1998	04/22/98	0.290	05/22/98	0.500	0.215	2150.00	05/21/98	2260.00		
1997	04/22/97	0.240	05/22/97	0.240	0.008	80.00	04/28/97	330.00	05/14/97	-670.00
1996	04/22/96	0.030	05/22/96	0.080	0.047	470.00	05/03/96	980.00		
1995	04/24/95	0.210	05/22/95	0.320	0.111	1110.00	05/22/95	1110.00		
1994	04/22/94	0.210	05/20/94	0.410	0.193	1930.00	05/20/94	1930.00	04/25/94	-0.00
1993	04/22/93	0.160	05/21/93	0.400	0.238	2380.00	05/10/93	3050.00		
1992	04/22/92	0.510	05/21/92	0.270	-0.245	-2450.00	04/24/92	340.00	05/20/92	-3030.00
1991	04/22/91	0.720	05/21/91	0.630	-0.084	-840.00			04/30/91	-1190.00
1990	04/23/90	0.570	05/22/90	0.600	0.028	280.00	05/18/90	360.00	05/08/90	-150.00

Percentage Correct	81									
Average Profit on Winning Trades					0.127	1267.69		Winners		13
Average Loss on Trades					-0.118	-1176.67		Losers		3
Average Net Profit Per Trade					0.081	809.37		Total trades		16

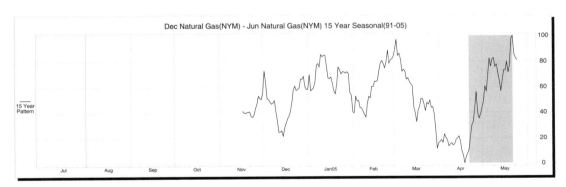

The seasonal pattern for May/April (Figure 2-40) depicts not only the overall tendencies and trends but also how this process tends to begin in November. The summary table details how the March contract, for example, has regularly outperformed January as the latter becomes front month.

Figure 2-31

Moore Research Center, Inc. — *Buy Dec Natural Gas(NYM) / Sell Jul Natural Gas(NYM)*

Enter on approximately 05/14 - Exit on approximately 06/28

CONT YEAR	ENTRY DATE	ENTRY PRICE	EXIT DATE	EXIT PRICE	PROFIT	PROFIT AMOUNT	BEST EQUITY DATE	BEST EQUITY AMOUNT	WORST EQUITY DATE	WORST EQUITY AMOUNT
2004	05/14/04	0.340	06/28/04	0.570	0.230	2300.00	06/28/04	2300.00	05/25/04	-140.00
2003	05/14/03	0.140	06/26/03	0.540	0.404	4040.00	06/12/03	4230.00		
2002	05/14/02	0.520	06/26/02	0.670	0.152	1520.00	06/21/02	1680.00		
2001	05/14/01	0.410	06/27/01	0.780	0.363	3630.00	06/27/01	3630.00	05/15/01	-70.00
2000	05/15/00	0.230	06/28/00	0.110	-0.120	-1200.00	05/16/00	220.00	06/27/00	-2570.00
1999	05/14/99	0.360	06/28/99	0.400	0.041	410.00	05/24/99	620.00	06/09/99	-320.00
1998	05/14/98	0.410	06/26/98	0.420	0.008	80.00	06/10/98	1730.00	06/25/98	-160.00
1997	05/14/97	0.170	06/24/97	0.200	0.034	340.00	06/11/97	1540.00	05/27/97	-30.00
1996	05/14/96	0.050	06/24/96	0.100	0.052	520.00	06/21/96	780.00	05/20/96	-480.00
1995	05/15/95	0.200	06/23/95	0.300	0.103	1030.00	06/23/95	1030.00	05/18/95	-80.00
1994	05/16/94	0.340	06/23/94	0.350	0.010	100.00	05/27/94	1020.00	06/15/94	-1490.00
1993	05/14/93	0.390	06/23/93	0.680	0.285	2850.00	06/23/93	2850.00	05/20/93	-430.00
1992	05/14/92	0.400	06/23/92	0.490	0.085	850.00	06/01/92	900.00	05/20/92	-390.00
1991	05/14/91	0.640	06/20/91	0.670	0.032	320.00	06/20/91	320.00	06/12/91	-610.00
1990	05/14/90	0.520	06/20/90	0.630	0.106	1060.00	06/20/90	1060.00		

Percentage Correct		93								
Average Profit on Winning Trades					0.136	1360.71		Winners		14
Average Loss on Trades					-0.120	-1200.00		Losers		1
Average Net Profit Per Trade					0.119	1190.00		Total trades		15

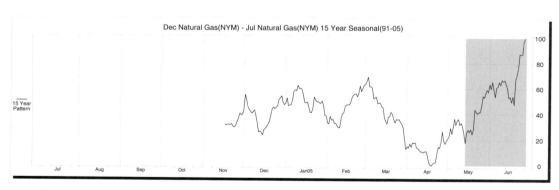

Dec Natural Gas(NYM) - Jul Natural Gas(NYM) 15 Year Seasonal(91-05)

The long April/short May strategy in the summary table (and Figure 2-37) shows how the process is temporarily interrupted during the first half of December, perhaps because the initial phase of liquidation was overdone with the coldest month of the year dead ahead. But thereafter and throughout the remainder of the heating season, bear spreads have been the rule. Once again, notice (in Figure 2-26) the cluster of entry dates around December 20-21.

Figure 2-32

Moore Research Center, Inc.

Buy Feb Natural Gas(NYM) / Sell Nov Natural Gas(NYM)

Enter on approximately 06/06 - Exit on approximately 07/22

CONT YEAR	ENTRY DATE	ENTRY PRICE	EXIT DATE	EXIT PRICE	PROFIT	PROFIT AMOUNT	BEST EQUITY DATE	BEST EQUITY AMOUNT	WORST EQUITY DATE	WORST EQUITY AMOUNT
2005	06/07/04	0.280	07/22/04	0.400	0.115	1150.00	07/20/04	1630.00	06/17/04	-350.00
2004	06/06/03	0.060	07/22/03	0.280	0.224	2240.00	07/22/03	2240.00		
2003	06/06/02	0.270	07/22/02	0.400	0.135	1350.00	07/17/02	1500.00	06/17/02	-70.00
2002	06/06/01	0.140	07/20/01	0.320	0.182	1820.00	07/20/01	1820.00	06/18/01	-350.00
2001	06/06/00	-0.150	07/21/00	-0.080	0.063	630.00	07/21/00	630.00	06/27/00	-890.00
2000	06/07/99	0.060	07/22/99	0.110	0.048	480.00	07/14/99	940.00	06/09/99	-40.00
1999	06/08/98	0.140	07/22/98	0.220	0.082	820.00	07/22/98	820.00	06/30/98	-1280.00
1998	06/06/97	0.080	07/22/97	0.100	0.018	180.00	06/11/97	250.00	06/24/97	-130.00
1997	06/06/96	-0.010	07/22/96	0.000	0.004	40.00	07/22/96	40.00	07/12/96	-1490.00
1996	06/06/95	0.030	07/21/95	0.140	0.112	1120.00	07/21/95	1120.00	06/14/95	-120.00
1995	06/06/94	0.000	07/22/94	0.050	0.047	470.00	07/22/94	470.00	07/01/94	-290.00
1994	06/07/93	-0.080	07/22/93	0.010	0.096	960.00	07/21/93	960.00	06/09/93	-150.00
1993	06/08/92	-0.070	07/22/92	-0.060	0.010	100.00	06/29/92	380.00	07/15/92	-20.00
1992	06/06/91	0.090	07/22/91	0.140	0.050	500.00	07/11/91	680.00	06/14/91	-100.00
1991	06/06/90	0.170	07/20/90	0.220	0.049	490.00	07/11/90	670.00	06/07/90	-80.00

Percentage Correct	100									
Average Profit on Winning Trades					0.082	823.33		Winners		15
Average Loss on Trades								Losers		0
Average Net Profit Per Trade					0.082	823.33		Total trades		15

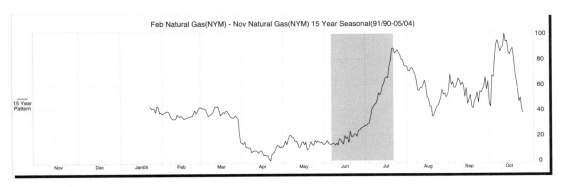

Feb Natural Gas(NYM) - Nov Natural Gas(NYM) 15 Year Seasonal(91/90-05/04)

The greatest difficulty and the well-deserved fear in trading those bear spreads is the potential for an unexpected or unexpectedly severe cold snap. In fact, as illustrated in the strategy table for the multi-month May/April spread (Figure 2-40), the most severe drawdowns in such bear spreads have tended to occur during or within a day or two of January, the coldest month of the year. The most notable exception? The enormous drawdown on the last day of February 2003 — just before the Iraq incursion.

Figure 2-33

Buy Dec Natural Gas(NYM) / Sell Sep Natural Gas(NYM)

Enter on approximately 06/19 - Exit on approximately 07/22

CONT YEAR	ENTRY DATE	ENTRY PRICE	EXIT DATE	EXIT PRICE	PROFIT	PROFIT AMOUNT	BEST EQUITY DATE	BEST EQUITY AMOUNT	WORST EQUITY DATE	WORST EQUITY AMOUNT
2004	06/21/04	0.440	07/22/04	0.610	0.174	1740.00	07/20/04	2670.00		
2003	06/19/03	0.280	07/22/03	0.470	0.195	1950.00	07/22/03	1950.00		
2002	06/19/02	0.560	07/22/02	0.630	0.065	650.00	07/12/02	1760.00		
2001	06/19/01	0.410	07/20/01	0.590	0.178	1780.00	07/06/01	3000.00		
2000	06/19/00	0.100	07/21/00	0.140	0.043	430.00	06/20/00	750.00	06/27/00	-220.00
1999	06/21/99	0.330	07/22/99	0.370	0.036	360.00	07/20/99	1100.00	06/29/99	-400.00
1998	06/19/98	0.380	07/22/98	0.580	0.202	2020.00	07/22/98	2020.00	06/30/98	-850.00
1997	06/19/97	0.250	07/22/97	0.300	0.052	520.00	07/22/97	520.00	06/24/97	-160.00
1996	06/19/96	0.030	07/22/96	0.110	0.084	840.00	07/22/96	840.00	07/15/96	-1070.00
1995	06/19/95	0.190	07/21/95	0.320	0.125	1250.00	07/21/95	1250.00		
1994	06/20/94	0.180	07/22/94	0.310	0.131	1310.00	07/22/94	1310.00	07/01/94	-340.00
1993	06/21/93	0.350	07/22/93	0.440	0.095	950.00	07/20/93	1080.00	07/08/93	-0.00
1992	06/19/92	0.500	07/22/92	0.380	-0.125	-1250.00	06/29/92	80.00	07/22/92	-1250.00
1991	06/19/91	0.610	07/22/91	0.700	0.091	910.00	07/16/91	1040.00		
1990	06/19/90	0.550	07/20/90	0.630	0.078	780.00	07/20/90	780.00	07/06/90	-450.00

Percentage Correct		93								
Average Profit on Winning Trades					0.111	1106.43		Winners		14
Average Loss on Trades					-0.125	-1250.00		Losers		1
Average Net Profit Per Trade					0.095	949.33		Total trades		15

HYPOTHETICAL PERFORMANCE RESULTS HAVE MANY INHERENT LIMITATIONS, SOME OF WHICH ARE DESCRIBED BELOW. NO REPRESENTATION IS BEING MADE THAT ANY ACCOUNT WILL OR IS LIKELY TO ACHIEVE PROFITS OR LOSSES SIMILAR TO THOSE SHOWN. IN FACT, THERE ARE FREQUENTLY SHARP DIFFERENCES BETWEEN HYPOTHETICAL PERFORMANCE RESULTS AND THE ACTUAL RESULTS SUBSEQUENTLY ACHIEVED BY ANY PARTICULAR TRADING PROGRAM. ONE OF THE LIMITATIONS OF HYPOTHETICAL PERFORMANCE RESULTS IS THAT THEY ARE GENERALLY PREPARED WITH THE BENEFIT OF HINDSIGHT. IN ADDITION, HYPOTHETICAL TRADING DOES NOT INVOLVE FINANCIAL RISK, AND NO HYPOTHETICAL TRADING RECORD CAN COMPLETELY ACCOUNT FOR THE IMPACT OF FINANCIAL RISK IN ACTUAL TRADING. FOR EXAMPLE, THE ABILITY TO WITHSTAND LOSSES OR ADHERE TO A PARTICULAR TRADING PROGRAM IN SPITE OF TRADING LOSSES ARE MATERIAL POINTS WHICH CAN ALSO ADVERSELY AFFECT ACTUAL TRADING RESULTS. THERE ARE NUMEROUS OTHER FACTORS RELATED TO THE MARKETS IN GENERAL OR TO THE IMPLEMENTATION OF ANY SPECIFIC TRADING PROGRAM WHICH CANNOT BE FULLY ACCOUNTED FOR IN THE PREPARATION OF HYPOTHETICAL PERFORMANCE RESULTS AND ALL OF WHICH CAN ADVERSELY AFFECT ACTUAL TRADING RESULTS. RESULTS NOT ADJUSTED FOR COMMISSION AND SLIPPAGE.

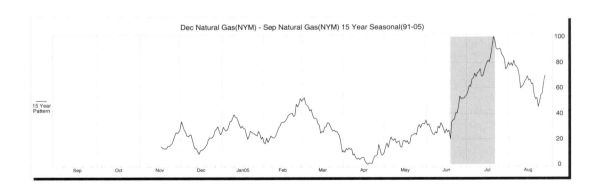

Dec Natural Gas(NYM) - Sep Natural Gas(NYM) 15 Year Seasonal(91-05)

Figure 2-34

Buy Nov Natural Gas(NYM) / Sell Oct Natural Gas(NYM)

Enter on approximately 08/29 - Exit on approximately 09/14

CONT YEAR	ENTRY DATE	ENTRY PRICE	EXIT DATE	EXIT PRICE	PROFIT	PROFIT AMOUNT	BEST EQUITY DATE	BEST EQUITY AMOUNT	WORST EQUITY DATE	WORST EQUITY AMOUNT
2004	08/30/04	0.620	09/14/04	0.790	0.172	1720.00	09/10/04	3540.00	09/01/04	-240.00
2003	08/29/03	0.250	09/12/03	0.260	0.019	190.00	09/02/03	220.00	09/10/03	-400.00
2002	08/29/02	0.300	09/13/02	0.370	0.070	700.00	09/11/02	900.00		
2001	08/29/01	0.290	09/14/01	0.350	0.060	600.00	09/14/01	600.00	09/07/01	-100.00
2000	08/29/00	0.050	09/14/00	0.110	0.063	630.00	09/11/00	700.00	08/30/00	-50.00
1999	08/30/99	0.100	09/14/99	0.170	0.072	720.00	09/14/99	720.00		
1998	08/31/98	0.220	09/14/98	0.260	0.042	420.00	09/11/98	560.00	09/01/98	-190.00
1997	08/29/97	0.100	09/12/97	0.130	0.027	270.00	09/10/97	350.00		
1996	08/29/96	0.130	09/13/96	0.200	0.069	690.00	09/10/96	1100.00		
1995	08/29/95	0.100	09/14/95	0.130	0.031	310.00	09/12/95	410.00	08/30/95	-70.00
1994	08/29/94	0.210	09/14/94	0.240	0.029	290.00	09/09/94	420.00		
1993	08/30/93	0.060	09/14/93	0.100	0.037	370.00	09/10/93	440.00		
1992	08/31/92	0.000	09/14/92	0.080	0.092	920.00	09/14/92	920.00		
1991	08/29/91	0.240	09/13/91	0.270	0.026	260.00	09/13/91	260.00	09/10/91	-440.00
1990	08/29/90	0.270	09/14/90	0.280	0.015	150.00	09/05/90	510.00	09/12/90	-80.00

Percentage Correct	100								
Average Profit on Winning Trades				0.055	549.33		Winners		15
Average Loss on Trades							Losers		0
Average Net Profit Per Trade				0.055	549.33		Total trades		15

HYPOTHETICAL PERFORMANCE RESULTS HAVE MANY INHERENT LIMITATIONS, SOME OF WHICH ARE DESCRIBED BELOW. NO REPRESENTATION IS BEING MADE THAT ANY ACCOUNT WILL OR IS LIKELY TO ACHIEVE PROFITS OR LOSSES SIMILAR TO THOSE SHOWN. IN FACT, THERE ARE FREQUENTLY SHARP DIFFERENCES BETWEEN HYPOTHETICAL PERFORMANCE RESULTS AND THE ACTUAL RESULTS SUBSEQUENTLY ACHIEVED BY ANY PARTICULAR TRADING PROGRAM. ONE OF THE LIMITATIONS OF HYPOTHETICAL PERFORMANCE RESULTS IS THAT THEY ARE GENERALLY PREPARED WITH THE BENEFIT OF HINDSIGHT. IN ADDITION, HYPOTHETICAL TRADING DOES NOT INVOLVE FINANCIAL RISK, AND NO HYPOTHETICAL TRADING RECORD CAN COMPLETELY ACCOUNT FOR THE IMPACT OF FINANCIAL RISK IN ACTUAL TRADING. FOR EXAMPLE, THE ABILITY TO WITHSTAND LOSSES OR ADHERE TO A PARTICULAR TRADING PROGRAM IN SPITE OF TRADING LOSSES ARE MATERIAL POINTS WHICH CAN ALSO ADVERSELY AFFECT ACTUAL TRADING RESULTS. THERE ARE NUMEROUS OTHER FACTORS RELATED TO THE MARKETS IN GENERAL OR TO THE IMPLEMENTATION OF ANY SPECIFIC TRADING PROGRAM WHICH CANNOT BE FULLY ACCOUNTED FOR IN THE PREPARATION OF HYPOTHETICAL PERFORMANCE RESULTS AND ALL OF WHICH CAN ADVERSELY AFFECT ACTUAL TRADING RESULTS. RESULTS NOT ADJUSTED FOR COMMISSION AND SLIPPAGE.

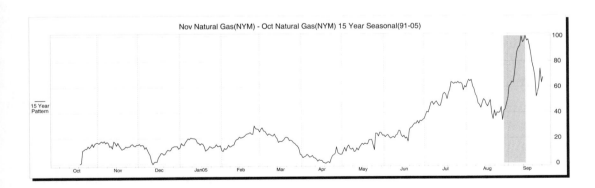

Nov Natural Gas(NYM) - Oct Natural Gas(NYM) 15 Year Seasonal(91-05)

Figure 2-35

Buy Nov Natural Gas(NYM) / Sell Dec Natural Gas(NYM)

Enter on approximately 10/11 - Exit on approximately 10/26

CONT YEAR	ENTRY DATE	ENTRY PRICE	EXIT DATE	EXIT PRICE	PROFIT	PROFIT AMOUNT	BEST EQUITY DATE	BEST EQUITY AMOUNT	WORST EQUITY DATE	WORST EQUITY AMOUNT
2004	10/11/04	-1.170	10/26/04	-0.960	0.210	2100.00	10/22/04	2820.00	10/12/04	-940.00
2003	10/13/03	-0.410	10/24/03	-0.260	0.148	1480.00	10/24/03	1480.00	10/17/03	-170.00
2002	10/11/02	-0.190	10/25/02	-0.160	0.030	300.00	10/25/02	300.00	10/18/02	-330.00
2001	10/11/01	-0.300	10/26/01	-0.140	0.160	1600.00	10/26/01	1600.00	10/18/01	-120.00
2000	10/11/00	-0.090	10/26/00	-0.080	0.002	20.00	10/26/00	20.00	10/16/00	-370.00
1999	10/11/99	-0.180	10/26/99	-0.130	0.051	510.00	10/25/99	820.00	10/18/99	-320.00
1998	10/12/98	-0.290	10/26/98	-0.270	0.016	160.00	10/16/98	470.00		
1997	10/13/97	-0.100	10/24/97	-0.090	0.013	130.00	10/17/97	420.00		
1996	10/11/96	-0.180	10/25/96	-0.050	0.133	1330.00	10/25/96	1330.00		
1995	10/11/95	-0.130	10/24/95	-0.030	0.101	1010.00	10/24/95	1010.00	10/12/95	-20.00
1994	10/11/94	-0.310	10/24/94	-0.250	0.065	650.00	10/20/94	750.00	10/12/94	-90.00
1993	10/11/93	-0.160	10/22/93	-0.150	0.007	70.00	10/19/93	350.00		
1992	10/12/92	-0.050	10/23/92	0.150	0.205	2050.00	10/23/92	2050.00	10/13/92	-350.00
1991	10/11/91	-0.180	10/24/91	-0.290	-0.109	-1090.00	10/21/91	400.00	10/24/91	-1090.00
1990	10/11/90	-0.540	10/22/90	-0.400	0.150	1500.00	10/22/90	1500.00	10/12/90	-60.00

Percentage Correct		93								
Average Profit on Winning Trades					0.092	922.14		Winners		14
Average Loss on Trades					-0.109	-1090.00		Losers		1
Average Net Profit Per Trade					0.079	788.00		Total trades		15

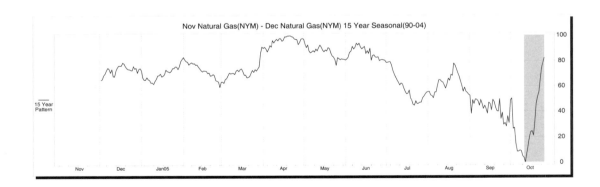

Nov Natural Gas(NYM) - Dec Natural Gas(NYM) 15 Year Seasonal(90-04)

15 Year Pattern

Figure 2-36

Moore Research Center, Inc.	**Buy Mar Natural Gas(NYM) / Sell Jan Natural Gas(NYM)**

Enter on approximately 11/22 - Exit on approximately 11/30

CONT YEAR	ENTRY DATE	ENTRY PRICE	EXIT DATE	EXIT PRICE	PROFIT	PROFIT AMOUNT	BEST EQUITY DATE	BEST EQUITY AMOUNT	WORST EQUITY DATE	WORST EQUITY AMOUNT
2005	11/22/04	-0.060	11/30/04	-0.060	0.005	50.00	11/30/04	50.00	11/24/04	-2150.00
2004	11/24/03	-0.050	11/26/03	-0.040	0.012	120.00	11/26/03	120.00	11/25/03	-200.00
2003	11/22/02	-0.180	11/27/02	-0.150	0.030	300.00	11/26/02	320.00		
2002	11/26/01	0.000	11/30/01	0.090	0.091	910.00	11/29/01	1140.00		
2001	11/22/00	-0.980	11/30/00	-0.750	0.231	2310.00	11/29/00	3390.00		
2000	11/22/99	-0.020	11/30/99	0.000	0.015	150.00	11/30/99	150.00	11/23/99	-130.00
1999	11/23/98	-0.060	11/30/98	0.020	0.088	880.00	11/30/98	880.00	11/24/98	-250.00
1998	11/24/97	-0.280	11/26/97	-0.240	0.048	480.00	11/26/97	480.00		
1997	11/22/96	-0.810	11/27/96	-0.790	0.019	190.00	11/27/96	190.00	11/26/96	-390.00
1996	11/22/95	-0.280	11/30/95	-0.190	0.096	960.00	11/30/95	960.00		
1995	11/22/94	-0.030	11/30/94	0.050	0.089	890.00	11/30/94	890.00		
1994	11/22/93	-0.240	11/30/93	-0.180	0.057	570.00	11/30/93	570.00		
1993	11/23/92	-0.500	11/30/92	-0.460	0.036	360.00	11/25/92	480.00		
1992	11/22/91	-0.580	11/29/91	-0.590	-0.004	-40.00	11/26/91	160.00	11/27/91	-60.00
1991	11/23/90	-0.700	11/30/90	-0.570	0.129	1290.00	11/30/90	1290.00	11/26/90	-200.00

Percentage Correct	93									
Average Profit on Winning Trades					0.068	675.71		Winners		14
Average Loss on Trades					-0.004	-40.00		Losers		1
Average Net Profit Per Trade					0.063	628.00		Total trades		15

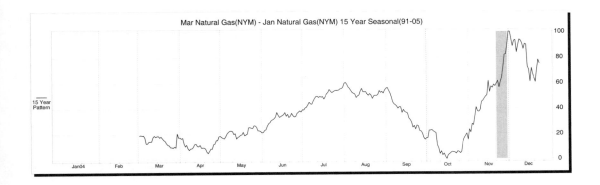

Mar Natural Gas(NYM) - Jan Natural Gas(NYM) 15 Year Seasonal(91-05)

Figure 2-37

Buy Apr Natural Gas(NYM) / Sell May Natural Gas(NYM)

Moore Research Center, Inc.

Enter on approximately 11/29 - Exit on approximately 12/15

CONT YEAR	ENTRY DATE	ENTRY PRICE	EXIT DATE	EXIT PRICE	PROFIT	PROFIT AMOUNT	BEST EQUITY DATE	BEST EQUITY AMOUNT	WORST EQUITY DATE	WORST EQUITY AMOUNT
2005	11/29/04	0.140	12/15/04	0.050	-0.090	-900.00			12/15/04	-900.00
2004	12/01/03	0.050	12/15/03	0.290	0.240	2400.00	12/10/03	2600.00		
2003	12/02/02	0.050	12/13/02	0.140	0.090	900.00	12/13/02	900.00	12/03/02	-100.00
2002	11/29/01	-0.050	12/14/01	-0.040	0.002	20.00	12/04/01	150.00	12/07/01	-70.00
2001	11/29/00	0.210	12/15/00	0.410	0.199	1990.00	12/11/00	4540.00		
2000	11/29/99	-0.010	12/15/99	0.010	0.023	230.00	12/14/99	290.00	12/06/99	-90.00
1999	11/30/98	-0.010	12/15/98	0.000	0.017	170.00	12/14/98	200.00	12/02/98	-50.00
1998	12/01/97	0.040	12/15/97	0.010	-0.027	-270.00			12/04/97	-300.00
1997	12/02/96	0.080	12/13/96	0.240	0.157	1570.00	12/13/96	1570.00		
1996	11/29/95	0.000	12/15/95	0.090	0.097	970.00	12/15/95	970.00		
1995	11/29/94	0.000	12/15/94	0.000	0.003	30.00	12/08/94	60.00	12/02/94	-40.00
1994	11/29/93	0.000	12/15/93	0.000	0.003	30.00	12/14/93	30.00	12/06/93	-70.00
1993	11/30/92	0.000	12/15/92	0.010	0.010	100.00	12/10/92	150.00	12/01/92	-80.00
1992	11/29/91	0.000	12/13/91	0.000	0.010	100.00	12/12/91	100.00	12/06/91	-0.00
1991	11/29/90	0.000	12/14/90	0.000	0.005	50.00	12/12/90	110.00	12/06/90	-100.00

Percentage Correct		87								
Average Profit on Winning Trades					0.066	658.46		Winners		13
Average Loss on Trades					-0.059	-585.00		Losers		2
Average Net Profit Per Trade					0.049	492.67		Total trades		15

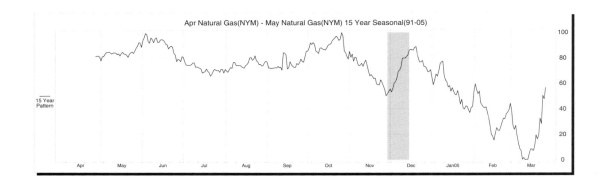

Apr Natural Gas(NYM) - May Natural Gas(NYM) 15 Year Seasonal(91-05)

Figure 2-38

Buy Jun Natural Gas(NYM) / Sell Mar Natural Gas(NYM)

Enter on approximately 12/20 - Exit on approximately 02/16

CONT YEAR	ENTRY DATE	ENTRY PRICE	EXIT DATE	EXIT PRICE	PROFIT	PROFIT AMOUNT	BEST EQUITY DATE	BEST EQUITY AMOUNT	WORST EQUITY DATE	WORST EQUITY AMOUNT
2005	12/20/04	-0.430	02/16/05	0.210	0.653	6530.00	02/16/05	6530.00		
2004	12/22/03	-1.080	02/13/04	-0.160	0.922	9220.00	02/11/04	10370.00	01/09/04	-5890.00
2003	12/20/02	-0.610	02/14/03	-0.500	0.105	1050.00	01/06/03	3500.00	02/03/03	-1610.00
2002	12/20/01	0.080	02/15/02	0.200	0.120	1200.00	01/28/02	1830.00	12/21/01	-450.00
2001	12/20/00	-2.810	02/16/01	-0.060	2.748	27480.00	02/15/01	27570.00	12/29/00	-5800.00
2000	12/20/99	-0.070	02/16/00	0.040	0.123	1230.00	01/05/00	1520.00	02/02/00	-1090.00
1999	12/21/98	0.000	02/16/99	0.070	0.073	730.00	02/01/99	1050.00	01/04/99	-540.00
1998	12/22/97	-0.090	02/13/98	0.080	0.174	1740.00	01/28/98	1950.00		
1997	12/20/96	-0.980	02/14/97	0.000	0.983	9830.00	02/14/97	9830.00		
1996	12/20/95	-0.470	02/16/96	-0.460	0.019	190.00	01/22/96	3400.00	01/31/96	-2240.00
1995	12/20/94	0.030	02/16/95	0.110	0.083	830.00	01/25/95	1040.00	12/30/94	-670.00
1994	12/20/93	0.000	02/16/94	-0.170	-0.179	-1790.00	12/21/93	150.00	02/01/94	-4630.00
1993	12/21/92	-0.080	02/16/93	-0.030	0.047	470.00	02/02/93	1500.00	12/23/92	-250.00
1992	12/20/91	-0.050	02/14/92	0.080	0.141	1410.00	02/14/92	1410.00	12/30/91	-30.00
1991	12/20/90	-0.070	02/15/91	0.050	0.130	1300.00	02/13/91	1730.00	12/26/90	-400.00

Percentage Correct	93									
Average Profit on Winning Trades					0.452	4515.00		Winners		14
Average Loss on Trades					-0.179	-1790.00		Losers		1
Average Net Profit Per Trade					0.409	4094.67		Total trades		15

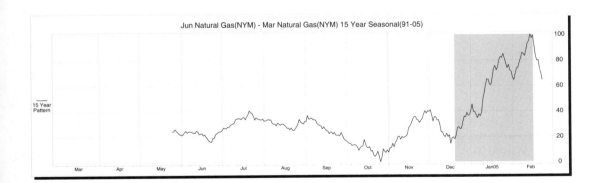

Jun Natural Gas(NYM) - Mar Natural Gas(NYM) 15 Year Seasonal(91-05)

Figure 2-39

Moore Research Center, Inc.	*Buy Jun Natural Gas(NYM) / Sell Feb Natural Gas(NYM)*

Enter on approximately 12/21 - Exit on approximately 01/23

CONT YEAR	ENTRY DATE	ENTRY PRICE	EXIT DATE	EXIT PRICE	PROFIT	PROFIT AMOUNT	BEST EQUITY DATE	BEST EQUITY AMOUNT	WORST EQUITY DATE	WORST EQUITY AMOUNT
2005	12/21/04	-0.410	01/21/05	0.000	0.411	4110.00	01/12/05	5000.00	12/22/04	-10.00
2004	12/22/03	-1.430	01/23/04	-0.770	0.668	6680.00	01/15/04	8900.00	01/09/04	-3280.00
2003	12/23/02	-0.750	01/23/03	-0.580	0.172	1720.00	01/06/03	4320.00	12/24/02	-200.00
2002	12/21/01	0.020	01/23/02	0.250	0.233	2330.00	01/23/02	2330.00		
2001	12/21/00	-3.920	01/23/01	-1.520	2.399	23990.00	01/17/01	24760.00	12/29/00	-4550.00
2000	12/21/99	-0.080	01/21/00	0.020	0.104	1040.00	01/07/00	2060.00		
1999	12/21/98	0.000	01/22/99	0.110	0.113	1130.00	01/22/99	1130.00	01/04/99	-680.00
1998	12/22/97	-0.130	01/23/98	0.070	0.217	2170.00	01/23/98	2170.00		
1997	12/23/96	-1.410	01/23/97	-0.700	0.713	7130.00	12/30/96	7600.00		
1996	12/21/95	-0.920	01/23/96	-0.600	0.317	3170.00	01/16/96	6580.00	01/03/96	-2390.00
1995	12/21/94	0.040	01/23/95	0.120	0.084	840.00	01/13/95	1370.00	12/27/94	-710.00
1994	12/21/93	0.000	01/21/94	-0.270	-0.285	-2850.00			01/17/94	-3830.00
1993	12/21/92	-0.220	01/22/93	-0.050	0.166	1660.00	01/19/93	2180.00	12/23/92	-860.00
1992	12/23/91	-0.150	01/23/92	0.100	0.261	2610.00	01/23/92	2610.00	12/24/91	-50.00
1991	12/21/90	-0.390	01/22/91	-0.060	0.326	3260.00	01/22/91	3260.00	12/26/90	-420.00

Percentage Correct	93									
Average Profit on Winning Trades					0.442	4417.14		Winners		14
Average Loss on Trades					-0.285	-2850.00		Losers		1
Average Net Profit Per Trade					0.393	3932.67		Total trades		15

HYPOTHETICAL PERFORMANCE RESULTS HAVE MANY INHERENT LIMITATIONS, SOME OF WHICH ARE DESCRIBED BELOW. NO REPRESENTATION IS BEING MADE THAT ANY ACCOUNT WILL OR IS LIKELY TO ACHIEVE PROFITS OR LOSSES SIMILAR TO THOSE SHOWN. IN FACT, THERE ARE FREQUENTLY SHARP DIFFERENCES BETWEEN HYPOTHETICAL PERFORMANCE RESULTS AND THE ACTUAL RESULTS SUBSEQUENTLY ACHIEVED BY ANY PARTICULAR TRADING PROGRAM. ONE OF THE LIMITATIONS OF HYPOTHETICAL PERFORMANCE RESULTS IS THAT THEY ARE GENERALLY PREPARED WITH THE BENEFIT OF HINDSIGHT. IN ADDITION, HYPOTHETICAL TRADING DOES NOT INVOLVE FINANCIAL RISK, AND NO HYPOTHETICAL TRADING RECORD CAN COMPLETELY ACCOUNT FOR THE IMPACT OF FINANCIAL RISK IN ACTUAL TRADING. FOR EXAMPLE, THE ABILITY TO WITHSTAND LOSSES OR ADHERE TO A PARTICULAR TRADING PROGRAM IN SPITE OF TRADING LOSSES ARE MATERIAL POINTS WHICH CAN ALSO ADVERSELY AFFECT ACTUAL TRADING RESULTS. THERE ARE NUMEROUS OTHER FACTORS RELATED TO THE MARKETS IN GENERAL OR TO THE IMPLEMENTATION OF ANY SPECIFIC TRADING PROGRAM WHICH CANNOT BE FULLY ACCOUNTED FOR IN THE PREPARATION OF HYPOTHETICAL PERFORMANCE RESULTS AND ALL OF WHICH CAN ADVERSELY AFFECT ACTUAL TRADING RESULTS. RESULTS NOT ADJUSTED FOR COMMISSION AND SLIPPAGE.

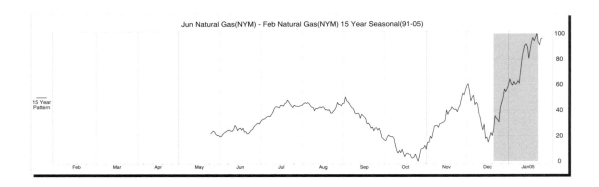

Jun Natural Gas(NYM) - Feb Natural Gas(NYM) 15 Year Seasonal(91-05)

Figure 2-40

Buy May Natural Gas(NYM) / Sell Apr Natural Gas(NYM)

Moore Research Center, Inc.

Enter on approximately 12/21 - Exit on approximately 03/12

CONT YEAR	ENTRY DATE	ENTRY PRICE	EXIT DATE	EXIT PRICE	PROFIT	PROFIT AMOUNT	BEST EQUITY DATE	BEST EQUITY AMOUNT	WORST EQUITY DATE	WORST EQUITY AMOUNT
2005	12/21/04	-0.020	03/11/05	0.110	0.143	1430.00	03/07/05	1620.00		
2004	12/22/03	-0.200	03/12/04	0.080	0.291	2910.00	03/11/04	2950.00	01/09/04	-1370.00
2003	12/23/02	-0.130	03/12/03	-0.060	0.072	720.00	03/12/03	720.00	02/28/03	-18930.00
2002	12/21/01	0.030	03/12/02	0.040	0.008	80.00	01/23/02	610.00		
2001	12/21/00	-0.640	03/12/01	0.040	0.690	6900.00	03/09/01	7130.00	12/29/00	-1500.00
2000	12/21/99	0.000	03/10/00	0.020	0.040	400.00	03/07/00	480.00	02/02/00	-400.00
1999	12/21/98	0.010	03/12/99	0.030	0.016	160.00	02/01/99	260.00	01/04/99	-170.00
1998	12/22/97	-0.020	03/12/98	0.030	0.055	550.00	03/09/98	650.00		
1997	12/23/96	-0.210	03/12/97	0.070	0.288	2880.00	03/10/97	3030.00	01/08/97	-1030.00
1996	12/21/95	-0.170	03/12/96	-0.060	0.115	1150.00	01/15/96	1390.00	02/26/96	-200.00
1995	12/21/94	0.010	03/10/95	0.050	0.041	410.00	02/15/95	550.00	12/30/94	-150.00
1994	12/21/93	0.010	03/11/94	0.030	0.026	260.00	03/11/94	260.00	02/01/94	-1400.00
1993	12/21/92	-0.010	03/12/93	-0.040	-0.031	-310.00	02/01/93	360.00	02/23/93	-540.00
1992	12/23/91	0.000	03/12/92	0.000	0.009	90.00	03/10/92	270.00		
1991	12/21/90	0.000	03/12/91	0.010	0.015	150.00	01/30/91	400.00	01/23/91	-130.00

Percentage Correct	93									
Average Profit on Winning Trades					0.129	1292.14		Winners		14
Average Loss on Trades					-0.031	-310.00		Losers		1
Average Net Profit Per Trade					0.119	1185.33		Total trades		15

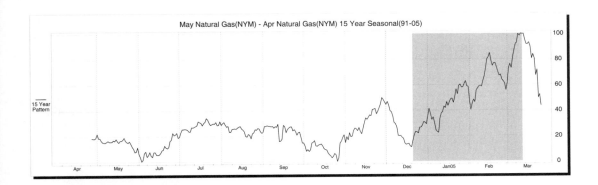

May Natural Gas(NYM) - Apr Natural Gas(NYM) 15 Year Seasonal(91-05)

15 Year Pattern

Inter-market Spreads

NYMEX recognizes a variety of spreads between and among its several energy markets. Many have commercial applications but are too complex or esoteric for most speculative traders. But there are a few straightforward, easily understood, and widely traded spreads.

Products: Gasoline versus Heating Oil

Figure 2-41: Gasoline vs Heating Oil Spread Strategies

Moore Research Center, Inc.	Gasoline vs Heating Oil Spread Strategies							
Seasonal Strategy	Entry Date	Exit Date	Win Pct	Win Yrs	Loss Years	Total Years	Average Profit	Ave Pft Per Day
Buy Jul Unleaded Reg.(NYM)	2/23	5/04	87	13	2	15	926	13
Sell Jul Heating Oil #2(NYM)			80	16	4	20	1115	16
Buy Jan Heating Oil #2(NYM)	8/07	9/12	87	13	2	15	632	17
Sell Jan Unleaded Reg.(NYM)			85	17	3	20	551	15
Buy Mar Unleaded Reg.(NYM)	12/19	2/03	87	13	2	15	1365	29
Sell Mar Heating Oil #2(NYM)			90	18	2	20	1428	30
Buy Jun Unleaded Reg.(NYM)	2/08	3/29	93	14	1	15	782	16
Sell Jun Heating Oil #2(NYM)			90	18	2	20	668	13
Buy Jul Unleaded Reg.(NYM)	2/24	3/29	100	15	0	15	620	18
Sell Jul Heating Oil #2(NYM)			100	20	0	20	670	20
Buy Jun Unleaded Reg.(NYM)	2/25	5/26	87	13	2	15	1445	16
Sell Jun Heating Oil #2(NYM)			80	16	4	20	1579	17
Buy Jun Unleaded Reg.(NYM)	4/12	4/27	93	14	1	15	515	32
Sell Jun Heating Oil #2(NYM)			85	17	3	20	592	37
Buy Jul Heating Oil #2(NYM)	5/28	6/21	93	14	1	15	1323	53
Sell Jul Unleaded Reg.(NYM)			89	17	2	19	1201	48
Buy Dec Unleaded Reg.(NYM)	10/06	11/05	87	13	2	15	1075	35
Sell Dec Heating Oil #2(NYM)			85	17	3	20	883	28
Buy Jan Unleaded Reg.(NYM)	10/12	10/31	87	13	2	15	401	20
Sell Jan Heating Oil #2(NYM)			80	16	4	20	319	16
Buy May Unleaded Reg.(NYM)	12/05	2/03	93	14	1	15	830	14
Sell May Heating Oil #2(NYM)			95	19	1	20	899	15
Buy Apr Unleaded Reg.(NYM)	12/11	1/31	93	14	1	15	944	18
Sell Apr Heating Oil #2(NYM)			95	19	1	20	980	19

The inverse relationship between gasoline and heating oil consumption, for example, generates logical spreads. Rising demand for one offsets falling demand for the other and is reflected in the changing value of each product. Refiners alter their production in response to changes in those product values. Because such transitions are seasonal, changes in product values tend to drive reliable, often dynamic seasonal spread movement.

The US vacation and driving season opens the last Monday of May. The pattern of trading in these product spreads early in the year may best be illustrated by their July relationship (Figure 2-42). The seasonal pattern in Figure 2-43 depicts how product values most favor heating oil at the expense of gasoline during October/November when driving conditions are deteriorating but market anxiety about heating oil supply is peaking. But as winter gets underway, those product values reverse, as illustrated in Figure 2-44. Inventories of heating oil compete with new production from refineries running at capacity to supply the

Figure 2-42

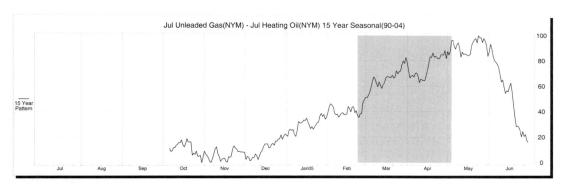

Moore Research Center, Inc.		**Buy Jul Unleaded Reg.(NYM) / Sell Jul Heating Oil #2(NYM)**								
		Enter on approximately 02/23 - Exit on approximately 05/04								
CONT YEAR	ENTRY DATE	ENTRY PRICE	EXIT DATE	EXIT PRICE	PROFIT	PROFIT AMOUNT	BEST EQUITY DATE	BEST EQUITY AMOUNT	WORST EQUITY DATE	WORST EQUITY AMOUNT
2005	02/23/05	10.30	05/04/05	1.96	-8.34	-3502.80	03/28/05	819.00	05/04/05	-3502.80
2004	02/23/04	18.59	05/04/04	27.86	9.28	3897.60	05/04/04	3897.60	03/09/04	-1033.20
2003	02/24/03	14.99	05/02/03	8.57	-6.41	-2692.20	03/07/03	592.20	05/02/03	-2692.20
2002	02/25/02	10.69	05/03/02	11.35	0.67	281.40	03/19/02	1394.40	02/26/02	-197.40
2001	02/23/01	14.87	05/04/01	25.04	10.17	4271.40	05/04/01	4271.40	03/05/01	-856.80
2000	02/23/00	12.35	05/04/00	18.93	6.58	2763.60	05/04/00	2763.60	04/10/00	-445.20
1999	02/23/99	6.60	05/04/99	10.09	3.49	1465.80	05/04/99	1465.80	02/24/99	-168.00
1998	02/23/98	7.11	05/04/98	8.55	1.44	604.80	04/17/98	709.80	03/10/98	-407.40
1997	02/24/97	6.28	05/02/97	6.39	0.10	42.00	03/19/97	924.00	04/10/97	-197.40
1996	02/23/96	8.07	05/03/96	12.65	4.59	1927.80	04/25/96	2692.20	03/05/96	-109.20
1995	02/23/95	8.17	05/04/95	10.35	2.17	911.40	05/01/95	1117.20	03/10/95	-466.20
1994	02/23/94	2.52	05/04/94	2.78	0.25	105.00	04/06/94	495.60	04/28/94	-96.60
1993	02/23/93	4.24	05/04/93	5.36	1.13	474.60	03/04/93	525.00	02/24/93	-71.40
1992	02/24/92	7.79	05/04/92	8.88	1.08	453.60	03/05/92	558.60	04/14/92	-739.20
1991	02/25/91	6.71	05/03/91	13.57	6.86	2881.20	05/02/91	2948.40		
1990	02/23/90	7.21	05/04/90	9.39	2.17	911.40	04/24/90	1167.60	02/27/90	-348.60
1989	02/23/89	6.60	05/04/89	18.37	11.77	4943.40	05/02/89	5623.80	03/02/89	-100.80
1988	02/23/88	3.57	05/04/88	3.55	-0.02	-8.40	03/17/88	281.40	04/21/88	-189.00
1987	02/23/87	5.25	05/04/87	3.28	-1.96	-823.20	03/23/87	420.00	05/04/87	-823.20
1986	02/24/86	0.29	05/02/86	8.35	8.06	3385.20	05/01/86	3532.20	02/25/86	-420.00

Percentage Correct	87					
Average Profit on Winning Trades				3.68	1544.63	Winners	13
Average Loss on Trades				-7.38	-3097.50	Losers	2
Average Net Profit Per Trade				2.20	925.68	Total trades	15
Percentage Correct	80					
Average Profit on Winning Trades				4.36	1832.51	Winners	16
Average Loss on Trades				-4.18	-1756.65	Losers	4
Average Net Profit Per Trade				2.65	1114.68	Total trades	20

retail market. By January, the industry increasingly worries about potentially excess heating oil at the end of winter.

February marks the beginning of another transition. The heating season is ending, and driving conditions will soon improve. Refiners begin a switchover. The focus must now be not only on gasoline rather than heating oil but on gasoline formulated for summer driving, stocks of which are nonexistent. Thus, by February, gasoline for delivery after April — when

Figure 2-43

Buy Jan Heating Oil #2(NYM) / Sell Jan Unleaded Reg.(NYM)

Enter on approximately 08/07 - Exit on approximately 09/12

CONT YEAR	ENTRY DATE	ENTRY PRICE	EXIT DATE	EXIT PRICE	PROFIT	PROFIT AMOUNT	BEST EQUITY DATE	BEST EQUITY AMOUNT	WORST EQUITY DATE	WORST EQUITY AMOUNT
2005	08/09/04	3.08	09/10/04	4.70	1.61	676.20	09/09/04	840.00	08/13/04	-693.00
2004	08/07/03	4.02	09/12/03	1.24	-2.78	-1167.60	08/22/03	54.60	09/12/03	-1167.60
2003	08/07/02	-0.18	09/12/02	1.87	2.06	865.20	09/06/02	1134.00	08/09/02	-130.20
2002	08/07/01	2.32	09/10/01	5.28	2.96	1243.20	08/28/01	1482.60		
2001	08/07/00	3.25	09/12/00	12.95	9.71	4078.20	09/12/00	4078.20	08/08/00	-25.20
2000	08/09/99	-1.50	09/10/99	-1.42	0.07	29.40	08/26/99	159.60	09/03/99	-273.00
1999	08/07/98	-2.29	09/11/98	-1.17	1.13	474.60	09/10/98	499.80	08/24/98	-369.60
1998	08/07/97	0.33	09/12/97	-0.10	-0.45	-189.00	08/14/97	352.80	09/02/97	-537.60
1997	08/07/96	2.14	09/12/96	4.53	2.40	1008.00	09/03/96	1041.60		
1996	08/07/95	0.21	09/12/95	0.67	0.45	189.00	09/05/95	310.80	08/10/95	-210.00
1995	08/08/94	-2.89	09/12/94	-1.63	1.27	533.40	09/06/94	827.40		
1994	08/09/93	3.89	09/10/93	4.94	1.05	441.00	09/10/93	441.00		
1993	08/07/92	5.73	09/11/92	7.16	1.42	596.40	09/11/92	596.40	08/11/92	-336.00
1992	08/07/91	4.78	09/12/91	6.21	1.44	604.80	08/20/91	1381.80		
1991	08/07/90	4.20	09/12/90	4.42	0.23	96.60	09/10/90	1331.40	08/29/90	-84.00
1990	08/07/89	3.89	09/12/89	4.04	0.16	67.20	08/21/89	411.60	08/08/89	-33.60
1989	08/08/88	4.07	09/12/88	4.22	0.15	63.00	08/12/88	197.40	08/29/88	-130.20
1988	08/07/87	3.69	09/11/87	4.12	0.42	176.40	09/01/87	365.40	08/20/87	-273.00
1987	08/07/86	4.17	09/12/86	3.76	-0.40	-168.00	08/26/86	470.40	09/09/86	-369.60
1986	08/07/85	5.15	09/12/85	8.50	3.35	1407.00	09/10/85	1932.00	08/19/85	-357.00

Percentage Correct	87								
Average Profit on Winning Trades				1.98	833.54		Winners	13	
Average Loss on Trades				-1.61	-678.30		Losers	2	
Average Net Profit Per Trade				1.50	631.96		Total trades	15	
Percentage Correct	85								
Average Profit on Winning Trades				1.76	738.21		Winners	17	
Average Loss on Trades				-1.21	-508.20		Losers	3	
Average Net Profit Per Trade				1.31	551.25		Total trades	20	

Jan Heating Oil(NYM) - Jan Unleaded Gas(NYM) 15 Year Seasonal(91-05)

heating season is over and stricter emission standards take effect — has regularly and aggressively begun to outperform heating oil.

Of the first several strategies in the summary table (Figure 2-41), two exit at the end of March, the last month before higher emission standards begin taking effect. The first (February 8 through March 29) would have worked for all 18 years 1987-2004. The second (entry February 24) would have worked for all 20 years in which gasoline futures have traded

---

Figure 2-44

Buy Mar Unleaded Reg.(NYM) / Sell Mar Heating Oil #2(NYM)

Enter on approximately 12/19 - Exit on approximately 02/03

CONT YEAR	ENTRY DATE	ENTRY PRICE	EXIT DATE	EXIT PRICE	PROFIT	PROFIT AMOUNT	BEST EQUITY DATE	BEST EQUITY AMOUNT	WORST EQUITY DATE	WORST EQUITY AMOUNT
2005	12/20/04	-13.81	02/03/05	-0.81	13.00	5460.00	02/01/05	5825.40	12/21/04	-210.00
2004	12/19/03	0.46	02/03/04	8.73	8.26	3469.20	02/03/04	3469.20		
2003	12/19/02	3.32	02/03/03	3.87	0.55	231.00	12/23/02	546.00	01/23/03	-642.60
2002	12/19/01	1.19	02/01/02	5.03	3.84	1612.80	01/28/02	1894.20		
2001	12/19/00	-4.62	02/02/01	7.31	11.94	5014.80	02/02/01	5014.80	12/27/00	-856.80
2000	12/20/99	3.81	02/03/00	0.65	-3.16	-1327.20	01/12/00	361.20	01/20/00	-1793.40
1999	12/21/98	2.60	02/03/99	4.92	2.31	970.20	02/02/99	1117.20	12/23/98	-168.00
1998	12/19/97	4.70	02/03/98	4.90	0.20	84.00	01/09/98	504.00	01/21/98	-365.40
1997	12/19/96	-0.26	02/03/97	3.06	3.34	1402.80	02/03/97	1402.80	12/20/96	-88.20
1996	12/19/95	0.43	02/02/96	0.48	0.04	16.80	01/26/96	781.20	12/22/95	-487.20
1995	12/19/94	2.34	02/03/95	7.91	5.56	2335.20	01/31/95	2868.60		
1994	12/20/93	-2.39	02/03/94	-6.29	-3.91	-1642.20	12/21/93	37.80	02/02/94	-2066.40
1993	12/21/92	-0.85	02/03/93	-0.12	0.73	306.60	01/25/93	995.40	12/23/92	-260.40
1992	12/19/91	0.50	02/03/92	4.25	3.75	1575.00	02/03/92	1575.00	01/13/92	-201.60
1991	12/19/90	-3.39	02/01/91	-1.08	2.31	970.20	01/17/91	1856.40	01/15/91	-214.20
1990	12/19/89	-4.00	02/02/90	5.96	9.96	4183.20	02/01/90	4183.20		
1989	12/19/88	-2.18	02/03/89	-1.14	1.05	441.00	01/24/89	1453.20	12/28/88	-449.40
1988	12/21/87	-3.24	02/03/88	-1.27	1.97	827.40	02/01/88	1075.20	01/07/88	-550.20
1987	12/19/86	0.40	02/03/87	0.42	0.01	4.20	01/02/87	109.20	01/16/87	-1251.60
1986	12/19/85	-5.17	02/03/86	1.07	6.25	2625.00	01/24/86	3402.00	12/27/85	-625.80

Percentage Correct	87					
Average Profit on Winning Trades		4.29	1803.74	Winners	13
Average Loss on Trades		-3.53	-1484.70	Losers	2
Average Net Profit Per Trade		3.25	1365.28	Total trades	15

Percentage Correct	90					
Average Profit on Winning Trades		4.17	1751.63	Winners	18
Average Loss on Trades		-3.53	-1484.70	Losers	2
Average Net Profit Per Trade		3.40	1428.00	Total trades	20

— further highlighting how critical is the month of March. The two spreads that encompass February through May (Figures 2-42 and 2-47) portray the extent of the seasonal move during which gasoline is being accumulated and heating oil liquidated.

With an eye toward the seasonal pattern for the July relationship, note the July strategy May 28 through June 21 (Figure 2-49). The traditional opening of the US driving and vacation season turns out to be the climax to all its preparations. By the end of May, gasoline

Figure 2-45

Buy Jun Unleaded Reg.(NYM) / Sell Jun Heating Oil #2(NYM)

Enter on approximately 02/08 - Exit on approximately 03/29

CONT YEAR	ENTRY DATE	ENTRY PRICE	EXIT DATE	EXIT PRICE	PROFIT	PROFIT AMOUNT	BEST EQUITY DATE	BEST EQUITY AMOUNT	WORST EQUITY DATE	WORST EQUITY AMOUNT
2005	02/08/05	12.28	03/29/05	10.78	-1.50	-630.00	02/14/05	1205.40	03/01/05	-2062.20
2004	02/09/04	19.53	03/29/04	22.62	3.09	1297.80	03/26/04	1520.40	03/09/04	-945.00
2003	02/10/03	16.96	03/28/03	18.34	1.38	579.60	03/07/03	651.00	03/20/03	-1104.60
2002	02/08/02	12.24	03/28/02	15.31	3.07	1289.40	03/19/02	1663.20	02/26/02	-495.60
2001	02/08/01	16.46	03/29/01	20.03	3.57	1499.40	03/29/01	1499.40	03/05/01	-743.40
2000	02/08/00	12.61	03/29/00	16.76	4.15	1743.00	03/09/00	2381.40		
1999	02/08/99	7.58	03/29/99	8.92	1.33	558.60	03/29/99	558.60	02/24/99	-558.60
1998	02/09/98	7.29	03/27/98	8.32	1.03	432.60	03/26/98	508.20	03/09/98	-436.80
1997	02/10/97	7.38	03/27/97	8.61	1.24	520.80	03/19/97	1138.20		
1996	02/08/96	7.27	03/29/96	10.53	3.26	1369.20	03/25/96	1444.80		
1995	02/08/95	8.09	03/29/95	10.75	2.66	1117.20	03/29/95	1117.20	03/10/95	-348.60
1994	02/08/94	2.86	03/29/94	3.54	0.68	285.60	03/24/94	457.80	02/15/94	-180.60
1993	02/08/93	4.85	03/29/93	5.07	0.21	88.20	02/10/93	147.00	02/25/93	-562.80
1992	02/10/92	8.57	03/27/92	8.80	0.23	96.60	03/04/92	621.60	03/20/92	-260.40
1991	02/08/91	7.72	03/28/91	11.26	3.53	1482.60	03/11/91	2356.20		
1990	02/08/90	10.80	03/29/90	10.98	0.19	79.80	03/29/90	79.80	02/27/90	-1255.80
1989	02/08/89	7.75	03/29/89	11.73	3.98	1671.60	03/29/89	1671.60	02/15/89	-693.00
1988	02/08/88	3.60	03/29/88	3.81	0.21	88.20	03/17/88	302.40	03/23/88	-159.60
1987	02/09/87	4.93	03/27/87	5.92	0.99	415.80	03/25/87	676.20	02/18/87	-163.80
1986	02/10/86	4.17	03/27/86	2.70	-1.48	-621.60			02/25/86	-2322.60

					PROFIT	AMOUNT				
Percentage Correct	93									
Average Profit on Winning Trades					2.10	882.90	Winners			14
Average Loss on Trades					-1.50	-630.00	Losers			1
Average Net Profit Per Trade					1.86	782.04	Total trades			15
Percentage Correct	90									
Average Profit on Winning Trades					1.93	812.00	Winners			18
Average Loss on Trades					-1.49	-625.80	Losers			2
Average Net Profit Per Trade					1.59	668.22	Total trades			20

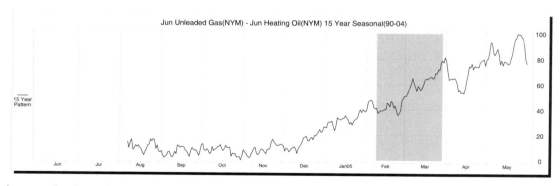

Jun Unleaded Gas(NYM) - Jun Heating Oil(NYM) 15 Year Seasonal(90-04)

inventories have been accumulated and refineries are already producing at capacity. This strategy reflects exhaustion.

The most reliable period during which heating oil outperforms gasoline actually comes as driving season, and therefore gasoline consumption, peaks (Figure 2-43). As is March, so too is September a transition. Refiners begin to switch their attention to building inventories of heating oil. As driving season ends, gasoline consumption will decline.

Figure 2-46

Moore Research Center, Inc. — Buy Jul Unleaded Reg.(NYM) / Sell Jul Heating Oil #2(NYM)

Enter on approximately 02/24 - Exit on approximately 03/29

CONT YEAR	ENTRY DATE	ENTRY PRICE	EXIT DATE	EXIT PRICE	PROFIT	PROFIT AMOUNT	BEST EQUITY DATE	BEST EQUITY AMOUNT	WORST EQUITY DATE	WORST EQUITY AMOUNT
2005	02/24/05	10.18	03/29/05	10.67	0.50	210.00	03/28/05	873.60	03/01/05	-970.20
2004	02/24/04	18.54	03/29/04	20.46	1.92	806.40	03/26/04	1029.00	03/09/04	-1016.40
2003	02/24/03	14.99	03/28/03	15.54	0.56	235.20	03/07/03	592.20	03/20/03	-1386.00
2002	02/25/02	10.69	03/28/02	13.31	2.63	1104.60	03/19/02	1394.40	02/26/02	-197.40
2001	02/26/01	14.48	03/29/01	17.32	2.84	1192.80	03/29/01	1192.80	03/05/01	-693.00
2000	02/24/00	12.53	03/29/00	14.76	2.24	940.80	03/27/00	1423.80		
1999	02/24/99	6.21	03/29/99	8.23	2.02	848.40	03/29/99	848.40		
1998	02/24/98	6.90	03/27/98	7.47	0.57	239.40	03/23/98	373.80	03/10/98	-319.20
1997	02/24/97	6.28	03/27/97	7.39	1.11	466.20	03/19/97	924.00		
1996	02/26/96	7.88	03/29/96	9.32	1.45	609.00	03/29/96	609.00	03/05/96	-29.40
1995	02/24/95	8.23	03/29/95	9.75	1.52	638.40	03/29/95	638.40	03/10/95	-487.20
1994	02/24/94	2.78	03/29/94	3.17	0.38	159.60	03/24/94	294.00	03/15/94	-29.40
1993	02/24/93	4.07	03/29/93	5.16	1.09	457.80	03/04/93	596.40		
1992	02/24/92	7.79	03/27/92	8.39	0.59	247.80	03/05/92	558.60	03/18/92	-33.60
1991	02/25/91	6.71	03/28/91	9.44	2.74	1150.80	03/11/91	1974.00		
1990	02/26/90	7.03	03/29/90	9.52	2.48	1041.60	03/29/90	1041.60	02/27/90	-273.00
1989	02/24/89	6.50	03/29/89	11.08	4.58	1923.60	03/29/89	1923.60	03/02/89	-58.80
1988	02/24/88	3.85	03/29/88	3.88	0.02	8.40	03/17/88	159.60	03/23/88	-163.80
1987	02/24/87	5.00	03/27/87	5.88	0.88	369.60	03/23/87	525.00		
1986	02/24/86	0.29	03/27/86	2.07	1.77	743.40	02/26/86	961.80	02/25/86	-420.00

Percentage Correct	100								
Average Profit on Winning Trades			1.48	620.48		Winners			15
Average Loss on Trades						Losers			0
Average Net Profit Per Trade			1.48	620.48		Total trades			15
Percentage Correct	100								
Average Profit on Winning Trades			1.59	669.69		Winners			20
Average Loss on Trades						Losers			0
Average Net Profit Per Trade			1.59	669.69		Total trades			20

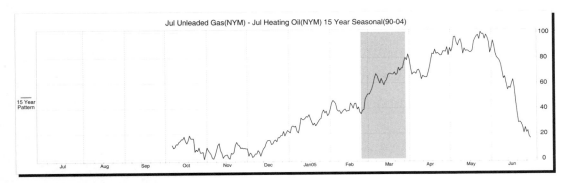

Jul Unleaded Gas(NYM) - Jul Heating Oil(NYM) 15 Year Seasonal(90-04)

To paraphrase Sherlock Holmes, consider the dog that does not bark. Of all the strategies in the summary table above, only two depict periods during which heating oil regularly outperforms gasoline. Of those two, the most reliable and dynamic reflects the market's exhaustion in accumulating gasoline rather than in accumulation of heating oil. The explanation may be two- or even threefold. Refiners running at capacity to meet demand for gasoline may create such an excess of heating oil in the offseason that there is less urgency. Gasoline consumption is universal and continues to grow while that for heating oil is more

Figure 2-47

Buy Jun Unleaded Reg.(NYM) / Sell Jun Heating Oil #2(NYM)

Enter on approximately 02/25 - Exit on approximately 05/26

CONT YEAR	ENTRY DATE	ENTRY PRICE	EXIT DATE	EXIT PRICE	PROFIT	PROFIT AMOUNT	BEST EQUITY DATE	BEST EQUITY AMOUNT	WORST EQUITY DATE	WORST EQUITY AMOUNT
2005	02/25/05	9.76	05/26/05	-0.05	-9.81	-4120.20	03/28/05	1029.00	05/26/05	-4120.20
2004	02/25/04	20.79	05/26/04	39.95	19.16	8047.20	05/20/04	9034.20	03/09/04	-1478.40
2003	02/25/03	15.90	05/23/03	16.25	0.34	142.80	03/07/03	1096.20	05/05/03	-3032.40
2002	02/25/02	11.59	05/24/02	13.06	1.47	617.40	03/19/02	1940.40	05/09/02	-806.40
2001	02/26/01	16.54	05/25/01	32.45	15.92	6686.40	05/23/01	7484.40	03/05/01	-777.00
2000	02/25/00	14.56	05/26/00	23.84	9.29	3901.80	05/08/00	4174.80	04/11/00	-961.80
1999	02/25/99	6.67	05/26/99	9.53	2.86	1201.20	05/04/99	1684.20	02/26/99	-25.20
1998	02/25/98	7.60	05/26/98	9.31	1.71	718.20	05/12/98	814.80	03/09/98	-562.80
1997	02/25/97	8.05	05/23/97	9.39	1.35	567.00	03/19/97	856.80	04/10/97	-537.60
1996	02/26/96	8.82	05/24/96	10.25	1.43	600.60	04/25/96	3326.40	03/11/96	-50.40
1995	02/27/95	9.55	05/26/95	15.34	5.79	2431.80	05/17/95	2856.00	03/10/95	-966.00
1994	02/25/94	3.42	05/26/94	3.67	0.25	105.00	05/23/94	369.60	05/11/94	-642.60
1993	02/25/93	3.52	05/26/93	3.63	0.11	46.20	05/04/93	1045.80		
1992	02/25/92	8.75	05/26/92	6.63	-2.11	-886.20	03/04/92	546.00	04/14/92	-1491.00
1991	02/25/91	8.05	05/24/91	11.90	3.84	1612.80	05/09/91	3729.60		
1990	02/26/90	8.56	05/25/90	13.75	5.19	2179.80	05/25/90	2179.80	04/12/90	-462.00
1989	02/27/89	6.89	05/26/89	17.18	10.30	4326.00	05/02/89	7035.00	03/02/89	-310.80
1988	02/25/88	4.17	05/26/88	4.16	-0.02	-8.40	05/18/88	411.60	04/26/88	-651.00
1987	02/25/87	4.97	05/26/87	2.92	-2.04	-856.80	03/25/87	663.60	05/11/87	-1209.60
1986	02/25/86	-1.35	05/23/86	8.79	10.15	4263.00	05/13/86	5527.20		

Percentage Correct	87									
Average Profit on Winning Trades					4.89	2052.18		Winners		13
Average Loss on Trades					-5.96	-2503.20		Losers		2
Average Net Profit Per Trade					3.44	1444.80		Total trades		15
Percentage Correct	80									
Average Profit on Winning Trades					5.57	2340.45		Winners		16
Average Loss on Trades					-3.50	-1467.90		Losers		4
Average Net Profit Per Trade					3.76	1578.78		Total trades		20

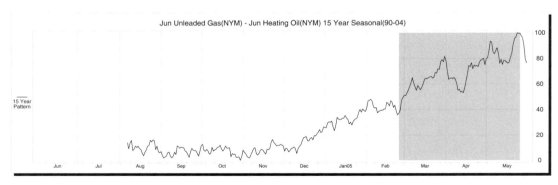

Jun Unleaded Gas(NYM) - Jun Heating Oil(NYM) 15 Year Seasonal(90-04)

regional and replaceable. Finally, even though gasoline consumption declines after early September and continues to do so into the dead of winter, emission standards change again in September — creating demand for the reformulated gasoline produced thereafter.

Thus, even as the industry's efforts to accumulate inventories of heating oil is peaking, heating oil's value as a product to refiners starts to ebb. In fact, strategies for both a

Figure 2-48

Moore Research Center, Inc.

Buy Jun Unleaded Reg.(NYM) / Sell Jun Heating Oil #2(NYM)

Enter on approximately 04/12 - Exit on approximately 04/27

CONT YEAR	ENTRY DATE	ENTRY PRICE	EXIT DATE	EXIT PRICE	PROFIT	PROFIT AMOUNT	BEST EQUITY DATE	BEST EQUITY AMOUNT	WORST EQUITY DATE	WORST EQUITY AMOUNT
2005	04/12/05	8.59	04/27/05	7.43	-1.16	-487.20	04/26/05	1192.80	04/15/05	-1894.20
2004	04/12/04	23.84	04/27/04	25.96	2.11	886.20	04/27/04	886.20	04/16/04	-793.80
2003	04/14/03	12.15	04/25/03	13.03	0.88	369.60	04/17/03	651.00	04/15/03	-201.60
2002	04/12/02	12.78	04/26/02	13.32	0.54	226.80	04/16/02	877.80	04/25/02	-302.40
2001	04/12/01	22.50	04/27/01	28.70	6.20	2604.00	04/27/01	2604.00	04/16/01	-436.80
2000	04/12/00	13.34	04/27/00	13.54	0.20	84.00	04/18/00	520.80	04/26/00	-67.20
1999	04/12/99	9.24	04/27/99	9.43	0.19	79.80	04/19/99	138.60	04/14/99	-231.00
1998	04/13/98	7.64	04/27/98	8.34	0.70	294.00	04/17/98	634.20		
1997	04/14/97	7.42	04/25/97	7.78	0.36	151.20	04/21/97	361.20	04/17/97	-46.20
1996	04/12/96	12.52	04/26/96	16.34	3.82	1604.40	04/25/96	1772.40	04/16/96	-226.80
1995	04/12/95	10.30	04/27/95	11.91	1.62	680.40	04/27/95	680.40	04/13/95	-88.20
1994	04/12/94	3.69	04/26/94	3.72	0.04	16.80	04/26/94	16.80	04/21/94	-302.40
1993	04/12/93	4.59	04/27/93	4.68	0.10	42.00	04/20/93	369.60	04/26/93	-37.80
1992	04/13/92	6.32	04/27/92	8.14	1.82	764.40	04/27/92	764.40	04/14/92	-474.60
1991	04/12/91	13.52	04/26/91	14.48	0.96	403.20	04/18/91	756.00	04/23/91	-100.80
1990	04/12/90	7.46	04/27/90	9.42	1.96	823.20	04/24/90	1801.80		
1989	04/12/89	15.64	04/27/89	22.42	6.79	2851.80	04/26/89	3095.40	04/14/89	-67.20
1988	04/12/88	3.75	04/27/88	3.19	-0.55	-231.00	04/13/88	168.00	04/26/88	-470.40
1987	04/13/87	4.75	04/27/87	3.85	-0.90	-378.00			04/23/87	-806.40
1986	04/14/86	5.32	04/25/86	7.85	2.53	1062.60	04/25/86	1062.60	04/17/86	-33.60

Percentage Correct	93									
Average Profit on Winning Trades					1.40	586.20		Winners		14
Average Loss on Trades					-1.16	-487.20		Losers		1
Average Net Profit Per Trade					1.23	514.64		Total trades		15
Percentage Correct	85									
Average Profit on Winning Trades					1.81	761.44		Winners		17
Average Loss on Trades					-0.87	-365.40		Losers		3
Average Net Profit Per Trade					1.41	592.41		Total trades		20

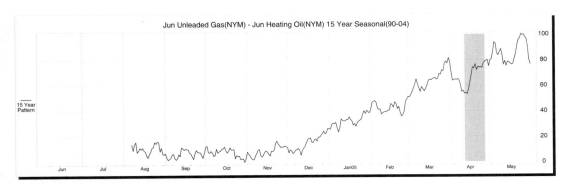

Jun Unleaded Gas(NYM) - Jun Heating Oil(NYM) 15 Year Seasonal(90-04)

December (Figure 2-50) and a January relationship (Figure 2-51) illustrate how gasoline actually outperforms heating oil during October — before winter even begins!

Remember that refiners in several large-producing US states are subject to tax on year-end inventories, which provide financial incentive to pump as much product into the pipeline as possible by year end. Remember that one effect has been to create a cluster of

Figure 2-49

Buy Jul Heating Oil #2(NYM) / Sell Jul Unleaded Reg.(NYM)

Enter on approximately 05/28 - Exit on approximately 06/21

CONT YEAR	ENTRY DATE	ENTRY PRICE	EXIT DATE	EXIT PRICE	PROFIT	PROFIT AMOUNT	BEST EQUITY DATE	BEST EQUITY AMOUNT	WORST EQUITY DATE	WORST EQUITY AMOUNT
2004	05/28/04	-28.45	06/21/04	-16.83	11.63	4884.60	06/17/04	5388.60	06/01/04	-180.60
2003	05/28/03	-11.48	06/20/03	-9.48	2.00	840.00	06/19/03	1054.20	06/11/03	-1188.60
2002	05/28/02	-11.60	06/21/02	-10.67	0.92	386.40	06/21/02	386.40	06/17/02	-424.20
2001	05/29/01	-18.03	06/21/01	-2.85	15.18	6375.60	06/21/01	6375.60		
2000	05/30/00	-25.65	06/21/00	-25.32	0.32	134.40	06/06/00	907.20	06/16/00	-2797.20
1999	05/28/99	-9.29	06/21/99	-7.28	2.01	844.20	06/21/99	844.20	06/08/99	-58.80
1998	05/28/98	-10.07	06/19/98	-8.35	1.72	722.40	06/10/98	1150.80	06/03/98	-403.20
1997	05/28/97	-7.72	06/20/97	-4.14	3.58	1503.60	06/20/97	1503.60		
1996	05/28/96	-9.30	06/21/96	-7.38	1.93	810.60	06/19/96	1037.40	06/11/96	-294.00
1995	05/30/95	-11.57	06/21/95	-12.18	-0.62	-260.40	06/01/95	554.40	06/20/95	-894.60
1994	05/31/94	-3.97	06/21/94	-3.36	0.61	256.20	06/16/94	432.60	06/06/94	-562.80
1993	05/28/93	-3.92	06/21/93	-2.70	1.22	512.40	06/11/93	978.60		
1992	05/28/92	-6.04	06/19/92	-3.88	2.16	907.20	06/19/92	907.20	06/03/92	-189.00
1991	05/28/91	-10.71	06/21/91	-6.80	3.92	1646.40	06/21/91	1646.40	06/10/91	-92.40
1990	05/29/90	-12.99	06/21/90	-12.32	0.67	281.40	06/11/90	1608.60	06/18/90	-298.20
1989	05/30/89	-16.29	06/21/89	-11.12	5.17	2171.40	06/21/89	2171.40	05/31/89	-210.00
1988	05/31/88	-4.28	06/21/88	-6.71	-2.43	-1020.60	06/03/88	218.40	06/21/88	-1020.60
1987	05/28/87	-3.60	06/19/87	-2.85	0.74	310.80	06/17/87	357.00	06/09/87	-411.60
1986	05/28/86	-8.51	06/20/86	-4.91	3.60	1512.00	06/19/86	2129.40		

Percentage Correct	93									
Average Profit on Winning Trades					3.42	1436.10		Winners		14
Average Loss on Trades					-0.62	-260.40		Losers		1
Average Net Profit Per Trade					3.15	1323.00		Total trades		15
Percentage Correct	89									
Average Profit on Winning Trades					3.38	1417.62		Winners		17
Average Loss on Trades					-1.52	-640.50		Losers		2
Average Net Profit Per Trade					2.86	1200.98		Total trades		19

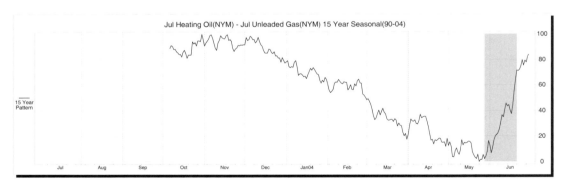

Jul Heating Oil(NYM) - Jul Unleaded Gas(NYM) 15 Year Seasonal(90-04)

seasonal dates on or near December 10-11, perhaps as the flush climaxes. Thus, three strategies, all with entries clustered within a few days of December 10-11, again portray exhaustion — this time of demand for heating oil. Going into and through January, normally the coldest month of the year, the industry's efforts are usually focused on aggressively selling heating oil into the retail market and liquidating inventories — preferably by the end of March and heating season. Traders may note that March forward relationships tend to be less vulnerable to unexpectedly severe cold snaps.

Figure 2-50

Buy Dec Unleaded Reg.(NYM) / Sell Dec Heating Oil #2(NYM)

Enter on approximately 10/06 - Exit on approximately 11/05

CONT YEAR	ENTRY DATE	ENTRY PRICE	EXIT DATE	EXIT PRICE	PROFIT	PROFIT AMOUNT	BEST EQUITY DATE	BEST EQUITY AMOUNT	WORST EQUITY DATE	WORST EQUITY AMOUNT
2004	10/06/04	-4.90	11/05/04	-8.72	-3.82	-1604.40	10/07/04	256.20	10/21/04	-4972.80
2003	10/06/03	-0.80	11/05/03	-0.23	0.57	239.40	10/29/03	684.60	10/13/03	-562.80
2002	10/07/02	-0.83	11/05/02	2.26	3.11	1306.20	11/04/02	2074.80	10/22/02	-239.40
2001	10/08/01	-3.83	11/05/01	-3.77	0.07	29.40	10/22/01	268.80	10/30/01	-802.20
2000	10/06/00	-9.56	11/03/00	-5.21	4.35	1827.00	11/03/00	1827.00	10/11/00	-777.00
1999	10/06/99	3.98	11/05/99	3.53	-0.44	-184.80	11/01/99	71.40	10/27/99	-571.20
1998	10/06/98	3.21	11/05/98	3.69	0.48	201.60	11/02/98	726.60	10/08/98	-205.80
1997	10/06/97	0.25	11/05/97	1.02	0.76	319.20	10/24/97	525.00	10/09/97	-96.60
1996	10/07/96	-10.11	11/05/96	-0.81	9.31	3910.20	11/05/96	3910.20		
1995	10/06/95	-0.31	11/03/95	-0.21	0.10	42.00	10/20/95	163.80	10/26/95	-243.60
1994	10/06/94	4.68	11/04/94	7.52	2.83	1188.60	10/28/94	2129.40		
1993	10/06/93	-5.46	11/05/93	-4.21	1.25	525.00	10/15/93	789.60		
1992	10/06/92	-6.07	11/05/92	-1.72	4.35	1827.00	11/03/92	1936.20	10/19/92	-394.80
1991	10/07/91	-5.92	11/05/91	-4.68	1.24	520.80	11/05/91	520.80	10/14/91	-571.20
1990	10/08/90	-11.13	11/05/90	3.08	14.22	5972.40	11/05/90	5972.40	10/12/90	-142.80
1989	10/06/89	-5.17	11/03/89	-7.98	-2.82	-1184.40	10/27/89	474.60	11/03/89	-1184.40
1988	10/06/88	-1.60	11/04/88	2.26	3.87	1625.40	10/25/88	2360.40	10/11/88	-319.20
1987	10/06/87	-4.91	11/05/87	-4.32	0.59	247.80	11/05/87	247.80	10/07/87	-197.40
1986	10/06/86	-1.38	11/05/86	-1.03	0.35	147.00	10/10/86	1079.40	10/07/86	-54.60
1985	10/07/85	-8.20	11/05/85	-6.54	1.66	697.20	10/18/85	1444.80	10/29/85	-567.00

Percentage Correct	87									
Average Profit on Winning Trades					3.28	1377.60		Winners		13
Average Loss on Trades					-2.13	-894.60		Losers		2
Average Net Profit Per Trade					2.56	1074.64		Total trades		15
Percentage Correct	85									
Average Profit on Winning Trades					2.89	1213.31		Winners		17
Average Loss on Trades					-2.36	-991.20		Losers		3
Average Net Profit Per Trade					2.10	882.63		Total trades		20

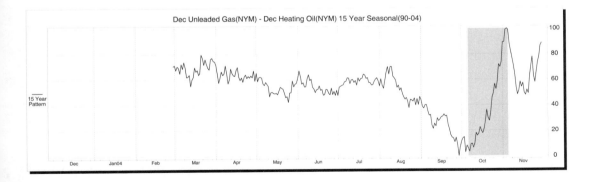

Dec Unleaded Gas(NYM) - Dec Heating Oil(NYM) 15 Year Seasonal(90-04)

Figure 2-51

Buy Jan Unleaded Reg.(NYM) / Sell Jan Heating Oil #2(NYM)

Enter on approximately 10/12 - Exit on approximately 10/31

CONT YEAR	ENTRY DATE	ENTRY PRICE	EXIT DATE	EXIT PRICE	PROFIT	PROFIT AMOUNT	BEST EQUITY DATE	BEST EQUITY AMOUNT	WORST EQUITY DATE	WORST EQUITY AMOUNT
2005	10/12/04	-7.86	10/29/04	-12.81	-4.95	-2079.00			10/25/04	-3397.80
2004	10/13/03	-3.44	10/31/03	-1.56	1.89	793.80	10/28/03	1104.60		
2003	10/14/02	-2.35	10/31/02	-2.09	0.26	109.20	10/25/02	999.60	10/17/02	-273.00
2002	10/12/01	-3.54	10/31/01	-4.69	-1.14	-478.80	10/22/01	189.00	10/30/01	-819.00
2001	10/12/00	-11.60	10/31/00	-7.24	4.36	1831.20	10/31/00	1831.20		
2000	10/12/99	2.95	10/29/99	3.01	0.07	29.40	10/20/99	88.20	10/27/99	-399.00
1999	10/12/98	3.06	10/30/98	3.26	0.20	84.00	10/15/98	210.00	10/19/98	-243.60
1998	10/13/97	-0.25	10/31/97	0.60	0.86	361.20	10/24/97	457.80	10/21/97	-71.40
1997	10/14/96	-6.76	10/31/96	-3.59	3.17	1331.40	10/31/96	1331.40		
1996	10/12/95	-0.57	10/31/95	-0.48	0.09	37.80	10/20/95	180.60	10/26/95	-180.60
1995	10/12/94	5.75	10/31/94	6.25	0.51	214.20	10/14/94	378.00	10/19/94	-386.40
1994	10/12/93	-4.85	10/29/93	-4.28	0.57	239.40	10/20/93	315.00		
1993	10/12/92	-6.94	10/30/92	-5.09	1.86	781.20	10/30/92	781.20	10/19/92	-197.40
1992	10/14/91	-7.82	10/31/91	-7.44	0.37	155.40	10/28/91	432.60		
1991	10/12/90	-10.93	10/31/90	-4.73	6.21	2608.20	10/31/90	2608.20		
1990	10/12/89	-6.88	10/31/89	-6.32	0.56	235.20	10/27/89	928.20	10/20/89	-33.60
1989	10/12/88	-4.21	10/31/88	-1.55	2.66	1117.20	10/25/88	1541.40	10/14/88	-105.00
1988	10/12/87	-5.39	10/30/87	-5.26	0.13	54.60	10/27/87	239.40	10/19/87	-21.00
1987	10/13/86	-0.35	10/31/86	-0.86	-0.51	-214.20	10/16/86	4.20	10/21/86	-499.80
1986	10/14/85	-8.34	10/31/85	-10.31	-1.97	-827.40	10/22/85	109.20	10/29/85	-1398.60

Percentage Correct		87								
Average Profit on Winning Trades					1.57	659.72		Winners		13
Average Loss on Trades					-3.04	-1278.90		Losers		2
Average Net Profit Per Trade					0.96	401.24		Total trades		15
Percentage Correct		80								
Average Profit on Winning Trades					1.49	623.96		Winners		16
Average Loss on Trades					-2.14	-899.85		Losers		4
Average Net Profit Per Trade					0.76	319.20		Total trades		20

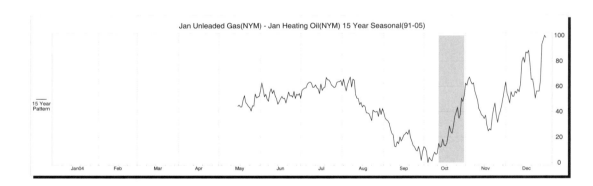

Jan Unleaded Gas(NYM) - Jan Heating Oil(NYM) 15 Year Seasonal(91-05)

Figure 2-52

Buy May Unleaded Reg.(NYM) / Sell May Heating Oil #2(NYM)

Enter on approximately 12/05 - Exit on approximately 02/03

CONT YEAR	ENTRY DATE	ENTRY PRICE	EXIT DATE	EXIT PRICE	PROFIT	PROFIT AMOUNT	BEST EQUITY DATE	BEST EQUITY AMOUNT	WORST EQUITY DATE	WORST EQUITY AMOUNT
2005	12/06/04	10.51	02/03/05	12.59	2.07	869.40	01/28/05	1444.80	12/21/04	-1419.60
2004	12/05/03	15.25	02/03/04	18.67	3.42	1436.40	02/02/04	1717.80	12/18/03	-386.40
2003	12/05/02	12.84	02/03/03	16.56	3.71	1558.20	02/03/03	1558.20	12/06/02	-193.20
2002	12/05/01	9.02	02/01/02	11.55	2.53	1062.60	01/28/02	1482.60	12/10/01	-331.80
2001	12/05/00	8.68	02/02/01	16.14	7.46	3133.20	02/02/01	3133.20	12/08/00	-617.40
2000	12/06/99	10.74	02/03/00	12.85	2.11	886.20	02/03/00	886.20	12/30/99	-403.20
1999	12/07/98	6.27	02/03/99	7.78	1.52	638.40	02/02/99	718.20	12/23/98	-277.20
1998	12/05/97	7.25	02/03/98	7.26	0.02	8.40	12/26/97	331.80	01/26/98	-399.00
1997	12/05/96	6.80	02/03/97	9.16	2.36	991.20	02/03/97	991.20	12/11/96	-113.40
1996	12/05/95	6.53	02/02/96	7.39	0.86	361.20	01/19/96	508.20	12/08/95	-142.80
1995	12/05/94	5.69	02/03/95	8.57	2.89	1213.80	01/31/95	1806.00	12/19/94	-168.00
1994	12/06/93	2.27	02/03/94	2.52	0.25	105.00	12/07/93	126.00	12/27/93	-390.60
1993	12/07/92	5.50	02/03/93	4.46	-1.04	-436.80	01/15/93	260.40	02/02/93	-470.40
1992	12/05/91	8.37	02/03/92	8.96	0.60	252.00	12/31/91	613.20	01/09/92	-571.20
1991	12/05/90	6.73	02/01/91	7.60	0.87	365.40	01/10/91	1281.00	12/07/90	-58.80
1990	12/05/89	5.14	02/02/90	12.53	7.39	3103.80	02/02/90	3103.80		
1989	12/05/88	3.44	02/03/89	7.00	3.56	1495.20	01/19/89	2196.60	12/14/88	-470.40
1988	12/07/87	1.82	02/03/88	2.85	1.02	428.40	02/01/88	499.80	01/05/88	-189.00
1987	12/05/86	3.04	02/03/87	3.77	0.72	302.40	01/06/87	768.60	12/10/86	-121.80
1986	12/05/85	3.70	02/03/86	4.17	0.47	197.40	01/17/86	655.20	12/27/85	-693.00

Percentage Correct		93								
Average Profit on Winning Trades					2.19	920.10		Winners		14
Average Loss on Trades					-1.04	-436.80		Losers		1
Average Net Profit Per Trade					1.98	829.64		Total trades		15
Percentage Correct		95								
Average Profit on Winning Trades					2.31	968.87		Winners		19
Average Loss on Trades					-1.04	-436.80		Losers		1
Average Net Profit Per Trade					2.14	898.59		Total trades		20

May Unleaded Gas(NYM) - May Heating Oil(NYM) 15 Year Seasonal(91-05)

Figure 2-53

Buy Apr Unleaded Reg.(NYM) / Sell Apr Heating Oil #2(NYM)

Enter on approximately 12/11 - Exit on approximately 01/31

CONT YEAR	ENTRY DATE	ENTRY PRICE	EXIT DATE	EXIT PRICE	PROFIT	PROFIT AMOUNT	BEST EQUITY DATE	BEST EQUITY AMOUNT	WORST EQUITY DATE	WORST EQUITY AMOUNT
2005	12/13/04	4.89	01/31/05	9.60	4.71	1978.20	01/28/05	2003.40	12/21/04	-1386.00
2004	12/11/03	11.59	01/30/04	15.17	3.57	1499.40	01/29/04	1654.80	12/18/03	-281.40
2003	12/11/02	11.53	01/31/03	13.14	1.61	676.20	12/23/02	772.80	12/31/02	-289.80
2002	12/11/01	7.89	01/31/02	11.06	3.16	1327.20	01/28/02	1818.60	12/18/01	-126.00
2001	12/11/00	3.12	01/31/01	13.86	10.74	4510.80	01/31/01	4510.80		
2000	12/13/99	9.11	01/31/00	9.78	0.68	285.60	01/12/00	323.40	01/20/00	-760.20
1999	12/11/98	6.06	01/29/99	7.31	1.25	525.00	01/29/99	525.00	12/23/98	-420.00
1998	12/11/97	6.31	01/30/98	7.34	1.03	432.60	12/26/97	684.60	01/21/98	-12.60
1997	12/11/96	4.13	01/31/97	6.27	2.14	898.80	01/23/97	966.00		
1996	12/11/95	5.26	01/31/96	5.53	0.26	109.20	01/19/96	495.60	12/22/95	-226.80
1995	12/12/94	6.55	01/31/95	10.68	4.14	1738.80	01/31/95	1738.80	12/16/94	-449.40
1994	12/13/93	1.01	01/31/94	-0.39	-1.41	-592.20	01/06/94	134.40	01/31/94	-592.20
1993	12/11/92	3.58	01/29/93	3.67	0.09	37.80	01/15/93	495.60	12/28/92	-184.80
1992	12/11/91	5.79	01/31/92	7.06	1.26	529.20	01/02/92	1075.20	01/13/92	-105.00
1991	12/11/90	5.89	01/31/91	6.37	0.49	205.80	01/09/91	924.00	12/26/90	-441.00
1990	12/11/89	0.23	01/31/90	8.07	7.84	3292.80	01/31/90	3292.80		
1989	12/12/88	0.53	01/31/89	2.13	1.60	672.00	01/24/89	1495.20	12/14/88	-147.00
1988	12/11/87	0.07	01/29/88	0.89	0.82	344.40	01/29/88	344.40	01/07/88	-441.00
1987	12/11/86	1.10	01/30/87	1.53	0.44	184.80	01/06/87	722.40	01/23/87	-109.20
1986	12/11/85	-0.12	01/31/86	2.09	2.23	936.60	01/21/86	1537.20	12/27/85	-508.20

Percentage Correct	93									
Average Profit on Winning Trades					2.51	1053.90		Winners		14
Average Loss on Trades					-1.41	-592.20		Losers		1
Average Net Profit Per Trade					2.25	944.16		Total trades		15
Percentage Correct	95									
Average Profit on Winning Trades					2.53	1062.38		Winners		19
Average Loss on Trades					-1.41	-592.20		Losers		1
Average Net Profit Per Trade					2.33	979.65		Total trades		20

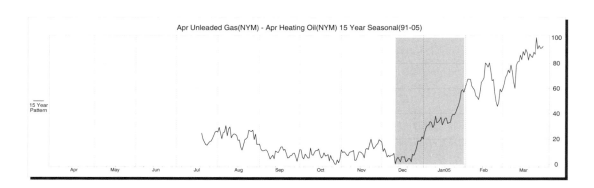

Apr Unleaded Gas(NYM) - Apr Heating Oil(NYM) 15 Year Seasonal(91-05)

Chapter 2: Energy

Cracks: Crude Oil versus Products

Refiners produce or buy crude oil (petroleum in its natural state), refine its molecules via a catalytic cracking process, and sell the derivative petroleum products. As mentioned previously, those products fall into six basic groups: kerosene, jet fuel, diesel fuel, gasoline, residuals (such as asphalt at the heavy end and butane at the light end), and distillates. The distillates are fuels used primarily by railroads, in agricultural machinery, and for heating. Heating oil accounts for perhaps 40% of total distillate fuel production.

Refining Crack Spreads. A crack spread defines value added by the refining operation. In other words, it is the value of the products minus the price of crude oil. The price of crude varies according to type, such as light, heavy, sour, or sweet. As noted earlier, seasonal demands for end product can affect these spreads; but, on average, a barrel of crude yields 50-55% gasoline and 20-25% heating oil. Although none are precise and all ignore lesser volume products, three standard crack spreads are used in most analyses. The 5-3-2 spread reflects 5 barrels of crude oil to produce 3 barrels of gasoline and 2 barrels of heating oil. Another standard is the 2-1-1. Perhaps the most widely used is the 3-2-1, however, reflecting 3 barrels of crude oil to produce 2 barrels of gasoline and 1 of heating oil.

NYMEX futures contracts for products call for 42,000 gallons whereas those for crude oil are for 1,000 barrels. But a barrel holds 42 gallons. Thus, a simple conversion creates the following formula for calculating the 3-2-1 crack spread:

$$[0.42(HO + 2HU)/3 - CL] = \text{crack spread}$$

where   **HO = price of heating oil futures in cents/gallon;**
                    HU = price of gasoline futures in cents/gallon; and
                    CL = price of crude oil futures in dollars/barrel

The crack spread is expressed in dollars/barrel and, in reflecting value added to a barrel of crude, quantifies the refiner's margin. Most are calculated using the same delivery month, though some analysts prefer to use a crude oil one month forward of products to factor in storage. In the years 1985-1999, 3-2-1 crack spreads rarely narrowed to less than $2.00/barrel nor, depending on the delivery month, widened beyond $6.00. Since 2000, however, they have widened, sometimes exceeding $10.00.

But the crack is not only an analytical tool. It is also a viable trading vehicle. Commercial refiners who want to protect, or hedge, a profitable margin for future operations might sell a wide crack spread — selling product futures and buying crude oil futures. Speculators who believe that potential new demand will increase product values might buy a narrow crack spread — buying product futures and selling crude oil futures.

Simple Crack Spreads. Most speculators find refiner crack spreads too large, too cumbersome, too complex. Instead, they can focus on one product and trade one contract of it against one of crude oil. The benefits to such 1-1 crack spreads are simplicity and focus. Traders who expect increasing seasonal demand for heating oil to increase its product value, for example, can simply buy one contract of heating oil and simultaneously sell one contract of crude oil. Such a spread is focused on heating oil and unencumbered by the potential drag of excess gasoline.

For analytical purposes, these simple 1-1 crack spreads can be calculated by simple formula, such as the following for heating oil:

$$0.42HO - CL = \text{crack spread}$$

Here again, the spread is expressed in dollars/barrel. These simple cracks are shorthand values and must be compared historically, although they too tend to fall into ranges similar to those for the refiner crack spreads.

Figure 2-54: Heating Oil Crack Strategies

Moore Research Center, Inc.	Heating Oil Crack Spread Strategies							
Seasonal Strategy	Entry Date	Exit Date	Win Pct	Win Yrs	Loss Years	Total Years	Average Profit	Ave Pft Per Day
Buy Dec Heating Oil #2(NYM)	7/24	8/21	80	12	3	15	542	19
Sell Dec Crude Oil(NYM)			80	16	4	20	445	15
Buy Apr Crude Oil(NYM)	12/21	2/19	87	13	2	15	585	10
Sell Apr Heating Oil #2(NYM)			85	17	3	20	579	9
Buy Apr Crude Oil(NYM)	1/09	2/16	80	12	3	15	366	9
Sell Apr Heating Oil #2(NYM)			80	16	4	20	401	10
Buy Nov Heating Oil #2(NYM)	8/09	9/09	87	13	2	15	547	17
Sell Nov Crude Oil(NYM)			85	17	3	20	527	16
Buy Feb Crude Oil(NYM)	12/12	1/15	87	13	2	15	715	20
Sell Feb Heating Oil #2(NYM)			85	17	3	20	822	23
Buy Mar Crude Oil(NYM)	12/21	1/31	80	12	3	15	598	14
Sell Mar Heating Oil #2(NYM)			80	16	4	20	722	17

For trading purposes, the proper way to reflect spread movement — and how it affects a trader's equity account — is to calculate them as equity spreads. To do so simply requires multiplying price/unit by contract size for each side and then subtracting the short side. For example, if HO is 143.00 cents/gallon, or $1.4300/gallon, and CL is $46.22/barrel, then:

HO = $1.4300/gallon x 42,000 gallons = $60,060
CL = $46.22/barrel x 1,000 barrels = $46,220
HO/CL spread = $13,840

Note these spreads are expressed in simple dollar values. Traders who calculate the difference in contract equity values daily will know exactly how the spread affects the balance in their trading account.

Seasonal patterns suggest how heating oil's product value tends to be low in summer, when consumption is least and stocks build up almost as if a byproduct while refiners are producing at capacity for gasoline. But that product value normally sees its most reliable increase from late July into early September. The strategy table for the December heating oil crack spread suggests that only every few years does this spread tend to move vigorously. Further, the lesser number of strategies in which heating oil outperforms crude oil and the bare threshold of reliability in those that do suggest that, despite the seasonal accumulation of heating oil before winter, competition with gasoline for product value is fierce when refineries switch gasoline formulations. Though the seasonal effect recurs regularly, the larger moves may be driven more by special situations.

Generally more reliable and dynamic have been those crack spreads that capture heating oil's declining product value as winter progresses. Figure 2-56 is typical of how these crack spreads begin to narrow in earnest immediately after the cluster of dates around

Figure 2-55

Buy Dec Heating Oil #2(NYM) / Sell Dec Crude Oil(NYM)

Enter on approximately 07/24 - Exit on approximately 08/21

CONT YEAR	ENTRY DATE	ENTRY PRICE	EXIT DATE	EXIT PRICE		PROFIT AMOUNT	BEST EQUITY DATE	BEST EQUITY AMOUNT	WORST EQUITY DATE	WORST EQUITY AMOUNT
2004	07/26/04	7996	08/20/04	7202		-793.20	08/05/04	455.80	08/16/04	-839.40
2003	07/24/03	4675	08/21/03	4950		275.80	08/01/03	840.20	08/18/03	-233.00
2002	07/24/02	3607	08/21/02	4315		707.20	08/21/02	707.20	08/06/02	-222.00
2001	07/24/01	4462	08/21/01	5076		614.00	08/16/01	1074.00		
2000	07/24/00	5106	08/21/00	7310		2204.40	08/21/00	2204.40		
1999	07/26/99	2429	08/20/99	3180		750.40	08/19/99	819.80	07/27/99	-34.40
1998	07/24/98	2745	08/21/98	2258		-487.60			08/21/98	-487.60
1997	07/24/97	3713	08/21/97	3746		32.20	08/04/97	701.80		
1996	07/24/96	4604	08/21/96	4978		374.60	08/19/96	411.60	07/29/96	-88.40
1995	07/24/95	3931	08/21/95	4272		340.80	08/18/95	398.20	07/25/95	-60.40
1994	07/25/94	3732	08/19/94	3824		92.80	08/01/94	497.80	08/05/94	-197.40
1993	07/26/93	4345	08/20/93	4709		363.40	08/13/93	383.40	08/05/93	-246.60
1992	07/24/92	5696	08/21/92	4731		-964.20			08/21/92	-964.20
1991	07/24/91	4935	08/21/91	5781		846.00	08/20/91	1678.40		
1990	07/24/90	4433	08/21/90	8203		3770.20	08/21/90	3770.20	07/30/90	-384.00
1989	07/24/89	3742	08/21/89	4237		495.40	08/21/89	495.40	07/31/89	-314.20
1988	07/25/88	3381	08/19/88	3457		76.00	08/02/88	165.00	07/29/88	-289.80
1987	07/24/87	3385	08/21/87	2890		-494.80	07/28/87	242.80	08/21/87	-494.80
1986	07/24/86	3681	08/21/86	3938		257.00	07/30/86	366.40	08/05/86	-223.00
1985	07/24/85	4689	08/21/85	5121		431.40	08/08/85	575.60		

Percentage Correct	80								
Average Profit on Winning Trades			864.32		Winners	12
Average Loss on Trades			-748.33		Losers	3
Average Net Profit Per Trade			541.79		Total trades	15
Percentage Correct	80					
Average Profit on Winning Trades			726.97		Winners	16
Average Loss on Trades			-684.95		Losers	4
Average Net Profit Per Trade			444.59		Total trades	20

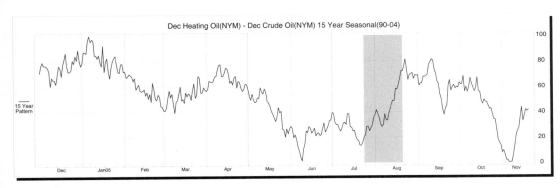

Dec Heating Oil(NYM) - Dec Crude Oil(NYM) 15 Year Seasonal(90-04)

December 10-11 and then continue counterintuitively throughout the heating season. Part of the reason may be the return of demand from refiners after running down inventories into year end. But the effect is much like time decay: As the number of remaining cold days declines, so too does the value of heating oil. Normally, the greatest danger to these spreads is the occasional unexpectedly severe cold snap. It is worth noting that adversity tends to be softened in spreads between contracts for delivery toward the end of the heating season. Note

Figure 2-56

Buy Apr Crude Oil(NYM) / Sell Apr Heating Oil #2(NYM)

Enter on approximately 12/21 - Exit on approximately 02/19

CONT YEAR	ENTRY DATE	ENTRY PRICE	EXIT DATE	EXIT PRICE		PROFIT AMOUNT	BEST EQUITY DATE	BEST EQUITY AMOUNT	WORST EQUITY DATE	WORST EQUITY AMOUNT
2005	12/21/04	-7942	02/18/05	-6615		1327.60	02/07/05	2662.40	12/22/04	-46.00
2004	12/22/03	-4102	02/19/04	-3215		887.40	02/19/04	887.40	01/09/04	-1118.20
2003	12/23/02	-3541	02/19/03	-6109		-2568.00	01/21/03	216.40	02/07/03	-3306.00
2002	12/21/01	-2841	02/19/02	-1854		987.20	02/15/02	1019.20	12/26/01	-128.40
2001	12/21/00	-5287	02/16/01	-2244		3043.40	02/16/01	3043.40	12/29/00	-1143.60
2000	12/21/99	-2082	02/18/00	-1735		346.40	02/15/00	687.40	01/20/00	-1006.00
1999	12/21/98	-2607	02/19/99	-1103		1503.80	02/12/99	1555.40	12/23/98	-31.00
1998	12/22/97	-2973	02/19/98	-2958		15.20	02/10/98	317.40	01/22/98	-194.40
1997	12/23/96	-3423	02/19/97	-2152		1271.20	02/19/97	1271.20		
1996	12/21/95	-3390	02/16/96	-3331		59.00	01/25/96	503.20	02/14/96	-285.00
1995	12/21/94	-3200	02/17/95	-1312		1887.60	02/16/95	1890.60	12/30/94	-175.00
1994	12/21/93	-3681	02/18/94	-4181		-500.20	12/22/93	101.00	02/10/94	-869.20
1993	12/21/92	-3816	02/19/93	-3514		302.20	01/21/93	587.20	12/23/92	-98.80
1992	12/23/91	-3360	02/19/92	-3260		99.80	12/31/91	710.00	02/10/92	-259.00
1991	12/21/90	-3977	02/19/91	-3865		112.20	01/03/91	882.40	01/16/91	-669.20
1990	12/21/89	-3344	02/16/90	-1610		1733.80	02/06/90	2170.60	12/29/89	-515.40
1989	12/21/88	-3225	02/17/89	-2434		791.20	02/14/89	870.80	12/28/88	-261.20
1988	12/21/87	-2791	02/19/88	-2232		559.20	02/18/88	673.00	01/07/88	-284.60
1987	12/22/86	-2389	02/19/87	-2262		127.40	02/11/87	294.20	01/14/87	-885.40
1986	12/23/85	-4233	02/19/86	-4638		-405.60	01/17/86	1155.20	02/19/86	-405.60

Percentage Correct	87				
Average Profit on Winning Trades		911.00	Winners	13
Average Loss on Trades		-1534.10	Losers	2
Average Net Profit Per Trade		584.99	Total trades	15

Percentage Correct	85				
Average Profit on Winning Trades		885.56	Winners	17
Average Loss on Trades		-1157.93	Losers	3
Average Net Profit Per Trade		579.04	Total trades	20

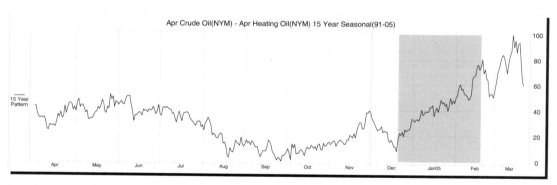

Apr Crude Oil(NYM) - Apr Heating Oil(NYM) 15 Year Seasonal(91-05)

also that several entries and exits tend to occur near front month expires — typically around the twentieth of the month for crude oil and the last business day of the month for products.

Figure 2-57

Buy Apr Crude Oil(NYM) / Sell Apr Heating Oil #2(NYM)

Enter on approximately 01/09 - Exit on approximately 02/16

CONT YEAR	ENTRY DATE	ENTRY PRICE	EXIT DATE	EXIT PRICE		PROFIT AMOUNT	BEST EQUITY DATE	BEST EQUITY AMOUNT	WORST EQUITY DATE	WORST EQUITY AMOUNT
2005	01/10/05	-5812	02/16/05	-6727		-915.20	02/07/05	531.80	01/26/05	-1713.00
2004	01/09/04	-5220	02/13/04	-4007		1213.60	02/06/04	1814.60		
2003	01/09/03	-3931	02/14/03	-5556		-1625.40	01/21/03	606.40	02/07/03	-2916.00
2002	01/09/02	-2090	02/15/02	-1822		267.80	02/15/02	267.80	01/17/02	-720.20
2001	01/09/01	-4778	02/16/01	-2244		2534.40	02/16/01	2534.40	01/10/01	-100.80
2000	01/10/00	-1987	02/16/00	-1582		405.40	02/15/00	593.00	01/20/00	-1100.40
1999	01/11/99	-2430	02/16/99	-1166		1263.40	02/12/99	1378.00		
1998	01/09/98	-2911	02/13/98	-2856		55.20	02/10/98	255.20	01/22/98	-256.60
1997	01/09/97	-3249	02/14/97	-2679		570.00	02/05/97	938.60	01/13/97	-3.80
1996	01/09/96	-3502	02/16/96	-3331		170.80	01/25/96	615.00	02/14/96	-173.20
1995	01/09/95	-3054	02/15/95	-1309		1744.20	02/16/95	1744.20		
1994	01/10/94	-3624	02/16/94	-3980		-356.40			02/10/94	-926.20
1993	01/11/93	-3508	02/16/93	-3448		59.40	01/21/93	278.40	02/08/93	-94.60
1992	01/09/92	-3174	02/14/92	-3113		60.60	01/22/92	171.60	02/10/92	-445.40
1991	01/09/91	-4088	02/15/91	-4051		37.00	01/11/91	557.80	01/16/91	-558.40
1990	01/09/90	-2895	02/16/90	-1610		1285.20	02/06/90	1722.00	01/11/90	-256.20
1989	01/09/89	-3452	02/16/89	-2438		1013.40	02/14/89	1097.00	01/10/89	-28.40
1988	01/11/88	-2726	02/16/88	-2412		313.80	02/01/88	484.60		
1987	01/09/87	-2908	02/13/87	-2311		597.00	02/11/87	813.00	01/14/87	-366.60
1986	01/09/86	-3674	02/14/86	-4350		-675.80	01/17/86	596.80	02/14/86	-675.80

Percentage Correct	80			
Average Profit on Winning Trades		698.48	Winners	12
Average Loss on Trades		-965.67	Losers	3
Average Net Profit Per Trade		365.65	Total trades	15

Percentage Correct	80			
Average Profit on Winning Trades		724.45	Winners	16
Average Loss on Trades		-893.20	Losers	4
Average Net Profit Per Trade		400.92	Total trades	20

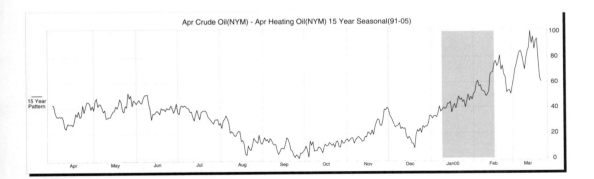

Apr Crude Oil(NYM) - Apr Heating Oil(NYM) 15 Year Seasonal(91-05)

Chapter 2: Energy

71

Figure 2-58

Buy Nov Heating Oil #2(NYM) / Sell Nov Crude Oil(NYM)

Enter on approximately 08/09 - Exit on approximately 09/09

CONT YEAR	ENTRY DATE	ENTRY PRICE	EXIT DATE	EXIT PRICE		PROFIT AMOUNT	BEST EQUITY DATE	BEST EQUITY AMOUNT	WORST EQUITY DATE	WORST EQUITY AMOUNT
2004	08/09/04	6780	09/09/04	7345		564.80	09/09/04	564.80	08/31/04	-1171.20
2003	08/11/03	4377	09/09/03	3534		-842.40			09/08/03	-864.20
2002	08/09/02	2939	09/09/02	3630		691.00	09/05/02	882.00		
2001	08/09/01	4444	09/07/01	5763		1319.00	08/28/01	1337.20		
2000	08/09/00	5611	09/08/00	8533		2922.20	08/31/00	3234.40		
1999	08/09/99	2502	09/09/99	2681		179.00	08/24/99	466.20	08/13/99	-127.80
1998	08/10/98	2056	09/09/98	2385		329.80	09/09/98	329.80	08/24/98	-322.20
1997	08/11/97	3590	09/09/97	3180		-410.60	08/14/97	171.20	09/04/97	-543.80
1996	08/09/96	4219	09/09/96	4609		390.00	08/29/96	805.80	08/12/96	-89.00
1995	08/09/95	3813	09/08/95	3894		81.40	09/05/95	349.40	08/29/95	-47.80
1994	08/09/94	3004	09/09/94	3473		468.80	09/06/94	686.60		
1993	08/09/93	3950	09/09/93	4631		681.40	09/09/93	681.40	08/10/93	-75.00
1992	08/10/92	4426	09/09/92	4512		86.40	08/31/92	202.00	08/21/92	-272.80
1991	08/09/91	4696	09/09/91	5026		329.40	08/20/91	1415.80	08/13/91	-186.00
1990	08/09/90	4806	09/07/90	6221		1414.80	08/23/90	5125.60		
1989	08/09/89	3498	09/08/89	4572		1074.00	09/08/89	1074.00		
1988	08/09/88	3088	09/09/88	3372		283.60	09/07/88	440.20		
1987	08/10/87	2876	09/09/87	2981		104.80	09/09/87	104.80	08/24/87	-351.80
1986	08/11/86	3442	09/09/86	2745		-697.20	08/26/86	142.20	09/09/86	-697.20
1985	08/09/85	4677	09/09/85	6247		1570.20	09/09/85	1570.20	08/19/85	-384.20

Percentage Correct	87						
Average Profit on Winning Trades		727.54		Winners	13		
Average Loss on Trades		-626.50		Losers	2		
Average Net Profit Per Trade		547.00		Total trades	15		
Percentage Correct	85						
Average Profit on Winning Trades		734.74		Winners	17		
Average Loss on Trades		-650.07		Losers	3		
Average Net Profit Per Trade		527.02		Total trades	20		

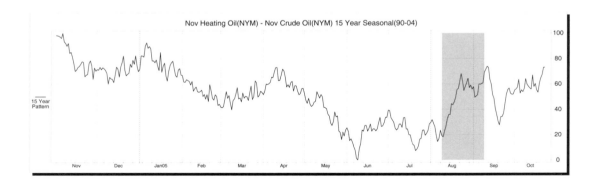

Nov Heating Oil(NYM) - Nov Crude Oil(NYM) 15 Year Seasonal(90-04)

Figure 2-59

Moore Research Center, Inc. — Buy Feb Crude Oil(NYM) / Sell Feb Heating Oil #2(NYM)

Enter on approximately 12/12 - Exit on approximately 01/15

CONT YEAR	ENTRY DATE	ENTRY PRICE	EXIT DATE	EXIT PRICE		PROFIT AMOUNT	BEST EQUITY DATE	BEST EQUITY AMOUNT	WORST EQUITY DATE	WORST EQUITY AMOUNT
2005	12/13/04	-11506	01/14/05	-8358		3148.00	01/05/05	3723.00	12/17/04	-2387.40
2004	12/12/03	-6030	01/15/04	-5616		414.40	01/15/04	414.40	01/09/04	-2063.00
2003	12/12/02	-5114	01/15/03	-4951		163.20	01/08/03	726.20	12/19/02	-790.40
2002	12/12/01	-3083	01/15/02	-2969		113.80	01/09/02	671.40	12/19/01	-968.60
2001	12/12/00	-9805	01/12/01	-5318		4486.40	01/12/01	4486.40	12/27/00	-1147.40
2000	12/13/99	-2124	01/14/00	-2980		-855.80			01/06/00	-933.20
1999	12/14/98	-2474	01/15/99	-1565		909.20	01/15/99	909.20	12/18/98	-323.00
1998	12/12/97	-3560	01/15/98	-3077		483.00	01/13/98	631.80		
1997	12/12/96	-5326	01/15/97	-4046		1279.40	01/14/97	1279.40	12/16/96	-336.60
1996	12/12/95	-4844	01/15/96	-4006		837.80	01/15/96	837.80	12/27/95	-1112.40
1995	12/12/94	-3643	01/13/95	-2086		1557.00	01/13/95	1557.00	12/14/94	-192.40
1994	12/13/93	-4069	01/14/94	-6749		-2679.80	12/22/93	107.40	01/14/94	-2679.80
1993	12/14/92	-3959	01/15/93	-3545		413.40	01/07/93	413.60	12/23/92	-976.20
1992	12/12/91	-4244	01/15/92	-3851		392.60	01/02/92	2078.40	12/17/91	-231.80
1991	12/12/90	-5572	01/15/91	-5504		67.60	01/04/91	1785.60	01/14/91	-1020.00
1990	12/12/89	-6533	01/15/90	-4772		1761.00	01/15/90	1761.00	12/29/89	-3252.00
1989	12/12/88	-5057	01/13/89	-3759		1298.40	01/13/89	1298.40	12/16/88	-300.00
1988	12/14/87	-4522	01/15/88	-4289		232.80	12/30/87	378.60	01/08/88	-734.40
1987	12/12/86	-3509	01/15/87	-4136		-627.60	12/19/86	507.40	01/14/87	-629.20
1986	12/12/85	-6777	01/15/86	-3725		3051.80	01/14/86	3311.20	12/23/85	-472.00

Percentage Correct	87									
Average Profit on Winning Trades						1097.37		Winners		13
Average Loss on Trades						-1767.80		Losers		2
Average Net Profit Per Trade						715.35		Total trades		15
Percentage Correct	85									
Average Profit on Winning Trades						1212.34		Winners		17
Average Loss on Trades						-1387.73		Losers		3
Average Net Profit Per Trade						822.33		Total trades		20

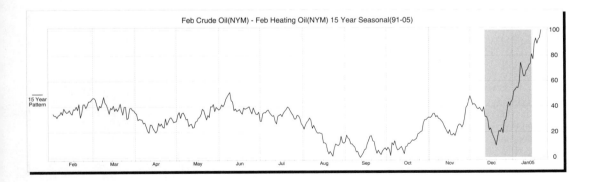

Feb Crude Oil(NYM) - Feb Heating Oil(NYM) 15 Year Seasonal(91-05)

Figure 2-60

Buy Mar Crude Oil(NYM) / Sell Mar Heating Oil #2(NYM)

Moore Research Center, Inc.

Enter on approximately 12/21 - Exit on approximately 01/31

CONT YEAR	ENTRY DATE	ENTRY PRICE	EXIT DATE	EXIT PRICE		PROFIT AMOUNT	BEST EQUITY DATE	BEST EQUITY AMOUNT	WORST EQUITY DATE	WORST EQUITY AMOUNT
2005	12/21/04	-11086	01/31/05	-8420		2666.20	01/03/05	3782.40		
2004	12/22/03	-5524	01/30/04	-5405		118.80	01/30/04	118.80	01/21/04	-1971.60
2003	12/23/02	-4577	01/31/03	-5659		-1082.20	01/21/03	668.40	01/30/03	-1137.00
2002	12/21/01	-3200	01/31/02	-2847		353.00	01/09/02	985.40	12/26/01	-184.40
2001	12/21/00	-7355	01/31/01	-3243		4112.00	01/31/01	4112.00	12/29/00	-1415.60
2000	12/21/99	-2344	01/31/00	-3583		-1239.00	01/11/00	107.60	01/20/00	-2085.00
1999	12/21/98	-2677	01/29/99	-1286		1390.60	01/25/99	1496.40	12/23/98	-53.00
1998	12/22/97	-3228	01/30/98	-2996		232.00	01/28/98	277.40	01/22/98	-22.40
1997	12/23/96	-4347	01/31/97	-3637		709.80	01/21/97	1178.80		
1996	12/21/95	-4632	01/31/96	-4104		527.60	01/25/96	1398.40	12/27/95	-314.40
1995	12/21/94	-3343	01/31/95	-1497		1846.00	01/31/95	1846.00	12/30/94	-325.00
1994	12/21/93	-4001	01/31/94	-5621		-1620.00	12/22/93	120.00	01/31/94	-1620.00
1993	12/21/92	-4202	01/29/93	-3487		715.60	01/21/93	916.20	12/23/92	-265.20
1992	12/23/91	-3783	01/31/92	-3700		83.20	01/02/92	1143.60	01/13/92	-353.60
1991	12/21/90	-5096	01/31/91	-4937		159.40	01/04/91	1629.80	01/25/91	-202.80
1990	12/21/89	-4742	01/31/90	-1495		3247.00	01/31/90	3247.00	12/27/89	-985.60
1989	12/21/88	-4173	01/31/89	-3718		455.40	01/26/89	1372.20	12/28/88	-328.80
1988	12/21/87	-3644	01/29/88	-2880		764.00	01/29/88	764.00	01/07/88	-518.00
1987	12/22/86	-2683	01/30/87	-3237		-553.60			01/14/87	-1319.80
1986	12/23/85	-5938	01/31/86	-4388		1550.40	01/17/86	2649.20	12/27/85	-201.20

Percentage Correct	80									
Average Profit on Winning Trades						1076.18		Winners		12
Average Loss on Trades						-1313.73		Losers		3
Average Net Profit Per Trade						598.20		Total trades		15
Percentage Correct	80									
Average Profit on Winning Trades						1183.19		Winners		16
Average Loss on Trades						-1123.70		Losers		4
Average Net Profit Per Trade						721.81		Total trades		20

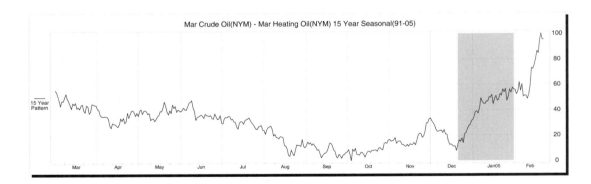

Mar Crude Oil(NYM) - Mar Heating Oil(NYM) 15 Year Seasonal(91-05)

Figure 2-61: Gasoline Crack Strategies

▲▲ Moore Research Center, Inc.			**Gasoline Crack Spread Strategies**					
Seasonal Strategy	Entry Date	Exit Date	Win Pct	Win Yrs	Loss Years	Total Years	Average Profit	Ave Pft Per Day
Buy Jul Unleaded Reg.(NYM)	2/24	4/27	93	14	1	15	983	16
Sell Jul Crude Oil(NYM)			90	18	2	20	1133	18
Buy Jun Unleaded Reg.(NYM)	2/13	3/30	93	14	1	15	884	19
Sell Jun Crude Oil(NYM)			95	19	1	20	918	20
Buy Jun Unleaded Reg.(NYM)	3/03	3/30	80	12	3	15	734	26
Sell Jun Crude Oil(NYM)			85	17	3	20	777	28
Buy Aug Crude Oil(NYM)	5/29	6/29	93	14	1	15	751	23
Sell Aug Unleaded Reg.(NYM)			89	17	2	19	732	23
Buy Dec Unleaded Reg.(NYM)	10/07	10/24	80	12	3	15	454	25
Sell Dec Crude Oil(NYM)			80	16	4	20	490	27
Buy May Unleaded Reg.(NYM)	12/03	1/27	93	14	1	15	571	10
Sell May Crude Oil(NYM)			95	19	1	20	605	11
Buy Apr Unleaded Reg.(NYM)	12/11	1/16	80	12	3	15	423	11
Sell Apr Crude Oil(NYM)			85	17	3	20	515	14
Buy Mar Unleaded Reg.(NYM)	12/11	2/03	93	14	1	15	851	15
Sell Mar Crude Oil(NYM)			90	18	2	20	745	14

Notice how the series of gasoline cracks differ from that of heating oil cracks. The proportion of strategies in which product value reliably and productively increases is nearly opposite. Whereas declining product values generate the more reliable seasonal strategies for heating oil cracks, increasing product values generate most seasonal gasoline cracks.

Seasonal patterns complement those for other spreads, illustrating how gasoline's product value tends to be least going into winter. Figure 2-62 depicts how, in December, it has begun slowly but consistently to increase. From February through April, refiners switch to summer blends, improving driving conditions increase daily consumption, and the industry accumulates inventories for the vacation and driving season. During this transition, gasoline's product value tends not only to increase — vigorously, reliably, persistently — but to accelerate. Notice in this strategy encompassing most of the seasonal trend that the only loss in the 17 years 1988-2004 would have been incurred — surprise! — in 2003.

This same seasonal pattern also depicts how (again counterintuitively!) gasoline's product value deflates after inventories are sufficient and refineries are back running at capacity. Although the August gasoline crack is the best trading vehicle with which to take advantage, the pattern for the July crack suggests how product value collapses after the driving season opens, traditionally the last Monday in May.

Figure 2-62

Buy Jul Unleaded Reg.(NYM) / Sell Jul Crude Oil(NYM)

Enter on approximately 02/24 - Exit on approximately 04/27

CONT YEAR	ENTRY DATE	ENTRY PRICE	EXIT DATE	EXIT PRICE	PROFIT AMOUNT	BEST EQUITY DATE	BEST EQUITY AMOUNT	WORST EQUITY DATE	WORST EQUITY AMOUNT
2005	02/24/05	9395	04/27/05	12267	2872.20	04/01/05	5050.40	02/28/05	-862.20
2004	02/24/04	10272	04/27/04	12443	2171.80	04/27/04	2171.80	03/09/04	-1096.00
2003	02/24/03	9640	04/25/03	7802	-1837.80	03/07/03	1442.80	04/10/03	-2212.20
2002	02/25/02	6426	04/26/02	7135	709.40	03/19/02	1920.60	02/26/02	-23.60
2001	02/26/01	8191	04/27/01	12858	4666.60	04/24/01	5065.80	03/05/01	-524.00
2000	02/24/00	6871	04/27/00	8104	1233.80	03/08/00	1339.40	04/05/00	-375.60
1999	02/24/99	4217	04/27/99	4634	417.40	03/31/99	1530.60		
1998	02/24/98	5605	04/27/98	6282	676.60	04/17/98	812.60	03/09/98	-299.80
1997	02/24/97	5155	04/25/97	5460	305.80	03/25/97	831.20		
1996	02/26/96	5809	04/26/96	7527	1717.40	04/25/96	1861.60	03/08/96	-146.40
1995	02/24/95	5543	04/27/95	5733	190.60	04/18/95	240.00	03/10/95	-818.60
1994	02/24/94	4680	04/26/94	4734	53.80	03/31/94	258.00	03/28/94	-250.00
1993	02/24/93	4797	04/27/93	4891	94.00	03/04/93	522.60		
1992	02/24/92	6057	04/27/92	6202	145.20	04/01/92	500.20	04/14/92	-547.80
1991	02/25/91	6045	04/26/91	7377	1332.20	04/18/91	1871.80	02/26/91	-15.00
1990	02/26/90	4894	04/27/90	5605	710.80	04/24/90	1419.40	03/09/90	-457.60
1989	02/24/89	5211	04/27/89	9073	3862.40	04/27/89	3862.40	03/02/89	-284.60
1988	02/24/88	3459	04/27/88	3515	56.40	04/13/88	190.60	03/02/88	-199.00
1987	02/24/87	4343	04/27/87	4012	-331.40	03/24/87	406.00	04/22/87	-590.20
1986	02/24/86	2990	04/25/86	6600	3610.40	04/25/86	3610.40	02/25/86	-220.00

Percentage Correct	93								
Average Profit on Winning Trades					1184.77		Winners		14
Average Loss on Trades					-1837.80		Losers		1
Average Net Profit Per Trade					983.27		Total trades		15
Percentage Correct	90								
Average Profit on Winning Trades					1379.27		Winners		18
Average Loss on Trades					-1084.60		Losers		2
Average Net Profit Per Trade					1132.88		Total trades		20

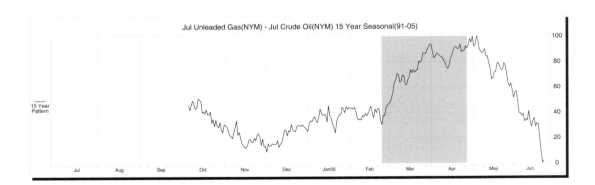

Jul Unleaded Gas(NYM) - Jul Crude Oil(NYM) 15 Year Seasonal(91-05)

Figure 2-63

Buy Jun Unleaded Reg.(NYM) / Sell Jun Crude Oil(NYM)

Enter on approximately 02/13 - Exit on approximately 03/30

CONT YEAR	ENTRY DATE	ENTRY PRICE	EXIT DATE	EXIT PRICE		PROFIT AMOUNT	BEST EQUITY DATE	BEST EQUITY AMOUNT	WORST EQUITY DATE	WORST EQUITY AMOUNT
2005	02/14/05	10000	03/30/05	13691		3691.00	03/30/05	3691.00	02/28/05	-1356.40
2004	02/13/04	11069	03/30/04	11960		891.40	03/30/04	891.40	03/09/04	-1745.00
2003	02/13/03	9805	03/28/03	10007		201.80	03/07/03	2246.20	03/21/03	-1137.80
2002	02/13/02	7209	03/28/02	8427		1218.20	03/19/02	1877.40	02/26/02	-709.80
2001	02/13/01	8726	03/30/01	11196		2470.40	03/30/01	2470.40	03/05/01	-664.60
2000	02/14/00	7082	03/30/00	7950		867.60	03/08/00	1829.60	02/18/00	-366.60
1999	02/16/99	4365	03/30/99	5587		1222.40	03/30/99	1222.40	02/24/99	-310.80
1998	02/13/98	5851	03/30/98	6105		253.80	03/26/98	290.60	03/09/98	-513.60
1997	02/13/97	5619	03/27/97	6043		424.40	03/25/97	791.20	02/24/97	-151.00
1996	02/13/96	5764	03/29/96	6520		756.40	03/29/96	756.40	02/20/96	-41.60
1995	02/13/95	5560	03/30/95	5596		36.40	02/22/95	479.00	03/10/95	-1036.20
1994	02/14/94	4413	03/30/94	4823		410.40	03/23/94	514.20		
1993	02/16/93	4791	03/30/93	5003		212.00	03/04/93	373.60	02/24/93	-171.00
1992	02/13/92	6688	03/30/92	6179		-509.00	02/19/92	187.00	03/25/92	-683.20
1991	02/13/91	6612	03/28/91	7732		1119.80	03/11/91	1889.00	02/14/91	-175.00
1990	02/13/90	5130	03/30/90	6373		1243.00	03/29/90	1384.80	03/09/90	-504.80
1989	02/13/89	4809	03/30/89	7201		2392.00	03/30/89	2392.00	02/21/89	-158.60
1988	02/16/88	3516	03/30/88	3702		186.80	03/30/88	186.80	03/08/88	-180.40
1987	02/13/87	4139	03/30/87	4278		139.20	03/24/87	590.40	02/17/87	-81.60
1986	02/13/86	3528	03/27/86	4665		1137.00	03/26/86	1397.00	02/25/86	-675.00

Percentage Correct		93								
Average Profit on Winning Trades						984.00		Winners		14
Average Loss on Trades						-509.00		Losers		1
Average Net Profit Per Trade						884.47		Total trades		15
Percentage Correct		95								
Average Profit on Winning Trades						993.37		Winners		19
Average Loss on Trades						-509.00		Losers		1
Average Net Profit Per Trade						918.25		Total trades		20

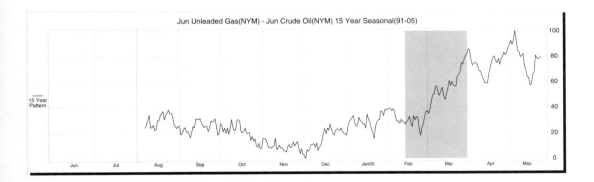

Jun Unleaded Gas(NYM) - Jun Crude Oil(NYM) 15 Year Seasonal(91-05)

Figure 2-64

Moore Research Center, Inc.

Buy Jun Unleaded Reg.(NYM) / Sell Jun Crude Oil(NYM)

Enter on approximately 03/03 - Exit on approximately 03/30

CONT YEAR	ENTRY DATE	ENTRY PRICE	EXIT DATE	EXIT PRICE		PROFIT AMOUNT	BEST EQUITY DATE	BEST EQUITY AMOUNT	WORST EQUITY DATE	WORST EQUITY AMOUNT
2005	03/03/05	10473	03/30/05	13691		3218.00	03/30/05	3218.00	03/14/05	-886.20
2004	03/03/04	10540	03/30/04	11960		1419.80	03/30/04	1419.80	03/09/04	-1216.60
2003	03/03/03	10574	03/28/03	10007		-566.80	03/07/03	1477.60	03/21/03	-1906.40
2002	03/04/02	7272	03/28/02	8427		1155.40	03/19/02	1814.60		
2001	03/05/01	8061	03/30/01	11196		3135.00	03/30/01	3135.00		
2000	03/03/00	8107	03/30/00	7950		-157.20	03/08/00	804.80	03/16/00	-827.20
1999	03/03/99	4439	03/30/99	5587		1148.60	03/30/99	1148.60		
1998	03/03/98	5812	03/30/98	6105		292.80	03/26/98	329.60	03/09/98	-474.60
1997	03/03/97	5736	03/27/97	6043		307.20	03/25/97	674.00		
1996	03/04/96	5956	03/29/96	6520		564.00	03/29/96	564.00	03/08/96	-87.00
1995	03/03/95	5189	03/30/95	5596		407.80	03/29/95	414.00	03/10/95	-664.80
1994	03/03/94	4632	03/30/94	4823		190.80	03/23/94	294.60	03/28/94	-135.00
1993	03/03/93	4933	03/30/93	5003		70.20	03/04/93	231.80	03/23/93	-268.60
1992	03/03/92	6648	03/30/92	6179		-469.00	03/05/92	182.80	03/25/92	-643.20
1991	03/04/91	7437	03/28/91	7732		295.20	03/11/91	1064.40		
1990	03/05/90	5298	03/30/90	6373		1075.40	03/29/90	1217.20	03/09/90	-672.40
1989	03/03/89	4984	03/30/89	7201		2217.80	03/30/89	2217.80		
1988	03/03/88	3410	03/30/88	3702		292.00	03/30/88	292.00	03/08/88	-75.20
1987	03/03/87	4208	03/30/87	4278		69.40	03/24/87	520.60		
1986	03/03/86	3798	03/27/86	4665		867.00	03/26/86	1127.00	03/13/86	-874.00

Percentage Correct	80			PROFIT		WINNERS	
Average Profit on Winning Trades			1017.07		Winners	12
Average Loss on Trades			-397.67		Losers	3
Average Net Profit Per Trade			734.12		Total trades	15
Percentage Correct	85					
Average Profit on Winning Trades			983.91		Winners	17
Average Loss on Trades			-397.67		Losers	3
Average Net Profit Per Trade			776.67		Total trades	20

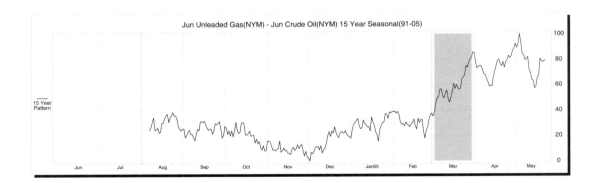

Jun Unleaded Gas(NYM) - Jun Crude Oil(NYM) 15 Year Seasonal(91-05)

Figure 2-65

Buy Aug Crude Oil(NYM) / Sell Aug Unleaded Reg.(NYM)

Enter on approximately 05/29 - Exit on approximately 06/29

CONT YEAR	ENTRY DATE	ENTRY PRICE	EXIT DATE	EXIT PRICE		PROFIT AMOUNT	BEST EQUITY DATE	BEST EQUITY AMOUNT	WORST EQUITY DATE	WORST EQUITY AMOUNT
2004	06/01/04	-12406	06/29/04	-11376		1030.00	06/04/04	2446.80	06/24/04	-614.40
2003	05/29/03	-6615	06/27/03	-6346		268.60	06/24/03	891.60	06/11/03	-534.40
2002	05/29/02	-6562	06/28/02	-6169		393.60	05/31/02	507.00	06/18/02	-488.80
2001	05/29/01	-9396	06/29/01	-4645		4750.60	06/28/01	4770.40		
2000	05/30/00	-10238	06/29/00	-9855		382.60	06/29/00	382.60	06/15/00	-1647.80
1999	06/01/99	-3678	06/29/99	-4374		-696.80			06/29/99	-696.80
1998	05/29/98	-6021	06/29/98	-5687		334.60	06/08/98	616.40	06/18/98	-504.60
1997	05/29/97	-4970	06/27/97	-4728		242.20	06/23/97	892.40		
1996	05/29/96	-5396	06/28/96	-4351		1044.60	06/26/96	1551.60	06/11/96	-348.60
1995	05/30/95	-5811	06/29/95	-5788		23.40	06/26/95	531.80	06/20/95	-553.60
1994	05/31/94	-4397	06/29/94	-3384		1013.40	06/22/94	1192.20	06/01/94	-169.80
1993	06/01/93	-4419	06/29/93	-4170		249.60	06/10/93	732.40	06/25/93	-4.40
1992	05/29/92	-5675	06/29/92	-4002		1673.00	06/29/92	1673.00	06/08/92	-70.60
1991	05/29/91	-5885	06/28/91	-5472		413.80	06/21/91	743.20	06/11/91	-235.80
1990	05/29/90	-6679	06/29/90	-6538		140.60	06/11/90	1827.80	06/25/90	-439.80
1989	05/30/89	-6937	06/29/89	-4373		2564.20	06/29/89	2564.20	05/31/89	-75.20
1988	05/31/88	-3500	06/29/88	-5272		-1771.80	06/06/88	298.40	06/29/88	-1771.80
1987	05/29/87	-3561	06/29/87	-2847		714.40	06/29/87	714.40	06/09/87	-232.40
1986	05/29/86	-5086	06/27/86	-3942		1144.20	06/27/86	1144.20		

Percentage Correct	93			
Average Profit on Winning Trades		854.33	Winners	14
Average Loss on Trades		-696.80	Losers	1
Average Net Profit Per Trade		750.92	Total trades	15

Percentage Correct	89			
Average Profit on Winning Trades		963.73	Winners	17
Average Loss on Trades		-1234.30	Losers	2
Average Net Profit Per Trade		732.36	Total trades	19

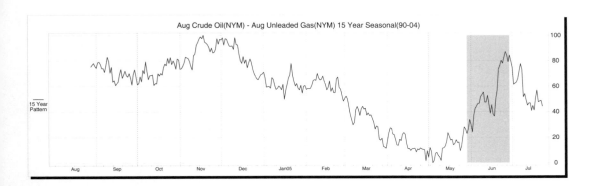

Aug Crude Oil(NYM) - Aug Unleaded Gas(NYM) 15 Year Seasonal(90-04)

Chapter 2: Energy

79

Figure 2-66

Buy Dec Unleaded Reg.(NYM) / Sell Dec Crude Oil(NYM)

Enter on approximately 10/07 - Exit on approximately 10/24

CONT YEAR	ENTRY DATE	ENTRY PRICE	EXIT DATE	EXIT PRICE		PROFIT AMOUNT	BEST EQUITY DATE	BEST EQUITY AMOUNT	WORST EQUITY DATE	WORST EQUITY AMOUNT
2004	10/07/04	6249	10/22/04	5327		-922.40			10/18/04	-2141.40
2003	10/07/03	3980	10/24/03	4347		367.00	10/09/03	932.20	10/22/03	-132.20
2002	10/07/02	3590	10/24/02	4035		444.60	10/08/02	541.60	10/22/02	-126.80
2001	10/08/01	3079	10/24/01	3097		17.60	10/24/01	17.60	10/17/01	-554.60
2000	10/09/00	4215	10/24/00	5262		1046.20	10/24/00	1046.20		
1999	10/07/99	3610	10/22/99	3749		139.60	10/20/99	479.60	10/13/99	-65.60
1998	10/07/98	3842	10/23/98	4195		352.60	10/20/98	567.60	10/08/98	-119.20
1997	10/07/97	3620	10/24/97	4020		400.40	10/23/97	473.60	10/10/97	-43.00
1996	10/07/96	2636	10/24/96	3567		931.40	10/24/96	931.40	10/16/96	-220.60
1995	10/09/95	3652	10/24/95	3390		-262.20			10/18/95	-437.00
1994	10/07/94	5179	10/24/94	7065		1886.60	10/20/94	2065.20	10/10/94	-15.00
1993	10/07/93	2984	10/22/93	2796		-188.00	10/15/93	392.40	10/22/93	-188.00
1992	10/07/92	2611	10/23/92	2754		142.80	10/09/92	313.80	10/19/92	-114.60
1991	10/07/91	3223	10/24/91	3575		352.20	10/24/91	352.20	10/16/91	-251.40
1990	10/08/90	1156	10/24/90	3259		2103.60	10/24/90	2103.60	10/11/90	-349.60
1989	10/09/89	2628	10/24/89	2250		-378.20	10/10/89	211.20	10/24/89	-378.20
1988	10/07/88	2781	10/24/88	5117		2336.00	10/24/88	2336.00	10/11/88	-209.80
1987	10/07/87	1730	10/23/87	2066		336.60	10/23/87	336.60		
1986	10/07/86	2227	10/24/86	2557		329.80	10/16/86	664.80		
1985	10/07/85	3026	10/24/85	3388		362.20	10/22/85	1079.80		

Percentage Correct	80			682.05		Winners	12
Average Profit on Winning Trades				682.05		Winners	12
Average Loss on Trades				-457.53		Losers	3
Average Net Profit Per Trade				454.13		Total trades	15
Percentage Correct	80						
Average Profit on Winning Trades				721.82		Winners	16
Average Loss on Trades				-437.70		Losers	4
Average Net Profit Per Trade				489.92		Total trades	20

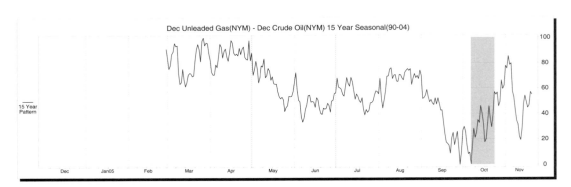

Dec Unleaded Gas(NYM) - Dec Crude Oil(NYM) 15 Year Seasonal(90-04)

15 Year Pattern

This crack illustrates the first attempt at recovery in gasoline's product value after the industry's intense focus on accumulating heating oil inventories begins to exhaust itself. That dynamic is suggested by the time period, the erratic pattern, the threshold reliability, and the modesty of movement. Note, however, how most drawdowns have been even more modest.

Figure 2-67

Buy May Unleaded Reg.(NYM) / Sell May Crude Oil(NYM)

Moore Research Center, Inc.

Enter on approximately 12/03 - Exit on approximately 01/27

CONT YEAR	ENTRY DATE	ENTRY PRICE	EXIT DATE	EXIT PRICE		PROFIT AMOUNT	BEST EQUITY DATE	BEST EQUITY AMOUNT	WORST EQUITY DATE	WORST EQUITY AMOUNT
2005	12/03/04	9653	01/27/05	11168		1514.60	01/26/05	1750.60	12/29/04	-1457.20
2004	12/03/03	9253	01/27/04	10490		1237.80	01/09/04	1741.40	12/04/03	-100.80
2003	12/03/02	8060	01/27/03	9158		1098.40	01/03/03	1338.40	12/04/02	-190.40
2002	12/03/01	6496	01/25/02	7620		1124.40	01/25/02	1124.40	12/06/01	-323.60
2001	12/04/00	7507	01/26/01	9176		1669.00	01/10/01	2453.60	12/08/00	-858.00
2000	12/03/99	6327	01/27/00	6533		206.00	12/08/99	311.20	12/10/99	-317.20
1999	12/03/98	4934	01/27/99	4691		-243.20	12/29/98	171.40	01/21/99	-566.80
1998	12/03/97	5781	01/27/98	5855		73.80	01/09/98	226.80	12/11/97	-282.40
1997	12/03/96	5709	01/27/97	5811		102.40	12/26/96	494.00	01/20/97	-200.00
1996	12/04/95	5519	01/26/96	5703		183.60	01/19/96	463.00	01/12/96	-141.20
1995	12/05/94	5416	01/27/95	5997		581.40	01/26/95	618.20	12/19/94	-226.20
1994	12/03/93	4411	01/27/94	4482		70.60	01/26/94	183.40	12/27/93	-527.60
1993	12/03/92	5339	01/27/93	5396		56.60	01/05/93	307.60	01/13/93	-63.80
1992	12/03/91	6149	01/27/92	6214		64.60	12/24/91	432.40	01/09/92	-344.20
1991	12/03/90	6265	01/25/91	7095		830.00	01/09/91	1315.00	01/04/91	-504.00
1990	12/04/89	5000	01/26/90	6360		1359.80	01/16/90	1917.80	12/14/89	-269.00
1989	12/05/88	4083	01/27/89	5432		1349.00	01/24/89	1685.80	12/14/88	-413.60
1988	12/03/87	3026	01/27/88	3227		201.20	01/15/88	242.20	12/30/87	-235.00
1987	12/03/86	3227	01/27/87	3666		438.80	01/12/87	1048.00	12/08/86	-328.00
1986	12/03/85	4502	01/27/86	4689		187.40	12/10/85	674.00	12/18/85	-374.00

Percentage Correct	93								
Average Profit on Winning Trades			629.51		Winners	14
Average Loss on Trades			-243.20		Losers	1
Average Net Profit Per Trade			571.33		Total trades	15
Percentage Correct	95					
Average Profit on Winning Trades			649.97		Winners	19
Average Loss on Trades			-243.20		Losers	1
Average Net Profit Per Trade			605.31		Total trades	20

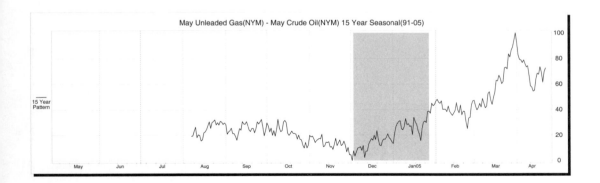

May Unleaded Gas(NYM) - May Crude Oil(NYM) 15 Year Seasonal(91-05)

Figure 2-68

Moore Research Center, Inc. — *Buy Apr Unleaded Reg.(NYM) / Sell Apr Crude Oil(NYM)*

Enter on approximately 12/11 - Exit on approximately 01/16

CONT YEAR	ENTRY DATE	ENTRY PRICE	EXIT DATE	EXIT PRICE		PROFIT AMOUNT	BEST EQUITY DATE	BEST EQUITY AMOUNT	WORST EQUITY DATE	WORST EQUITY AMOUNT
2005	12/13/04	9324	01/14/05	8856		-467.60	12/15/04	81.40	12/29/04	-1651.40
2004	12/11/03	8922	01/16/04	10590		1668.00	01/09/04	2048.00		
2003	12/11/02	8277	01/16/03	8700		422.80	12/24/02	891.60	01/07/03	-241.60
2002	12/11/01	6315	01/16/02	7065		750.20	01/03/02	979.40		
2001	12/11/00	6910	01/16/01	9224		2314.40	01/10/01	3168.60	12/12/00	-34.60
2000	12/13/99	5982	01/14/00	6241		259.40	01/12/00	298.60	12/30/99	-403.60
1999	12/11/98	4861	01/15/99	4391		-470.60	12/17/98	101.00	01/15/99	-470.60
1998	12/11/97	5702	01/16/98	5830		128.60	01/09/98	506.20		
1997	12/11/96	5559	01/16/97	5434		-125.00	12/26/96	296.60	01/14/97	-363.40
1996	12/11/95	5528	01/16/96	5674		146.20	12/28/95	314.00	01/12/96	-193.20
1995	12/12/94	5918	01/16/95	6226		308.20	01/16/95	308.20	12/19/94	-454.80
1994	12/13/93	4180	01/14/94	4239		59.20	12/17/93	267.60	12/27/93	-322.20
1993	12/11/92	5011	01/15/93	5341		330.20	01/06/93	444.80		
1992	12/11/91	6030	01/16/92	6049		18.60	12/24/91	270.00	01/09/92	-470.80
1991	12/11/90	5969	01/16/91	6977		1008.60	01/09/91	1517.00	01/04/91	-551.40
1990	12/11/89	3642	01/16/90	5644		2002.00	01/16/90	2002.00	12/14/89	-130.00
1989	12/12/88	3445	01/16/89	4289		844.60	01/16/89	844.60	12/14/88	-118.40
1988	12/11/87	2696	01/15/88	2846		150.40	01/15/88	150.40	12/29/87	-310.60
1987	12/11/86	2884	01/16/87	3504		620.40	01/12/87	1002.40	12/15/86	-224.00
1986	12/11/85	4449	01/16/86	4788		339.00	01/16/86	339.00	12/18/85	-680.00

Percentage Correct	80			PROFIT		
Average Profit on Winning Trades			617.87	Winners	12
Average Loss on Trades			-354.40	Losers	3
Average Net Profit Per Trade			423.41	Total trades	15
Percentage Correct	85				
Average Profit on Winning Trades			668.87	Winners	17
Average Loss on Trades			-354.40	Losers	3
Average Net Profit Per Trade			515.38	Total trades	20

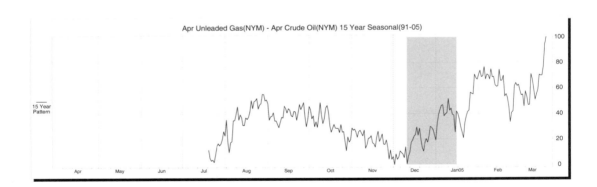

Apr Unleaded Gas(NYM) - Apr Crude Oil(NYM) 15 Year Seasonal(91-05)

15 Year Pattern

Figure 2-69

Buy Mar Unleaded Reg.(NYM) / Sell Mar Crude Oil(NYM)

Enter on approximately 12/11 - Exit on approximately 02/03

CONT YEAR	ENTRY DATE	ENTRY PRICE	EXIT DATE	EXIT PRICE		PROFIT AMOUNT	BEST EQUITY DATE	BEST EQUITY AMOUNT	WORST EQUITY DATE	WORST EQUITY AMOUNT
2005	12/13/04	6194	02/03/05	6823		629.20	01/26/05	2625.20	12/29/04	-1857.40
2004	12/11/03	5628	02/03/04	7963		2335.00	01/09/04	3207.20		
2003	12/11/02	5304	02/03/03	7426		2121.40	02/03/03	2121.40	01/07/03	-351.60
2002	12/11/01	3773	02/01/02	4963		1189.80	01/03/02	1278.40		
2001	12/11/00	4211	02/02/01	6379		2168.00	01/08/01	3778.40	12/12/00	-54.60
2000	12/13/99	4166	02/03/00	4965		799.60	02/03/00	799.60	12/30/99	-605.60
1999	12/11/98	3871	02/03/99	3290		-580.80	12/15/98	76.80	01/21/99	-1290.80
1998	12/11/97	4696	02/03/98	4899		203.20	01/29/98	794.20		
1997	12/11/96	4314	02/03/97	4557		243.00	12/26/96	261.60	01/15/97	-510.20
1996	12/11/95	4432	02/02/96	4771		338.40	12/28/95	436.40	01/12/96	-337.20
1995	12/12/94	4591	02/03/95	5307		716.40	01/18/95	906.60	12/19/94	-255.80
1994	12/13/93	3019	02/03/94	3430		411.00	12/17/93	416.80	12/27/93	-416.60
1993	12/11/92	3380	02/03/93	3527		147.00	01/06/93	762.60		
1992	12/11/91	3940	02/03/92	5312		1371.80	02/03/92	1371.80	01/09/92	-116.60
1991	12/11/90	3657	02/01/91	4330		673.20	01/18/91	1620.40	12/31/90	-994.60
1990	12/11/89	2948	02/02/90	3952		1004.40	01/16/90	2126.40	12/13/89	-160.80
1989	12/12/88	3125	02/03/89	3121		-3.40	01/24/89	541.00	12/14/88	-222.40
1988	12/11/87	2254	02/03/88	2436		182.40	01/27/88	188.20	12/30/87	-324.80
1987	12/11/86	2538	02/03/87	2913		375.00	01/12/87	837.60	12/16/86	-301.80
1986	12/11/85	3874	02/03/86	4455		580.80	01/24/86	1422.80	12/18/85	-839.00

Percentage Correct	93			
Average Profit on Winning Trades		953.36	Winners	14
Average Loss on Trades		-580.80	Losers	1
Average Net Profit Per Trade		851.08	Total trades	15

Percentage Correct	90			
Average Profit on Winning Trades		860.53	Winners	18
Average Loss on Trades		-292.10	Losers	2
Average Net Profit Per Trade		745.27	Total trades	20

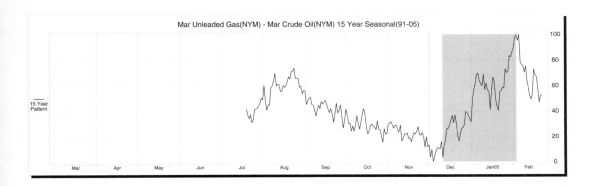

Mar Unleaded Gas(NYM) - Mar Crude Oil(NYM) 15 Year Seasonal(91-05)

Chapter 2: Energy

83

Complex Crack Spreads

Besides refiners hedging profit margins (see page 67), many industry professionals also trade the energy markets in crack spreads of various complexity. Illustrated below are seasonal patterns for the more common combinations, using the underlying cash markets.

Figure 2-70: 2/1/1 Crack Seasonal Pattern

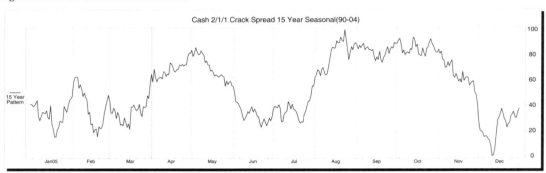

Figure 2-71: 3/2/1 Crack Seasonal Pattern

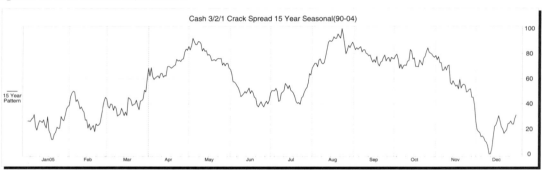

Figure 2-72: 5/3/2 Crack Seasonal Pattern

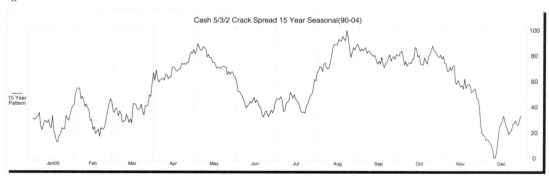

Chapter 3: Grains

As instrumental as was grain cultivation to the advance of civilization, so too was grain trading in the evolution of futures markets. The former finally allowed humans to settle and socialize rather than simply to hunt and gather. The latter eventually required a marketplace, price discovery, enforceable agreements, and mechanisms for delivery. Ancient Greek and Roman markets developed a practice of contracting for future delivery of commodities. Japan's Dojima Rice Market is said to have implemented forward contracting of rice in the early 1700s.

Modern futures trading began in the mid 1800s as Chicago, strategically located at the base of the Great Lakes in the fertile Midwest, developed into a grain terminal. But farmers who brought grain to market at a certain time each year too often found the supply of grain exceeded the immediate needs of users, who would then bid the lowest price. When immediate demand could not absorb a glut at any price, grain was dumped in the street. At other times of the year or in years of crop failure, supplies were exhausted, prices soared, and people went hungry. Forward contracts in corn were first used by river merchants who bought corn after harvest but had to store it until dry enough to transport on rivers free of ice. To reduce the risk of storing grain through winter, merchants traveled to Chicago to contract for spring delivery, assuring themselves of both buyer and price.

The Chicago Board of Trade (CBOT) was founded in 1848 to serve as a central marketplace, with forward contracts gaining popularity shortly thereafter. According to the CBOT, the earliest recorded forward contract for corn was made March 13, 1851, with 3,000 bushels to be delivered in June at a price one cent per bushel below that on March 13. By 1865, the CBOT developed standardized agreements called futures contracts. With the launch of futures contracts in essentially their current form for corn, oats, and wheat on the first business day of 1877, futures trading became more formalized and speculative activity began to grow.

Although corn, oats, and/or wheat are now or have traded on exchanges on six continents, this chapter will focus on primary markets in the United States. Contracts for corn, oats, and soft red winter wheat are little changed from those launched in the 19th century that propelled the CBOT into a global financial institution. The Kansas City Board of Trade (KCBT) launched its contract for hard red winter wheat, which accounts for the bulk of US wheat production and is the primary ingredient in the world's bread, in June 1876. The Minneapolis Grain Exchange (MGEX) launched its contract for hard red spring, one of the highest-protein classes of wheat, in January 1883.

Intra-market Spreads

Spreads between delivery months in a grain market are of two basic types. The spread between delivery months of the same crop marketing year can reflect supply and demand conditions by how much it differs from full carrying charges — the cost to store, insure, and finance the actual grain over time. The spread between delivery months of different crop years can reflect not only those conditions current but also the difference between those already known about one crop and those unknown about a future crop.

Corn

The bulk of the US corn crop is planted April/May and harvested October/November. The crop marketing year runs October-September.

Figure 3-1: Cash Corn Seasonal Pattern

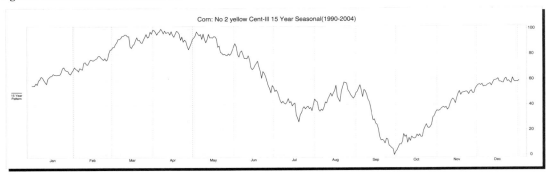

The seasonal pattern for the cash market assumes a logical path. Price and perceptions of supply tend to be inversely related, with price often lowest when supply is greatest, at harvest. As supply declines, price tends to rise. Going into May, the decline in supplies can make the market anxious about the potential for new production. But by the time the bulk of the crop in the Corn Belt is planted, both acreage and early growing conditions are better known. Barring disastrous weather, price tends to decline as prospects for new-crop production grow. As harvest approaches, old-crop carryover is increasingly burdensome.

Carrying Charges. A normal market with adequate supply and sufficient storage would price the spread between a nearby and any deferred contract at a calculable relationship — the cost to carry the commodity from the nearby to delivery against the deferred. For example, December is the first contract of the corn crop marketing year and is usually priced lowest because supply is then largest. A primary function of grain futures is to discourage dumping at harvest and to ensure supply throughout the year. To do so, the market prices grain for progressively deferred delivery at a progressively higher price to help defray the expense of holding, or carrying, the commodity through time. That total expense, or full carrying charges, includes the entire cost of storage, insurance, and financing for a given period of time. The maximum rate for storage in exchange-approved warehouses is set by the exchange. Insurance is minimal and can be included in the storage rate. The cost of finance is traditionally calculated using the prime rate plus 1%, about what is available to a credit-worthy borrower.

Full carry, except in an extreme circumstance, limits spreads between delivery months of the same crop year. Were such a spread to exceed full carry, traders would simultaneously buy the nearby and sell the deferred, accept delivery of the nearby, store the grain, and then redeliver against the deferred for a risk-free profit — as abhorrent to markets as a vacuum is to nature! In fact, such spreads rarely reach more than 70-80% of full carry. Commercials tend to calculate interest as the cost of opportunity, employing the 90-day Bankers' Acceptance Rate rather than the usually higher rate of prime plus 1%. Speculators will also step in front of full carry, assuming positions in these so-called carrying-charge spreads which benefit not only from theoretically defined and limited risk but also from unlimited potential reward.

Figure 3-2

Buy May Corn(CBOT) / Sell Dec Corn(CBOT)

Enter on approximately 06/25 - Exit on approximately 09/27

CONT YEAR	ENTRY DATE	ENTRY PRICE	EXIT DATE	EXIT PRICE	PROFIT	PROFIT AMOUNT	BEST EQUITY DATE	BEST EQUITY AMOUNT	WORST EQUITY DATE	WORST EQUITY AMOUNT
2005	06/25/04	10.75	09/27/04	17.50	6.75	337.50	09/24/04	337.50		
2004	06/25/03	10.25	09/26/03	12.25	2.00	100.00	07/23/03	237.50	09/04/03	-162.50
2003	06/25/02	7.75	09/27/02	11.50	3.75	187.50	09/24/02	200.00	08/14/02	-137.50
2002	06/25/01	18.25	09/27/01	19.25	1.00	50.00	09/19/01	75.00	07/17/01	-262.50
2001	06/26/00	17.75	09/27/00	19.00	1.25	62.50	07/21/00	112.50	06/29/00	-25.00
2000	06/25/99	14.75	09/27/99	16.75	2.00	100.00	07/09/99	200.00	08/04/99	-25.00
1999	06/25/98	11.75	09/25/98	20.00	8.25	412.50	09/17/98	437.50		
1998	06/25/97	12.00	09/26/97	13.75	1.75	87.50	07/25/97	125.00		
1997	06/25/96	6.50	09/27/96	13.75	7.25	362.50	07/22/96	462.50		
1996	06/26/95	7.50	09/27/95	11.00	3.50	175.00	09/14/95	187.50	07/21/95	-75.00
1995	06/27/94	13.00	09/27/94	17.25	4.25	212.50	09/19/94	212.50	06/28/94	-37.50
1994	06/25/93	12.25	09/27/93	12.50	0.25	12.50	09/01/93	112.50	07/16/93	-162.50
1993	06/25/92	9.75	09/25/92	14.75	5.00	250.00	08/10/92	300.00	07/01/92	-62.50
1992	06/25/91	13.00	09/27/91	13.25	0.25	12.50	07/08/91	75.00	07/31/91	-225.00
1991	06/25/90	11.50	09/27/90	15.50	4.00	200.00	09/17/90	250.00	07/03/90	-100.00
1990	06/26/89	7.75	09/27/89	13.50	5.75	287.50	08/03/89	300.00	07/03/89	-12.50
1989	06/27/88	-0.25	09/27/88	8.75	9.00	450.00	09/19/88	537.50	07/15/88	-137.50
1988	06/25/87	9.75	09/25/87	15.00	5.25	262.50	08/04/87	350.00		
1987	06/25/86	13.25	09/26/86	14.75	1.50	75.00	09/03/86	325.00		
1986	06/25/85	13.50	09/27/85	15.75	2.25	112.50	09/03/85	200.00	07/17/85	-125.00

Percentage Correct		100								
Average Profit on Winning Trades					3.42	170.83		Winners		15
Average Loss on Trades								Losers		0
Average Net Profit Per Trade					3.42	170.83		Total trades		15
Percentage Correct		100								
Average Profit on Winning Trades					3.75	187.50		Winners		20
Average Loss on Trades								Losers		0
Average Net Profit Per Trade					3.75	187.50		Total trades		20

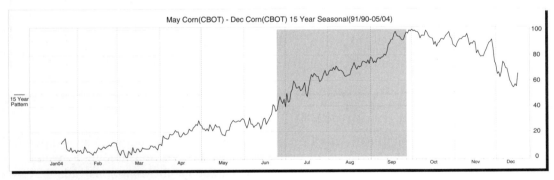

May Corn(CBOT) - Dec Corn(CBOT) 15 Year Seasonal(91/90-05/04)

Such special situations, with their low risk-/high potential-reward profile, occur infrequently and unpredictably. Spreads within the same crop year far more normally trade quietly and at some smaller percentage of full carry, narrowing slowly on strong demand/tight supply and widening on weak demand/abundant supply. In fact, they usually widen throughout the growing season, often from planting all the way to harvest as prospects for the new-crop production improve. Statistics for this May/December spread illustrate the tradeoff of volatility in exchange for persistence and reliability. Although sometimes the spread widened only minimally, it did so in each of the last 20 years — and with no daily closing drawdown exceeding 5.25 cents/bushel.

Figure 3-3: Old-crop/New-crop Corn Strategies

Moore Research Center, Inc.	Old-crop/New-crop Corn Strategies							
Seasonal Strategy	Entry Date	Exit Date	Win Pct	Win Yrs	Loss Years	Total Years	Average Profit	Ave Pft Per Day
Buy Dec Corn(CBOT)	5/08	8/07	93	14	1	15	272	3
Sell Sep Corn(CBOT)			90	18	2	20	263	3
Buy Dec Corn(CBOT)	5/21	6/29	87	13	2	15	173	4
Sell Jul Corn(CBOT)			85	17	3	20	166	4
Buy Jul Corn(CBOT)	6/25	8/07	80	12	3	15	261	6
Sell Sep Corn(CBOT)			80	16	4	20	321	7
Buy "Red" Dec Corn(CBOT)	8/16	9/20	93	14	1	15	350	10
Sell Dec Corn(CBOT)			90	18	2	20	293	8

Old-crop/new-crop. The function of spreads that bridge crop years is to smooth the transition from one to the other. When a commodity is in short supply, the nearby can trade at a premium to the deferred in what is called an inverted market. Typical of such spreads is the old-crop/new-crop relationship, wherein an inversion effectively offers a negative return for holding inventory. Thus, corn contracts from the previous crop year tend to be priced higher than December in order to lure supply from storage when tighter than it presumably will be at harvest.

Figure 3-4: New-crop Dec/Old-crop Jul Corn Pattern

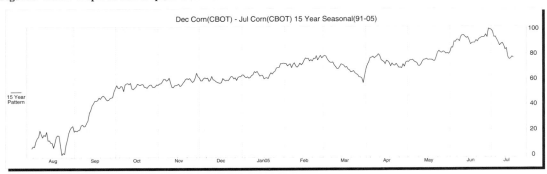

Long old-crop July/short new-crop December is a classic bullish corn spread. Under the most extreme conditions of adverse weather or tight supply, the potential amount by which old-crop can rise over new-crop is limited only by the market's ability to ration available supply to most efficient demand. But such potential occurs rarely. In most conditions, as illustrated by the seasonal pattern above for December over July of the same calendar year, the market tends progressively to favor new-crop over old-crop after planting begins.

Just as December represents new-crop and July old-crop, the September contract represents carryover — physical supplies unused from last harvest that must be carried over as excess into the new crop year. Under normal conditions, that carryover becomes ever

---

Figure 3-5

Buy Dec Corn(CBOT) / Sell Sep Corn(CBOT)

Enter on approximately 05/08 - Exit on approximately 08/07

CONT YEAR	ENTRY DATE	ENTRY PRICE	EXIT DATE	EXIT PRICE	PROFIT	PROFIT AMOUNT	BEST EQUITY DATE	BEST EQUITY AMOUNT	WORST EQUITY DATE	WORST EQUITY AMOUNT
2004	05/10/04	-2.75	08/06/04	11.00	13.75	687.50	08/06/04	687.50	05/21/04	-50.00
2003	05/08/03	1.25	08/07/03	8.00	6.75	337.50	08/07/03	337.50	05/13/03	-100.00
2002	05/08/02	9.75	08/07/02	11.00	1.25	62.50	08/07/02	62.50	06/11/02	-62.50
2001	05/08/01	11.25	08/07/01	11.75	0.50	25.00	07/13/01	50.00	06/21/01	-50.00
2000	05/08/00	8.75	08/07/00	12.25	3.50	175.00	06/29/00	175.00		
1999	05/10/99	8.00	08/06/99	12.00	4.00	200.00	07/23/99	225.00	06/24/99	-25.00
1998	05/08/98	5.25	08/07/98	9.75	4.50	225.00	08/07/98	225.00	06/08/98	-112.50
1997	05/08/97	-1.00	08/07/97	3.00	4.00	200.00	08/07/97	200.00	06/16/97	-162.50
1996	05/08/96	-51.00	08/07/96	-23.75	27.25	1362.50	08/07/96	1362.50	05/17/96	-912.50
1995	05/08/95	3.25	08/07/95	0.00	-3.25	-162.50	06/07/95	112.50	07/25/95	-237.50
1994	05/09/94	-8.00	08/05/94	2.50	10.50	525.00	08/03/94	625.00	06/07/94	-25.00
1993	05/10/93	4.50	08/06/93	5.00	0.50	25.00	07/01/93	287.50		
1992	05/08/92	-0.50	08/07/92	2.25	2.75	137.50	06/29/92	300.00		
1991	05/08/91	0.50	08/07/91	3.75	3.25	162.50	08/02/91	287.50	05/29/91	-75.00
1990	05/08/90	-7.00	08/07/90	-4.75	2.25	112.50	07/03/90	362.50		
1989	05/08/89	-3.25	08/07/89	2.00	5.25	262.50	08/04/89	287.50	05/25/89	-150.00
1988	05/09/88	9.50	08/05/88	7.75	-1.75	-87.50	06/01/88	162.50	06/23/88	-425.00
1987	05/08/87	4.00	08/07/87	11.25	7.25	362.50	08/07/87	362.50	05/26/87	-125.00
1986	05/08/86	-5.50	08/07/86	6.50	12.00	600.00	08/06/86	675.00	05/13/86	-175.00
1985	05/08/85	-3.75	08/07/85	-3.00	0.75	37.50	08/05/85	112.50	07/18/85	-400.00

Percentage Correct	93									
Average Profit on Winning Trades					6.05	302.68		Winners		14
Average Loss on Trades					-3.25	-162.50		Losers		1
Average Net Profit Per Trade					5.43	271.67		Total trades		15
Percentage Correct	90									
Average Profit on Winning Trades					6.11	305.56		Winners		18
Average Loss on Trades					-2.50	-125.00		Losers		2
Average Net Profit Per Trade					5.25	262.50		Total trades		20

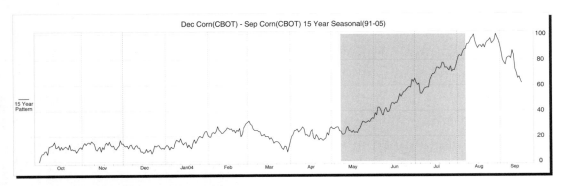

Dec Corn(CBOT) - Sep Corn(CBOT) 15 Year Seasonal(91-05)

more burdensome as the growing season progresses. Also of note is the last spread in the table, "Red" December over December. After the current crop is made and matures into harvest, its production potential becomes secure and known compared to the completely unknown of next year's "Red" crop.

Figure 3-6

Buy Dec Corn(CBOT) / Sell Jul Corn(CBOT)

Moore Research Center, Inc.

Enter on approximately 05/21 - Exit on approximately 06/29

CONT YEAR	ENTRY DATE	ENTRY PRICE	EXIT DATE	EXIT PRICE	PROFIT	PROFIT AMOUNT	BEST EQUITY DATE	BEST EQUITY AMOUNT	WORST EQUITY DATE	WORST EQUITY AMOUNT
2004	05/21/04	-9.00	06/29/04	9.50	18.50	925.00	06/23/04	937.50		
2003	05/21/03	-0.50	06/27/03	-3.50	-3.00	-150.00	06/05/03	62.50	06/26/03	-212.50
2002	05/21/02	15.50	06/28/02	18.00	2.50	125.00	06/25/02	162.50		
2001	05/21/01	18.50	06/29/01	19.50	1.00	50.00	06/29/01	50.00	06/21/01	-25.00
2000	05/22/00	18.75	06/29/00	21.25	2.50	125.00	06/29/00	125.00	05/24/00	-25.00
1999	05/21/99	13.75	06/29/99	14.50	0.75	37.50	05/24/99	37.50	06/25/99	-225.00
1998	05/21/98	12.00	06/29/98	14.00	2.00	100.00	06/26/98	100.00	06/05/98	-300.00
1997	05/21/97	-14.75	06/27/97	-10.75	4.00	200.00	06/27/97	200.00	06/19/97	-350.00
1996	05/21/96	-159.25	06/28/96	-155.00	4.25	212.50	06/05/96	3250.00		
1995	05/22/95	9.00	06/29/95	6.00	-3.00	-150.00	06/07/95	162.50	06/29/95	-150.00
1994	05/23/94	-7.75	06/29/94	-6.50	1.25	62.50	06/29/94	62.50	06/22/94	-337.50
1993	05/21/93	11.00	06/29/93	15.75	4.75	237.50	06/29/93	237.50	06/02/93	-25.00
1992	05/21/92	2.00	06/29/92	10.50	8.50	425.00	06/29/92	425.00		
1991	05/21/91	-2.75	06/28/91	1.00	3.75	187.50	06/11/91	387.50		
1990	05/21/90	-11.75	06/29/90	-7.75	4.00	200.00	06/25/90	450.00		
1989	05/22/89	-16.75	06/29/89	-17.25	-0.50	-25.00	06/14/89	250.00	05/30/89	-500.00
1988	05/23/88	17.50	06/29/88	23.75	6.25	312.50	06/29/88	312.50	06/23/88	-725.00
1987	05/21/87	5.75	06/29/87	11.25	5.50	275.00	06/15/87	425.00	05/28/87	-300.00
1986	05/21/86	-41.25	06/27/86	-38.50	2.75	137.50	05/23/86	200.00	06/23/86	-262.50
1985	05/21/85	-18.25	06/28/85	-17.50	0.75	37.50	05/24/85	100.00	06/19/85	-325.00

Percentage Correct		87								
Average Profit on Winning Trades					4.44	222.12		Winners		13
Average Loss on Trades					-3.00	-150.00		Losers		2
Average Net Profit Per Trade					3.45	172.50		Total trades		15
Percentage Correct		85								
Average Profit on Winning Trades					4.29	214.71		Winners		17
Average Loss on Trades					-2.17	-108.33		Losers		3
Average Net Profit Per Trade					3.33	166.25		Total trades		20

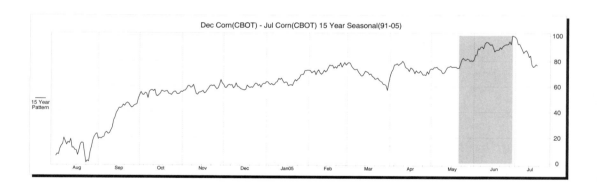

Dec Corn(CBOT) - Jul Corn(CBOT) 15 Year Seasonal(91-05)

Figure 3-7

Buy Jul Corn(CBOT) / Sell Sep Corn(CBOT)

Enter on approximately 06/25 - Exit on approximately 08/07

CONT YEAR	ENTRY DATE	ENTRY PRICE	EXIT DATE	EXIT PRICE	PROFIT	PROFIT AMOUNT	BEST EQUITY DATE	BEST EQUITY AMOUNT	WORST EQUITY DATE	WORST EQUITY AMOUNT
2005	06/25/04	16.25	08/06/04	30.75	14.50	725.00	08/06/04	725.00		
2004	06/25/03	12.75	08/07/03	25.00	12.25	612.50	08/01/03	662.50	06/26/03	-12.50
2003	06/25/02	20.00	08/07/02	20.25	0.25	12.50	07/02/02	237.50	08/05/02	-75.00
2002	06/25/01	35.50	08/07/01	31.75	-3.75	-187.50	07/02/01	62.50	07/17/01	-387.50
2001	06/26/00	34.75	08/07/00	39.00	4.25	212.50	08/02/00	225.00		
2000	06/25/99	26.50	08/06/99	29.75	3.25	162.50	07/15/99	450.00		
1999	06/25/98	22.00	08/07/98	33.75	11.75	587.50	08/06/98	612.50		
1998	06/25/97	14.25	08/07/97	18.00	3.75	187.50	07/28/97	212.50		
1997	06/25/96	-31.50	08/07/96	-10.25	21.25	1062.50	07/22/96	1112.50	07/10/96	-587.50
1996	06/26/95	12.25	08/07/95	12.50	0.25	12.50	06/27/95	75.00	07/25/95	-350.00
1995	06/25/94	9.75	08/05/94	22.00	12.25	612.50	08/01/94	725.00		
1994	06/25/93	23.25	08/06/93	19.25	-4.00	-200.00	06/29/93	62.50	07/26/93	-387.50
1993	06/25/92	17.25	08/07/92	22.25	5.00	250.00	07/23/92	275.00	07/02/92	-112.50
1992	06/25/91	20.00	08/07/91	16.75	-3.25	-162.50	07/12/91	100.00	07/31/91	-200.00
1991	06/25/90	12.75	08/07/90	13.25	0.50	25.00	06/26/90	62.50	07/18/90	-225.00
1990	06/26/89	4.00	08/07/89	16.25	12.25	612.50	08/03/89	662.50		
1989	06/27/88	-1.50	08/05/88	5.50	7.00	350.00	07/28/88	837.50	07/15/88	-350.00
1988	06/25/87	17.00	08/07/87	30.25	13.25	662.50	08/07/87	662.50		
1987	06/25/86	9.75	08/07/86	27.25	17.50	875.00	08/06/86	925.00		
1986	06/25/85	8.75	08/07/85	8.75	0.00	0.00	08/05/85	100.00	07/18/85	-462.50

Percentage Correct	80									
Average Profit on Winning Trades					7.44	371.88		Winners		12
Average Loss on Trades					-3.67	-183.33		Losers		3
Average Net Profit Per Trade					5.22	260.83		Total trades		15
Percentage Correct	80									
Average Profit on Winning Trades					8.70	435.16		Winners		16
Average Loss on Trades					-2.75	-137.50		Losers		4
Average Net Profit Per Trade					6.41	320.63		Total trades		20

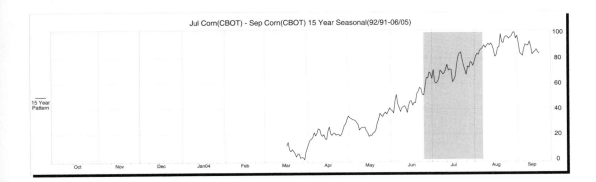

Jul Corn(CBOT) - Sep Corn(CBOT) 15 Year Seasonal(92/91-06/05)

Figure 3-8

Buy "Red" Dec Corn(CBOT) / Sell Dec Corn(CBOT)

Enter on approximately 08/16 - Exit on approximately 09/20

CONT YEAR	ENTRY DATE	ENTRY PRICE	EXIT DATE	EXIT PRICE	PROFIT	PROFIT AMOUNT	BEST EQUITY DATE	BEST EQUITY AMOUNT	WORST EQUITY DATE	WORST EQUITY AMOUNT
2005	08/16/04	25.75	09/20/04	34.50	8.75	437.50	09/20/04	437.50	08/23/04	-262.50
2004	08/18/03	7.00	09/19/03	13.00	6.00	300.00	09/18/03	375.00	09/04/03	-500.00
2003	08/16/02	-25.50	09/20/02	-11.75	13.75	687.50	09/20/02	687.50	09/11/02	-437.50
2002	08/16/01	23.50	09/20/01	32.25	8.75	437.50	09/19/01	475.00	08/31/01	-112.50
2001	08/16/00	42.75	09/20/00	43.00	0.25	12.50	09/19/00	50.00	08/29/00	-87.50
2000	08/16/99	25.00	09/20/99	33.25	8.25	412.50	09/17/99	475.00	08/17/99	-87.50
1999	08/17/98	33.50	09/18/98	42.25	8.75	437.50	09/15/98	437.50		
1998	08/18/97	-0.75	09/19/97	8.75	9.50	475.00	09/19/97	475.00	08/25/97	-262.50
1997	08/16/96	-42.50	09/20/96	-12.50	30.00	1500.00	09/20/96	1500.00	08/26/96	-200.00
1996	08/16/95	-20.50	09/20/95	-33.50	-13.00	-650.00	08/17/95	25.00	09/18/95	-712.50
1995	08/16/94	23.75	09/20/94	28.50	4.75	237.50	09/19/94	275.00	09/06/94	-37.50
1994	08/16/93	-0.25	09/20/93	4.25	4.50	225.00	09/01/93	562.50	08/23/93	-75.00
1993	08/17/92	21.50	09/18/92	25.00	3.50	175.00	08/28/92	225.00	08/24/92	-87.50
1992	08/16/91	0.25	09/20/91	1.25	1.00	50.00	08/20/91	525.00	09/16/91	-300.00
1991	08/16/90	10.00	09/20/90	20.25	10.25	512.50	09/14/90	637.50		
1990	08/16/89	4.00	09/20/89	5.50	1.50	75.00	09/01/89	175.00	09/14/89	-175.00
1989	08/16/88	-30.25	09/20/88	-20.25	10.00	500.00	09/19/88	750.00	09/06/88	-87.50
1988	08/17/87	24.50	09/18/87	15.50	-9.00	-450.00	08/21/87	37.50	09/18/87	-450.00
1987	08/18/86	21.25	09/19/86	22.75	1.50	75.00	09/03/86	575.00		
1986	08/16/85	-0.25	09/20/85	7.75	8.00	400.00	09/13/85	600.00	08/23/85	-125.00

Percentage Correct	93									
Average Profit on Winning Trades					8.43	421.43		Winners		14
Average Loss on Trades					-13.00	-650.00		Losers		1
Average Net Profit Per Trade					7.00	350.00		Total trades		15

Percentage Correct	90									
Average Profit on Winning Trades					7.72	386.11		Winners		18
Average Loss on Trades					-11.00	-550.00		Losers		2
Average Net Profit Per Trade					5.85	292.50		Total trades		20

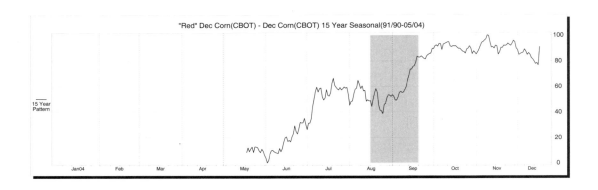

"Red" Dec Corn(CBOT) - Dec Corn(CBOT) 15 Year Seasonal(91/90-05/04)

Oats

Most domestically grown oats are sown April/May and harvested July/August. The crop marketing year runs from July-June. The seasonal pattern for cash oats illustrates how prices tend to bottom when supply is largest, in August, and to peak when the market is most anxious about future supply, between March and early May.

Figure 3-9: Cash Oats Seasonal Pattern

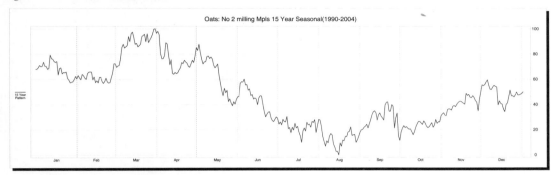

Oats: No 2 milling Mpls 15 Year Seasonal(1990-2004)

Figure 3-10: Oats Spread Strategies

Moore Research Center, Inc.	Oats(CBOT) Spread Strategies							
Seasonal Strategy	Entry Date	Exit Date	Win Pct	Win Yrs	Loss Years	Total Years	Average Profit	Ave Pft Per Day
Buy Sep Oats(CBOT)	3/12	4/18	80	12	3	15	154	4
Sell May Oats(CBOT)			80	16	4	20	166	4
Buy May Oats(CBOT)	4/29	5/11	100	15	0	15	189	15
Sell Jul Oats(CBOT)			100	20	0	20	174	13
Buy Jul Oats(CBOT)	6/13	7/13	93	14	1	15	438	14
Sell Dec Oats(CBOT)			80	16	4	20	323	10

Although oats was one of the original formalized futures contracts, its primary use was as livestock feed. But acreage devoted to oats declined as first horse and later dairy cattle populations declined. It has now devolved into a minor crop. With little volume and open interest in its futures market, intramarket spreads tend to be illiquid. By far the most reliable have been delivery plays, in which commercial firms buy and hold the nearby going into and through First Notice Day and then take delivery. Thus, the contract in strong hands tends to outperform all others.

Figure 3-11

| | | | Moore Research Center, Inc. | *Buy Sep Oats(CBOT) / Sell May Oats(CBOT)* | | | | | | |

Enter on approximately 03/12 - Exit on approximately 04/18

CONT YEAR	ENTRY DATE	ENTRY PRICE	EXIT DATE	EXIT PRICE	PROFIT	PROFIT AMOUNT	BEST EQUITY DATE	BEST EQUITY AMOUNT	WORST EQUITY DATE	WORST EQUITY AMOUNT
2004	03/12/04	5.50	04/16/04	10.00	4.50	225.00	04/15/04	337.50	03/17/04	-12.50
2003	03/12/03	-26.00	04/17/03	-34.50	-8.50	-425.00	03/13/03	400.00	04/09/03	-675.00
2002	03/12/02	-64.00	04/18/02	-36.75	27.25	1362.50	04/18/02	1362.50	04/09/02	-537.50
2001	03/12/01	6.00	04/18/01	6.25	0.25	12.50	03/15/01	62.50	04/02/01	-37.50
2000	03/13/00	1.75	04/18/00	-1.50	-3.25	-162.50			04/17/00	-200.00
1999	03/12/99	4.00	04/16/99	-2.50	-6.50	-325.00	04/06/99	75.00	04/16/99	-325.00
1998	03/12/98	8.75	04/17/98	11.25	2.50	125.00	04/17/98	125.00	03/24/98	-75.00
1997	03/12/97	-5.50	04/18/97	-4.75	0.75	37.50	04/04/97	187.50		
1996	03/12/96	-38.50	04/18/96	-20.25	18.25	912.50	04/15/96	1112.50	03/14/96	-100.00
1995	03/13/95	9.00	04/18/95	9.25	0.25	12.50	04/12/95	37.50	04/03/95	-87.50
1994	03/14/94	8.75	04/18/94	9.25	0.50	25.00	04/04/94	37.50	03/24/94	-50.00
1993	03/12/93	0.25	04/16/93	3.75	3.50	175.00	04/16/93	175.00	03/19/93	-75.00
1992	03/12/92	9.00	04/16/92	9.25	0.25	12.50	03/20/92	87.50		
1991	03/12/91	9.00	04/18/91	13.25	4.25	212.50	04/15/91	237.50		
1990	03/12/90	11.75	04/18/90	14.00	2.25	112.50	04/17/90	125.00		
1989	03/13/89	6.00	04/18/89	10.00	4.00	200.00	04/12/89	425.00	03/15/89	-12.50
1988	03/14/88	-5.50	04/18/88	5.25	10.75	537.50	04/15/88	650.00	03/18/88	-262.50
1987	03/12/87	-7.75	04/16/87	-18.00	-10.25	-512.50			04/03/87	-750.00
1986	03/12/86	-3.00	04/18/86	10.25	13.25	662.50	04/18/86	662.50	03/13/86	-12.50
1985	03/12/85	-9.25	04/18/85	-7.00	2.25	112.50	03/28/85	150.00	03/18/85	-25.00

Percentage Correct	80									
Average Profit on Winning Trades					5.38	268.75		Winners		12
Average Loss on Trades					-6.08	-304.17		Losers		3
Average Net Profit Per Trade					3.08	154.17		Total trades		15
Percentage Correct	80									
Average Profit on Winning Trades					5.92	296.09		Winners		16
Average Loss on Trades					-7.13	-356.25		Losers		4
Average Net Profit Per Trade					3.31	165.63		Total trades		20

HYPOTHETICAL PERFORMANCE RESULTS HAVE MANY INHERENT LIMITATIONS, SOME OF WHICH ARE DESCRIBED BELOW. NO REPRESENTATION IS BEING MADE THAT ANY ACCOUNT WILL OR IS LIKELY TO ACHIEVE PROFITS OR LOSSES SIMILAR TO THOSE SHOWN. IN FACT, THERE ARE FREQUENTLY SHARP DIFFERENCES BETWEEN HYPOTHETICAL PERFORMANCE RESULTS AND THE ACTUAL RESULTS SUBSEQUENTLY ACHIEVED BY ANY PARTICULAR TRADING PROGRAM. ONE OF THE LIMITATIONS OF HYPOTHETICAL PERFORMANCE RESULTS IS THAT THEY ARE GENERALLY PREPARED WITH THE BENEFIT OF HINDSIGHT. IN ADDITION, HYPOTHETICAL TRADING DOES NOT INVOLVE FINANCIAL RISK, AND NO HYPOTHETICAL TRADING RECORD CAN COMPLETELY ACCOUNT FOR THE IMPACT OF FINANCIAL RISK IN ACTUAL TRADING. FOR EXAMPLE, THE ABILITY TO WITHSTAND LOSSES OR ADHERE TO A PARTICULAR TRADING PROGRAM IN SPITE OF TRADING LOSSES ARE MATERIAL POINTS WHICH CAN ALSO ADVERSELY AFFECT ACTUAL TRADING RESULTS. THERE ARE NUMEROUS OTHER FACTORS RELATED TO THE MARKETS IN GENERAL OR TO THE IMPLEMENTATION OF ANY SPECIFIC TRADING PROGRAM WHICH CANNOT BE FULLY ACCOUNTED FOR IN THE PREPARATION OF HYPOTHETICAL PERFORMANCE RESULTS AND ALL OF WHICH CAN ADVERSELY AFFECT ACTUAL TRADING RESULTS. RESULTS NOT ADJUSTED FOR COMMISSION AND SLIPPAGE.

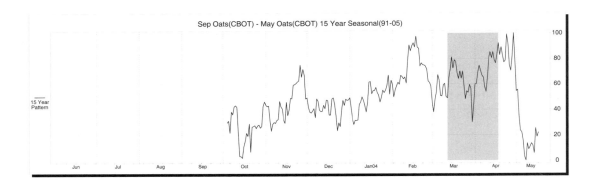

Sep Oats(CBOT) - May Oats(CBOT) 15 Year Seasonal(91-05)

Figure 3-12

Buy May Oats(CBOT) / Sell Jul Oats(CBOT)

Enter on approximately 04/29 - Exit on approximately 05/11

CONT YEAR	ENTRY DATE	ENTRY PRICE	EXIT DATE	EXIT PRICE	PROFIT	PROFIT AMOUNT	BEST EQUITY DATE	BEST EQUITY AMOUNT	WORST EQUITY DATE	WORST EQUITY AMOUNT
2004	04/29/04	-7.25	05/11/04	-5.00	2.25	112.50	05/10/04	162.50		
2003	04/29/03	15.50	05/09/03	17.25	1.75	87.50	05/05/03	462.50	04/30/03	-325.00
2002	04/29/02	25.50	05/10/02	45.50	20.00	1000.00	05/10/02	1000.00		
2001	04/30/01	-2.75	05/11/01	-2.00	0.75	37.50	05/08/01	37.50	05/01/01	-25.00
2000	05/01/00	3.00	05/11/00	5.12	2.13	106.25	05/10/00	112.50		
1999	04/29/99	1.75	05/11/99	3.25	1.50	75.00	04/30/99	125.00	05/10/99	-50.00
1998	04/29/98	-6.25	05/11/98	-2.50	3.75	187.50	05/11/98	187.50		
1997	04/29/97	4.75	05/09/97	8.50	3.75	187.50	05/08/97	250.00		
1996	04/29/96	-13.00	05/10/96	-3.50	9.50	475.00	05/01/96	675.00		
1995	05/01/95	-5.75	05/11/95	-5.50	0.25	12.50	05/02/95	37.50		
1994	04/29/94	-6.25	05/11/94	-4.50	1.75	87.50	05/05/94	112.50		
1993	04/29/93	-3.00	05/11/93	-2.00	1.00	50.00	05/05/93	75.00		
1992	04/29/92	-5.75	05/11/92	-2.75	3.00	150.00	05/11/92	150.00		
1991	04/29/91	-6.50	05/10/91	-2.00	4.50	225.00	05/10/91	225.00		
1990	04/30/90	-8.00	05/11/90	-7.25	0.75	37.50	05/11/90	37.50	05/03/90	-100.00
1989	05/01/89	-9.25	05/11/89	-8.00	1.25	62.50	05/08/89	225.00		
1988	04/29/88	-6.00	05/11/88	-5.50	0.50	25.00	05/06/88	150.00		
1987	04/29/87	12.50	05/11/87	20.50	8.00	400.00	05/07/87	787.50		
1986	04/29/86	-8.00	05/09/86	-6.00	2.00	100.00	05/09/86	100.00		
1985	04/29/85	2.50	05/10/85	3.75	1.25	62.50	05/07/85	87.50		

Percentage Correct	100									
Average Profit on Winning Trades					3.78	188.75		Winners		15
Average Loss on Trades								Losers		0
Average Net Profit Per Trade					3.78	188.75		Total trades		15
Percentage Correct	100									
Average Profit on Winning Trades					3.48	174.06		Winners		20
Average Loss on Trades								Losers		0
Average Net Profit Per Trade					3.48	174.06		Total trades		20

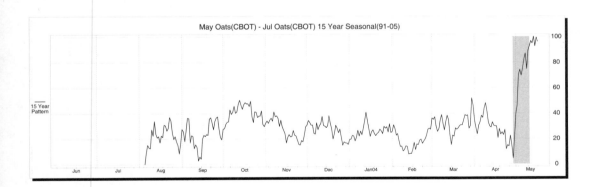

May Oats(CBOT) - Jul Oats(CBOT) 15 Year Seasonal(91-05)

Figure 3-13

Moore Research Center, Inc. — Buy Jul Oats(CBOT) / Sell Dec Oats(CBOT)

Enter on approximately 06/13 - Exit on approximately 07/13

CONT YEAR	ENTRY DATE	ENTRY PRICE	EXIT DATE	EXIT PRICE	PROFIT	PROFIT AMOUNT	BEST EQUITY DATE	BEST EQUITY AMOUNT	WORST EQUITY DATE	WORST EQUITY AMOUNT
2004	06/14/04	-10.75	07/13/04	-6.25	4.50	225.00	07/13/04	225.00	06/29/04	-175.00
2003	06/13/03	7.75	07/11/03	26.00	18.25	912.50	07/11/03	912.50		
2002	06/13/02	39.25	07/12/02	65.25	26.00	1300.00	07/12/02	1300.00	06/27/02	-87.50
2001	06/13/01	-5.75	07/13/01	23.25	29.00	1450.00	07/12/01	1762.50		
2000	06/13/00	-13.00	07/13/00	-12.50	0.50	25.00	06/15/00	62.50	07/03/00	-137.50
1999	06/14/99	3.75	07/13/99	-1.00	-4.75	-237.50			06/29/99	-462.50
1998	06/15/98	-12.50	07/13/98	-11.25	1.25	62.50	07/13/98	62.50	06/22/98	-75.00
1997	06/13/97	6.00	07/11/97	21.75	15.75	787.50	07/11/97	787.50	06/16/97	-25.00
1996	06/13/96	22.50	07/12/96	36.00	13.50	675.00	07/12/96	675.00	06/27/96	-500.00
1995	06/13/95	-11.50	07/13/95	-6.50	5.00	250.00	07/12/95	250.00		
1994	06/13/94	-11.00	07/13/94	-3.75	7.25	362.50	06/24/94	950.00		
1993	06/14/93	-6.00	07/13/93	-5.50	0.50	25.00	06/21/93	75.00	06/30/93	-100.00
1992	06/15/92	-10.25	07/13/92	-6.25	4.00	200.00	07/09/92	200.00	06/30/92	-175.00
1991	06/13/91	-15.25	07/12/91	-8.75	6.50	325.00	07/12/91	325.00		
1990	06/13/90	-20.00	07/13/90	-15.75	4.25	212.50	07/12/90	212.50	06/28/90	-62.50
1989	06/13/89	-16.00	07/13/89	-19.25	-3.25	-162.50	06/14/89	12.50	07/03/89	-200.00
1988	06/13/88	0.00	07/13/88	3.25	3.25	162.50	06/16/88	237.50	07/11/88	-1075.00
1987	06/15/87	-8.25	07/13/87	-8.50	-0.25	-12.50	06/24/87	75.00	06/19/87	-200.00
1986	06/13/86	-6.50	07/11/86	-9.50	-3.00	-150.00	06/23/86	75.00	06/30/86	-400.00
1985	06/13/85	-1.50	07/12/85	-0.50	1.00	50.00	06/21/85	275.00		

Percentage Correct	93									
Average Profit on Winning Trades					9.73	486.61		Winners	14	
Average Loss on Trades					-4.75	-237.50		Losers	1	
Average Net Profit Per Trade					8.77	438.33		Total trades	15	
Percentage Correct	80									
Average Profit on Winning Trades					8.78	439.06		Winners	16	
Average Loss on Trades					-2.81	-140.63		Losers	4	
Average Net Profit Per Trade					6.46	323.13		Total trades	20	

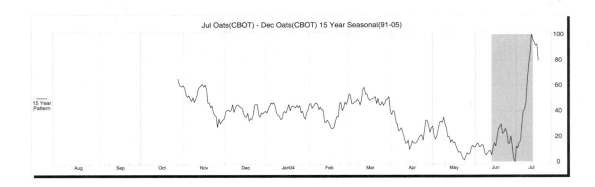

Jul Oats(CBOT) - Dec Oats(CBOT) 15 Year Seasonal(91-05)

15 Year Pattern

Wheat

Wheat is divided into two major *types*: winter and spring. Winter wheat is seeded in September/October, enters dormancy over winter, reemerges in spring, and is harvested mostly June/July. Spring wheat is planted April-June and harvested August/September. The USDA crop marketing year runs July-June.

Wheat is also divided into five main *classes*: hard red winter, soft red winter, hard red spring, durum, and white. Hard red winter, flour from which is primarily used in bread, accounts for about half of all US production. The bulk of the crop is grown in the arid Great Plains, and it is the only wheat deliverable at the KCBT. Soft red winter, flour from which is used in snack foods and pastries, is grown in the Midwest and east toward the Atlantic. Although the exchange accepts other classes for delivery at differentials, soft red winter wheat underlies the CBOT contract. Hard red spring, also used for breads, is grown in northern states with severe winters.

Figure 3-14: Cash KCBT Wheat Seasonal Pattern

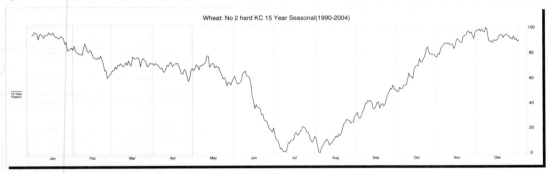

Cash markets for both classes of winter wheat tend to follow the same pattern. Prices tend to reach a seasonal bottom in July/August, between the harvests of winter and spring wheat, and then to rise through the primary export season. Prices often peak by December as winter wheat enters dormancy and just before Southern Hemisphere crops enter export channels. In the new year, the US market then suffers from renewed producer selling in a new tax year, logistical difficulties, surging export competition, and finally the approach of another harvest.

Carrying Charges. Going into and through harvest, the market tends to increase premiums for deferred contracts in order to encourage storage and defray its costs. As the last contract of the crop marketing year, May tends to be the regular recipient of widening premiums in order to ensure supply throughout the year. Note (in Figure 3-15) that in only 2 of the last 20 years would any daily closing drawdown have even reached 5.00 cents/bushel.

Figure 3-15

Moore Research Center, Inc. — Buy May Wheat(CBOT) / Sell Sep Wheat(CBOT)

Enter on approximately 07/12 - Exit on approximately 08/20

CONT YEAR	ENTRY DATE	ENTRY PRICE	EXIT DATE	EXIT PRICE	PROFIT	PROFIT AMOUNT	BEST EQUITY DATE	BEST EQUITY AMOUNT	WORST EQUITY DATE	WORST EQUITY AMOUNT
2005	07/12/04	27.50	08/20/04	28.50	1.00	50.00	08/09/04	250.00	07/19/04	-75.00
2004	07/14/03	0.25	08/20/03	6.00	5.75	287.50	07/30/03	475.00	08/18/03	-137.50
2003	07/12/02	5.75	08/20/02	16.75	11.00	550.00	08/20/02	550.00	07/25/02	-87.50
2002	07/12/01	29.75	08/20/01	34.75	5.00	250.00	08/15/01	262.50	07/16/01	-187.50
2001	07/12/00	42.50	08/18/00	47.00	4.50	225.00	08/15/00	225.00	07/14/00	-62.50
2000	07/12/99	39.00	08/20/99	39.75	0.75	37.50	08/13/99	62.50	07/23/99	-75.00
1999	07/13/98	35.75	08/20/98	40.00	4.25	212.50	08/07/98	262.50	07/20/98	-50.00
1998	07/14/97	22.00	08/20/97	28.25	6.25	312.50	08/15/97	550.00	07/22/97	-37.50
1997	07/12/96	-31.00	08/20/96	-22.50	8.50	425.00	07/24/96	1150.00		
1996	07/12/95	-24.00	08/18/95	-16.75	7.25	362.50	08/10/95	437.50	07/21/95	-1212.50
1995	07/12/94	11.75	08/19/94	17.50	5.75	287.50	08/18/94	300.00	07/28/94	-62.50
1994	07/12/93	16.50	08/20/93	1.00	-15.50	-775.00	07/14/93	12.50	08/19/93	-850.00
1993	07/13/92	4.00	08/20/92	18.00	14.00	700.00	08/20/92	700.00	07/17/92	-225.00
1992	07/12/91	16.00	08/20/91	18.25	2.25	112.50	07/29/91	112.50	08/16/91	-200.00
1991	07/12/90	21.00	08/20/90	28.25	7.25	362.50	08/10/90	475.00	07/13/90	-150.00
1990	07/12/89	-4.25	08/18/89	9.50	13.75	687.50	08/18/89	687.50	07/14/89	-112.50
1989	07/12/88	-9.50	08/19/88	-11.75	-2.25	-112.50	07/25/88	450.00	08/19/88	-112.50
1988	07/13/87	7.75	08/20/87	22.50	14.75	737.50	08/07/87	862.50	07/22/87	-125.00
1987	07/14/86	-19.50	08/20/86	-9.00	10.50	525.00	08/20/86	525.00		
1986	07/12/85	-5.25	08/20/85	14.75	20.00	1000.00	08/20/85	1000.00	07/15/85	-37.50

Percentage Correct	93									
Average Profit on Winning Trades					5.96	298.21	Winners	14		
Average Loss on Trades					-15.50	-775.00	Losers	1		
Average Net Profit Per Trade					4.53	226.67	Total trades	15		
Percentage Correct	90									
Average Profit on Winning Trades					7.92	395.83	Winners	18		
Average Loss on Trades					-8.88	-443.75	Losers	2		
Average Net Profit Per Trade					6.24	311.88	Total trades	20		

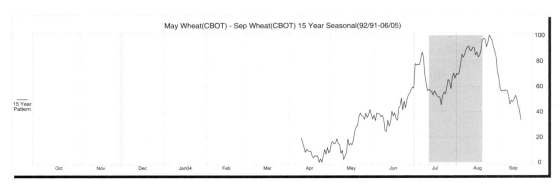

May Wheat(CBOT) - Sep Wheat(CBOT) 15 Year Seasonal(92/91-06/05)

Old-crop/new-crop. US supplies peak by the end of spring wheat harvest in early September. During the primary US export season, demand grows and physical supply declines. When winter wheat is planted in September/October, the market can begin to calculate the production potential of a new crop — however many months from fruition. The seasonal pattern below illustrates how old-crop has tended to outperform new-crop during export and planting seasons.

Figure 3-16: Dec/Jul CBOT Wheat Seasonal Pattern

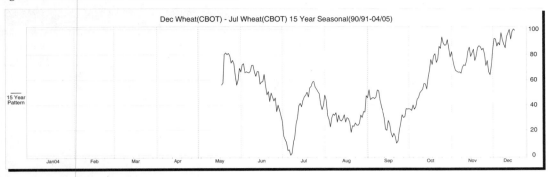

The most prominent feature of the seasonal spread landscape, however, appears as the export season draws to a close. As winter arrives and temperatures freeze, the tender wheat shoots go dormant until warm weather returns. The blanket of snow which normally covers the winter wheat regions serves to insulate and protect the crop. With inadequate snow cover, wheat can heave — severing the stem from the root as the soil alternately freezes and thaws. Thus is the new crop vulnerable through winter.

In contrast, old-crop begins to suffer the initial effects of the notorious "February Break." Export competition from Southern Hemisphere producers surges. The new calendar year is also a new US tax year. Producers already prevented from working frozen fields instead haul grain and convert it to income. But inland rivers freeze and flood, creating transportation bottlenecks. Barge traffic slows and grain supply builds in the interior. Ocean-going freighters can find navigation on the St. Lawrence Seaway difficult, hindering traffic from Great Lakes' terminals to export destinations. With domestic consumption accounting for perhaps only 60% of total US production, large amounts of old-crop wheat with nowhere else to go are placed in position for delivery against March futures. Thus, beginning as early as mid November, new-crop winter wheat — both hard red and soft red — has begun to outperform old-crop. Both the seasonal pattern and the listings of seasonal strategies below testify to how reliable the dynamic has been and how it tends to intensify in the new calendar year.

Figure 3-17: Jul/Mar CBOT Wheat Seasonal Pattern

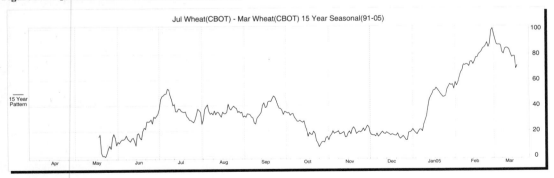

Figure 3-18: Old-crop/New-crop Wheat Strategies

Moore Research Center, Inc.		*Old-crop/New-crop Wheat Strategies*						
Seasonal Strategy	Entry Date	Exit Date	Win Pct	Win Yrs	Loss Years	Total Years	Average Profit	Ave Pft Per Day
Buy Dec Wheat(CBOT)	9/23	10/22	87	13	2	15	312	10
Sell Jul Wheat(CBOT)			80	16	4	20	301	10
Buy Jul Wheat(CBOT)	11/17	2/16	100	15	0	15	649	7
Sell Mar Wheat(CBOT)			95	19	1	20	533	6
Buy Jul Wheat(CBOT)	12/17	2/28	93	14	1	15	412	6
Sell May Wheat(CBOT)			85	17	3	20	374	5
Buy Jul Wheat(KCBT)	12/20	2/08	87	13	2	15	405	8
Sell Mar Wheat(KCBT)			85	17	3	20	381	7
Buy Jul Wheat(CBOT)	12/22	2/12	100	15	0	15	600	11
Sell Mar Wheat(CBOT)			95	19	1	20	557	11
Buy Jul Wheat(KCBT)	12/23	2/28	93	14	1	15	311	5
Sell May Wheat(KCBT)			90	18	2	20	298	4
Buy Dec Wheat(CBOT)	1/07	2/28	93	14	1	15	344	6
Sell May Wheat(CBOT)			90	18	2	20	367	7
Buy Jul Wheat(CBOT)	1/09	2/08	93	14	1	15	406	13
Sell Mar Wheat(CBOT)			90	18	2	20	418	13

As has often been the case during the decades of disinflation (1980-2000), bull spreads have tended to be harder to find, less reliable, and of shorter duration. The first strategy in the table above, the only presentable long old-crop/short new-crop bull spread found, would have succeeded in 16 of the last 20 years. In contrast, all but one of the new-crop/old-crop spreads would have succeeded in each of the last 17 or 18 years through 2004.

Figure 3-19: Old-crop Dec/New-crop Jul Wheat Monthly

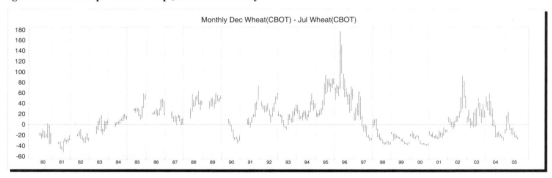

Figure 3-20

Buy Dec Wheat(CBOT) / Sell Jul Wheat(CBOT)

Enter on approximately 09/23 - Exit on approximately 10/22

CONT YEAR	ENTRY DATE	ENTRY PRICE	EXIT DATE	EXIT PRICE	PROFIT	PROFIT AMOUNT	BEST EQUITY DATE	BEST EQUITY AMOUNT	WORST EQUITY DATE	WORST EQUITY AMOUNT
2004	09/23/04	-18.25	10/22/04	-17.50	0.75	37.50	10/13/04	75.00	09/30/04	-212.50
2003	09/23/03	16.00	10/22/03	17.00	1.00	50.00	09/25/03	287.50	10/14/03	-675.00
2002	09/23/02	44.00	10/22/02	73.25	29.25	1462.50	10/18/02	1550.00	10/10/02	-700.00
2001	09/24/01	-25.25	10/22/01	-10.75	14.50	725.00	10/17/01	1000.00		
2000	09/25/00	-37.50	10/20/00	-36.75	0.75	37.50	10/10/00	100.00		
1999	09/23/99	-35.75	10/22/99	-35.25	0.50	25.00	09/29/99	75.00	10/11/99	-37.50
1998	09/23/98	-35.00	10/22/98	-32.75	2.25	112.50	10/19/98	187.50	09/30/98	-12.50
1997	09/23/97	-21.50	10/22/97	-22.00	-0.50	-25.00	09/25/97	125.00	10/01/97	-112.50
1996	09/23/96	41.50	10/22/96	42.00	0.50	25.00	09/30/96	787.50	09/25/96	-50.00
1995	09/25/95	81.50	10/20/95	75.75	-5.75	-287.50			10/11/95	-975.00
1994	09/23/94	33.50	10/21/94	45.00	11.50	575.00	10/11/94	1250.00		
1993	09/23/93	3.75	10/22/93	23.25	19.50	975.00	10/21/93	1050.00		
1992	09/23/92	24.25	10/22/92	33.75	9.50	475.00	10/19/92	712.50		
1991	09/23/91	19.50	10/22/91	27.75	8.25	412.50	10/22/91	412.50	10/03/91	-262.50
1990	09/24/90	-27.75	10/22/90	-26.25	1.50	75.00	10/08/90	275.00		
1989	09/25/89	44.25	10/20/89	48.25	4.00	200.00	09/29/89	712.50		
1988	09/23/88	50.50	10/21/88	49.00	-1.50	-75.00	10/13/88	637.50	10/21/88	-75.00
1987	09/23/87	16.00	10/22/87	6.50	-9.50	-475.00	09/25/87	112.50	10/21/87	-512.50
1986	09/23/86	28.00	10/22/86	46.00	18.00	900.00	10/22/86	900.00	09/25/86	-112.50
1985	09/23/85	14.00	10/22/85	29.75	15.75	787.50	10/22/85	787.50	09/30/85	-162.50

Percentage Correct		87								
Average Profit on Winning Trades					7.67	383.65		Winners		13
Average Loss on Trades					-3.13	-156.25		Losers		2
Average Net Profit Per Trade					6.23	311.67		Total trades		15
Percentage Correct		80								
Average Profit on Winning Trades					8.59	429.69		Winners		16
Average Loss on Trades					-4.31	-215.63		Losers		4
Average Net Profit Per Trade					6.01	300.63		Total trades		20

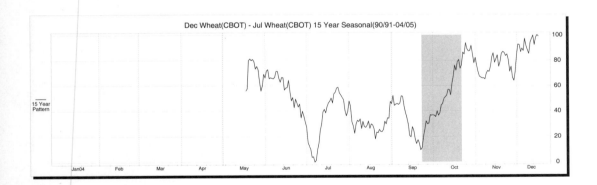

Dec Wheat(CBOT) - Jul Wheat(CBOT) 15 Year Seasonal(90/91-04/05)

15 Year Pattern

Figure 3-21

Moore Research Center, Inc.				**Buy Jul Wheat(CBOT) / Sell Mar Wheat(CBOT)**						
				Enter on approximately 11/17 - Exit on approximately 02/16						
CONT YEAR	ENTRY DATE	ENTRY PRICE	EXIT DATE	EXIT PRICE	PROFIT	PROFIT AMOUNT	BEST EQUITY DATE	BEST EQUITY AMOUNT	WORST EQUITY DATE	WORST EQUITY AMOUNT
2005	11/17/04	13.00	02/16/05	14.00	1.00	50.00	11/22/04	125.00	11/30/04	-25.00
2004	11/17/03	-45.00	02/13/04	-0.75	44.25	2212.50	02/02/04	2350.00		
2003	11/18/02	-65.50	02/14/03	-11.75	53.75	2687.50	01/10/03	3250.00		
2002	11/19/01	3.00	02/15/02	8.75	5.75	287.50	02/12/02	362.50	01/04/02	-600.00
2001	11/17/00	21.25	02/16/01	23.25	2.00	100.00	01/30/01	112.50	12/01/00	-75.00
2000	11/17/99	20.25	02/16/00	22.75	2.50	125.00	02/14/00	125.00	11/23/99	-50.00
1999	11/17/98	19.25	02/16/99	20.00	0.75	37.50	12/11/98	87.50	11/18/98	-25.00
1998	11/17/97	13.50	02/13/98	18.75	5.25	262.50	02/11/98	287.50	12/01/97	-162.50
1997	11/18/96	-40.00	02/14/97	-16.75	23.25	1162.50	02/10/97	1350.00	12/19/96	-612.50
1996	11/17/95	-76.25	02/16/96	-64.75	11.50	575.00	01/05/96	1025.00	11/24/95	-387.50
1995	11/17/94	-51.75	02/16/95	-29.25	22.50	1125.00	01/19/95	1225.00	12/27/94	-525.00
1994	11/17/93	-24.25	02/16/94	-23.00	1.25	62.50	02/08/94	62.50	01/06/94	-1062.50
1993	11/17/92	-45.00	02/16/93	-40.00	5.00	250.00	12/07/92	462.50	01/21/93	-550.00
1992	11/18/91	-34.75	02/14/92	-23.75	11.00	550.00	02/14/92	550.00	12/26/91	-1500.00
1991	11/19/90	15.50	02/15/91	20.50	5.00	250.00	02/14/91	250.00	12/17/90	-312.50
1990	11/17/89	-50.00	02/16/90	-39.50	10.50	525.00	02/01/90	1162.50	12/11/89	-250.00
1989	11/17/88	-37.50	02/16/89	-23.50	14.00	700.00	02/14/89	1075.00	01/06/89	-687.50
1988	11/17/87	-12.25	02/16/88	2.00	14.25	712.50	02/16/88	712.50	12/18/87	-400.00
1987	11/17/86	-26.00	02/13/87	-23.50	2.50	125.00	02/12/87	125.00	01/21/87	-662.50
1986	11/18/85	-50.00	02/14/86	-72.75	-22.75	-1137.50	11/26/85	337.50	02/13/86	-1212.50
Percentage Correct	100									
Average Profit on Winning Trades					12.98	649.17		Winners		15
Average Loss on Trades								Losers		0
Average Net Profit Per Trade					12.98	649.17		Total trades		15
Percentage Correct	95									
Average Profit on Winning Trades					12.42	621.05		Winners		19
Average Loss on Trades					-22.75	-1137.50		Losers		1
Average Net Profit Per Trade					10.66	533.13		Total trades		20

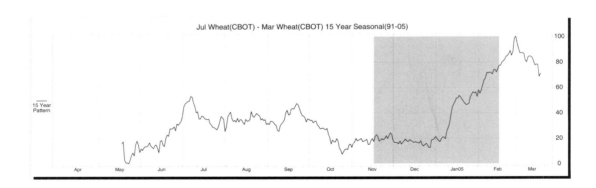

Jul Wheat(CBOT) - Mar Wheat(CBOT) 15 Year Seasonal(91-05)

Chapter 3: Grains

Figure 3-22

Buy Jul Wheat(CBOT) / Sell May Wheat(CBOT)

Enter on approximately 12/17 - Exit on approximately 02/28

CONT YEAR	ENTRY DATE	ENTRY PRICE	EXIT DATE	EXIT PRICE	PROFIT	PROFIT AMOUNT	BEST EQUITY DATE	BEST EQUITY AMOUNT	WORST EQUITY DATE	WORST EQUITY AMOUNT
2005	12/17/04	6.75	02/28/05	6.25	-0.50	-25.00	02/17/05	50.00	02/08/05	-100.00
2004	12/17/03	-20.00	02/27/04	1.50	21.50	1075.00	02/27/04	1075.00	12/18/03	-75.00
2003	12/17/02	-33.75	02/28/03	-5.50	28.25	1412.50	01/13/03	1662.50		
2002	12/17/01	-0.50	02/28/02	6.50	7.00	350.00	02/28/02	350.00	01/04/02	-187.50
2001	12/18/00	10.00	02/28/01	11.00	1.00	50.00	02/26/01	87.50	12/27/00	-50.00
2000	12/17/99	10.25	02/28/00	10.75	0.50	25.00	02/24/00	75.00	01/25/00	-37.50
1999	12/17/98	10.25	02/26/99	10.50	0.25	12.50	12/31/98	25.00	12/30/98	-62.50
1998	12/17/97	6.00	02/27/98	9.75	3.75	187.50	01/22/98	250.00	12/26/97	-50.00
1997	12/17/96	-22.25	02/28/97	-10.75	11.50	575.00	02/27/97	675.00	12/19/96	-225.00
1996	12/18/95	-38.00	02/28/96	-32.25	5.75	287.50	02/27/96	412.50	02/14/96	-225.00
1995	12/19/94	-30.25	02/28/95	-15.75	14.50	725.00	02/28/95	725.00	12/27/94	-275.00
1994	12/17/93	-12.75	02/28/94	-10.25	2.50	125.00	12/20/93	175.00	01/07/94	-425.00
1993	12/17/92	-22.50	02/26/93	-17.75	4.75	237.50	02/12/93	262.50	01/19/93	-287.50
1992	12/17/91	-29.25	02/28/92	-14.25	15.00	750.00	02/28/92	750.00	12/27/91	-550.00
1991	12/17/90	2.75	02/28/91	10.50	7.75	387.50	02/22/91	400.00		
1990	12/18/89	-29.50	02/28/90	-17.25	12.25	612.50	01/31/90	712.50	12/20/89	-62.50
1989	12/19/88	-31.25	02/28/89	-28.50	2.75	137.50	02/06/89	762.50	01/11/89	-375.00
1988	12/17/87	-12.25	02/26/88	4.50	16.75	837.50	02/19/88	962.50	01/29/88	-112.50
1987	12/17/86	-16.75	02/27/87	-22.25	-5.50	-275.00	02/12/87	125.00	02/27/87	-275.00
1986	12/17/85	-31.50	02/28/86	-31.50	0.00	0.00	01/24/86	837.50	01/02/86	-112.50

Percentage Correct	93									
Average Profit on Winning Trades					8.86	442.86		Winners		14
Average Loss on Trades					-0.50	-25.00		Losers		1
Average Net Profit Per Trade					8.23	411.67		Total trades		15
Percentage Correct	85									
Average Profit on Winning Trades					9.16	458.09		Winners		17
Average Loss on Trades					-2.00	-100.00		Losers		3
Average Net Profit Per Trade					7.49	374.38		Total trades		20

HYPOTHETICAL PERFORMANCE RESULTS HAVE MANY INHERENT LIMITATIONS, SOME OF WHICH ARE DESCRIBED BELOW. NO REPRESENTATION IS BEING MADE THAT ANY ACCOUNT WILL OR IS LIKELY TO ACHIEVE PROFITS OR LOSSES SIMILAR TO THOSE SHOWN. IN FACT, THERE ARE FREQUENTLY SHARP DIFFERENCES BETWEEN HYPOTHETICAL PERFORMANCE RESULTS AND THE ACTUAL RESULTS SUBSEQUENTLY ACHIEVED BY ANY PARTICULAR TRADING PROGRAM. ONE OF THE LIMITATIONS OF HYPOTHETICAL PERFORMANCE RESULTS IS THAT THEY ARE GENERALLY PREPARED WITH THE BENEFIT OF HINDSIGHT. IN ADDITION, HYPOTHETICAL TRADING DOES NOT INVOLVE FINANCIAL RISK, AND NO HYPOTHETICAL TRADING RECORD CAN COMPLETELY ACCOUNT FOR THE IMPACT OF FINANCIAL RISK IN ACTUAL TRADING. FOR EXAMPLE, THE ABILITY TO WITHSTAND LOSSES OR ADHERE TO A PARTICULAR TRADING PROGRAM IN SPITE OF TRADING LOSSES ARE MATERIAL POINTS WHICH CAN ALSO ADVERSELY AFFECT ACTUAL TRADING RESULTS. THERE ARE NUMEROUS OTHER FACTORS RELATED TO THE MARKETS IN GENERAL OR TO THE IMPLEMENTATION OF ANY SPECIFIC TRADING PROGRAM WHICH CANNOT BE FULLY ACCOUNTED FOR IN THE PREPARATION OF HYPOTHETICAL PERFORMANCE RESULTS AND ALL OF WHICH CAN ADVERSELY AFFECT ACTUAL TRADING RESULTS. RESULTS NOT ADJUSTED FOR COMMISSION AND SLIPPAGE.

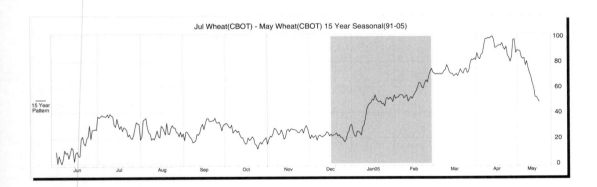

Jul Wheat(CBOT) - May Wheat(CBOT) 15 Year Seasonal(91-05)

Figure 3-23

Moore Research Center, Inc.

Buy Jul Wheat(KCBT) / Sell Mar Wheat(KCBT)

Enter on approximately 12/20 - Exit on approximately 02/08

CONT YEAR	ENTRY DATE	ENTRY PRICE	EXIT DATE	EXIT PRICE	PROFIT	PROFIT AMOUNT	BEST EQUITY DATE	BEST EQUITY AMOUNT	WORST EQUITY DATE	WORST EQUITY AMOUNT
2005	12/20/04	-12.75	02/08/05	-21.00	-8.25	-412.50	01/03/05	212.50	01/19/05	-537.50
2004	12/22/03	-17.50	02/06/04	-1.50	16.00	800.00	02/04/04	875.00	01/02/04	-37.50
2003	12/20/02	-52.25	02/07/03	-16.75	35.50	1775.00	01/13/03	2325.00	12/23/02	-50.00
2002	12/20/01	10.50	02/08/02	11.75	1.25	62.50	01/30/02	150.00	01/04/02	-12.50
2001	12/20/00	16.25	02/08/01	21.50	5.25	262.50	02/08/01	262.50	12/29/00	-62.50
2000	12/20/99	20.00	02/08/00	21.75	1.75	87.50	02/03/00	100.00	01/14/00	-37.50
1999	12/21/98	15.00	02/08/99	19.50	4.50	225.00	02/03/99	262.50		
1998	12/22/97	14.25	02/06/98	16.00	1.75	87.50	01/21/98	187.50	12/26/97	-112.50
1997	12/20/96	-60.75	02/07/97	-59.50	1.25	62.50	12/31/96	675.00	01/23/97	-125.00
1996	12/20/95	-55.75	02/08/96	-59.25	-3.50	-175.00	01/05/96	825.00	01/26/96	-862.50
1995	12/20/94	-48.00	02/08/95	-31.00	17.00	850.00	01/19/95	1337.50	12/27/94	-412.50
1994	12/20/93	-45.00	02/08/94	-17.00	28.00	1400.00	02/08/94	1400.00	12/28/93	-62.50
1993	12/21/92	-34.00	02/08/93	-27.50	6.50	325.00	02/08/93	325.00	01/19/93	-450.00
1992	12/20/91	-50.25	02/07/92	-40.50	9.75	487.50	01/16/92	875.00	12/27/91	-687.50
1991	12/20/90	7.50	02/08/91	12.25	4.75	237.50	02/06/91	287.50	12/21/90	-25.00
1990	12/20/89	-41.00	02/08/90	-24.00	17.00	850.00	02/02/90	987.50	12/22/89	-25.00
1989	12/20/88	-30.25	02/08/89	-12.75	17.50	875.00	02/02/89	1100.00	01/05/89	-262.50
1988	12/21/87	-13.00	02/08/88	-6.25	6.75	337.50	01/22/88	675.00		
1987	12/22/86	-15.00	02/06/87	-25.50	-10.50	-525.00	12/24/86	37.50	02/05/87	-537.50
1986	12/20/85	-44.75	02/07/86	-44.50	0.25	12.50	01/24/86	187.50	01/16/86	-550.00

Percentage Correct	87									
Average Profit on Winning Trades					10.25	512.50		Winners		13
Average Loss on Trades					-5.88	-293.75		Losers		2
Average Net Profit Per Trade					8.10	405.00		Total trades		15
Percentage Correct	85									
Average Profit on Winning Trades					10.28	513.97		Winners		17
Average Loss on Trades					-7.42	-370.83		Losers		3
Average Net Profit Per Trade					7.63	381.25		Total trades		20

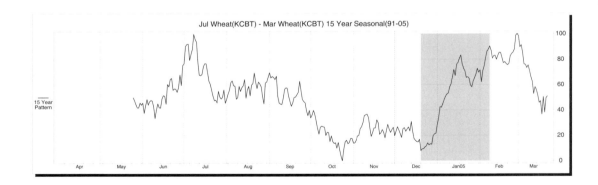

Jul Wheat(KCBT) - Mar Wheat(KCBT) 15 Year Seasonal(91-05)

Figure 3-24

Buy Jul Wheat(CBOT) / Sell Mar Wheat(CBOT)

Enter on approximately 12/22 - Exit on approximately 02/12

CONT YEAR	ENTRY DATE	ENTRY PRICE	EXIT DATE	EXIT PRICE	PROFIT	PROFIT AMOUNT	BEST EQUITY DATE	BEST EQUITY AMOUNT	WORST EQUITY DATE	WORST EQUITY AMOUNT
2005	12/22/04	14.25	02/11/05	14.50	0.25	12.50	02/04/05	62.50	12/23/04	-62.50
2004	12/22/03	-16.75	02/12/04	-2.75	14.00	700.00	02/02/04	937.50	01/02/04	-125.00
2003	12/23/02	-38.75	02/12/03	-3.00	35.75	1787.50	01/10/03	1912.50		
2002	12/26/01	-2.50	02/12/02	10.25	12.75	637.50	02/12/02	637.50	01/04/02	-325.00
2001	12/22/00	21.00	02/12/01	23.00	2.00	100.00	01/30/01	125.00	12/27/00	-50.00
2000	12/22/99	20.50	02/11/00	22.00	1.50	75.00	02/07/00	100.00	12/30/99	-25.00
1999	12/22/98	19.75	02/12/99	20.00	0.25	12.50	01/13/99	62.50	12/24/98	-25.00
1998	12/22/97	14.00	02/12/98	19.25	5.25	262.50	02/11/98	262.50	01/02/98	-75.00
1997	12/23/96	-50.00	02/12/97	-15.25	34.75	1737.50	02/10/97	1850.00	12/26/96	-37.50
1996	12/22/95	-67.75	02/12/96	-57.00	10.75	537.50	01/05/96	600.00	01/29/96	-500.00
1995	12/22/94	-54.50	02/10/95	-34.75	19.75	987.50	01/19/95	1362.50	12/27/94	-387.50
1994	12/22/93	-29.00	02/11/94	-26.75	2.25	112.50	02/08/94	300.00	01/06/94	-825.00
1993	12/22/92	-41.25	02/12/93	-40.75	0.50	25.00	12/29/92	262.50	01/21/93	-737.50
1992	12/23/91	-60.00	02/12/92	-29.50	30.50	1525.00	02/12/92	1525.00	12/26/91	-237.50
1991	12/24/90	10.25	02/12/91	20.00	9.75	487.50	02/08/91	487.50	01/02/91	-25.00
1990	12/22/89	-52.00	02/12/90	-41.25	10.75	537.50	02/01/90	1262.50		
1989	12/22/88	-43.75	02/10/89	-18.50	25.25	1262.50	02/06/89	1312.50	01/06/89	-375.00
1988	12/22/87	-18.50	02/12/88	-1.25	17.25	862.50	02/11/88	950.00		
1987	12/22/86	-30.50	02/12/87	-23.50	7.00	350.00	02/12/87	350.00	01/21/87	-437.50
1986	12/23/85	-48.00	02/12/86	-65.50	-17.50	-875.00			02/12/86	-875.00

Percentage Correct	100						
Average Profit on Winning Trades			12.00	600.00		Winners	15
Average Loss on Trades						Losers	0
Average Net Profit Per Trade			12.00	600.00		Total trades	15
Percentage Correct	95						
Average Profit on Winning Trades			12.64	632.24		Winners	19
Average Loss on Trades			-17.50	-875.00		Losers	1
Average Net Profit Per Trade			11.14	556.88		Total trades	20

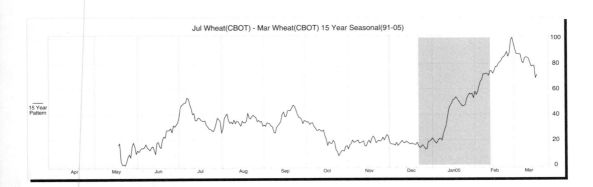

Jul Wheat(CBOT) - Mar Wheat(CBOT) 15 Year Seasonal(91-05)

Figure 3-25

Moore Research Center, Inc.

Buy Jul Wheat(KCBT) / Sell May Wheat(KCBT)

Enter on approximately 12/23 - Exit on approximately 02/28

CONT YEAR	ENTRY DATE	ENTRY PRICE	EXIT DATE	EXIT PRICE	PROFIT	PROFIT AMOUNT	BEST EQUITY DATE	BEST EQUITY AMOUNT	WORST EQUITY DATE	WORST EQUITY AMOUNT
2005	12/23/04	-2.50	02/28/05	-13.00	-10.50	-525.00			02/25/05	-650.00
2004	12/23/03	-12.50	02/27/04	-0.75	11.75	587.50	02/04/04	625.00	01/02/04	-312.50
2003	12/23/02	-30.75	02/28/03	-7.00	23.75	1187.50	01/13/03	1475.00		
2002	12/26/01	4.75	02/28/02	7.50	2.75	137.50	12/31/01	137.50		
2001	12/26/00	7.75	02/28/01	8.75	1.00	50.00	02/15/01	150.00	12/29/00	-125.00
2000	12/23/99	10.25	02/28/00	10.50	0.25	12.50	02/18/00	62.50	01/14/00	-50.00
1999	12/23/98	7.00	02/26/99	9.75	2.75	137.50	02/12/99	175.00		
1998	12/23/97	7.50	02/27/98	9.50	2.00	100.00	01/02/98	137.50	01/07/98	-112.50
1997	12/23/96	-24.75	02/28/97	-22.25	2.50	125.00	01/17/97	437.50	02/24/97	-237.50
1996	12/26/95	-23.50	02/28/96	-22.50	1.00	50.00	01/05/96	287.50	02/05/96	-525.00
1995	12/23/94	-33.50	02/28/95	-13.75	19.75	987.50	02/23/95	1062.50	12/27/94	-50.00
1994	12/23/93	-18.75	02/28/94	-7.75	11.00	550.00	02/28/94	550.00	01/06/94	-200.00
1993	12/23/92	-15.75	02/26/93	-10.75	5.00	250.00	02/12/93	375.00	01/19/93	-200.00
1992	12/23/91	-31.50	02/28/92	-14.00	17.50	875.00	02/28/92	875.00	12/27/91	-300.00
1991	12/24/90	3.50	02/28/91	6.25	2.75	137.50	01/18/91	175.00	01/02/91	-75.00
1990	12/26/89	-23.00	02/28/90	-14.00	9.00	450.00	01/31/90	600.00		
1989	12/23/88	-26.00	02/28/89	-13.50	12.50	625.00	02/02/89	912.50		
1988	12/23/87	-5.50	02/26/88	2.75	8.25	412.50	02/24/88	425.00		
1987	12/23/86	-8.75	02/27/87	-17.75	-9.00	-450.00	01/16/87	62.50	02/27/87	-450.00
1986	12/23/85	-30.50	02/28/86	-25.50	5.00	250.00	01/31/86	1037.50	01/02/86	-112.50

Percentage Correct	93									
Average Profit on Winning Trades					7.41	370.54		Winners		14
Average Loss on Trades					-10.50	-525.00		Losers		1
Average Net Profit Per Trade					6.22	310.83		Total trades		15
Percentage Correct	90									
Average Profit on Winning Trades					7.69	384.72		Winners		18
Average Loss on Trades					-9.75	-487.50		Losers		2
Average Net Profit Per Trade					5.95	297.50		Total trades		20

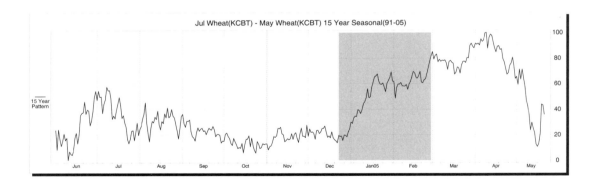

Jul Wheat(KCBT) - May Wheat(KCBT) 15 Year Seasonal(91-05)

15 Year Pattern

Figure 3-26

Buy Dec Wheat(CBOT) / Sell May Wheat(CBOT)

Enter on approximately 01/07 - Exit on approximately 02/28

CONT YEAR	ENTRY DATE	ENTRY PRICE	EXIT DATE	EXIT PRICE	PROFIT	PROFIT AMOUNT	BEST EQUITY DATE	BEST EQUITY AMOUNT	WORST EQUITY DATE	WORST EQUITY AMOUNT
2005	01/07/05	21.75	02/28/05	18.00	-3.75	-187.50	01/11/05	25.00	02/08/05	-212.50
2004	01/07/04	-1.50	02/27/04	12.00	13.50	675.00	02/27/04	675.00		
2003	01/07/03	1.25	02/28/03	9.25	8.00	400.00	01/13/03	612.50	01/08/03	-25.00
2002	01/07/02	9.00	02/28/02	20.75	11.75	587.50	02/28/02	587.50	01/10/02	-37.50
2001	01/08/01	33.50	02/28/01	35.50	2.00	100.00	01/25/01	250.00	01/12/01	-12.50
2000	01/07/00	34.50	02/28/00	34.75	0.25	12.50	01/10/00	62.50	01/21/00	-50.00
1999	01/07/99	33.25	02/26/99	35.50	2.25	112.50	02/25/99	187.50	02/08/99	-62.50
1998	01/07/98	22.00	02/27/98	27.25	5.25	262.50	02/26/98	287.50		
1997	01/07/97	-6.50	02/28/97	1.25	7.75	387.50	02/19/97	537.50	01/09/97	-112.50
1996	01/08/96	-21.50	02/28/96	-20.75	0.75	37.50	02/27/96	175.00	02/16/96	-650.00
1995	01/09/95	-9.25	02/28/95	-0.25	9.00	450.00	02/27/95	475.00	02/02/95	-62.50
1994	01/07/94	-12.00	02/28/94	-0.75	11.25	562.50	01/18/94	562.50		
1993	01/07/93	-13.00	02/26/93	-6.50	6.50	325.00	02/12/93	387.50	01/19/93	-125.00
1992	01/07/92	-22.25	02/28/92	0.50	22.75	1137.50	02/28/92	1137.50	02/04/92	-112.50
1991	01/07/91	27.00	02/28/91	33.00	6.00	300.00	02/28/91	300.00	01/10/91	-25.00
1990	01/08/90	-11.75	02/28/90	1.25	13.00	650.00	01/31/90	725.00		
1989	01/09/89	-23.25	02/28/89	-9.25	14.00	700.00	02/14/89	1187.50	01/10/89	-62.50
1988	01/07/88	2.00	02/26/88	20.50	18.50	925.00	02/19/88	1100.00	01/29/88	-150.00
1987	01/07/87	-10.00	02/27/87	-16.00	-6.00	-300.00	02/23/87	112.50	02/20/87	-325.00
1986	01/07/86	-21.75	02/28/86	-17.75	4.00	200.00	01/24/86	975.00		

Percentage Correct		93								
Average Profit on Winning Trades					7.64	382.14		Winners		14
Average Loss on Trades					-3.75	-187.50		Losers		1
Average Net Profit Per Trade					6.88	344.17		Total trades		15
Percentage Correct		90								
Average Profit on Winning Trades					8.69	434.72		Winners		18
Average Loss on Trades					-4.88	-243.75		Losers		2
Average Net Profit Per Trade					7.34	366.88		Total trades		20

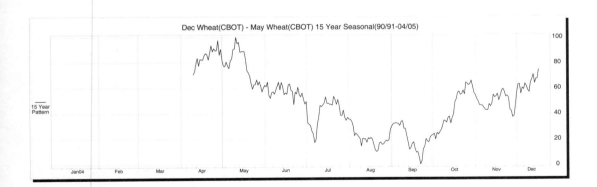

Dec Wheat(CBOT) - May Wheat(CBOT) 15 Year Seasonal(90/91-04/05)

Chapter 3: Grains

Figure 3-27

Buy Jul Wheat(CBOT) / Sell Mar Wheat(CBOT)

Enter on approximately 01/09 - Exit on approximately 02/08

CONT YEAR	ENTRY DATE	ENTRY PRICE	EXIT DATE	EXIT PRICE	PROFIT	PROFIT AMOUNT	BEST EQUITY DATE	BEST EQUITY AMOUNT	WORST EQUITY DATE	WORST EQUITY AMOUNT
2005	01/10/05	13.50	02/08/05	13.50	0.00	0.00	02/04/05	100.00		
2004	01/09/04	-4.25	02/06/04	0.25	4.50	225.00	02/02/04	312.50	01/16/04	-12.50
2003	01/09/03	-10.00	02/07/03	-8.50	1.50	75.00	01/10/03	475.00		
2002	01/09/02	-8.25	02/08/02	9.00	17.25	862.50	02/04/02	887.50		
2001	01/09/01	21.50	02/08/01	23.25	1.75	87.50	01/30/01	100.00	01/11/01	-37.50
2000	01/10/00	21.25	02/08/00	21.75	0.50	25.00	02/07/00	62.50	01/25/00	-25.00
1999	01/11/99	20.50	02/08/99	21.00	0.50	25.00	01/13/99	25.00	01/29/99	-50.00
1998	01/09/98	15.25	02/06/98	18.25	3.00	150.00	01/22/98	162.50	01/12/98	-37.50
1997	01/09/97	-43.50	02/07/97	-17.00	26.50	1325.00	02/07/97	1325.00		
1996	01/09/96	-63.75	02/08/96	-59.75	4.00	200.00	01/22/96	300.00	01/29/96	-700.00
1995	01/09/95	-43.50	02/08/95	-28.50	15.00	750.00	01/19/95	812.50	01/10/95	-62.50
1994	01/10/94	-44.50	02/08/94	-23.00	21.50	1075.00	02/08/94	1075.00		
1993	01/11/93	-48.25	02/08/93	-41.75	6.50	325.00	02/08/93	325.00	01/21/93	-387.50
1992	01/09/92	-55.50	02/07/92	-39.50	16.00	800.00	01/16/92	1025.00		
1991	01/09/91	16.75	02/08/91	20.00	3.25	162.50	02/08/91	162.50	01/10/91	-62.50
1990	01/09/90	-47.25	02/08/90	-34.25	13.00	650.00	02/01/90	1025.00	01/11/90	-25.00
1989	01/09/89	-50.50	02/08/89	-21.00	29.50	1475.00	02/06/89	1650.00		
1988	01/11/88	-10.00	02/08/88	-8.75	1.25	62.50	01/22/88	137.50	01/29/88	-175.00
1987	01/09/87	-33.75	02/06/87	-31.00	2.75	137.50	02/06/87	137.50	01/21/87	-275.00
1986	01/09/86	-55.25	02/07/86	-56.25	-1.00	-50.00	01/27/86	356.25	01/30/86	-187.50

Percentage Correct		93								
Average Profit on Winning Trades					8.70	434.82		Winners		14
Average Loss on Trades					0.00	0.00		Losers		1
Average Net Profit Per Trade					8.12	405.83		Total trades		15
Percentage Correct		90								
Average Profit on Winning Trades					9.35	467.36		Winners		18
Average Loss on Trades					-0.50	-25.00		Losers		2
Average Net Profit Per Trade					8.36	418.13		Total trades		20

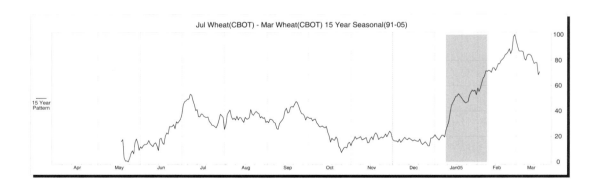

Jul Wheat(CBOT) - Mar Wheat(CBOT) 15 Year Seasonal(91-05)

Inter-market Spreads

Members of the grains complex are related, but their uses and crop cycles differ. Thus, the pace, timing, even the direction of their price movements can differ.

Inter-exchange

For example, crop cycles for winter and spring wheat are offset, with supplies of winter wheat greatest at the end of harvest in July, just before spring wheat harvest when supplies are least. These offset crop cycles at least partly explain why spring wheat has tended to outperform winter wheat, especially soft red, throughout the first half of the calendar year.

Figure 3-28: July MGE/CBOT Wheat Seasonal Pattern

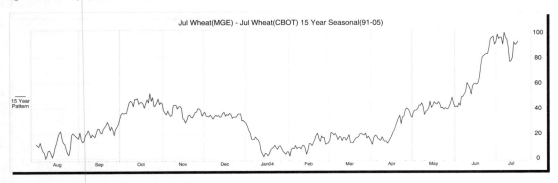

But then notice how the month of July tends to be a seasonal pivot, with especially hard red winter wheat tending to outperform spring wheat during the latter half of the calendar year. The pivotal nature of July is not only illustrated in the seasonal pattern for December contracts but also quantified in the table of strategies.

Figure 3-29: Dec KCBT/MGE Wheat Seasonal Pattern

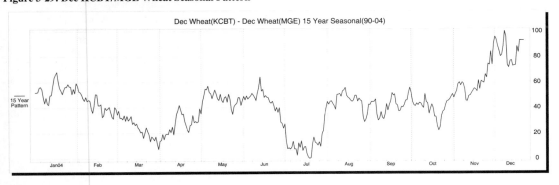

Even differences between the two classes of winter wheat tend to drive spreads between them. Hard red winter grows in regions more subject to the vagaries of weather, helping explain the tendency for July hard red to outperform its soft red counterpart from emergence in March/April into the most intense part of harvest in June. Exporters have also tended to prefer the higher quality of hard red winter, partly explaining the tendency for the December contract of hard red to outperform its soft red counterpart from September into deliveries.

Figure 3-30: July KCBT/CBOT Wheat Seasonal Pattern

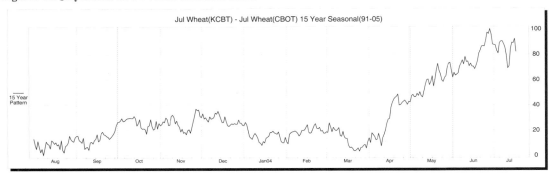

Jul Wheat(KCBT) - Jul Wheat(CBOT) 15 Year Seasonal(91-05)

Figure 3-31: December KCBT/CBOT Wheat Seasonal Pattern

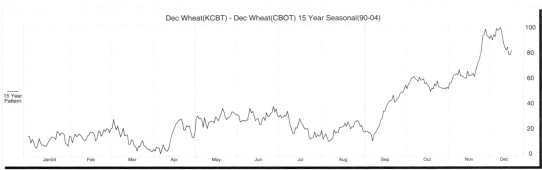

Dec Wheat(KCBT) - Dec Wheat(CBOT) 15 Year Seasonal(90-04)

Figure 3-32: Inter-exchange Wheat Strategies

Moore Research Center, Inc.	Inter-exchange Wheat Strategies							
Seasonal Strategy	Entry Date	Exit Date	Win Pct	Win Yrs	Loss Years	Total Years	Average Profit	Ave Pft Per Day
Buy Mar Wheat(MGE)	1/11	2/22	87	13	2	15	563	13
Sell Mar Wheat(CBOT)			85	17	3	20	436	10
Buy Mar Wheat(KCBT)	1/11	2/22	87	13	2	15	493	11
Sell Mar Wheat(CBOT)			80	16	2	20	401	9
Buy Sep Wheat(MGE)	6/02	7/03	93	14	1	15	258	8
Sell Sep Wheat(KCBT)			90	18	2	20	306	10
Buy Dec Wheat(KCBT)	7/17	8/14	100	15	0	15	269	9
Sell Dec Wheat(MGE)			100	20	0	20	263	9
Buy Dec Wheat(CBOT)	7/19	8/06	93	14	1	15	329	17
Sell Dec Wheat(MGE)			95	19	1	20	304	16
Buy Dec Wheat(KCBT)	9/05	11/26	87	13	2	15	533	6
Sell Dec Wheat(CBOT)			80	16	4	20	309	4

Figure 3-33

Buy Mar Wheat(MGE) / Sell Mar Wheat(CBOT)

Enter on approximately 01/11 - Exit on approximately 02/22

CONT YEAR	ENTRY DATE	ENTRY PRICE	EXIT DATE	EXIT PRICE	PROFIT	PROFIT AMOUNT	BEST EQUITY DATE	BEST EQUITY AMOUNT	WORST EQUITY DATE	WORST EQUITY AMOUNT
2005	01/11/05	37.75	02/22/05	40.50	2.75	137.50	02/09/05	650.00	02/15/05	-62.50
2004	01/12/04	13.00	02/20/04	51.50	38.50	1925.00	02/20/04	1925.00		
2003	01/13/03	54.00	02/21/03	56.25	2.25	112.50	01/27/03	787.50	02/18/03	-425.00
2002	01/11/02	-1.00	02/22/02	16.75	17.75	887.50	02/07/02	1087.50		
2001	01/11/01	44.50	02/22/01	58.75	14.25	712.50	02/22/01	712.50	01/18/01	-37.50
2000	01/11/00	64.50	02/22/00	59.50	-5.00	-250.00			02/11/00	-487.50
1999	01/11/99	78.00	02/22/99	80.25	2.25	112.50	01/26/99	600.00		
1998	01/12/98	40.25	02/20/98	48.50	8.25	412.50	02/19/98	512.50	01/27/98	-425.00
1997	01/13/97	2.50	02/21/97	30.75	28.25	1412.50	02/12/97	1475.00		
1996	01/11/96	-3.00	02/22/96	23.50	26.50	1325.00	02/22/96	1325.00	01/30/96	-750.00
1995	01/11/95	-9.00	02/22/95	-7.25	1.75	87.50	01/26/95	375.00	01/13/95	-100.00
1994	01/11/94	6.75	02/22/94	8.50	1.75	87.50	01/14/94	137.50	02/02/94	-475.00
1993	01/11/93	-26.25	02/22/93	-32.25	-6.00	-300.00			01/21/93	-550.00
1992	01/13/92	-19.00	02/21/92	12.50	31.50	1575.00	02/20/92	1600.00		
1991	01/11/91	5.75	02/22/91	10.00	4.25	212.50	02/22/91	212.50	01/31/91	-275.00
1990	01/11/90	-12.50	02/22/90	-9.25	3.25	162.50	01/19/90	500.00		
1989	01/11/89	-23.25	02/22/89	-11.50	11.75	587.50	02/06/89	875.00	01/20/89	-62.50
1988	01/11/88	-26.50	02/22/88	-16.75	9.75	487.50	02/18/88	487.50	01/26/88	-37.50
1987	01/12/87	-12.25	02/20/87	-11.25	1.00	50.00	02/13/87	462.50	01/26/87	-300.00
1986	01/13/86	26.00	02/21/86	5.75	-20.25	-1012.50			02/18/86	-1350.00

Percentage Correct	87								
Average Profit on Winning Trades			13.85	692.31		Winners	13		
Average Loss on Trades			-5.50	-275.00		Losers	2		
Average Net Profit Per Trade			11.27	563.33		Total trades	15		
Percentage Correct	85								
Average Profit on Winning Trades			12.10	605.15		Winners	17		
Average Loss on Trades			-10.42	-520.83		Losers	3		
Average Net Profit Per Trade			8.73	436.25		Total trades	20		

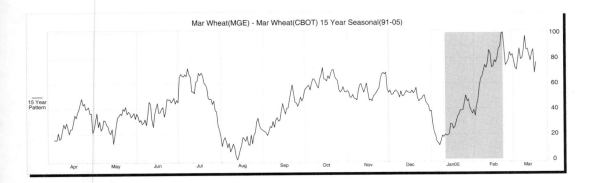

Mar Wheat(MGE) - Mar Wheat(CBOT) 15 Year Seasonal(91-05)

Figure 3-34

Buy Mar Wheat(KCBT) / Sell Mar Wheat(CBOT)

Enter on approximately 01/11 - Exit on approximately 02/22

CONT YEAR	ENTRY DATE	ENTRY PRICE	EXIT DATE	EXIT PRICE	PROFIT	PROFIT AMOUNT	BEST EQUITY DATE	BEST EQUITY AMOUNT	WORST EQUITY DATE	WORST EQUITY AMOUNT
2005	01/11/05	31.25	02/22/05	35.50	4.25	212.50	01/19/05	437.50		
2004	01/12/04	10.50	02/20/04	10.75	0.25	12.50	02/18/04	87.50	02/09/04	-487.50
2003	01/13/03	22.50	02/21/03	31.25	8.75	437.50	01/27/03	700.00		
2002	01/11/02	-15.25	02/22/02	8.00	23.25	1162.50	02/22/02	1162.50		
2001	01/11/01	47.75	02/22/01	49.50	1.75	87.50	02/22/01	87.50	02/14/01	-175.00
2000	01/11/00	26.25	02/22/00	31.00	4.75	237.50	02/22/00	237.50		
1999	01/11/99	36.00	02/22/99	32.50	-3.50	-175.00	01/26/99	162.50	02/19/99	-287.50
1998	01/12/98	10.75	02/20/98	16.50	5.75	287.50	02/19/98	300.00	01/28/98	-75.00
1997	01/13/97	27.00	02/21/97	59.75	32.75	1637.50	02/12/97	1825.00		
1996	01/11/96	-0.50	02/22/96	34.00	34.50	1725.00	02/22/96	1725.00	01/12/96	-12.50
1995	01/11/95	-2.75	02/22/95	12.00	14.75	737.50	02/21/95	812.50	01/18/95	-12.50
1994	01/11/94	-3.00	02/22/94	-1.25	1.75	87.50	02/22/94	87.50	02/04/94	-362.50
1993	01/11/93	-11.50	02/22/93	-20.00	-8.50	-425.00			01/21/93	-475.00
1992	01/13/92	-6.00	02/21/92	14.25	20.25	1012.50	02/20/92	1050.00		
1991	01/11/91	5.75	02/22/91	12.75	7.00	350.00	02/22/91	350.00	01/30/91	-162.50
1990	01/11/90	-0.25	02/22/90	-3.25	-3.00	-150.00	01/19/90	312.50	02/14/90	-187.50
1989	01/11/89	-8.50	02/22/89	-3.50	5.00	250.00	02/08/89	462.50	01/19/89	-50.00
1988	01/11/88	-12.75	02/22/88	0.75	13.50	675.00	02/22/88	675.00	01/26/88	-62.50
1987	01/12/87	-24.00	02/20/87	-11.75	12.25	612.50	02/19/87	800.00	01/26/87	-275.00
1986	01/13/86	-5.00	02/21/86	-20.00	-15.00	-750.00	01/15/86	175.00	02/21/86	-750.00

Percentage Correct	87							
Average Profit on Winning Trades			12.29	614.42		Winners	13
Average Loss on Trades			-6.00	-300.00		Losers	2
Average Net Profit Per Trade			9.85	492.50		Total trades	15
Percentage Correct	80							
Average Profit on Winning Trades			11.91	595.31		Winners	16
Average Loss on Trades			-7.50	-375.00		Losers	4
Average Net Profit Per Trade			8.03	401.25		Total trades	20

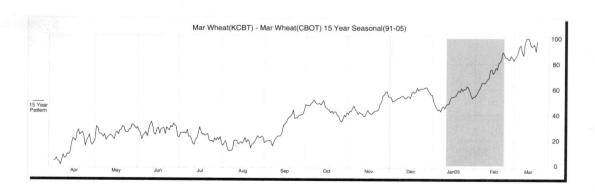

Mar Wheat(KCBT) - Mar Wheat(CBOT) 15 Year Seasonal(91-05)

Figure 3-35

Buy Sep Wheat(MGE) / Sell Sep Wheat(KCBT)

Enter on approximately 06/02 - Exit on approximately 07/03

CONT YEAR	ENTRY DATE	ENTRY PRICE	EXIT DATE	EXIT PRICE	PROFIT	PROFIT AMOUNT	BEST EQUITY DATE	BEST EQUITY AMOUNT	WORST EQUITY DATE	WORST EQUITY AMOUNT
2004	06/02/04	16.00	07/02/04	23.75	7.75	387.50	06/29/04	750.00		
2003	06/02/03	26.00	07/03/03	28.75	2.75	137.50	06/25/03	212.50	06/12/03	-375.00
2002	06/03/02	2.50	07/03/02	11.50	9.00	450.00	07/03/02	450.00	06/13/02	-687.50
2001	06/04/01	6.00	07/03/01	17.25	11.25	562.50	07/03/01	562.50	06/18/01	-75.00
2000	06/02/00	27.00	07/03/00	27.25	0.25	12.50	06/05/00	50.00	06/29/00	-725.00
1999	06/02/99	44.75	07/02/99	55.25	10.50	525.00	06/24/99	662.50	06/14/99	-87.50
1998	06/02/98	45.50	07/02/98	49.75	4.25	212.50	07/02/98	212.50	06/08/98	-600.00
1997	06/02/97	-2.50	07/03/97	19.00	21.50	1075.00	06/27/97	1400.00		
1996	06/03/96	-23.25	07/03/96	-22.00	1.25	62.50	06/05/96	325.00	06/12/96	-287.50
1995	06/02/95	-1.75	07/03/95	-1.50	0.25	12.50	06/21/95	150.00	06/15/95	-275.00
1994	06/02/94	-0.75	07/01/94	-2.00	-1.25	-62.50	06/03/94	87.50	06/10/94	-162.50
1993	06/02/93	2.75	07/02/93	9.75	7.00	350.00	07/02/93	350.00	06/18/93	-362.50
1992	06/02/92	-4.25	07/02/92	-3.00	1.25	62.50	06/12/92	312.50	06/08/92	-125.00
1991	06/03/91	-5.00	07/03/91	-3.75	1.25	62.50	06/24/91	212.50	06/13/91	-112.50
1990	06/04/90	3.50	07/03/90	4.00	0.50	25.00	06/26/90	137.50	06/05/90	-50.00
1989	06/02/89	-15.50	07/03/89	-10.75	4.75	237.50	06/19/89	275.00	06/13/89	-112.50
1988	06/02/88	1.00	07/01/88	32.50	31.50	1575.00	06/29/88	2725.00	06/06/88	-62.50
1987	06/02/87	-5.75	07/02/87	2.25	8.00	400.00	06/18/87	500.00	06/03/87	-62.50
1986	06/02/86	27.25	07/03/86	22.25	-5.00	-250.00	06/30/86	350.00	07/03/86	-250.00
1985	06/03/85	28.75	07/03/85	34.50	5.75	287.50	07/02/85	287.50	06/05/85	-87.50

Percentage Correct	93									
Average Profit on Winning Trades					5.63	281.25		Winners		14
Average Loss on Trades					-1.25	-62.50		Losers		1
Average Net Profit Per Trade					5.17	258.33		Total trades		15
Percentage Correct	90									
Average Profit on Winning Trades					7.15	357.64		Winners		18
Average Loss on Trades					-3.13	-156.25		Losers		2
Average Net Profit Per Trade					6.13	306.25		Total trades		20

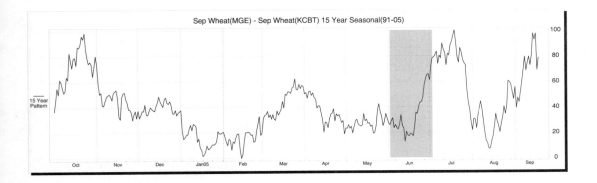

Sep Wheat(MGE) - Sep Wheat(KCBT) 15 Year Seasonal(91-05)

Figure 3-36

Moore Research Center, Inc. — Buy Dec Wheat(KCBT) / Sell Dec Wheat(MGE)

Enter on approximately 07/17 - Exit on approximately 08/14

CONT YEAR	ENTRY DATE	ENTRY PRICE	EXIT DATE	EXIT PRICE	PROFIT	PROFIT AMOUNT	BEST EQUITY DATE	BEST EQUITY AMOUNT	WORST EQUITY DATE	WORST EQUITY AMOUNT
2004	07/19/04	-14.25	08/13/04	-14.00	0.25	12.50	08/05/04	287.50	07/27/04	-87.50
2003	07/17/03	-21.50	08/14/03	-8.50	13.00	650.00	08/14/03	650.00	07/29/03	-200.00
2002	07/17/02	-14.50	08/14/02	-11.50	3.00	150.00	08/06/02	650.00		
2001	07/17/01	-10.25	08/14/01	-7.00	3.25	162.50	08/13/01	225.00	07/26/01	-162.50
2000	07/17/00	-22.50	08/14/00	-11.75	10.75	537.50	08/14/00	537.50	07/18/00	-125.00
1999	07/19/99	-55.00	08/13/99	-39.50	15.50	775.00	08/12/99	887.50		
1998	07/17/98	-43.00	08/14/98	-42.50	0.50	25.00	08/04/98	850.00		
1997	07/17/97	-15.75	08/14/97	-9.75	6.00	300.00	08/08/97	425.00	07/21/97	-200.00
1996	07/17/96	16.75	08/14/96	17.50	0.75	37.50	08/08/96	87.50	07/26/96	-237.50
1995	07/17/95	-4.50	08/14/95	2.50	7.00	350.00	08/14/95	350.00	07/19/95	-300.00
1994	07/18/94	1.75	08/12/94	6.25	4.50	225.00	08/04/94	325.00	07/21/94	-150.00
1993	07/19/93	-7.00	08/13/93	-2.25	4.75	237.50	08/12/93	250.00	07/21/93	-50.00
1992	07/17/92	1.50	08/14/92	4.75	3.25	162.50	08/07/92	237.50		
1991	07/17/91	3.25	08/14/91	10.75	7.50	375.00	08/13/91	387.50		
1990	07/17/90	1.25	08/14/90	2.00	0.75	37.50	07/23/90	100.00	07/26/90	-12.50
1989	07/17/89	3.00	08/14/89	6.75	3.75	187.50	08/07/89	325.00	07/20/89	-75.00
1988	07/18/88	-25.50	08/12/88	-25.00	0.50	25.00	07/20/88	475.00	08/01/88	-12.50
1987	07/17/87	-5.50	08/14/87	-1.00	4.50	225.00	07/27/87	325.00	07/21/87	-62.50
1986	07/17/86	-19.00	08/14/86	-15.25	3.75	187.50	08/04/86	262.50	07/18/86	-62.50
1985	07/17/85	-33.50	08/14/85	-21.75	11.75	587.50	08/14/85	587.50		

Percentage Correct	100									
Average Profit on Winning Trades					5.38	269.17		Winners		15
Average Loss on Trades								Losers		0
Average Net Profit Per Trade					5.38	269.17		Total trades		15
Percentage Correct	100									
Average Profit on Winning Trades					5.25	262.50		Winners		20
Average Loss on Trades								Losers		0
Average Net Profit Per Trade					5.25	262.50		Total trades		20

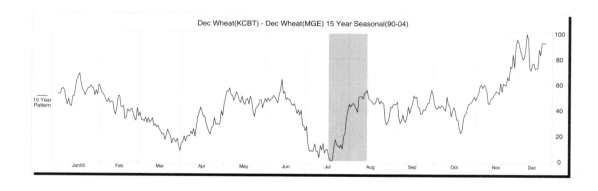

Dec Wheat(KCBT) - Dec Wheat(MGE) 15 Year Seasonal(90-04)

15 Year Pattern

Figure 3-37

Buy Dec Wheat(CBOT) / Sell Dec Wheat(MGE)

Enter on approximately 07/19 - Exit on approximately 08/06

CONT YEAR	ENTRY DATE	ENTRY PRICE	EXIT DATE	EXIT PRICE	PROFIT	PROFIT AMOUNT	BEST EQUITY DATE	BEST EQUITY AMOUNT	WORST EQUITY DATE	WORST EQUITY AMOUNT
2004	07/19/04	-41.75	08/06/04	-29.75	12.00	600.00	08/05/04	612.50	07/21/04	-162.50
2003	07/21/03	-15.50	08/06/03	-8.50	7.00	350.00	08/04/03	350.00	07/29/03	-50.00
2002	07/19/02	-35.00	08/06/02	-33.25	1.75	87.50	08/06/02	87.50	08/01/02	-262.50
2001	07/19/01	-36.50	08/06/01	-44.50	-8.00	-400.00			07/26/01	-437.50
2000	07/19/00	-59.25	08/04/00	-54.00	5.25	262.50	08/02/00	512.50		
1999	07/19/99	-76.75	08/06/99	-57.75	19.00	950.00	08/04/99	1012.50		
1998	07/20/98	-58.50	08/06/98	-52.00	6.50	325.00	08/03/98	475.00	07/23/98	-50.00
1997	07/21/97	-34.00	08/06/97	-19.00	15.00	750.00	07/28/97	850.00		
1996	07/19/96	-15.75	08/06/96	-3.00	12.75	637.50	08/06/96	637.50	07/26/96	-212.50
1995	07/19/95	-17.00	08/04/95	-9.00	8.00	400.00	08/01/95	800.00		
1994	07/19/94	-2.50	08/05/94	3.25	5.75	287.50	08/01/94	362.50	07/22/94	-112.50
1993	07/19/93	-8.00	08/06/93	-4.00	4.00	200.00	08/02/93	300.00		
1992	07/20/92	8.25	08/06/92	15.75	7.50	375.00	08/06/92	375.00		
1991	07/19/91	9.25	08/06/91	11.25	2.00	100.00	07/31/91	187.50	08/01/91	-75.00
1990	07/19/90	7.50	08/06/90	7.75	0.25	12.50	07/30/90	12.50	08/01/90	-137.50
1989	07/19/89	-5.75	08/04/89	5.25	11.00	550.00	08/04/89	550.00		
1988	07/19/88	-24.75	08/05/88	-22.25	2.50	125.00	07/20/88	275.00	08/01/88	-137.50
1987	07/20/87	2.25	08/06/87	3.25	1.00	50.00	07/27/87	300.00	07/21/87	-100.00
1986	07/21/86	-12.00	08/06/86	-11.75	0.25	12.50	07/30/86	125.00	07/24/86	-37.50
1985	07/19/85	-31.00	08/06/85	-23.00	8.00	400.00	08/05/85	525.00	07/24/85	-250.00

Percentage Correct		93								
Average Profit on Winning Trades					7.63	381.25		Winners		14
Average Loss on Trades					-8.00	-400.00		Losers		1
Average Net Profit Per Trade					6.58	329.17		Total trades		15
Percentage Correct		95								
Average Profit on Winning Trades					6.82	340.79		Winners		19
Average Loss on Trades					-8.00	-400.00		Losers		1
Average Net Profit Per Trade					6.08	303.75		Total trades		20

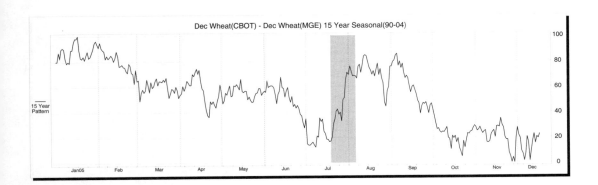

Dec Wheat(CBOT) - Dec Wheat(MGE) 15 Year Seasonal(90-04)

Figure 3-38

Buy Dec Wheat(KCBT) / Sell Dec Wheat(CBOT)

Enter on approximately 09/05 - Exit on approximately 11/26

CONT YEAR	ENTRY DATE	ENTRY PRICE	EXIT DATE	EXIT PRICE	PROFIT	PROFIT AMOUNT	BEST EQUITY DATE	BEST EQUITY AMOUNT	WORST EQUITY DATE	WORST EQUITY AMOUNT
2004	09/07/04	18.25	11/26/04	48.50	30.25	1512.50	11/09/04	1637.50		
2003	09/05/03	-1.50	11/26/03	7.25	8.75	437.50	10/08/03	487.50	11/13/03	-562.50
2002	09/05/02	51.75	11/26/02	54.25	2.50	125.00	10/11/02	2562.50	11/12/02	-1112.50
2001	09/05/01	22.25	11/26/01	6.25	-16.00	-800.00	09/19/01	350.00	11/19/01	-1112.50
2000	09/05/00	40.75	11/24/00	57.75	17.00	850.00	11/24/00	850.00	09/07/00	-100.00
1999	09/07/99	18.25	11/26/99	29.00	10.75	537.50	11/26/99	537.50		
1998	09/08/98	24.75	11/25/98	35.75	11.00	550.00	11/17/98	600.00	09/10/98	-75.00
1997	09/05/97	6.00	11/26/97	16.25	10.25	512.50	11/26/97	512.50	09/12/97	-62.50
1996	09/05/96	7.75	11/26/96	37.00	29.25	1462.50	10/24/96	1725.00	09/09/96	-475.00
1995	09/05/95	6.00	11/24/95	9.75	3.75	187.50	10/24/95	787.50	09/07/95	-300.00
1994	09/06/94	2.50	11/25/94	14.00	11.50	575.00	11/09/94	762.50	09/09/94	-37.50
1993	09/07/93	1.75	11/26/93	22.25	20.50	1025.00	11/26/93	1025.00	10/21/93	-125.00
1992	09/08/92	-7.50	11/25/92	-13.25	-5.75	-287.50	09/15/92	250.00	11/23/92	-387.50
1991	09/05/91	-3.50	11/26/91	7.75	11.25	562.50	11/18/91	612.50	09/11/91	-25.00
1990	09/05/90	-3.00	11/26/90	12.00	15.00	750.00	11/26/90	750.00		
1989	09/05/89	0.50	11/24/89	5.50	5.00	250.00	11/22/89	262.50	10/16/89	-437.50
1988	09/06/88	-11.25	11/25/88	-8.00	3.25	162.50	11/17/88	525.00	10/06/88	-75.00
1987	09/08/87	-8.25	11/25/87	-7.75	0.50	25.00	11/03/87	375.00	11/23/87	-212.50
1986	09/05/86	-8.00	11/26/86	-29.00	-21.00	-1050.00			10/27/86	-1537.50
1985	09/05/85	18.00	11/26/85	-6.25	-24.25	-1212.50	09/11/85	150.00	11/22/85	-1425.00

Percentage Correct	87									
Average Profit on Winning Trades					13.98	699.04		Winners		13
Average Loss on Trades					-10.88	-543.75		Losers		2
Average Net Profit Per Trade					10.67	533.33		Total trades		15
Percentage Correct	80									
Average Profit on Winning Trades					11.91	595.31		Winners		16
Average Loss on Trades					-16.75	-837.50		Losers		4
Average Net Profit Per Trade					6.18	308.75		Total trades		20

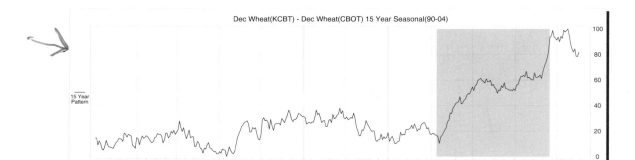

Dec Wheat(KCBT) - Dec Wheat(CBOT) 15 Year Seasonal(90-04)

Chapter 3: Grains

Inter-commodity

There is also interplay among the grains. Although wheat is higher in protein content, it is also substitutable for corn as a livestock feed at appropriate values. But their demand profiles differ. Domestic consumption accounts for perhaps 80% of US corn production whereas about 40% of US wheat production must be exported. Given the logistical difficulties and competition for wheat exports from the Southern Hemisphere, corn tends to outperform wheat at least into deliveries against March contracts.

Figure 3-39: May Corn/Wheat Seasonal Pattern

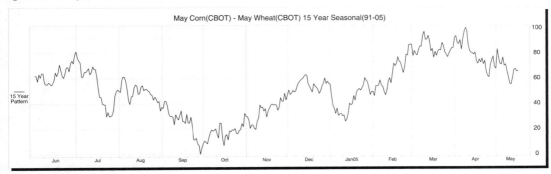

But the primary driver of seasonal spreads for these two cereal grains is that crop cycles for (winter) wheat and corn differ. For example, winter wheat is planted as corn is harvested. In July, the wheat market suffers a harvest glut just when the corn market is most anxious about tight old-crop supplies and moisture for pollination. The first three strategies in the table below quantify how old-crop corn also tends to outperform both old- and new-crop wheat through corn planting in April/May and into wheat harvest June/July.

Figure 3-40: Corn/Wheat Spread Strategies

Moore Research Center, Inc.	Corn vs Wheat Strategies							
Seasonal Strategy	Entry Date	Exit Date	Win Pct	Win Yrs	Loss Years	Total Years	Average Profit	Ave Pft Per Day
Buy May Corn(CBOT)	2/10	2/19	87	13	2	15	333	33
Sell May Wheat(CBOT)			85	17	3	20	319	32
Buy Jul Corn(CBOT)	5/12	6/01	87	13	2	15	405	19
Sell Jul Wheat(MGE)			85	17	3	20	466	22
Buy Sep Corn(CBOT)	5/12	6/17	87	13	2	15	408	11
Sell Sep Wheat(CBOT)			85	17	3	20	517	14
Buy Dec Wheat(CBOT)	6/30	7/23	87	13	2	15	534	22
Sell Dec Corn(CBOT)			85	17	3	20	548	23
Buy Sep Wheat(CBOT)	7/07	7/22	87	13	2	15	685	43
Sell Sep Corn(CBOT)			85	17	3	20	654	41
Buy Sep Wheat(KCBT)	7/07	8/27	80	12	3	15	654	13
Sell Sep Corn(CBOT)			85	17	3	20	797	14
Buy Dec Wheat(KCBT)	7/15	9/30	87	13	2	15	1072	14
Sell Dec Corn(CBOT)			90	18	2	20	1028	13

Figure 3-41: Dec Wheat/Corn Seasonal Pattern

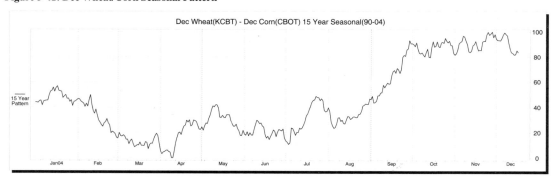

But tendencies reverse on or about First Notice Day of deliveries against July contracts — the best representative of old-crop corn and the first for new-crop wheat. By then, wheat supplies will be peaking and export season begins. In contrast, barring extremely adverse weather, the new corn crop will shortly thereafter be made. New supply will be assured, carryover will become increasingly burdensome. Furthermore, if large wheat supplies force wheat prices too low or tight corn supplies force corn prices too high, spreads that are too narrow make wheat an economically viable substitute for corn in livestock rations.

Figure 3-42: May Wheat/Corn Monthly

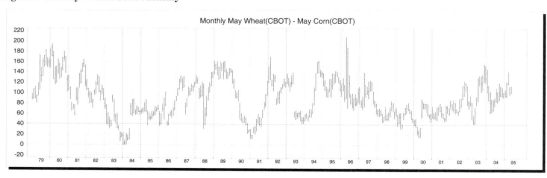

Figure 3-43: Dec KCBT Wheat/Corn Monthly

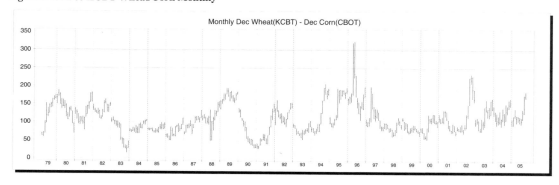

Chapter 3: Grains

Figure 3-44

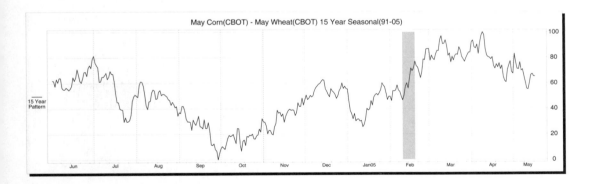

Moore Research Center, Inc.

Buy May Corn(CBOT) / Sell May Wheat(CBOT)

Enter on approximately 02/10 - Exit on approximately 02/19

CONT YEAR	ENTRY DATE	ENTRY PRICE	EXIT DATE	EXIT PRICE	PROFIT	PROFIT AMOUNT	BEST EQUITY DATE	BEST EQUITY AMOUNT	WORST EQUITY DATE	WORST EQUITY AMOUNT
2005	02/10/05	-98.50	02/18/05	-96.25	2.25	112.50	02/16/05	150.00	02/14/05	-112.50
2004	02/10/04	-105.50	02/19/04	-88.25	17.25	862.50	02/18/04	987.50		
2003	02/10/03	-90.75	02/19/03	-89.00	1.75	87.50	02/13/03	312.50	02/18/03	-25.00
2002	02/11/02	-74.75	02/19/02	-71.00	3.75	187.50	02/15/02	237.50		
2001	02/12/01	-55.75	02/16/01	-57.00	-1.25	-62.50			02/15/01	-175.00
2000	02/10/00	-48.50	02/18/00	-47.50	1.00	50.00	02/17/00	200.00	02/11/00	-162.50
1999	02/10/99	-52.00	02/19/99	-44.00	8.00	400.00	02/16/99	450.00		
1998	02/10/98	-66.25	02/19/98	-56.25	10.00	500.00	02/18/98	537.50	02/11/98	-37.50
1997	02/10/97	-79.50	02/19/97	-72.50	7.00	350.00	02/19/97	350.00	02/11/97	-387.50
1996	02/12/96	-123.75	02/16/96	-117.75	6.00	300.00	02/16/96	300.00		
1995	02/10/95	-124.75	02/17/95	-118.75	6.00	300.00	02/15/95	312.50		
1994	02/10/94	-62.50	02/18/94	-60.50	2.00	100.00	02/16/94	275.00		
1993	02/10/93	-123.75	02/19/93	-116.50	7.25	362.50	02/19/93	362.50		
1992	02/10/92	-170.50	02/19/92	-136.75	33.75	1687.50	02/19/92	1687.50		
1991	02/11/91	-11.50	02/19/91	-16.25	-4.75	-237.50			02/14/91	-375.00
1990	02/12/90	-121.25	02/16/90	-115.25	6.00	300.00	02/16/90	300.00		
1989	02/10/89	-157.00	02/17/89	-145.00	12.00	600.00	02/17/89	600.00		
1988	02/10/88	-125.00	02/19/88	-119.50	5.50	275.00	02/19/88	275.00	02/16/88	-275.00
1987	02/10/87	-110.75	02/19/87	-115.75	-5.00	-250.00	02/11/87	12.50	02/19/87	-250.00
1986	02/10/86	-47.25	02/19/86	-38.00	9.25	462.50	02/19/86	462.50	02/11/86	-237.50

Percentage Correct	87					
Average Profit on Winning Trades		8.15	407.69	Winners	13
Average Loss on Trades		-3.00	-150.00	Losers	2
Average Net Profit Per Trade		6.67	333.33	Total trades	15

Percentage Correct	85					
Average Profit on Winning Trades		8.16	408.09	Winners	17
Average Loss on Trades		-3.67	-183.33	Losers	3
Average Net Profit Per Trade		6.39	319.38	Total trades	20

May Corn(CBOT) - May Wheat(CBOT) 15 Year Seasonal(91-05)

15 Year Pattern

Figure 3-45

Buy Jul Corn(CBOT) / Sell Jul Wheat(MGE)

Enter on approximately 05/12 - Exit on approximately 06/01

CONT YEAR	ENTRY DATE	ENTRY PRICE	EXIT DATE	EXIT PRICE	PROFIT	PROFIT AMOUNT	BEST EQUITY DATE	BEST EQUITY AMOUNT	WORST EQUITY DATE	WORST EQUITY AMOUNT
2004	05/12/04	-114.25	06/01/04	-102.50	11.75	587.50	06/01/04	587.50	05/24/04	-262.50
2003	05/12/03	-123.75	05/30/03	-117.75	6.00	300.00	05/28/03	700.00		
2002	05/13/02	-79.75	05/31/02	-90.00	-10.25	-512.50	05/14/02	25.00	05/31/02	-512.50
2001	05/14/01	-138.00	06/01/01	-134.75	3.25	162.50	05/24/01	462.50		
2000	05/12/00	-92.50	06/01/00	-98.75	-6.25	-312.50	05/18/00	50.00	05/30/00	-562.50
1999	05/12/99	-110.50	06/01/99	-106.50	4.00	200.00	05/28/99	462.50		
1998	05/12/98	-118.75	06/01/98	-118.00	0.75	37.50	05/22/98	162.50	05/27/98	-262.50
1997	05/12/97	-133.50	05/30/97	-120.00	13.50	675.00	05/29/97	962.50		
1996	05/13/96	-155.50	05/31/96	-103.50	52.00	2600.00	05/30/96	2650.00	05/14/96	-12.50
1995	05/12/95	-137.25	06/01/95	-124.50	12.75	637.50	05/17/95	1100.00		
1994	05/12/94	-82.00	06/01/94	-57.75	24.25	1212.50	06/01/94	1212.50		
1993	05/12/93	-73.75	06/01/93	-73.00	0.75	37.50	05/26/93	75.00	05/19/93	-337.50
1992	05/12/92	-117.50	06/01/92	-116.50	1.00	50.00	05/22/92	412.50	05/19/92	-37.50
1991	05/13/91	-45.50	05/31/91	-37.75	7.75	387.50	05/31/91	387.50		
1990	05/14/90	-71.75	06/01/90	-71.50	0.25	12.50	05/25/90	350.00	05/16/90	-575.00
1989	05/12/89	-155.25	06/01/89	-143.50	11.75	587.50	06/01/89	587.50		
1988	05/12/88	-105.75	06/01/88	-118.75	-13.00	-650.00	05/17/88	37.50	05/24/88	-687.50
1987	05/12/87	-107.00	06/01/87	-83.75	23.25	1162.50	06/01/87	1162.50		
1986	05/12/86	-80.00	05/30/86	-42.75	37.25	1862.50	05/29/86	2100.00	05/13/86	-50.00
1985	05/13/85	-87.25	05/31/85	-81.50	5.75	287.50	05/28/85	325.00		

Percentage Correct	87				
Average Profit on Winning Trades		10.62	530.77	Winners	13
Average Loss on Trades		-8.25	-412.50	Losers	2
Average Net Profit Per Trade		8.10	405.00	Total trades	15

Percentage Correct	85				
Average Profit on Winning Trades		12.71	635.29	Winners	17
Average Loss on Trades		-9.83	-491.67	Losers	3
Average Net Profit Per Trade		9.32	466.25	Total trades	20

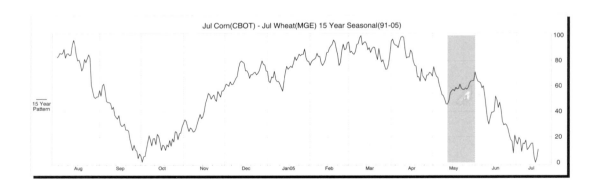

Jul Corn(CBOT) - Jul Wheat(MGE) 15 Year Seasonal(91-05)

15 Year Pattern

Figure 3-46

Moore Research Center, Inc.	Buy Sep Corn(CBOT) / Sell Sep Wheat(CBOT)

Enter on approximately 05/12 - Exit on approximately 06/17

CONT YEAR	ENTRY DATE	ENTRY PRICE	EXIT DATE	EXIT PRICE	PROFIT	PROFIT AMOUNT	BEST EQUITY DATE	BEST EQUITY AMOUNT	WORST EQUITY DATE	WORST EQUITY AMOUNT
2004	05/12/04	-82.75	06/17/04	-80.50	2.25	112.50	06/02/04	912.50	05/24/04	-575.00
2003	05/12/03	-87.00	06/17/03	-84.50	2.50	125.00	06/16/03	187.50	06/10/03	-875.00
2002	05/13/02	-62.75	06/17/02	-81.00	-18.25	-912.50	05/22/02	100.00	06/14/02	-1100.00
2001	05/14/01	-79.25	06/15/01	-68.75	10.50	525.00	06/06/01	687.50		
2000	05/12/00	-41.50	06/16/00	-59.25	-17.75	-887.50	05/18/00	225.00	06/14/00	-987.50
1999	05/12/99	-52.50	06/17/99	-46.50	6.00	300.00	05/26/99	737.50		
1998	05/12/98	-62.50	06/17/98	-46.00	16.50	825.00	06/17/98	825.00		
1997	05/12/97	-137.25	06/17/97	-100.00	37.25	1862.50	06/16/97	1950.00		
1996	05/13/96	-169.50	06/17/96	-119.50	50.00	2500.00	06/12/96	3762.50		
1995	05/12/95	-111.25	06/16/95	-106.00	5.25	262.50	05/17/95	650.00	06/05/95	-250.00
1994	05/12/94	-72.00	06/17/94	-63.00	9.00	450.00	06/01/94	675.00	06/08/94	-375.00
1993	05/12/93	-62.50	06/17/93	-62.00	0.50	25.00	05/13/93	75.00	05/19/93	-350.00
1992	05/12/92	-108.75	06/17/92	-102.00	6.75	337.50	05/20/92	962.50	06/09/92	-175.00
1991	05/13/91	-59.75	06/17/91	-57.75	2.00	100.00	05/31/91	537.50	06/12/91	-337.50
1990	05/14/90	-65.25	06/15/90	-55.25	10.00	500.00	06/12/90	737.50	05/16/90	-287.50
1989	05/12/89	-156.25	06/16/89	-151.25	5.00	250.00	05/19/89	450.00	05/24/89	-187.50
1988	05/12/88	-107.00	06/17/88	-75.25	31.75	1587.50	06/17/88	1587.50	06/06/88	-1600.00
1987	05/12/87	-110.00	06/17/87	-69.75	40.25	2012.50	06/17/87	2012.50		
1986	05/12/86	-68.50	06/17/86	-46.50	22.00	1100.00	06/17/86	1100.00	05/13/86	-225.00
1985	05/13/85	-56.75	06/17/85	-71.50	-14.75	-737.50	05/16/85	175.00	06/17/85	-737.50

Percentage Correct	87								
Average Profit on Winning Trades				12.19	609.62		Winners		13
Average Loss on Trades				-18.00	-900.00		Losers		2
Average Net Profit Per Trade				8.17	408.33		Total trades		15
Percentage Correct	85								
Average Profit on Winning Trades				15.15	757.35		Winners		17
Average Loss on Trades				-16.92	-845.83		Losers		3
Average Net Profit Per Trade				10.34	516.88		Total trades		20

HYPOTHETICAL PERFORMANCE RESULTS HAVE MANY INHERENT LIMITATIONS, SOME OF WHICH ARE DESCRIBED BELOW. NO REPRESENTATION IS BEING MADE THAT ANY ACCOUNT WILL OR IS LIKELY TO ACHIEVE PROFITS OR LOSSES SIMILAR TO THOSE SHOWN. IN FACT, THERE ARE FREQUENTLY SHARP DIFFERENCES BETWEEN HYPOTHETICAL PERFORMANCE RESULTS AND THE ACTUAL RESULTS SUBSEQUENTLY ACHIEVED BY ANY PARTICULAR TRADING PROGRAM. ONE OF THE LIMITATIONS OF HYPOTHETICAL PERFORMANCE RESULTS IS THAT THEY ARE GENERALLY PREPARED WITH THE BENEFIT OF HINDSIGHT. IN ADDITION, HYPOTHETICAL TRADING DOES NOT INVOLVE FINANCIAL RISK, AND NO HYPOTHETICAL TRADING RECORD CAN COMPLETELY ACCOUNT FOR THE IMPACT OF FINANCIAL RISK IN ACTUAL TRADING. FOR EXAMPLE, THE ABILITY TO WITHSTAND LOSSES OR ADHERE TO A PARTICULAR TRADING PROGRAM IN SPITE OF TRADING LOSSES ARE MATERIAL POINTS WHICH CAN ALSO ADVERSELY AFFECT ACTUAL TRADING RESULTS. THERE ARE NUMEROUS OTHER FACTORS RELATED TO THE MARKETS IN GENERAL OR TO THE IMPLEMENTATION OF ANY SPECIFIC TRADING PROGRAM WHICH CANNOT BE FULLY ACCOUNTED FOR IN THE PREPARATION OF HYPOTHETICAL PERFORMANCE RESULTS AND ALL OF WHICH CAN ADVERSELY AFFECT ACTUAL TRADING RESULTS. RESULTS NOT ADJUSTED FOR COMMISSION AND SLIPPAGE.

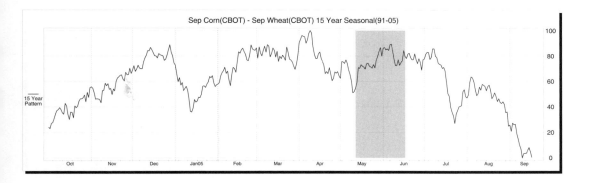

Sep Corn(CBOT) - Sep Wheat(CBOT) 15 Year Seasonal(91-05)

15 Year Pattern

Figure 3-47

Buy Dec Wheat(CBOT) / Sell Dec Corn(CBOT)

Enter on approximately 06/30 - Exit on approximately 07/23

CONT YEAR	ENTRY DATE	ENTRY PRICE	EXIT DATE	EXIT PRICE	PROFIT	PROFIT AMOUNT	BEST EQUITY DATE	BEST EQUITY AMOUNT	WORST EQUITY DATE	WORST EQUITY AMOUNT
2004	06/30/04	90.25	07/23/04	110.25	20.00	1000.00	07/23/04	1000.00	07/01/04	-325.00
2003	06/30/03	96.75	07/23/03	144.50	47.75	2387.50	07/23/03	2387.50	07/08/03	-100.00
2002	07/01/02	82.25	07/23/02	91.25	9.00	450.00	07/17/02	1025.00		
2001	07/02/01	66.25	07/23/01	77.00	10.75	537.50	07/20/01	562.50	07/11/01	-725.00
2000	06/30/00	81.00	07/21/00	64.75	-16.25	-812.50			07/21/00	-812.50
1999	06/30/99	53.25	07/23/99	54.25	1.00	50.00	07/09/99	512.50		
1998	06/30/98	43.75	07/23/98	49.00	5.25	262.50	07/06/98	537.50		
1997	06/30/97	107.00	07/23/97	122.50	15.50	775.00	07/23/97	775.00	07/18/97	-562.50
1996	07/01/96	124.50	07/23/96	127.50	3.00	150.00	07/11/96	862.50	07/15/96	-237.50
1995	06/30/95	170.00	07/21/95	185.25	15.25	762.50	07/21/95	762.50	07/10/95	-1325.00
1994	06/30/94	92.25	07/22/94	118.50	26.25	1312.50	07/19/94	1462.50		
1993	06/30/93	60.50	07/23/93	73.00	12.50	625.00	07/23/93	625.00	07/13/93	-187.50
1992	06/30/92	104.75	07/23/92	119.00	14.25	712.50	07/17/92	837.50	07/02/92	-512.50
1991	07/01/91	58.75	07/23/91	52.50	-6.25	-312.50			07/17/91	-587.50
1990	07/02/90	57.25	07/23/90	59.50	2.25	112.50	07/18/90	500.00	07/03/90	-50.00
1989	06/30/89	164.00	07/21/89	170.50	6.50	325.00	07/20/89	462.50	07/06/89	-637.50
1988	06/30/88	60.50	07/22/88	75.75	15.25	762.50	07/19/88	1012.50	07/05/88	-375.00
1987	06/30/87	79.50	07/23/87	97.25	17.75	887.50	07/06/87	1112.50		
1986	06/30/86	69.00	07/23/86	92.00	23.00	1150.00	07/23/86	1150.00	07/02/86	-262.50
1985	07/01/85	78.00	07/23/85	74.50	-3.50	-175.00	07/22/85	25.00	07/16/85	-250.00

Percentage Correct	87					Winners	13
Average Profit on Winning Trades				14.06	702.88	Winners	13
Average Loss on Trades				-11.25	-562.50	Losers	2
Average Net Profit Per Trade				10.68	534.17	Total trades	15
Percentage Correct	85						
Average Profit on Winning Trades				14.43	721.32	Winners	17
Average Loss on Trades				-8.67	-433.33	Losers	3
Average Net Profit Per Trade				10.96	548.13	Total trades	20

HYPOTHETICAL PERFORMANCE RESULTS HAVE MANY INHERENT LIMITATIONS, SOME OF WHICH ARE DESCRIBED BELOW. NO REPRESENTATION IS BEING MADE THAT ANY ACCOUNT WILL OR IS LIKELY TO ACHIEVE PROFITS OR LOSSES SIMILAR TO THOSE SHOWN. IN FACT, THERE ARE FREQUENTLY SHARP DIFFERENCES BETWEEN HYPOTHETICAL PERFORMANCE RESULTS AND THE ACTUAL RESULTS SUBSEQUENTLY ACHIEVED BY ANY PARTICULAR TRADING PROGRAM. ONE OF THE LIMITATIONS OF HYPOTHETICAL PERFORMANCE RESULTS IS THAT THEY ARE GENERALLY PREPARED WITH THE BENEFIT OF HINDSIGHT. IN ADDITION, HYPOTHETICAL TRADING DOES NOT INVOLVE FINANCIAL RISK, AND NO HYPOTHETICAL TRADING RECORD CAN COMPLETELY ACCOUNT FOR THE IMPACT OF FINANCIAL RISK IN ACTUAL TRADING. FOR EXAMPLE, THE ABILITY TO WITHSTAND LOSSES OR ADHERE TO A PARTICULAR TRADING PROGRAM IN SPITE OF TRADING LOSSES ARE MATERIAL POINTS WHICH CAN ALSO ADVERSELY AFFECT ACTUAL TRADING RESULTS. THERE ARE NUMEROUS OTHER FACTORS RELATED TO THE MARKETS IN GENERAL OR TO THE IMPLEMENTATION OF ANY SPECIFIC TRADING PROGRAM WHICH CANNOT BE FULLY ACCOUNTED FOR IN THE PREPARATION OF HYPOTHETICAL PERFORMANCE RESULTS AND ALL OF WHICH CAN ADVERSELY AFFECT ACTUAL TRADING RESULTS. RESULTS NOT ADJUSTED FOR COMMISSION AND SLIPPAGE.

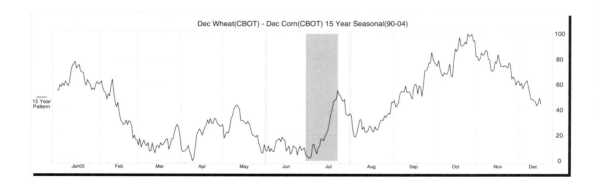

Dec Wheat(CBOT) - Dec Corn(CBOT) 15 Year Seasonal(90-04)

Figure 3-48

Buy Sep Wheat(CBOT) / Sell Sep Corn(CBOT)

Enter on approximately 07/07 - Exit on approximately 07/22

CONT YEAR	ENTRY DATE	ENTRY PRICE	EXIT DATE	EXIT PRICE	PROFIT	PROFIT AMOUNT	BEST EQUITY DATE	BEST EQUITY AMOUNT	WORST EQUITY DATE	WORST EQUITY AMOUNT
2004	07/07/04	94.50	07/22/04	103.50	9.00	450.00	07/22/04	450.00	07/15/04	-187.50
2003	07/07/03	86.75	07/22/03	124.75	38.00	1900.00	07/18/03	2137.50	07/08/03	-100.00
2002	07/08/02	87.75	07/22/02	93.75	6.00	300.00	07/17/02	787.50		
2001	07/09/01	56.50	07/20/01	74.25	17.75	887.50	07/20/01	887.50	07/11/01	-412.50
2000	07/07/00	64.00	07/21/00	59.50	-4.50	-225.00	07/11/00	362.50	07/21/00	-225.00
1999	07/07/99	55.00	07/22/99	48.25	-6.75	-337.50	07/09/99	125.00	07/22/99	-337.50
1998	07/07/98	39.00	07/22/98	39.75	0.75	37.50	07/20/98	225.00	07/08/98	-275.00
1997	07/07/97	92.50	07/22/97	102.25	9.75	487.50	07/22/97	487.50	07/16/97	-550.00
1996	07/08/96	75.50	07/22/96	104.75	29.25	1462.50	07/22/96	1462.50	07/12/96	-150.00
1995	07/07/95	135.00	07/21/95	184.25	49.25	2462.50	07/21/95	2462.50	07/10/95	-37.50
1994	07/07/94	84.75	07/22/94	107.50	22.75	1137.50	07/20/94	1300.00		
1993	07/07/93	57.75	07/22/93	69.25	11.50	575.00	07/21/93	625.00	07/13/93	-137.50
1992	07/07/92	94.50	07/22/92	115.00	20.50	1025.00	07/17/92	1125.00	07/10/92	-25.00
1991	07/08/91	40.00	07/22/91	41.75	1.75	87.50	07/12/91	462.50	07/16/91	-175.00
1990	07/09/90	40.25	07/20/90	40.75	0.50	25.00	07/18/90	262.50	07/10/90	-112.50
1989	07/07/89	141.25	07/21/89	156.25	15.00	750.00	07/20/89	825.00		
1988	07/07/88	53.75	07/22/88	72.00	18.25	912.50	07/08/88	1200.00	07/18/88	-175.00
1987	07/07/87	94.25	07/22/87	98.00	3.75	187.50	07/09/87	187.50	07/20/87	-162.50
1986	07/07/86	67.25	07/22/86	89.25	22.00	1100.00	07/22/86	1100.00		
1985	07/08/85	63.25	07/22/85	60.50	-2.75	-137.50	07/10/85	25.00	07/18/85	-400.00

Percentage Correct		87								
Average Profit on Winning Trades					16.67	833.65		Winners		13
Average Loss on Trades					-5.63	-281.25		Losers		2
Average Net Profit Per Trade					13.70	685.00		Total trades		15
Percentage Correct		85								
Average Profit on Winning Trades					16.22	811.03		Winners		17
Average Loss on Trades					-4.67	-233.33		Losers		3
Average Net Profit Per Trade					13.09	654.38		Total trades		20

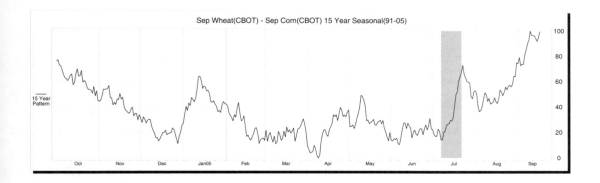

Sep Wheat(CBOT) - Sep Corn(CBOT) 15 Year Seasonal(91-05)

15 Year Pattern

Figure 3-49

Buy Sep Wheat(KCBT) / Sell Sep Corn(CBOT)

Enter on approximately 07/07 - Exit on approximately 08/27

CONT YEAR	ENTRY DATE	ENTRY PRICE	EXIT DATE	EXIT PRICE	PROFIT	PROFIT AMOUNT	BEST EQUITY DATE	BEST EQUITY AMOUNT	WORST EQUITY DATE	WORST EQUITY AMOUNT
2004	07/07/04	119.25	08/27/04	104.25	-15.00	-750.00	07/22/04	837.50	08/18/04	-1337.50
2003	07/07/03	82.50	08/27/03	131.50	49.00	2450.00	08/15/03	3925.00	07/08/03	-225.00
2002	07/08/02	108.25	08/27/02	144.00	35.75	1787.50	08/27/02	1787.50		
2001	07/09/01	93.00	08/27/01	81.00	-12.00	-600.00	07/23/01	512.50	08/15/01	-900.00
2000	07/07/00	105.50	08/25/00	110.00	4.50	225.00	08/25/00	225.00	08/07/00	-562.50
1999	07/07/99	80.25	08/27/99	82.25	2.00	100.00	08/02/99	362.50	08/04/99	-537.50
1998	07/07/98	63.25	08/27/98	73.00	9.75	487.50	08/17/98	612.50	07/29/98	-450.00
1997	07/07/97	96.00	08/27/97	111.25	15.25	762.50	08/08/97	1525.00	07/16/97	-250.00
1996	07/08/96	108.25	08/27/96	112.75	4.50	225.00	07/18/96	1637.50	07/12/96	-562.50
1995	07/07/95	158.75	08/25/95	175.25	16.50	825.00	07/21/95	2162.50	07/10/95	-362.50
1994	07/07/94	94.75	08/26/94	156.75	62.00	3100.00	08/26/94	3100.00		
1993	07/07/93	58.00	08/27/93	78.50	20.50	1025.00	07/27/93	1125.00	07/13/93	-25.00
1992	07/07/92	93.75	08/27/92	95.50	1.75	87.50	07/21/92	800.00	08/17/92	-712.50
1991	07/08/91	43.25	08/27/91	57.25	14.00	700.00	08/26/91	862.50	07/17/91	-325.00
1990	07/09/90	38.75	08/27/90	26.50	-12.25	-612.50	07/18/90	100.00	08/23/90	-975.00
1989	07/07/89	152.00	08/25/89	170.25	18.25	912.50	08/09/89	1350.00		
1988	07/07/88	55.75	08/26/88	106.25	50.50	2525.00	08/23/88	2562.50	07/18/88	-262.50
1987	07/07/87	85.75	08/27/87	110.75	25.00	1250.00	08/25/87	1450.00	07/20/87	-50.00
1986	07/07/86	62.25	08/27/86	87.00	24.75	1237.50	08/04/86	1487.50	07/08/86	-12.50
1985	07/08/85	61.25	08/27/85	65.25	4.00	200.00	08/16/85	462.50	07/17/85	-212.50

Percentage Correct	80									
Average Profit on Winning Trades					19.63	981.25		Winners		12
Average Loss on Trades					-13.08	-654.17		Losers		3
Average Net Profit Per Trade					13.08	654.17		Total trades		15
Percentage Correct	85									
Average Profit on Winning Trades					21.06	1052.94		Winners		17
Average Loss on Trades					-13.08	-654.17		Losers		3
Average Net Profit Per Trade					15.94	796.88		Total trades		20

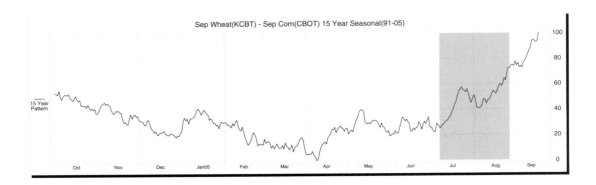

Sep Wheat(KCBT) - Sep Corn(CBOT) 15 Year Seasonal(91-05)

Figure 3-50

Buy Dec Wheat(KCBT) / Sell Dec Corn(CBOT)

Enter on approximately 07/15 - Exit on approximately 09/30

CONT YEAR	ENTRY DATE	ENTRY PRICE	EXIT DATE	EXIT PRICE	PROFIT	PROFIT AMOUNT	BEST EQUITY DATE	BEST EQUITY AMOUNT	WORST EQUITY DATE	WORST EQUITY AMOUNT
2004	07/15/04	125.25	09/30/04	131.25	6.00	300.00	09/21/04	1262.50	08/18/04	-1562.50
2003	07/15/03	109.50	09/30/03	136.50	27.00	1350.00	08/15/03	2637.50		
2002	07/15/02	114.75	09/30/02	223.75	109.00	5450.00	09/30/02	5450.00	07/24/02	-87.50
2001	07/16/01	99.25	09/28/01	78.00	-21.25	-1062.50	07/23/01	312.50	09/14/01	-1400.00
2000	07/17/00	107.00	09/29/00	122.25	15.25	762.50	09/29/00	762.50	08/07/00	-462.50
1999	07/15/99	77.25	09/30/99	86.00	8.75	437.50	08/02/99	787.50	07/21/99	-137.50
1998	07/15/98	72.50	09/30/98	94.25	21.75	1087.50	09/24/98	1475.00	07/29/98	-500.00
1997	07/15/97	105.50	09/30/97	107.25	1.75	87.50	07/25/97	1625.00	07/16/97	-62.50
1996	07/15/96	143.75	09/30/96	145.25	1.50	75.00	07/18/96	1250.00	09/12/96	-1912.50
1995	07/17/95	181.00	09/29/95	189.00	8.00	400.00	08/01/95	462.50	08/17/95	-850.00
1994	07/15/94	114.00	09/30/94	195.25	81.25	4062.50	09/30/94	4062.50		
1993	07/15/93	62.75	09/30/93	78.25	15.50	775.00	09/01/93	912.50	07/16/93	-37.50
1992	07/15/92	114.75	09/30/92	127.25	12.50	625.00	09/30/92	625.00	08/17/92	-1375.00
1991	07/15/91	49.75	09/30/91	86.75	37.00	1850.00	09/27/91	1900.00	08/02/91	-487.50
1990	07/16/90	55.25	09/28/90	52.75	-2.50	-125.00	07/18/90	300.00	09/04/90	-887.50
1989	07/17/89	165.00	09/29/89	166.50	1.50	75.00	08/09/89	1075.00	09/22/89	-412.50
1988	07/15/88	60.50	09/30/88	122.75	62.25	3112.50	09/26/88	3612.50	07/18/88	-75.00
1987	07/15/87	92.25	09/30/87	105.50	13.25	662.50	08/25/87	1200.00	07/20/87	-362.50
1986	07/15/86	72.25	09/30/86	72.75	0.50	25.00	09/04/86	1187.50	09/29/86	-12.50
1985	07/15/85	72.75	09/30/85	85.00	12.25	612.50	09/06/85	1025.00	08/05/85	-175.00

Percentage Correct	87									
Average Profit on Winning Trades					26.56	1327.88		Winners		13
Average Loss on Trades					-11.88	-593.75		Losers		2
Average Net Profit Per Trade					21.43	1071.67		Total trades		15
Percentage Correct	90									
Average Profit on Winning Trades					24.17	1208.33		Winners		18
Average Loss on Trades					-11.88	-593.75		Losers		2
Average Net Profit Per Trade					20.56	1028.13		Total trades		20

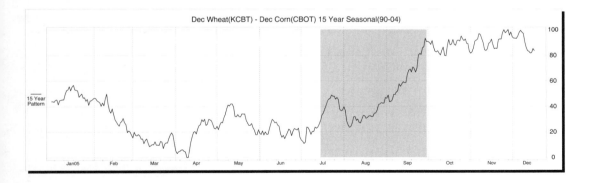

Dec Wheat(KCBT) - Dec Corn(CBOT) 15 Year Seasonal(90-04)

Sometimes spreads are traded with multiple contracts on one or both sides as a way to balance equity in the attempt to wring out even more risk. For example, if wheat was priced at $4.00 and corn at $2.00, a trader might spread one wheat contract against two corn contracts. In much the same way, traders can spread corn and oats. Perhaps the most traditional relationship has been one-to-one. But, depending on relative prices, the equity can be more evenly balanced by spreading one corn against two oats or even two corn against three oats. Note the differences and similarities in the seasonal patterns for the three different relationships.

Figure 3-51: Jul Corn/Oats Seasonal Pattern

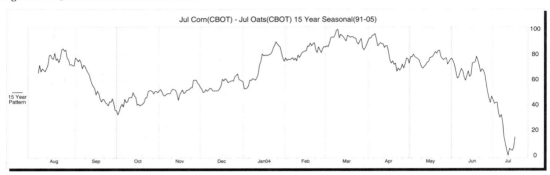

Figure 3-52: Jul Corn/2 Oats Seasonal Pattern

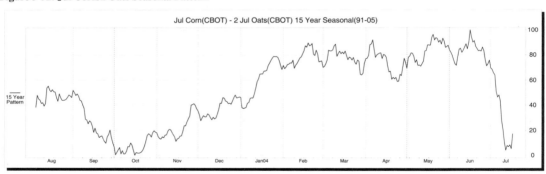

Figure 3-53: Jul 2 Corn/3 Oats Seasonal Pattern

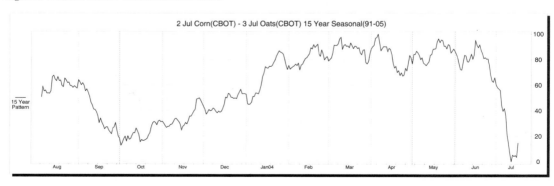

Chapter 3: Grains

Now compare seasonal strategies in their various combinations.

Figure 3-54: Oats vs Corn Spread Strategies

	Oats vs Corn Strategies							
Seasonal Strategy	Entry Date	Exit Date	Win Pct	Win Yrs	Loss Years	Total Years	Average Profit	Ave Pft Per Day
Buy 2 May Corn(CBOT)	1/03	2/14	87	13	2	15	979	23
Sell 3 May Oats(CBOT)			85	17	3	20	1086	25
Buy Jul Corn(CBOT)	1/03	2/19	87	13	2	15	613	13
Sell 2 Jul Oats(CBOT)			90	18	2	20	735	15
Buy May Corn(CBOT)	1/05	4/11	80	12	3	15	615	6
Sell 2 May Oats(CBOT)			85	17	3	20	1096	11
Buy 2 Mar Corn(CBOT)	1/08	1/25	87	13	2	15	737	41
Sell 3 Mar Oats(CBOT)			85	17	3	20	782	43
Buy Mar Corn(CBOT)	1/10	1/25	93	14	1	15	432	27
Sell 2 Mar Oats(CBOT)			85	17	3	20	429	27
Buy 3 Dec Oats(CBOT)	4/06	4/24	87	13	2	15	976	51
Sell 2 Dec Corn(CBOT)			90	18	2	20	866	46
Buy 3 Sep Oats(CBOT)	6/22	7/31	100	15	0	15	1513	38
Sell 2 Sep Corn(CBOT)			85	17	3	20	1262	32
Buy Sep Oats(CBOT)	6/24	7/25	93	14	1	15	758	24
Sell Sep Corn(CBOT)			90	18	2	20	533	17

Figure 3-55: Sep 3 Oats/2 Corn Monthly

Figure 3-56: Sep Oats/Corn Monthly

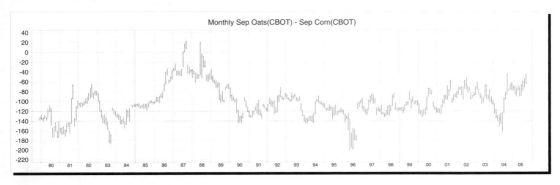

Figure 3-57

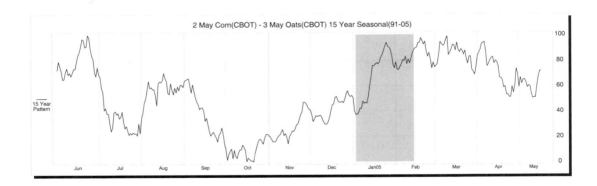

Buy 2 May Corn(CBOT) / Sell 3 May Oats(CBOT)

Moore Research Center, Inc.

Enter on approximately 01/03 - Exit on approximately 02/14

CONT YEAR	ENTRY DATE	ENTRY PRICE	EXIT DATE	EXIT PRICE	PROFIT	PROFIT AMOUNT	BEST EQUITY DATE	BEST EQUITY AMOUNT	WORST EQUITY DATE	WORST EQUITY AMOUNT
2005	01/03/05	-44.75	02/14/05	-55.50	-10.75	-537.50	01/07/05	462.50	02/01/05	-1400.00
2004	01/05/04	46.75	02/13/04	120.00	73.25	3662.50	02/13/04	3662.50	01/07/04	-312.50
2003	01/03/03	-119.00	02/14/03	-103.25	15.75	787.50	02/14/03	787.50	01/13/03	-1287.50
2002	01/03/02	-149.50	02/14/02	-133.00	16.50	825.00	01/16/02	3587.50		
2001	01/03/01	117.25	02/14/01	118.25	1.00	50.00	01/10/01	87.50	01/12/01	-575.00
2000	01/03/00	74.75	02/14/00	113.50	38.75	1937.50	02/10/00	2150.00		
1999	01/04/99	105.50	02/12/99	122.25	16.75	837.50	02/12/99	837.50		
1998	01/05/98	74.50	02/13/98	106.50	32.00	1600.00	01/26/98	1925.00	01/08/98	-325.00
1997	01/03/97	44.00	02/14/97	78.00	34.00	1700.00	01/30/97	2175.00	01/07/97	-775.00
1996	01/03/96	16.25	02/14/96	103.50	87.25	4362.50	02/13/96	4500.00		
1995	01/03/95	80.00	02/14/95	111.50	31.50	1575.00	02/08/95	1625.00	01/04/95	-37.50
1994	01/03/94	199.25	02/14/94	200.00	0.75	37.50	01/06/94	437.50	01/31/94	-887.50
1993	01/04/93	11.50	02/12/93	19.75	8.25	412.50	01/27/93	612.50	01/08/93	-250.00
1992	01/03/92	98.00	02/14/92	32.50	-65.50	-3275.00	01/15/92	862.50	02/10/92	-3475.00
1991	01/03/91	134.25	02/14/91	148.50	14.25	712.50	01/31/91	1325.00	01/09/91	-487.50
1990	01/03/90	7.50	02/14/90	49.50	42.00	2100.00	01/22/90	2600.00		
1989	01/03/89	-161.00	02/14/89	-90.50	70.50	3525.00	02/13/89	3925.00	01/18/89	-400.00
1988	01/04/88	-149.25	02/12/88	-122.25	27.00	1350.00	02/11/88	1675.00	01/06/88	-637.50
1987	01/05/87	-141.00	02/13/87	-160.50	-19.50	-975.00	01/12/87	937.50	02/12/87	-1537.50
1986	01/03/86	81.75	02/14/86	102.50	20.75	1037.50	02/03/86	1912.50		

Percentage Correct	87									
Average Profit on Winning Trades					28.46	1423.08		Winners		13
Average Loss on Trades					-38.13	-1906.25		Losers		2
Average Net Profit Per Trade					19.58	979.17		Total trades		15
Percentage Correct	85									
Average Profit on Winning Trades					31.19	1559.56		Winners		17
Average Loss on Trades					-31.92	-1595.83		Losers		3
Average Net Profit Per Trade					21.73	1086.25		Total trades		20

2 May Corn(CBOT) - 3 May Oats(CBOT) 15 Year Seasonal(91-05)

15 Year Pattern

Chapter 3: Grains

Figure 3-58

Buy Jul Corn(CBOT) / Sell 2 Jul Oats(CBOT)

Enter on approximately 01/03 - Exit on approximately 02/19

CONT YEAR	ENTRY DATE	ENTRY PRICE	EXIT DATE	EXIT PRICE	PROFIT	PROFIT AMOUNT	BEST EQUITY DATE	BEST EQUITY AMOUNT	WORST EQUITY DATE	WORST EQUITY AMOUNT
2005	01/03/05	-91.25	02/18/05	-82.75	8.50	425.00	01/11/05	737.50	02/08/05	-225.00
2004	01/05/04	-56.00	02/19/04	-20.25	35.75	1787.50	02/19/04	1787.50	01/06/04	-150.00
2003	01/03/03	-118.75	02/19/03	-128.75	-10.00	-500.00	01/07/03	275.00	01/17/03	-1137.50
2002	01/03/02	-122.50	02/19/02	-108.50	14.00	700.00	01/17/02	1837.50		
2001	01/03/01	-5.00	02/16/01	1.00	6.00	300.00	02/14/01	362.50	01/12/01	-212.50
2000	01/03/00	-8.75	02/18/00	9.75	18.50	925.00	02/16/00	1037.50	01/05/00	-37.50
1999	01/04/99	-3.50	02/19/99	7.75	11.25	562.50	02/18/99	575.00	01/11/99	-100.00
1998	01/05/98	-43.50	02/19/98	-25.50	18.00	900.00	01/26/98	1050.00	01/08/98	-100.00
1997	01/03/97	-62.75	02/19/97	-33.25	29.50	1475.00	01/30/97	1762.50	01/07/97	-375.00
1996	01/03/96	-112.25	02/16/96	-64.50	47.75	2387.50	02/13/96	2475.00		
1995	01/03/95	-30.25	02/17/95	-10.75	19.50	975.00	02/14/95	1012.50		
1994	01/03/94	20.25	02/18/94	20.75	0.50	25.00	02/11/94	300.00	01/11/94	-275.00
1993	01/04/93	-63.00	02/19/93	-46.75	16.25	812.50	02/18/93	825.00	01/07/93	-150.00
1992	01/03/92	-18.50	02/19/92	-57.75	-39.25	-1962.50	01/15/92	100.00	02/10/92	-3037.50
1991	01/03/91	4.25	02/19/91	12.00	7.75	387.50	01/31/91	637.50	01/09/91	-300.00
1990	01/03/90	-88.00	02/16/90	-56.25	31.75	1587.50	01/22/90	1800.00		
1989	01/03/89	-196.25	02/17/89	-153.75	42.50	2125.00	02/16/89	2325.00	01/18/89	-387.50
1988	01/04/88	-138.50	02/19/88	-129.25	9.00	450.00	01/19/88	762.50	01/06/88	-400.00
1987	01/05/87	-119.00	02/19/87	-116.50	2.50	125.00	01/12/87	200.00	02/11/87	-837.50
1986	01/03/86	-24.75	02/19/86	-0.50	24.25	1212.50	02/03/86	1275.00	01/06/86	-25.00

Percentage Correct	87									
Average Profit on Winning Trades					17.94	897.12		Winners		13
Average Loss on Trades					-24.63	-1231.25		Losers		2
Average Net Profit Per Trade					12.27	613.33		Total trades		15
Percentage Correct	90									
Average Profit on Winning Trades					19.07	953.47		Winners		18
Average Loss on Trades					-24.63	-1231.25		Losers		2
Average Net Profit Per Trade					14.70	735.00		Total trades		20

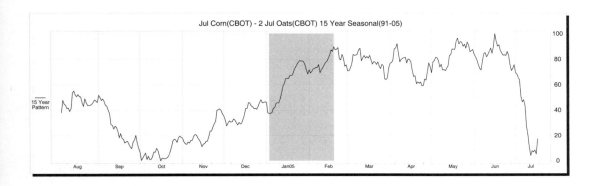

Jul Corn(CBOT) - 2 Jul Oats(CBOT) 15 Year Seasonal(91-05)

Figure 3-59

Buy May Corn(CBOT) / Sell 2 May Oats(CBOT)

Moore Research Center, Inc.

Enter on approximately 01/05 - Exit on approximately 04/11

CONT YEAR	ENTRY DATE	ENTRY PRICE	EXIT DATE	EXIT PRICE	PROFIT	PROFIT AMOUNT	BEST EQUITY DATE	BEST EQUITY AMOUNT	WORST EQUITY DATE	WORST EQUITY AMOUNT
2005	01/05/05	-100.75	04/11/05	-110.25	-9.50	-475.00	02/25/05	1412.50	03/30/05	-2112.50
2004	01/05/04	-54.25	04/08/04	-21.50	32.75	1637.50	02/26/04	2062.50	01/07/04	-162.50
2003	01/06/03	-154.75	04/11/03	-119.75	35.00	1750.00	03/13/03	2162.50	02/24/03	-1625.00
2002	01/07/02	-165.25	04/11/02	-145.25	20.00	1000.00	01/16/02	1975.00	04/05/02	-3387.50
2001	01/05/01	-0.50	04/11/01	-9.50	-9.00	-450.00	03/01/01	525.00	03/30/01	-462.50
2000	01/05/00	-19.50	04/11/00	-17.75	1.75	87.50	02/16/00	1037.50		
1999	01/05/99	-2.00	04/09/99	-15.75	-13.75	-687.50	02/16/99	587.50	04/08/99	-750.00
1998	01/05/98	-41.25	04/09/98	-12.00	29.25	1462.50	04/03/98	2162.50	01/08/98	-87.50
1997	01/06/97	-64.75	04/11/97	-42.00	22.75	1137.50	04/04/97	1800.00	01/07/97	-137.50
1996	01/05/96	-97.25	04/11/96	-39.00	58.25	2912.50	04/09/96	3012.50		
1995	01/05/95	-24.00	04/11/95	-20.50	3.50	175.00	02/08/95	925.00	04/07/95	-100.00
1994	01/05/94	31.50	04/11/94	31.75	0.25	12.50	01/06/94	137.50	03/28/94	-800.00
1993	01/05/93	-67.75	04/08/93	-59.75	8.00	400.00	03/12/93	1062.50	01/08/93	-162.50
1992	01/06/92	-18.75	04/10/92	-15.00	3.75	187.50	01/15/92	300.00	02/10/92	-2750.00
1991	01/07/91	5.75	04/11/91	7.25	1.50	75.00	01/31/91	862.50	04/01/91	-600.00
1990	01/05/90	-74.50	04/11/90	-30.75	43.75	2187.50	04/10/90	2262.50		
1989	01/05/89	-196.75	04/11/89	-101.50	95.25	4762.50	04/11/89	4762.50	01/18/89	-425.00
1988	01/05/88	-167.75	04/11/88	-127.75	40.00	2000.00	03/30/88	2862.50	01/06/88	-275.00
1987	01/05/87	-148.00	04/10/87	-133.50	14.50	725.00	03/10/87	2075.00	02/12/87	-862.50
1986	01/06/86	-28.50	04/11/86	31.75	60.25	3012.50	04/09/86	3337.50		

Percentage Correct	80								
Average Profit on Winning Trades					18.06	903.13	Winners		12
Average Loss on Trades					-10.75	-537.50	Losers		3
Average Net Profit Per Trade					12.30	615.00	Total trades		15
Percentage Correct	85								
Average Profit on Winning Trades					27.68	1383.82	Winners		17
Average Loss on Trades					-10.75	-537.50	Losers		3
Average Net Profit Per Trade					21.91	1095.63	Total trades		20

HYPOTHETICAL PERFORMANCE RESULTS HAVE MANY INHERENT LIMITATIONS, SOME OF WHICH ARE DESCRIBED BELOW. NO REPRESENTATION IS BEING MADE THAT ANY ACCOUNT WILL OR IS LIKELY TO ACHIEVE PROFITS OR LOSSES SIMILAR TO THOSE SHOWN. IN FACT, THERE ARE FREQUENTLY SHARP DIFFERENCES BETWEEN HYPOTHETICAL PERFORMANCE RESULTS AND THE ACTUAL RESULTS SUBSEQUENTLY ACHIEVED BY ANY PARTICULAR TRADING PROGRAM. ONE OF THE LIMITATIONS OF HYPOTHETICAL PERFORMANCE RESULTS IS THAT THEY ARE GENERALLY PREPARED WITH THE BENEFIT OF HINDSIGHT. IN ADDITION, HYPOTHETICAL TRADING DOES NOT INVOLVE FINANCIAL RISK, AND NO HYPOTHETICAL TRADING RECORD CAN COMPLETELY ACCOUNT FOR THE IMPACT OF FINANCIAL RISK IN ACTUAL TRADING. FOR EXAMPLE, THE ABILITY TO WITHSTAND LOSSES OR ADHERE TO A PARTICULAR TRADING PROGRAM IN SPITE OF TRADING LOSSES ARE MATERIAL POINTS WHICH CAN ALSO ADVERSELY AFFECT ACTUAL TRADING RESULTS. THERE ARE NUMEROUS OTHER FACTORS RELATED TO THE MARKETS IN GENERAL OR TO THE IMPLEMENTATION OF ANY SPECIFIC TRADING PROGRAM WHICH CANNOT BE FULLY ACCOUNTED FOR IN THE PREPARATION OF HYPOTHETICAL PERFORMANCE RESULTS AND ALL OF WHICH CAN ADVERSELY AFFECT ACTUAL TRADING RESULTS. RESULTS NOT ADJUSTED FOR COMMISSION AND SLIPPAGE.

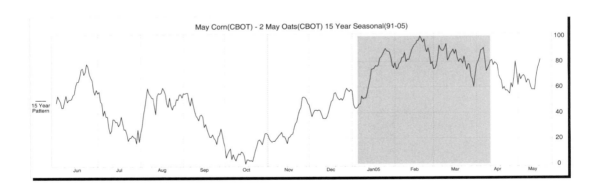

May Corn(CBOT) - 2 May Oats(CBOT) 15 Year Seasonal(91-05)

15 Year Pattern

Figure 3-60

Buy 2 Mar Corn(CBOT) / Sell 3 Mar Oats(CBOT)

Enter on approximately 01/08 - Exit on approximately 01/25

CONT YEAR	ENTRY DATE	ENTRY PRICE	EXIT DATE	EXIT PRICE	PROFIT	PROFIT AMOUNT	BEST EQUITY DATE	BEST EQUITY AMOUNT	WORST EQUITY DATE	WORST EQUITY AMOUNT
2005	01/10/05	-71.00	01/25/05	-106.00	-35.00	-1750.00			01/18/05	-2650.00
2004	01/08/04	36.25	01/23/04	79.25	43.00	2150.00	01/21/04	2512.50		
2003	01/08/03	-148.50	01/24/03	-141.75	6.75	337.50	01/24/03	337.50	01/10/03	-1762.50
2002	01/08/02	-188.25	01/25/02	-161.75	26.50	1325.00	01/16/02	2387.50		
2001	01/08/01	117.00	01/25/01	113.50	-3.50	-175.00	01/10/01	187.50	01/12/01	-500.00
2000	01/10/00	88.50	01/25/00	110.00	21.50	1075.00	01/24/00	1200.00		
1999	01/08/99	109.00	01/25/99	110.75	1.75	87.50	01/13/99	175.00	01/11/99	-162.50
1998	01/08/98	68.50	01/23/98	107.75	39.25	1962.50	01/23/98	1962.50		
1997	01/08/97	42.25	01/24/97	78.25	36.00	1800.00	01/20/97	2075.00		
1996	01/08/96	46.75	01/25/96	78.00	31.25	1562.50	01/25/96	1562.50	01/15/96	-487.50
1995	01/09/95	98.00	01/25/95	105.00	7.00	350.00	01/19/95	562.50	01/11/95	-62.50
1994	01/10/94	193.50	01/25/94	194.00	0.50	25.00	01/17/94	237.50	01/19/94	-262.50
1993	01/08/93	-7.00	01/25/93	7.75	14.75	737.50	01/25/93	737.50		
1992	01/08/92	92.00	01/24/92	105.25	13.25	662.50	01/15/92	1062.50		
1991	01/08/91	136.25	01/25/91	154.25	18.00	900.00	01/25/91	900.00	01/09/91	-400.00
1990	01/08/90	25.75	01/25/90	67.50	41.75	2087.50	01/22/90	2250.00		
1989	01/09/89	-134.75	01/25/89	-135.25	-0.50	-25.00	01/11/89	12.50	01/18/89	-1875.00
1988	01/08/88	-180.50	01/25/88	-176.50	4.00	200.00	01/19/88	525.00	01/14/88	-275.00
1987	01/08/87	-176.25	01/23/87	-159.50	16.75	837.50	01/22/87	1000.00		
1986	01/08/86	80.75	01/24/86	110.50	29.75	1487.50	01/24/86	1487.50		

Percentage Correct	87									
Average Profit on Winning Trades					19.96	998.08		Winners		13
Average Loss on Trades					-19.25	-962.50		Losers		2
Average Net Profit Per Trade					14.73	736.67		Total trades		15
Percentage Correct	85									
Average Profit on Winning Trades					20.69	1034.56		Winners		17
Average Loss on Trades					-13.00	-650.00		Losers		3
Average Net Profit Per Trade					15.64	781.88		Total trades		20

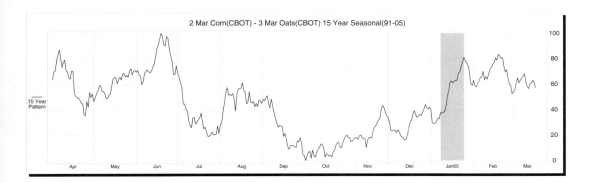

2 Mar Corn(CBOT) - 3 Mar Oats(CBOT) 15 Year Seasonal(91-05)

Figure 3-61

Buy Mar Corn(CBOT) / Sell 2 Mar Oats(CBOT)

Enter on approximately 01/10 - Exit on approximately 01/25

CONT YEAR	ENTRY DATE	ENTRY PRICE	EXIT DATE	EXIT PRICE	PROFIT	PROFIT AMOUNT	BEST EQUITY DATE	BEST EQUITY AMOUNT	WORST EQUITY DATE	WORST EQUITY AMOUNT
2005	01/10/05	-116.25	01/25/05	-137.00	-20.75	-1037.50			01/18/05	-1587.50
2004	01/12/04	-60.00	01/23/04	-39.50	20.50	1025.00	01/21/04	1262.50		
2003	01/10/03	-200.75	01/24/03	-173.00	27.75	1387.50	01/24/03	1387.50		
2002	01/10/02	-182.75	01/25/02	-177.50	5.25	262.50	01/16/02	875.00	01/24/02	-237.50
2001	01/10/01	4.00	01/25/01	4.50	0.50	25.00	01/16/01	137.50	01/12/01	-287.50
2000	01/10/00	-10.50	01/25/00	-2.50	8.00	400.00	01/24/00	487.50		
1999	01/11/99	-2.75	01/25/99	2.00	4.75	237.50	01/13/99	300.00		
1998	01/12/98	-37.25	01/23/98	-20.00	17.25	862.50	01/23/98	862.50		
1997	01/10/97	-52.50	01/24/97	-38.75	13.75	687.50	01/20/97	887.50	01/13/97	-12.50
1996	01/10/96	-88.25	01/25/96	-66.75	21.50	1075.00	01/25/96	1075.00	01/15/96	-437.50
1995	01/10/95	-12.75	01/25/95	-7.75	5.00	250.00	01/19/95	375.00	01/11/95	-12.50
1994	01/10/94	27.75	01/25/94	29.50	1.75	87.50	01/12/94	125.00	01/13/94	-162.50
1993	01/11/93	-75.00	01/25/93	-67.25	7.75	387.50	01/25/93	387.50		
1992	01/10/92	-20.75	01/24/92	-17.75	3.00	150.00	01/15/92	450.00		
1991	01/10/91	8.50	01/25/91	22.00	13.50	675.00	01/23/91	725.00		
1990	01/10/90	-52.00	01/25/90	-34.75	17.25	862.50	01/22/90	950.00		
1989	01/10/89	-188.50	01/25/89	-180.25	8.25	412.50	01/25/89	412.50	01/18/89	-825.00
1988	01/11/88	-182.25	01/25/88	-185.00	-2.75	-137.50	01/19/88	100.00	01/15/88	-362.50
1987	01/12/87	-158.00	01/23/87	-159.50	-1.50	-75.00	01/22/87	37.50	01/15/87	-362.50
1986	01/10/86	-27.75	01/24/86	-7.00	20.75	1037.50	01/24/86	1037.50		

Percentage Correct	93			
Average Profit on Winning Trades		10.73	536.61	Winners	14
Average Loss on Trades		-20.75	-1037.50	Losers	1
Average Net Profit Per Trade		8.63	431.67	Total trades	15
Percentage Correct	85			
Average Profit on Winning Trades		11.56	577.94	Winners	17
Average Loss on Trades		-8.33	-416.67	Losers	3
Average Net Profit Per Trade		8.57	428.75	Total trades	20

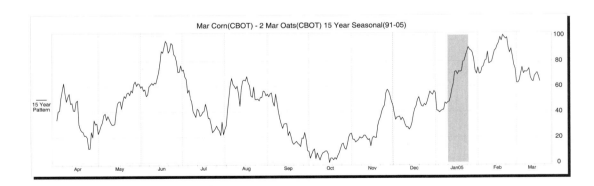

Mar Corn(CBOT) - 2 Mar Oats(CBOT) 15 Year Seasonal(91-05)

Figure 3-62

Buy 3 Dec Oats(CBOT) / Sell 2 Dec Corn(CBOT)

Enter on approximately 04/06 - Exit on approximately 04/24

CONT YEAR	ENTRY DATE	ENTRY PRICE	EXIT DATE	EXIT PRICE	PROFIT	PROFIT AMOUNT	BEST EQUITY DATE	BEST EQUITY AMOUNT	WORST EQUITY DATE	WORST EQUITY AMOUNT
2005	04/06/05	-10.00	04/22/05	-15.00	-5.00	-250.00	04/13/05	650.00	04/22/05	-250.00
2004	04/06/04	-105.00	04/23/04	-59.00	46.00	2300.00	04/23/04	2300.00	04/08/04	-50.00
2003	04/07/03	-46.50	04/24/03	-33.00	13.50	675.00	04/24/03	675.00	04/08/03	-50.00
2002	04/08/02	-34.25	04/24/02	-56.00	-21.75	-1087.50			04/22/02	-1462.50
2001	04/06/01	-108.50	04/24/01	-83.25	25.25	1262.50	04/24/01	1262.50	04/09/01	-300.00
2000	04/06/00	-123.50	04/24/00	-117.50	6.00	300.00	04/24/00	300.00	04/07/00	-100.00
1999	04/06/99	-128.50	04/23/99	-118.50	10.00	500.00	04/12/99	975.00		
1998	04/06/98	-115.50	04/24/98	-88.75	26.75	1337.50	04/20/98	1662.50		
1997	04/07/97	-90.50	04/24/97	-62.00	28.50	1425.00	04/17/97	1487.50		
1996	04/08/96	-23.00	04/24/96	60.75	83.75	4187.50	04/24/96	4187.50		
1995	04/06/95	-83.25	04/24/95	-76.50	6.75	337.50	04/18/95	1125.00		
1994	04/06/94	-103.00	04/22/94	-101.50	1.50	75.00	04/18/94	212.50	04/13/94	-612.50
1993	04/06/93	-56.75	04/23/93	-23.50	33.25	1662.50	04/20/93	2212.50		
1992	04/06/92	-53.75	04/24/92	-24.25	29.50	1475.00	04/24/92	1475.00	04/10/92	-137.50
1991	04/08/91	-83.00	04/24/91	-74.25	8.75	437.50	04/24/91	437.50	04/16/91	-475.00
1990	04/06/90	-4.00	04/24/90	6.00	10.00	500.00	04/23/90	600.00	04/09/90	-237.50
1989	04/06/89	94.50	04/24/89	110.00	15.50	775.00	04/21/89	1000.00	04/12/89	-725.00
1988	04/06/88	69.25	04/22/88	74.75	5.50	275.00	04/20/88	737.50	04/07/88	-37.50
1987	04/06/87	52.50	04/24/87	54.50	2.00	100.00	04/24/87	100.00	04/08/87	-362.50
1986	04/07/86	-71.75	04/24/86	-51.00	20.75	1037.50	04/24/86	1037.50	04/09/86	-450.00

Percentage Correct	87							
Average Profit on Winning Trades				24.58	1228.85		Winners	13
Average Loss on Trades				-13.38	-668.75		Losers	2
Average Net Profit Per Trade				19.52	975.83		Total trades	15
Percentage Correct	90							
Average Profit on Winning Trades				20.74	1036.81		Winners	18
Average Loss on Trades				-13.38	-668.75		Losers	2
Average Net Profit Per Trade				17.33	866.25		Total trades	20

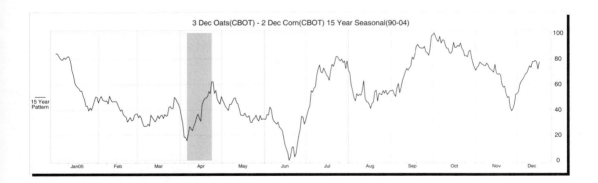

3 Dec Oats(CBOT) - 2 Dec Corn(CBOT) 15 Year Seasonal(90-04)

15 Year Pattern

Figure 3-63

Buy 3 Sep Oats(CBOT) / Sell 2 Sep Corn(CBOT)

Enter on approximately 06/22 - Exit on approximately 07/31

CONT YEAR	ENTRY DATE	ENTRY PRICE	EXIT DATE	EXIT PRICE	PROFIT	PROFIT AMOUNT	BEST EQUITY DATE	BEST EQUITY AMOUNT	WORST EQUITY DATE	WORST EQUITY AMOUNT
2004	06/22/04	-102.50	07/30/04	-69.25	33.25	1662.50	07/28/04	2137.50	07/02/04	-512.50
2003	06/23/03	-53.25	07/31/03	7.25	60.50	3025.00	07/31/03	3025.00	06/24/03	-687.50
2002	06/24/02	16.75	07/31/02	41.00	24.25	1212.50	07/17/02	3050.00	07/26/02	-50.00
2001	06/22/01	-75.50	07/31/01	-16.00	59.50	2975.00	07/25/01	4500.00	07/09/01	-162.50
2000	06/22/00	-79.75	07/31/00	-41.00	38.75	1937.50	07/26/00	2062.50	06/29/00	-150.00
1999	06/22/99	-101.00	07/30/99	-82.50	18.50	925.00	07/13/99	2312.50		
1998	06/22/98	-124.00	07/31/98	-110.25	13.75	687.50	07/06/98	1050.00	06/23/98	-312.50
1997	06/23/97	-44.50	07/31/97	-23.25	21.25	1062.50	07/08/97	1075.00	06/24/97	-162.50
1996	06/24/96	-165.50	07/31/96	-131.75	33.75	1687.50	07/22/96	2887.50	07/01/96	-787.50
1995	06/22/95	-101.50	07/31/95	-55.00	46.50	2325.00	07/31/95	2325.00	06/26/95	-500.00
1994	06/22/94	-123.25	07/29/94	-94.00	29.25	1462.50	07/28/94	1887.50	06/28/94	-1062.50
1993	06/22/93	-50.25	07/30/93	-50.00	0.25	12.50	06/30/93	762.50	07/20/93	-250.00
1992	06/22/92	-104.00	07/31/92	-48.25	55.75	2787.50	07/31/92	2787.50	06/30/92	-475.00
1991	06/24/91	-142.50	07/31/91	-125.25	17.25	862.50	07/12/91	3787.50		
1990	06/22/90	-133.25	07/31/90	-132.00	1.25	62.50	07/26/90	262.50	07/17/90	-1287.50
1989	06/22/89	-8.50	07/31/89	-53.50	-45.00	-2250.00			07/31/89	-2250.00
1988	06/22/88	299.00	07/29/88	264.50	-34.50	-1725.00	06/27/88	6150.00	07/22/88	-7200.00
1987	06/22/87	73.75	07/31/87	167.25	93.50	4675.00	07/31/87	4675.00		
1986	06/23/86	-66.25	07/31/86	-29.00	37.25	1862.50	07/31/86	1862.50	06/25/86	-437.50
1985	06/24/85	-85.25	07/31/85	-85.50	-0.25	-12.50	07/02/85	625.00	07/29/85	-412.50

Percentage Correct		100								
Average Profit on Winning Trades					30.25	1512.50		Winners		15
Average Loss on Trades								Losers		0
Average Net Profit Per Trade					30.25	1512.50		Total trades		15
Percentage Correct		85								
Average Profit on Winning Trades					34.38	1719.12		Winners		17
Average Loss on Trades					-26.58	-1329.17		Losers		3
Average Net Profit Per Trade					25.24	1261.88		Total trades		20

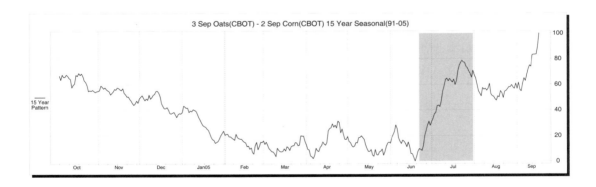

3 Sep Oats(CBOT) - 2 Sep Corn(CBOT) 15 Year Seasonal(91-05)

15 Year Pattern

Figure 3-64

Buy Sep Oats(CBOT) / Sell Sep Corn(CBOT)

Moore Research Center, Inc.

Enter on approximately 06/24 - Exit on approximately 07/25

CONT YEAR	ENTRY DATE	ENTRY PRICE	EXIT DATE	EXIT PRICE	PROFIT	PROFIT AMOUNT	BEST EQUITY DATE	BEST EQUITY AMOUNT	WORST EQUITY DATE	WORST EQUITY AMOUNT
2004	06/24/04	-127.25	07/23/04	-98.00	29.25	1462.50	07/22/04	1612.50	06/25/04	-75.00
2003	06/24/03	-100.50	07/25/03	-75.00	25.50	1275.00	07/24/03	1325.00		
2002	06/24/02	-69.75	07/25/02	-68.50	1.25	62.50	07/17/02	925.00	07/24/02	-175.00
2001	06/25/01	-88.50	07/25/01	-68.25	20.25	1012.50	07/24/01	1037.50	07/10/01	-425.00
2000	06/26/00	-94.00	07/25/00	-75.50	18.50	925.00	07/19/00	962.50	06/27/00	-87.50
1999	06/24/99	-104.50	07/23/99	-95.00	9.50	475.00	07/13/99	1212.50		
1998	06/24/98	-129.00	07/24/98	-110.75	18.25	912.50	07/24/98	912.50		
1997	06/24/97	-98.25	07/25/97	-89.00	9.25	462.50	07/08/97	700.00	07/15/97	-37.50
1996	06/24/96	-185.00	07/25/96	-159.25	25.75	1287.50	07/22/96	1525.00	07/01/96	-700.00
1995	06/26/95	-128.00	07/25/95	-120.00	8.00	400.00	07/24/95	500.00	07/12/95	-125.00
1994	06/24/94	-127.75	07/25/94	-103.00	24.75	1237.50	07/21/94	1312.50	06/28/94	-250.00
1993	06/24/93	-90.50	07/23/93	-96.00	-5.50	-275.00	06/29/93	137.50	07/19/93	-437.50
1992	06/24/92	-118.00	07/24/92	-91.25	26.75	1337.50	07/24/92	1337.50	07/01/92	-237.50
1991	06/24/91	-126.50	07/25/91	-117.00	9.50	475.00	07/12/91	1475.00		
1990	06/25/90	-138.00	07/25/90	-131.75	6.25	312.50	07/25/90	312.50	06/29/90	-325.00
1989	06/26/89	-88.00	07/25/89	-85.75	2.25	112.50	07/25/89	112.50	07/06/89	-750.00
1988	06/24/88	16.50	07/25/88	-48.50	-65.00	-3250.00	06/27/88	250.00	07/22/88	-3450.00
1987	06/24/87	-39.00	07/24/87	-11.25	27.75	1387.50	07/24/87	1387.50		
1986	06/24/86	-87.50	07/25/86	-72.50	15.00	750.00	07/21/86	1000.00	06/25/86	-37.50
1985	06/24/85	-114.75	07/25/85	-108.75	6.00	300.00	07/22/85	350.00	06/26/85	-25.00

Percentage Correct		93								
Average Profit on Winning Trades					16.63	831.25		Winners		14
Average Loss on Trades					-5.50	-275.00		Losers		1
Average Net Profit Per Trade					15.15	757.50		Total trades		15
Percentage Correct		90								
Average Profit on Winning Trades					15.76	788.19		Winners		18
Average Loss on Trades					-35.25	-1762.50		Losers		2
Average Net Profit Per Trade					10.66	533.13		Total trades		20

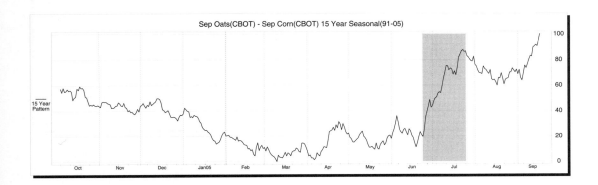

Sep Oats(CBOT) - Sep Corn(CBOT) 15 Year Seasonal(91-05)

15 Year Pattern

Figure 3-65: Jul Corn/Oats Monthly

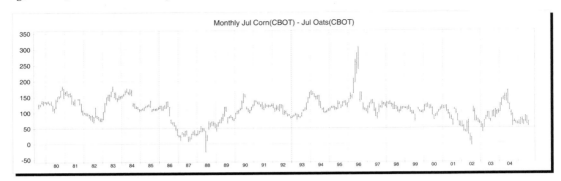

Figure 3-66: Jul Corn/2 Oats Monthly

Figure 3-67: Jul 2 Corn/3 Oats Monthly

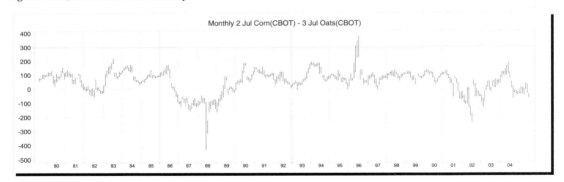

Chapter 4: Soybean Complex

Soybeans have been grown in China for perhaps 5,000 years. Marco Polo is thought to have first introduced soy foods to Europe upon his return in 1295. Few soybeans were produced outside the Orient, however, until the early 1900s when the West began finally to recognize the value of soybeans as a source of high-protein meal and of edible oil. Because the whole soybean is of limited use, in fact, demand derives principally from its two primary products. Thus, the term soybean complex refers to the interrelationship of soybeans with soymeal and soyoil.

The United States began producing a significant crop of soybeans only after a trade embargo by China cut off soybean supplies in the 1930s. Acreage restrictions to reduce oversupply of other crops during the Great Depression further stimulated soybeans as an alternative, as did trade restrictions during World War II that prompted growth of a domestic oilseed industry. After the war, growing populations and rising affluence steadily increased demand for meats, which in turn expanded demand for livestock feeds including soymeal.

The United States thus emerged in the 1950s as a primary soybean producer and by the 1970s was producing about two-thirds of the world's total. But a series of US crop problems, growing global demand, and finally a US grain embargo drove global consumers to seek and invest in alternative sources. The emergence of first Brazil and later Argentina in the 1980s as major producers had profound market implications. The world had a new crop harvested every six months, and US exports faced stiff competition. In 2003/04, total production in South America surpassed that in the United States.

Processing, or crushing, a 60-pound bushel of soybeans yields 44 pounds of (48% protein) soymeal and 11 pounds of soyoil, and 5 pounds of waste, primarily hulls. The CBOT launched its futures contract for soybean futures in 1936, for soyoil in 1950, and for soymeal in 1951. The CBOT launched a futures contract for South American soybeans in May 2005.

Intra-market Spreads

As with grains, spreads between delivery months in the soybean complex are of two basic types. Spreads within the same crop marketing year reflect supply and demand by how they differ from full carry. In normal conditions, deferred contracts command a premium that is a greater percentage of full carry when supply is more than sufficient for demand. In more extraordinary conditions, when supply is tight but demand robust, the nearby contracts can command a premium that is limited only by how well it rations supply to most efficient demand.

Spreads between delivery months of different crop years are more likely to display significant premiums or discounts, however, because crop problems in one year or the other can create a supply imbalance. Spreads must then perform the vital function of helping manage the transition from one to the other by offering financial incentives that attract greater demand to greater supply.

Soybeans

Because the US Soybean Belt roughly coincides with the Corn Belt but also extends southward along the Mississippi River, soybeans compete with both corn and cotton for acreage. The bulk of the crop is planted from late April through early June and harvested from late September through early November. Although the USDA crop marketing year runs September through August, so few soybeans are harvested in time for delivery against it that the industry considers September a "bastard" delivery month — claimed by neither old- nor new-crop.

Figure 4-1: Cash Soybean Seasonal Pattern

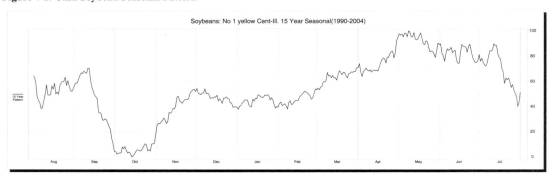

Cash prices for soybeans tend to follow a predictable pattern. Prices are usually lowest in October when harvest activity is most intense and supply at its peak. By November, the stream of new supply slows and a post-harvest recovery is led by commercial demand from processors crushing at capacity for soymeal. The market then weakens in the new calendar year as producers sell into the new tax year; logistics slow distribution to export destinations; domestic consumption of soymeal peaks; and South American crops that will replace US soybeans in export markets mature. After falling in the so-called February Break, prices rise into planting. With supply nearing its annual nadir, price tends to remain subject to crop scares until mid July. But, barring disastrous weather, the market normally declines into August as pods are set on plants and as demand slows when processors reduce activity to perform pre-harvest maintenance. After firming into early September when processors return and need soybeans to crush, prices decline again into harvest.

Figure 4-2: Jul/Nov Soybeans Seasonal Pattern

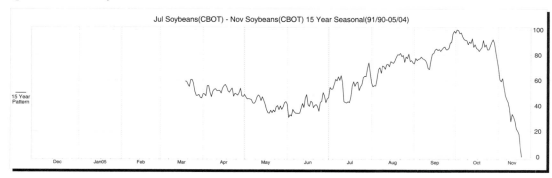

Chapter 4: Soybean Complex

Carrying charges. Soybeans do tend to build carrying charges into price structure but not so reliably as do corn and wheat. Greater volatility may be partially responsible. But it may also be that demand for soybeans is greatest during and immediately after harvest and that South America's crop will be available when domestic supplies are tightest. Thus, as evidenced by the marginal performance seen below, the market is less consistently willing to pay a premium to ensure plentiful supplies late in the crop marketing year.

Figure 4-3: Soybean Carrying-charge Strategies

Moore Research Center, Inc.	Soybean Carrying- charge Spread Strategies							
Seasonal Strategy	Entry Date	Exit Date	Win Pct	Win Yrs	Loss Years	Total Years	Average Profit	Ave Pft Per Day
Buy Jul Soybeans(CBOT) Sell Nov Soybeans(CBOT)	7/15	10/03	73 80	11 16	4 4	15 20	290 451	4 6
Buy Jul Soybeans(CBOT) Sell Nov Soybeans(CBOT)	7/16	9/28	80 75	12 15	3 5	15 20	258 448	3 6

Figure 4-4

Moore Research Center, Inc.	Buy Jul Soybeans(CBOT) / Sell Nov Soybeans(CBOT)									
Enter on approximately 07/15 - Exit on approximately 10/03										
CONT YEAR	ENTRY DATE	ENTRY PRICE	EXIT DATE	EXIT PRICE	PROFIT	PROFIT AMOUNT	BEST EQUITY DATE	BEST EQUITY AMOUNT	WORST EQUITY DATE	WORST EQUITY AMOUNT
2005	07/15/04	5.50	10/01/04	25.75	20.25	1012.50	09/24/04	1237.50		
2004	07/15/03	10.25	10/03/03	-30.75	-41.00	-2050.00	08/07/03	262.50	09/29/03	-2562.50
2003	07/15/02	-6.25	10/03/02	7.25	13.50	675.00	07/29/02	687.50	08/14/02	-425.00
2002	07/16/01	2.75	10/03/01	20.25	17.50	875.00	09/28/01	1087.50	07/17/01	-400.00
2001	07/17/00	38.75	10/03/00	35.00	-3.75	-187.50	07/24/00	75.00	09/11/00	-337.50
2000	07/15/99	30.75	10/01/99	27.50	-3.25	-162.50	07/16/99	150.00	09/10/99	-350.00
1999	07/15/98	24.00	10/02/98	40.00	16.00	800.00	09/02/98	900.00	07/17/98	-25.00
1998	07/15/97	22.62	10/03/97	21.00	-1.63	-81.25	08/18/97	331.25	09/17/97	-231.25
1997	07/15/96	8.75	10/03/96	19.25	10.50	525.00	07/26/96	612.50	07/16/96	-162.50
1996	07/17/95	15.75	10/03/95	30.50	14.75	737.50	09/06/95	825.00		
1995	07/15/94	24.75	10/03/94	35.75	11.00	550.00	10/03/94	550.00	07/19/94	-112.50
1994	07/15/93	2.00	10/01/93	22.50	20.50	1025.00	10/01/93	1025.00	07/23/93	-200.00
1993	07/15/92	27.00	10/02/92	29.75	2.75	137.50	08/19/92	150.00	08/07/92	-250.00
1992	07/15/91	35.00	10/03/91	35.75	0.75	37.50	07/18/91	62.50	08/02/91	-825.00
1991	07/16/90	35.75	10/03/90	44.75	9.00	450.00	10/02/90	512.50	08/01/90	-150.00
1990	07/17/89	20.00	10/03/89	39.50	19.50	975.00	09/28/89	1025.00	07/19/89	-50.00
1989	07/15/88	-59.00	10/03/88	4.00	63.00	3150.00	09/28/88	3550.00		
1988	07/15/87	23.50	10/02/87	24.00	0.50	25.00	07/21/87	137.50	08/12/87	-475.00
1987	07/15/86	24.50	10/03/86	25.25	0.75	37.50	08/07/86	512.50	09/19/86	-50.00
1986	07/15/85	31.75	10/03/85	41.50	9.75	487.50	09/27/85	550.00	08/06/85	-425.00
Percentage Correct	73									
Average Profit on Winning Trades					12.41	620.45		Winners		11
Average Loss on Trades					-12.41	-620.31		Losers		4
Average Net Profit Per Trade					5.79	289.58		Total trades		15
Percentage Correct	80									
Average Profit on Winning Trades					14.38	718.75		Winners		16
Average Loss on Trades					-12.41	-620.31		Losers		4
Average Net Profit Per Trade					9.02	450.94		Total trades		20

Figure 4-5

Buy Jul Soybeans(CBOT) / Sell Nov Soybeans(CBOT)

Enter on approximately 07/16 - Exit on approximately 09/28

CONT YEAR	ENTRY DATE	ENTRY PRICE	EXIT DATE	EXIT PRICE	PROFIT	PROFIT AMOUNT	BEST EQUITY DATE	BEST EQUITY AMOUNT	WORST EQUITY DATE	WORST EQUITY AMOUNT
2005	07/16/04	7.50	09/28/04	29.00	21.50	1075.00	09/24/04	1137.50	07/20/04	-75.00
2004	07/16/03	10.00	09/26/03	-29.25	-39.25	-1962.50	08/07/03	275.00	09/24/03	-2037.50
2003	07/16/02	-6.75	09/27/02	4.00	10.75	537.50	07/29/02	712.50	08/14/02	-400.00
2002	07/16/01	2.75	09/28/01	24.50	21.75	1087.50	09/28/01	1087.50	07/17/01	-400.00
2001	07/17/00	38.75	09/28/00	33.50	-5.25	-262.50	07/24/00	75.00	09/11/00	-337.50
2000	07/16/99	33.75	09/28/99	27.25	-6.50	-325.00			09/10/99	-500.00
1999	07/16/98	24.75	09/28/98	38.00	13.25	662.50	09/02/98	862.50	07/17/98	-62.50
1998	07/16/97	24.00	09/26/97	26.50	2.50	125.00	08/18/97	262.50	09/17/97	-300.00
1997	07/16/96	5.50	09/27/96	13.75	8.25	412.50	07/26/96	775.00		
1996	07/17/95	15.75	09/28/95	30.00	14.25	712.50	09/06/95	825.00		
1995	07/18/94	24.75	09/28/94	32.25	7.50	375.00	09/21/94	450.00	07/19/94	-112.50
1994	07/16/93	4.00	09/28/93	21.00	17.00	850.00	09/28/93	850.00	07/23/93	-300.00
1993	07/16/92	28.00	09/28/92	28.50	0.50	25.00	08/19/92	100.00	08/07/92	-300.00
1992	07/16/91	31.50	09/27/91	33.25	1.75	87.50	07/18/91	237.50	08/02/91	-650.00
1991	07/16/90	35.75	09/28/90	45.00	9.25	462.50	09/28/90	462.50	08/01/90	-150.00
1990	07/17/89	20.00	09/28/89	40.50	20.50	1025.00	09/28/89	1025.00	07/19/89	-50.00
1989	07/18/88	-59.00	09/28/88	12.00	71.00	3550.00	09/28/88	3550.00		
1988	07/16/87	24.25	09/28/87	22.00	-2.25	-112.50	07/21/87	100.00	08/12/87	-512.50
1987	07/16/86	26.50	09/26/86	26.50	0.00	0.00	08/07/86	412.50	09/19/86	-150.00
1986	07/16/85	30.00	09/27/85	42.75	12.75	637.50	09/27/85	637.50	08/06/85	-337.50

Percentage Correct	80								
Average Profit on Winning Trades					10.69	534.38		Winners	12
Average Loss on Trades					-17.00	-850.00		Losers	3
Average Net Profit Per Trade					5.15	257.50		Total trades	15
Percentage Correct	75								
Average Profit on Winning Trades					15.50	775.00		Winners	15
Average Loss on Trades					-10.65	-532.50		Losers	5
Average Net Profit Per Trade					8.96	448.13		Total trades	20

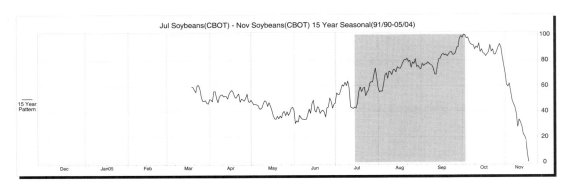

Jul Soybeans(CBOT) - Nov Soybeans(CBOT) 15 Year Seasonal(91/90-05/04)

These strategies quantify the borderline tendency for this market to increase the percentage of full carry into its price structure from mid July into harvest. They also offer a classic example of how slightly different entry and/or exit can affect performance. The first holds up over 20 years but not 15 whereas the second holds up over 15 but not 20. The tendency exists and is tradable but imprecise. Flexibility in entry and exit matters.

Old-crop/new-crop. The all-time "granddaddy" of spreads may still be July/November 1973 Soybeans. From barely $0.20/bushel in October 1972, July's premium over November soared by June 1973 to $5.33. In less than 8 months, this spread with initial margin of probably less than $100 moved more than $25,000. Talk about annualized returns!

Figure 4-6: Jul73/Nov73 Soybeans

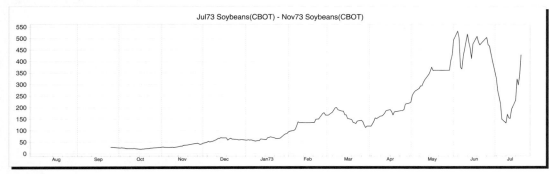

That was an exceptional example of a tendency that still holds — and logically so. Although May now is considered the last true old-crop contract because it is too early to deliver South American soybeans against and July is still most identified with old-crop tightness, the August contract helps better illustrate typical old-crop/new-crop spread movement late into the crop year.

Figure 4-7: Aug/Nov Soybeans Seasonal Pattern

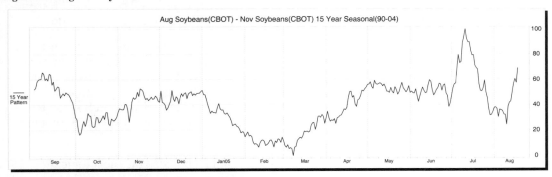

Under the pressure of new supply the cash market usually declines into harvest, dragging delivery months (such as August) for that current crop year lower but affecting those (such as November) for the following crop year very little. Likewise, the post-harvest recovery in cash most affects the current crop year, as do all the negative pressures associated with the February Break. But, because domestic consumption is heaviest during cold weather and US exports greatest when South American supplies are lowest, the last half of the crop year (March-August) begins with far less than half the crop supply from harvest. With the potential for tight stocks before another crop can be harvested, a primary function of all old-crop/new-crop relationships is to ensure supply at least until the market feels more secure that the new crop will be made. Thus, the market tends to place an increasing premium on declining old-crop supplies even as new-crop production potential grows. Market anxiety and

Figure 4-8: Old-crop/New-crop Soybeans Strategies

Moore Research Center, Inc.	Old-crop/New-crop Soybeans Spread Strategies							
Seasonal Strategy	Entry Date	Exit Date	Win Pct	Win Yrs	Loss Years	Total Years	Average Profit	Ave Pft Per Day
Buy "Red" Nov Soybeans(CBOT)	9/11	10/20	80	12	3	15	351	9
Sell Nov Soybeans(CBOT)			80	16	4	20	464	12
Buy Nov Soybeans(CBOT)	12/10	2/04	80	12	3	15	178	3
Sell May Soybeans(CBOT)			80	16	4	20	369	6
Buy May Soybeans(CBOT)	3/08	3/27	87	13	2	15	464	23
Sell Nov Soybeans(CBOT)			85	17	3	20	361	18
Buy Jul Soybeans(CBOT)	3/08	6/09	80	12	3	15	458	5
Sell Nov Soybeans(CBOT)			80	16	4	20	428	5
Buy Aug Soybeans(CBOT)	5/26	7/10	93	14	1	15	485	11
Sell Mar Soybeans(CBOT)			95	19	1	20	541	12
Buy May Soybeans(CBOT)	7/17	7/31	80	12	3	15	319	21
Sell Sep Soybeans(CBOT)			80	16	4	20	427	28

crop scares often peak in July. Barring disastrous weather, the market thereafter breathes in relief as pods are set, the crop is made, and harvest soon begins.

Notice the first strategy in the table directly compares market perceptions of two crop years, with November contracts best representing harvest. The current November is most closely associated with the cash market entering harvest, such that it usually suffers first and most, whereas the "Red" November contract represents unknown future possibilities and is usually least affected. Of special note, however, is what happened to the spread in 2003 (see Figure 4-9) when unexpected and late weather problems sharply reduced crop yield. Except in that year of extraordinary events, drawdowns and losses suffered were mostly moderate.

The second strategy, which begins after the post-harvest recovery, reflects pressures on old-crop contracts associated with the notorious February Break discussed above. The next two strategies suggest how old-crop/new-crop relationships pivot around the transition into the second half of the crop year, when market focus shifts to the potential for both new production and tight old-crop stocks. The strategy quantifying the typical March surge in favor of old-crop has not always generated a large move, but neither has it suffered frequent or severe drawdowns.

Perhaps the most impressive, certainly the most reliable, but also the most logical strategy has been the August/March spread from late May into mid July. It has held up over not only the last 15 but also the last 20 years. It has suffered the occasional severe drawdown, but volatility can be expected as market anxieties peak when crop scares are most frequent.

The final strategy identifies the typical peak in old-crop/new-crop dynamics and the exhaustion thereafter. Once the market believes the new crop will likely reach production potential, prospective carryover becomes progressively more burdensome. During a period when volatility is often at its own seasonal peak, the strategy has suffered drawdowns in only about half of the last 20 years and both drawdowns and losses have usually been modest.

Chapter 4: Soybean Complex

Figure 4-9

Buy "Red" Nov Soybeans(CBOT) / Sell Nov Soybeans(CBOT)

Enter on approximately 09/11 - Exit on approximately 10/20

CONT YEAR	ENTRY DATE	ENTRY PRICE	EXIT DATE	EXIT PRICE	PROFIT	PROFIT AMOUNT	BEST EQUITY DATE	BEST EQUITY AMOUNT	WORST EQUITY DATE	WORST EQUITY AMOUNT
2005	09/13/04	10.50	10/20/04	24.00	13.50	675.00	10/12/04	1387.50		
2004	09/11/03	-74.75	10/20/03	-158.75	-84.00	-4200.00	09/16/03	212.50	10/14/03	-5862.50
2003	09/11/02	-49.50	10/18/02	-36.25	13.25	662.50	10/09/02	1337.50		
2002	09/13/01	4.50	10/19/01	23.75	19.25	962.50	10/19/01	962.50	09/17/01	-37.50
2001	09/11/00	31.00	10/20/00	40.25	9.25	462.50	10/13/00	662.50		
2000	09/13/99	30.25	10/20/99	33.25	3.00	150.00	09/15/99	325.00		
1999	09/11/98	51.00	10/20/98	44.00	-7.00	-350.00	09/17/98	200.00	10/16/98	-475.00
1998	09/11/97	-4.25	10/20/97	-3.00	1.25	62.50	09/30/97	737.50	10/13/97	-337.50
1997	09/11/96	-65.00	10/18/96	-10.50	54.50	2725.00	10/14/96	2750.00	09/12/96	-50.00
1996	09/11/95	11.75	10/20/95	1.00	-10.75	-537.50	09/13/95	412.50	09/21/95	-650.00
1995	09/12/94	31.75	10/20/94	50.75	19.00	950.00	10/05/94	1112.50		
1994	09/13/93	-16.00	10/20/93	3.75	19.75	987.50	10/04/93	1262.50	09/23/93	-200.00
1993	09/11/92	29.25	10/20/92	33.25	4.00	200.00	10/02/92	487.50	09/15/92	-62.50
1992	09/11/91	-2.75	10/18/91	33.75	36.50	1825.00	10/15/91	2175.00	09/16/91	-737.50
1991	09/11/90	-4.50	10/19/90	9.25	13.75	687.50	10/15/90	937.50	10/08/90	-500.00
1990	09/11/89	-2.00	10/20/89	17.25	19.25	962.50	10/13/89	1325.00		
1989	09/12/88	-115.50	10/20/88	-65.00	50.50	2525.00	10/20/88	2525.00	09/14/88	-500.00
1988	09/11/87	7.50	10/20/87	19.50	12.00	600.00	10/19/87	1050.00	09/18/87	-512.50
1987	09/11/86	24.25	10/20/86	19.25	-5.00	-250.00	10/07/86	62.50	10/03/86	-287.50
1986	09/11/85	30.00	10/18/85	33.50	3.50	175.00	10/02/85	300.00	09/17/85	-312.50

Percentage Correct	80									
Average Profit on Winning Trades					17.25	862.50		Winners		12
Average Loss on Trades					-33.92	-1695.83		Losers		3
Average Net Profit Per Trade					7.02	350.83		Total trades		15
Percentage Correct	80									
Average Profit on Winning Trades					18.27	913.28		Winners		16
Average Loss on Trades					-26.69	-1334.38		Losers		4
Average Net Profit Per Trade					9.28	463.75		Total trades		20

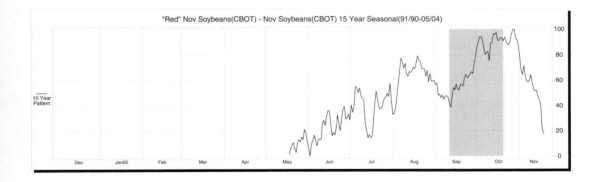

"Red" Nov Soybeans(CBOT) - Nov Soybeans(CBOT) 15 Year Seasonal(91/90-05/04)

Figure 4-10

Buy Nov Soybeans(CBOT) / Sell May Soybeans(CBOT)

Enter on approximately 12/10 - Exit on approximately 02/04

CONT YEAR	ENTRY DATE	ENTRY PRICE	EXIT DATE	EXIT PRICE	PROFIT	PROFIT AMOUNT	BEST EQUITY DATE	BEST EQUITY AMOUNT	WORST EQUITY DATE	WORST EQUITY AMOUNT
2004	12/10/03	-154.25	02/04/04	-169.25	-15.00	-750.00	12/23/03	1137.50	01/14/04	-1000.00
2003	12/10/02	-46.75	02/04/03	-38.75	8.00	400.00	01/21/03	712.50	01/02/03	-337.50
2002	12/10/01	9.75	02/04/02	8.00	-1.75	-87.50	12/13/01	25.00	01/14/02	-200.00
2001	12/11/00	1.50	02/02/01	7.25	5.75	287.50	02/01/01	475.00	12/28/00	-125.00
2000	12/10/99	12.50	02/04/00	17.25	4.75	237.50	01/21/00	362.50	12/17/99	-25.00
1999	12/10/98	12.50	02/04/99	14.75	2.25	112.50	12/15/98	125.00	01/13/99	-225.00
1998	12/10/97	-33.50	02/04/98	-13.75	19.75	987.50	02/02/98	1050.00		
1997	12/10/96	-24.75	02/04/97	-52.75	-28.00	-1400.00			01/17/97	-1762.50
1996	12/11/95	-34.75	02/02/96	-32.50	2.25	112.50	02/02/96	112.50	01/03/96	-1162.50
1995	12/12/94	16.50	02/03/95	18.75	2.25	112.50	01/05/95	200.00	12/23/94	-112.50
1994	12/10/93	-56.50	02/04/94	-41.50	15.00	750.00	02/04/94	750.00	12/30/93	-450.00
1993	12/10/92	12.00	02/02/93	13.50	1.50	75.00	12/30/92	75.00	01/12/93	-200.00
1992	12/10/91	18.00	02/04/92	20.00	2.00	100.00	01/29/92	375.00	12/17/91	-225.00
1991	12/10/90	1.00	02/04/91	25.25	24.25	1212.50	01/30/91	1350.00		
1990	12/11/89	8.75	02/02/90	19.25	10.50	525.00	01/04/90	800.00		
1989	12/12/88	-85.00	02/03/89	-41.75	43.25	2162.50	01/30/89	2700.00	12/21/88	-887.50
1988	12/10/87	-34.50	02/04/88	14.00	48.50	2425.00	02/01/88	2550.00		
1987	12/10/86	-3.75	02/04/87	-14.75	-11.00	-550.00	12/12/86	137.50	01/27/87	-637.50
1986	12/10/85	-21.75	02/04/86	-15.50	6.25	312.50	12/20/85	912.50	01/15/86	-562.50
1985	12/10/84	0.25	02/04/85	7.50	7.25	362.50	01/04/85	900.00	01/28/85	-75.00

Percentage Correct		80								
Average Profit on Winning Trades					8.19	409.38		Winners		12
Average Loss on Trades					-14.92	-745.83		Losers		3
Average Net Profit Per Trade					3.57	178.33		Total trades		15
Percentage Correct		80								
Average Profit on Winning Trades					12.72	635.94		Winners		16
Average Loss on Trades					-13.94	-696.88		Losers		4
Average Net Profit Per Trade					7.39	369.38		Total trades		20

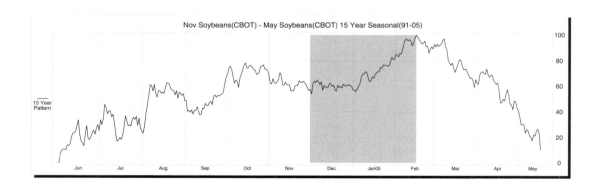

Nov Soybeans(CBOT) - May Soybeans(CBOT) 15 Year Seasonal(91-05)

Figure 4-11

Moore Research Center, Inc.

Buy May Soybeans(CBOT) / Sell Nov Soybeans(CBOT)

Enter on approximately 03/08 - Exit on approximately 03/27

CONT YEAR	ENTRY DATE	ENTRY PRICE	EXIT DATE	EXIT PRICE	PROFIT	PROFIT AMOUNT	BEST EQUITY DATE	BEST EQUITY AMOUNT	WORST EQUITY DATE	WORST EQUITY AMOUNT
2004	03/08/04	187.50	03/26/04	245.50	58.00	2900.00	03/22/04	4087.50		
2003	03/10/03	49.50	03/27/03	61.50	12.00	600.00	03/27/03	600.00		
2002	03/08/02	-11.25	03/27/02	-1.50	9.75	487.50	03/26/02	512.50		
2001	03/08/01	-11.00	03/27/01	-3.50	7.50	375.00	03/27/01	375.00		
2000	03/08/00	-17.50	03/27/00	-24.50	-7.00	-350.00	03/13/00	37.50	03/27/00	-350.00
1999	03/08/99	-22.25	03/26/99	-19.50	2.75	137.50	03/16/99	287.50		
1998	03/09/98	12.75	03/27/98	18.00	5.25	262.50	03/26/98	400.00		
1997	03/10/97	116.50	03/27/97	141.00	24.50	1225.00	03/27/97	1225.00	03/12/97	-525.00
1996	03/08/96	-3.50	03/27/96	11.00	14.50	725.00	03/27/96	725.00		
1995	03/08/95	-25.00	03/27/95	-23.75	1.25	62.50	03/17/95	62.50	03/24/95	-37.50
1994	03/08/94	28.25	03/25/94	38.00	9.75	487.50	03/24/94	537.50		
1993	03/08/93	-14.25	03/26/93	-13.75	0.50	25.00	03/23/93	50.00	03/16/93	-37.50
1992	03/09/92	-26.75	03/27/92	-25.50	1.25	62.50	03/24/92	175.00		
1991	03/08/91	-28.00	03/27/91	-32.00	-4.00	-200.00			03/15/91	-375.00
1990	03/08/90	-24.25	03/27/90	-21.00	3.25	162.50	03/22/90	250.00	03/19/90	-12.50
1989	03/08/89	29.00	03/27/89	31.75	2.75	137.50	03/23/89	312.50	03/10/89	-12.50
1988	03/08/88	-21.75	03/25/88	-19.25	2.50	125.00	03/10/88	175.00	03/17/88	-62.50
1987	03/09/87	15.25	03/27/87	11.50	-3.75	-187.50			03/12/87	-200.00
1986	03/10/86	18.25	03/27/86	20.00	1.75	87.50	03/21/86	187.50	03/12/86	-250.00
1985	03/08/85	-7.25	03/27/85	-5.50	1.75	87.50	03/25/85	262.50	03/19/85	-137.50

Percentage Correct	87									
Average Profit on Winning Trades					11.56	577.88		Winners	13	
Average Loss on Trades					-5.50	-275.00		Losers	2	
Average Net Profit Per Trade					9.28	464.17		Total trades	15	
Percentage Correct	85									
Average Profit on Winning Trades					9.35	467.65		Winners	17	
Average Loss on Trades					-4.92	-245.83		Losers	3	
Average Net Profit Per Trade					7.21	360.63		Total trades	20	

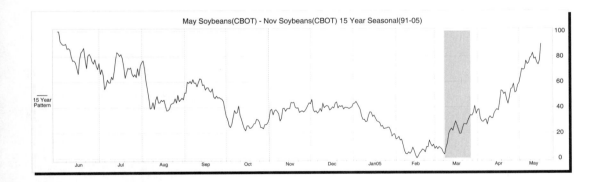

May Soybeans(CBOT) - Nov Soybeans(CBOT) 15 Year Seasonal(91-05)

15 Year Pattern

Figure 4-12

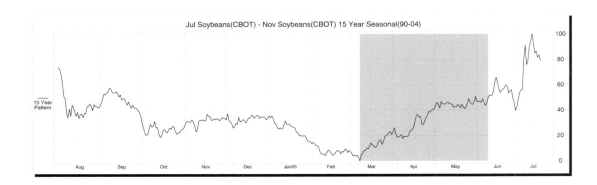

Buy Jul Soybeans(CBOT) / Sell Nov Soybeans(CBOT)

Enter on approximately 03/08 - Exit on approximately 06/09

CONT YEAR	ENTRY DATE	ENTRY PRICE	EXIT DATE	EXIT PRICE	PROFIT	PROFIT AMOUNT	BEST EQUITY DATE	BEST EQUITY AMOUNT	WORST EQUITY DATE	WORST EQUITY AMOUNT
2004	03/08/04	178.00	06/09/04	173.00	-5.00	-250.00	04/30/04	4512.50	06/03/04	-2975.00
2003	03/10/03	47.75	06/09/03	57.00	9.25	462.50	05/13/03	1900.00		
2002	03/08/02	-5.75	06/07/02	30.25	36.00	1800.00	06/06/02	1912.50		
2001	03/08/01	-3.25	06/08/01	18.00	21.25	1062.50	05/31/01	1100.00		
2000	03/08/00	-8.25	06/09/00	-7.50	0.75	37.50	05/30/00	62.50	03/27/00	-287.50
1999	03/08/99	-13.25	06/09/99	-10.75	2.50	125.00	03/16/99	162.50	04/05/99	-125.00
1998	03/09/98	17.25	06/09/98	34.50	17.25	862.50	06/08/98	900.00	03/20/98	-12.50
1997	03/10/97	116.50	06/09/97	132.00	15.50	775.00	05/30/97	3962.50	03/12/97	-375.00
1996	03/08/96	5.00	06/07/96	33.25	28.25	1412.50	04/26/96	1962.50	03/19/96	-12.50
1995	03/08/95	-14.50	06/09/95	-19.00	-4.50	-225.00	03/22/95	87.50	05/30/95	-250.00
1994	03/08/94	29.75	06/09/94	30.25	0.50	25.00	05/11/94	1112.50	06/02/94	-387.50
1993	03/08/93	-9.50	06/09/93	5.50	15.00	750.00	06/09/93	750.00	03/11/93	-12.50
1992	03/09/92	-16.50	06/09/92	-15.00	1.50	75.00	04/07/92	175.00	03/27/92	-12.50
1991	03/08/91	-14.75	06/07/91	-11.00	3.75	187.50	05/30/91	262.50	03/15/91	-350.00
1990	03/08/90	-11.25	06/08/90	-16.00	-4.75	-237.50	03/22/90	237.50	06/07/90	-325.00
1989	03/08/89	37.75	06/09/89	75.50	37.75	1887.50	06/08/89	2537.50	04/06/89	-1487.50
1988	03/08/88	-12.75	06/09/88	-5.50	7.25	362.50	06/08/88	562.50	05/16/88	-387.50
1987	03/09/87	13.25	06/09/87	-8.75	-22.00	-1100.00			05/14/87	-1662.50
1986	03/10/86	21.75	06/09/86	25.50	3.75	187.50	06/09/86	187.50	05/08/86	-1037.50
1985	03/08/85	2.25	06/07/85	9.50	7.25	362.50	06/04/85	400.00	04/29/85	-812.50

Percentage Correct		80								
Average Profit on Winning Trades					12.63	631.25		Winners		12
Average Loss on Trades					-4.75	-237.50		Losers		3
Average Net Profit Per Trade					9.15	457.50		Total trades		15
Percentage Correct		80								
Average Profit on Winning Trades					12.97	648.44		Winners		16
Average Loss on Trades					-9.06	-453.13		Losers		4
Average Net Profit Per Trade					8.56	428.13		Total trades		20

Figure 4-13

Buy Aug Soybeans(CBOT) / Sell Mar Soybeans(CBOT)

Moore Research Center, Inc.

Enter on approximately 05/26 - Exit on approximately 07/10

CONT YEAR	ENTRY DATE	ENTRY PRICE	EXIT DATE	EXIT PRICE	PROFIT	PROFIT AMOUNT	BEST EQUITY DATE	BEST EQUITY AMOUNT	WORST EQUITY DATE	WORST EQUITY AMOUNT
2004	05/26/04	114.25	07/09/04	159.00	44.75	2237.50	07/06/04	2412.50	05/28/04	-1112.50
2003	05/27/03	57.75	07/10/03	67.25	9.50	475.00	07/10/03	475.00	06/12/03	-762.50
2002	05/28/02	11.25	07/10/02	34.50	23.25	1162.50	07/09/02	1237.50	06/19/02	-37.50
2001	05/29/01	-5.50	07/10/01	-5.25	0.25	12.50	06/20/01	312.50	07/03/01	-50.00
2000	05/26/00	-20.25	07/10/00	-13.25	7.00	350.00	06/26/00	962.50	06/06/00	-150.00
1999	05/26/99	-28.00	07/09/99	-16.50	11.50	575.00	07/09/99	575.00	06/30/99	-50.00
1998	05/26/98	5.50	07/10/98	20.25	14.75	737.50	07/10/98	737.50	06/26/98	-562.50
1997	05/27/97	117.00	07/10/97	137.75	20.75	1037.50	05/30/97	1087.50	07/02/97	-2262.50
1996	05/28/96	11.50	07/10/96	19.50	8.00	400.00	06/12/96	475.00	06/25/96	-100.00
1995	05/26/95	-25.25	07/10/95	-21.50	3.75	187.50	07/10/95	187.50	06/12/95	-212.50
1994	05/26/94	17.50	07/08/94	24.50	7.00	350.00	07/08/94	350.00	06/15/94	-612.50
1993	05/26/93	-8.50	07/09/93	-8.00	0.50	25.00	07/02/93	37.50	06/07/93	-262.50
1992	05/26/92	-26.25	07/10/92	-25.00	1.25	62.50	05/29/92	87.50	06/30/92	-137.50
1991	05/28/91	-33.50	07/10/91	-23.75	9.75	487.50	07/09/91	575.00		
1990	05/29/90	-27.50	07/10/90	-44.00	-16.50	-825.00			06/29/90	-825.00
1989	05/26/89	28.00	07/10/89	28.50	0.50	25.00	06/26/89	1025.00	06/13/89	-237.50
1988	05/26/88	-25.75	07/08/88	22.00	47.75	2387.50	06/22/88	4287.50	05/27/88	-25.00
1987	05/26/87	-20.00	07/10/87	-8.75	11.25	562.50	07/10/87	562.50	06/17/87	-725.00
1986	05/27/86	-4.00	07/10/86	7.25	11.25	562.50	07/10/86	562.50	06/03/86	-50.00
1985	05/28/85	-26.75	07/10/85	-26.50	0.25	12.50	06/17/85	812.50		

Percentage Correct	93				
Average Profit on Winning Trades		11.57	578.57	Winners	14
Average Loss on Trades		-16.50	-825.00	Losers	1
Average Net Profit Per Trade		9.70	485.00	Total trades	15

Percentage Correct	95				
Average Profit on Winning Trades		12.26	613.16	Winners	19
Average Loss on Trades		-16.50	-825.00	Losers	1
Average Net Profit Per Trade		10.83	541.25	Total trades	20

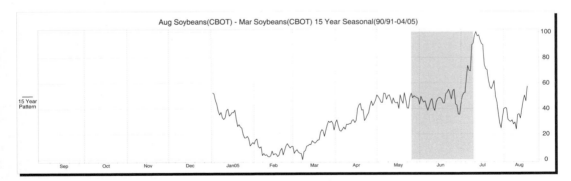

Aug Soybeans(CBOT) - Mar Soybeans(CBOT) 15 Year Seasonal(90/91-04/05)

H - Q

X

Figure 4-14

Buy May Soybeans(CBOT) / Sell Sep Soybeans(CBOT)

Enter on approximately 07/17 - Exit on approximately 07/31

CONT YEAR	ENTRY DATE	ENTRY PRICE	EXIT DATE	EXIT PRICE	PROFIT	PROFIT AMOUNT	BEST EQUITY DATE	BEST EQUITY AMOUNT	WORST EQUITY DATE	WORST EQUITY AMOUNT
2005	07/19/04	-2.25	07/30/04	15.50	17.75	887.50	07/30/04	887.50	07/20/04	-162.50
2004	07/17/03	-15.50	07/31/03	-1.50	14.00	700.00	07/31/03	700.00		
2003	07/17/02	-22.25	07/31/02	-19.25	3.00	150.00	07/30/02	700.00	07/22/02	-87.50
2002	07/17/01	-5.00	07/31/01	3.75	8.75	437.50	07/20/01	537.50		
2001	07/17/00	34.00	07/31/00	40.00	6.00	300.00	07/31/00	300.00		
2000	07/19/99	30.25	07/30/99	28.00	-2.25	-112.50	07/22/99	137.50	07/23/99	-212.50
1999	07/17/98	8.50	07/31/98	23.00	14.50	725.00	07/31/98	725.00		
1998	07/17/97	-25.75	07/31/97	-10.00	15.75	787.50	07/31/97	787.50	07/25/97	-525.00
1997	07/17/96	-1.00	07/31/96	2.50	3.50	175.00	07/22/96	300.00		
1996	07/17/95	18.25	07/31/95	31.50	13.25	662.50	07/31/95	662.50		
1995	07/18/94	4.75	07/29/94	13.00	8.25	412.50	07/28/94	525.00		
1994	07/19/93	3.00	07/30/93	7.50	4.50	225.00	07/30/93	225.00		
1993	07/17/92	28.25	07/31/92	16.75	-11.50	-575.00			07/31/92	-575.00
1992	07/17/91	33.50	07/31/91	36.75	3.25	162.50	07/30/91	275.00	07/22/91	-50.00
1991	07/17/90	42.75	07/31/90	39.75	-3.00	-150.00			07/25/90	-200.00
1990	07/17/89	9.25	07/31/89	13.75	4.50	225.00	07/31/89	225.00	07/19/89	-475.00
1989	07/18/88	-54.00	07/29/88	16.50	70.50	3525.00	07/28/88	3525.00		
1988	07/17/87	26.75	07/31/87	23.00	-3.75	-187.50	07/20/87	125.00	07/24/87	-287.50
1987	07/17/86	23.50	07/31/86	24.75	1.25	62.50	07/30/86	150.00	07/18/86	-50.00
1986	07/17/85	31.00	07/31/85	33.50	2.50	125.00	07/23/85	125.00	07/30/85	-150.00

Percentage Correct	80									
Average Profit on Winning Trades					9.38	468.75		Winners		12
Average Loss on Trades					-5.58	-279.17		Losers		3
Average Net Profit Per Trade					6.38	319.17		Total trades		15
Percentage Correct	80									
Average Profit on Winning Trades					11.95	597.66		Winners		16
Average Loss on Trades					-5.13	-256.25		Losers		4
Average Net Profit Per Trade					8.54	426.88		Total trades		20

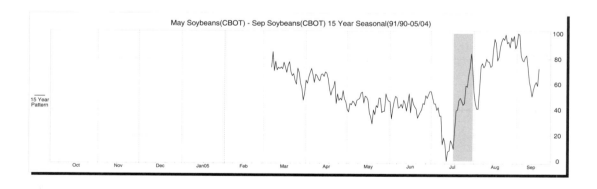

May Soybeans(CBOT) - Sep Soybeans(CBOT) 15 Year Seasonal(91/90-05/04)

Soymeal

Soybean meal normally accounts for 60-70% of soybean product value. In its primary use as a high-protein supplement in livestock and poultry feed rations, it has no commercially viable substitute. Because consumption is greatest during the cold of winter, processors crush aggressively for soymeal during and after harvest. The marketing year logically runs October through September.

Figure 4-15: Cash Soymeal Seasonal Pattern

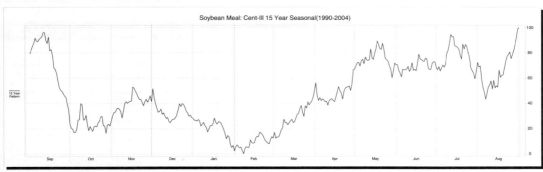

Commercial activity in soymeal is greatest during the fourth quarter, when processors produce at capacity. Because soymeal can turn rancid, it is considered a nonstorable commodity. Thus, prices tend to be lowest October through February because supply is greatest, cannot accumulate, and must therefore be sold aggressively. By March, processors prepare for lower domestic consumption and export competition from South America by slowing their rate of crush. But even reduced domestic consumption provides persistent underlying demand. Without large stocks in reserve, the market must bid price up enough to maintain a stream of new supply. As physical supplies of soybeans tighten, cash soymeal prices tend to rise into September.

Carrying charges. Because soymeal is a nonstorable commodity, the market tends not to build significant carrying charges into its price structure. In fact, one primary feature of spreads between delivery months of the same crop year in soymeal is their tendency toward bull spreads during that crop year, as illustrated in Figure 4-16.

Figure 4-16: Dec/Jul Soymeal Seasonal Pattern

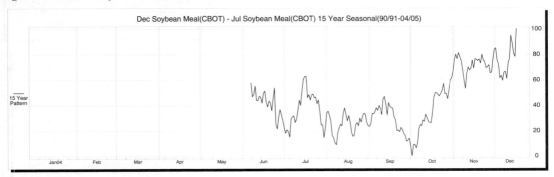

Figure 4-17: Soybean Meal Carrying-charge Strategies

Moore Research Center, Inc.									
Soybean Meal Carrying-charge Spread Strategies									
Seasonal Strategy	Entry Date	Exit Date	Win Pct	Win Yrs	Loss Years	Total Years	Average Profit	Ave Pft Per Day	
Buy Dec Soybean Meal(CBOT)	10/2	11/2	87	13	2	15	322	10	
Sell Jul Soybean Meal(CBOT)			90	18	2	20	322	10	
Buy Jul Soybean Meal(CBOT)	3/26	6/26	93	14	1	15	419	5	
Sell Sep Soybean Meal(CBOT)			95	19	1	20	443	5	

Figure 4-18

Moore Research Center, Inc. — **Buy Dec Soybean Meal(CBOT) / Sell Jul Soybean Meal(CBOT)**

Enter on approximately 10/02 - Exit on approximately 11/02

CONT YEAR	ENTRY DATE	ENTRY PRICE	EXIT DATE	EXIT PRICE	PROFIT	PROFIT AMOUNT	BEST EQUITY DATE	BEST EQUITY AMOUNT	WORST EQUITY DATE	WORST EQUITY AMOUNT
2004	10/04/04	-9.09	11/02/04	-8.80	0.30	30.00	10/20/04	200.00	10/05/04	-160.00
2003	10/02/03	8.50	10/31/03	22.79	14.30	1430.00	10/23/03	2620.00	10/03/03	-130.00
2002	10/02/02	-2.00	11/01/02	3.20	5.20	520.00	11/01/02	520.00	10/04/02	-50.00
2001	10/02/01	3.19	11/02/01	12.20	9.00	900.00	11/02/01	900.00		
2000	10/02/00	-0.70	11/02/00	2.80	3.50	350.00	10/31/00	480.00	10/09/00	-140.00
1999	10/04/99	-4.29	11/02/99	-2.09	2.20	220.00	11/02/99	220.00	10/22/99	-170.00
1998	10/02/98	-15.60	11/02/98	-13.29	2.30	230.00	10/19/98	250.00	10/05/98	-30.00
1997	10/02/97	4.80	10/31/97	6.79	2.00	200.00	10/13/97	280.00	10/22/97	-340.00
1996	10/02/96	5.09	11/01/96	8.19	3.10	310.00	10/25/96	550.00		
1995	10/02/95	-5.09	11/02/95	-1.09	4.00	400.00	10/30/95	500.00	10/06/95	-70.00
1994	10/03/94	-11.80	11/02/94	-13.90	-2.10	-210.00	10/11/94	200.00	11/02/94	-210.00
1993	10/04/93	-6.60	11/02/93	-0.39	6.20	620.00	11/02/93	620.00		
1992	10/02/92	-2.70	11/02/92	-2.39	0.30	30.00	10/22/92	120.00	10/14/92	-130.00
1991	10/02/91	5.80	11/01/91	7.90	2.10	210.00	11/01/91	210.00	10/15/91	-310.00
1990	10/02/90	-6.69	11/02/90	-10.80	-4.10	-410.00	10/08/90	420.00	10/31/90	-470.00
1989	10/02/89	3.59	11/02/89	4.40	0.80	80.00	10/05/89	360.00	10/13/89	-130.00
1988	10/03/88	16.00	11/02/88	16.40	0.40	40.00	10/04/88	290.00	10/24/88	-1200.00
1987	10/02/87	8.20	11/02/87	17.60	9.40	940.00	11/02/87	940.00	10/12/87	-480.00
1986	10/02/86	-2.90	10/31/86	-0.20	2.70	270.00	10/31/86	270.00	10/10/86	-250.00
1985	10/02/85	-8.00	11/01/85	-5.19	2.80	280.00	10/09/85	410.00	10/28/85	-10.00

Percentage Correct	87								
Average Profit on Winning Trades					4.19	419.23	Winners		13
Average Loss on Trades					-3.10	-310.00	Losers		2
Average Net Profit Per Trade					3.22	322.00	Total trades		15
Percentage Correct	90								
Average Profit on Winning Trades					3.92	392.22	Winners		18
Average Loss on Trades					-3.10	-310.00	Losers		2
Average Net Profit Per Trade					3.22	322.00	Total trades		20

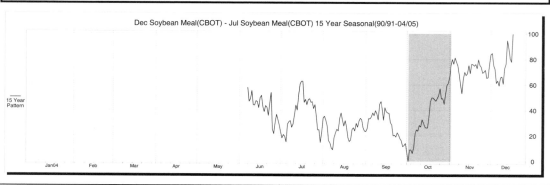

Dec Soybean Meal(CBOT) - Jul Soybean Meal(CBOT) 15 Year Seasonal(90/91-04/05)

Figure 4-19

Buy Jul Soybean Meal(CBOT) / Sell Sep Soybean Meal(CBOT)

Enter on approximately 03/26 - Exit on approximately 06/26

CONT YEAR	ENTRY DATE	ENTRY PRICE	EXIT DATE	EXIT PRICE	PROFIT	PROFIT AMOUNT	BEST EQUITY DATE	BEST EQUITY AMOUNT	WORST EQUITY DATE	WORST EQUITY AMOUNT
2004	03/26/04	31.60	06/25/04	49.19	17.60	1760.00	06/25/04	1760.00	06/02/04	-1320.00
2003	03/26/03	9.19	06/26/03	9.50	0.30	30.00	04/21/03	770.00	06/12/03	-550.00
2002	03/26/02	3.00	06/26/02	6.39	3.40	340.00	06/06/02	620.00	04/01/02	-110.00
2001	03/26/01	3.40	06/26/01	7.79	4.40	440.00	05/25/01	780.00	04/03/01	-10.00
2000	03/27/00	-1.00	06/26/00	13.00	14.00	1400.00	06/23/00	1440.00	04/04/00	-10.00
1999	03/26/99	-2.59	06/25/99	2.69	5.30	530.00	06/23/99	570.00	04/07/99	-80.00
1998	03/26/98	-2.19	06/26/98	-0.09	2.10	210.00	06/08/98	810.00	03/31/98	-110.00
1997	03/26/97	26.89	06/26/97	37.19	10.30	1030.00	06/23/97	1710.00	04/11/97	-740.00
1996	03/26/96	1.00	06/26/96	3.80	2.80	280.00	04/18/96	340.00	04/09/96	-40.00
1995	03/27/95	-3.79	06/26/95	-3.59	0.20	20.00	05/18/95	70.00	04/26/95	-70.00
1994	03/28/94	3.00	06/24/94	0.19	-2.80	-280.00	05/18/94	60.00	06/17/94	-390.00
1993	03/26/93	-1.90	06/25/93	-0.09	1.80	180.00	05/21/93	350.00	04/12/93	-30.00
1992	03/26/92	-2.30	06/26/92	-1.80	0.50	50.00	06/02/92	210.00	03/27/92	-40.00
1991	03/26/91	-3.30	06/26/91	-0.50	2.80	280.00	06/21/91	430.00	03/28/91	-60.00
1990	03/26/90	-3.79	06/26/90	-3.59	0.20	20.00	06/22/90	90.00	03/27/90	-50.00
1989	03/27/89	5.90	06/26/89	16.60	10.70	1070.00	06/26/89	1070.00	04/03/89	-370.00
1988	03/28/88	-0.80	06/24/88	10.50	11.30	1130.00	06/23/88	1400.00	04/19/88	-170.00
1987	03/26/87	0.59	06/26/87	3.19	2.60	260.00	06/10/87	300.00	05/15/87	-400.00
1986	03/26/86	4.19	06/26/86	5.30	1.10	110.00	06/25/86	110.00	05/08/86	-540.00
1985	03/26/85	-5.20	06/26/85	-5.20	0.00	0.00	04/16/85	50.00	05/13/85	-90.00

Percentage Correct	93									
Average Profit on Winning Trades					4.69	469.29		Winners		14
Average Loss on Trades					-2.80	-280.00		Losers		1
Average Net Profit Per Trade					4.19	419.33		Total trades		15
Percentage Correct	95									
Average Profit on Winning Trades					4.81	481.05		Winners		19
Average Loss on Trades					-2.80	-280.00		Losers		1
Average Net Profit Per Trade					4.43	443.00		Total trades		20

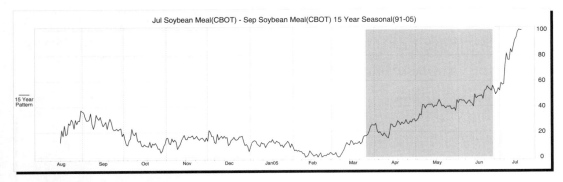

Jul Soybean Meal(CBOT) - Sep Soybean Meal(CBOT) 15 Year Seasonal(91-05)

This dynamic tends to appear immediately in the new crop year. Nearby contracts are pressured most going into harvest on expectations of new supply. But then livestock feeders and exporters buy aggressively, and these relationships pivot on the surge in demand. With little reason to offer storage incentives, drawdowns have usually been modest.

The most reliable, enduring bull spreads begin typically but counterintuitively in March. With both domestic consumption and exports soon to decline seasonally, processors slow their rate of crush. A market unable to rely on inventories must depend on a constant stream of new supply. Underlying demand in the cash market consistently favors nearby contracts at the expense of deferred.

Old-crop/new-crop. These relationships mirror, perhaps even drive, those in soybeans. But they also tend to be more consistent.

Figure 4-20: Jul/Dec Soymeal Seasonal Pattern

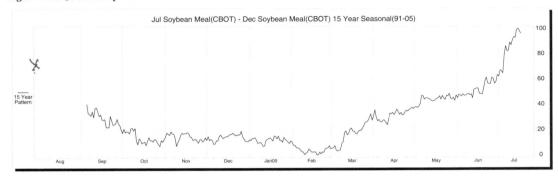

Figure 4-21: Soymeal Old-crop/New-crop Strategies

Moore Research Center, Inc.	Soybean Meal Old-crop/New-crop Spread Strategies							
Seasonal Strategy	Entry Date	Exit Date	Win Pct	Win Yrs	Loss Years	Total Years	Average Profit	Ave Pft Per Day
Buy Aug Soybean Meal(CBOT)	4/4	7/11	100	15	0	15	619	6
Sell Mar Soybean Meal(CBOT)			100	20	0	20	667	7
Buy Jul Soybean Meal(CBOT)	4/23	6/26	93	14	1	15	381	6
Sell Dec Soybean Meal(CBOT)			95	19	1	20	502	8
Buy Aug Soybean Meal(CBOT)	5/23	7/11	93	14	1	15	623	12
Sell Mar Soybean Meal(CBOT)			95	19	1	20	646	13

The seasonal pattern suggests smooth and steady movement. That tendency is not only reflected in the impressive reliability of these old-crop/new-crop spread strategies but also reinforced by the modesty of most drawdowns. For example, the first and longest strategy in the table has not only an impeccable 20-year history but suffered drawdown greater than $3.50/ton in only 4 of those years.

Figure 4-22: Jul/Dec Soymeal Monthly

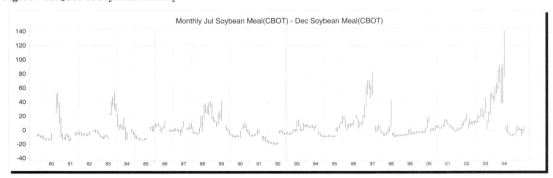

Figure 4-23

Buy Aug Soybean Meal(CBOT) / Sell Mar Soybean Meal(CBOT)

Enter on approximately 04/04 - Exit on approximately 07/11

CONT YEAR	ENTRY DATE	ENTRY PRICE	EXIT DATE	EXIT PRICE	PROFIT	PROFIT AMOUNT	BEST EQUITY DATE	BEST EQUITY AMOUNT	WORST EQUITY DATE	WORST EQUITY AMOUNT
2004	04/05/04	76.50	07/09/04	83.19	6.70	670.00	07/06/04	1460.00	06/03/04	-4200.00
2003	04/04/03	15.30	07/11/03	24.50	9.20	920.00	05/01/03	930.00	06/12/03	-220.00
2002	04/04/02	3.69	07/11/02	18.70	15.00	1500.00	07/11/02	1500.00	04/12/02	-40.00
2001	04/04/01	1.90	07/11/01	7.80	5.90	590.00	06/08/01	870.00	04/30/01	-60.00
2000	04/04/00	-5.50	07/11/00	8.50	14.00	1400.00	07/11/00	1400.00		
1999	04/05/99	-9.30	07/09/99	-4.89	4.40	440.00	07/06/99	470.00	04/22/99	-350.00
1998	04/06/98	-8.90	07/10/98	1.59	10.50	1050.00	07/10/98	1050.00		
1997	04/04/97	50.39	07/11/97	55.29	4.90	490.00	05/07/97	1230.00	07/02/97	-1760.00
1996	04/04/96	3.09	07/11/96	5.90	2.80	280.00	04/26/96	920.00	04/09/96	-290.00
1995	04/27/95	-11.30	07/11/95	-11.00	0.30	30.00	06/27/95	250.00	05/03/95	-40.00
1994	04/04/94	1.19	07/11/94	3.90	2.70	270.00	05/11/94	340.00	06/17/94	-90.00
1993	04/05/93	-4.59	07/09/93	-1.50	3.10	310.00	06/09/93	500.00	04/12/93	-100.00
1992	04/06/92	-18.90	07/10/92	-18.20	0.70	70.00	04/09/92	210.00	06/30/92	-300.00
1991	04/04/91	-13.00	07/11/91	-3.50	9.50	950.00	06/21/91	1030.00		
1990	04/04/90	-14.09	07/11/90	-10.90	3.20	320.00	06/13/90	400.00	04/17/90	-120.00
1989	04/04/89	6.80	07/11/89	13.40	6.60	660.00	06/26/89	1390.00	04/07/89	-250.00
1988	04/04/88	-8.50	07/11/88	19.69	28.20	2820.00	06/23/88	3120.00	04/19/88	-200.00
1987	04/06/87	-3.00	07/10/87	0.69	3.70	370.00	07/08/87	390.00	05/15/87	-880.00
1986	04/04/86	0.79	07/11/86	1.00	0.20	20.00	04/18/86	300.00	05/08/86	-610.00
1985	04/04/85	-17.59	07/11/85	-15.80	1.80	180.00	07/08/85	190.00	05/24/85	-170.00

Percentage Correct	100									
Average Profit on Winning Trades					6.19	619.33		Winners		15
Average Loss on Trades								Losers		0
Average Net Profit Per Trade					6.19	619.33		Total trades		15
Percentage Correct	100									
Average Profit on Winning Trades					6.67	667.00		Winners		20
Average Loss on Trades								Losers		0
Average Net Profit Per Trade					6.67	667.00		Total trades		20

HYPOTHETICAL PERFORMANCE RESULTS HAVE MANY INHERENT LIMITATIONS, SOME OF WHICH ARE DESCRIBED BELOW. NO REPRESENTATION IS BEING MADE THAT ANY ACCOUNT WILL OR IS LIKELY TO ACHIEVE PROFITS OR LOSSES SIMILAR TO THOSE SHOWN. IN FACT, THERE ARE FREQUENTLY SHARP DIFFERENCES BETWEEN HYPOTHETICAL PERFORMANCE RESULTS AND THE ACTUAL RESULTS SUBSEQUENTLY ACHIEVED BY ANY PARTICULAR TRADING PROGRAM. ONE OF THE LIMITATIONS OF HYPOTHETICAL PERFORMANCE RESULTS IS THAT THEY ARE GENERALLY PREPARED WITH THE BENEFIT OF HINDSIGHT. IN ADDITION, HYPOTHETICAL TRADING DOES NOT INVOLVE FINANCIAL RISK, AND NO HYPOTHETICAL TRADING RECORD CAN COMPLETELY ACCOUNT FOR THE IMPACT OF FINANCIAL RISK IN ACTUAL TRADING. FOR EXAMPLE, THE ABILITY TO WITHSTAND LOSSES OR ADHERE TO A PARTICULAR TRADING PROGRAM IN SPITE OF TRADING LOSSES ARE MATERIAL POINTS WHICH CAN ALSO ADVERSELY AFFECT ACTUAL TRADING RESULTS. THERE ARE NUMEROUS OTHER FACTORS RELATED TO THE MARKETS IN GENERAL OR TO THE IMPLEMENTATION OF ANY SPECIFIC TRADING PROGRAM WHICH CANNOT BE FULLY ACCOUNTED FOR IN THE PREPARATION OF HYPOTHETICAL PERFORMANCE RESULTS AND ALL OF WHICH CAN ADVERSELY AFFECT ACTUAL TRADING RESULTS. RESULTS NOT ADJUSTED FOR COMMISSION AND SLIPPAGE.

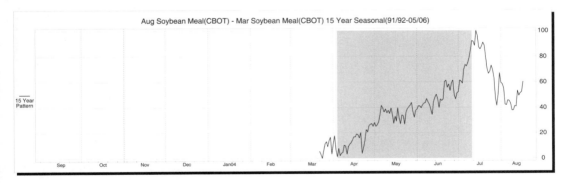

Aug Soybean Meal(CBOT) - Mar Soybean Meal(CBOT) 15 Year Seasonal(91/92-05/06)

Figure 4-24

Buy Jul Soybean Meal(CBOT) / Sell Dec Soybean Meal(CBOT)

Enter on approximately 04/23 - Exit on approximately 06/26

CONT YEAR	ENTRY DATE	ENTRY PRICE	EXIT DATE	EXIT PRICE	PROFIT	PROFIT AMOUNT	BEST EQUITY DATE	BEST EQUITY AMOUNT	WORST EQUITY DATE	WORST EQUITY AMOUNT
2004	04/23/04	70.80	06/25/04	80.30	9.50	950.00	05/11/04	1720.00	06/03/04	-3360.00
2003	04/23/03	22.40	06/26/03	25.80	3.40	340.00	05/13/03	840.00	06/12/03	-730.00
2002	04/23/02	8.90	06/26/02	12.19	3.30	330.00	06/05/02	720.00	05/10/02	-410.00
2001	04/23/01	7.50	06/26/01	11.50	4.00	400.00	06/08/01	790.00	04/27/01	-210.00
2000	04/24/00	-2.09	06/26/00	16.30	18.40	1840.00	06/23/00	1850.00	05/03/00	-20.00
1999	04/23/99	-7.29	06/25/99	-0.30	7.00	700.00	06/23/99	740.00	05/04/99	-10.00
1998	04/23/98	-4.90	06/26/98	-2.00	2.90	290.00	06/08/98	1040.00	04/29/98	-90.00
1997	04/23/97	49.89	06/26/97	52.49	2.60	260.00	05/06/97	2040.00	06/09/97	-360.00
1996	04/23/96	7.49	06/26/96	9.30	1.80	180.00	04/26/96	260.00	05/29/96	-380.00
1995	04/24/95	-9.00	06/26/95	-8.59	0.40	40.00	05/10/95	100.00	06/12/95	-110.00
1994	04/25/94	7.00	06/24/94	3.19	-3.80	-380.00	05/11/94	90.00	06/17/94	-730.00
1993	04/23/93	-4.00	06/25/93	-1.59	2.40	240.00	05/21/93	550.00		
1992	04/23/92	-18.89	06/26/92	-18.80	0.10	10.00	06/22/92	140.00	05/04/92	-170.00
1991	04/23/91	-6.30	06/26/91	-1.29	5.00	500.00	06/21/91	700.00	04/29/91	-80.00
1990	04/23/90	-9.40	06/26/90	-9.29	0.10	10.00	05/29/90	230.00	04/24/90	-80.00
1989	04/24/89	10.09	06/26/89	27.60	17.50	1750.00	06/26/89	1750.00	05/02/89	-170.00
1988	04/25/88	-5.09	06/24/88	16.50	21.60	2160.00	06/23/88	2560.00	04/27/88	-130.00
1987	04/23/87	-1.50	06/26/87	2.40	3.90	390.00	06/26/87	390.00	05/15/87	-590.00
1986	04/23/86	4.80	06/26/86	4.90	0.10	10.00	06/12/86	80.00	05/08/86	-920.00
1985	04/23/85	-13.80	06/26/85	-13.60	0.20	20.00	06/20/85	150.00	05/24/85	-60.00

Percentage Correct	93									
Average Profit on Winning Trades					4.35	435.00		Winners		14
Average Loss on Trades					-3.80	-380.00		Losers		1
Average Net Profit Per Trade					3.81	380.67		Total trades		15
Percentage Correct	95									
Average Profit on Winning Trades					5.48	548.42		Winners		19
Average Loss on Trades					-3.80	-380.00		Losers		1
Average Net Profit Per Trade					5.02	502.00		Total trades		20

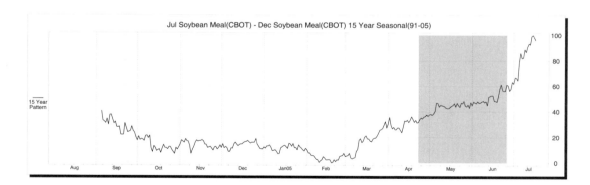

Jul Soybean Meal(CBOT) - Dec Soybean Meal(CBOT) 15 Year Seasonal(91-05)

Figure 4-25

Buy Aug Soybean Meal(CBOT) / Sell Mar Soybean Meal(CBOT)

Enter on approximately 05/23 - Exit on approximately 07/11

CONT YEAR	ENTRY DATE	ENTRY PRICE	EXIT DATE	EXIT PRICE	PROFIT	PROFIT AMOUNT	BEST EQUITY DATE	BEST EQUITY AMOUNT	WORST EQUITY DATE	WORST EQUITY AMOUNT
2004	05/24/04	43.50	07/09/04	83.19	39.70	3970.00	07/06/04	4760.00	06/03/04	-900.00
2003	05/23/03	17.39	07/11/03	24.50	7.10	710.00	07/11/03	710.00	06/12/03	-430.00
2002	05/23/02	9.79	07/11/02	18.70	8.90	890.00	07/11/02	890.00		
2001	05/23/01	6.10	07/11/01	7.80	1.70	170.00	06/08/01	450.00		
2000	05/23/00	0.19	07/11/00	8.50	8.30	830.00	07/11/00	830.00	05/26/00	-40.00
1999	05/24/99	-9.60	07/09/99	-4.89	4.70	470.00	07/06/99	500.00		
1998	05/26/98	-7.19	07/10/98	1.59	8.80	880.00	07/10/98	880.00		
1997	05/23/97	49.60	07/11/97	55.29	5.70	570.00	07/11/97	570.00	07/02/97	-1680.00
1996	05/23/96	3.59	07/11/96	5.90	2.30	230.00	06/27/96	550.00	05/29/96	-150.00
1995	05/23/95	-11.69	07/11/95	-11.00	0.70	70.00	06/27/95	290.00		
1994	05/23/94	2.80	07/11/94	3.90	1.10	110.00	07/11/94	110.00	06/17/94	-250.00
1993	05/24/93	-1.10	07/09/93	-1.50	-0.40	-40.00	06/09/93	150.00	06/17/93	-140.00
1992	05/26/92	-19.00	07/10/92	-18.20	0.80	80.00	06/22/92	120.00	06/30/92	-290.00
1991	05/23/91	-6.69	07/11/91	-3.50	3.20	320.00	06/21/91	400.00	06/10/91	-20.00
1990	05/23/90	-11.69	07/11/90	-10.90	0.80	80.00	06/13/90	160.00	07/02/90	-160.00
1989	05/23/89	10.40	07/11/89	13.40	3.00	300.00	06/26/89	1030.00		
1988	05/23/88	0.69	07/11/88	19.69	19.00	1900.00	06/23/88	2200.00	05/26/88	-200.00
1987	05/26/87	-6.40	07/10/87	0.69	7.10	710.00	07/08/87	730.00	06/08/87	-240.00
1986	05/23/86	-3.00	07/11/86	1.00	4.00	400.00	07/11/86	400.00	06/19/86	-70.00
1985	05/23/85	-18.59	07/11/85	-15.80	2.80	280.00	07/08/85	290.00	05/24/85	-70.00

Percentage Correct		93								
Average Profit on Winning Trades					6.70	670.00		Winners		14
Average Loss on Trades					-0.40	-40.00		Losers		1
Average Net Profit Per Trade					6.23	622.67		Total trades		15
Percentage Correct		95								
Average Profit on Winning Trades					6.83	682.63		Winners		19
Average Loss on Trades					-0.40	-40.00		Losers		1
Average Net Profit Per Trade					6.46	646.50		Total trades		20

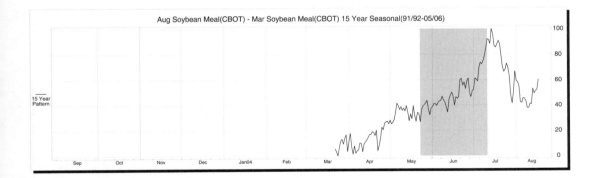

Aug Soybean Meal(CBOT) - Mar Soybean Meal(CBOT) 15 Year Seasonal(91/92-05/06)

Soyoil

Demand for soyoil is greatest as an edible oil in shortening, margarine, salad, and cooking oils. It also has industrial applications in manufacturing chemicals, paints, varnishes, lubricants, adhesives, and sealants. Unlike soymeal, however, soyoil has several competitors in both markets.

Figure 4-26: Cash Soyoil Seasonal Pattern

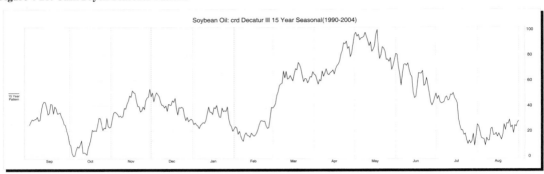

While processors are crushing aggressively for meal during and after soybean harvest, oil stocks build almost as if it were a byproduct. Thus, cash prices have often been weakest during October. In February, oil tends to maintain its product value relatively better than meal as the industry prepares to slow down its crushing activity, thereby easing the supply pressure on oil. Prices then tend to make their seasonal high in May, just before South American products flood export markets. Barring weather problems — oil content usually suffers most in drought conditions, the market thereafter normally begins to decline into harvest not only of soybeans but also of such oilseed competitors as palm nuts, cotton, flax, and canola.

Carrying charges. Even though soyoil is storable, the market does little to defray storage costs — perhaps because stocks inevitably build as if a byproduct. The seasonal pattern suggests deferred contracts do normally outperform harvest contracts such as December throughout the growing season.

Figure 4-27: Jul/Dec Soyoil Seasonal Pattern

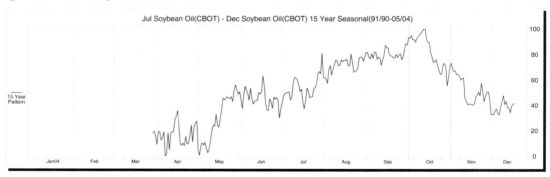

For example, note how deferred July tends to increase relative to December from planting season in April/May into harvest in October. It did so, in fact, from May 13 through October 1 in 13 of the 15 years from 1990-2004. The average move for that 140-day window, however, was less than 0.40 cents/pound — less than $2/day on a 60,000-pound tank car filled with soyoil.

Old-crop/new-crop. Even more reliable have been the spread movements between crops. By May, export competition begins to grow as, first, South American soyoil becomes available and then, in July/August, Malaysian palm oil.

Figure 4-28: New-crop Jan/Old-crop Sep Soyoil Pattern

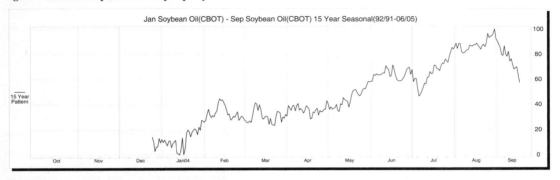

Figure 4-29: Soybean Oil Old-crop/New-crop Strategies

Moore Research Center, Inc.	Soybean Oil Old-crop/New-crop Spread Strategies							
Seasonal Strategy	Entry Date	Exit Date	Win Pct	Win Yrs	Loss Years	Total Years	Average Profit	Ave Pft Per Day
Buy Dec Soybean Oil(CBOT)	5/04	7/26	100	15	0	15	264	3
Sell Aug Soybean Oil(CBOT)			100	20	0	20	243	3
Buy Jan Soybean Oil(CBOT)	5/16	8/17	93	14	1	15	277	3
Sell Sep Soybean Oil(CBOT)			95	19	1	20	301	3
Buy Jan Soybean Oil(CBOT)	6/06	8/25	93	14	1	15	172	2
Sell Sep Soybean Oil(CBOT)			95	19	1	20	225	3

In contrast to those for soymeal, seasonal patterns and strategies for old-crop/new-crop soyoil relationships suggest that, even as the new soybean crop grows, stocks of soyoil become progressively burdensome. In fact, old-crop contracts have consistently underperformed new-crop all the way into deliveries. These spreads may not always generate large moves, but their reliability, the typically minimal margin required, and the usually mosquito bite–sized drawdowns make them worth considering each year.

Figure 4-30

	Moore Research Center, Inc.				*Buy Dec Soybean Oil(CBOT) / Sell Aug Soybean Oil(CBOT)*					

Enter on approximately 05/04 - Exit on approximately 07/26

CONT YEAR	ENTRY DATE	ENTRY PRICE	EXIT DATE	EXIT PRICE	PROFIT	PROFIT AMOUNT	BEST EQUITY DATE	BEST EQUITY AMOUNT	WORST EQUITY DATE	WORST EQUITY AMOUNT
2004	05/04/04	-4.40	07/26/04	-2.22	2.17	1302.00	07/26/04	1302.00	07/09/04	-144.00
2003	05/05/03	-0.78	07/25/03	-0.71	0.08	48.00	06/12/03	294.00	07/11/03	-240.00
2002	05/06/02	0.49	07/26/02	0.50	0.02	12.00	05/10/02	18.00	06/14/02	-72.00
2001	05/04/01	0.58	07/26/01	0.68	0.10	60.00	07/17/01	108.00	05/08/01	-30.00
2000	05/04/00	0.66	07/26/00	0.82	0.15	90.00	07/19/00	96.00	06/26/00	-30.00
1999	05/04/99	0.44	07/26/99	0.52	0.08	48.00	05/26/99	78.00	07/06/99	-12.00
1998	05/04/98	-0.49	07/24/98	0.51	1.01	606.00	06/26/98	660.00	05/08/98	-60.00
1997	05/05/97	0.14	07/25/97	0.48	0.35	210.00	06/04/97	246.00	07/11/97	-30.00
1996	05/06/96	0.51	07/26/96	0.78	0.26	156.00	07/12/96	198.00	05/08/96	-30.00
1995	05/04/95	-0.30	07/26/95	-0.21	0.08	48.00	05/19/95	192.00	06/21/95	-48.00
1994	05/04/94	-2.41	07/26/94	-0.99	1.42	852.00	06/29/94	1224.00		
1993	05/04/93	0.46	07/26/93	0.48	0.01	6.00	06/17/93	54.00	07/19/93	-60.00
1992	05/04/92	0.64	07/24/92	0.64	0.01	6.00	05/07/92	78.00	06/02/92	-66.00
1991	05/06/91	0.66	07/26/91	0.71	0.06	36.00	07/16/91	102.00	07/03/91	-36.00
1990	05/04/90	-0.73	07/26/90	0.08	0.81	486.00	07/20/90	552.00	05/18/90	-192.00
1989	05/04/89	0.76	07/26/89	0.78	0.01	6.00	05/15/89	78.00	06/26/89	-162.00
1988	05/04/88	0.58	07/26/88	0.76	0.18	108.00	06/03/88	156.00	07/01/88	-252.00
1987	05/04/87	0.62	07/24/87	0.65	0.04	24.00	06/30/87	138.00	05/08/87	-36.00
1986	05/05/86	0.35	07/25/86	0.80	0.45	270.00	07/16/86	324.00	05/23/86	-192.00
1985	05/06/85	-2.30	07/26/85	-1.50	0.80	480.00	07/26/85	480.00	06/06/85	-606.00

Percentage Correct	100									
Average Profit on Winning Trades					0.44	264.40		Winners		15
Average Loss on Trades								Losers		0
Average Net Profit Per Trade					0.44	264.40		Total trades		15
Percentage Correct	100									
Average Profit on Winning Trades					0.40	242.70		Winners		20
Average Loss on Trades								Losers		0
Average Net Profit Per Trade					0.40	242.70		Total trades		20

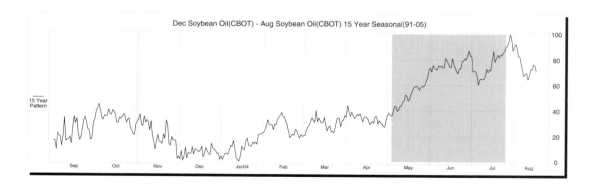

Dec Soybean Oil(CBOT) - Aug Soybean Oil(CBOT) 15 Year Seasonal(91-05)

15 Year Pattern

Figure 4-31

Buy Jan Soybean Oil(CBOT) / Sell Sep Soybean Oil(CBOT)

Moore Research Center, Inc.

Enter on approximately 05/16 - Exit on approximately 08/17

CONT YEAR	ENTRY DATE	ENTRY PRICE	EXIT DATE	EXIT PRICE	PROFIT	PROFIT AMOUNT	BEST EQUITY DATE	BEST EQUITY AMOUNT	WORST EQUITY DATE	WORST EQUITY AMOUNT
2005	05/17/04	-2.88	08/17/04	-1.07	1.82	1092.00	08/03/04	1416.00	07/09/04	-438.00
2004	05/16/03	-0.78	08/15/03	-0.02	0.76	456.00	08/15/03	456.00	07/11/03	-126.00
2003	05/16/02	0.53	08/16/02	-0.02	-0.56	-336.00	05/31/02	12.00	08/16/02	-336.00
2002	05/16/01	0.52	08/17/01	0.66	0.13	78.00	08/02/01	120.00		
2001	05/16/00	0.82	08/17/00	0.88	0.06	36.00	08/04/00	102.00	06/26/00	-60.00
2000	05/17/99	0.71	08/17/99	0.75	0.04	24.00	08/11/99	54.00	07/06/99	-78.00
1999	05/18/98	-0.44	08/17/98	0.35	0.81	486.00	07/10/98	624.00	05/22/98	-84.00
1998	05/16/97	0.33	08/15/97	0.67	0.35	210.00	08/14/97	252.00	07/07/97	-138.00
1997	05/16/96	0.29	08/16/96	0.76	0.46	276.00	07/31/96	324.00		
1996	05/16/95	-0.16	08/17/95	-0.05	0.10	60.00	05/19/95	132.00	07/31/95	-204.00
1995	05/16/94	-1.92	08/17/94	-0.30	1.63	978.00	08/15/94	1032.00	05/18/94	-12.00
1994	05/17/93	0.39	08/17/93	0.49	0.10	60.00	06/17/93	78.00	07/20/93	-42.00
1993	05/18/92	0.57	08/17/92	0.58	0.02	12.00	07/17/92	84.00	06/16/92	-72.00
1992	05/16/91	0.64	08/16/91	0.67	0.03	18.00	07/16/91	114.00	07/29/91	-84.00
1991	05/16/90	-0.77	08/17/90	0.41	1.18	708.00	08/17/90	708.00	06/12/90	-168.00
1990	05/16/89	0.73	08/17/89	0.89	0.17	102.00	08/16/89	108.00	06/26/89	-198.00
1989	05/16/88	0.60	08/17/88	1.03	0.43	258.00	08/17/88	258.00	06/22/88	-522.00
1988	05/18/87	0.60	08/17/87	0.64	0.03	18.00	07/16/87	48.00	05/29/87	-54.00
1987	05/16/86	0.31	08/15/86	0.85	0.55	330.00	07/22/86	336.00	05/22/86	-84.00
1986	05/16/85	-1.85	08/16/85	0.06	1.91	1146.00	08/13/85	1266.00	06/10/85	-522.00

Percentage Correct		93								
Average Profit on Winning Trades					0.53	321.00		Winners		14
Average Loss on Trades					-0.56	-336.00		Losers		1
Average Net Profit Per Trade					0.46	277.20		Total trades		15
Percentage Correct		95								
Average Profit on Winning Trades					0.56	334.11		Winners		19
Average Loss on Trades					-0.56	-336.00		Losers		1
Average Net Profit Per Trade					0.50	300.60		Total trades		20

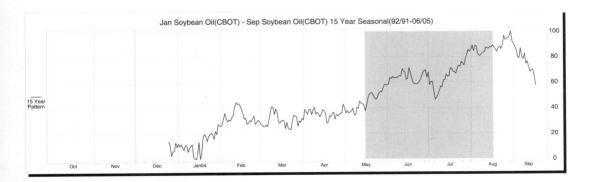

Jan Soybean Oil(CBOT) - Sep Soybean Oil(CBOT) 15 Year Seasonal(92/91-06/05)

Chapter 4: Soybean Complex

Figure 4-32

Buy Jan Soybean Oil(CBOT) / Sell Sep Soybean Oil(CBOT)

Moore Research Center, Inc.

Enter on approximately 06/06 - Exit on approximately 08/25

CONT YEAR	ENTRY DATE	ENTRY PRICE	EXIT DATE	EXIT PRICE	PROFIT	PROFIT AMOUNT	BEST EQUITY DATE	BEST EQUITY AMOUNT	WORST EQUITY DATE	WORST EQUITY AMOUNT
2005	06/07/04	-2.16	08/25/04	-1.65	0.51	306.00	08/03/04	978.00	07/09/04	-876.00
2004	06/06/03	-0.55	08/25/03	-0.03	0.53	318.00	08/21/03	336.00	07/11/03	-264.00
2003	06/06/02	0.36	08/23/02	-0.15	-0.52	-312.00	06/28/02	90.00	08/23/02	-312.00
2002	06/06/01	0.60	08/24/01	0.60	0.01	6.00	08/02/01	78.00	08/03/01	-36.00
2001	06/06/00	0.89	08/25/00	0.91	0.02	12.00	08/04/00	60.00	06/26/00	-102.00
2000	06/07/99	0.69	08/25/99	0.83	0.14	84.00	08/25/99	84.00	07/06/99	-66.00
1999	06/08/98	-0.05	08/25/98	0.35	0.42	252.00	07/10/98	390.00	06/10/98	-216.00
1998	06/06/97	0.50	08/25/97	0.75	0.25	150.00	08/14/97	150.00	07/07/97	-240.00
1997	06/06/96	0.48	08/23/96	0.86	0.37	222.00	08/23/96	222.00	06/13/96	-42.00
1996	06/06/95	-0.15	08/25/95	0.16	0.31	186.00	08/25/95	186.00	07/31/95	-210.00
1995	06/06/94	-1.11	08/25/94	-0.23	0.89	534.00	08/15/94	546.00	06/09/94	-30.00
1994	06/07/93	0.44	08/25/93	0.48	0.04	24.00	06/17/93	48.00	07/20/93	-72.00
1993	06/08/92	0.50	08/25/92	0.62	0.13	78.00	07/17/92	126.00	06/16/92	-30.00
1992	06/06/91	0.66	08/23/91	0.71	0.05	30.00	07/16/91	102.00	07/29/91	-96.00
1991	06/06/90	-0.90	08/24/90	0.26	1.16	696.00	08/20/90	798.00	06/12/90	-90.00
1990	06/06/89	0.69	08/25/89	0.94	0.26	156.00	08/24/89	168.00	06/26/89	-174.00
1989	06/06/88	0.73	08/25/88	1.00	0.27	162.00	08/23/88	198.00	06/22/88	-600.00
1988	06/08/87	0.57	08/25/87	0.60	0.02	12.00	08/24/87	72.00	08/06/87	-36.00
1987	06/06/86	0.41	08/25/86	0.71	0.30	180.00	07/22/86	270.00		
1986	06/06/85	-2.70	08/23/85	-0.37	2.33	1398.00	08/13/85	1782.00	06/10/85	-6.00

Percentage Correct	93				
Average Profit on Winning Trades		0.35	207.00	Winners	14
Average Loss on Trades		-0.52	-312.00	Losers	1
Average Net Profit Per Trade		0.29	172.40	Total trades	15
Percentage Correct	95				
Average Profit on Winning Trades		0.42	252.95	Winners	19
Average Loss on Trades		-0.52	-312.00	Losers	1
Average Net Profit Per Trade		0.37	224.70	Total trades	20

HYPOTHETICAL PERFORMANCE RESULTS HAVE MANY INHERENT LIMITATIONS, SOME OF WHICH ARE DESCRIBED BELOW. NO REPRESENTATION IS BEING MADE THAT ANY ACCOUNT WILL OR IS LIKELY TO ACHIEVE PROFITS OR LOSSES SIMILAR TO THOSE SHOWN. IN FACT, THERE ARE FREQUENTLY SHARP DIFFERENCES BETWEEN HYPOTHETICAL PERFORMANCE RESULTS AND THE ACTUAL RESULTS SUBSEQUENTLY ACHIEVED BY ANY PARTICULAR TRADING PROGRAM. ONE OF THE LIMITATIONS OF HYPOTHETICAL PERFORMANCE RESULTS IS THAT THEY ARE GENERALLY PREPARED WITH THE BENEFIT OF HINDSIGHT. IN ADDITION, HYPOTHETICAL TRADING DOES NOT INVOLVE FINANCIAL RISK, AND NO HYPOTHETICAL TRADING RECORD CAN COMPLETELY ACCOUNT FOR THE IMPACT OF FINANCIAL RISK IN ACTUAL TRADING. FOR EXAMPLE, THE ABILITY TO WITHSTAND LOSSES OR ADHERE TO A PARTICULAR TRADING PROGRAM IN SPITE OF TRADING LOSSES ARE MATERIAL POINTS WHICH CAN ALSO ADVERSELY AFFECT ACTUAL TRADING RESULTS. THERE ARE NUMEROUS OTHER FACTORS RELATED TO THE MARKETS IN GENERAL OR TO THE IMPLEMENTATION OF ANY SPECIFIC TRADING PROGRAM WHICH CANNOT BE FULLY ACCOUNTED FOR IN THE PREPARATION OF HYPOTHETICAL PERFORMANCE RESULTS AND ALL OF WHICH CAN ADVERSELY AFFECT ACTUAL TRADING RESULTS. RESULTS NOT ADJUSTED FOR COMMISSION AND SLIPPAGE.

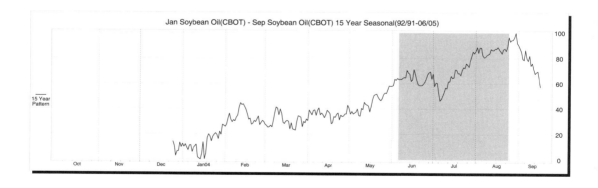

Jan Soybean Oil(CBOT) - Sep Soybean Oil(CBOT) 15 Year Seasonal(92/91-06/05)

15 Year Pattern

Chapter 4: Soybean Complex

Inter-market Spreads

The CBOT recognizes several spreads between and among members of the soy complex. All reflect relationships derived from crushing the soybean into meal and oil and thus have commercial application. Because these contracts differ in size and pricing, however, most speculative traders perceive them to be complex and esoteric. Some of these tradable relationships involve multiple contracts, others one-to-one.

Board Crush and Its Reverse

The standard 60-pound bushel of soybeans yields 44 pounds of 48% protein soymeal (the CBOT revised the contract specifications from 44% in October 1992) and 11 pounds of soyoil. Because this yield relationship is relatively constant, the soybean-processing industry can accurately measure cost versus income to calculate profitability — a critical factor in determining the rate at which domestic soybeans are processed. Thus, the formula for the Gross Processing Margin measures the difference in the cost of soybeans and the value of its products. This crush margin, which reflects value added to a bushel of soybeans by crushing into products and is expressed in dollars and cents per bushel, is calculated as follows:

Crush margin = (0.022SM + 0.11BO) - S

where SM is the price of soymeal expressed in dollars/ton; BO is the price of soyoil expressed in cents/pound; and S is the price of soybeans expressed in dollars and cents/bushel

The crush relationship yields not only a formula by which to calculate this margin but also a futures spread vehicle, referred to as the Board Crush and its opposite, the Reverse Board Crush, used by processors to hedge and speculators to trade. Processors wanting to protect a profitable crush margin could put on the Board Crush — going long soybean futures to hedge against a cost increase and short product futures to hedge against a revenue decrease. In contrast, those who expect the crush margin to increase could put on the Reverse Board Crush — going long the products and short soybeans. Both the Board Crush and its Reverse are otherwise beyond the scope of this volume. Suffice it here to say that the CBOT recognizes such spreads in ratios of both 1 futures contract of soybeans versus 1 of soymeal and also 1 of soyoil and the more precise 10 futures contracts of soybeans versus 11 of soymeal and 9 of soyoil.

Product Spreads

The CBOT also recognizes simpler spreads both between soybeans and each of its products and between the products themselves. Even these are not so readily traded because dissimilar contract size and pricing make spread orders impossible. Nonetheless, changes in their relationships are dynamic enough to be tradable.

Source versus Product. Under normal conditions, soyoil accounts for 35-40% of total product value. In extreme conditions, however, soyoil as a percentage of product value can range from as little as 30% to as much as 50%. (To calculate the value of soyoil in a bushel of soybeans, convert the oil price/pound to its bushel equivalent by multiplying by 11, the number of pounds of oil per bushel of soybeans. Thus, if the price of soyoil is $0.2100/pound, then the value of oil would be $2.31/bushel.)

If soyoil normally accounts for 35-40% of product value, then soymeal normally accounts for 60-65%, within a larger range of 50-70%. Thus, the equity values of soymeal and soybeans are more evenly balanced. (To calculate the value of soymeal in a bushel of soybeans, multiply the meal price/ton by the conversion factor 0.022, thereby accounting for

48 pounds of meal per bushel of soybeans and 2,000 pounds/ton. Thus, if the price of soymeal is $190/ton, then the value of soymeal would be $4.18/bushel.)

Figure 4-33: Jan Soyoil/Soybeans Seasonal Pattern

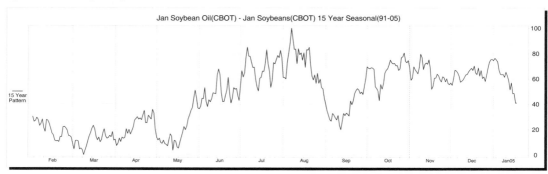

Figure 4-34: Jan Soymeal/Soybeans Seasonal Pattern

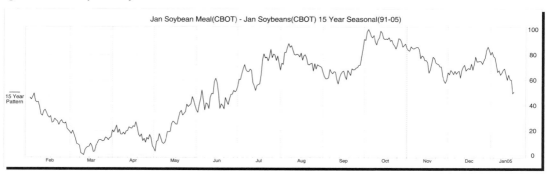

Figure 4-35: Soybeans versus Soy Products Strategies

Moore Research Center, Inc.	*Soybeans versus Soy Product Spread Strategies*							
Seasonal Strategy	Entry Date	Exit Date	Win Pct	Win Yrs	Loss Years	Total Years	Average Profit	Ave Pft Per Day
Buy Jul Soybeans(CBOT)	2/09	5/01	80	12	3	15	563	7
Sell Jul Soybean Meal(CBOT)			80	16	4	20	524	6
Buy Jul Soybeans(CBOT)	4/27	5/10	87	13	2	15	475	34
Sell Jul Soybean Oil(CBOT)			90	18	2	20	503	36
Buy Dec Soybean Meal(CBOT)	6/21	8/07	80	12	3	15	587	12
Sell Nov Soybeans(CBOT)			85	17	3	20	790	16
Buy Sep Soybean Meal(CBOT)	6/23	7/28	80	12	3	15	564	16
Sell Sep Soybeans(CBOT)			85	17	3	20	890	25
Buy Dec Soybean Meal(CBOT)	7/15	7/29	87	13	2	15	294	20
Sell Nov Soybeans(CBOT)			90	18	2	20	577	38
Buy Sep Soybean Oil(CBOT)	7/16	8/07	87	13	2	15	690	30
Sell Sep Soybeans(CBOT)			90	18	2	20	726	32
Buy Mar Soybeans(CBOT)	8/12	9/04	87	13	2	15	550	23
Sell Mar Soybean Oil(CBOT)			90	18	2	20	599	25
Buy Jan Soybean Meal(CBOT)	9/27	10/05	80	12	3	15	346	38
Sell Jan Soybeans(CBOT)			85	17	3	20	329	37

Figure 4-36

Buy Jul Soybeans(CBOT) / Sell Jul Soybean Meal(CBOT)

Enter on approximately 02/09 - Exit on approximately 05/01

CONT YEAR	ENTRY DATE	ENTRY PRICE	EXIT DATE	EXIT PRICE		PROFIT AMOUNT	BEST EQUITY DATE	BEST EQUITY AMOUNT	WORST EQUITY DATE	WORST EQUITY AMOUNT
2004	02/09/04	16433	04/30/04	19050		2617.50	03/22/04	3695.00	02/18/04	-165.00
2003	02/10/03	11180	05/01/03	12045		865.00	04/09/03	1240.00	02/12/03	-262.50
2002	02/11/02	7257	05/01/02	7403		145.00	03/15/02	737.50	02/28/02	-125.00
2001	02/09/01	7145	05/01/01	6482		-662.50	03/08/01	682.50	04/23/01	-817.50
2000	02/09/00	9400	05/01/00	10248		847.50	04/03/00	1185.00	02/25/00	-322.50
1999	02/09/99	12260	04/30/99	11115		-1145.00			03/05/99	-1762.50
1998	02/09/98	15355	05/01/98	16238		882.50	04/21/98	920.00	03/04/98	-505.00
1997	02/10/97	13990	05/01/97	15460		1470.00	03/10/97	1830.00	02/11/97	-10.00
1996	02/09/96	13685	05/01/96	15665		1980.00	05/01/96	1980.00	03/08/96	-545.00
1995	02/09/95	12323	05/01/95	12610		287.50	03/06/95	662.50	04/04/95	-400.00
1994	02/09/94	14673	04/29/94	14725		52.50	03/23/94	482.50	04/15/94	-845.00
1993	02/09/93	10690	04/30/93	10893		202.50	04/07/93	727.50	02/11/93	-27.50
1992	02/10/92	11565	05/01/92	11723		157.50	03/06/92	950.00	04/07/92	-322.50
1991	02/11/91	12338	05/01/91	11968		-370.00	03/08/91	980.00	04/30/91	-412.50
1990	02/09/90	12045	05/01/90	13165		1120.00	04/27/90	1585.00		
1989	02/09/89	14700	05/01/89	14865		165.00	03/02/89	1250.00	04/04/89	-485.00
1988	02/09/88	13453	04/29/88	14615		1162.50	04/29/88	1162.50	03/09/88	-695.00
1987	02/09/87	10748	05/01/87	11028		280.00	05/01/87	280.00	03/23/87	-370.00
1986	02/10/86	11860	05/01/86	11295		-565.00			02/28/86	-1417.50
1985	02/11/85	15845	05/01/85	16833		987.50	04/25/85	1582.50	03/04/85	-582.50

Percentage Correct	80									
Average Profit on Winning Trades						885.63		Winners		12
Average Loss on Trades						-725.83		Losers		3
Average Net Profit Per Trade						563.33		Total trades		15
Percentage Correct	80									
Average Profit on Winning Trades						826.41		Winners		16
Average Loss on Trades						-685.63		Losers		4
Average Net Profit Per Trade						524.00		Total trades		20

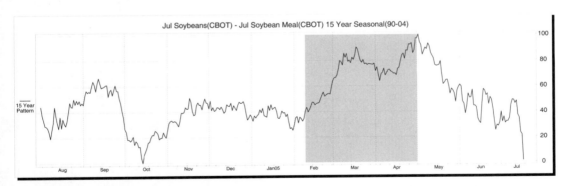

Jul Soybeans(CBOT) - Jul Soybean Meal(CBOT) 15 Year Seasonal(90-04)

These spreads can generate significant moves not only because product value can change but also because contract equity values are unbalanced. Thus, if the complex as a whole trends in one direction, the equity value of the soybean contract will tend to gain or lose more simply because it is larger than that of either product.

Figure 4-37

Moore Research Center, Inc.

Buy Jul Soybeans(CBOT) / Sell Jul Soybean Oil(CBOT)

Enter on approximately 04/27 - Exit on approximately 05/10

CONT YEAR	ENTRY DATE	ENTRY PRICE	EXIT DATE	EXIT PRICE		PROFIT AMOUNT	BEST EQUITY DATE	BEST EQUITY AMOUNT	WORST EQUITY DATE	WORST EQUITY AMOUNT
2004	04/27/04	29355	05/10/04	31197		1842.00	05/07/04	2228.00	04/28/04	-209.00
2003	04/28/03	17351	05/09/03	18370		1019.50	05/02/03	1119.50		
2002	04/29/02	13411	05/10/02	13446		34.50	05/09/02	261.50	05/03/02	-104.50
2001	04/27/01	12382	05/10/01	12894		512.50	05/04/01	809.00		
2000	04/27/00	16396	05/10/00	17742		1346.00	05/10/00	1346.00	04/28/00	-263.50
1999	04/27/99	12460	05/10/99	12646		186.50	04/28/99	244.00	05/07/99	-62.50
1998	04/27/98	14875	05/08/98	14877		2.00	05/06/98	489.50	05/04/98	-83.50
1997	04/28/97	28101	05/09/97	29630		1529.00	05/07/97	1595.00		
1996	04/29/96	23554	05/10/96	24194		640.50	05/08/96	790.00	04/30/96	-207.50
1995	04/27/95	13601	05/10/95	13676		75.00	05/10/95	75.00	05/01/95	-110.50
1994	04/28/94	16537	05/10/94	16110		-426.50			05/05/94	-516.50
1993	04/27/93	16873	05/10/93	17323		450.00	05/07/93	617.00	04/28/93	-108.00
1992	04/27/92	17198	05/08/92	17461		263.00	05/07/92	414.00		
1991	04/29/91	16922	05/10/91	16541		-381.00	05/03/91	341.00	05/10/91	-381.00
1990	04/27/90	18198	05/10/90	18235		37.00	05/02/90	235.50	05/04/90	-357.00
1989	04/27/89	22734	05/10/89	22941		207.00	05/05/89	789.00	04/28/89	-287.00
1988	04/27/88	20453	05/10/88	21552		1099.00	05/10/88	1099.00		
1987	04/27/87	16565	05/08/87	17641		1076.00	05/08/87	1076.00		
1986	04/28/86	15804	05/09/86	16181		377.00	05/06/86	389.00	05/01/86	-28.50
1985	04/29/85	11025	05/10/85	11200		175.00	05/02/85	282.00	05/06/85	-285.00

Percentage Correct	87		
Average Profit on Winning Trades	610.58	Winners	13
Average Loss on Trades	-403.75	Losers	2
Average Net Profit Per Trade	475.33	Total trades	15
Percentage Correct	90		
Average Profit on Winning Trades	603.97	Winners	18
Average Loss on Trades	-403.75	Losers	2
Average Net Profit Per Trade	503.20	Total trades	20

HYPOTHETICAL PERFORMANCE RESULTS HAVE MANY INHERENT LIMITATIONS, SOME OF WHICH ARE DESCRIBED BELOW. NO REPRESENTATION IS BEING MADE THAT ANY ACCOUNT WILL OR IS LIKELY TO ACHIEVE PROFITS OR LOSSES SIMILAR TO THOSE SHOWN. IN FACT, THERE ARE FREQUENTLY SHARP DIFFERENCES BETWEEN HYPOTHETICAL PERFORMANCE RESULTS AND THE ACTUAL RESULTS SUBSEQUENTLY ACHIEVED BY ANY PARTICULAR TRADING PROGRAM. ONE OF THE LIMITATIONS OF HYPOTHETICAL PERFORMANCE RESULTS IS THAT THEY ARE GENERALLY PREPARED WITH THE BENEFIT OF HINDSIGHT. IN ADDITION, HYPOTHETICAL TRADING DOES NOT INVOLVE FINANCIAL RISK, AND NO HYPOTHETICAL TRADING RECORD CAN COMPLETELY ACCOUNT FOR THE IMPACT OF FINANCIAL RISK IN ACTUAL TRADING. FOR EXAMPLE, THE ABILITY TO WITHSTAND LOSSES OR ADHERE TO A PARTICULAR TRADING PROGRAM IN SPITE OF TRADING LOSSES ARE MATERIAL POINTS WHICH CAN ALSO ADVERSELY AFFECT ACTUAL TRADING RESULTS. THERE ARE NUMEROUS OTHER FACTORS RELATED TO THE MARKETS IN GENERAL OR TO THE IMPLEMENTATION OF ANY SPECIFIC TRADING PROGRAM WHICH CANNOT BE FULLY ACCOUNTED FOR IN THE PREPARATION OF HYPOTHETICAL PERFORMANCE RESULTS AND ALL OF WHICH CAN ADVERSELY AFFECT ACTUAL TRADING RESULTS. RESULTS NOT ADJUSTED FOR COMMISSION AND SLIPPAGE.

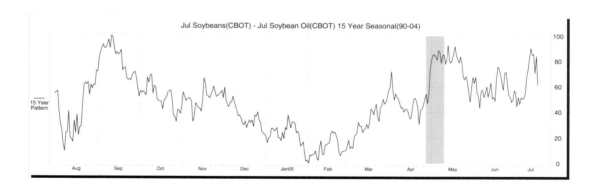

Jul Soybeans(CBOT) - Jul Soybean Oil(CBOT) 15 Year Seasonal(90-04)

164 Chapter 4: Soybean Complex

Figure 4-38

Buy Dec Soybean Meal(CBOT) / Sell Nov Soybeans(CBOT)

Enter on approximately 06/21 - Exit on approximately 08/07

CONT YEAR	ENTRY DATE	ENTRY PRICE	EXIT DATE	EXIT PRICE		PROFIT AMOUNT	BEST EQUITY DATE	BEST EQUITY AMOUNT	WORST EQUITY DATE	WORST EQUITY AMOUNT
2004	06/21/04	-12780	08/06/04	-10818		1962.50	08/04/04	2110.00	06/29/04	-337.50
2003	06/23/03	-11308	08/07/03	-10055		1252.50	07/31/03	1507.50	06/25/03	-135.00
2002	06/21/02	-8168	08/07/02	-9885		-1717.50			07/22/02	-2052.50
2001	06/21/01	-6743	08/07/01	-8730		-1987.50	06/25/01	190.00	07/17/01	-2430.00
2000	06/21/00	-8970	08/07/00	-7678		1292.50	08/07/00	1292.50		
1999	06/21/99	-9580	08/06/99	-9290		290.00	07/28/99	1532.50	06/23/99	-42.50
1998	06/22/98	-14148	08/07/98	-12658		1490.00	08/07/98	1490.00	06/26/98	-472.50
1997	06/23/97	-11448	08/07/97	-10575		872.50	07/11/97	1230.00	06/24/97	-10.00
1996	06/21/96	-14135	08/07/96	-13933		202.50	07/05/96	885.00	07/15/96	-1132.50
1995	06/21/95	-12853	08/07/95	-11925		927.50	06/30/95	992.50	07/17/95	-197.50
1994	06/21/94	-13435	08/05/94	-10873		2562.50	07/27/94	2930.00		
1993	06/21/93	-11465	08/06/93	-12500		-1035.00			07/09/93	-2155.00
1992	06/22/92	-10735	08/07/92	-8210		2525.00	08/07/92	2525.00	06/25/92	-270.00
1991	06/21/91	-11228	08/07/91	-11100		127.50	07/08/91	1380.00	08/02/91	-1577.50
1990	06/21/90	-12790	08/07/90	-12753		37.50	07/24/90	375.00	07/02/90	-1100.00
1989	06/21/89	-13055	08/07/89	-11035		2020.00	08/03/89	2502.50	07/05/89	-825.00
1988	06/21/88	-19425	08/05/88	-17950		1475.00	07/26/88	4135.00	07/15/88	-1335.00
1987	06/22/87	-10605	08/07/87	-9728		877.50	08/07/87	877.50	07/02/87	-550.00
1986	06/23/86	-10598	08/07/86	-9348		1250.00	08/07/86	1250.00	07/16/86	-137.50
1985	06/21/85	-14750	08/07/85	-13383		1367.50	08/06/85	1482.50	06/25/85	-175.00

Percentage Correct	80								
Average Profit on Winning Trades					1128.54		Winners	12
Average Loss on Trades					-1580.00		Losers	3
Average Net Profit Per Trade					586.83		Total trades	15
Percentage Correct	85								
Average Profit on Winning Trades					1207.79		Winners	17
Average Loss on Trades					-1580.00		Losers	3
Average Net Profit Per Trade					789.63		Total trades	20

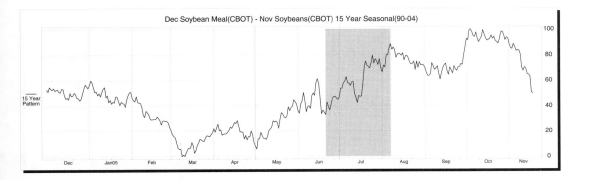

Dec Soybean Meal(CBOT) - Nov Soybeans(CBOT) 15 Year Seasonal(90-04)

Figure 4-39

Moore Research Center, Inc.

Buy Sep Soybean Meal(CBOT) / Sell Sep Soybeans(CBOT)

Enter on approximately 06/23 - Exit on approximately 07/28

CONT YEAR	ENTRY DATE	ENTRY PRICE	EXIT DATE	EXIT PRICE		PROFIT AMOUNT	BEST EQUITY DATE	BEST EQUITY AMOUNT	WORST EQUITY DATE	WORST EQUITY AMOUNT
2004	06/23/04	-11175	07/28/04	-10245		930.00	07/09/04	2025.00	06/25/04	-370.00
2003	06/23/03	-11543	07/28/03	-10123		1420.00	07/18/03	1722.50		
2002	06/24/02	-8205	07/26/02	-9445		-1240.00	06/26/02	135.00	07/22/02	-1970.00
2001	06/25/01	-6240	07/27/01	-8315		-2075.00			07/17/01	-2770.00
2000	06/23/00	-8232	07/28/00	-7507		725.00	07/17/00	1087.50	06/29/00	-55.00
1999	06/23/99	-9685	07/28/99	-8153		1532.50	07/28/99	1532.50		
1998	06/23/98	-14835	07/28/98	-13780		1055.00	07/24/98	1402.50	07/08/98	-230.00
1997	06/23/97	-11180	07/28/97	-10365		815.00	07/02/97	1335.00	06/24/97	-232.50
1996	06/24/96	-13905	07/26/96	-13360		545.00	07/26/96	545.00	07/15/96	-1567.50
1995	06/23/95	-12740	07/28/95	-12600		140.00	06/30/95	697.50	07/17/95	-552.50
1994	06/23/94	-13178	07/28/94	-10945		2232.50	07/21/94	2317.50	06/28/94	-425.00
1993	06/23/93	-11728	07/28/93	-12110		-382.50	06/25/93	62.50	07/09/93	-1910.00
1992	06/23/92	-12263	07/28/92	-10548		1715.00	07/23/92	1915.00	06/25/92	-72.50
1991	06/24/91	-11153	07/26/91	-10908		245.00	07/08/91	1425.00		
1990	06/25/90	-13303	07/27/90	-12503		800.00	07/24/90	1037.50	07/02/90	-575.00
1989	06/23/89	-12650	07/28/89	-10843		1807.50	07/28/89	1807.50	07/05/89	-1355.00
1988	06/23/88	-20325	07/28/88	-14605		5720.00	07/28/88	5720.00	06/27/88	-705.00
1987	06/23/87	-10593	07/28/87	-10288		305.00	07/17/87	1120.00	07/02/87	-150.00
1986	06/23/86	-10853	07/28/86	-10603		250.00	07/01/86	582.50	07/16/86	-85.00
1985	06/24/85	-15398	07/26/85	-14148		1250.00	07/24/85	1342.50	06/26/85	-102.50

Percentage Correct	80							
Average Profit on Winning Trades				1012.92		Winners	12
Average Loss on Trades				-1232.50		Losers	3
Average Net Profit Per Trade				563.83		Total trades	15
Percentage Correct	85							
Average Profit on Winning Trades				1263.97		Winners	17
Average Loss on Trades				-1232.50		Losers	3
Average Net Profit Per Trade				889.50		Total trades	20

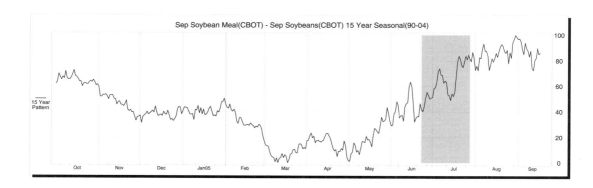

Sep Soybean Meal(CBOT) - Sep Soybeans(CBOT) 15 Year Seasonal(90-04)

Chapter 4: Soybean Complex

Figure 4-40

Buy Dec Soybean Meal(CBOT) / Sell Nov Soybeans(CBOT)

Enter on approximately 07/15 - Exit on approximately 07/29

CONT YEAR	ENTRY DATE	ENTRY PRICE	EXIT DATE	EXIT PRICE		PROFIT AMOUNT	BEST EQUITY DATE	BEST EQUITY AMOUNT	WORST EQUITY DATE	WORST EQUITY AMOUNT
2004	07/15/04	-12135	07/29/04	-11118		1017.50	07/28/04	1137.50	07/19/04	-52.50
2003	07/15/03	-10373	07/29/03	-10025		347.50	07/24/03	557.50		
2002	07/15/02	-9603	07/29/02	-9230		372.50	07/29/02	372.50	07/22/02	-617.50
2001	07/16/01	-8698	07/27/01	-8683		15.00	07/20/01	585.00	07/17/01	-475.00
2000	07/17/00	-7815	07/28/00	-7913		-97.50			07/24/00	-350.00
1999	07/15/99	-8373	07/29/99	-8145		227.50	07/28/99	325.00	07/23/99	-832.50
1998	07/15/98	-13650	07/29/98	-13563		87.50	07/22/98	437.50	07/17/98	-250.00
1997	07/15/97	-11061	07/29/97	-10905		156.25	07/25/97	658.75		
1996	07/15/96	-15268	07/29/96	-13763		1505.00	07/26/96	1815.00		
1995	07/17/95	-13050	07/28/95	-12345		705.00	07/19/95	742.50		
1994	07/15/94	-11128	07/29/94	-10748		380.00	07/27/94	622.50		
1993	07/15/93	-13150	07/29/93	-12418		732.50	07/28/93	752.50	07/16/93	-225.00
1992	07/15/92	-9418	07/29/92	-9143		275.00	07/23/92	545.00		
1991	07/15/91	-10215	07/29/91	-11790		-1575.00	07/19/91	155.00	07/29/91	-1575.00
1990	07/16/90	-12845	07/27/90	-12585		260.00	07/24/90	430.00		
1989	07/17/89	-12155	07/28/89	-11215		940.00	07/28/89	940.00	07/19/89	-215.00
1988	07/15/88	-20760	07/29/88	-15605		5155.00	07/26/88	5470.00		
1987	07/15/87	-10240	07/29/87	-10148		92.50	07/17/87	435.00	07/28/87	-245.00
1986	07/15/86	-10555	07/29/86	-10475		80.00	07/24/86	255.00	07/16/86	-180.00
1985	07/15/85	-14498	07/29/85	-13625		872.50	07/24/85	912.50		

Percentage Correct	87									
Average Profit on Winning Trades						467.79		Winners		13
Average Loss on Trades						-836.25		Losers		2
Average Net Profit Per Trade						293.92		Total trades		15
Percentage Correct	90									
Average Profit on Winning Trades						734.51		Winners		18
Average Loss on Trades						-836.25		Losers		2
Average Net Profit Per Trade						577.44		Total trades		20

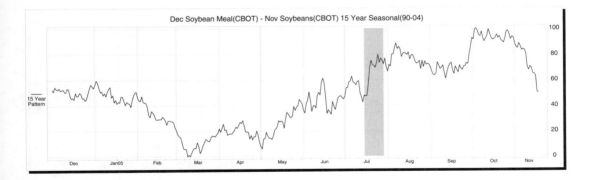

Dec Soybean Meal(CBOT) - Nov Soybeans(CBOT) 15 Year Seasonal(90-04)

Figure 4-41

Moore Research Center, Inc.

Buy Sep Soybean Oil(CBOT) / Sell Sep Soybeans(CBOT)

Enter on approximately 07/16 - Exit on approximately 08/07

CONT YEAR	ENTRY DATE	ENTRY PRICE	EXIT DATE	EXIT PRICE		PROFIT AMOUNT	BEST EQUITY DATE	BEST EQUITY AMOUNT	WORST EQUITY DATE	WORST EQUITY AMOUNT
2004	07/16/04	-17160	08/06/04	-14981		2179.50	08/06/04	2179.50	07/20/04	-666.00
2003	07/16/03	-14579	08/07/03	-14239		340.00	07/18/03	410.50	07/28/03	-310.00
2002	07/16/02	-15798	08/07/02	-15478		320.50	07/29/02	1397.00	07/22/02	-607.00
2001	07/16/01	-14580	08/07/01	-14070		510.00	08/02/01	876.50	07/17/01	-330.50
2000	07/17/00	-12853	08/07/00	-12743		110.50	08/01/00	132.00	07/21/00	-686.50
1999	07/16/99	-11454	08/06/99	-13944		-2490.00			08/04/99	-2727.00
1998	07/16/98	-14958	08/07/98	-12682		2276.50	08/07/98	2276.50	07/17/98	-838.00
1997	07/16/97	-19198	08/07/97	-19956		-758.00	07/17/97	299.00	08/01/97	-1621.50
1996	07/16/96	-24576	08/07/96	-22764		1812.00	08/05/96	1960.00		
1995	07/17/95	-15525	08/07/95	-13848		1676.50	08/04/95	1678.50		
1994	07/18/94	-14719	08/05/94	-13565		1153.50	08/05/94	1153.50		
1993	07/16/93	-21361	08/06/93	-19569		1792.50	08/06/93	1792.50	07/19/93	-639.00
1992	07/16/92	-16695	08/07/92	-15984		711.50	08/07/92	711.50	07/29/92	-100.00
1991	07/16/91	-15801	08/07/91	-15660		140.50	07/18/91	916.00	08/02/91	-2711.00
1990	07/16/90	-16045	08/07/90	-15475		570.00	08/02/90	1265.00	07/19/90	-323.50
1989	07/17/89	-20203	08/07/89	-18319		1884.00	08/03/89	2475.50	07/19/89	-330.00
1988	07/18/88	-27725	08/05/88	-27091		634.00	07/28/88	5348.00		
1987	07/16/87	-16172	08/07/87	-15750		422.00	08/06/87	717.00	07/28/87	-792.00
1986	07/16/86	-15548	08/07/86	-14819		729.00	08/05/86	741.50	07/21/86	-195.00
1985	07/16/85	-12193	08/07/85	-11686		506.50	07/31/85	1123.00		

Percentage Correct	87		
Average Profit on Winning Trades		1045.65	
Average Loss on Trades		-1624.00	
Average Net Profit Per Trade		689.70	

Winners	13
Losers	2
Total trades	15

Percentage Correct	90		
Average Profit on Winning Trades		987.17	
Average Loss on Trades		-1624.00	
Average Net Profit Per Trade		726.05	

Winners	18
Losers	2
Total trades	20

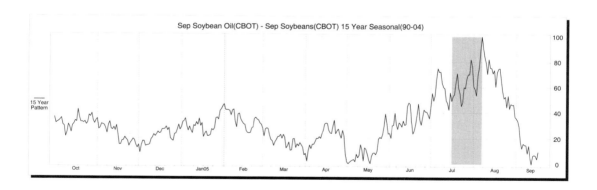

Sep Soybean Oil(CBOT) - Sep Soybeans(CBOT) 15 Year Seasonal(90-04)

Figure 4-42

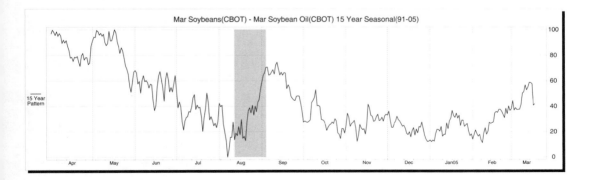

	Moore Research Center, Inc.			*Buy Mar Soybeans(CBOT) / Sell Mar Soybean Oil(CBOT)*						
			Enter on approximately 08/12 - Exit on approximately 09/04							

CONT YEAR	ENTRY DATE	ENTRY PRICE	EXIT DATE	EXIT PRICE		PROFIT AMOUNT	BEST EQUITY DATE	BEST EQUITY AMOUNT	WORST EQUITY DATE	WORST EQUITY AMOUNT
2005	08/12/04	16548	09/03/04	16175		-373.00	08/23/04	619.50	08/16/04	-420.50
2004	08/12/03	15875	09/04/03	16747		872.50	08/25/03	1452.00	08/13/03	-102.50
2003	08/12/02	15186	09/04/02	15457		270.50	08/14/02	670.50	08/20/02	-678.50
2002	08/13/01	14105	09/04/01	14415		310.00	09/04/01	310.00	08/24/01	-546.00
2001	08/14/00	14332	09/01/00	15913		1580.50	08/31/00	1691.50		
2000	08/12/99	13285	09/03/99	14748		1463.00	09/03/99	1463.00		
1999	08/12/98	13366	09/04/98	12113		-1253.00			09/04/98	-1253.00
1998	08/12/97	17355	09/04/97	18413		1058.50	09/04/97	1058.50	08/15/97	-187.00
1997	08/12/96	23769	09/04/96	24005		236.50	08/29/96	703.50	08/19/96	-296.00
1996	08/14/95	15393	09/01/95	16440		1047.50	09/01/95	1047.50	08/15/95	-102.00
1995	08/12/94	14511	09/02/94	14763		252.50	08/19/94	609.00	08/15/94	-21.50
1994	08/12/93	18937	09/03/93	19150		212.50	08/25/93	721.00	08/16/93	-245.00
1993	08/12/92	16067	09/04/92	16627		560.00	08/24/92	707.00		
1992	08/12/91	16911	09/04/91	18103		1192.00	09/04/91	1192.00	08/19/91	-906.50
1991	08/13/90	16988	09/04/90	17813		825.00	08/28/90	1337.00		
1990	08/14/89	18174	09/01/89	18248		74.00	08/22/89	401.00	08/16/89	-163.00
1989	08/12/88	26165	09/02/88	27805		1640.00	09/02/88	1640.00	08/23/88	-985.00
1988	08/12/87	15635	09/04/87	16373		738.50	09/04/87	738.50		
1987	08/12/86	15217	09/04/86	16126		909.00	09/04/86	909.00	08/13/86	-41.50
1986	08/12/85	12888	09/04/85	13253		365.00	09/04/85	365.00	08/20/85	-124.50

Percentage Correct	87									
Average Profit on Winning Trades						760.08		Winners		13
Average Loss on Trades						-813.00		Losers		2
Average Net Profit Per Trade						550.33		Total trades		15
Percentage Correct	90									
Average Profit on Winning Trades						755.97		Winners		18
Average Loss on Trades						-813.00		Losers		2
Average Net Profit Per Trade						599.07		Total trades		20

Mar Soybeans(CBOT) - Mar Soybean Oil(CBOT) 15 Year Seasonal(91-05)

15 Year Pattern

Figure 4-43

Buy Jan Soybean Meal(CBOT) / Sell Jan Soybeans(CBOT)

Enter on approximately 09/27 - Exit on approximately 10/05

CONT YEAR	ENTRY DATE	ENTRY PRICE	EXIT DATE	EXIT PRICE		PROFIT AMOUNT	BEST EQUITY DATE	BEST EQUITY AMOUNT	WORST EQUITY DATE	WORST EQUITY AMOUNT
2005	09/27/04	-10673	10/05/04	-10865		-192.50	10/04/04	72.50	10/05/04	-192.50
2004	09/29/03	-13925	10/03/03	-14098		-172.50	09/30/03	37.50	10/02/03	-567.50
2003	09/27/02	-10500	10/04/02	-10040		460.00	10/02/02	485.00		
2002	09/27/01	-7503	10/05/01	-6663		840.00	10/05/01	840.00		
2001	09/27/00	-8275	10/05/00	-7905		370.00	10/05/00	370.00		
2000	09/27/99	-9830	10/05/99	-9698		132.50	10/01/99	215.00	09/28/99	-117.50
1999	09/28/98	-13495	10/05/98	-13423		72.50	10/01/98	395.00		
1998	09/29/97	-11670	10/03/97	-11895		-225.00			10/03/97	-225.00
1997	09/27/96	-14015	10/04/96	-12778		1237.50	10/04/96	1237.50		
1996	09/27/95	-12955	10/05/95	-12858		97.50	10/03/95	100.00	09/29/95	-80.00
1995	09/27/94	-11498	10/05/94	-10823		675.00	10/05/94	675.00		
1994	09/27/93	-12615	10/05/93	-11808		807.50	10/05/93	807.50		
1993	09/28/92	-8838	10/05/92	-8420		417.50	10/05/92	417.50		
1992	09/27/91	-11083	10/04/91	-10933		150.00	10/01/91	160.00	10/02/91	-17.50
1991	09/27/90	-13148	10/05/90	-12635		512.50	10/05/90	512.50	09/28/90	-30.00
1990	09/27/89	-11023	10/05/89	-10768		255.00	10/05/89	255.00	10/02/89	-10.00
1989	09/27/88	-15630	10/05/88	-15165		465.00	10/05/88	465.00		
1988	09/28/87	-10363	10/05/87	-10335		27.50	09/30/87	70.00	10/02/87	-5.00
1987	09/29/86	-9515	10/03/86	-9320		195.00	10/03/86	195.00	10/01/86	-92.50
1986	09/27/85	-12560	10/04/85	-12103		457.50	10/04/85	457.50	09/30/85	-117.50

Percentage Correct	80			
Average Profit on Winning Trades		481.04	Winners	12
Average Loss on Trades		-196.67	Losers	3
Average Net Profit Per Trade		345.50	Total trades	15
Percentage Correct	85			
Average Profit on Winning Trades		421.91	Winners	17
Average Loss on Trades		-196.67	Losers	3
Average Net Profit Per Trade		329.13	Total trades	20

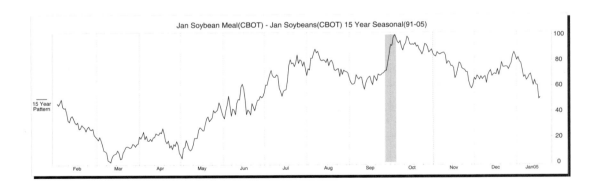

Jan Soybean Meal(CBOT) - Jan Soybeans(CBOT) 15 Year Seasonal(91-05)

Product versus Product. Only in unusual conditions, such as when oil content is reduced by drought, does the equity value of any soyoil contract reach or exceed that of soymeal. Thus, via SPAN (Standard Portfolio Analysis of Risk) the CBOT recognizes the relationship between soy products in a ratio of 3 soyoil to 2 soymeal. Spreads in this ratio are also beyond the scope of this volume.

Figure 4-44: Aug Soymeal/Soyoil Seasonal Pattern

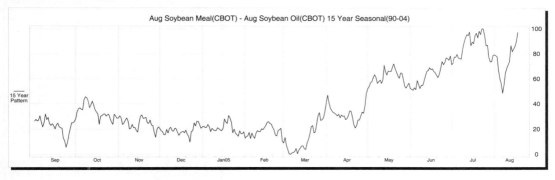

Figure 4-45: Soymeal/Soyoil Strategies

Moore Research Center, Inc.	Soymeal/Soyoil Spread Strategies							
Seasonal Strategy	Entry Date	Exit Date	Win Pct	Win Yrs	Loss Years	Total Years	Average Profit	Ave Pft Per Day
Buy Aug Soybean Meal(CBOT)	4/24	7/14	93	14	1	15	971	12
Sell Aug Soybean Oil(CBOT)			95	19	1	20	1128	14
Buy Jul Soybean Meal(CBOT)	4/29	6/24	87	13	2	15	814	14
Sell Jul Soybean Oil(CBOT)			90	18	2	20	1084	19
Buy Oct Soybean Meal(CBOT)	6/08	9/06	80	12	3	15	470	5
Sell Oct Soybean Oil(CBOT)			85	17	3	20	778	9
Buy Dec Soybean Meal(CBOT)	7/01	9/14	80	12	3	15	281	4
Sell Dec Soybean Oil(CBOT)			85	17	3	20	703	9
Buy Dec Soybean Meal(CBOT)	8/07	10/13	80	12	3	15	921	14
Sell Dec Soybean Oil(CBOT)			80	16	4	20	1057	16

But contracts for these products can also be traded one against another (with fractional margin credit). Because of its greater product value and thus contract size, soymeal tends to lead their more persistent and consistent seasonal trends.

The most reliable strategy, with the longest, smoothest seasonal trend, reflects an old-crop relationship during the latter half of the crop marketing year when supply is well known and the pattern of consumption well established. Still, several years would have suffered severe drawdowns prior to their eventual outcome. One might then be wary of the new-crop relationships during the usual peak in market anxiety over the vulnerability of the new crop to weather. Nonetheless, the peak in commercial activity and demand for soymeal comes during and after harvest — when soyoil will face competition from other oilseeds and stocks will build as if a byproduct.

Figure 4-46

Buy Aug Soybean Meal(CBOT) / Sell Aug Soybean Oil(CBOT)

Enter on approximately 04/24 - Exit on approximately 07/14

CONT YEAR	ENTRY DATE	ENTRY PRICE	EXIT DATE	EXIT PRICE		PROFIT AMOUNT	BEST EQUITY DATE	BEST EQUITY AMOUNT	WORST EQUITY DATE	WORST EQUITY AMOUNT
2004	04/26/04	9702	07/14/04	11042		1340.00	07/09/04	2854.00	05/28/04	-1532.00
2003	04/24/03	4752	07/14/03	5744		992.00	06/27/03	1426.00		
2002	04/24/02	5584	07/12/02	6912		1328.00	07/05/02	1782.00	05/28/02	-480.00
2001	04/24/01	5530	07/13/01	6698		1168.00	06/29/01	2274.00	04/25/01	-348.00
2000	04/24/00	6048	07/14/00	6486		438.00	05/12/00	2094.00		
1999	04/26/99	1196	07/14/99	3582		2386.00	06/18/99	2934.00		
1998	04/24/98	-938	07/14/98	1154		2092.00	06/24/98	3400.00	05/11/98	-1126.00
1997	04/24/97	10982	07/14/97	12032		1050.00	05/19/97	2260.00	07/02/97	-2158.00
1996	04/24/96	9672	07/12/96	10040		368.00	07/12/96	368.00	05/29/96	-2150.00
1995	04/24/95	1968	07/14/95	1424		-544.00	05/23/95	546.00	07/06/95	-1340.00
1994	04/25/94	2128	07/14/94	3736		1608.00	06/15/94	1818.00	05/16/94	-1020.00
1993	04/26/93	5640	07/14/93	7672		2032.00	07/14/93	2032.00		
1992	04/24/92	5764	07/14/92	5946		182.00	05/13/92	384.00	06/05/92	-636.00
1991	04/24/91	5192	07/12/91	5258		66.00	06/19/91	592.00	05/08/91	-366.00
1990	04/24/90	3550	07/13/90	3604		54.00	05/01/90	1880.00	06/08/90	-842.00
1989	04/24/89	8170	07/14/89	9370		1200.00	07/14/89	1200.00	05/22/89	-1180.00
1988	04/25/88	6110	07/14/88	8980		2870.00	06/21/88	7770.00	04/26/88	-238.00
1987	04/24/87	5866	07/14/87	6852		986.00	06/15/87	2872.00	05/06/87	-232.00
1986	04/24/86	4562	07/14/86	4994		432.00	07/14/86	432.00	05/23/86	-966.00
1985	04/24/85	-5248	07/12/85	-2746		2502.00	07/12/85	2502.00	06/11/85	-460.00

Percentage Correct	93			
Average Profit on Winning Trades		1078.86	Winners	14
Average Loss on Trades		-544.00	Losers	1
Average Net Profit Per Trade		970.67	Total trades	15
Percentage Correct	95			
Average Profit on Winning Trades		1215.47	Winners	19
Average Loss on Trades		-544.00	Losers	1
Average Net Profit Per Trade		1127.50	Total trades	20

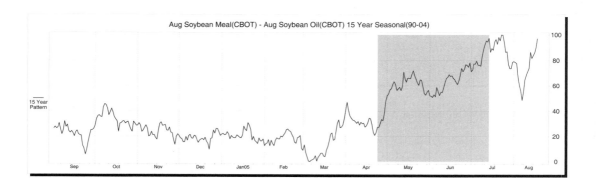

Aug Soybean Meal(CBOT) - Aug Soybean Oil(CBOT) 15 Year Seasonal(90-04)

Chapter 4: Soybean Complex

Figure 4-47

Buy Jul Soybean Meal(CBOT) / Sell Jul Soybean Oil(CBOT)

Enter on approximately 04/29 - Exit on approximately 06/24

CONT YEAR	ENTRY DATE	ENTRY PRICE	EXIT DATE	EXIT PRICE		PROFIT AMOUNT	BEST EQUITY DATE	BEST EQUITY AMOUNT	WORST EQUITY DATE	WORST EQUITY AMOUNT
2004	04/29/04	10458	06/24/04	12960		2502.00	05/11/04	2854.00	05/28/04	-1808.00
2003	04/29/03	6068	06/24/03	6104		36.00	05/02/03	502.00	05/15/03	-848.00
2002	04/29/02	5936	06/24/02	6088		152.00	05/16/02	416.00	05/28/02	-472.00
2001	04/30/01	6146	06/22/01	7406		1260.00	06/08/01	1910.00		
2000	05/01/00	6986	06/23/00	7342		356.00	05/12/00	1276.00	06/20/00	-42.00
1999	04/29/99	1544	06/24/99	3446		1902.00	06/18/99	2664.00	05/04/99	-100.00
1998	04/29/98	-1216	06/24/98	2460		3676.00	06/24/98	3676.00	05/11/98	-888.00
1997	04/29/97	12714	06/24/97	13652		938.00	05/19/97	2186.00	06/09/97	-172.00
1996	04/29/96	8546	06/24/96	9116		570.00	06/21/96	672.00	05/29/96	-920.00
1995	05/01/95	880	06/23/95	922		42.00	05/23/95	1498.00	06/21/95	-192.00
1994	04/29/94	1760	06/24/94	3312		1552.00	06/15/94	2124.00	05/16/94	-650.00
1993	04/29/93	5914	06/24/93	6316		402.00	05/07/93	586.00		
1992	04/29/92	5872	06/24/92	5674		-198.00	05/13/92	276.00	06/05/92	-720.00
1991	04/29/91	4874	06/24/91	5622		748.00	06/19/91	968.00	05/08/91	-70.00
1990	04/30/90	4718	06/22/90	2990		-1728.00	05/01/90	504.00	06/08/90	-2298.00
1989	05/01/89	8146	06/23/89	9452		1306.00	06/19/89	1746.00	05/22/89	-854.00
1988	04/29/88	6330	06/24/88	12290		5960.00	06/21/88	7974.00	05/02/88	-134.00
1987	04/29/87	6288	06/24/87	7538		1250.00	06/15/87	2786.00	05/06/87	-550.00
1986	04/29/86	4524	06/24/86	4844		320.00	06/12/86	592.00	05/23/86	-906.00
1985	04/29/85	-6288	06/24/85	-5662		626.00	05/15/85	1528.00	06/11/85	-554.00

Percentage Correct	87									
Average Profit on Winning Trades						1087.38		Winners		13
Average Loss on Trades						-963.00		Losers		2
Average Net Profit Per Trade						814.00		Total trades		15
Percentage Correct	90									
Average Profit on Winning Trades						1311.00		Winners		18
Average Loss on Trades						-963.00		Losers		2
Average Net Profit Per Trade						1083.60		Total trades		20

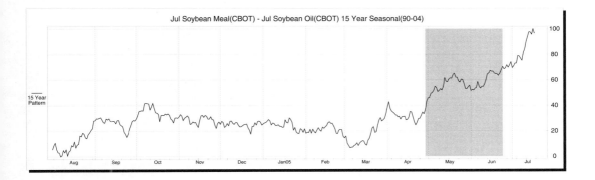

Jul Soybean Meal(CBOT) - Jul Soybean Oil(CBOT) 15 Year Seasonal(90-04)

Figure 4-48

Buy Oct Soybean Meal(CBOT) / Sell Oct Soybean Oil(CBOT)

Enter on approximately 06/08 - Exit on approximately 09/06

CONT YEAR	ENTRY DATE	ENTRY PRICE	EXIT DATE	EXIT PRICE		PROFIT AMOUNT	BEST EQUITY DATE	BEST EQUITY AMOUNT	WORST EQUITY DATE	WORST EQUITY AMOUNT
2004	06/08/04	6202	09/03/04	1628		-4574.00	06/25/04	1488.00	09/03/04	-4574.00
2003	06/09/03	4422	09/05/03	6274		1852.00	08/25/03	2306.00	07/08/03	-1274.00
2002	06/10/02	4626	09/06/02	5584		958.00	07/02/02	1430.00	08/23/02	-440.00
2001	06/08/01	6320	09/06/01	6622		302.00	06/29/01	620.00	08/08/01	-1404.00
2000	06/08/00	6852	09/06/00	7282		430.00	09/05/00	642.00	07/17/00	-1794.00
1999	06/08/99	3340	09/03/99	4608		1268.00	09/03/99	1268.00	07/09/99	-690.00
1998	06/08/98	-930	09/04/98	-1780		-850.00	06/24/98	3220.00	09/04/98	-850.00
1997	06/09/97	8240	09/05/97	10248		2008.00	09/05/97	2008.00	07/03/97	-2010.00
1996	06/10/96	7270	09/06/96	10416		3146.00	08/29/96	3304.00	06/12/96	-380.00
1995	06/08/95	2130	09/06/95	3174		1044.00	09/05/95	1140.00	07/07/95	-976.00
1994	06/08/94	2958	09/06/94	2002		-956.00	06/15/94	1066.00	09/02/94	-960.00
1993	06/08/93	5952	09/03/93	6324		372.00	07/19/93	2598.00	07/01/93	-274.00
1992	06/08/92	7034	09/04/92	7892		858.00	09/02/92	1274.00	06/10/92	-88.00
1991	06/10/91	5282	09/06/91	6222		940.00	09/04/91	1494.00	08/20/91	-432.00
1990	06/08/90	3390	09/06/90	3642		252.00	07/03/90	1170.00	08/01/90	-1164.00
1989	06/08/89	5830	09/06/89	7402		1572.00	07/14/89	2614.00		
1988	06/08/88	11048	09/06/88	11362		314.00	06/21/88	2202.00	07/20/88	-4608.00
1987	06/08/87	6742	09/04/87	6752		10.00	06/15/87	1832.00	08/03/87	-1452.00
1986	06/09/86	4024	09/05/86	7244		3220.00	09/04/86	3284.00	06/25/86	-258.00
1985	06/10/85	-3450	09/06/85	-52		3398.00	09/06/85	3398.00	06/11/85	-472.00

Percentage Correct	80								
Average Profit on Winning Trades			1119.17		Winners	12
Average Loss on Trades			-2126.67		Losers	3
Average Net Profit Per Trade			470.00		Total trades	15
Percentage Correct	85						
Average Profit on Winning Trades			1290.82		Winners	17
Average Loss on Trades			-2126.67		Losers	3
Average Net Profit Per Trade			778.20		Total trades	20

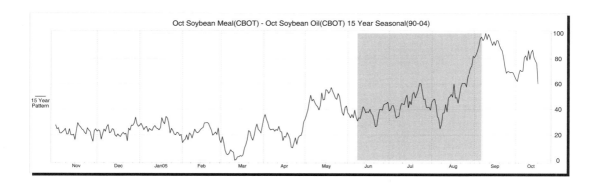

Oct Soybean Meal(CBOT) - Oct Soybean Oil(CBOT) 15 Year Seasonal(90-04)

Chapter 4: Soybean Complex

Figure 4-49

	Buy Dec Soybean Meal(CBOT) / Sell Dec Soybean Oil(CBOT)

Enter on approximately 07/01 - Exit on approximately 09/14

CONT YEAR	ENTRY DATE	ENTRY PRICE	EXIT DATE	EXIT PRICE		PROFIT AMOUNT	BEST EQUITY DATE	BEST EQUITY AMOUNT	WORST EQUITY DATE	WORST EQUITY AMOUNT
2004	07/01/04	6150	09/14/04	3142		-3008.00	07/09/04	920.00	09/03/04	-4178.00
2003	07/01/03	3410	09/12/03	5582		2172.00	08/25/03	3284.00	07/08/03	-136.00
2002	07/01/02	5734	09/13/02	5882		148.00	09/11/02	750.00	08/23/02	-1646.00
2001	07/02/01	6656	09/14/01	6892		236.00	09/13/01	378.00	08/08/01	-2028.00
2000	07/03/00	5470	09/14/00	7262		1792.00	09/05/00	1928.00	07/17/00	-574.00
1999	07/01/99	3454	09/14/99	4232		778.00	09/07/99	1748.00	07/09/99	-780.00
1998	07/01/98	480	09/14/98	-2068		-2548.00	07/17/98	754.00	09/14/98	-2548.00
1997	07/01/97	5984	09/12/97	7296		1312.00	09/05/97	2164.00	07/03/97	-552.00
1996	07/01/96	7910	09/13/96	9946		2036.00	09/11/96	2450.00	07/02/96	-126.00
1995	07/03/95	2500	09/14/95	3566		1066.00	09/05/95	1160.00	07/07/95	-908.00
1994	07/01/94	3294	09/14/94	1166		-2128.00	07/11/94	782.00	09/14/94	-2128.00
1993	07/01/93	5688	09/14/93	5816		128.00	07/19/93	2764.00		
1992	07/01/92	7150	09/14/92	7364		214.00	09/02/92	870.00	07/08/92	-168.00
1991	07/01/91	4904	09/13/91	6730		1826.00	09/13/91	1826.00	07/09/91	-202.00
1990	07/02/90	4542	09/14/90	4728		186.00	07/03/90	398.00	08/01/90	-2066.00
1989	07/03/89	6888	09/14/89	7066		178.00	07/14/89	1040.00	08/09/89	-550.00
1988	07/01/88	8648	09/14/88	11550		2902.00	09/13/88	3030.00	07/20/88	-2278.00
1987	07/01/87	5842	09/14/87	7210		1368.00	09/14/87	1368.00	08/03/87	-758.00
1986	07/01/86	3924	09/12/86	6562		2638.00	09/04/86	3024.00	07/09/86	-150.00
1985	07/01/85	-2152	09/13/85	610		2762.00	09/12/85	2932.00		

Percentage Correct	80					
Average Profit on Winning Trades				991.17	Winners	12
Average Loss on Trades				-2561.33	Losers	3
Average Net Profit Per Trade				280.67	Total trades	15
Percentage Correct	85					
Average Profit on Winning Trades				1278.94	Winners	17
Average Loss on Trades				-2561.33	Losers	3
Average Net Profit Per Trade				702.90	Total trades	20

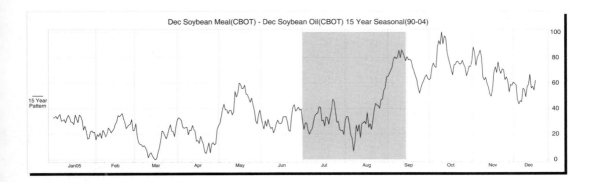

Dec Soybean Meal(CBOT) - Dec Soybean Oil(CBOT) 15 Year Seasonal(90-04)

Figure 4-50

Buy Dec Soybean Meal(CBOT) / Sell Dec Soybean Oil(CBOT)

Enter on approximately 08/07 - Exit on approximately 10/13

CONT YEAR	ENTRY DATE	ENTRY PRICE	EXIT DATE	EXIT PRICE		PROFIT AMOUNT	BEST EQUITY DATE	BEST EQUITY AMOUNT	WORST EQUITY DATE	WORST EQUITY AMOUNT
2003	08/07/03	4224	10/13/03	5684		1460.00	08/25/03	2470.00		
2002	08/07/02	4460	10/11/02	5042		582.00	09/18/02	2078.00	08/23/02	-372.00
2001	08/07/01	4720	10/12/01	7062		2342.00	10/08/01	2806.00	08/08/01	-92.00
2000	08/07/00	5168	10/13/00	7186		2018.00	09/22/00	2586.00		
1999	08/09/99	4428	10/13/99	5658		1230.00	10/13/99	1230.00	08/27/99	-710.00
1998	08/07/98	28	10/13/98	298		270.00	10/13/98	270.00	09/18/98	-2702.00
1997	08/07/97	7518	10/13/97	8666		1148.00	10/13/97	1148.00	09/30/97	-2140.00
1996	08/07/96	8020	10/11/96	9784		1764.00	09/26/96	2866.00		
1995	08/07/95	2454	10/13/95	4094		1640.00	09/21/95	1852.00	08/17/95	-180.00
1994	08/08/94	2778	10/13/94	1688		-1090.00	08/19/94	328.00	09/14/94	-1612.00
1993	08/09/93	6660	10/13/93	5638		-1022.00	08/11/93	330.00	09/28/93	-1924.00
1992	08/07/92	7104	10/13/92	6690		-414.00	09/02/92	916.00	10/13/92	-414.00
1991	08/07/91	4736	10/11/91	6056		1320.00	10/01/91	2294.00		
1990	08/07/90	3172	10/12/90	5502		2330.00	10/08/90	2624.00	08/13/90	-192.00
1989	08/07/89	6638	10/13/89	6868		230.00	09/12/89	688.00	09/27/89	-392.00
1988	08/08/88	8538	10/13/88	11388		2850.00	10/05/88	3530.00		
1987	08/07/87	5526	10/13/87	6348		822.00	09/16/87	1740.00	08/25/87	-128.00
1986	08/07/86	4994	10/13/86	6208		1214.00	09/04/86	1954.00		
1985	08/07/85	-1352	10/11/85	2438		3790.00	10/11/85	3790.00		
1984	08/07/84	1130	10/12/84	-218		-1348.00	08/10/84	472.00	10/04/84	-1570.00

Percentage Correct	80							
Average Profit on Winning Trades			1361.17		Winners	12		
Average Loss on Trades			-842.00		Losers	3		
Average Net Profit Per Trade			920.53		Total trades	15		
Percentage Correct	80							
Average Profit on Winning Trades			1563.13		Winners	16		
Average Loss on Trades			-968.50		Losers	4		
Average Net Profit Per Trade			1056.80		Total trades	20		

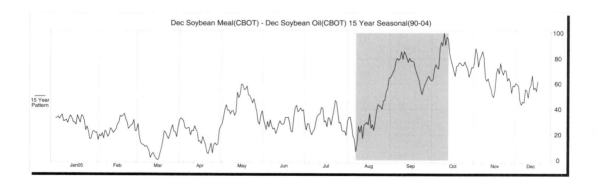

Dec Soybean Meal(CBOT) - Dec Soybean Oil(CBOT) 15 Year Seasonal(90-04)

Chapter 5: Soybeans vs Grains

Soybeans lend themselves to inter-commodity, even inter-exchange (or inter-market) spreads, against wheat and corn. Such spreads track easily because both pricing and contract size are uniform. Because they would be difficult to execute, however, few if any brokerage firms accept spread orders; and exchanges do not reduce margin requirements. Nonetheless, spreads between these related markets can mitigate risks associated with so-called fat-tail events (of low probability but disastrous result) such as overnight grain embargoes, abrupt currency adjustments, or financial crises.

Although soybeans cannot be used interchangeably with either wheat or corn, they do have common characteristics of supply and demand. All are annual crops; all have protein content; all are used in processed foods; all provide animal feed; all are exported. Soybeans and corn compete directly for acreage across their primary production belts. Soybeans and wheat compete in smaller regions but can also be double-cropped — with soybeans planted immediately after winter wheat is harvested.

Soybeans/Corn

The hearts of the Corn and Soybean Belts overlap from southern Minnesota through Iowa, Illinois, and Indiana. Most producers therein plant both, but agricultural economics — both market-oriented and government-sponsored — dictate how much of each. As the chart below illustrates, those economics have historically been in rough equilibrium when the price ratio of soybeans to corn fluctuated near the range of 2.20-2.40.

Figure 5-1: 30-year Monthly SX/CZ Price Ratio

A ratio much below that range suggested soybeans were cheap (excess supply/weak demand) relative to corn (short supply/strong demand), thereby encouraging producers to plant more acreage to corn and fewer to soybeans. Conversely, a ratio much above that range suggested soybean prices were high relative to corn, enabling soybeans to buy acreage at the expense of corn. Left to the market, the ratio itself would tend to be self-correcting, with supply/demand in each market eventually returning to an equilibrium.

Of course, the influence of that ratio on prices is secular rather than seasonal. Although corn and soybeans compete for acreage and have many similar uses, differences in their crop cycles drive seasonal trends between them. For example, corn requires a longer growing season. In the Midwestern Corn Belt, corn planted after mid May tends to begin losing yield potential. Thus, producers who grow both usually have all their corn in the ground before planting soybeans. Further, to pollinate properly, the corn crop absolutely requires moisture

---

in early to mid July; otherwise, yield suffers. The more drought-tolerant soybean plant most needs moisture when it sets pods in early August. Finally, most producers complete their soybean harvest and only then switch equipment to harvest corn.

Figure 5-2: Nov Soybeans/Dec Corn Seasonal Pattern

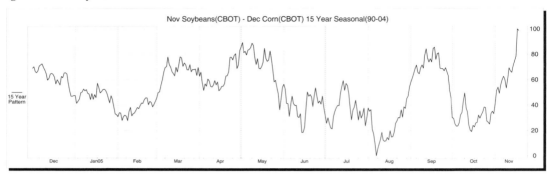

Figure 5-3: July Soybeans/July Corn Seasonal Pattern

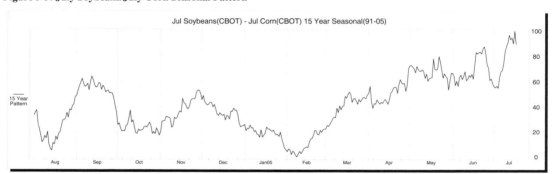

Figure 5-4: Soybeans versus Corn Strategies

Moore Research Center, Inc.	Soybeans versus Corn Spread Strategies							
Seasonal Strategy	Entry Date	Exit Date	Win Pct	Win Yrs	Loss Years	Total Years	Average Profit	Ave Pft Per Day
Buy 2 Mar Corn(CBOT) Sell Mar Soybeans(CBOT)	12/24	2/09	87 85	13 17	2 3	15 20	593 601	12 13
Buy Sep Soybeans(CBOT) Sell Sep Corn(CBOT)	2/11	5/01	80 85	12 17	3 3	15 20	1146 1232	14 15
Buy Sep Soybeans(CBOT) Sell 2 Sep Corn(CBOT)	2/11	5/01	93 95	14 19	1 1	15 20	1165 1149	15 14
Buy Jul Soybeans(CBOT) Sell Jul Corn(CBOT)	2/24	5/01	87 85	13 17	2 3	15 20	1291 1208	19 18
Buy Jul Soybeans(CBOT) Sell 2 Jul Corn(CBOT)	2/28	4/27	87 80	13 16	2 4	15 20	836 709	14 12
Buy Jul Soybeans(CBOT) Sell Jul Corn(CBOT)	4/15	5/03	87 85	13 17	2 3	15 20	709 683	37 36
Buy Sep Corn(CBOT) Sell Sep Soybeans(CBOT)	7/13	7/31	93 85	14 17	1 3	15 20	654 751	34 40

Figure 5-4 Soybeans versus Corn Strategies continued

▲▲ Moore Research Center, Inc.		**Soybeans versus Corn Spread Strategies**							
Seasonal Strategy	Entry Date	Exit Date	Win Pct	Win Yrs	Loss Years	Total Years	Average Profit	Ave Pft Per Day
Buy Nov Soybeans(CBOT)	8/13	9/12	80	12	3	15	1012	33
Sell Dec Corn(CBOT)			80	16	4	20	867	28
Buy Mar Soybeans(CBOT)	8/18	9/05	87	13	2	15	717	38
Sell 2 Mar Corn(CBOT)			90	18	2	20	646	34
Buy Dec Corn(CBOT)	9/16	10/04	93	14	1	15	574	30
Sell Nov Soybeans(CBOT)			90	18	2	20	541	28
Buy Mar Soybeans(CBOT)	10/31	12/09	93	14	1	15	638	16
Sell 2 Mar Corn(CBOT)			90	18	2	20	618	15

Such differences in timing can generate their own pressures and market dynamics. The most prominent feature of these spreads early in each calendar year is the decline into and recovery from the February Break. The strategy listed first in the table above — in which the alert reader will note spreads two (2) contracts of corn against one (1) of soybeans — quantifies how soybeans have typically suffered more pressure than corn ever since first Brazil and then Argentina became major global producers. South American soybean crops are made beginning in February and domestic US soymeal consumption declines seasonally going into summer.

But by mid February the market has usually discounted both. Attention turns to the new crop and to how far into the future old-crop supplies must stretch. Corn is planted first; all else being equal, many producers would prefer to plant corn. Thus, soybeans tend to outperform corn as planting season gets underway in order to ensure sufficient soybean acreage. The September relationships also benefit from that contract representing corn carryover. The more acreage to and the better planting conditions are for corn, the more excessive may the market eventually view old-crop supplies. The comparison of a 1:1 spread with that of a 2:1 implies that weakness in corn adds significantly to performance.

Various strategies between July contracts also serve to remind that, while corn is consumed at a more even pace throughout the year, soybeans have already undergone the heaviest consumption of the marketing year. Thus, old-crop supplies of US soybeans, measured in percent of production, are much tighter than those of corn.

Corn pollinates in mid July. Barring disastrous hot, dry weather, both corn and soybeans tend to decline at least during the last half of the month. Soybeans tend to decline harder, however, both because it is the larger contract and because the market must still discount the crop being made in early August.

By mid August, soybeans have set pods, yield is nearly determined, and speculative bullish excess cleansed from the market. Thus are conditions often created for soybeans to bounce from a pre-harvest low — which, in some years, can be lower than the harvest low itself. Soybeans stocks are low, and processors return in September from maintenance and vacation shutdowns in need of soybeans to crush going into the season of greatest soymeal demand. Further, commercial consumers begin to price their future needs at low, pre-harvest levels. Thus, soybeans have tended to outperform corn, which normally struggles at best going into harvest, from mid August into early/mid September, only after which will new soybeans become available.

Figure 5-5

Moore Research Center, Inc.				Buy 2 Mar Corn(CBOT) / Sell Mar Soybeans(CBOT)						
Enter on approximately 12/24 - Exit on approximately 02/09										
CONT YEAR	ENTRY DATE	ENTRY PRICE	EXIT DATE	EXIT PRICE	PROFIT	PROFIT AMOUNT	BEST EQUITY DATE	BEST EQUITY AMOUNT	WORST EQUITY DATE	WORST EQUITY AMOUNT
2005	12/27/04	-139.00	02/09/05	-120.75	18.25	912.50	02/07/05	1512.50		
2004	12/24/03	-293.50	02/09/04	-279.00	14.50	725.00	02/02/04	2150.00	12/26/03	-1350.00
2003	12/26/02	-76.75	02/07/03	-76.25	0.50	25.00	02/07/03	25.00	01/02/03	-1512.50
2002	12/26/01	-10.75	02/08/02	-19.50	-8.75	-437.50	01/02/02	475.00	01/14/02	-700.00
2001	12/26/00	-58.50	02/09/01	-35.75	22.75	1137.50	02/08/01	1312.50		
2000	12/27/99	-59.00	02/09/00	-58.75	0.25	12.50	01/13/00	575.00	01/28/00	-875.00
1999	12/24/98	-110.00	02/09/99	-65.50	44.50	2225.00	02/09/99	2225.00	01/05/99	-337.50
1998	12/24/97	-150.00	02/09/98	-145.75	4.25	212.50	01/16/98	2000.00	12/30/97	-112.50
1997	12/24/96	-169.75	02/07/97	-196.00	-26.25	-1312.50	12/26/96	362.50	01/21/97	-1750.00
1996	12/26/95	-16.50	02/09/96	6.00	22.50	1125.00	02/09/96	1125.00	01/17/96	-862.50
1995	12/27/94	-111.75	02/09/95	-86.75	25.00	1250.00	02/06/95	1637.50		
1994	12/27/93	-106.25	02/09/94	-87.50	18.75	937.50	01/10/94	1262.50	01/19/94	-412.50
1993	12/24/92	-142.75	02/09/93	-141.25	1.50	75.00	01/04/93	312.50	02/03/93	-287.50
1992	12/24/91	-58.00	02/07/92	-41.00	17.00	850.00	02/07/92	850.00	01/09/92	-150.00
1991	12/24/90	-111.25	02/08/91	-88.25	23.00	1150.00	01/29/91	1850.00	12/26/90	-62.50
1990	12/26/89	-105.75	02/09/90	-87.75	18.00	900.00	01/25/90	1300.00		
1989	12/27/88	-240.75	02/09/89	-216.00	24.75	1237.50	01/25/89	1600.00	01/04/89	-962.50
1988	12/24/87	-236.25	02/09/88	-202.75	33.50	1675.00	02/02/88	1787.50	01/06/88	-762.50
1987	12/24/86	-167.00	02/09/87	-184.75	-17.75	-887.50			01/29/87	-1112.50
1986	12/24/85	-53.25	02/07/86	-49.25	4.00	200.00	01/13/86	775.00	01/08/86	-212.50

Percentage Correct	87									
Average Profit on Winning Trades					16.37	818.27		Winners		13
Average Loss on Trades					-17.50	-875.00		Losers		2
Average Net Profit Per Trade					11.85	592.50		Total trades		15
Percentage Correct	85									
Average Profit on Winning Trades					17.24	861.76		Winners		17
Average Loss on Trades					-17.58	-879.17		Losers		3
Average Net Profit Per Trade					12.01	600.63		Total trades		20

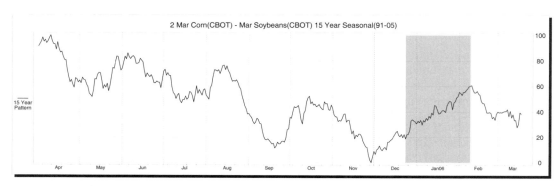

2 Mar Corn(CBOT) - Mar Soybeans(CBOT) 15 Year Seasonal(91-05)

As soybean harvest begins in earnest in last-half September, however, soybeans have regularly come under increasing harvest pressure. As they do so, corn meanders. By the end of October, soybean harvest is over and corn harvest in full swing. Soybeans normally enjoy a post-harvest recovery on strong demand from processors crushing at capacity to meet surging soymeal demand. In contrast, new-crop corn remains under pressure into December deliveries.

Figure 5-6

Buy Sep Soybeans(CBOT) / Sell Sep Corn(CBOT)

Enter on approximately 02/11 - Exit on approximately 05/01

CONT YEAR	ENTRY DATE	ENTRY PRICE	EXIT DATE	EXIT PRICE	PROFIT	PROFIT AMOUNT	BEST EQUITY DATE	BEST EQUITY AMOUNT	WORST EQUITY DATE	WORST EQUITY AMOUNT
2005	02/11/05	311.00	04/29/05	401.75	90.75	4537.50	03/15/05	5437.50		
2004	02/11/04	442.00	04/30/04	497.75	55.75	2787.50	03/23/04	6600.00	02/12/04	-325.00
2003	02/11/03	302.00	05/01/03	356.25	54.25	2712.50	05/01/03	2712.50	03/06/03	-537.50
2002	02/11/02	216.00	05/01/02	246.50	30.50	1525.00	03/28/02	2300.00		
2001	02/12/01	224.50	05/01/01	215.25	-9.25	-462.50	03/06/01	350.00	04/19/01	-1212.50
2000	02/11/00	283.75	05/01/00	320.75	37.00	1850.00	05/01/00	1850.00	02/25/00	-325.00
1999	02/11/99	274.50	04/30/99	268.50	-6.00	-300.00			02/25/99	-1350.00
1998	02/11/98	392.75	05/01/98	367.25	-25.50	-1275.00			04/09/98	-1937.50
1997	02/11/97	449.00	05/01/97	482.50	33.50	1675.00	03/10/97	2737.50		
1996	02/12/96	402.75	05/01/96	421.75	19.00	950.00	04/22/96	1525.00	03/19/96	-400.00
1995	02/13/95	324.50	05/01/95	335.75	11.25	562.50	03/20/95	1100.00		
1994	02/11/94	375.00	04/29/94	382.75	7.75	387.50	03/23/94	962.50	04/04/94	-625.00
1993	02/11/93	344.00	04/30/93	356.00	12.00	600.00	04/07/93	1037.50	02/22/93	-25.00
1992	02/11/92	315.50	05/01/92	345.25	29.75	1487.50	03/19/92	1562.50		
1991	02/11/91	347.00	05/01/91	350.00	3.00	150.00	03/08/91	825.00	03/25/91	-675.00
1990	02/12/90	342.50	05/01/90	372.25	29.75	1487.50	04/27/90	1925.00	02/26/90	-450.00
1989	02/13/89	449.50	05/01/89	463.25	13.75	687.50	03/22/89	2525.00		
1988	02/11/88	422.50	04/29/88	487.50	65.00	3250.00	04/29/88	3250.00	03/10/88	-712.50
1987	02/11/87	314.25	05/01/87	347.00	32.75	1637.50	05/01/87	1637.50	02/23/87	-350.00
1986	02/11/86	307.75	05/01/86	315.50	7.75	387.50	04/30/86	912.50	02/25/86	-400.00
Percentage Correct		80								
Average Profit on Winning Trades					32.04	1602.08		Winners		12
Average Loss on Trades					-13.58	-679.17		Losers		3
Average Net Profit Per Trade					22.92	1145.83		Total trades		15
Percentage Correct		85								
Average Profit on Winning Trades					31.38	1569.12		Winners		17
Average Loss on Trades					-13.58	-679.17		Losers		3
Average Net Profit Per Trade					24.64	1231.88		Total trades		20

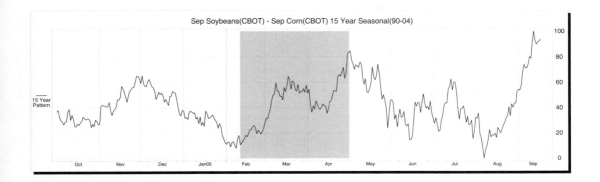

Sep Soybeans(CBOT) - Sep Corn(CBOT) 15 Year Seasonal(90-04)

15 Year Pattern

Chapter 5: Soybeans vs Grains

181

Figure 5-7

Buy Sep Soybeans(CBOT) / Sell 2 Sep Corn(CBOT)

Enter on approximately 02/11 - Exit on approximately 05/01

CONT YEAR	ENTRY DATE	ENTRY PRICE	EXIT DATE	EXIT PRICE	PROFIT	PROFIT AMOUNT	BEST EQUITY DATE	BEST EQUITY AMOUNT	WORST EQUITY DATE	WORST EQUITY AMOUNT
2005	02/11/05	90.50	04/29/05	180.25	89.75	4487.50	04/21/05	4662.50		
2004	02/11/04	155.00	04/30/04	179.00	24.00	1200.00	03/25/04	5475.00	02/12/04	-200.00
2003	02/11/03	56.50	05/01/03	125.00	68.50	3425.00	05/01/03	3425.00	03/06/03	-375.00
2002	02/11/02	-7.50	05/01/02	36.50	44.00	2200.00	04/24/02	2987.50		
2001	02/12/01	-9.50	05/01/01	-0.25	9.25	462.50	04/30/01	475.00	04/16/01	-812.50
2000	02/11/00	40.00	05/01/00	68.75	28.75	1437.50	04/24/00	1625.00	03/10/00	-225.00
1999	02/11/99	39.75	04/30/99	45.25	5.50	275.00	04/30/99	275.00	03/17/99	-1187.50
1998	02/11/98	109.50	05/01/98	110.00	0.50	25.00	04/27/98	87.50	03/13/98	-1675.00
1997	02/11/97	182.25	05/01/97	201.50	19.25	962.50	03/10/97	1387.50	03/24/97	-925.00
1996	02/12/96	84.25	05/01/96	47.50	-36.75	-1837.50	02/14/96	87.50	04/15/96	-2525.00
1995	02/13/95	72.25	05/01/95	73.00	0.75	37.50	03/20/95	837.50	04/26/95	-362.50
1994	02/11/94	86.00	04/29/94	116.50	30.50	1525.00	04/25/94	2025.00		
1993	02/11/93	110.00	04/30/93	119.50	9.50	475.00	04/27/93	1075.00		
1992	02/11/92	46.00	05/01/92	93.00	47.00	2350.00	05/01/92	2350.00		
1991	02/11/91	90.75	05/01/91	99.75	9.00	450.00	05/01/91	450.00	03/14/91	-887.50
1990	02/12/90	93.25	05/01/90	96.00	2.75	137.50	03/09/90	712.50	04/19/90	-950.00
1989	02/13/89	180.00	05/01/89	196.50	16.50	825.00	03/22/89	2275.00		
1988	02/11/88	207.00	04/29/88	269.75	62.75	3137.50	04/29/88	3137.50	03/10/88	-450.00
1987	02/11/87	152.00	05/01/87	162.00	10.00	500.00	04/09/87	725.00	03/24/87	-587.50
1986	02/11/86	88.50	05/01/86	106.50	18.00	900.00	04/25/86	1350.00	02/12/86	-250.00

Percentage Correct	93									
Average Profit on Winning Trades					27.59	1379.46		Winners		14
Average Loss on Trades					-36.75	-1837.50		Losers		1
Average Net Profit Per Trade					23.30	1165.00		Total trades		15
Percentage Correct	95									
Average Profit on Winning Trades					26.12	1305.92		Winners		19
Average Loss on Trades					-36.75	-1837.50		Losers		1
Average Net Profit Per Trade					22.98	1148.75		Total trades		20

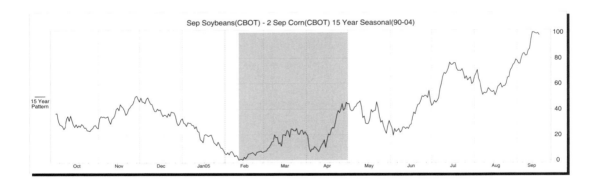

Sep Soybeans(CBOT) - 2 Sep Corn(CBOT) 15 Year Seasonal(90-04)

Figure 5-8

Buy Jul Soybeans(CBOT) / Sell Jul Corn(CBOT)

Enter on approximately 02/24 - Exit on approximately 05/01

CONT YEAR	ENTRY DATE	ENTRY PRICE	EXIT DATE	EXIT PRICE	PROFIT	PROFIT AMOUNT	BEST EQUITY DATE	BEST EQUITY AMOUNT	WORST EQUITY DATE	WORST EQUITY AMOUNT
2005	02/24/05	355.75	04/29/05	412.75	57.00	2850.00	03/15/05	4687.50		
2004	02/24/04	607.25	04/30/04	691.50	84.25	4212.50	03/22/04	6000.00	02/26/04	-125.00
2003	02/24/03	332.00	05/01/03	400.00	68.00	3400.00	05/01/03	3400.00	03/06/03	-700.00
2002	02/25/02	230.25	05/01/02	261.25	31.00	1550.00	04/24/02	2475.00		
2001	02/26/01	227.50	05/01/01	229.75	2.25	112.50	03/06/01	787.50	04/17/01	-525.00
2000	02/24/00	289.75	05/01/00	323.75	34.00	1700.00	05/01/00	1700.00	03/02/00	-300.00
1999	02/24/99	251.00	04/30/99	267.75	16.75	837.50	04/14/99	1212.50	02/25/99	-75.00
1998	02/24/98	383.25	05/01/98	390.75	7.50	375.00	04/27/98	512.50	04/13/98	-425.00
1997	02/24/97	488.25	05/01/97	580.25	92.00	4600.00	04/30/97	5275.00		
1996	02/26/96	380.25	05/01/96	351.25	-29.00	-1450.00			04/29/96	-2675.00
1995	02/24/95	330.50	05/01/95	331.00	0.50	25.00	03/20/95	725.00	04/27/95	-525.00
1994	02/24/94	396.25	04/29/94	404.50	8.25	412.50	03/23/94	550.00	04/05/94	-1012.50
1993	02/24/93	351.50	04/30/93	358.75	7.25	362.50	04/26/93	750.00		
1992	02/24/92	322.75	05/01/92	337.00	14.25	712.50	05/01/92	712.50	04/07/92	-387.50
1991	02/25/91	347.00	05/01/91	340.25	-6.75	-337.50	03/08/91	537.50	03/25/91	-1250.00
1990	02/26/90	328.50	05/01/90	358.75	30.25	1512.50	04/27/90	1987.50		
1989	02/24/89	493.00	05/01/89	469.75	-23.25	-1162.50	03/22/89	1250.00	04/07/89	-1925.00
1988	02/24/88	433.00	04/29/88	487.25	54.25	2712.50	04/29/88	2712.50	03/10/88	-1112.50
1987	02/24/87	324.50	05/01/87	352.00	27.50	1375.00	04/30/87	1412.50	03/23/87	-150.00
1986	02/24/86	299.75	05/01/86	306.75	7.00	350.00	04/30/86	925.00	04/04/86	-287.50

Percentage Correct		87								
Average Profit on Winning Trades					32.54	1626.92		Winners		13
Average Loss on Trades					-17.88	-893.75		Losers		2
Average Net Profit Per Trade					25.82	1290.83		Total trades		15
Percentage Correct		85								
Average Profit on Winning Trades					31.88	1594.12		Winners		17
Average Loss on Trades					-19.67	-983.33		Losers		3
Average Net Profit Per Trade					24.15	1207.50		Total trades		20

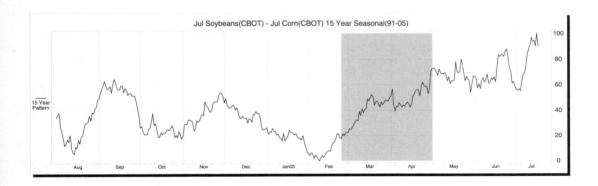

Jul Soybeans(CBOT) - Jul Corn(CBOT) 15 Year Seasonal(91-05)

15 Year Pattern

Figure 5-9

	Moore Research Center, Inc.		**Buy Jul Soybeans(CBOT) / Sell 2 Jul Corn(CBOT)**							

Enter on approximately 02/28 - Exit on approximately 04/27

CONT YEAR	ENTRY DATE	ENTRY PRICE	EXIT DATE	EXIT PRICE	PROFIT	PROFIT AMOUNT	BEST EQUITY DATE	BEST EQUITY AMOUNT	WORST EQUITY DATE	WORST EQUITY AMOUNT
2005	02/28/05	165.50	04/27/05	199.75	34.25	1712.50	03/15/05	2437.50	03/01/05	-75.00
2004	03/01/04	332.50	04/27/04	363.50	31.00	1550.00	03/23/04	3587.50	04/12/04	-1225.00
2003	02/28/03	103.25	04/25/03	133.50	30.25	1512.50	04/17/03	1800.00	03/06/03	-1375.00
2002	02/28/02	16.75	04/26/02	63.50	46.75	2337.50	04/24/02	2975.00		
2001	02/28/01	1.75	04/27/01	19.25	17.50	875.00	04/24/01	1050.00	04/16/01	-225.00
2000	02/28/00	57.00	04/27/00	76.50	19.50	975.00	04/24/00	1325.00	03/15/00	-512.50
1999	03/01/99	36.75	04/27/99	48.25	11.50	575.00	04/14/99	762.50	03/12/99	-675.00
1998	03/02/98	99.25	04/27/98	138.75	39.50	1975.00	04/27/98	1975.00	03/12/98	-250.00
1997	02/28/97	204.00	04/25/97	278.50	74.50	3725.00	04/25/97	3725.00		
1996	02/28/96	-5.50	04/26/96	-137.25	-131.75	-6587.50			04/26/96	-6587.50
1995	02/28/95	78.00	04/27/95	64.75	-13.25	-662.50	03/20/95	712.50	04/27/95	-662.50
1994	02/28/94	93.75	04/26/94	139.50	45.75	2287.50	04/25/94	2537.50	03/07/94	-175.00
1993	03/01/93	130.50	04/27/93	138.50	8.00	400.00	04/27/93	400.00	04/20/93	-612.50
1992	02/28/92	39.75	04/27/92	76.75	37.00	1850.00	04/27/92	1850.00	03/03/92	-137.50
1991	02/28/91	83.00	04/26/91	83.25	0.25	12.50	03/08/91	487.50	03/25/91	-1012.50
1990	02/28/90	77.00	04/27/90	85.50	8.50	425.00	03/09/90	1312.50	04/19/90	-1012.50
1989	02/28/89	217.50	04/27/89	193.50	-24.00	-1200.00	03/22/89	850.00	04/07/89	-1525.00
1988	03/01/88	222.25	04/27/88	268.00	45.75	2287.50	04/26/88	2287.50	03/09/88	-1050.00
1987	03/02/87	165.25	04/27/87	162.50	-2.75	-137.50	04/07/87	750.00	03/24/87	-450.00
1986	02/28/86	81.75	04/25/86	87.25	5.50	275.00	03/04/86	350.00	04/04/86	-762.50

Percentage Correct	87									
Average Profit on Winning Trades					30.44	1522.12		Winners		13
Average Loss on Trades					-72.50	-3625.00		Losers		2
Average Net Profit Per Trade					16.72	835.83		Total trades		15
Percentage Correct	80									
Average Profit on Winning Trades					28.47	1423.44		Winners		16
Average Loss on Trades					-42.94	-2146.88		Losers		4
Average Net Profit Per Trade					14.19	709.38		Total trades		20

HYPOTHETICAL PERFORMANCE RESULTS HAVE MANY INHERENT LIMITATIONS, SOME OF WHICH ARE DESCRIBED BELOW. NO REPRESENTATION IS BEING MADE THAT ANY ACCOUNT WILL OR IS LIKELY TO ACHIEVE PROFITS OR LOSSES SIMILAR TO THOSE SHOWN. IN FACT, THERE ARE FREQUENTLY SHARP DIFFERENCES BETWEEN HYPOTHETICAL PERFORMANCE RESULTS AND THE ACTUAL RESULTS SUBSEQUENTLY ACHIEVED BY ANY PARTICULAR TRADING PROGRAM. ONE OF THE LIMITATIONS OF HYPOTHETICAL PERFORMANCE RESULTS IS THAT THEY ARE GENERALLY PREPARED WITH THE BENEFIT OF HINDSIGHT. IN ADDITION, HYPOTHETICAL TRADING DOES NOT INVOLVE FINANCIAL RISK, AND NO HYPOTHETICAL TRADING RECORD CAN COMPLETELY ACCOUNT FOR THE IMPACT OF FINANCIAL RISK IN ACTUAL TRADING. FOR EXAMPLE, THE ABILITY TO WITHSTAND LOSSES OR ADHERE TO A PARTICULAR TRADING PROGRAM IN SPITE OF TRADING LOSSES ARE MATERIAL POINTS WHICH CAN ALSO ADVERSELY AFFECT ACTUAL TRADING RESULTS. THERE ARE NUMEROUS OTHER FACTORS RELATED TO THE MARKETS IN GENERAL OR TO THE IMPLEMENTATION OF ANY SPECIFIC TRADING PROGRAM WHICH CANNOT BE FULLY ACCOUNTED FOR IN THE PREPARATION OF HYPOTHETICAL PERFORMANCE RESULTS AND ALL OF WHICH CAN ADVERSELY AFFECT ACTUAL TRADING RESULTS. RESULTS NOT ADJUSTED FOR COMMISSION AND SLIPPAGE.

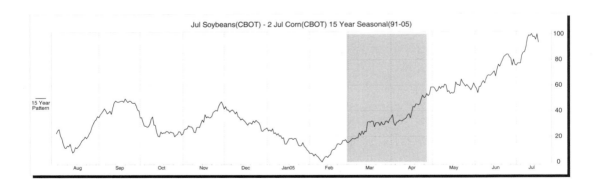

Jul Soybeans(CBOT) - 2 Jul Corn(CBOT) 15 Year Seasonal(91-05)

Figure 5-10

Buy Jul Soybeans(CBOT) / Sell Jul Corn(CBOT)

Enter on approximately 04/15 - Exit on approximately 05/03

CONT YEAR	ENTRY DATE	ENTRY PRICE	EXIT DATE	EXIT PRICE	PROFIT	PROFIT AMOUNT	BEST EQUITY DATE	BEST EQUITY AMOUNT	WORST EQUITY DATE	WORST EQUITY AMOUNT
2005	04/15/05	407.75	05/03/05	420.50	12.75	637.50	04/21/05	900.00	04/18/05	-200.00
2004	04/15/04	648.25	05/03/04	697.00	48.75	2437.50	05/03/04	2437.50	04/21/04	-1187.50
2003	04/15/03	367.50	05/02/03	398.50	31.00	1550.00	05/01/03	1625.00	04/23/03	-50.00
2002	04/15/02	256.50	05/03/02	260.25	3.75	187.50	04/24/02	1162.50		
2001	04/16/01	217.50	05/03/01	230.00	12.50	625.00	05/02/01	712.50	04/17/01	-25.00
2000	04/17/00	311.50	05/03/00	321.25	9.75	487.50	05/01/00	612.50	04/28/00	-212.50
1999	04/15/99	273.50	05/03/99	268.75	-4.75	-237.50	04/20/99	75.00	04/29/99	-387.50
1998	04/15/98	381.75	05/01/98	390.75	9.00	450.00	04/27/98	587.50		
1997	04/15/97	537.00	05/02/97	592.75	55.75	2787.50	04/30/97	2837.50		
1996	04/15/96	356.00	05/03/96	363.50	7.50	375.00	04/18/96	1137.50	04/29/96	-1462.50
1995	04/17/95	334.75	05/03/95	326.25	-8.50	-425.00			04/27/95	-737.50
1994	04/15/94	383.00	05/03/94	398.25	15.25	762.50	04/25/94	1175.00		
1993	04/15/93	356.50	05/03/93	360.75	4.25	212.50	04/26/93	500.00	04/20/93	-37.50
1992	04/15/92	324.25	05/01/92	337.00	12.75	637.50	05/01/92	637.50		
1991	04/15/91	334.00	05/03/91	337.00	3.00	150.00	04/24/91	500.00	04/29/91	-37.50
1990	04/16/90	331.75	05/03/90	357.00	25.25	1262.50	04/27/90	1825.00		
1989	04/17/89	478.00	05/03/89	476.75	-1.25	-62.50	04/21/89	575.00	04/28/89	-950.00
1988	04/15/88	460.50	05/03/88	484.50	24.00	1200.00	04/29/88	1337.50	04/21/88	-75.00
1987	04/15/87	344.50	05/01/87	352.00	7.50	375.00	04/30/87	412.50	04/21/87	-225.00
1986	04/15/86	304.25	05/02/86	309.25	5.00	250.00	04/30/86	700.00	04/16/86	-87.50

Percentage Correct		87								
Average Profit on Winning Trades					17.38	869.23		Winners		13
Average Loss on Trades					-6.63	-331.25		Losers		2
Average Net Profit Per Trade					14.18	709.17		Total trades		15
Percentage Correct		85								
Average Profit on Winning Trades					16.93	846.32		Winners		17
Average Loss on Trades					-4.83	-241.67		Losers		3
Average Net Profit Per Trade					13.66	683.13		Total trades		20

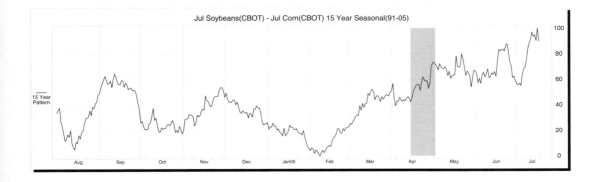

Jul Soybeans(CBOT) - Jul Corn(CBOT) 15 Year Seasonal(91-05)

Chapter 5: Soybeans vs Grains

185

Figure 5-11

Buy Sep Corn(CBOT) / Sell Sep Soybeans(CBOT)

Moore Research Center, Inc.

Enter on approximately 07/13 - Exit on approximately 07/31

CONT YEAR	ENTRY DATE	ENTRY PRICE	EXIT DATE	EXIT PRICE	PROFIT	PROFIT AMOUNT	BEST EQUITY DATE	BEST EQUITY AMOUNT	WORST EQUITY DATE	WORST EQUITY AMOUNT
2005	07/13/05	-472.00	07/29/05	-440.50	31.50	1575.00	07/19/05	1750.00		
2004	07/13/04	-411.75	07/30/04	-357.25	54.50	2725.00	07/30/04	2725.00	07/14/04	-1162.50
2003	07/14/03	-343.50	07/31/03	-313.25	30.25	1512.50	07/31/03	1512.50		
2002	07/15/02	-320.25	07/31/02	-306.75	13.50	675.00	07/29/02	1587.50	07/22/02	-212.50
2001	07/13/01	-299.75	07/31/01	-293.50	6.25	312.50	07/20/01	1025.00	07/17/01	-25.00
2000	07/13/00	-269.75	07/31/00	-264.25	5.50	275.00	07/31/00	275.00	07/21/00	-162.50
1999	07/13/99	-232.25	07/30/99	-227.75	4.50	225.00	07/16/99	300.00	07/23/99	-1587.50
1998	07/13/98	-369.00	07/31/98	-347.00	22.00	1100.00	07/24/98	1175.00	07/17/98	-400.00
1997	07/14/97	-425.50	07/31/97	-419.50	6.00	300.00	07/17/97	1412.50		
1996	07/15/96	-405.75	07/31/96	-392.75	13.00	650.00	07/30/96	937.50		
1995	07/13/95	-334.50	07/31/95	-324.25	10.25	512.50	07/31/95	512.50	07/17/95	-1037.50
1994	07/13/94	-370.00	07/29/94	-356.50	13.50	675.00	07/21/94	950.00		
1993	07/13/93	-463.25	07/30/93	-450.75	12.50	625.00	07/28/93	725.00	07/19/93	-1537.50
1992	07/13/92	-339.50	07/31/92	-335.25	4.25	212.50	07/23/92	462.50	07/29/92	-62.50
1991	07/15/91	-300.75	07/31/91	-332.00	-31.25	-1562.50	07/18/91	575.00	07/31/91	-1562.50
1990	07/13/90	-348.75	07/31/90	-339.00	9.75	487.50	07/27/90	1100.00		
1989	07/13/89	-407.00	07/31/89	-365.50	41.50	2075.00	07/31/89	2075.00	07/14/89	-512.50
1988	07/13/88	-585.25	07/29/88	-503.50	81.75	4087.50	07/26/88	5637.50	07/15/88	-2912.50
1987	07/13/87	-349.75	07/31/87	-361.00	-11.25	-562.50	07/17/87	387.50	07/28/87	-912.50
1986	07/14/86	-317.50	07/31/86	-335.00	-17.50	-875.00			07/21/86	-1362.50

Percentage Correct	93								
Average Profit on Winning Trades				16.25	812.50		Winners		14
Average Loss on Trades				-31.25	-1562.50		Losers		1
Average Net Profit Per Trade				13.08	654.17		Total trades		15
Percentage Correct	85								
Average Profit on Winning Trades				21.21	1060.29		Winners		17
Average Loss on Trades				-20.00	-1000.00		Losers		3
Average Net Profit Per Trade				15.03	751.25		Total trades		20

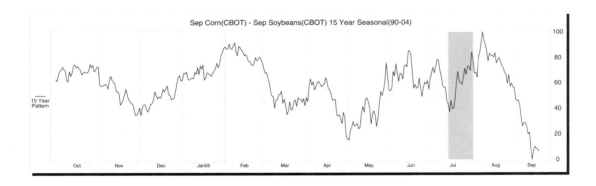

Sep Corn(CBOT) - Sep Soybeans(CBOT) 15 Year Seasonal(90-04)

15 Year Pattern

Figure 5-12

							BEST EQUITY DATE	BEST EQUITY AMOUNT	WORST EQUITY DATE	WORST EQUITY AMOUNT

Buy Nov Soybeans(CBOT) / Sell Dec Corn(CBOT)

Enter on approximately 08/13 - Exit on approximately 09/12

CONT YEAR	ENTRY DATE	ENTRY PRICE	EXIT DATE	EXIT PRICE	PROFIT	PROFIT AMOUNT	BEST EQUITY DATE	BEST EQUITY AMOUNT	WORST EQUITY DATE	WORST EQUITY AMOUNT
2004	08/13/04	352.50	09/10/04	349.75	-2.75	-137.50	09/01/04	2100.00	08/16/04	-837.50
2003	08/13/03	314.25	09/12/03	395.00	80.75	4037.50	09/12/03	4037.50		
2002	08/13/02	282.50	09/12/02	295.00	12.50	625.00	09/11/02	687.50	08/20/02	-1012.50
2001	08/13/01	281.00	09/10/01	243.50	-37.50	-1875.00	08/15/01	12.50	09/10/01	-1875.00
2000	08/14/00	277.00	09/12/00	311.50	34.50	1725.00	09/05/00	1887.50		
1999	08/13/99	231.25	09/10/99	298.00	66.75	3337.50	09/10/99	3337.50		
1998	08/13/98	313.50	09/11/98	321.25	7.75	387.50	08/19/98	487.50	09/09/98	-362.50
1997	08/13/97	349.00	09/12/97	367.00	18.00	900.00	09/09/97	1575.00	08/25/97	-287.50
1996	08/13/96	432.00	09/12/96	484.50	52.50	2625.00	09/12/96	2625.00	08/19/96	-112.50
1995	08/14/95	321.50	09/12/95	328.75	7.25	362.50	09/08/95	787.50	08/25/95	-162.50
1994	08/15/94	337.75	09/12/94	353.50	15.75	787.50	09/06/94	912.50		
1993	08/13/93	409.75	09/10/93	385.25	-24.50	-1225.00	08/30/93	1200.00	09/10/93	-1225.00
1992	08/13/92	325.50	09/11/92	331.00	5.50	275.00	09/08/92	512.50	08/19/92	-300.00
1991	08/13/91	303.25	09/12/91	341.50	38.25	1912.50	09/12/91	1912.50	08/19/91	-137.50
1990	08/13/90	378.25	09/12/90	407.00	28.75	1437.50	09/12/90	1437.50		
1989	08/14/89	339.25	09/12/89	350.50	11.25	562.50	08/22/89	837.50	08/16/89	-300.00
1988	08/15/88	581.00	09/12/88	583.00	2.00	100.00	09/08/88	1125.00	08/23/88	-2325.00
1987	08/13/87	333.50	09/11/87	354.75	21.25	1062.50	09/11/87	1062.50	08/14/87	-37.50
1986	08/13/86	300.25	09/12/86	314.25	14.00	700.00	09/04/86	725.00	08/20/86	-25.00
1985	08/13/85	294.75	09/12/85	289.50	-5.25	-262.50	08/15/85	112.50	08/26/85	-500.00

Percentage Correct	80									
Average Profit on Winning Trades					30.69	1534.38		Winners		12
Average Loss on Trades					-21.58	-1079.17		Losers		3
Average Net Profit Per Trade					20.23	1011.67		Total trades		15
Percentage Correct	80									
Average Profit on Winning Trades					26.05	1302.34		Winners		16
Average Loss on Trades					-17.50	-875.00		Losers		4
Average Net Profit Per Trade					17.34	866.88		Total trades		20

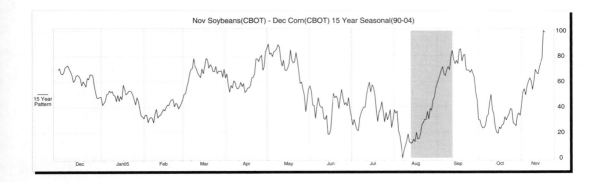

Nov Soybeans(CBOT) - Dec Corn(CBOT) 15 Year Seasonal(90-04)

Figure 5-13

Buy Mar Soybeans(CBOT) / Sell 2 Mar Corn(CBOT)

Enter on approximately 08/18 - Exit on approximately 09/05

CONT YEAR	ENTRY DATE	ENTRY PRICE	EXIT DATE	EXIT PRICE	PROFIT	PROFIT AMOUNT	BEST EQUITY DATE	BEST EQUITY AMOUNT	WORST EQUITY DATE	WORST EQUITY AMOUNT
2005	08/18/04	115.00	09/03/04	148.00	33.00	1650.00	09/02/04	1912.50	08/20/04	-850.00
2004	08/18/03	87.00	09/05/03	87.50	0.50	25.00	08/21/03	650.00	09/03/03	-412.50
2003	08/19/02	-15.50	09/05/02	-12.50	3.00	150.00	08/30/02	762.50	08/26/02	-137.50
2002	08/20/01	24.00	09/05/01	8.25	-15.75	-787.50	08/21/01	50.00	08/23/01	-862.50
2001	08/18/00	84.00	09/05/00	111.50	27.50	1375.00	09/05/00	1375.00		
2000	08/18/99	10.00	09/03/99	46.25	36.25	1812.50	09/03/99	1812.50		
1999	08/18/98	96.75	09/04/98	98.25	1.50	75.00	09/02/98	650.00	08/21/98	-250.00
1998	08/18/97	78.75	09/05/97	102.75	24.00	1200.00	09/05/97	1200.00	08/25/97	-912.50
1997	08/19/96	85.75	09/05/96	123.00	37.25	1862.50	09/05/96	1862.50		
1996	08/18/95	52.25	09/05/95	42.75	-9.50	-475.00			08/25/95	-837.50
1995	08/18/94	121.00	09/02/94	126.00	5.00	250.00	08/25/94	337.50	08/22/94	-75.00
1994	08/18/93	165.75	09/03/93	183.75	18.00	900.00	08/30/93	1025.00		
1993	08/18/92	95.50	09/04/92	108.75	13.25	662.50	09/04/92	662.50		
1992	08/19/91	68.00	09/05/91	88.00	20.00	1000.00	09/04/91	1212.50		
1991	08/20/90	143.00	09/05/90	164.00	21.00	1050.00	09/04/90	1050.00	08/21/90	-12.50
1990	08/18/89	110.25	09/05/89	115.00	4.75	237.50	08/24/89	662.50		
1989	08/18/88	284.00	09/02/88	287.00	3.00	150.00	09/02/88	150.00	08/23/88	-2025.00
1988	08/18/87	162.00	09/04/87	172.50	10.50	525.00	09/04/87	525.00	08/19/87	-112.50
1987	08/18/86	131.50	09/05/86	145.25	13.75	687.50	09/05/86	687.50	08/20/86	-275.00
1986	08/19/85	64.50	09/05/85	75.75	11.25	562.50	09/04/85	737.50	08/23/85	-25.00

Percentage Correct		87								
Average Profit on Winning Trades					18.48	924.04		Winners		13
Average Loss on Trades					-12.63	-631.25		Losers		2
Average Net Profit Per Trade					14.33	716.67		Total trades		15
Percentage Correct		90								
Average Profit on Winning Trades					15.75	787.50		Winners		18
Average Loss on Trades					-12.63	-631.25		Losers		2
Average Net Profit Per Trade					12.91	645.63		Total trades		20

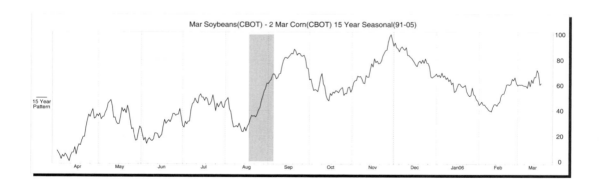

Mar Soybeans(CBOT) - 2 Mar Corn(CBOT) 15 Year Seasonal(91-05)

15 Year Pattern

Chapter 5: Soybeans vs Grains

Figure 5-14

Moore Research Center, Inc.

Buy Dec Corn(CBOT) / Sell Nov Soybeans(CBOT)

Enter on approximately 09/16 - Exit on approximately 10/04

CONT YEAR	ENTRY DATE	ENTRY PRICE	EXIT DATE	EXIT PRICE	PROFIT	PROFIT AMOUNT	BEST EQUITY DATE	BEST EQUITY AMOUNT	WORST EQUITY DATE	WORST EQUITY AMOUNT
2004	09/16/04	-341.00	10/04/04	-322.50	18.50	925.00	09/24/04	1137.50		
2003	09/16/03	-386.50	10/03/03	-455.00	-68.50	-3425.00			10/02/03	-4512.50
2002	09/16/02	-294.50	10/04/02	-281.75	12.75	637.50	10/02/02	700.00	09/26/02	-525.00
2001	09/17/01	-258.25	10/04/01	-239.50	18.75	937.50	09/28/01	1075.00		
2000	09/18/00	-299.00	10/04/00	-282.00	17.00	850.00	10/04/00	850.00	09/22/00	-150.00
1999	09/16/99	-280.25	10/04/99	-279.00	1.25	62.50	09/23/99	525.00	09/30/99	-137.50
1998	09/16/98	-317.25	10/02/98	-309.25	8.00	400.00	10/02/98	400.00	09/22/98	-300.00
1997	09/16/97	-383.25	10/03/97	-374.75	8.50	425.00	09/30/97	975.00		
1996	09/16/96	-478.50	10/04/96	-437.75	40.75	2037.50	10/04/96	2037.50	09/23/96	-350.00
1995	09/18/95	-347.25	10/04/95	-329.00	18.25	912.50	10/02/95	1112.50	09/21/95	-275.00
1994	09/16/94	-335.50	10/04/94	-318.50	17.00	850.00	10/04/94	850.00	09/27/94	-150.00
1993	09/16/93	-391.00	10/04/93	-368.50	22.50	1125.00	10/04/93	1125.00	09/23/93	-475.00
1992	09/16/92	-334.00	10/02/92	-316.00	18.00	900.00	10/02/92	900.00		
1991	09/16/91	-353.50	10/04/91	-328.00	25.50	1275.00	10/03/91	1362.50	09/18/91	-350.00
1990	09/17/90	-401.00	10/04/90	-387.00	14.00	700.00	10/02/90	1000.00	09/18/90	-312.50
1989	09/18/89	-340.50	10/04/89	-337.50	3.00	150.00	09/29/89	275.00	09/21/89	-537.50
1988	09/16/88	-569.00	10/04/88	-534.50	34.50	1725.00	09/29/88	2375.00		
1987	09/16/87	-354.75	10/02/87	-356.25	-1.50	-75.00	09/28/87	412.50	10/01/87	-275.00
1986	09/16/86	-312.50	10/03/86	-312.25	0.25	12.50	09/26/86	150.00	09/19/86	-462.50
1985	09/16/85	-290.75	10/04/85	-282.75	8.00	400.00	10/02/85	412.50	09/23/85	-537.50
Percentage Correct	93									
Average Profit on Winning Trades					17.20	859.82		Winners		14
Average Loss on Trades					-68.50	-3425.00		Losers		1
Average Net Profit Per Trade					11.48	574.17		Total trades		15
Percentage Correct	90									
Average Profit on Winning Trades					15.92	795.83		Winners		18
Average Loss on Trades					-35.00	-1750.00		Losers		2
Average Net Profit Per Trade					10.83	541.25		Total trades		20

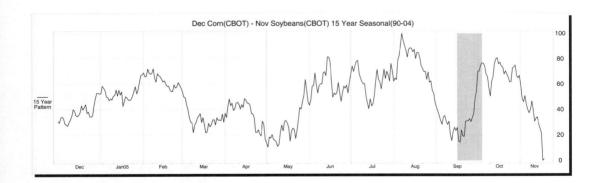

Dec Corn(CBOT) - Nov Soybeans(CBOT) 15 Year Seasonal(90-04)

Figure 5-15

Buy Mar Soybeans(CBOT) / Sell 2 Mar Corn(CBOT)

Enter on approximately 10/31 - Exit on approximately 12/09

CONT YEAR	ENTRY DATE	ENTRY PRICE	EXIT DATE	EXIT PRICE	PROFIT	PROFIT AMOUNT	BEST EQUITY DATE	BEST EQUITY AMOUNT	WORST EQUITY DATE	WORST EQUITY AMOUNT
2005	11/01/04	105.50	12/09/04	120.50	15.00	750.00	11/23/04	2125.00	11/05/04	-850.00
2004	10/31/03	279.00	12/09/03	288.00	9.00	450.00	11/03/03	812.50	11/26/03	-1487.50
2003	10/31/02	58.25	12/09/02	85.50	27.25	1362.50	12/02/02	1700.00		
2002	10/31/01	5.75	12/07/01	10.25	4.50	225.00	11/16/01	575.00	12/04/01	-25.00
2001	10/31/00	43.75	12/08/00	81.50	37.75	1887.50	12/08/00	1887.50	11/10/00	-537.50
2000	11/01/99	67.25	12/09/99	72.25	5.00	250.00	11/30/99	750.00	11/10/99	-437.50
1999	11/02/98	115.50	12/09/98	130.25	14.75	737.50	12/04/98	1462.50	11/03/98	-137.50
1998	10/31/97	123.25	12/09/97	146.00	22.75	1137.50	11/13/97	2325.00		
1997	10/31/96	128.50	12/09/96	154.75	26.25	1312.50	12/02/96	1937.50		
1996	10/31/95	17.25	12/08/95	29.00	11.75	587.50	12/05/95	612.50	11/02/95	-237.50
1995	10/31/94	110.50	12/09/94	112.50	2.00	100.00	11/28/94	1300.00		
1994	11/01/93	98.25	12/09/93	100.75	2.50	125.00	11/15/93	1012.50		
1993	11/02/92	119.75	12/09/92	133.00	13.25	662.50	12/09/92	662.50	11/05/92	-75.00
1992	10/31/91	56.50	12/09/91	66.00	9.50	475.00	11/27/91	875.00	11/11/91	-325.00
1991	10/31/90	146.00	12/07/90	136.00	-10.00	-500.00	11/01/90	100.00	11/13/90	-1812.50
1990	10/31/89	102.75	12/08/89	110.50	7.75	387.50	11/16/89	900.00		
1989	10/31/88	226.75	12/09/88	243.75	17.00	850.00	11/08/88	1050.00	11/18/88	-875.00
1988	11/02/87	174.75	12/09/87	213.75	39.00	1950.00	12/01/87	2812.50		
1987	10/31/86	140.75	12/09/86	155.75	15.00	750.00	12/05/86	912.50	11/04/86	-250.00
1986	10/31/85	55.00	12/09/85	32.25	-22.75	-1137.50	11/04/85	25.00	11/21/85	-2287.50

Percentage Correct		93								
Average Profit on Winning Trades					14.38	718.75		Winners		14
Average Loss on Trades					-10.00	-500.00		Losers		1
Average Net Profit Per Trade					12.75	637.50		Total trades		15
Percentage Correct		90								
Average Profit on Winning Trades					15.56	777.78		Winners		18
Average Loss on Trades					-16.38	-818.75		Losers		2
Average Net Profit Per Trade					12.36	618.13		Total trades		20

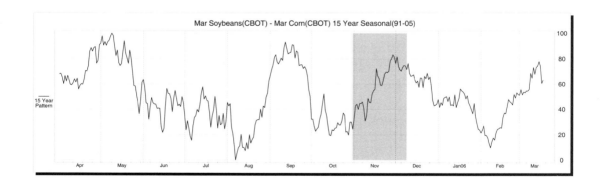

Mar Soybeans(CBOT) - Mar Corn(CBOT) 15 Year Seasonal(91-05)

Chapter 5: Soybeans vs Grains

Soybeans/Wheat

Offset crop cycles for soybeans and for winter wheat, those traded at the CBOT and KCBT, drive spreads between them. Soybeans are planted mostly May/June and harvested September/October. In contrast, winter wheat is harvested mostly May-July and planted September/October. Thus, wheat supply is heaviest when soybean supply is least, with the opposite also true. Spreads between July Soybeans and either of the July Wheat contracts are between old-crop soybeans and new-crop wheat. In contrast, those between November Soybeans and either of the December Wheat contracts, for example, are between new-crop soybeans and old-crop wheat.

Figure 5-17

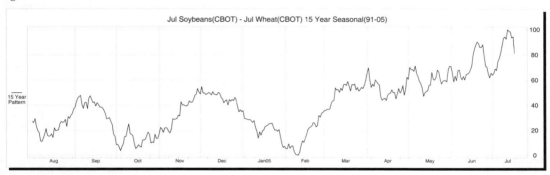

Once the February Break has flushed the soybeans market, old-crop soybeans tend to outperform new-crop wheat into winter wheat harvest. Physical supplies of soybeans are tight. In contrast, old-crop US wheat must then compete for exports with recently harvested Australian and Argentine crops even as harvest approaches.

Figure 5-18

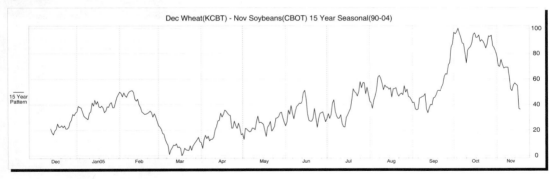

With exports normally accounting for perhaps 40% of total US wheat production, wheat's primary export season of July-December is crucial to the wheat market. Because soymeal tends normally to account for about 65% of soybean product value and soymeal is most heavily consumed during cold weather, October-March consumption is crucial to the soybean market. While wheat focuses on export demand, soybeans focus on harvest supply.

Figure 5-16

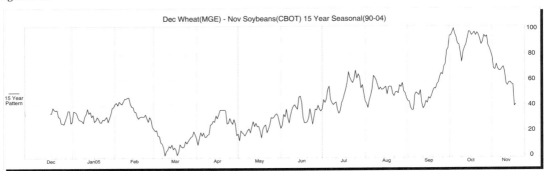

Thus, soybeans tend to outperform wheat from February/March into July, at which time the spreads tend to reverse and favor wheat into October and then again from December into February/March. Even spring wheat, planted April-June and harvested August/September, follows a similar pattern.

Spreads listed in the table below can now speak for themselves. Traders must carefully note, however, designations for each type and class of wheat at the three various exchanges — soft red winter at the Chicago Board of Trade (CBOT), hard red winter at the Kansas City Board of Trade (KCBT), and hard red spring at the Minneapolis Grain Exchange (MGE). Furthermore, these strategies will make far more sense to the reader who remembers that November is the first true new-crop contract for soybeans, July the first for winter wheat at the CBOT and KCBT, and September the first for spring wheat at the MGE. Also, keep in mind speculative liquidation of long positions going into deliveries — and the typical recoveries thereafter.

Figure 5-19: Soybeans versus Wheat Strategies

Moore Research Center, Inc.	Soybeans vs Wheat Spread Strategies							
Seasonal Strategy	Entry Date	Exit Date	Win Pct	Win Yrs	Loss Years	Total Years	Average Profit	Ave Pft Per Day
Buy Jul Wheat(MGE)	1/27	2/08	93	14	1	15	460	35
Sell Jul Soybeans(CBOT)			95	19	1	20	468	36
Buy May Soybeans(CBOT)	2/14	3/22	87	13	2	15	1422	38
Sell May Wheat(KCBT)			80	16	4	20	1230	33
Buy Jul Soybeans(CBOT)	2/23	3/21	80	12	3	15	1029	38
Sell Jul Wheat(KCBT)			80	16	4	20	918	34
Buy Jul Soybeans(CBOT)	2/24	3/21	80	12	3	15	919	35
Sell Jul Wheat(CBOT)			85	17	3	20	883	34
Buy May Soybeans(CBOT)	3/02	3/23	87	13	2	15	781	35
Sell May Wheat(KCBT)			80	16	4	20	613	28
Buy Jul Soybeans(CBOT)	6/05	6/21	87	13	2	15	723	43
Sell Jul Wheat(CBOT)			85	17	3	20	1056	62
Buy Dec Wheat(CBOT)	7/12	7/28	93	14	1	15	792	47
Sell Nov Soybeans(CBOT)			85	17	3	20	894	53
Buy Dec Wheat(MGE)	7/13	7/21	87	13	2	15	783	87
Sell Nov Soybeans(CBOT)			80	16	4	20	723	80

Figure 5-19 Soybeans versus Wheat Strategies continued

Seasonal Strategy	Entry Date	Exit Date	Win Pct	Win Yrs	Loss Years	Total Years	Average Profit	Ave Pft Per Day
						Soybeans vs Wheat Spread Strategies		
Buy Sep Wheat(CBOT)	7/13	7/28	93	14	1	15	1029	64
Sell Sep Soybeans(CBOT)			85	17	3	20	1120	70
Buy Mar Wheat(KCBT)	7/13	8/08	80	12	3	15	978	36
Sell Mar Soybeans(CBOT)			85	17	3	20	1087	40
Buy Sep Wheat(KCBT)	7/14	7/21	87	13	2	15	834	104
Sell Sep Soybeans(CBOT)			80	16	4	20	927	116
Buy Dec Wheat(MGE)	9/11	10/01	93	14	1	15	974	46
Sell Nov Soybeans(CBOT)			85	17	3	20	876	42
Buy Dec Wheat(KCBT)	9/11	10/21	87	13	2	15	979	24
Sell Nov Soybeans(CBOT)			85	17	3	20	1094	27
Buy Mar Wheat(KCBT)	9/16	10/01	87	13	2	15	782	49
Sell Mar Soybeans(CBOT)			80	16	4	20	673	42
Buy Dec Wheat(CBOT)	9/16	10/22	80	12	3	15	618	17
Sell Nov Soybeans(CBOT)			85	17	3	20	854	23
Buy Dec Wheat(MGE)	9/18	10/01	87	13	2	15	853	61
Sell Nov Soybeans(CBOT)			80	16	4	20	678	48
Buy Dec Wheat(CBOT)	9/21	10/01	87	13	2	15	638	58
Sell Nov Soybeans(CBOT)			85	17	3	20	632	57
Buy Jul Wheat(CBOT)	12/26	2/03	87	13	2	15	739	18
Sell Jul Soybeans(CBOT)			85	17	3	20	803	20
Buy Jul Wheat(KCBT)	12/26	2/08	80	12	3	15	743	17
Sell Jul Soybeans(CBOT)			85	17	3	20	874	19

Although exaggerated here because strategies for wheat at all three exchanges are included for comparison, traders will note that — as is usually true — the best seasonal strategies often exist in clusters rather than in splendid isolation.

Figure 5-20

Moore Research Center, Inc. — Buy Jul Wheat(MGE) / Sell Jul Soybeans(CBOT)

Enter on approximately 01/27 - Exit on approximately 02/08

CONT YEAR	ENTRY DATE	ENTRY PRICE	EXIT DATE	EXIT PRICE	PROFIT	PROFIT AMOUNT	BEST EQUITY DATE	BEST EQUITY AMOUNT	WORST EQUITY DATE	WORST EQUITY AMOUNT
2005	01/27/05	-189.75	02/08/05	-183.75	6.00	300.00	02/04/05	587.50		
2004	01/27/04	-432.50	02/06/04	-427.25	5.25	262.50	02/02/04	2250.00		
2003	01/27/03	-193.00	02/07/03	-178.25	14.75	737.50	02/07/03	737.50	01/28/03	-287.50
2002	01/28/02	-128.00	02/08/02	-121.50	6.50	325.00	02/01/02	475.00		
2001	01/29/01	-138.50	02/08/01	-130.50	8.00	400.00	02/08/01	400.00	02/02/01	-425.00
2000	01/27/00	-203.00	02/08/00	-182.50	20.50	1025.00	02/08/00	1025.00		
1999	01/27/99	-157.50	02/08/99	-156.75	0.75	37.50	01/29/99	175.00	02/02/99	-400.00
1998	01/27/98	-296.50	02/06/98	-309.25	-12.75	-637.50	01/30/98	312.50	02/06/98	-637.50
1997	01/27/97	-394.25	02/07/97	-380.75	13.50	675.00	02/06/97	862.50		
1996	01/29/96	-279.00	02/08/96	-266.00	13.00	650.00	02/08/96	650.00	01/31/96	-350.00
1995	01/27/95	-213.25	02/08/95	-212.75	0.50	25.00	01/31/95	425.00		
1994	01/27/94	-350.75	02/08/94	-330.00	20.75	1037.50	02/07/94	1137.50		
1993	01/27/93	-256.75	02/08/93	-248.50	8.25	412.50	02/05/93	475.00		
1992	01/27/92	-191.50	02/07/92	-162.50	29.00	1450.00	02/07/92	1450.00	01/28/92	-175.00
1991	01/28/91	-322.25	02/08/91	-318.25	4.00	200.00	01/30/91	425.00	02/06/91	-50.00
1990	01/29/90	-219.00	02/08/90	-216.50	2.50	125.00	02/05/90	300.00		
1989	01/27/89	-358.25	02/08/89	-348.25	10.00	500.00	02/08/89	500.00	01/31/89	-675.00
1988	01/27/88	-321.25	02/08/88	-313.00	8.25	412.50	02/02/88	650.00		
1987	01/27/87	-241.50	02/06/87	-229.00	12.50	625.00	02/06/87	625.00		
1986	01/27/86	-253.50	02/07/86	-237.75	15.75	787.50	02/07/86	787.50	01/30/86	-125.00

Percentage Correct	93									
Average Profit on Winning Trades					10.77	538.39		Winners	14	
Average Loss on Trades					-12.75	-637.50		Losers	1	
Average Net Profit Per Trade					9.20	460.00		Total trades	15	
Percentage Correct	95									
Average Profit on Winning Trades					10.51	525.66		Winners	19	
Average Loss on Trades					-12.75	-637.50		Losers	1	
Average Net Profit Per Trade					9.35	467.50		Total trades	20	

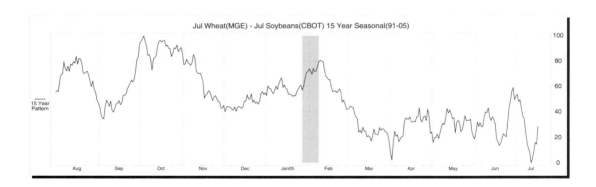

Jul Wheat(MGE) - Jul Soybeans(CBOT) 15 Year Seasonal(91-05)

15 Year Pattern

Figure 5-21

Buy May Soybeans(CBOT) / Sell May Wheat(KCBT)

Enter on approximately 02/14 - Exit on approximately 03/22

CONT YEAR	ENTRY DATE	ENTRY PRICE	EXIT DATE	EXIT PRICE	PROFIT	PROFIT AMOUNT	BEST EQUITY DATE	BEST EQUITY AMOUNT	WORST EQUITY DATE	WORST EQUITY AMOUNT
2005	02/14/05	213.25	03/22/05	278.00	64.75	3237.50	03/16/05	4837.50		
2004	02/17/04	466.00	03/22/04	627.50	161.50	8075.00	03/22/04	8075.00		
2003	02/14/03	222.75	03/21/03	256.75	34.00	1700.00	03/21/03	1700.00	03/06/03	-175.00
2002	02/14/02	149.25	03/22/02	182.50	33.25	1662.50	03/15/02	1812.50		
2001	02/14/01	130.25	03/22/01	130.50	0.25	12.50	03/06/01	462.50	03/14/01	-775.00
2000	02/14/00	205.25	03/22/00	243.00	37.75	1887.50	03/22/00	1887.50		
1999	02/16/99	196.00	03/22/99	196.25	0.25	12.50	03/22/99	12.50	03/05/99	-1375.00
1998	02/17/98	326.25	03/20/98	303.25	-23.00	-1150.00	02/18/98	162.50	03/13/98	-1225.00
1997	02/14/97	377.25	03/21/97	429.25	52.00	2600.00	03/10/97	3525.00	02/24/97	-312.50
1996	02/14/96	233.75	03/22/96	237.50	3.75	187.50	02/26/96	662.50	03/08/96	-1137.50
1995	02/14/95	207.50	03/22/95	221.50	14.00	700.00	03/17/95	1437.50	02/17/95	-200.00
1994	02/14/94	329.75	03/22/94	357.75	28.00	1400.00	03/22/94	1400.00	03/07/94	-275.00
1993	02/16/93	246.50	03/22/93	257.75	11.25	562.50	03/10/93	937.50	02/22/93	-62.50
1992	02/14/92	149.25	03/20/92	184.25	35.00	1750.00	03/13/92	2975.00		
1991	02/14/91	316.50	03/22/91	290.25	-26.25	-1312.50	03/08/91	462.50	03/22/91	-1312.50
1990	02/14/90	209.75	03/22/90	241.50	31.75	1587.50	03/09/90	1600.00	02/26/90	-262.50
1989	02/14/89	322.00	03/22/89	359.25	37.25	1862.50	03/22/89	1862.50	02/16/89	-150.00
1988	02/16/88	304.75	03/22/88	332.75	28.00	1400.00	03/22/88	1400.00	02/25/88	-50.00
1987	02/17/87	235.25	03/20/87	220.50	-14.75	-737.50			03/02/87	-975.00
1986	02/14/86	258.50	03/21/86	241.75	-16.75	-837.50	02/21/86	125.00	03/20/86	-925.00

Percentage Correct		87								
Average Profit on Winning Trades					36.60	1829.81		Winners		13
Average Loss on Trades					-24.63	-1231.25		Losers		2
Average Net Profit Per Trade					28.43	1421.67		Total trades		15
Percentage Correct		80								
Average Profit on Winning Trades					35.80	1789.84		Winners		16
Average Loss on Trades					-20.19	-1009.38		Losers		4
Average Net Profit Per Trade					24.60	1230.00		Total trades		20

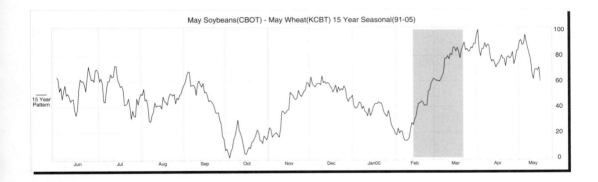

May Soybeans(CBOT) - May Wheat(KCBT) 15 Year Seasonal(91-05)

Figure 5-22

Moore Research Center, Inc.

Buy Jul Soybeans(CBOT) / Sell Jul Wheat(KCBT)

Enter on approximately 02/23 - Exit on approximately 03/21

CONT YEAR	ENTRY DATE	ENTRY PRICE	EXIT DATE	EXIT PRICE	PROFIT	PROFIT AMOUNT	BEST EQUITY DATE	BEST EQUITY AMOUNT	WORST EQUITY DATE	WORST EQUITY AMOUNT
2005	02/23/05	257.00	03/21/05	286.50	29.50	1475.00	03/16/05	3037.50	02/24/05	-312.50
2004	02/23/04	490.75	03/19/04	618.50	127.75	6387.50	03/19/04	6387.50		
2003	02/24/03	233.75	03/21/03	263.25	29.50	1475.00	03/21/03	1475.00	03/06/03	-462.50
2002	02/25/02	149.00	03/21/02	173.75	24.75	1237.50	03/15/02	1762.50		
2001	02/23/01	127.50	03/21/01	129.50	2.00	100.00	03/06/01	487.50	03/14/01	-775.00
2000	02/23/00	208.00	03/21/00	239.00	31.00	1550.00	03/21/00	1550.00		
1999	02/23/99	181.25	03/19/99	184.50	3.25	162.50	03/19/99	162.50	03/05/99	-737.50
1998	02/23/98	314.75	03/20/98	298.75	-16.00	-800.00			03/13/98	-937.50
1997	02/24/97	400.50	03/21/97	459.00	58.50	2925.00	03/10/97	4112.50		
1996	02/23/96	277.50	03/21/96	257.25	-20.25	-1012.50			03/08/96	-1962.50
1995	02/23/95	234.25	03/21/95	250.50	16.25	812.50	03/17/95	1262.50		
1994	02/23/94	352.50	03/21/94	364.50	12.00	600.00	03/14/94	800.00	03/04/94	-612.50
1993	02/23/93	263.50	03/19/93	286.75	23.25	1162.50	03/18/93	1312.50		
1992	02/24/92	205.75	03/20/92	216.50	10.75	537.50	03/13/92	1250.00	02/27/92	-475.00
1991	02/25/91	327.75	03/21/91	304.25	-23.50	-1175.00	03/08/91	200.00	03/20/91	-1337.50
1990	02/23/90	234.75	03/21/90	267.25	32.50	1625.00	03/09/90	1675.00	02/26/90	-112.50
1989	02/23/89	365.50	03/21/89	367.00	1.50	75.00	03/02/89	537.50	03/10/89	-637.50
1988	02/23/88	316.00	03/21/88	335.00	19.00	950.00	03/21/88	950.00	02/25/88	-387.50
1987	02/23/87	236.25	03/20/87	233.00	-3.25	-162.50	03/13/87	175.00	03/10/87	-250.00
1986	02/24/86	280.75	03/21/86	289.50	8.75	437.50	03/06/86	625.00	03/03/86	-150.00

Percentage Correct		80								
Average Profit on Winning Trades					30.71	1535.42		Winners		12
Average Loss on Trades					-19.92	-995.83		Losers		3
Average Net Profit Per Trade					20.58	1029.17		Total trades		15
Percentage Correct		80								
Average Profit on Winning Trades					26.89	1344.53		Winners		16
Average Loss on Trades					-15.75	-787.50		Losers		4
Average Net Profit Per Trade					18.36	918.13		Total trades		20

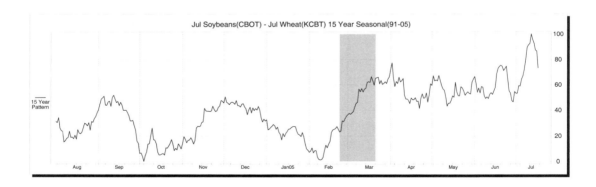

Jul Soybeans(CBOT) - Jul Wheat(KCBT) 15 Year Seasonal(91-05)

Figure 5-23

Buy Jul Soybeans(CBOT) / Sell Jul Wheat(CBOT)

Enter on approximately 02/24 - Exit on approximately 03/21

CONT YEAR	ENTRY DATE	ENTRY PRICE	EXIT DATE	EXIT PRICE	PROFIT	PROFIT AMOUNT	BEST EQUITY DATE	BEST EQUITY AMOUNT	WORST EQUITY DATE	WORST EQUITY AMOUNT
2005	02/24/05	248.75	03/21/05	279.75	31.00	1550.00	03/16/05	3100.00		
2004	02/24/04	511.00	03/19/04	620.25	109.25	5462.50	03/19/04	5462.50		
2003	02/24/03	250.75	03/21/03	286.75	36.00	1800.00	03/21/03	1800.00	03/06/03	-87.50
2002	02/25/02	158.25	03/21/02	178.25	20.00	1000.00	03/15/02	1687.50		
2001	02/26/01	171.25	03/21/01	171.50	0.25	12.50	03/06/01	487.50	03/14/01	-712.50
2000	02/24/00	243.50	03/21/00	265.50	22.00	1100.00	03/21/00	1100.00		
1999	02/24/99	206.00	03/19/99	211.75	5.75	287.50	03/19/99	287.50	03/05/99	-525.00
1998	02/24/98	320.50	03/20/98	311.00	-9.50	-475.00	02/25/98	150.00	03/13/98	-662.50
1997	02/24/97	415.25	03/21/97	460.00	44.75	2237.50	03/10/97	3912.50		
1996	02/26/96	299.75	03/21/96	283.00	-16.75	-837.50			03/04/96	-1450.00
1995	02/24/95	241.25	03/21/95	253.00	11.75	587.50	03/17/95	1075.00	02/27/95	-75.00
1994	02/24/94	350.25	03/21/94	363.75	13.50	675.00	03/14/94	862.50	03/04/94	-525.00
1993	02/24/93	260.00	03/19/93	282.25	22.25	1112.50	03/18/93	1250.00		
1992	02/24/92	213.00	03/20/92	223.25	10.25	512.50	03/19/92	1125.00	02/27/92	-450.00
1991	02/25/91	328.25	03/21/91	303.50	-24.75	-1237.50	03/08/91	87.50	03/20/91	-1387.50
1990	02/26/90	240.00	03/21/90	272.00	32.00	1600.00	03/20/90	1650.00	02/27/90	-12.50
1989	02/24/89	367.75	03/21/89	382.25	14.50	725.00	03/20/89	1025.00	03/01/89	-312.50
1988	02/24/88	312.00	03/21/88	334.50	22.50	1125.00	03/21/88	1125.00	02/25/88	-300.00
1987	02/24/87	222.00	03/20/87	225.50	3.50	175.00	03/17/87	400.00	02/26/87	-62.50
1986	02/24/86	278.25	03/21/86	283.25	5.00	250.00	03/06/86	587.50	03/03/86	-325.00

Percentage Correct	80									
Average Profit on Winning Trades					27.23	1361.46		Winners		12
Average Loss on Trades					-17.00	-850.00		Losers		3
Average Net Profit Per Trade					18.38	919.17		Total trades		15
Percentage Correct	85									
Average Profit on Winning Trades					23.78	1188.97		Winners		17
Average Loss on Trades					-17.00	-850.00		Losers		3
Average Net Profit Per Trade					17.66	883.13		Total trades		20

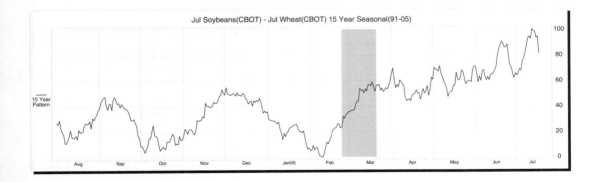

Jul Soybeans(CBOT) - Jul Wheat(CBOT) 15 Year Seasonal(91-05)

Figure 5-24

Buy May Soybeans(CBOT) / Sell May Wheat(KCBT)

Enter on approximately 03/02 - Exit on approximately 03/23

CONT YEAR	ENTRY DATE	ENTRY PRICE	EXIT DATE	EXIT PRICE	PROFIT	PROFIT AMOUNT	BEST EQUITY DATE	BEST EQUITY AMOUNT	WORST EQUITY DATE	WORST EQUITY AMOUNT
2005	03/02/05	275.75	03/23/05	278.25	2.50	125.00	03/16/05	1712.50	03/07/05	-112.50
2004	03/02/04	546.00	03/23/04	635.00	89.00	4450.00	03/23/04	4450.00	03/08/04	-25.00
2003	03/03/03	239.25	03/21/03	256.75	17.50	875.00	03/21/03	875.00	03/06/03	-1000.00
2002	03/04/02	164.75	03/22/02	182.50	17.75	887.50	03/15/02	1037.50		
2001	03/02/01	133.50	03/23/01	129.75	-3.75	-187.50	03/06/01	300.00	03/14/01	-937.50
2000	03/02/00	218.50	03/23/00	241.75	23.25	1162.50	03/22/00	1225.00		
1999	03/02/99	178.00	03/23/99	193.75	15.75	787.50	03/22/99	912.50	03/05/99	-475.00
1998	03/02/98	303.25	03/23/98	305.00	1.75	87.50	03/06/98	512.50	03/13/98	-75.00
1997	03/03/97	401.00	03/21/97	429.25	28.25	1412.50	03/10/97	2337.50		
1996	03/02/96	221.00	03/22/96	237.50	16.50	825.00	03/22/96	825.00	03/08/96	-500.00
1995	03/02/95	213.75	03/23/95	227.25	13.50	675.00	03/17/95	1125.00		
1994	03/02/94	335.25	03/23/94	363.00	27.75	1387.50	03/23/94	1387.50	03/07/94	-550.00
1993	03/02/93	258.50	03/23/93	266.00	7.50	375.00	03/23/93	375.00	03/08/93	-387.50
1992	03/02/92	182.75	03/23/92	186.50	3.75	187.50	03/13/92	1300.00		
1991	03/04/91	317.00	03/22/91	290.25	-26.75	-1337.50	03/08/91	437.50	03/22/91	-1337.50
1990	03/02/90	224.00	03/23/90	235.00	11.00	550.00	03/09/90	887.50		
1989	03/02/89	352.75	03/23/89	349.50	-3.25	-162.50	03/22/89	325.00	03/10/89	-837.50
1988	03/02/88	322.75	03/23/88	328.00	5.25	262.50	03/22/88	500.00	03/07/88	-875.00
1987	03/02/87	215.75	03/23/87	219.75	4.00	200.00	03/13/87	512.50		
1986	03/03/86	247.75	03/21/86	241.75	-6.00	-300.00	03/06/86	362.50	03/20/86	-387.50

Percentage Correct	87									
Average Profit on Winning Trades					20.37	1018.27		Winners		13
Average Loss on Trades					-15.25	-762.50		Losers		2
Average Net Profit Per Trade					15.62	780.83		Total trades		15
Percentage Correct	80									
Average Profit on Winning Trades					17.81	890.63		Winners		16
Average Loss on Trades					-9.94	-496.88		Losers		4
Average Net Profit Per Trade					12.26	613.13		Total trades		20

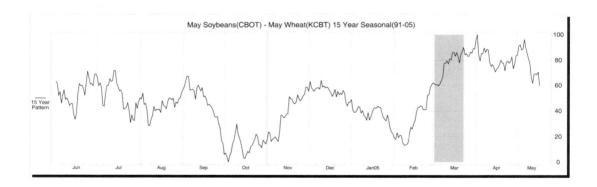

May Soybeans(CBOT) - May Wheat(KCBT) 15 Year Seasonal(91-05)

Figure 5-25

Moore Research Center, Inc.

Buy Jul Soybeans(CBOT) / Sell Jul Wheat(CBOT)

Enter on approximately 06/05 - Exit on approximately 06/21

CONT YEAR	ENTRY DATE	ENTRY PRICE	EXIT DATE	EXIT PRICE	PROFIT	PROFIT AMOUNT	BEST EQUITY DATE	BEST EQUITY AMOUNT	WORST EQUITY DATE	WORST EQUITY AMOUNT
2005	06/06/05	355.25	06/21/05	400.25	45.00	2250.00	06/21/05	2250.00	06/10/05	-125.00
2004	06/07/04	486.00	06/21/04	534.25	48.25	2412.50	06/21/04	2412.50		
2003	06/05/03	298.25	06/20/03	317.50	19.25	962.50	06/20/03	962.50	06/12/03	-537.50
2002	06/05/02	230.50	06/21/02	207.75	-22.75	-1137.50	06/06/02	112.50	06/20/02	-1712.50
2001	06/05/01	192.75	06/21/01	205.00	12.25	612.50	06/13/01	962.50		
2000	06/05/00	262.25	06/21/00	229.50	-32.75	-1637.50	06/06/00	62.50	06/20/00	-1750.00
1999	06/07/99	210.50	06/21/99	216.75	6.25	312.50	06/18/99	475.00	06/15/99	-312.50
1998	06/05/98	336.00	06/19/98	363.00	27.00	1350.00	06/19/98	1350.00	06/09/98	-250.00
1997	06/05/97	480.00	06/20/97	491.25	11.25	562.50	06/17/97	1462.50	06/09/97	-1825.00
1996	06/05/96	276.75	06/21/96	300.50	23.75	1187.50	06/21/96	1187.50	06/13/96	-625.00
1995	06/05/95	197.75	06/21/95	208.00	10.25	512.50	06/07/95	1012.50		
1994	06/06/94	327.50	06/21/94	352.00	24.50	1225.00	06/17/94	2412.50	06/07/94	-112.50
1993	06/07/93	305.25	06/21/93	340.50	35.25	1762.50	06/21/93	1762.50	06/14/93	-325.00
1992	06/05/92	239.75	06/19/92	246.00	6.25	312.50	06/12/92	925.00		
1991	06/05/91	288.00	06/21/91	291.00	3.00	150.00	06/20/91	175.00	06/12/91	-800.00
1990	06/05/90	260.25	06/21/90	265.00	4.75	237.50	06/11/90	762.50	06/15/90	-112.50
1989	06/05/89	310.75	06/21/89	339.25	28.50	1425.00	06/19/89	2062.50	06/12/89	-312.50
1988	06/06/88	496.25	06/21/88	657.00	160.75	8037.50	06/21/88	8037.50	06/08/88	-275.00
1987	06/05/87	300.25	06/19/87	299.75	-0.50	-25.00	06/15/87	1337.50	06/09/87	-337.50
1986	06/05/86	276.50	06/20/86	288.50	12.00	600.00	06/20/86	600.00		

Percentage Correct	87									
Average Profit on Winning Trades					20.94	1047.12		Winners		13
Average Loss on Trades					-27.75	-1387.50		Losers		2
Average Net Profit Per Trade					14.45	722.50		Total trades		15
Percentage Correct	85									
Average Profit on Winning Trades					28.13	1406.62		Winners		17
Average Loss on Trades					-18.67	-933.33		Losers		3
Average Net Profit Per Trade					21.11	1055.63		Total trades		20

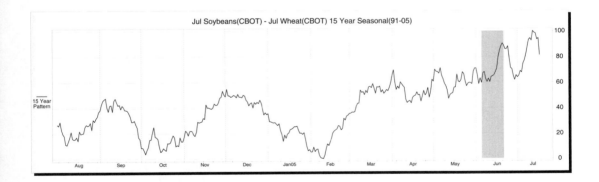

Jul Soybeans(CBOT) - Jul Wheat(CBOT) 15 Year Seasonal(91-05)

15 Year Pattern

Figure 5-26

Buy Dec Wheat(CBOT) / Sell Nov Soybeans(CBOT)

Enter on approximately 07/12 - Exit on approximately 07/28

CONT YEAR	ENTRY DATE	ENTRY PRICE	EXIT DATE	EXIT PRICE	PROFIT	PROFIT AMOUNT	BEST EQUITY DATE	BEST EQUITY AMOUNT	WORST EQUITY DATE	WORST EQUITY AMOUNT
2005	07/12/05	-367.00	07/28/05	-351.25	15.75	787.50	07/22/05	1600.00	07/13/05	-225.00
2004	07/12/04	-282.50	07/28/04	-248.25	34.25	1712.50	07/28/04	1712.50	07/14/04	-1400.00
2003	07/14/03	-201.00	07/28/03	-164.00	37.00	1850.00	07/23/03	2337.50		
2002	07/12/02	-195.50	07/26/02	-171.25	24.25	1212.50	07/26/02	1212.50	07/22/02	-537.50
2001	07/12/01	-220.50	07/27/01	-218.75	1.75	87.50	07/20/01	1612.50	07/13/01	-112.50
2000	07/12/00	-193.50	07/28/00	-190.25	3.25	162.50	07/17/00	350.00	07/21/00	-575.00
1999	07/12/99	-158.50	07/28/99	-155.75	2.75	137.50	07/28/99	137.50	07/23/99	-2212.50
1998	07/13/98	-306.75	07/28/98	-296.00	10.75	537.50	07/24/98	1137.50	07/17/98	-425.00
1997	07/14/97	-272.00	07/28/97	-248.75	23.25	1162.50	07/25/97	2137.50	07/15/97	-43.75
1996	07/12/96	-303.75	07/26/96	-283.25	20.50	1025.00	07/18/96	1762.50	07/15/96	-300.00
1995	07/12/95	-192.50	07/28/95	-167.50	25.00	1250.00	07/24/95	1812.50		
1994	07/12/94	-244.50	07/28/94	-219.50	25.00	1250.00	07/27/94	1487.50	07/13/94	-212.50
1993	07/12/93	-395.50	07/28/93	-367.75	27.75	1387.50	07/28/93	1387.50	07/19/93	-1300.00
1992	07/13/92	-233.50	07/28/92	-218.00	15.50	775.00	07/24/92	1175.00		
1991	07/12/91	-245.50	07/26/91	-274.75	-29.25	-1462.50	07/18/91	250.00	07/26/91	-1462.50
1990	07/12/90	-302.25	07/27/90	-284.25	18.00	900.00	07/24/90	1125.00	07/13/90	-62.50
1989	07/12/89	-235.50	07/28/89	-188.00	47.50	2375.00	07/28/89	2375.00	07/14/89	-850.00
1988	07/12/88	-477.25	07/28/88	-388.00	89.25	4462.50	07/28/88	4462.50	07/15/88	-4487.50
1987	07/13/87	-242.25	07/28/87	-263.75	-21.50	-1075.00	07/17/87	100.00	07/20/87	-1100.00
1986	07/14/86	-230.00	07/28/86	-243.25	-13.25	-662.50			07/21/86	-1300.00

Percentage Correct	93									
Average Profit on Winning Trades					19.05	952.68		Winners		14
Average Loss on Trades					-29.25	-1462.50		Losers		1
Average Net Profit Per Trade					15.83	791.67		Total trades		15
Percentage Correct	85									
Average Profit on Winning Trades					24.79	1239.71		Winners		17
Average Loss on Trades					-21.33	-1066.67		Losers		3
Average Net Profit Per Trade					17.88	893.75		Total trades		20

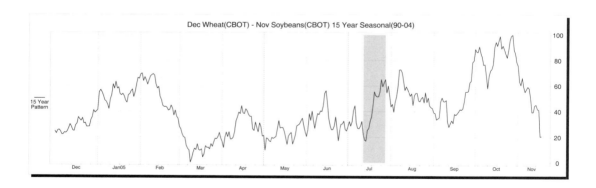

Dec Wheat(CBOT) - Nov Soybeans(CBOT) 15 Year Seasonal(90-04)

Figure 5-27

Buy Dec Wheat(MGE) / Sell Nov Soybeans(CBOT)

Enter on approximately 07/13 - Exit on approximately 07/21

CONT YEAR	ENTRY DATE	ENTRY PRICE	EXIT DATE	EXIT PRICE	PROFIT	PROFIT AMOUNT	BEST EQUITY DATE	BEST EQUITY AMOUNT	WORST EQUITY DATE	WORST EQUITY AMOUNT
2005	07/13/05	-359.50	07/21/05	-325.00	34.50	1725.00	07/21/05	1725.00	07/14/05	-75.00
2004	07/13/04	-247.25	07/21/04	-229.50	17.75	887.50	07/21/04	887.50	07/14/04	-1200.00
2003	07/14/03	-187.25	07/21/03	-153.50	33.75	1687.50	07/18/03	1725.00		
2002	07/15/02	-167.50	07/19/02	-162.00	5.50	275.00	07/17/02	750.00		
2001	07/13/01	-179.00	07/20/01	-151.50	27.50	1375.00	07/20/01	1375.00	07/17/01	-100.00
2000	07/13/00	-133.25	07/21/00	-148.50	-15.25	-762.50	07/17/00	275.00	07/21/00	-762.50
1999	07/13/99	-86.50	07/21/99	-119.75	-33.25	-1662.50	07/16/99	275.00	07/21/99	-1662.50
1998	07/13/98	-243.50	07/21/98	-231.25	12.25	612.50	07/14/98	662.50	07/17/98	-525.00
1997	07/14/97	-251.75	07/21/97	-209.25	42.50	2125.00	07/21/97	2125.00	07/15/97	-43.75
1996	07/15/96	-299.75	07/19/96	-266.25	33.50	1675.00	07/18/96	2487.50		
1995	07/13/95	-173.75	07/21/95	-155.75	18.00	900.00	07/20/95	1437.50		
1994	07/13/94	-245.50	07/21/94	-214.75	30.75	1537.50	07/20/94	1575.00		
1993	07/13/93	-397.00	07/21/93	-393.75	3.25	162.50	07/21/93	162.50	07/19/93	-825.00
1992	07/13/92	-239.25	07/21/92	-222.25	17.00	850.00	07/17/92	975.00		
1991	07/15/91	-257.00	07/19/91	-249.75	7.25	362.50	07/18/91	425.00	07/16/91	-600.00
1990	07/13/90	-311.50	07/20/90	-291.50	20.00	1000.00	07/20/90	1000.00		
1989	07/13/89	-235.75	07/21/89	-214.75	21.00	1050.00	07/18/89	1125.00	07/14/89	-512.50
1988	07/13/88	-468.25	07/21/88	-418.25	50.00	2500.00	07/21/88	2500.00	07/15/88	-3337.50
1987	07/13/87	-245.00	07/21/87	-255.25	-10.25	-512.50	07/17/87	175.00	07/20/87	-1075.00
1986	07/14/86	-217.50	07/21/86	-244.00	-26.50	-1325.00			07/21/86	-1325.00

Percentage Correct	87									
Average Profit on Winning Trades					21.81	1090.38		Winners		13
Average Loss on Trades					-24.25	-1212.50		Losers		2
Average Net Profit Per Trade					15.67	783.33		Total trades		15
Percentage Correct	80									
Average Profit on Winning Trades					23.41	1170.31		Winners		16
Average Loss on Trades					-21.31	-1065.63		Losers		4
Average Net Profit Per Trade					14.46	723.13		Total trades		20

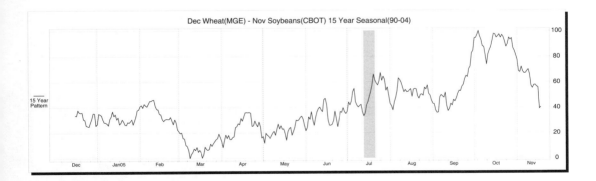

Dec Wheat(MGE) - Nov Soybeans(CBOT) 15 Year Seasonal(90-04)

15 Year Pattern

Figure 5-28

Buy Sep Wheat(CBOT) / Sell Sep Soybeans(CBOT)

Moore Research Center, Inc.

Enter on approximately 07/13 - Exit on approximately 07/28

CONT YEAR	ENTRY DATE	ENTRY PRICE	EXIT DATE	EXIT PRICE	PROFIT	PROFIT AMOUNT	BEST EQUITY DATE	BEST EQUITY AMOUNT	WORST EQUITY DATE	WORST EQUITY AMOUNT
2005	07/13/05	-377.00	07/28/05	-356.00	21.00	1050.00	07/22/05	1712.50	07/14/05	-37.50
2004	07/13/04	-317.00	07/28/04	-267.75	49.25	2462.50	07/28/04	2462.50	07/14/04	-975.00
2003	07/14/03	-236.75	07/28/03	-188.75	48.00	2400.00	07/23/03	2700.00		
2002	07/15/02	-223.75	07/26/02	-197.50	26.25	1312.50	07/26/02	1312.50	07/22/02	-350.00
2001	07/13/01	-237.50	07/27/01	-234.25	3.25	162.50	07/20/01	1625.00		
2000	07/13/00	-201.25	07/28/00	-199.75	1.50	75.00	07/28/00	75.00	07/21/00	-612.50
1999	07/13/99	-175.25	07/28/99	-167.75	7.50	375.00	07/28/99	375.00	07/23/99	-1912.50
1998	07/13/98	-334.25	07/28/98	-316.00	18.25	912.50	07/24/98	1462.50	07/17/98	-300.00
1997	07/14/97	-338.00	07/28/97	-307.00	31.00	1550.00	07/23/97	2362.50	07/15/97	-56.25
1996	07/15/96	-329.75	07/26/96	-308.50	21.25	1062.50	07/18/96	2100.00		
1995	07/13/95	-188.50	07/28/95	-168.00	20.50	1025.00	07/24/95	1787.50	07/17/95	-62.50
1994	07/13/94	-275.50	07/28/94	-241.00	34.50	1725.00	07/27/94	1837.50		
1993	07/13/93	-408.25	07/28/93	-374.25	34.00	1700.00	07/28/93	1700.00	07/19/93	-1237.50
1992	07/13/92	-238.25	07/28/92	-224.50	13.75	687.50	07/17/92	1125.00		
1991	07/15/91	-257.50	07/26/91	-278.75	-21.25	-1062.50	07/19/91	462.50	07/26/91	-1062.50
1990	07/13/90	-304.50	07/27/90	-290.75	13.75	687.50	07/24/90	925.00	07/19/90	-50.00
1989	07/13/89	-261.75	07/28/89	-216.50	45.25	2262.50	07/28/89	2262.50	07/14/89	-612.50
1988	07/13/88	-509.50	07/28/88	-391.50	118.00	5900.00	07/28/88	5900.00	07/15/88	-4175.00
1987	07/13/87	-252.25	07/28/87	-276.50	-24.25	-1212.50	07/17/87	187.50	07/28/87	-1212.50
1986	07/14/86	-231.50	07/28/86	-245.00	-13.50	-675.00			07/21/86	-1425.00

Percentage Correct	93									
Average Profit on Winning Trades					23.57	1178.57		Winners		14
Average Loss on Trades					-21.25	-1062.50		Losers		1
Average Net Profit Per Trade					20.58	1029.17		Total trades		15
Percentage Correct	85									
Average Profit on Winning Trades					29.82	1491.18		Winners		17
Average Loss on Trades					-19.67	-983.33		Losers		3
Average Net Profit Per Trade					22.40	1120.00		Total trades		20

HYPOTHETICAL PERFORMANCE RESULTS HAVE MANY INHERENT LIMITATIONS, SOME OF WHICH ARE DESCRIBED BELOW. NO REPRESENTATION IS BEING MADE THAT ANY ACCOUNT WILL OR IS LIKELY TO ACHIEVE PROFITS OR LOSSES SIMILAR TO THOSE SHOWN. IN FACT, THERE ARE FREQUENTLY SHARP DIFFERENCES BETWEEN HYPOTHETICAL PERFORMANCE RESULTS AND THE ACTUAL RESULTS SUBSEQUENTLY ACHIEVED BY ANY PARTICULAR TRADING PROGRAM. ONE OF THE LIMITATIONS OF HYPOTHETICAL PERFORMANCE RESULTS IS THAT THEY ARE GENERALLY PREPARED WITH THE BENEFIT OF HINDSIGHT. IN ADDITION, HYPOTHETICAL TRADING DOES NOT INVOLVE FINANCIAL RISK, AND NO HYPOTHETICAL TRADING RECORD CAN COMPLETELY ACCOUNT FOR THE IMPACT OF FINANCIAL RISK IN ACTUAL TRADING. FOR EXAMPLE, THE ABILITY TO WITHSTAND LOSSES OR ADHERE TO A PARTICULAR TRADING PROGRAM IN SPITE OF TRADING LOSSES ARE MATERIAL POINTS WHICH CAN ALSO ADVERSELY AFFECT ACTUAL TRADING RESULTS. THERE ARE NUMEROUS OTHER FACTORS RELATED TO THE MARKETS IN GENERAL OR TO THE IMPLEMENTATION OF ANY SPECIFIC TRADING PROGRAM WHICH CANNOT BE FULLY ACCOUNTED FOR IN THE PREPARATION OF HYPOTHETICAL PERFORMANCE RESULTS AND ALL OF WHICH CAN ADVERSELY AFFECT ACTUAL TRADING RESULTS. RESULTS NOT ADJUSTED FOR COMMISSION AND SLIPPAGE.

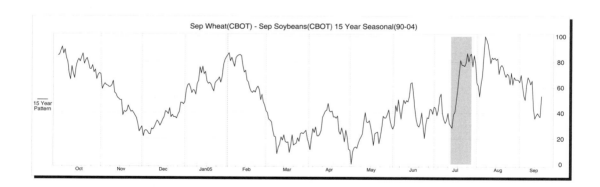

Sep Wheat(CBOT) - Sep Soybeans(CBOT) 15 Year Seasonal(90-04)

Figure 5-29

Buy Mar Wheat(KCBT) / Sell Mar Soybeans(CBOT)

Enter on approximately 07/13 - Exit on approximately 08/08

CONT YEAR	ENTRY DATE	ENTRY PRICE	EXIT DATE	EXIT PRICE	PROFIT	PROFIT AMOUNT	BEST EQUITY DATE	BEST EQUITY AMOUNT	WORST EQUITY DATE	WORST EQUITY AMOUNT
2006	07/13/05	-353.50	08/08/05	-318.25	35.25	1762.50	08/08/05	1762.50	07/14/05	-125.00
2005	07/13/04	-262.25	08/06/04	-214.25	48.00	2400.00	08/04/04	2762.50	07/14/04	-1012.50
2004	07/14/03	-206.50	08/08/03	-158.25	48.25	2412.50	08/06/03	2600.00		
2003	07/15/02	-181.25	08/08/02	-141.50	39.75	1987.50	08/08/02	1987.50		
2002	07/13/01	-182.50	08/08/01	-180.75	1.75	87.50	07/20/01	1400.00		
2001	07/13/00	-159.50	08/08/00	-170.50	-11.00	-550.00	07/14/00	87.50	07/21/00	-987.50
2000	07/13/99	-141.25	08/06/99	-173.50	-32.25	-1612.50	07/30/99	287.50	07/23/99	-2212.50
1999	07/13/98	-289.00	08/07/98	-251.50	37.50	1875.00	08/07/98	1875.00	07/17/98	-600.00
1998	07/14/97	-269.50	08/08/97	-248.50	21.00	1050.00	07/25/97	2250.00	07/31/97	-375.00
1997	07/15/96	-301.50	08/08/96	-292.25	9.25	462.50	07/18/96	2325.00		
1996	07/13/95	-195.25	08/08/95	-171.00	24.25	1212.50	08/01/95	1437.50	07/17/95	-162.50
1995	07/13/94	-260.00	08/08/94	-228.00	32.00	1600.00	08/04/94	1950.00		
1994	07/13/93	-397.50	08/06/93	-367.50	30.00	1500.00	08/06/93	1500.00	07/19/93	-1137.50
1993	07/13/92	-252.00	08/07/92	-230.50	21.50	1075.00	07/24/92	1137.50		
1992	07/15/91	-269.50	08/08/91	-281.50	-12.00	-600.00	07/18/91	425.00	08/02/91	-4000.00
1991	07/13/90	-326.25	08/08/90	-320.50	5.75	287.50	07/25/90	1387.50	08/06/90	-87.50
1990	07/13/89	-252.75	08/08/89	-172.25	80.50	4025.00	08/08/89	4025.00	07/14/89	-387.50
1989	07/13/88	-475.50	08/08/88	-468.00	7.50	375.00	07/26/88	4675.00	07/15/88	-3025.00
1988	07/13/87	-262.00	08/07/87	-234.50	27.50	1375.00	08/07/87	1375.00	07/20/87	-1250.00
1987	07/14/86	-258.00	08/08/86	-237.75	20.25	1012.50	08/07/86	1050.00	07/21/86	-1175.00

Percentage Correct	80									
Average Profit on Winning Trades					29.04	1452.08		Winners		12
Average Loss on Trades					-18.42	-920.83		Losers		3
Average Net Profit Per Trade					19.55	977.50		Total trades		15
Percentage Correct	85									
Average Profit on Winning Trades					28.82	1441.18		Winners		17
Average Loss on Trades					-18.42	-920.83		Losers		3
Average Net Profit Per Trade					21.74	1086.88		Total trades		20

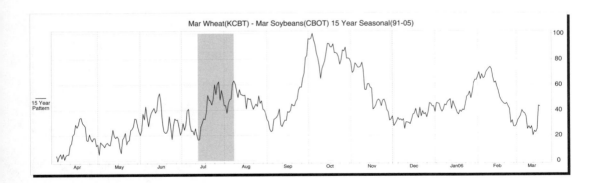

Mar Wheat(KCBT) - Mar Soybeans(CBOT) 15 Year Seasonal(91-05)

15 Year Pattern

Apr May Jun Jul Aug Sep Oct Nov Dec Jan06 Feb Mar

Figure 5-30

Buy Sep Wheat(KCBT) / Sell Sep Soybeans(CBOT)

Enter on approximately 07/14 - Exit on approximately 07/21

CONT YEAR	ENTRY DATE	ENTRY PRICE	EXIT DATE	EXIT PRICE	PROFIT	PROFIT AMOUNT	BEST EQUITY DATE	BEST EQUITY AMOUNT	WORST EQUITY DATE	WORST EQUITY AMOUNT
2005	07/14/05	-373.75	07/21/05	-339.75	34.00	1700.00	07/21/05	1700.00		
2004	07/14/04	-308.00	07/21/04	-269.00	39.00	1950.00	07/21/04	1950.00		
2003	07/14/03	-246.25	07/21/03	-204.50	41.75	2087.50	07/18/03	2237.50		
2002	07/15/02	-197.50	07/19/02	-192.50	5.00	250.00	07/17/02	475.00		
2001	07/16/01	-195.75	07/20/01	-176.25	19.50	975.00	07/20/01	975.00	07/17/01	-537.50
2000	07/14/00	-161.75	07/21/00	-175.75	-14.00	-700.00	07/17/00	37.50	07/21/00	-700.00
1999	07/14/99	-153.00	07/21/99	-177.25	-24.25	-1212.50	07/16/99	212.50	07/21/99	-1212.50
1998	07/14/98	-302.25	07/21/98	-293.25	9.00	450.00	07/21/98	450.00	07/17/98	-925.00
1997	07/14/97	-330.00	07/21/97	-292.00	38.00	1900.00	07/21/97	1900.00		
1996	07/15/96	-299.75	07/19/96	-267.50	32.25	1612.50	07/18/96	2525.00		
1995	07/14/95	-157.00	07/21/95	-141.25	15.75	787.50	07/20/95	962.50	07/17/95	-612.50
1994	07/14/94	-261.25	07/21/94	-231.75	29.50	1475.00	07/21/94	1475.00		
1993	07/14/93	-413.75	07/21/93	-409.75	4.00	200.00	07/21/93	200.00	07/19/93	-825.00
1992	07/14/92	-236.00	07/21/92	-222.75	13.25	662.50	07/21/92	662.50		
1991	07/15/91	-257.50	07/19/91	-250.00	7.50	375.00	07/18/91	437.50	07/16/91	-575.00
1990	07/16/90	-305.25	07/20/90	-298.25	7.00	350.00	07/20/90	350.00	07/19/90	-187.50
1989	07/14/89	-261.00	07/21/89	-232.00	29.00	1450.00	07/21/89	1450.00		
1988	07/14/88	-562.00	07/21/88	-454.00	108.00	5400.00	07/21/88	5400.00	07/15/88	-1425.00
1987	07/14/87	-267.75	07/21/87	-267.75	0.00	0.00	07/17/87	700.00	07/20/87	-475.00
1986	07/14/86	-246.50	07/21/86	-270.00	-23.50	-1175.00			07/21/86	-1175.00

Percentage Correct	87							
Average Profit on Winning Trades			22.19	1109.62		Winners	13
Average Loss on Trades			-19.13	-956.25		Losers	2
Average Net Profit Per Trade			16.68	834.17		Total trades	15
Percentage Correct	80							
Average Profit on Winning Trades			27.03	1351.56		Winners	16
Average Loss on Trades			-15.44	-771.88		Losers	4
Average Net Profit Per Trade			18.54	926.88		Total trades	20

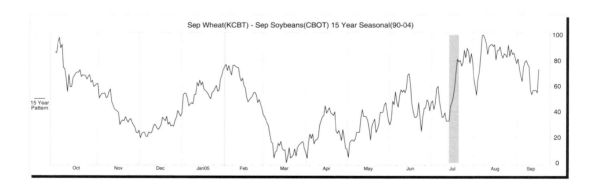

Sep Wheat(KCBT) - Sep Soybeans(CBOT) 15 Year Seasonal(90-04)

Figure 5-31

Buy Dec Wheat(MGE) / Sell Nov Soybeans(CBOT)

Enter on approximately 09/11 - Exit on approximately 10/01

CONT YEAR	ENTRY DATE	ENTRY PRICE	EXIT DATE	EXIT PRICE	PROFIT	PROFIT AMOUNT	BEST EQUITY DATE	BEST EQUITY AMOUNT	WORST EQUITY DATE	WORST EQUITY AMOUNT
2004	09/13/04	-188.00	10/01/04	-179.50	8.50	425.00	09/24/04	1837.50		
2003	09/11/03	-257.75	10/01/03	-320.75	-63.00	-3150.00	09/16/03	250.00	09/29/03	-3175.00
2002	09/11/02	-89.25	10/01/02	-26.75	62.50	3125.00	10/01/02	3125.00	09/16/02	-400.00
2001	09/13/01	-162.50	10/01/01	-149.50	13.00	650.00	09/28/01	900.00	09/17/01	-100.00
2000	09/11/00	-188.50	09/29/00	-166.00	22.50	1125.00	09/29/00	1125.00	09/12/00	-175.00
1999	09/13/99	-165.50	10/01/99	-155.75	9.75	487.50	09/24/99	1150.00		
1998	09/11/98	-210.50	10/01/98	-174.25	36.25	1812.50	10/01/98	1812.50	09/14/98	-162.50
1997	09/11/97	-239.00	10/01/97	-233.75	5.25	262.50	09/12/97	437.50	09/16/97	-562.50
1996	09/11/96	-385.00	10/01/96	-327.00	58.00	2900.00	10/01/96	2900.00	09/12/96	-450.00
1995	09/11/95	-154.75	09/29/95	-153.75	1.00	50.00	09/13/95	312.50	09/18/95	-1225.00
1994	09/12/94	-187.00	09/30/94	-134.25	52.75	2637.50	09/30/94	2637.50		
1993	09/13/93	-312.25	10/01/93	-294.75	17.50	875.00	10/01/93	875.00	09/23/93	-625.00
1992	09/11/92	-223.00	10/01/92	-192.75	30.25	1512.50	10/01/92	1512.50	09/15/92	-387.50
1991	09/11/91	-280.50	10/01/91	-260.00	20.50	1025.00	10/01/91	1025.00	09/18/91	-987.50
1990	09/11/90	-359.50	10/01/90	-342.00	17.50	875.00	10/01/90	875.00	09/14/90	-300.00
1989	09/11/89	-194.25	09/29/89	-175.50	18.75	937.50	09/29/89	937.50	09/21/89	-25.00
1988	09/12/88	-465.50	09/30/88	-398.25	67.25	3362.50	09/26/88	3937.50	09/14/88	-137.50
1987	09/11/87	-242.50	10/01/87	-262.50	-20.00	-1000.00	09/15/87	100.00	10/01/87	-1000.00
1986	09/11/86	-215.25	10/01/86	-227.00	-11.75	-587.50	09/15/86	100.00	09/22/86	-775.00
1985	09/11/85	-178.25	10/01/85	-174.25	4.00	200.00	09/27/85	437.50	09/23/85	-500.00

Percentage Correct	93									
Average Profit on Winning Trades					25.38	1268.75		Winners		14
Average Loss on Trades					-63.00	-3150.00		Losers		1
Average Net Profit Per Trade					19.48	974.17		Total trades		15
Percentage Correct	85									
Average Profit on Winning Trades					26.19	1309.56		Winners		17
Average Loss on Trades					-31.58	-1579.17		Losers		3
Average Net Profit Per Trade					17.53	876.25		Total trades		20

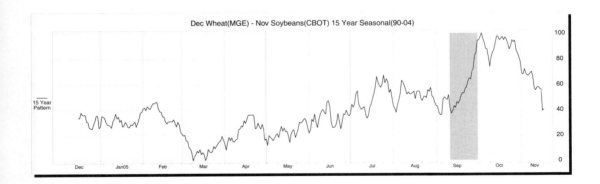

Dec Wheat(MGE) - Nov Soybeans(CBOT) 15 Year Seasonal(90-04)

15 Year Pattern

Figure 5-32

Buy Dec Wheat(KCBT) / Sell Nov Soybeans(CBOT)

Enter on approximately 09/11 - Exit on approximately 10/21

CONT YEAR	ENTRY DATE	ENTRY PRICE	EXIT DATE	EXIT PRICE	PROFIT	PROFIT AMOUNT	BEST EQUITY DATE	BEST EQUITY AMOUNT	WORST EQUITY DATE	WORST EQUITY AMOUNT
2004	09/13/04	-212.00	10/21/04	-191.25	20.75	1037.50	10/15/04	2325.00		
2003	09/11/03	-264.00	10/21/03	-389.75	-125.75	-6287.50	09/16/03	287.50	10/14/03	-7262.50
2002	09/11/02	-116.25	10/21/02	-71.75	44.50	2225.00	10/09/02	2937.50	09/16/02	-37.50
2001	09/13/01	-179.00	10/19/01	-130.75	48.25	2412.50	10/19/01	2412.50	09/17/01	-212.50
2000	09/11/00	-197.25	10/20/00	-159.75	37.50	1875.00	10/16/00	2812.50	09/22/00	-162.50
1999	09/13/99	-203.25	10/21/99	-202.00	1.25	62.50	09/24/99	1087.50	10/13/99	-1025.00
1998	09/11/98	-245.00	10/21/98	-230.75	14.25	712.50	10/05/98	2137.50		
1997	09/11/97	-259.25	10/21/97	-307.25	-48.00	-2400.00	09/23/97	400.00	10/13/97	-3962.50
1996	09/11/96	-368.25	10/21/96	-257.00	111.25	5562.50	10/14/96	6212.50	09/12/96	-537.50
1995	09/11/95	-151.75	10/20/95	-149.50	2.25	112.50	10/02/95	700.00	09/18/95	-1125.00
1994	09/12/94	-182.75	10/21/94	-142.25	40.50	2025.00	10/07/94	3612.50		
1993	09/13/93	-322.25	10/21/93	-285.00	37.25	1862.50	10/20/93	2100.00	09/23/93	-462.50
1992	09/11/92	-222.00	10/21/92	-205.25	16.75	837.50	10/02/92	1787.50	09/15/92	-162.50
1991	09/11/91	-269.00	10/21/91	-187.25	81.75	4087.50	10/21/91	4087.50	09/18/91	-725.00
1990	09/11/90	-354.25	10/19/90	-343.00	11.25	562.50	10/02/90	1250.00	09/12/90	-175.00
1989	09/11/89	-188.50	10/20/89	-160.25	28.25	1412.50	10/16/89	2200.00	09/21/89	-162.50
1988	09/12/88	-471.25	10/21/88	-364.00	107.25	5362.50	10/12/88	5375.00	09/14/88	-175.00
1987	09/11/87	-241.50	10/21/87	-238.50	3.00	150.00	09/25/87	400.00	10/01/87	-600.00
1986	09/11/86	-227.25	10/21/86	-228.25	-1.00	-50.00	10/14/86	400.00	09/22/86	-700.00
1985	09/11/85	-197.00	10/21/85	-190.50	6.50	325.00	10/16/85	462.50	09/23/85	-1162.50

Percentage Correct	87								
Average Profit on Winning Trades			35.96	1798.08		Winners	13
Average Loss on Trades			-86.88	-4343.75		Losers	2
Average Net Profit Per Trade			19.58	979.17		Total trades	15
Percentage Correct	85								
Average Profit on Winning Trades			36.03	1801.47		Winners	17
Average Loss on Trades			-58.25	-2912.50		Losers	3
Average Net Profit Per Trade			21.89	1094.38		Total trades	20

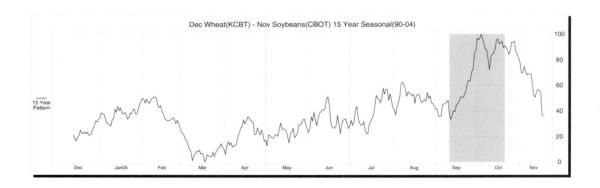

Dec Wheat(KCBT) - Nov Soybeans(CBOT) 15 Year Seasonal(90-04)

Chapter 5: Soybeans vs Grains

Figure 5-33

Buy Mar Wheat(KCBT) / Sell Mar Soybeans(CBOT)

Enter on approximately 09/16 - Exit on approximately 10/01

CONT YEAR	ENTRY DATE	ENTRY PRICE	EXIT DATE	EXIT PRICE	PROFIT	PROFIT AMOUNT	BEST EQUITY DATE	BEST EQUITY AMOUNT	WORST EQUITY DATE	WORST EQUITY AMOUNT
2005	09/16/04	-201.50	10/01/04	-205.75	-4.25	-212.50	09/24/04	1075.00	10/01/04	-212.50
2004	09/16/03	-251.25	10/01/03	-315.00	-63.75	-3187.50			10/01/03	-3187.50
2003	09/16/02	-129.00	10/01/02	-82.50	46.50	2325.00	10/01/02	2325.00		
2002	09/17/01	-181.50	10/01/01	-168.75	12.75	637.50	09/28/01	987.50		
2001	09/18/00	-191.00	09/29/00	-177.50	13.50	675.00	09/29/00	675.00	09/22/00	-750.00
2000	09/16/99	-198.25	10/01/99	-195.75	2.50	125.00	09/24/99	775.00	09/30/99	-12.50
1999	09/16/98	-245.25	10/01/98	-221.00	24.25	1212.50	10/01/98	1212.50		
1998	09/16/97	-261.50	10/01/97	-252.25	9.25	462.50	09/18/97	487.50		
1997	09/16/96	-388.50	10/01/96	-338.75	49.75	2487.50	10/01/96	2487.50	09/20/96	-37.50
1996	09/18/95	-194.50	09/29/95	-166.75	27.75	1387.50	09/29/95	1387.50		
1995	09/16/94	-173.25	09/30/94	-146.25	27.00	1350.00	09/30/94	1350.00	09/21/94	-175.00
1994	09/16/93	-324.50	10/01/93	-310.50	14.00	700.00	10/01/93	700.00	09/23/93	-900.00
1993	09/16/92	-231.75	10/01/92	-203.50	28.25	1412.50	10/01/92	1412.50		
1992	09/16/91	-297.00	10/01/91	-266.50	30.50	1525.00	10/01/91	1525.00	09/18/91	-300.00
1991	09/17/90	-363.75	10/01/90	-347.25	16.50	825.00	10/01/90	825.00	09/18/90	-450.00
1990	09/18/89	-204.25	09/29/89	-197.50	6.75	337.50	09/29/89	337.50	09/21/89	-650.00
1989	09/16/88	-462.00	09/30/88	-416.00	46.00	2300.00	09/26/88	2925.00		
1988	09/16/87	-250.25	10/01/87	-261.75	-11.50	-575.00	09/25/87	475.00	10/01/87	-575.00
1987	09/16/86	-244.50	10/01/86	-251.50	-7.00	-350.00			09/22/86	-612.50
1986	09/16/85	-228.00	10/01/85	-227.50	0.50	25.00	09/27/85	187.50	09/23/85	-787.50

Percentage Correct	87				
Average Profit on Winning Trades		23.27	1163.46	Winners	13
Average Loss on Trades		-34.00	-1700.00	Losers	2
Average Net Profit Per Trade		15.63	781.67	Total trades	15

Percentage Correct	80				
Average Profit on Winning Trades		22.23	1111.72	Winners	16
Average Loss on Trades		-21.63	-1081.25	Losers	4
Average Net Profit Per Trade		13.46	673.13	Total trades	20

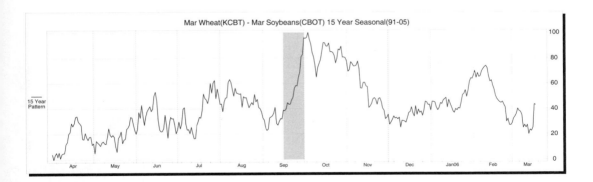

Mar Wheat(KCBT) - Mar Soybeans(CBOT) 15 Year Seasonal(91-05)

Figure 5-34

Buy Dec Wheat(CBOT) / Sell Nov Soybeans(CBOT)

Enter on approximately 09/16 - Exit on approximately 10/22

CONT YEAR	ENTRY DATE	ENTRY PRICE	EXIT DATE	EXIT PRICE	PROFIT	PROFIT AMOUNT	BEST EQUITY DATE	BEST EQUITY AMOUNT	WORST EQUITY DATE	WORST EQUITY AMOUNT
2004	09/16/04	-219.00	10/22/04	-221.50	-2.50	-125.00	10/15/04	1212.50	10/11/04	-850.00
2003	09/16/03	-257.25	10/22/03	-395.25	-138.00	-6900.00			10/14/03	-7937.50
2002	09/16/02	-171.75	10/22/02	-142.75	29.00	1450.00	10/18/02	1937.50		
2001	09/17/01	-205.50	10/22/01	-138.75	66.75	3337.50	10/19/01	3387.50	09/20/01	-112.50
2000	09/18/00	-232.25	10/20/00	-207.50	24.75	1237.50	10/16/00	1900.00	09/22/00	-650.00
1999	09/16/99	-216.75	10/22/99	-214.75	2.00	100.00	09/24/99	725.00	10/13/99	-1375.00
1998	09/16/98	-262.50	10/22/98	-261.50	1.00	50.00	10/05/98	1400.00	10/13/98	-250.00
1997	09/16/97	-274.25	10/22/97	-324.25	-50.00	-2500.00	09/23/97	512.50	10/13/97	-3700.00
1996	09/16/96	-376.00	10/22/96	-289.50	86.50	4325.00	10/14/96	5850.00	09/17/96	-75.00
1995	09/18/95	-179.75	10/20/95	-163.50	16.25	812.50	10/02/95	1700.00		
1994	09/16/94	-163.75	10/21/94	-151.25	12.50	625.00	10/07/94	2437.50	09/21/94	-137.50
1993	09/16/93	-319.75	10/22/93	-286.00	33.75	1687.50	10/20/93	1925.00	09/23/93	-900.00
1992	09/16/92	-214.75	10/22/92	-195.25	19.50	975.00	10/15/92	1812.50		
1991	09/16/91	-275.75	10/22/91	-194.75	81.00	4050.00	10/21/91	4162.50	09/18/91	-350.00
1990	09/17/90	-350.50	10/22/90	-347.50	3.00	150.00	10/02/90	825.00	09/18/90	-387.50
1989	09/18/89	-177.25	10/20/89	-156.50	20.75	1037.50	10/16/89	2050.00	09/21/89	-587.50
1988	09/16/88	-442.00	10/21/88	-355.25	86.75	4337.50	10/21/88	4337.50		
1987	09/16/87	-236.75	10/22/87	-234.50	2.25	112.50	10/12/87	462.50	10/01/87	-462.50
1986	09/16/86	-215.50	10/22/86	-197.75	17.75	887.50	10/21/86	1137.50	09/22/86	-687.50
1985	09/16/85	-219.50	10/22/85	-191.00	28.50	1425.00	10/17/85	1462.50	09/23/85	-600.00

Percentage Correct	80							
Average Profit on Winning Trades		31.33	1566.67		Winners	12
Average Loss on Trades		-63.50	-3175.00		Losers	3
Average Net Profit Per Trade		12.37	618.33		Total trades	15

Percentage Correct	85							
Average Profit on Winning Trades		31.29	1564.71		Winners	17
Average Loss on Trades		-63.50	-3175.00		Losers	3
Average Net Profit Per Trade		17.08	853.75		Total trades	20

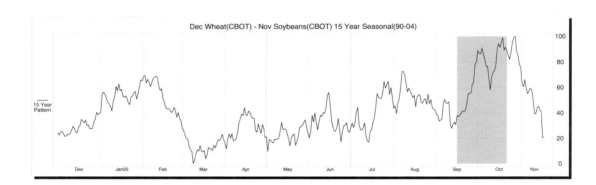

Dec Wheat(CBOT) - Nov Soybeans(CBOT) 15 Year Seasonal(90-04)

15 Year Pattern

Chapter 5: Soybeans vs Grains

Figure 5-35

Buy Dec Wheat(MGE) / Sell Nov Soybeans(CBOT)

Enter on approximately 09/18 - Exit on approximately 10/01

CONT YEAR	ENTRY DATE	ENTRY PRICE	EXIT DATE	EXIT PRICE	PROFIT	PROFIT AMOUNT	BEST EQUITY DATE	BEST EQUITY AMOUNT	WORST EQUITY DATE	WORST EQUITY AMOUNT
2004	09/20/04	-169.50	10/01/04	-179.50	-10.00	-500.00	09/24/04	912.50	10/01/04	-500.00
2003	09/18/03	-279.50	10/01/03	-320.75	-41.25	-2062.50			09/29/03	-2087.50
2002	09/18/02	-74.75	10/01/02	-26.75	48.00	2400.00	10/01/02	2400.00	09/19/02	-112.50
2001	09/18/01	-161.00	10/01/01	-149.50	11.50	575.00	09/28/01	825.00		
2000	09/18/00	-178.25	09/29/00	-166.00	12.25	612.50	09/29/00	612.50	09/22/00	-462.50
1999	09/20/99	-156.00	10/01/99	-155.75	0.25	12.50	09/24/99	675.00	09/30/99	-187.50
1998	09/18/98	-190.25	10/01/98	-174.25	16.00	800.00	10/01/98	800.00		
1997	09/18/97	-238.00	10/01/97	-233.75	4.25	212.50	09/23/97	375.00	09/19/97	-200.00
1996	09/18/96	-383.50	10/01/96	-327.00	56.50	2825.00	10/01/96	2825.00	09/20/96	-200.00
1995	09/18/95	-179.25	09/29/95	-153.75	25.50	1275.00	09/29/95	1275.00		
1994	09/19/94	-164.25	09/30/94	-134.25	30.00	1500.00	09/30/94	1500.00	09/21/94	-100.00
1993	09/20/93	-318.75	10/01/93	-294.75	24.00	1200.00	10/01/93	1200.00	09/23/93	-300.00
1992	09/18/92	-209.25	10/01/92	-192.75	16.50	825.00	10/01/92	825.00	09/24/92	-200.00
1991	09/18/91	-300.25	10/01/91	-260.00	40.25	2012.50	10/01/91	2012.50		
1990	09/18/90	-364.25	10/01/90	-342.00	22.25	1112.50	10/01/90	1112.50		
1989	09/18/89	-183.00	09/29/89	-175.50	7.50	375.00	09/29/89	375.00	09/21/89	-587.50
1988	09/19/88	-414.75	09/30/88	-398.25	16.50	825.00	09/26/88	1400.00	09/22/88	-262.50
1987	09/18/87	-247.50	10/01/87	-262.50	-15.00	-750.00	09/25/87	275.00	10/01/87	-750.00
1986	09/18/86	-223.75	10/01/86	-227.00	-3.25	-162.50	09/26/86	62.50	09/22/86	-350.00
1985	09/18/85	-183.75	10/01/85	-174.25	9.50	475.00	09/27/85	712.50	09/23/85	-225.00

Percentage Correct		87								
Average Profit on Winning Trades					23.63	1181.73		Winners		13
Average Loss on Trades					-25.63	-1281.25		Losers		2
Average Net Profit Per Trade					17.07	853.33		Total trades		15
Percentage Correct		80								
Average Profit on Winning Trades					21.30	1064.84		Winners		16
Average Loss on Trades					-17.38	-868.75		Losers		4
Average Net Profit Per Trade					13.56	678.13		Total trades		20

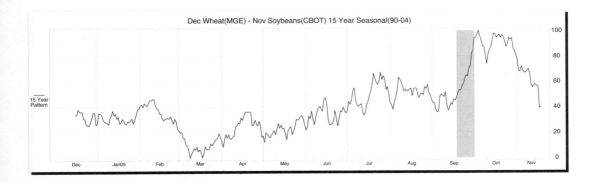

Dec Wheat(MGE) - Nov Soybeans(CBOT) 15 Year Seasonal(90-04)

Chapter 5: Soybeans vs Grains

209

Figure 5-36

Buy Dec Wheat(CBOT) / Sell Nov Soybeans(CBOT)

Enter on approximately 09/21 - Exit on approximately 10/01

CONT YEAR	ENTRY DATE	ENTRY PRICE	EXIT DATE	EXIT PRICE	PROFIT	PROFIT AMOUNT	BEST EQUITY DATE	BEST EQUITY AMOUNT	WORST EQUITY DATE	WORST EQUITY AMOUNT
2004	09/21/04	-207.50	10/01/04	-230.75	-23.25	-1162.50	09/24/04	287.50	10/01/04	-1162.50
2003	09/22/03	-305.75	10/01/03	-323.00	-17.25	-862.50	09/25/03	537.50	09/29/03	-1112.50
2002	09/23/02	-163.75	10/01/02	-145.50	18.25	912.50	10/01/02	912.50	09/25/02	-200.00
2001	09/21/01	-203.75	10/01/01	-185.75	18.00	900.00	09/28/01	1162.50		
2000	09/21/00	-244.25	09/29/00	-225.50	18.75	937.50	09/29/00	937.50	09/22/00	-50.00
1999	09/21/99	-214.75	10/01/99	-214.00	0.75	37.50	09/24/99	625.00	09/22/99	-37.50
1998	09/21/98	-253.25	10/01/98	-246.25	7.00	350.00	10/01/98	350.00	09/22/98	-112.50
1997	09/22/97	-271.25	10/01/97	-269.75	1.50	75.00	09/23/97	362.50	09/26/97	-162.50
1996	09/23/96	-372.25	10/01/96	-315.50	56.75	2837.50	10/01/96	2837.50		
1995	09/21/95	-172.75	09/29/95	-153.75	19.00	950.00	09/29/95	950.00		
1994	09/21/94	-166.50	09/30/94	-132.50	34.00	1700.00	09/30/94	1700.00		
1993	09/21/93	-320.50	10/01/93	-301.75	18.75	937.50	10/01/93	937.50	09/23/93	-862.50
1992	09/21/92	-201.25	10/01/92	-183.00	18.25	912.50	10/01/92	912.50	09/22/92	-100.00
1991	09/23/91	-265.25	10/01/91	-248.75	16.50	825.00	10/01/91	825.00	09/24/91	-12.50
1990	09/21/90	-341.25	10/01/90	-336.75	4.50	225.00	10/01/90	225.00	09/25/90	-75.00
1989	09/21/89	-189.00	09/29/89	-160.75	28.25	1412.50	09/29/89	1412.50		
1988	09/21/88	-417.75	09/30/88	-398.25	19.50	975.00	09/26/88	1687.50		
1987	09/21/87	-229.50	10/01/87	-246.00	-16.50	-825.00	09/25/87	87.50	10/01/87	-825.00
1986	09/22/86	-229.25	10/01/86	-218.75	10.50	525.00	09/26/86	575.00		
1985	09/23/85	-231.50	10/01/85	-212.00	19.50	975.00	10/01/85	975.00		

Percentage Correct	87			
Average Profit on Winning Trades		17.85	892.31	Winners	13
Average Loss on Trades		-20.25	-1012.50	Losers	2
Average Net Profit Per Trade		12.77	638.33	Total trades	15
Percentage Correct	85			
Average Profit on Winning Trades		18.22	911.03	Winners	17
Average Loss on Trades		-19.00	-950.00	Losers	3
Average Net Profit Per Trade		12.64	631.88	Total trades	20

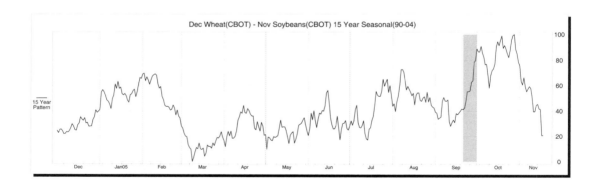

Dec Wheat(CBOT) - Nov Soybeans(CBOT) 15 Year Seasonal(90-04)

Figure 5-37

Buy Jul Wheat(CBOT) / Sell Jul Soybeans(CBOT)

Enter on approximately 12/26 - Exit on approximately 02/03

CONT YEAR	ENTRY DATE	ENTRY PRICE	EXIT DATE	EXIT PRICE	PROFIT	PROFIT AMOUNT	BEST EQUITY DATE	BEST EQUITY AMOUNT	WORST EQUITY DATE	WORST EQUITY AMOUNT
2005	12/27/04	-245.75	02/03/05	-204.75	41.00	2050.00	02/03/05	2050.00		
2004	12/26/03	-424.25	02/03/04	-413.50	10.75	537.50	01/07/04	1925.00	01/26/04	-1550.00
2003	12/26/02	-248.75	02/03/03	-247.25	1.50	75.00	01/10/03	975.00	01/02/03	-612.50
2002	12/26/01	-154.25	02/01/02	-139.50	14.75	737.50	01/04/02	987.50	01/16/02	-287.50
2001	12/26/00	-230.00	02/02/01	-189.50	40.50	2025.00	01/23/01	2862.50		
2000	12/27/99	-213.75	02/03/00	-242.75	-29.00	-1450.00	12/29/99	175.00	01/27/00	-2325.00
1999	12/28/98	-256.00	02/03/99	-230.00	26.00	1300.00	01/29/99	1737.50	01/05/99	-300.00
1998	12/26/97	-349.25	02/03/98	-329.00	20.25	1012.50	01/16/98	1537.50	12/30/97	-325.00
1997	12/26/96	-348.25	02/03/97	-394.75	-46.50	-2325.00	01/08/97	100.00	01/27/97	-2937.50
1996	12/26/95	-309.50	02/02/96	-295.00	14.50	725.00	01/30/96	750.00	01/16/96	-850.00
1995	12/27/94	-244.75	02/03/95	-225.75	19.00	950.00	01/18/95	1150.00		
1994	12/27/93	-367.75	02/03/94	-342.50	25.25	1262.50	02/03/94	1262.50	01/19/94	-175.00
1993	12/28/92	-275.50	02/03/93	-258.25	17.25	862.50	02/01/93	1250.00		
1992	12/26/91	-241.75	02/03/92	-195.25	46.50	2325.00	02/03/92	2325.00		
1991	12/26/90	-333.75	02/01/91	-313.75	20.00	1000.00	01/30/91	1012.50	01/22/91	-475.00
1990	12/26/89	-249.25	02/02/90	-234.50	14.75	737.50	01/25/90	900.00	12/28/89	-137.50
1989	12/27/88	-434.75	02/03/89	-376.25	58.50	2925.00	01/20/89	3625.00	01/06/89	-462.50
1988	12/28/87	-319.00	02/03/88	-301.75	17.25	862.50	02/02/88	1000.00	01/04/88	-800.00
1987	12/26/86	-253.75	02/03/87	-244.25	9.50	475.00	02/02/87	500.00	12/31/86	-125.00
1986	12/26/85	-277.00	02/03/86	-277.75	-0.75	-37.50	12/27/85	550.00	01/15/86	-1062.50

Percentage Correct	87							
Average Profit on Winning Trades					22.87	1143.27	Winners	13
Average Loss on Trades					-37.75	-1887.50	Losers	2
Average Net Profit Per Trade					14.78	739.17	Total trades	15
Percentage Correct	85							
Average Profit on Winning Trades					23.37	1168.38	Winners	17
Average Loss on Trades					-25.42	-1270.83	Losers	3
Average Net Profit Per Trade					16.05	802.50	Total trades	20

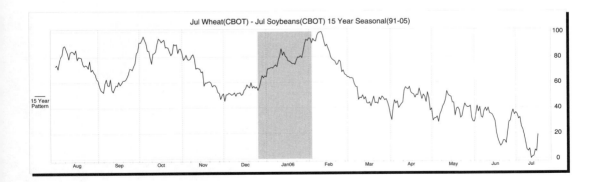

Jul Wheat(CBOT) - Jul Soybeans(CBOT) 15 Year Seasonal(91-05)

15 Year Pattern

Chapter 5: Soybeans vs Grains

211

Figure 5-38

Buy Jul Wheat(KCBT) / Sell Jul Soybeans(CBOT)

Enter on approximately 12/26 - Exit on approximately 02/08

CONT YEAR	ENTRY DATE	ENTRY PRICE	EXIT DATE	EXIT PRICE	PROFIT	PROFIT AMOUNT	BEST EQUITY DATE	BEST EQUITY AMOUNT	WORST EQUITY DATE	WORST EQUITY AMOUNT
2005	12/27/04	-237.00	02/08/05	-203.75	33.25	1662.50	02/07/05	1900.00		
2004	12/26/03	-421.25	02/06/04	-440.50	-19.25	-962.50	01/07/04	1862.50	01/26/04	-1487.50
2003	12/26/02	-224.50	02/07/03	-210.25	14.25	712.50	02/07/03	712.50	01/28/03	-787.50
2002	12/26/01	-143.25	02/08/02	-139.50	3.75	187.50	01/02/02	637.50	01/16/02	-662.50
2001	12/26/00	-182.50	02/08/01	-130.50	52.00	2600.00	01/26/01	2712.50		
2000	12/27/99	-186.50	02/08/00	-209.75	-23.25	-1162.50	12/29/99	175.00	01/27/00	-2350.00
1999	12/28/98	-221.75	02/08/99	-193.75	28.00	1400.00	01/29/99	1650.00	01/05/99	-425.00
1998	12/26/97	-341.25	02/06/98	-333.00	8.25	412.50	01/16/98	1650.00	12/30/97	-175.00
1997	12/26/96	-338.00	02/07/97	-383.50	-45.50	-2275.00			01/27/97	-2925.00
1996	12/26/95	-295.00	02/08/96	-267.50	27.50	1375.00	02/07/96	1512.50	01/03/96	-787.50
1995	12/27/94	-238.50	02/08/95	-226.75	11.75	587.50	01/18/95	1125.00		
1994	12/27/93	-369.00	02/08/94	-337.50	31.50	1575.00	02/07/94	1575.00	01/19/94	-212.50
1993	12/28/92	-276.25	02/08/93	-258.25	18.00	900.00	01/29/93	1012.50	01/12/93	-12.50
1992	12/26/91	-240.00	02/07/92	-168.50	71.50	3575.00	02/07/92	3575.00		
1991	12/26/90	-334.00	02/08/91	-323.00	11.00	550.00	01/31/91	925.00	01/22/91	-500.00
1990	12/26/89	-239.00	02/08/90	-230.00	9.00	450.00	01/25/90	850.00	12/28/89	-187.50
1989	12/27/88	-431.75	02/08/89	-346.50	85.25	4262.50	02/08/89	4262.50	01/06/89	-362.50
1988	12/28/87	-320.25	02/08/88	-301.75	18.50	925.00	02/08/88	925.00	01/04/88	-800.00
1987	12/26/86	-261.25	02/06/87	-247.50	13.75	687.50	02/06/87	687.50	12/31/86	-237.50
1986	12/26/85	-278.25	02/07/86	-278.00	0.25	12.50	12/27/85	512.50	01/15/86	-987.50

Percentage Correct		80								
Average Profit on Winning Trades					25.90	1294.79		Winners		12
Average Loss on Trades					-29.33	-1466.67		Losers		3
Average Net Profit Per Trade					14.85	742.50		Total trades		15
Percentage Correct		85								
Average Profit on Winning Trades					25.74	1286.76		Winners		17
Average Loss on Trades					-29.33	-1466.67		Losers		3
Average Net Profit Per Trade					17.48	873.75		Total trades		20

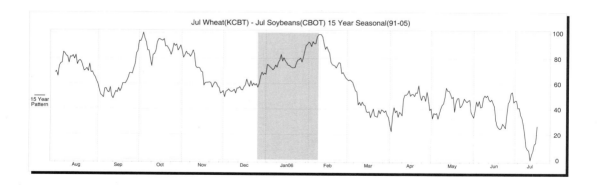

Jul Wheat(KCBT) - Jul Soybeans(CBOT) 15 Year Seasonal(91-05)

Chapter 6: Meats

Meat is the primary source of protein in human diets of developed nations and a growing source in those of developing nations. Health-conscious diets in the early twenty-first century have elevated fish and poultry, but beef and pork remain staples.

Domestic US beef and pork industries have undergone transformations over the decades, both in response to changing consumer tastes and to reflect increasing production efficiencies. Pork, for example, was once considered part of a rich man's diet; but greater economy of production made it more readily available and the shift toward leaner hogs boosted demand. Further, no longer are Midwestern farms dotted with hog houses: Production is now more concentrated in contained commercial facilities. Similarly with cattle: No longer do cowboys drive herds along dusty trails from ranch to railhead. Most cattle are now finished in commercial feedlots.

Beef production involves first breeding and then raising cattle. Cow-calf operations, still located mostly on Western ranches and in regions with harsh winters, produce calves, or feeder cattle. A young female can first be bred at 14-18 months of age. Gestation requires another 9 months. Feedlot operators buy calves and yearlings preferably when they weigh 650-850 pounds. Called feeder cattle by then, they are placed into feedlots and fed to desired market weight. Because beef production is both capital intensive and requires a lengthy start-up time, there has evolved over the last century a cattle cycle averaging about 12 years during which the size of the nation's herd expands and contracts in response to rising and falling prices.

Pork production cycles are shorter, largely because less time is required to bring a hog to market. A young female can first be bred at 7-8 months of age. Gestation requires less than 4 months. A newly born pig can reach market weight in 5-6 months. Concentrating production into large facilities with higher fixed costs has tended to smooth a seasonal production pattern still greatly influenced by weather and feed, which remains a primary cost. Pork products are moved into cold storage when production is heaviest and moved out during periods of high demand.

In 1964, the Chicago Mercantile Exchange (CME) launched the first-ever futures contract for a nonstorable commodity — live cattle. Although the contract has changed as the industry has evolved, it is still settled by delivery of live animals. In 1971, CME introduced a contract for feeder cattle, also settled by delivery. In order to better serve both long and short hedgers, this contract is now settled to an exchange-calculated cash index of feeder cattle prices. In 1969, CME launched the industry's second contract for a nonstorable commodity when it began trading live hogs, also settled by delivery. As the industry responded to changes in consumer preference, this contract evolved into lean hogs and is now also settled to an exchange-calculated cash index. Although contracts for various pork products have been listed at CME over the years, the one most attractive to the industry was that for frozen pork bellies, or bacon, first traded in 1961 and also settled by delivery.

Intra-market Spreads

The function of spreads between delivery months in the meats complex is to balance supply and demand over time, but their task is more difficult than those in other markets. With the exception of pork bellies, the underlying commodities are nonstorable. Thus, rather than simply derive carrying charges from current cash prices, markets for live cattle, feeder

---

cattle, and lean hogs build premiums and discounts into their price structures that anticipate seasonal disparities in supply and demand.

Live Cattle

Consider the apparent discrepancy between seasonal patterns of cash live cattle and of futures contracts, which can trade above or below cash. The seasonal pattern in cash cattle prices seems ideally to reflect dynamics in demand. Retail beef consumption is greatest in cold weather and least in hot weather. Thus, demand tends to be weakest in the heat of July/August, to rise through autumn, to peak in winter, and then to decline again into summer.

Figure 6-1: Cash Live Cattle Seasonal Pattern

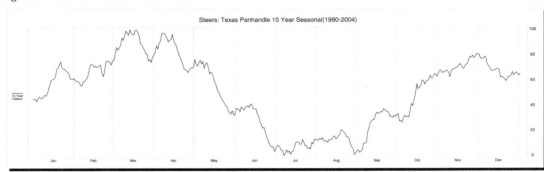

The pattern of supply tends to reinforce that pattern of demand. Most cow-calf operations are in regions with harsh winters. In order to increase the rate of survivability, cows are bred to calve in the spring. This seasonal breeding pattern helps effect a seasonal slaughter pattern. Weather helps reinforce a seasonal bulge in slaughter in another way. Animals in outdoor feedlots gain weight much more slowly during cold winter weather. Thus, demand tends to outstrip supply into a March/April peak — when consumption is still high, the industry is accumulating inventory for the opening of outdoor grilling season, but slaughter remains constrained. By mid April, however, the number of animals finally ready for market rises dramatically. Slaughter then peaks in May/June. With production highest just before consumption will be lowest, supply far outstrips demand and cash prices decline into their seasonal nadir.

Figure 6-2: August Live Cattle Seasonal Pattern

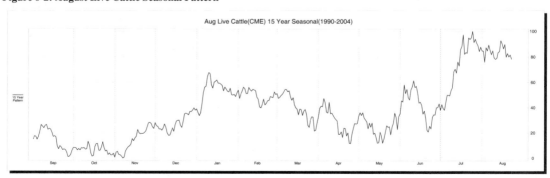

Compare that with the pattern of August futures. With retail beef consumption lowest and feed costs high during the heat of summer, feedlot operators typically work cattle inventories lower into August. Thus, the function of futures can be to bid prices high enough to maintain sufficient supply through summer. In addition, the federal government tends to begin purchasing beef for subsidized programs such as school lunches, and retail grocers accumulate some beef for the last holiday weekend of the season in early September.

Corn harvest is also a primary determinant in the pattern of supply. After being placed into a feedlot, feeder cattle require at least 3-4 months and as many as 7-8 to become market-ready. Feedlot inventories may be lowest in August; but, because feedlot operators want to feed as much freshly harvested corn as possible to as many animals as possible, they aggressively fill those feedlots September-November. In response, a pattern of slaughter has evolved such that numbers tend to be lowest December-March and, with cold weather slowing weight gain until spring, highest in May/June.

Figure 6-3: Dec/Jun Live Cattle Seasonal Pattern

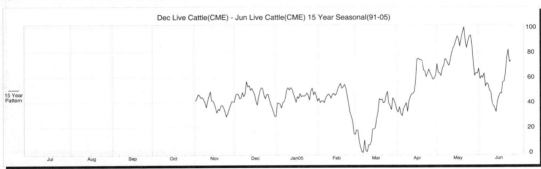

Thus, well-defined patterns both of supply and of demand tend to drive bull and bear spreads. Bear spreads tend to be most prominent and most regular from March through May, after the demand peak (consumption plus accumulation) and at the approach of the slaughter peak. As the seasonal pattern above suggests, the deferred December contract (representing low slaughter) outperforms June Cattle (representing peak slaughter) from March into May. The first strategy listed in the table below identifies the typically most reliable and most intense few weeks for this bear spread. As is true in certain markets, however, spreads during this period have tended to exhibit characteristics less of true bear spreads than of exhausted bull spreads — often with the nearby contract declining sharply but with little effect on the deferred.

Figure 6-4: Live Cattle Spread Summary

Moore Research Center, Inc.	Live Cattle Spread Strategies							
Seasonal Strategy	Entry Date	Exit Date	Win Pct	Win Yrs	Loss Years	Total Years	Average Profit	Ave Pft Per Day
Buy Dec Live Cattle(CME)	4/10	5/20	87	13	2	15	478	12
Sell Jun Live Cattle(CME)			85	17	3	20	408	10
Buy Oct Live Cattle(CME)	6/22	9/12	80	12	3	15	705	8
Sell Apr Live Cattle(CME)			80	16	4	20	767	9
Buy Oct Live Cattle(CME)	6/22	8/05	80	12	3	15	419	9
Sell Apr Live Cattle(CME)			80	16	4	20	524	12

Figure 6-4: Live Cattle Spread Summary continued

Moore Research Center, Inc.							Live Cattle Spread Strategies	
Seasonal Strategy	Entry Date	Exit Date	Win Pct	Win Yrs	Loss Years	Total Years	Average Profit	Ave Pft Per Day
Buy Dec Live Cattle(CME)	7/23	10/15	80	12	3	15	477	6
Sell Jun Live Cattle(CME)			85	17	3	20	635	7
Buy Dec Live Cattle(CME)	8/29	11/12	80	12	3	15	692	9
Sell Jun Live Cattle(CME)			80	16	4	20	774	10
Buy Feb Live Cattle(CME)	10/05	11/07	80	12	3	15	441	13
Sell Aug Live Cattle(CME)			80	16	4	20	422	12
Buy Apr Live Cattle(CME)	12/27	3/05	87	13	2	15	585	8
Sell Aug Live Cattle(CME)			90	18	2	20	631	9

Figure 6-5: Oct/Apr Live Cattle Seasonal Pattern

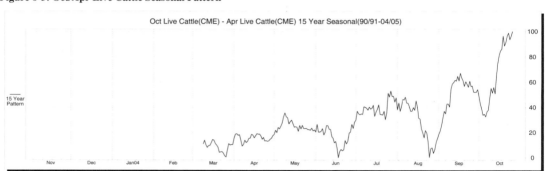

Oct Live Cattle(CME) - Apr Live Cattle(CME) 15 Year Seasonal(90/91-04/05)

For the remaining nine months of the year, bull spreads tend to predominate. The seasonal pattern for October/April Cattle illustrates how it can begin even as slaughter is peaking and then continue, albeit with a few interruptions along the way, into expiry of the October contract. The underlying fundamental cause, of course, is that slaughter tends generally to decline into December but demand to rise as temperatures cool and schools reopen.

Figure 6-6: Apr/Aug Live Cattle Seasonal Pattern

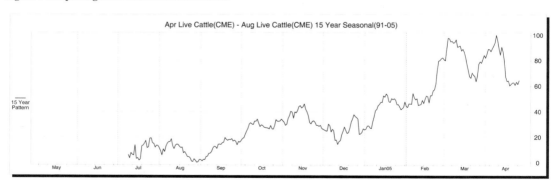

Apr Live Cattle(CME) - Aug Live Cattle(CME) 15 Year Seasonal(91-05)

Both the seasonal pattern above and the strategies listed in the table suggest that these bull spreads tend to move in surges, initially from peak slaughter into late July/early August and again often dramatically from late August into September. Not only have these bull spreads been reliable but they tend to suffer but little adversity. For example, the bull spread

Figure 6-7

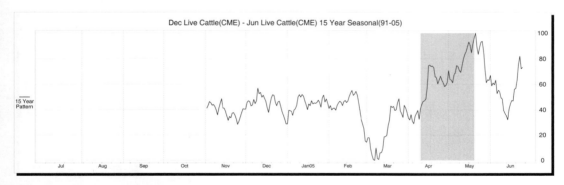

							BEST	BEST	WORST	WORST
CONT YEAR	ENTRY DATE	ENTRY PRICE	EXIT DATE	EXIT PRICE	PROFIT	PROFIT AMOUNT	EQUITY DATE	EQUITY AMOUNT	EQUITY DATE	EQUITY AMOUNT
2005	04/11/05	1.62	05/20/05	2.09	0.47	188.00	05/06/05	268.00	04/26/05	-652.00
2004	04/12/04	0.81	05/20/04	3.37	2.56	1024.00	04/22/04	1384.00	05/06/04	-1236.00
2003	04/10/03	0.04	05/20/03	-0.98	-1.03	-412.00	04/16/03	320.00	05/19/03	-412.00
2002	04/10/02	4.84	05/20/02	6.07	1.23	492.00	05/20/02	492.00	05/08/02	-232.00
2001	04/10/01	1.90	05/18/01	1.96	0.07	28.00	05/16/01	460.00		
2000	04/10/00	4.69	05/19/00	3.97	-0.72	-288.00	05/08/00	92.00	04/25/00	-312.00
1999	04/12/99	1.92	05/20/99	3.50	1.58	632.00	05/12/99	840.00		
1998	04/13/98	1.68	05/20/98	3.78	2.10	840.00	05/20/98	840.00	04/30/98	-312.00
1997	04/10/97	5.45	05/20/97	5.61	0.17	68.00	04/28/97	400.00	04/15/97	-372.00
1996	04/10/96	1.50	05/20/96	3.45	1.95	780.00	04/25/96	1340.00	05/06/96	-352.00
1995	04/10/95	0.79	05/19/95	2.29	1.50	600.00	05/11/95	1072.00	04/24/95	-332.00
1994	04/11/94	-0.47	05/20/94	5.22	5.71	2284.00	05/20/94	2284.00		
1993	04/12/93	-2.60	05/20/93	-1.94	0.65	260.00	04/20/93	632.00	05/10/93	-132.00
1992	04/10/92	-4.37	05/20/92	-3.64	0.72	288.00	04/22/92	428.00	05/08/92	-24.00
1991	04/10/91	-0.34	05/20/91	0.59	0.95	380.00	05/01/91	500.00	04/16/91	-52.00
1990	04/10/90	0.65	05/18/90	1.63	0.98	392.00	04/30/90	480.00	05/07/90	-200.00
1989	04/10/89	-2.09	05/19/89	0.39	2.50	1000.00	05/17/89	1120.00		
1988	04/11/88	-4.59	05/20/88	-4.21	0.38	152.00	04/25/88	1092.00		
1987	04/10/87	-4.50	05/20/87	-4.11	0.38	152.00	04/15/87	340.00	05/11/87	-1028.00
1986	04/10/86	-0.57	05/20/86	-2.32	-1.75	-700.00	04/16/86	60.00	05/09/86	-1244.00

Percentage Correct	87			
Average Profit on Winning Trades		1.51	604.92	Winners	13
Average Loss on Trades		-0.88	-350.00	Losers	2
Average Net Profit Per Trade		1.19	477.60	Total trades	15
Percentage Correct	85			
Average Profit on Winning Trades		1.41	562.35	Winners	17
Average Loss on Trades		-1.17	-466.67	Losers	3
Average Net Profit Per Trade		1.02	408.00	Total trades	20

for December/June (Figure 6-10) from late July into mid October suffered daily closing draw-down greater than or equal to 1.85 cents/pound in only two of the nineteen years 1985-2003.

But those often represent only the bull's initial legs. The relationship between April/August can perform as a proxy to illustrate how the market tends to build seasonal disparities in supply/demand into its price structure. As feedlots are being filled September-November, bull spreads begin their journey toward the typical spring peak in the cash market.

Figure 6-8

							BEST	BEST	WORST	WORST

Buy Oct Live Cattle(CME) / Sell Apr Live Cattle(CME)

Enter on approximately 06/22 - Exit on approximately 09/12

CONT YEAR	ENTRY DATE	ENTRY PRICE	EXIT DATE	EXIT PRICE	PROFIT	PROFIT AMOUNT	BEST EQUITY DATE	BEST EQUITY AMOUNT	WORST EQUITY DATE	WORST EQUITY AMOUNT
2004	06/22/04	2.03	09/10/04	-1.38	-3.41	-1364.00	06/24/04	340.00	09/09/04	-1832.00
2003	06/23/03	-5.78	09/12/03	7.75	13.53	5412.00	09/11/03	5552.00		
2002	06/24/02	-4.03	09/12/02	-3.59	0.43	172.00	07/18/02	700.00	08/26/02	-480.00
2001	06/22/01	-2.12	09/10/01	-5.25	-3.12	-1248.00	06/27/01	220.00	09/10/01	-1248.00
2000	06/22/00	-5.95	09/12/00	-5.53	0.42	168.00	08/23/00	532.00	07/25/00	-52.00
1999	06/22/99	-4.01	09/10/99	-2.55	1.47	588.00	09/07/99	696.00	07/20/99	-172.00
1998	06/22/98	-4.31	09/11/98	-3.39	0.92	368.00	09/11/98	368.00	08/21/98	-452.00
1997	06/23/97	-5.71	09/12/97	-5.39	0.32	128.00	07/28/97	748.00	07/08/97	-452.00
1996	06/24/96	0.29	09/12/96	6.15	5.85	2340.00	09/12/96	2340.00		
1995	06/22/95	-2.37	09/12/95	-1.56	0.81	324.00	08/02/95	660.00	08/25/95	-476.00
1994	06/22/94	-3.52	09/12/94	0.50	4.02	1608.00	08/03/94	2156.00	06/24/94	-24.00
1993	06/22/93	-1.53	09/10/93	-1.25	0.28	112.00	09/03/93	332.00	07/23/93	-740.00
1992	06/22/92	0.75	09/11/92	2.25	1.50	600.00	09/10/92	620.00	06/25/92	-268.00
1991	06/24/91	-1.25	09/12/91	-1.48	-0.23	-92.00	07/08/91	620.00	08/08/91	-888.00
1990	06/22/90	-0.82	09/12/90	2.82	3.66	1464.00	09/11/90	1504.00	07/02/90	-8.00
1989	06/22/89	-0.21	09/12/89	-1.54	-1.33	-532.00	07/26/89	896.00	09/11/89	-712.00
1988	06/22/88	-9.04	09/12/88	-3.48	5.57	2228.00	08/29/88	2780.00	06/23/88	-220.00
1987	06/22/87	-3.14	09/11/87	-0.85	2.30	920.00	09/11/87	920.00	07/23/87	-552.00
1986	06/23/86	-1.30	09/12/86	3.39	4.70	1880.00	09/09/86	1920.00		
1985	06/24/85	-3.67	09/12/85	-3.00	0.68	272.00	08/30/85	472.00	07/23/85	-568.00

Percentage Correct	80								
Average Profit on Winning Trades			2.77	1107.00		Winners	12
Average Loss on Trades			-2.25	-901.33		Losers	3
Average Net Profit Per Trade			1.76	705.33		Total trades	15
Percentage Correct	80						
Average Profit on Winning Trades			2.90	1161.50		Winners	16
Average Loss on Trades			-2.02	-809.00		Losers	4
Average Net Profit Per Trade			1.92	767.40		Total trades	20

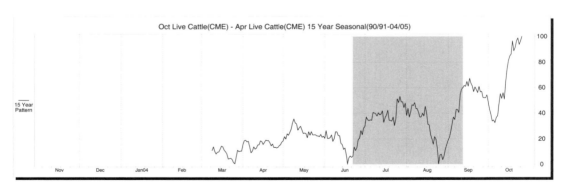

Oct Live Cattle(CME) - Apr Live Cattle(CME) 15 Year Seasonal(90/91-04/05)

Growing demand and declining supply combine to drive bull spreads into mid November before being interrupted by grocers featuring first turkey and then hams for the holidays. In addition, hog marketings tend to peak by early December, creating an abundance of competitive meat. But after the year-end holidays, demand returns to drive bull spreads at least into March if not April deliveries.

Figure 6-9

Buy Oct Live Cattle(CME) / Sell Apr Live Cattle(CME)

Enter on approximately 06/22 - Exit on approximately 08/05

CONT YEAR	ENTRY DATE	ENTRY PRICE	EXIT DATE	EXIT PRICE	PROFIT	PROFIT AMOUNT	BEST EQUITY DATE	BEST EQUITY AMOUNT	WORST EQUITY DATE	WORST EQUITY AMOUNT
2004	06/22/04	2.03	08/05/04	0.25	-1.78	-712.00	06/24/04	340.00	07/20/04	-932.00
2003	06/23/03	-5.78	08/05/03	0.84	6.63	2652.00	08/01/03	2864.00		
2002	06/24/02	-4.03	08/05/02	-3.20	0.83	332.00	07/18/02	700.00	06/25/02	-16.00
2001	06/22/01	-2.12	08/03/01	-4.34	-2.22	-888.00	06/27/01	220.00	08/02/01	-888.00
2000	06/22/00	-5.95	08/04/00	-5.20	0.75	300.00	07/18/00	380.00	07/25/00	-52.00
1999	06/22/99	-4.01	08/05/99	-3.67	0.35	140.00	07/26/99	308.00	07/20/99	-172.00
1998	06/22/98	-4.31	08/05/98	-4.29	0.02	8.00	07/08/98	220.00	08/03/98	-424.00
1997	06/23/97	-5.71	08/05/97	-5.09	0.62	248.00	07/28/97	748.00	07/08/97	-452.00
1996	06/24/96	0.29	08/05/96	2.64	2.35	940.00	07/25/96	1060.00		
1995	06/22/95	-2.37	08/04/95	-0.84	1.53	612.00	08/02/95	660.00		
1994	06/22/94	-3.52	08/05/94	1.65	5.17	2068.00	08/03/94	2156.00	06/24/94	-24.00
1993	06/22/93	-1.53	08/05/93	-1.50	0.03	12.00	06/28/93	180.00	07/23/93	-740.00
1992	06/22/92	0.75	08/05/92	1.28	0.53	212.00	07/16/92	320.00	06/25/92	-268.00
1991	06/24/91	-1.25	08/05/91	-1.87	-0.63	-252.00	07/08/91	620.00	08/01/91	-520.00
1990	06/22/90	-0.82	08/03/90	0.70	1.53	612.00	07/25/90	900.00	07/02/90	-8.00
1989	06/22/89	-0.21	08/04/89	1.75	1.97	788.00	07/26/89	896.00		
1988	06/22/88	-9.04	08/05/88	-3.85	5.20	2080.00	07/28/88	2112.00	06/23/88	-220.00
1987	06/22/87	-3.14	08/05/87	-2.40	0.75	300.00	08/04/87	512.00	07/23/87	-552.00
1986	06/23/86	-1.30	08/05/86	1.70	3.00	1200.00	08/04/86	1340.00		
1985	06/24/85	-3.67	08/05/85	-4.09	-0.42	-168.00	07/30/85	120.00	07/23/85	-568.00

Percentage Correct		80								
Average Profit on Winning Trades					1.70	678.00		Winners		12
Average Loss on Trades					-1.54	-617.33		Losers		3
Average Net Profit Per Trade					1.05	418.93		Total trades		15
Percentage Correct		80								
Average Profit on Winning Trades					1.95	781.50		Winners		16
Average Loss on Trades					-1.26	-505.00		Losers		4
Average Net Profit Per Trade					1.31	524.20		Total trades		20

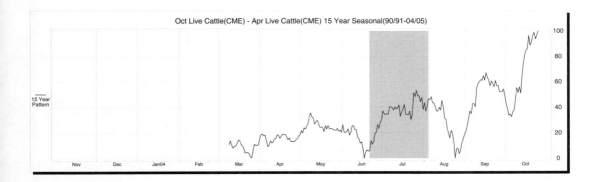

Oct Live Cattle(CME) - Apr Live Cattle(CME) 15 Year Seasonal(90/91-04/05)

Chapter 6: Meats

Figure 6-10

Buy Dec Live Cattle(CME) / Sell Jun Live Cattle(CME)

Enter on approximately 07/23 - Exit on approximately 10/15

CONT YEAR	ENTRY DATE	ENTRY PRICE	EXIT DATE	EXIT PRICE	PROFIT	PROFIT AMOUNT	BEST EQUITY DATE	BEST EQUITY AMOUNT	WORST EQUITY DATE	WORST EQUITY AMOUNT
2004	07/23/04	6.54	10/15/04	4.90	-1.65	-660.00	07/27/04	640.00	09/28/04	-1160.00
2003	07/23/03	5.69	10/15/03	16.96	11.27	4508.00	10/14/03	4520.00	07/24/03	-260.00
2002	07/23/02	2.44	10/15/02	2.79	0.35	140.00	08/09/02	500.00	08/23/02	-188.00
2001	07/23/01	1.26	10/15/01	-2.09	-3.37	-1348.00	07/25/01	112.00	10/15/01	-1348.00
2000	07/24/00	-1.56	10/13/00	-0.15	1.42	568.00	10/02/00	820.00	08/08/00	-152.00
1999	07/23/99	-0.45	10/15/99	0.95	1.40	560.00	09/27/99	880.00		
1998	07/23/98	-1.72	10/15/98	1.45	3.18	1272.00	09/15/98	1420.00	07/31/98	-328.00
1997	07/23/97	0.07	10/15/97	-3.64	-3.72	-1488.00	07/28/97	500.00	10/14/97	-1556.00
1996	07/23/96	0.86	10/15/96	1.67	0.81	324.00	09/30/96	1284.00		
1995	07/24/95	2.82	10/13/95	5.10	2.28	912.00	09/25/95	1044.00	08/10/95	-140.00
1994	07/25/94	2.75	10/14/94	4.25	1.50	600.00	10/14/94	600.00	08/29/94	-532.00
1993	07/23/93	1.39	10/15/93	1.70	0.30	120.00	09/10/93	420.00	10/11/93	-380.00
1992	07/23/92	2.25	10/15/92	4.57	2.32	928.00	10/14/92	980.00	07/28/92	-92.00
1991	07/23/91	2.07	10/15/91	3.71	1.65	660.00	10/04/91	980.00	08/08/91	-528.00
1990	07/23/90	2.75	10/15/90	2.90	0.15	60.00	10/01/90	520.00	08/24/90	-732.00
1989	07/24/89	1.41	10/13/89	2.73	1.31	524.00	10/11/89	592.00	09/05/89	-236.00
1988	07/25/88	-1.96	10/14/88	0.45	2.42	968.00	10/12/88	1028.00	08/03/88	-492.00
1987	07/23/87	-2.20	10/15/87	1.28	3.48	1392.00	10/13/87	1540.00		
1986	07/23/86	-0.19	10/15/86	1.57	1.78	712.00	10/13/86	800.00	09/24/86	-332.00
1985	07/23/85	-3.25	10/15/85	1.62	4.87	1948.00	10/08/85	2080.00	07/24/85	-100.00

Percentage Correct		80								
Average Profit on Winning Trades					2.22	887.67		Winners		12
Average Loss on Trades					-2.91	-1165.33		Losers		3
Average Net Profit Per Trade					1.19	477.07		Total trades		15
Percentage Correct		85								
Average Profit on Winning Trades					2.38	952.71		Winners		17
Average Loss on Trades					-2.91	-1165.33		Losers		3
Average Net Profit Per Trade					1.59	635.00		Total trades		20

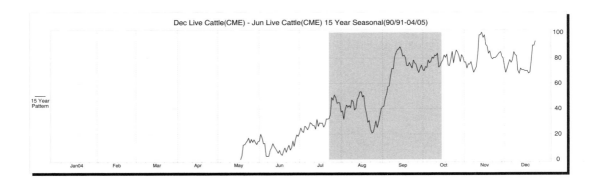

Dec Live Cattle(CME) - Jun Live Cattle(CME) 15 Year Seasonal(90/91-04/05)

Figure 6-11

Buy Dec Live Cattle(CME) / Sell Jun Live Cattle(CME)

Enter on approximately 08/29 - Exit on approximately 11/12

CONT YEAR	ENTRY DATE	ENTRY PRICE	EXIT DATE	EXIT PRICE	PROFIT	PROFIT AMOUNT	BEST EQUITY DATE	BEST EQUITY AMOUNT	WORST EQUITY DATE	WORST EQUITY AMOUNT
2004	08/30/04	4.45	11/12/04	5.32	0.87	348.00	09/16/04	600.00	11/01/04	-828.00
2003	08/29/03	8.40	11/12/03	20.81	12.42	4968.00	11/10/03	5028.00		
2002	08/29/02	2.28	11/12/02	2.85	0.57	228.00	09/16/02	500.00	10/18/02	-200.00
2001	08/29/01	0.34	11/12/01	-2.79	-3.15	-1260.00	09/05/01	100.00	11/12/01	-1260.00
2000	08/29/00	-1.25	11/10/00	-0.04	1.20	480.00	10/30/00	972.00	09/06/00	-140.00
1999	08/30/99	0.34	11/12/99	1.45	1.10	440.00	09/27/99	560.00	09/02/99	-100.00
1998	08/31/98	-1.30	11/12/98	-0.34	0.95	380.00	09/15/98	1248.00	09/03/98	-12.00
1997	08/29/97	-1.65	11/12/97	-3.50	-1.85	-740.00	09/03/97	180.00	11/10/97	-900.00
1996	08/29/96	3.01	11/12/96	3.92	0.90	360.00	09/30/96	424.00	10/15/96	-536.00
1995	08/29/95	3.17	11/10/95	5.10	1.93	772.00	09/25/95	904.00		
1994	08/29/94	1.42	11/11/94	5.13	3.71	1484.00	11/11/94	1484.00		
1993	08/30/93	2.04	11/12/93	1.14	-0.90	-360.00	09/10/93	160.00	11/04/93	-780.00
1992	08/31/92	2.89	11/12/92	4.75	1.85	740.00	10/26/92	900.00	09/15/92	-72.00
1991	08/29/91	2.17	11/12/91	4.40	2.23	892.00	10/04/91	940.00	11/04/91	-168.00
1990	08/29/90	1.17	11/12/90	5.30	4.13	1652.00	11/12/90	1652.00		
1989	08/29/89	2.00	11/10/89	3.21	1.22	488.00	10/18/89	608.00	09/05/89	-468.00
1988	08/29/88	-0.69	11/11/88	-0.85	-0.15	-60.00	10/12/88	520.00	09/21/88	-700.00
1987	08/31/87	-1.10	11/12/87	1.36	2.47	988.00	10/27/87	1340.00	09/01/87	-180.00
1986	08/29/86	0.67	11/12/86	3.32	2.66	1064.00	11/10/86	1252.00	09/24/86	-680.00
1985	08/29/85	-1.37	11/12/85	5.14	6.53	2612.00	11/01/85	2752.00	09/03/85	-156.00

Percentage Correct		80								
Average Profit on Winning Trades					2.66	1062.00		Winners		12
Average Loss on Trades					-1.97	-786.67		Losers		3
Average Net Profit Per Trade					1.73	692.27		Total trades		15
Percentage Correct		80								
Average Profit on Winning Trades					2.80	1118.50		Winners		16
Average Loss on Trades					-1.51	-605.00		Losers		4
Average Net Profit Per Trade					1.93	773.80		Total trades		20

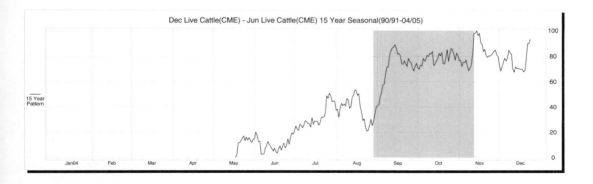

Dec Live Cattle(CME) - Jun Live Cattle(CME) 15 Year Seasonal(90/91-04/05)

15 Year Pattern

Figure 6-12

Moore Research Center, Inc.
Buy Feb Live Cattle(CME) / Sell Aug Live Cattle(CME)

Enter on approximately 10/05 - Exit on approximately 11/07

CONT YEAR	ENTRY DATE	ENTRY PRICE	EXIT DATE	EXIT PRICE	PROFIT	PROFIT AMOUNT	BEST EQUITY DATE	BEST EQUITY AMOUNT	WORST EQUITY DATE	WORST EQUITY AMOUNT
2005	10/05/04	7.12	11/05/04	5.54	-1.58	-632.00			11/02/04	-780.00
2004	10/06/03	10.28	11/07/03	17.96	7.69	3076.00	11/07/03	3076.00	10/22/03	-432.00
2003	10/07/02	3.84	11/07/02	7.37	3.53	1412.00	11/01/02	1588.00		
2002	10/05/01	1.29	11/07/01	2.34	1.05	420.00	11/01/01	732.00		
2001	10/05/00	1.09	11/07/00	2.32	1.23	492.00	11/06/00	580.00	10/06/00	-80.00
2000	10/05/99	1.46	11/05/99	1.94	0.48	192.00	11/05/99	192.00	10/15/99	-120.00
1999	10/05/98	0.75	11/06/98	1.81	1.07	428.00	10/13/98	508.00		
1998	10/06/97	0.56	11/07/97	-1.20	-1.77	-708.00			10/29/97	-788.00
1997	10/07/96	0.71	11/07/96	1.14	0.43	172.00	10/28/96	172.00	10/22/96	-340.00
1996	10/05/95	4.64	11/07/95	5.52	0.88	352.00	10/30/95	408.00	10/23/95	-20.00
1995	10/05/94	2.81	11/07/94	4.92	2.10	840.00	11/07/94	840.00		
1994	10/05/93	3.81	11/05/93	3.07	-0.74	-296.00			11/04/93	-480.00
1993	10/05/92	3.38	11/06/92	3.96	0.59	236.00	11/06/92	236.00	10/14/92	-84.00
1992	10/07/91	4.39	11/07/91	5.59	1.20	480.00	10/17/91	480.00	10/28/91	-140.00
1991	10/05/90	3.20	11/07/90	3.57	0.38	152.00	11/07/90	152.00	10/16/90	-192.00
1990	10/05/89	3.70	11/07/89	4.62	0.92	368.00	10/23/89	488.00	10/06/89	-0.00
1989	10/05/88	2.20	11/07/88	2.35	0.15	60.00	10/24/88	428.00	11/03/88	-48.00
1988	10/05/87	-0.28	11/06/87	-1.20	-0.92	-368.00	10/13/87	584.00	11/05/87	-380.00
1987	10/06/86	-0.17	11/07/86	1.45	1.63	652.00	11/03/86	740.00		
1986	10/07/85	0.70	11/07/85	3.50	2.80	1120.00	11/07/85	1120.00		

Percentage Correct	80									
Average Profit on Winning Trades					1.72	687.67		Winners		12
Average Loss on Trades					-1.36	-545.33		Losers		3
Average Net Profit Per Trade					1.10	441.07		Total trades		15
Percentage Correct	80									
Average Profit on Winning Trades					1.63	653.25		Winners		16
Average Loss on Trades					-1.25	-501.00		Losers		4
Average Net Profit Per Trade					1.06	422.40		Total trades		20

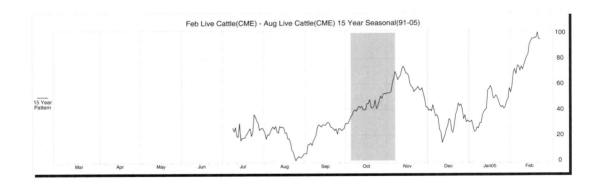

Feb Live Cattle(CME) - Aug Live Cattle(CME) 15 Year Seasonal(91-05)

Figure 6-13

Buy Apr Live Cattle(CME) / Sell Aug Live Cattle(CME)

Enter on approximately 12/27 - Exit on approximately 03/05

CONT YEAR	ENTRY DATE	ENTRY PRICE	EXIT DATE	EXIT PRICE	PROFIT	PROFIT AMOUNT	BEST EQUITY DATE	BEST EQUITY AMOUNT	WORST EQUITY DATE	WORST EQUITY AMOUNT
2005	12/27/04	7.08	03/04/05	7.79	0.72	288.00	01/11/05	480.00	12/29/04	-372.00
2004	12/29/03	3.96	03/05/04	6.06	2.10	840.00	03/05/04	840.00	02/17/04	-1660.00
2003	12/27/02	7.84	03/05/03	8.04	0.20	80.00	02/03/03	1152.00	03/04/03	-48.00
2002	12/27/01	3.54	03/05/02	4.45	0.90	360.00	02/06/02	700.00	01/11/02	-100.00
2001	12/27/00	4.40	03/05/01	8.28	3.88	1552.00	03/01/01	1668.00	01/04/01	-148.00
2000	12/27/99	1.86	03/04/00	2.81	0.95	380.00	03/04/00	380.00	02/14/00	-500.00
1999	12/28/98	-0.40	03/05/99	4.34	4.75	1900.00	03/03/99	1912.00	12/29/98	-52.00
1998	12/29/97	-0.07	03/05/98	-3.17	-3.09	-1236.00	12/31/97	32.00	02/23/98	-1548.00
1997	12/27/96	2.77	03/05/97	4.72	1.96	784.00	02/26/97	1272.00	02/04/97	-616.00
1996	12/27/95	5.08	03/05/96	1.00	-4.08	-1632.00	12/29/95	108.00	03/04/96	-1752.00
1995	12/27/94	7.57	03/03/95	10.29	2.72	1088.00	03/03/95	1088.00	12/28/94	-72.00
1994	12/27/93	3.04	03/04/94	3.95	0.90	360.00	03/04/94	360.00	02/04/94	-500.00
1993	12/28/92	5.38	03/05/93	9.23	3.85	1540.00	02/24/93	1576.00		
1992	12/27/91	5.39	03/05/92	8.79	3.40	1360.00	02/07/92	1520.00		
1991	12/27/90	3.40	03/05/91	6.17	2.77	1108.00	03/05/91	1108.00	01/14/91	-492.00
1990	12/27/89	4.06	03/05/90	5.65	1.58	632.00	02/12/90	992.00	01/04/90	-36.00
1989	12/27/88	4.01	03/03/89	5.14	1.13	452.00	02/27/89	632.00	01/20/89	-860.00
1988	12/28/87	2.36	03/05/88	4.42	2.05	820.00	02/22/88	1212.00		
1987	12/29/86	1.62	03/05/87	4.89	3.27	1308.00	02/23/87	1788.00	12/31/86	-40.00
1986	12/27/85	1.40	03/05/86	2.98	1.58	632.00	02/26/86	888.00	01/03/86	-340.00

Percentage Correct	87									
Average Profit on Winning Trades					2.24	895.38		Winners		13
Average Loss on Trades					-3.59	-1434.00		Losers		2
Average Net Profit Per Trade					1.46	584.80		Total trades		15
Percentage Correct	90									
Average Profit on Winning Trades					2.15	860.22		Winners		18
Average Loss on Trades					-3.59	-1434.00		Losers		2
Average Net Profit Per Trade					1.58	630.80		Total trades		20

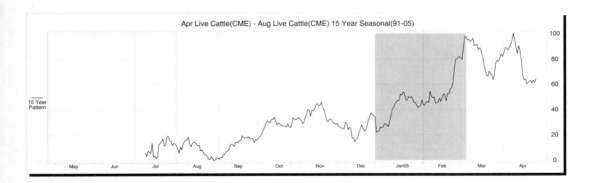

Apr Live Cattle(CME) - Aug Live Cattle(CME) 15 Year Seasonal(91-05)

Feeder Cattle

Fresh beef supply peaks with peak slaughter in May/June. Beef consumption is lowest in July/August. With feed supply tightest and often most costly then also, feedlot operators want minimal numbers of cattle going into August. Thus, demand for feeder cattle tends to be weakest March-May because feeders placed then could reach market weight in July/August.

Figure 6-14: Feeder Cattle Index Seasonal Pattern

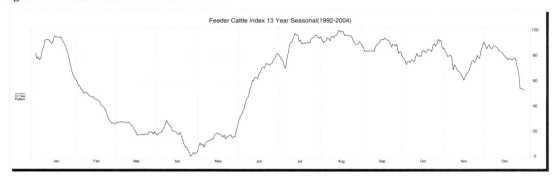

But by mid/late May, the market begins to anticipate the need to replenish those depleted feedlot inventories in order to be at capacity during and after corn harvest. Further, the market will need to bid high enough to entice feeders off spring and summer grass. Thus, prices tend to rise into July/August as demand begins to accelerate. Prices then remain high through corn harvest and, in some locations, into a seasonal peak in December/January. Demand then softens with feedlots full and the market anticipating another flush of cattle into May/June.

Figure 6-15: Aug/Oct Feeder Cattle Seasonal Pattern

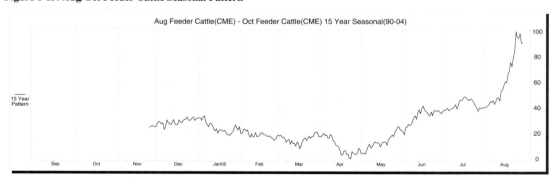

Figure 6-16: Jan/Mar Feeder Cattle Seasonal Pattern

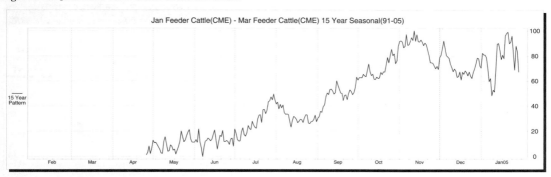

Jan Feeder Cattle(CME) - Mar Feeder Cattle(CME) 15 Year Seasonal(91-05)

Figure 6-17: Feeder Cattle Spread Strategy Summary

Moore Research Center, Inc.		Feeder Cattle Spread Strategies							
Seasonal Strategy	Entry Date	Exit Date	Win Pct	Win Yrs	Loss Years	Total Years	Average Profit	Ave Pft Per Day
Buy Apr Feeder Cattle(CME)	3/23	4/18	93	14	1	15	370	14
Sell May Feeder Cattle(CME)			95	19	1	20	429	16
Buy Aug Feeder Cattle(CME)	6/03	8/22	87	13	2	15	560	7
Sell Oct Feeder Cattle(CME)			85	17	3	20	617	8
Buy Nov Feeder Cattle(CME)	6/18	9/10	80	12	3	15	487	6
Sell Mar Feeder Cattle(CME)			85	17	3	20	518	6
Buy Jan Feeder Cattle(CME)	8/17	11/10	93	14	1	15	325	4
Sell Mar Feeder Cattle(CME)			95	19	1	20	288	3

As the table above suggests, only bull spreads have been particularly reliable. For example, the April contract tends to underperform May during much of winter as the market anticipates weakness in the cash market March-May. But the April contract then tends to recover sharply and has regularly outperformed the May contract throughout March and into mid April. In fact, as the first strategy in the table quantifies (see Figure 6-18), that spread from late March would not have suffered any daily closing drawdown of as much as 0.625 cents/pound in the 20 years 1985-2004.

As the seasonal patterns illustrate, however, it is as demand returns when feedlots begin to replenish numbers that the bull spreads have moved most dramatically and persistently. Note the pattern for August/October does indeed bottom in April/May and begins to anticipate the typical return of demand. But note also how it accelerates higher during August, almost as if there were a "sudden realization" of a supply squeeze every year. The pattern of January/March Feeders illustrates the overall trend in bull spreads into mid November, essentially the end of corn harvest. The last strategy quantifies just how persistent and how reliable has been the move. Not only did the January contract outperform between the dates listed in each of the 19 contract years 1986-2004 but the strategy did so without suffering any daily closing drawdown greater 0.85 cents/pound.

Figure 6-18

Buy Apr Feeder Cattle(CME) / Sell May Feeder Cattle(CME)

Enter on approximately 03/23 - Exit on approximately 04/18

CONT YEAR	ENTRY DATE	ENTRY PRICE	EXIT DATE	EXIT PRICE	PROFIT	PROFIT AMOUNT	BEST EQUITY DATE	BEST EQUITY AMOUNT	WORST EQUITY DATE	WORST EQUITY AMOUNT
2005	03/23/05	1.65	04/18/05	4.08	2.43	1215.00	04/18/05	1215.00	03/28/05	-210.00
2004	03/23/04	1.65	04/16/04	3.73	2.08	1040.00	04/08/04	1085.00		
2003	03/24/03	-0.36	04/17/03	0.87	1.25	625.00	04/17/03	625.00		
2002	03/25/02	-0.10	04/18/02	0.85	0.95	475.00	04/11/02	500.00	03/26/02	-15.00
2001	03/23/01	-0.55	04/18/01	0.09	0.65	325.00	04/11/01	690.00	03/28/01	-40.00
2000	03/23/00	-0.11	04/18/00	0.09	0.22	110.00	04/17/00	185.00	03/28/00	-40.00
1999	03/23/99	-0.12	04/16/99	0.05	0.17	85.00	04/15/99	185.00	04/06/99	-250.00
1998	03/23/98	0.12	04/17/98	0.14	0.02	10.00	03/30/98	310.00	04/03/98	-40.00
1997	03/24/97	-0.53	04/18/97	0.46	1.00	500.00	04/08/97	715.00	04/14/97	-25.00
1996	03/25/96	-1.17	04/18/96	-0.88	0.29	145.00	04/11/96	300.00	04/17/96	-305.00
1995	03/23/95	0.20	04/18/95	-0.01	-0.22	-110.00	04/10/95	350.00	04/18/95	-110.00
1994	03/23/94	0.12	04/18/94	0.50	0.38	190.00	04/12/94	215.00	04/04/94	-135.00
1993	03/23/93	0.93	04/16/93	1.28	0.35	175.00	04/16/93	175.00	04/06/93	-150.00
1992	03/23/92	1.45	04/16/92	1.97	0.53	265.00	04/14/92	265.00	03/27/92	-75.00
1991	03/25/91	1.42	04/18/91	2.42	1.00	500.00	04/18/91	500.00	03/28/91	-50.00
1990	03/23/90	0.67	04/18/90	1.84	1.18	590.00	04/18/90	590.00	03/28/90	-70.00
1989	03/23/89	-0.23	04/18/89	-0.07	0.15	75.00	04/12/89	155.00	04/14/89	-145.00
1988	03/23/88	1.95	04/18/88	2.86	0.92	460.00	04/14/88	685.00		
1987	03/23/87	1.35	04/16/87	2.04	0.70	350.00	04/16/87	350.00	04/03/87	-290.00
1986	03/24/86	-1.35	04/18/86	1.75	3.10	1550.00	04/18/86	1550.00	03/27/86	-190.00

Percentage Correct	93								
Average Profit on Winning Trades				0.81	404.29		Winners	14	
Average Loss on Trades				-0.22	-110.00		Losers	1	
Average Net Profit Per Trade				0.74	370.00		Total trades	15	
Percentage Correct	95								
Average Profit on Winning Trades				0.91	457.11		Winners	19	
Average Loss on Trades				-0.22	-110.00		Losers	1	
Average Net Profit Per Trade				0.86	428.75		Total trades	20	

HYPOTHETICAL PERFORMANCE RESULTS HAVE MANY INHERENT LIMITATIONS, SOME OF WHICH ARE DESCRIBED BELOW. NO REPRESENTATION IS BEING MADE THAT ANY ACCOUNT WILL OR IS LIKELY TO ACHIEVE PROFITS OR LOSSES SIMILAR TO THOSE SHOWN. IN FACT, THERE ARE FREQUENTLY SHARP DIFFERENCES BETWEEN HYPOTHETICAL PERFORMANCE RESULTS AND THE ACTUAL RESULTS SUBSEQUENTLY ACHIEVED BY ANY PARTICULAR TRADING PROGRAM. ONE OF THE LIMITATIONS OF HYPOTHETICAL PERFORMANCE RESULTS IS THAT THEY ARE GENERALLY PREPARED WITH THE BENEFIT OF HINDSIGHT. IN ADDITION, HYPOTHETICAL TRADING DOES NOT INVOLVE FINANCIAL RISK, AND NO HYPOTHETICAL TRADING RECORD CAN COMPLETELY ACCOUNT FOR THE IMPACT OF FINANCIAL RISK IN ACTUAL TRADING. FOR EXAMPLE, THE ABILITY TO WITHSTAND LOSSES OR ADHERE TO A PARTICULAR TRADING PROGRAM IN SPITE OF TRADING LOSSES ARE MATERIAL POINTS WHICH CAN ALSO ADVERSELY AFFECT ACTUAL TRADING RESULTS. THERE ARE NUMEROUS OTHER FACTORS RELATED TO THE MARKETS IN GENERAL OR TO THE IMPLEMENTATION OF ANY SPECIFIC TRADING PROGRAM WHICH CANNOT BE FULLY ACCOUNTED FOR IN THE PREPARATION OF HYPOTHETICAL PERFORMANCE RESULTS AND ALL OF WHICH CAN ADVERSELY AFFECT ACTUAL TRADING RESULTS. RESULTS NOT ADJUSTED FOR COMMISSION AND SLIPPAGE.

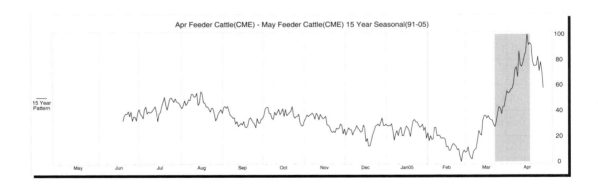

Apr Feeder Cattle(CME) - May Feeder Cattle(CME) 15 Year Seasonal(91-05)

Figure 6-19

Buy Aug Feeder Cattle(CME) / Sell Oct Feeder Cattle(CME)

Enter on approximately 06/03 - Exit on approximately 08/22

CONT YEAR	ENTRY DATE	ENTRY PRICE	EXIT DATE	EXIT PRICE	PROFIT	PROFIT AMOUNT	BEST EQUITY DATE	BEST EQUITY AMOUNT	WORST EQUITY DATE	WORST EQUITY AMOUNT
2004	06/03/04	2.36	08/20/04	5.04	2.68	1340.00	08/20/04	1340.00	07/27/04	-610.00
2003	06/03/03	-0.38	08/22/03	3.45	3.83	1915.00	08/22/03	1915.00	06/19/03	-210.00
2002	06/03/02	0.20	08/22/02	0.26	0.07	35.00	08/20/02	340.00	06/28/02	-375.00
2001	06/04/01	0.46	08/22/01	0.55	0.08	40.00	06/19/01	225.00	08/09/01	-560.00
2000	06/05/00	-0.73	08/21/00	-0.73	0.00	0.00	07/06/00	90.00	08/14/00	-235.00
1999	06/03/99	-0.47	08/20/99	-0.76	-0.29	-145.00	06/17/99	425.00	08/16/99	-345.00
1998	06/03/98	-0.45	08/21/98	0.60	1.05	525.00	08/21/98	525.00		
1997	06/03/97	-0.14	08/22/97	1.15	1.30	650.00	08/22/97	650.00	07/15/97	-215.00
1996	06/03/96	-0.25	08/21/96	0.28	0.53	265.00	07/16/96	625.00	08/13/96	-350.00
1995	06/05/95	0.35	08/22/95	0.93	0.58	290.00	07/19/95	650.00		
1994	06/03/94	-0.12	08/22/94	2.09	2.23	1115.00	08/03/94	1190.00		
1993	06/03/93	1.20	08/20/93	1.76	0.57	285.00	08/13/93	675.00		
1992	06/03/92	1.42	08/21/92	2.31	0.89	445.00	07/24/92	510.00	06/04/92	-65.00
1991	06/03/91	1.15	08/22/91	2.42	1.28	640.00	07/24/91	710.00	06/24/91	-115.00
1990	06/04/90	1.36	08/22/90	3.36	2.00	1000.00	08/20/90	1415.00	06/15/90	-185.00
1989	06/05/89	-0.23	08/22/89	1.79	2.03	1015.00	08/15/89	1155.00	06/08/89	-60.00
1988	06/03/88	-0.07	08/19/88	0.53	0.61	305.00	08/02/88	390.00	06/22/88	-860.00
1987	06/03/87	0.77	08/21/87	0.36	-0.40	-200.00	07/17/87	190.00	08/06/87	-735.00
1986	06/03/86	1.65	08/20/86	4.66	3.02	1510.00	08/20/86	1510.00	06/09/86	-125.00
1985	06/03/85	0.35	08/20/85	2.96	2.62	1310.00	08/19/85	1350.00	07/23/85	-585.00

Percentage Correct	87			
Average Profit on Winning Trades		1.31	657.31	Winners	13
Average Loss on Trades		-0.15	-72.50	Losers	2
Average Net Profit Per Trade		1.12	560.00	Total trades	15
Percentage Correct	85			
Average Profit on Winning Trades		1.49	746.18	Winners	17
Average Loss on Trades		-0.23	-115.00	Losers	3
Average Net Profit Per Trade		1.23	617.00	Total trades	20

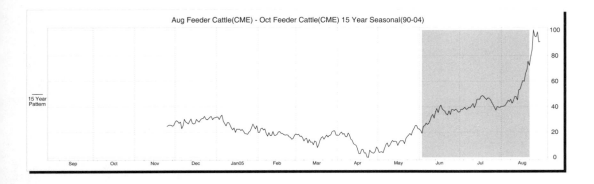

Aug Feeder Cattle(CME) - Oct Feeder Cattle(CME) 15 Year Seasonal(90-04)

15 Year Pattern

Figure 6-20

Buy Nov Feeder Cattle(CME) / Sell Mar Feeder Cattle(CME)

Enter on approximately 06/18 - Exit on approximately 09/10

CONT YEAR	ENTRY DATE	ENTRY PRICE	EXIT DATE	EXIT PRICE	PROFIT	PROFIT AMOUNT	BEST EQUITY DATE	BEST EQUITY AMOUNT	WORST EQUITY DATE	WORST EQUITY AMOUNT
2004	06/18/04	8.84	09/10/04	8.04	-0.80	-400.00	08/16/04	775.00	07/16/04	-1140.00
2003	06/18/03	2.57	09/10/03	7.21	4.64	2320.00	09/10/03	2320.00	06/19/03	-15.00
2002	06/18/02	1.67	09/10/02	3.04	1.38	690.00	09/06/02	815.00	07/08/02	-385.00
2001	06/18/01	0.90	09/10/01	1.67	0.77	385.00	06/28/01	600.00	08/27/01	-360.00
2000	06/19/00	-0.51	09/08/00	-0.54	-0.03	-15.00	07/20/00	285.00	07/03/00	-180.00
1999	06/18/99	0.15	09/10/99	0.34	0.20	100.00	07/30/99	510.00	09/02/99	-125.00
1998	06/18/98	-0.90	09/10/98	-0.75	0.15	75.00	07/01/98	685.00	07/23/98	-365.00
1997	06/18/97	0.34	09/10/97	-0.68	-1.03	-515.00	06/23/97	160.00	09/02/97	-640.00
1996	06/18/96	-0.95	09/10/96	0.41	1.37	685.00	09/09/96	800.00	07/15/96	-525.00
1995	06/19/95	0.50	09/08/95	2.42	1.92	960.00	09/08/95	960.00		
1994	06/20/94	0.27	09/09/94	1.94	1.68	840.00	08/04/94	1415.00	06/21/94	-150.00
1993	06/18/93	2.20	09/10/93	2.85	0.65	325.00	09/02/93	400.00	07/06/93	-240.00
1992	06/18/92	0.69	09/10/92	2.95	2.25	1125.00	08/19/92	1235.00	06/24/92	-25.00
1991	06/18/91	1.00	09/10/91	1.46	0.47	235.00	07/18/91	360.00	08/12/91	-365.00
1990	06/18/90	1.29	09/10/90	2.29	1.00	500.00	09/10/90	500.00	07/03/90	-275.00
1989	06/19/89	0.40	09/08/89	0.71	0.32	160.00	07/31/89	610.00	07/07/89	-250.00
1988	06/20/88	-2.89	09/09/88	-0.06	2.83	1415.00	08/29/88	1635.00		
1987	06/18/87	0.10	09/10/87	0.80	0.70	350.00	09/09/87	415.00	07/23/87	-450.00
1986	06/18/86	-0.79	09/10/86	1.04	1.85	925.00	09/09/86	925.00	07/11/86	-125.00
1985	06/18/85	-2.40	09/10/85	-1.98	0.42	210.00	08/12/85	685.00	07/24/85	-225.00

Percentage Correct	80								
Average Profit on Winning Trades			1.37	686.67		Winners	12		
Average Loss on Trades			-0.62	-310.00		Losers	3		
Average Net Profit Per Trade			0.97	487.33		Total trades	15		
Percentage Correct	85								
Average Profit on Winning Trades			1.33	664.71		Winners	17		
Average Loss on Trades			-0.62	-310.00		Losers	3		
Average Net Profit Per Trade			1.04	518.50		Total trades	20		

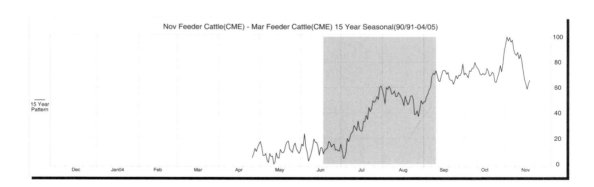

Nov Feeder Cattle(CME) - Mar Feeder Cattle(CME) 15 Year Seasonal(90/91-04/05)

Figure 6-21

Buy Jan Feeder Cattle(CME) / Sell Mar Feeder Cattle(CME)

Enter on approximately 08/17 - Exit on approximately 11/10

CONT YEAR	ENTRY DATE	ENTRY PRICE	EXIT DATE	EXIT PRICE	PROFIT	PROFIT AMOUNT	BEST EQUITY DATE	BEST EQUITY AMOUNT	WORST EQUITY DATE	WORST EQUITY AMOUNT
2005	08/17/04	4.95	11/10/04	3.42	-1.53	-765.00			11/05/04	-1100.00
2004	08/18/03	2.32	11/10/03	6.11	3.80	1900.00	11/06/03	2400.00	09/02/03	-425.00
2003	08/19/02	0.85	11/08/02	1.92	1.07	535.00	10/23/02	1000.00	09/13/02	-40.00
2002	08/17/01	0.75	11/09/01	1.00	0.25	125.00	10/29/01	135.00	09/27/01	-375.00
2001	08/17/00	0.07	11/10/00	0.43	0.35	175.00	10/31/00	360.00	09/06/00	-105.00
2000	08/17/99	0.60	11/10/99	0.85	0.25	125.00	09/30/99	260.00	11/04/99	-165.00
1999	08/17/98	-0.45	11/10/98	0.25	0.70	350.00	10/28/98	700.00	08/20/98	-100.00
1998	08/18/97	0.11	11/10/97	0.25	0.13	65.00	09/15/97	150.00	10/29/97	-95.00
1997	08/19/96	0.31	11/08/96	0.57	0.25	125.00	11/04/96	315.00	10/15/96	-160.00
1996	08/17/95	0.80	11/10/95	2.19	1.40	700.00	10/31/95	810.00	08/24/95	-125.00
1995	08/17/94	1.34	11/10/94	2.07	0.73	365.00	11/10/94	365.00	10/05/94	-235.00
1994	08/17/93	1.50	11/10/93	1.61	0.12	60.00	10/22/93	300.00	10/11/93	-65.00
1993	08/17/92	1.15	11/10/92	2.09	0.95	475.00	11/09/92	500.00		
1992	08/19/91	1.34	11/08/91	1.76	0.42	210.00	11/01/91	400.00	10/02/91	-375.00
1991	08/17/90	1.39	11/09/90	2.25	0.85	425.00	10/03/90	600.00	08/29/90	-100.00
1990	08/17/89	1.09	11/10/89	1.45	0.35	175.00	10/13/89	350.00	08/28/89	-215.00
1989	08/17/88	0.04	11/10/88	0.46	0.42	210.00	10/17/88	660.00	08/22/88	-115.00
1988	08/17/87	0.46	11/10/87	0.51	0.05	25.00	10/21/87	380.00	10/30/87	-235.00
1987	08/18/86	0.10	11/10/86	0.97	0.88	440.00	10/17/86	640.00	08/20/86	-35.00
1986	08/19/85	-0.09	11/08/85	-0.01	0.08	40.00	09/03/85	125.00	09/19/85	-375.00

Percentage Correct	93									
Average Profit on Winning Trades					0.81	402.50		Winners		14
Average Loss on Trades					-1.53	-765.00		Losers		1
Average Net Profit Per Trade					0.65	324.67		Total trades		15
Percentage Correct	95									
Average Profit on Winning Trades					0.69	343.42		Winners		19
Average Loss on Trades					-1.53	-765.00		Losers		1
Average Net Profit Per Trade					0.58	288.00		Total trades		20

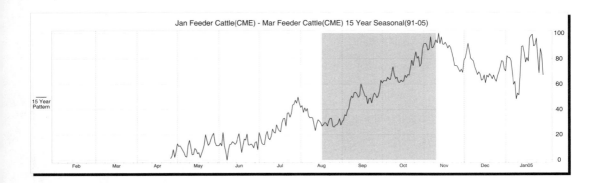

Jan Feeder Cattle(CME) - Mar Feeder Cattle(CME) 15 Year Seasonal(91-05)

15 Year Pattern

Lean Hogs

Like live cattle, hogs have well-defined patterns both of supply and of demand that tend to reinforce each other in creating a seasonal price pattern. And also like cattle, futures prices can and do trade above and below cash prices.

Figure 6-22: Lean Hog Index Seasonal Pattern

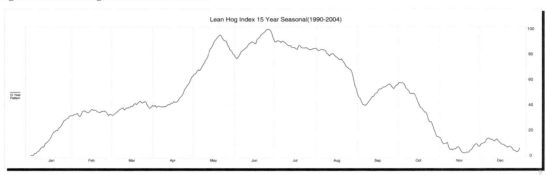

Because feed is a primary cost, hog producers like to feed as much cheap corn as possible to as many hogs as possible. Thus, producers make an effort to have as many hogs as possible available to feed during and immediately after corn harvest in October/November. In fact, the heaviest hog marketings of the year have traditionally come immediately after US Thanksgiving (last Thursday of November). With both weights and numbers peaking, pork production is usually highest November/December. From thence, slaughter begins to decline into its typical nadir in May/June and to remain low at least through July — during which time feed prices can also be high. With numbers lower and weight gain slower, pork production is normally lowest during the heat of May-August.

Just when production is least, demand tends to be greatest. Consumers eat less heavy, red meat during the heat of summer. Families on vacation prefer the convenience of processed meats. As tomatoes ripen, bacon is in peak demand. In contrast, grocers feature turkey at Thanksgiving — just when production is peaking.

Figure 6-23: Feb/Dec Lean Hogs Seasonal Pattern

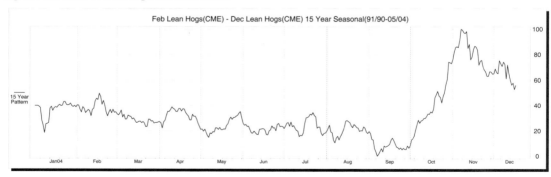

Of all the more reliable spreads, the only time in which characteristics of a bear spread seem truly to be exhibited is during corn harvest when both slaughter weights and numbers

Figure 6-24: Lean Hogs Spread Strategies

Seasonal Strategy	Entry Date	Exit Date	Win Pct	Win Yrs	Loss Years	Total Years	Average Profit	Ave Pft Per Day
Lean Hogs Spread Strategies								
Buy Feb Lean Hogs(CME)	10/15	11/07	87	13	2	15	583	24
Sell Dec Lean Hogs(CME)			85	17	3	20	456	19
Buy Jun Lean Hogs(CME)	11/07	1/10	100	15	0	15	979	15
Sell Feb Lean Hogs(CME)			100	20	0	20	871	13
Buy Apr Lean Hogs(CME)	12/06	1/08	100	15	0	15	603	18
Sell Feb Lean Hogs(CME)			95	19	1	20	549	16
Buy Jun Lean Hogs(CME)	12/07	3/09	93	14	1	15	608	7
Sell Apr Lean Hogs(CME)			95	19	1	20	601	6
Buy Jul Lean Hogs(CME)	12/31	3/13	93	14	1	15	852	12
Sell Dec Lean Hogs(CME)			95	19	1	20	843	12
Buy Jul Lean Hogs(CME)	2/15	5/11	93	14	1	15	942	11
Sell Dec Lean Hogs(CME)			95	19	1	20	1003	12
Buy Jun Lean Hogs(CME)	2/17	3/10	87	13	2	15	482	22
Sell Oct Lean Hogs(CME)			90	18	2	20	468	21
Buy Aug Lean Hogs(CME)	4/03	7/26	93	14	1	15	1045	9
Sell Dec Lean Hogs(CME)			90	18	2	20	1185	10
Buy Aug Lean Hogs(CME)	4/06	5/23	87	13	2	15	336	7
Sell Oct Lean Hogs(CME)			90	18	2	20	439	9
Buy Aug Lean Hogs(CME)	7/14	8/07	93	14	1	15	489	20
Sell Oct Lean Hogs(CME)			95	19	1	20	621	25

Moore Research Center, Inc.

rise. For example, December and February Hogs meander along closely together until early October when the more nearby December begins dramatically to underperform.

But now peruse the next three spreads in the table. In each case, the deferred contract has regularly outperformed the more nearby, also. Now refer back to the seasonal pattern for the cash market: Prices tend to make a seasonal low in November, or at the latest at the end of December when slaughter begins its long seasonal decline. How then to explain that, for example, the June contract has outperformed the more nearby April from early December into early March in 19 of the 20 years 1985-2004? In most markets, the more nearby would tend to lead an uptrend, thereby driving bull spreads.

This would seem to confirm that most hog spreads perform less as bull or bear than as the market's attempt to reflect seasonal disparities of supply and demand in the price structure, placing a premium on hogs in those months of low supply/high demand. What singular characteristic do these most reliable of all spread strategies exhibit? Contract months of lower slaughter usually outperform those of higher slaughter — no matter what time of year, no matter in which direction the market is moving.

Compare the table's fourth and fifth strategies. June outperforms April while July outperforms December. The common denominator? As slaughter turns the corner and begins to decline, the market begins building into its price structure a slaughter level lower in June than in April but greater again in December than in July. The second and third strategies in the table that exit early in January quantify how reliable is that turn in slaughter.

Figure 6-25: Jul/Dec Lean Hogs Seasonal Pattern

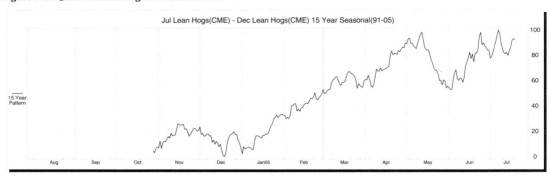

As slaughter declines, the market continues generally to infuse increasing premiums into the months of least slaughter and highest demand — June, July, August — over those of greater slaughter and lesser demand such as October and December. It tends to continue into August, but it does so in surges and not without moderate interruptions along the way. In fact, some of the strategy tables illustrate a tendency toward volatility in April and May, especially. Nonetheless, because slaughter is lowest when demand for pork is highest, the industry moves pork into cold storage during winter and spring. Thus, these spreads are not solely dependent on declining slaughter but do have underlying demand from accumulation of inventory.

Figure 6-26: Feb/Dec Lean Hogs Monthly

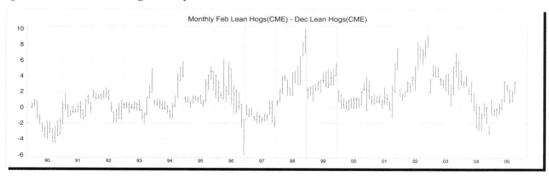

Figure 6-27: Jul/Dec Lean Hogs Monthly

Figure 6-28

Buy Feb Lean Hogs(CME) / Sell Dec Lean Hogs(CME)

Enter on approximately 10/15 - Exit on approximately 11/07

CONT YEAR	ENTRY DATE	ENTRY PRICE	EXIT DATE	EXIT PRICE	PROFIT	PROFIT AMOUNT	BEST EQUITY DATE	BEST EQUITY AMOUNT	WORST EQUITY DATE	WORST EQUITY AMOUNT
2005	10/15/04	0.02	11/05/04	-0.65	-0.67	-268.00	10/22/04	232.00	10/27/04	-400.00
2004	10/15/03	1.97	11/07/03	6.35	4.37	1748.00	11/07/03	1748.00	10/17/03	-140.00
2003	10/15/02	5.45	11/07/02	6.37	0.93	372.00	10/29/02	820.00		
2002	10/15/01	1.46	11/07/01	2.90	1.43	572.00	10/24/01	572.00	10/17/01	-48.00
2001	10/16/00	0.89	11/07/00	3.05	2.15	860.00	11/07/00	860.00	10/17/00	-168.00
2000	10/15/99	4.04	11/05/99	4.77	0.72	288.00	11/05/99	288.00	10/25/99	-480.00
1999	10/15/98	3.17	11/06/98	7.11	3.95	1580.00	11/06/98	1580.00		
1998	10/15/97	-0.29	11/07/97	0.92	1.23	492.00	11/07/97	492.00	10/28/97	-32.00
1997	10/15/96	1.00	11/07/96	0.03	-0.98	-392.00	10/22/96	360.00	11/06/96	-568.00
1996	10/16/95	3.51	11/07/95	5.21	1.70	680.00	11/07/95	680.00	10/26/95	-236.00
1995	10/17/94	3.63	11/07/94	5.20	1.57	628.00	11/07/94	628.00	11/01/94	-96.00
1994	10/15/93	0.26	11/05/93	1.64	1.39	556.00	11/03/93	652.00	10/18/93	-24.00
1993	10/15/92	-1.71	11/06/92	0.42	2.13	852.00	11/06/92	852.00	10/26/92	-56.00
1992	10/15/91	-0.66	11/07/91	1.22	1.90	760.00	11/04/91	900.00	10/16/91	-168.00
1991	10/15/90	-3.51	11/07/90	-3.46	0.05	20.00	10/31/90	424.00	10/23/90	-400.00
1990	10/16/89	-0.50	11/07/89	-0.15	0.35	140.00	11/07/89	140.00	10/24/89	-456.00
1989	10/17/88	4.11	11/07/88	4.92	0.81	324.00	10/31/88	712.00		
1988	10/15/87	-2.46	11/06/87	-1.14	1.32	528.00	11/05/87	692.00	10/22/87	-312.00
1987	10/15/86	-3.10	11/07/86	-5.14	-2.03	-812.00			11/07/86	-812.00
1986	10/15/85	-1.39	11/07/85	-0.90	0.48	192.00	11/06/85	192.00	10/31/85	-284.00

Percentage Correct	87									
Average Profit on Winning Trades					1.81	723.69		Winners		13
Average Loss on Trades					-0.83	-330.00		Losers		2
Average Net Profit Per Trade					1.46	583.20		Total trades		15
Percentage Correct	85									
Average Profit on Winning Trades					1.56	623.06		Winners		17
Average Loss on Trades					-1.23	-490.67		Losers		3
Average Net Profit Per Trade					1.14	456.00		Total trades		20

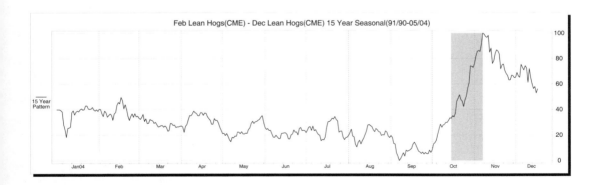

Feb Lean Hogs(CME) - Dec Lean Hogs(CME) 15 Year Seasonal(91/90-05/04)

15 Year Pattern

Figure 6-29

Moore Research Center, Inc. — *Buy Jun Lean Hogs(CME) / Sell Feb Lean Hogs(CME)*

Enter on approximately 11/07 - Exit on approximately 01/10

CONT YEAR	ENTRY DATE	ENTRY PRICE	EXIT DATE	EXIT PRICE	PROFIT	PROFIT AMOUNT	BEST EQUITY DATE	BEST EQUITY AMOUNT	WORST EQUITY DATE	WORST EQUITY AMOUNT
2005	11/08/04	-0.39	01/10/05	2.00	2.40	960.00	01/07/05	1020.00	11/30/04	-472.00
2004	11/07/03	5.70	01/09/04	9.20	3.50	1400.00	11/25/03	2020.00		
2003	11/07/02	10.15	01/10/03	11.84	1.70	680.00	12/12/02	1512.00	11/11/02	-120.00
2002	11/07/01	8.54	01/10/02	9.86	1.32	528.00	12/12/01	1340.00	12/31/01	-412.00
2001	11/07/00	5.75	01/10/01	7.25	1.50	600.00	01/10/01	600.00	12/11/00	-368.00
2000	11/08/99	8.94	01/10/00	10.00	1.05	420.00	01/10/00	420.00	12/02/99	-1072.00
1999	11/09/98	11.78	01/08/99	14.64	2.87	1148.00	12/16/98	3228.00	11/10/98	-4.00
1998	11/07/97	3.53	01/09/98	6.42	2.89	1156.00	01/09/98	1156.00	11/13/97	-132.00
1997	11/07/96	-0.85	01/10/97	1.70	2.55	1020.00	01/10/97	1020.00	12/02/96	-652.00
1996	11/07/95	7.39	01/10/96	7.94	0.55	220.00	11/28/95	340.00	12/13/95	-668.00
1995	11/07/94	7.82	01/10/95	8.04	0.22	88.00	01/06/95	716.00	12/28/94	-576.00
1994	11/08/93	3.73	01/10/94	10.00	6.26	2504.00	12/28/93	2624.00		
1993	11/09/92	2.10	01/08/93	5.75	3.66	1464.00	01/06/93	1620.00	11/16/92	-4.00
1992	11/07/91	3.92	01/10/92	6.01	2.08	832.00	01/09/92	872.00	11/11/91	-288.00
1991	11/07/90	0.73	01/10/91	4.90	4.16	1664.00	01/10/91	1664.00	11/13/90	-244.00
1990	11/07/89	0.87	01/10/90	2.28	1.42	568.00	01/10/90	568.00	11/24/89	-968.00
1989	11/07/88	3.96	01/10/89	5.10	1.15	460.00	11/18/88	616.00	12/23/88	-304.00
1988	11/09/87	0.33	01/08/88	1.66	1.33	532.00	01/08/88	532.00	11/24/87	-1040.00
1987	11/07/86	-3.48	01/09/87	-2.60	0.88	352.00	01/02/87	608.00	11/18/86	-920.00
1986	11/07/85	-3.28	01/10/86	-1.21	2.06	824.00	01/02/86	1012.00	12/09/85	-480.00

Percentage Correct	100								
Average Profit on Winning Trades			2.45	978.93		Winners	15		
Average Loss on Trades						Losers	0		
Average Net Profit Per Trade			2.45	978.93		Total trades	15		
Percentage Correct	100								
Average Profit on Winning Trades			2.18	871.00		Winners	20		
Average Loss on Trades						Losers	0		
Average Net Profit Per Trade			2.18	871.00		Total trades	20		

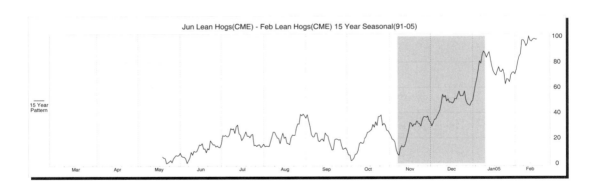

Jun Lean Hogs(CME) - Feb Lean Hogs(CME) 15 Year Seasonal(91-05)

15 Year Pattern

Figure 6-30

Moore Research Center, Inc.

Buy Apr Lean Hogs(CME) / Sell Feb Lean Hogs(CME)

Enter on approximately 12/06 - Exit on approximately 01/08

CONT YEAR	ENTRY DATE	ENTRY PRICE	EXIT DATE	EXIT PRICE	PROFIT	PROFIT AMOUNT	BEST EQUITY DATE	BEST EQUITY AMOUNT	WORST EQUITY DATE	WORST EQUITY AMOUNT
2005	12/06/04	-2.64	01/07/05	0.89	3.55	1420.00	01/05/05	1468.00		
2004	12/08/03	2.71	01/08/04	3.48	0.76	304.00	12/23/03	424.00	12/31/03	-496.00
2003	12/06/02	5.39	01/08/03	6.30	0.90	360.00	12/26/02	420.00	12/18/02	-120.00
2002	12/06/01	4.32	01/08/02	4.94	0.63	252.00	01/08/02	252.00	12/24/01	-696.00
2001	12/06/00	-0.59	01/08/01	1.54	2.15	860.00	01/08/01	860.00	12/08/00	-40.00
2000	12/06/99	0.55	01/07/00	2.08	1.53	612.00	01/06/00	632.00	12/09/99	-200.00
1999	12/07/98	4.10	01/08/99	4.14	0.05	20.00	12/21/98	1232.00		
1998	12/08/97	-2.96	01/08/98	-1.25	1.72	688.00	01/05/98	960.00	12/11/97	-212.00
1997	12/06/96	-5.03	01/08/97	-1.60	3.44	1376.00	01/08/97	1376.00		
1996	12/06/95	-0.29	01/08/96	0.60	0.91	364.00	01/08/96	364.00	12/13/95	-288.00
1995	12/06/94	1.32	01/06/95	2.21	0.89	356.00	01/06/95	356.00	12/28/94	-732.00
1994	12/06/93	0.36	01/07/94	2.39	2.02	808.00	01/05/94	872.00	12/07/93	-40.00
1993	12/07/92	-2.69	01/08/93	-0.53	2.16	864.00	01/08/93	864.00	12/11/92	-56.00
1992	12/06/91	-2.58	01/08/92	-1.19	1.39	556.00	01/08/92	556.00	12/20/91	-268.00
1991	12/06/90	-3.00	01/08/91	-2.50	0.51	204.00	12/26/90	488.00	12/11/90	-108.00
1990	12/06/89	-5.74	01/08/90	-4.34	1.40	560.00	01/05/90	804.00		
1989	12/06/88	-1.38	01/06/89	-1.64	-0.27	-108.00	12/30/88	136.00	12/23/88	-304.00
1988	12/07/87	-4.57	01/08/88	-3.17	1.39	556.00	01/08/88	556.00	12/08/87	-72.00
1987	12/08/86	-7.80	01/08/87	-6.51	1.30	520.00	12/31/86	1124.00		
1986	12/06/85	-6.76	01/08/86	-5.74	1.02	408.00	12/30/85	812.00	12/09/85	-24.00

Percentage Correct	100									
Average Profit on Winning Trades					1.51	602.93		Winners		15
Average Loss on Trades								Losers		0
Average Net Profit Per Trade					1.51	602.93		Total trades		15
Percentage Correct	95									
Average Profit on Winning Trades					1.46	583.58		Winners		19
Average Loss on Trades					-0.27	-108.00		Losers		1
Average Net Profit Per Trade					1.37	549.00		Total trades		20

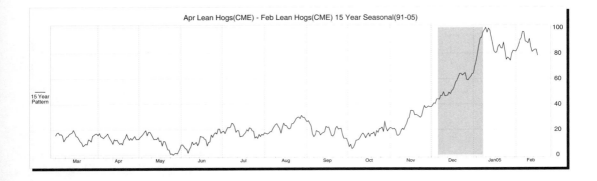

Apr Lean Hogs(CME) - Feb Lean Hogs(CME) 15 Year Seasonal(91-05)

Figure 6-31

Buy Jun Lean Hogs(CME) / Sell Apr Lean Hogs(CME)

Enter on approximately 12/07 - Exit on approximately 03/09

CONT YEAR	ENTRY DATE	ENTRY PRICE	EXIT DATE	EXIT PRICE	PROFIT	PROFIT AMOUNT	BEST EQUITY DATE	BEST EQUITY AMOUNT	WORST EQUITY DATE	WORST EQUITY AMOUNT
2005	12/07/04	1.29	03/09/05	6.08	4.78	1912.00	03/09/05	1912.00	12/27/04	-532.00
2004	12/08/03	5.70	03/09/04	5.85	0.15	60.00	01/13/04	508.00	02/23/04	-620.00
2003	12/09/02	7.25	03/07/03	10.17	2.93	1172.00	03/07/03	1172.00	01/09/03	-760.00
2002	12/07/01	6.98	03/08/02	8.64	1.67	668.00	03/07/02	708.00	01/02/02	-1012.00
2001	12/07/00	5.72	03/09/01	6.10	0.38	152.00	02/08/01	524.00	03/05/01	-856.00
2000	12/07/99	6.70	03/09/00	9.20	2.50	1000.00	03/07/00	1220.00		
1999	12/07/98	9.72	03/09/99	12.40	2.67	1068.00	12/14/98	1476.00	02/09/99	-300.00
1998	12/08/97	8.00	03/09/98	8.17	0.18	72.00	03/03/98	500.00	01/23/98	-600.00
1997	12/09/96	2.75	03/07/97	6.68	3.93	1572.00	03/07/97	1572.00	12/27/96	-100.00
1996	12/07/95	6.92	03/08/96	6.05	-0.87	-348.00	01/16/96	584.00	03/08/96	-348.00
1995	12/07/94	7.28	03/09/95	8.78	1.49	596.00	03/08/95	636.00	01/20/95	-212.00
1994	12/07/93	7.94	03/09/94	8.65	0.70	280.00	03/09/94	280.00	02/02/94	-912.00
1993	12/07/92	5.75	03/09/93	7.40	1.66	664.00	02/23/93	888.00	12/16/92	-32.00
1992	12/09/91	6.89	03/09/92	7.11	0.22	88.00	12/17/91	288.00	01/23/92	-856.00
1991	12/07/90	4.99	03/08/91	5.39	0.40	160.00	02/21/91	976.00	12/17/90	-292.00
1990	12/07/89	4.72	03/09/90	6.15	1.43	572.00	02/21/90	1128.00	12/19/89	-164.00
1989	12/07/88	5.83	03/09/89	6.32	0.49	196.00	02/07/89	540.00	12/30/88	-268.00
1988	12/07/87	4.16	03/09/88	5.50	1.34	536.00	03/08/88	768.00	12/14/87	-244.00
1987	12/08/86	2.57	03/09/87	2.97	0.41	164.00	01/09/87	456.00	01/27/87	-164.00
1986	12/09/85	2.34	03/07/86	5.95	3.61	1444.00	03/06/86	1672.00	12/10/85	-8.00

Percentage Correct		93								
Average Profit on Winning Trades					1.69	676.00		Winners		14
Average Loss on Trades					-0.87	-348.00		Losers		1
Average Net Profit Per Trade					1.52	607.73		Total trades		15
Percentage Correct		95								
Average Profit on Winning Trades					1.63	651.37		Winners		19
Average Loss on Trades					-0.87	-348.00		Losers		1
Average Net Profit Per Trade					1.50	601.40		Total trades		20

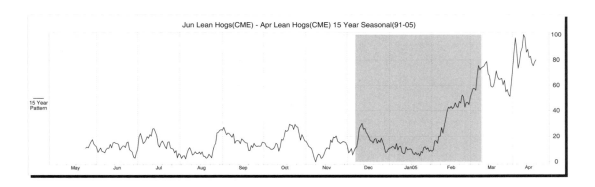

Jun Lean Hogs(CME) - Apr Lean Hogs(CME) 15 Year Seasonal(91-05)

Figure 6-32

Moore Research Center, Inc.

Buy Jul Lean Hogs(CME) / Sell Dec Lean Hogs(CME)

Enter on approximately 12/31 - Exit on approximately 03/13

CONT YEAR	ENTRY DATE	ENTRY PRICE	EXIT DATE	EXIT PRICE	PROFIT	PROFIT AMOUNT	BEST EQUITY DATE	BEST EQUITY AMOUNT	WORST EQUITY DATE	WORST EQUITY AMOUNT
2005	01/03/05	16.26	03/11/05	17.52	1.25	500.00	03/11/05	500.00	02/02/05	-1580.00
2004	12/31/03	8.14	03/12/04	12.11	3.97	1588.00	03/11/04	1720.00	01/27/04	-388.00
2003	12/31/02	9.65	03/13/03	10.12	0.47	188.00	02/05/03	680.00	01/08/03	-460.00
2002	12/31/01	10.36	03/13/02	14.54	4.18	1672.00	03/08/02	1692.00		
2001	01/02/01	12.65	03/13/01	15.16	2.52	1008.00	03/13/01	1008.00	02/12/01	-740.00
2000	01/03/00	7.36	03/13/00	12.39	5.03	2012.00	03/10/00	2160.00		
1999	12/31/98	-3.54	03/12/99	0.54	4.10	1640.00	02/19/99	1968.00	01/04/99	-252.00
1998	12/31/97	7.03	03/13/98	5.03	-2.00	-800.00	01/23/98	384.00	02/25/98	-1552.00
1997	12/31/96	11.40	03/13/97	11.42	0.01	4.00	01/27/97	824.00	03/11/97	-212.00
1996	01/02/96	5.50	03/13/96	6.09	0.60	240.00	02/26/96	540.00	01/17/96	-540.00
1995	01/03/95	2.12	03/13/95	5.03	2.92	1168.00	02/23/95	1200.00	01/05/95	-20.00
1994	12/31/93	4.59	03/11/94	5.82	1.24	496.00	02/22/94	1164.00		
1993	12/31/92	5.17	03/12/93	7.92	2.76	1104.00	03/08/93	1708.00	01/07/93	-40.00
1992	12/31/91	0.89	03/13/92	1.72	0.83	332.00	02/10/92	1072.00		
1991	12/31/90	8.04	03/13/91	12.12	4.08	1632.00	03/08/91	2108.00	01/09/91	-124.00
1990	01/02/90	5.14	03/13/90	10.07	4.94	1976.00	03/12/90	2144.00		
1989	01/03/89	4.24	03/13/89	4.53	0.28	112.00	01/06/89	300.00	02/10/89	-780.00
1988	12/31/87	5.64	03/11/88	7.20	1.55	620.00	01/11/88	1136.00	03/01/88	-16.00
1987	12/31/86	6.92	03/13/87	9.95	3.03	1212.00	03/09/87	1284.00	01/09/87	-296.00
1986	12/31/85	4.42	03/13/86	4.82	0.40	160.00	01/29/86	812.00	01/09/86	-596.00

Percentage Correct	93								
Average Profit on Winning Trades					2.43	970.29		Winners	14
Average Loss on Trades					-2.00	-800.00		Losers	1
Average Net Profit Per Trade					2.13	852.27		Total trades	15
Percentage Correct	95								
Average Profit on Winning Trades					2.32	929.68		Winners	19
Average Loss on Trades					-2.00	-800.00		Losers	1
Average Net Profit Per Trade					2.11	843.20		Total trades	20

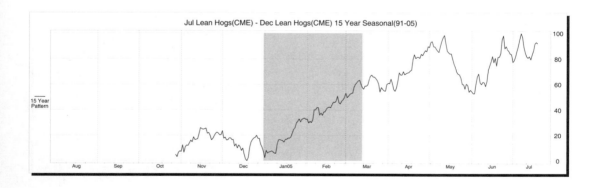

Jul Lean Hogs(CME) - Dec Lean Hogs(CME) 15 Year Seasonal(91-05)

Figure 6-33

Buy Jul Lean Hogs(CME) / Sell Dec Lean Hogs(CME)

Enter on approximately 02/15 - Exit on approximately 05/11

CONT YEAR	ENTRY DATE	ENTRY PRICE	EXIT DATE	EXIT PRICE	PROFIT	PROFIT AMOUNT	BEST EQUITY DATE	BEST EQUITY AMOUNT	WORST EQUITY DATE	WORST EQUITY AMOUNT
2005	02/15/05	14.22	05/11/05	15.39	1.18	472.00	04/11/05	1484.00		
2004	02/17/04	9.82	05/11/04	18.89	9.07	3628.00	05/11/04	3628.00	02/25/04	-140.00
2003	02/18/03	9.89	05/09/03	12.64	2.75	1100.00	05/02/03	1212.00	04/01/03	-1940.00
2002	02/15/02	13.50	05/10/02	14.14	0.65	260.00	03/08/02	440.00	04/15/02	-1860.00
2001	02/15/01	12.17	05/11/01	15.47	3.31	1324.00	04/16/01	1452.00		
2000	02/15/00	8.45	05/11/00	14.92	6.48	2592.00	05/05/00	2800.00		
1999	02/16/99	0.69	05/11/99	6.36	5.67	2268.00	05/10/99	2372.00	03/15/99	-380.00
1998	02/17/98	5.82	05/11/98	7.67	1.84	736.00	05/11/98	736.00	02/25/98	-1072.00
1997	02/18/97	11.89	05/09/97	13.19	1.30	520.00	04/18/97	612.00	04/08/97	-832.00
1996	02/15/96	5.93	05/10/96	7.29	1.36	544.00	04/16/96	1336.00	02/21/96	-188.00
1995	02/15/95	3.64	05/11/95	1.43	-2.21	-884.00	03/20/95	740.00	05/08/95	-1336.00
1994	02/15/94	6.84	05/11/94	6.90	0.06	24.00	04/22/94	1232.00	03/16/94	-476.00
1993	02/16/93	8.26	05/11/93	8.32	0.05	20.00	04/01/93	1408.00	03/12/93	-136.00
1992	02/18/92	2.62	05/11/92	4.70	2.08	832.00	04/09/92	948.00	03/30/92	-820.00
1991	02/15/91	10.10	05/10/91	11.82	1.73	692.00	03/28/91	1356.00	02/21/91	-148.00
1990	02/15/90	7.78	05/11/90	11.75	3.96	1584.00	05/07/90	2604.00		
1989	02/15/89	2.86	05/11/89	3.64	0.78	312.00	03/03/89	824.00	03/23/89	-308.00
1988	02/16/88	7.09	05/11/88	8.91	1.82	728.00	03/31/88	808.00	03/01/88	-596.00
1987	02/17/87	7.53	05/11/87	13.03	5.50	2200.00	04/24/87	2536.00	02/18/87	-108.00
1986	02/18/86	3.75	05/09/86	6.53	2.78	1112.00	05/06/86	1444.00	04/07/86	-960.00

Percentage Correct	93									
Average Profit on Winning Trades					2.68	1072.29		Winners		14
Average Loss on Trades					-2.21	-884.00		Losers		1
Average Net Profit Per Trade					2.35	941.87		Total trades		15
Percentage Correct	95									
Average Profit on Winning Trades					2.76	1102.53		Winners		19
Average Loss on Trades					-2.21	-884.00		Losers		1
Average Net Profit Per Trade					2.51	1003.20		Total trades		20

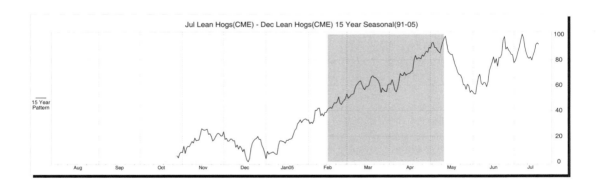

Jul Lean Hogs(CME) - Dec Lean Hogs(CME) 15 Year Seasonal(91-05)

Figure 6-34

Buy Jun Lean Hogs(CME) / Sell Oct Lean Hogs(CME)

Enter on approximately 02/17 - Exit on approximately 03/10

CONT YEAR	ENTRY DATE	ENTRY PRICE	EXIT DATE	EXIT PRICE	PROFIT	PROFIT AMOUNT	BEST EQUITY DATE	BEST EQUITY AMOUNT	WORST EQUITY DATE	WORST EQUITY AMOUNT
2005	02/17/05	15.24	03/10/05	15.67	0.42	168.00	03/04/05	708.00	02/18/05	-240.00
2004	02/17/04	13.25	03/10/04	15.54	2.30	920.00	03/10/04	920.00	02/25/04	-172.00
2003	02/18/03	11.17	03/10/03	9.67	-1.50	-600.00	03/03/03	160.00	03/07/03	-608.00
2002	02/19/02	14.69	03/08/02	15.26	0.57	228.00	03/07/02	240.00	02/26/02	-172.00
2001	02/20/01	13.54	03/09/01	16.25	2.70	1080.00	03/09/01	1080.00	02/21/01	-20.00
2000	02/17/00	8.31	03/10/00	12.95	4.63	1852.00	03/10/00	1852.00	02/23/00	-260.00
1999	02/17/99	0.00	03/10/99	0.53	0.53	212.00	03/10/99	212.00	02/24/99	-160.00
1998	02/17/98	4.30	03/10/98	4.60	0.30	120.00	03/09/98	280.00	02/25/98	-1000.00
1997	02/18/97	11.20	03/10/97	10.67	-0.53	-212.00	02/26/97	660.00	03/10/97	-212.00
1996	02/20/96	9.03	03/08/96	10.97	1.93	772.00	03/07/96	800.00	02/21/96	-168.00
1995	02/17/95	5.77	03/10/95	6.63	0.87	348.00	02/28/95	492.00		
1994	02/17/94	8.56	03/10/94	9.01	0.45	180.00	02/22/94	392.00	03/02/94	-236.00
1993	02/17/93	11.08	03/10/93	13.54	2.46	984.00	03/09/93	1056.00		
1992	02/18/92	5.40	03/10/92	6.65	1.25	500.00	03/06/92	596.00	02/24/92	-80.00
1991	02/19/91	11.31	03/08/91	13.00	1.69	676.00	03/08/91	676.00	02/21/91	-360.00
1990	02/20/90	9.04	03/09/90	11.29	2.24	896.00	03/09/90	896.00	02/21/90	-48.00
1989	02/17/89	5.40	03/10/89	5.47	0.07	28.00	03/01/89	448.00		
1988	02/17/88	7.46	03/10/88	7.66	0.20	80.00	03/08/88	216.00	03/04/88	-488.00
1987	02/17/87	8.52	03/10/87	10.67	2.16	864.00	03/09/87	1052.00		
1986	02/18/86	4.92	03/10/86	5.57	0.64	256.00	02/25/86	516.00		

Percentage Correct	87									
Average Profit on Winning Trades					1.55	618.46		Winners		13
Average Loss on Trades					-1.02	-406.00		Losers		2
Average Net Profit Per Trade					1.20	481.87		Total trades		15
Percentage Correct	90									
Average Profit on Winning Trades					1.41	564.67		Winners		18
Average Loss on Trades					-1.02	-406.00		Losers		2
Average Net Profit Per Trade					1.17	467.60		Total trades		20

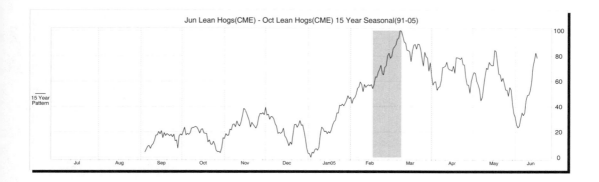

Jun Lean Hogs(CME) - Oct Lean Hogs(CME) 15 Year Seasonal(91-05)

15 Year Pattern

Chapter 6: Meats

Figure 6-35

Buy Aug Lean Hogs(CME) / Sell Dec Lean Hogs(CME)

Enter on approximately 04/03 - Exit on approximately 07/26

CONT YEAR	ENTRY DATE	ENTRY PRICE	EXIT DATE	EXIT PRICE	PROFIT	PROFIT AMOUNT	BEST EQUITY DATE	BEST EQUITY AMOUNT	WORST EQUITY DATE	WORST EQUITY AMOUNT
2004	04/05/04	11.71	07/26/04	13.76	2.05	820.00	05/28/04	2692.00		
2003	04/03/03	6.65	07/25/03	7.47	0.83	332.00	06/05/03	2960.00	07/24/03	-88.00
2002	04/03/02	10.35	07/26/02	10.97	0.63	252.00	05/15/02	800.00	04/11/02	-1160.00
2001	04/03/01	10.37	07/26/01	14.77	4.41	1764.00	06/26/01	2024.00		
2000	04/03/00	10.05	07/26/00	14.24	4.20	1680.00	07/07/00	2080.00	04/11/00	-152.00
1999	04/05/99	1.29	07/26/99	9.60	8.30	3320.00	07/26/99	3320.00	06/25/99	-712.00
1998	04/03/98	2.75	07/24/98	5.15	2.40	960.00	06/19/98	1628.00	04/06/98	-260.00
1997	04/03/97	8.40	07/25/97	11.84	3.45	1380.00	06/27/97	1592.00	04/08/97	-272.00
1996	04/03/96	3.82	07/26/96	6.79	2.97	1188.00	07/26/96	1188.00	07/01/96	-1396.00
1995	04/03/95	3.10	07/26/95	5.52	2.41	964.00	07/24/95	1008.00	05/08/95	-1144.00
1994	04/04/94	4.78	07/26/94	6.64	1.87	748.00	04/22/94	748.00	06/03/94	-1264.00
1993	04/05/93	6.40	07/26/93	2.46	-3.94	-1576.00	06/24/93	556.00	07/20/93	-1844.00
1992	04/03/92	0.93	07/24/92	4.05	3.11	1244.00	07/17/92	1832.00	06/03/92	-384.00
1991	04/03/91	8.45	07/26/91	11.41	2.96	1184.00	07/24/91	1268.00	06/12/91	-1220.00
1990	04/03/90	7.67	07/26/90	11.21	3.55	1420.00	07/23/90	1904.00		
1989	04/03/89	1.57	07/26/89	6.36	4.79	1916.00	07/25/89	2028.00	05/26/89	-332.00
1988	04/04/88	4.64	07/26/88	3.68	-0.95	-380.00	06/01/88	1344.00	06/23/88	-3072.00
1987	04/03/87	5.39	07/24/87	12.34	6.94	2776.00	07/22/87	2904.00		
1986	04/03/86	0.71	07/25/86	8.38	7.66	3064.00	07/03/86	3268.00	04/07/86	-224.00
1985	04/03/85	2.76	07/26/85	4.36	1.60	640.00	07/26/85	640.00	06/21/85	-880.00

Percentage Correct	93							
Average Profit on Winning Trades		3.08	1232.57		Winners	14
Average Loss on Trades		-3.94	-1576.00		Losers	1
Average Net Profit Per Trade		2.61	1045.33		Total trades	15

Percentage Correct	90							
Average Profit on Winning Trades		3.56	1425.11		Winners	18
Average Loss on Trades		-2.45	-978.00		Losers	2
Average Net Profit Per Trade		2.96	1184.80		Total trades	20

HYPOTHETICAL PERFORMANCE RESULTS HAVE MANY INHERENT LIMITATIONS, SOME OF WHICH ARE DESCRIBED BELOW. NO REPRESENTATION IS BEING MADE THAT ANY ACCOUNT WILL OR IS LIKELY TO ACHIEVE PROFITS OR LOSSES SIMILAR TO THOSE SHOWN. IN FACT, THERE ARE FREQUENTLY SHARP DIFFERENCES BETWEEN HYPOTHETICAL PERFORMANCE RESULTS AND THE ACTUAL RESULTS SUBSEQUENTLY ACHIEVED BY ANY PARTICULAR TRADING PROGRAM. ONE OF THE LIMITATIONS OF HYPOTHETICAL PERFORMANCE RESULTS IS THAT THEY ARE GENERALLY PREPARED WITH THE BENEFIT OF HINDSIGHT. IN ADDITION, HYPOTHETICAL TRADING DOES NOT INVOLVE FINANCIAL RISK, AND NO HYPOTHETICAL TRADING RECORD CAN COMPLETELY ACCOUNT FOR THE IMPACT OF FINANCIAL RISK IN ACTUAL TRADING. FOR EXAMPLE, THE ABILITY TO WITHSTAND LOSSES OR ADHERE TO A PARTICULAR TRADING PROGRAM IN SPITE OF TRADING LOSSES ARE MATERIAL POINTS WHICH CAN ALSO ADVERSELY AFFECT ACTUAL TRADING RESULTS. THERE ARE NUMEROUS OTHER FACTORS RELATED TO THE MARKETS IN GENERAL OR TO THE IMPLEMENTATION OF ANY SPECIFIC TRADING PROGRAM WHICH CANNOT BE FULLY ACCOUNTED FOR IN THE PREPARATION OF HYPOTHETICAL PERFORMANCE RESULTS AND ALL OF WHICH CAN ADVERSELY AFFECT ACTUAL TRADING RESULTS. RESULTS NOT ADJUSTED FOR COMMISSION AND SLIPPAGE.

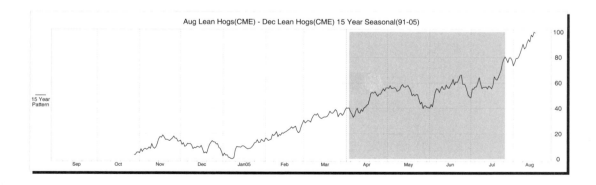

Aug Lean Hogs(CME) - Dec Lean Hogs(CME) 15 Year Seasonal(91-05)

15 Year Pattern

Figure 6-36

Buy Aug Lean Hogs(CME) / Sell Oct Lean Hogs(CME)

Enter on approximately 04/06 - Exit on approximately 05/23

CONT YEAR	ENTRY DATE	ENTRY PRICE	EXIT DATE	EXIT PRICE	PROFIT	PROFIT AMOUNT	BEST EQUITY DATE	BEST EQUITY AMOUNT	WORST EQUITY DATE	WORST EQUITY AMOUNT
2005	04/06/05	10.45	05/23/05	9.32	-1.12	-448.00	04/20/05	552.00	05/19/05	-460.00
2004	04/06/04	10.67	05/21/04	11.13	0.45	180.00	04/30/04	608.00	04/19/04	-320.00
2003	04/07/03	7.85	05/23/03	9.85	2.00	800.00	05/19/03	1160.00	04/10/03	-160.00
2002	04/08/02	7.53	05/23/02	8.89	1.37	548.00	05/17/02	848.00	04/11/02	-552.00
2001	04/06/01	7.97	05/23/01	8.62	0.65	260.00	04/27/01	504.00		
2000	04/06/00	7.02	05/23/00	8.09	1.08	432.00	05/09/00	852.00	04/07/00	-100.00
1999	04/06/99	1.82	05/21/99	3.50	1.67	668.00	05/07/99	888.00	04/14/99	-140.00
1998	04/06/98	2.85	05/22/98	4.78	1.93	772.00	05/15/98	848.00		
1997	04/07/97	5.93	05/23/97	7.46	1.53	612.00	05/07/97	828.00	04/08/97	-184.00
1996	04/08/96	4.78	05/23/96	6.37	1.60	640.00	05/16/96	908.00	04/10/96	-336.00
1995	04/06/95	3.85	05/23/95	3.21	-0.63	-252.00	04/12/95	176.00	05/08/95	-780.00
1994	04/06/94	5.38	05/23/94	5.46	0.07	28.00	04/22/94	560.00	05/20/94	-168.00
1993	04/06/93	7.12	05/21/93	8.19	1.08	432.00	05/20/93	440.00	05/11/93	-76.00
1992	04/06/92	3.92	05/22/92	4.39	0.48	192.00	05/08/92	472.00		
1991	04/08/91	6.47	05/23/91	6.92	0.44	176.00	04/30/91	364.00	05/10/91	-64.00
1990	04/06/90	7.31	05/23/90	10.34	3.02	1208.00	05/22/90	1324.00	04/16/90	-256.00
1989	04/06/89	4.35	05/23/89	4.61	0.26	104.00	04/13/89	292.00	05/17/89	-204.00
1988	04/06/88	6.07	05/23/88	7.30	1.22	488.00	05/16/88	624.00	04/13/88	-448.00
1987	04/06/87	5.87	05/22/87	7.57	1.69	676.00	04/24/87	1120.00		
1986	04/07/86	2.85	05/23/86	6.01	3.15	1260.00	05/23/86	1260.00		

Percentage Correct	87									
Average Profit on Winning Trades					1.10	441.54		Winners		13
Average Loss on Trades					-0.88	-350.00		Losers		2
Average Net Profit Per Trade					0.84	336.00		Total trades		15
Percentage Correct	90									
Average Profit on Winning Trades					1.32	526.44		Winners		18
Average Loss on Trades					-0.88	-350.00		Losers		2
Average Net Profit Per Trade					1.10	438.80		Total trades		20

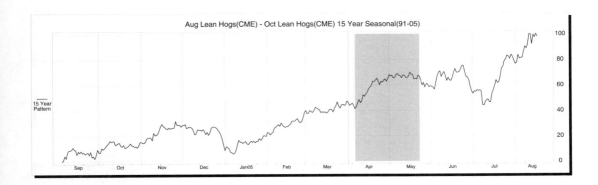

Aug Lean Hogs(CME) - Oct Lean Hogs(CME) 15 Year Seasonal(91-05)

15 Year Pattern

Chapter 6: Meats

Figure 6-37

Buy Aug Lean Hogs(CME) / Sell Oct Lean Hogs(CME)

Enter on approximately 07/14 - Exit on approximately 08/07

CONT YEAR	ENTRY DATE	ENTRY PRICE	EXIT DATE	EXIT PRICE	PROFIT	PROFIT AMOUNT	BEST EQUITY DATE	BEST EQUITY AMOUNT	WORST EQUITY DATE	WORST EQUITY AMOUNT
2004	07/14/04	8.30	08/06/04	8.50	0.20	80.00	07/23/04	720.00	07/27/04	-308.00
2003	07/14/03	5.85	08/07/03	6.57	0.72	288.00	07/30/03	612.00	08/01/03	-320.00
2002	07/15/02	8.75	08/07/02	9.80	1.05	420.00	08/02/02	808.00	07/19/02	-352.00
2001	07/16/01	9.29	08/07/01	11.67	2.38	952.00	08/06/01	1060.00	07/20/01	-140.00
2000	07/14/00	8.85	08/07/00	8.92	0.07	28.00	08/02/00	740.00	07/19/00	-100.00
1999	07/14/99	4.13	08/06/99	5.01	0.89	356.00	07/28/99	956.00		
1998	07/14/98	4.55	08/07/98	8.04	3.50	1400.00	08/07/98	1400.00		
1997	07/14/97	6.50	08/07/97	7.75	1.25	500.00	07/25/97	584.00		
1996	07/15/96	4.93	08/07/96	6.96	2.03	812.00	07/26/96	1352.00		
1995	07/14/95	5.21	08/07/95	5.64	0.42	168.00	07/24/95	488.00		
1994	07/14/94	3.71	08/05/94	6.12	2.40	960.00	08/03/94	1144.00		
1993	07/14/93	4.49	08/06/93	3.03	-1.45	-580.00	07/19/93	232.00	08/06/93	-580.00
1992	07/14/92	6.28	08/07/92	6.99	0.70	280.00	08/07/92	280.00	08/04/92	-544.00
1991	07/15/91	9.51	08/07/91	11.85	2.34	936.00	08/05/91	1136.00	07/16/91	-120.00
1990	07/16/90	7.91	08/07/90	9.75	1.83	732.00	07/23/90	932.00		
1989	07/14/89	6.72	08/07/89	7.50	0.77	308.00	07/27/89	928.00		
1988	07/14/88	4.03	08/05/88	7.98	3.95	1580.00	08/03/88	1640.00	07/15/88	-124.00
1987	07/14/87	11.68	08/07/87	13.01	1.33	532.00	08/07/87	532.00	07/31/87	-596.00
1986	07/14/86	4.92	08/07/86	10.51	5.58	2232.00	08/07/86	2232.00		
1985	07/15/85	6.12	08/07/85	7.23	1.11	444.00	08/07/85	444.00	07/31/85	-464.00

Percentage Correct	93									
Average Profit on Winning Trades					1.41	565.14		Winners		14
Average Loss on Trades					-1.45	-580.00		Losers		1
Average Net Profit Per Trade					1.22	488.80		Total trades		15
Percentage Correct	95									
Average Profit on Winning Trades					1.71	684.63		Winners		19
Average Loss on Trades					-1.45	-580.00		Losers		1
Average Net Profit Per Trade					1.55	621.40		Total trades		20

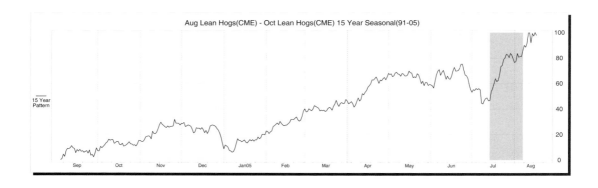

Aug Lean Hogs(CME) - Oct Lean Hogs(CME) 15 Year Seasonal(91-05)

Pork Bellies

Frozen pork bellies, which are slabs of bacon, are the only storable commodity in the meats complex. However, they are more like a grain crop. Contract specifications require that deliverable bellies cannot be stored prior to the preceding November 1. Thus, each "crop" of bellies begins moving into cold storage in November and must be moved out by the end of deliveries against the August contract.

Figure 6-38: Aug Pork Bellies Seasonal Pattern

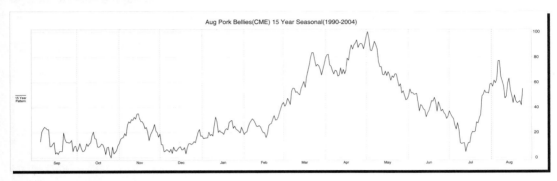

The peak in demand for bacon is the bacon-lettuce-tomato season of summer. Thus, the industry stores bellies aggressively until slaughter is too low and hog prices too high. This accumulation, or in-movement, drives prices higher into March and tends to keep them at an elevated plateau until May, at which time grocers begin featuring by then plentiful beef and in-movement ends. As stocks move out of storage, prices tend to cascade lower in anticipation of deliveries against the July contract — typically the heaviest of the season. The market tends then to recover into August in order to prevent a supply squeeze just as tomatoes ripen and pork consumption peaks.

Figure 6-39: Feb/Aug Pork Bellies Seasonal Pattern

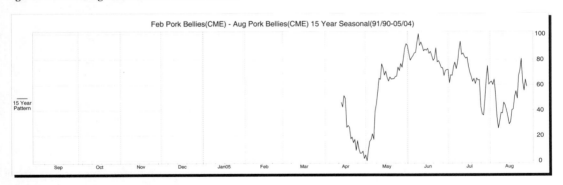

Spreads between delivery months of the same "crop year" of pork bellies are not tradable, lacking in both reliability and intensity. The "old-crop/new-crop" spread between August and the following February contract may seem to help the market make the transition from one to the other, but the new-crop represented by the February contract is more concept than substance.

Inter-market Spreads

Spreads between members of the meats complex tend to be exceptionally tradable. Those between live cattle and hogs, for example, reflect not only competition between meats but also the contrast in slaughter patterns. Those between feeder cattle and live cattle and between hogs and pork bellies are also commercially viable hedging vehicles.

Cattle versus Hogs

Inverse patterns of both supply and demand drive spreads throughout the year. Cattle slaughter is greatest in May/June, when hog slaughter is least. Cattle slaughter declines while hog slaughter rises. Cattle slaughter is least in December, when hog slaughter is greatest. Retail pork consumption is greatest in August, when beef consumption is least.

Figure 6-40: Jun Lean Hogs/Live Cattle Seasonal Pattern

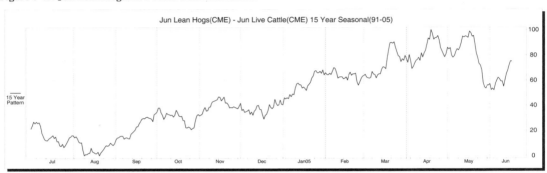

Figure 6-41: Lean Hogs/Live Cattle Spread Strategies

Moore Research Center, Inc.			Hogs versus Cattle Spread Strategies					
Seasonal Strategy	Entry Date	Exit Date	Win Pct	Win Yrs	Loss Years	Total Years	Average Profit	Ave Pft Per Day
Buy Apr Live Cattle(CME)	1/30	2/26	80	12	3	15	581	21
Sell Apr Lean Hogs(CME)			80	16	4	20	620	42
Buy Jun Lean Hogs(CME)	2/25	4/19	80	12	3	15	1179	22
Sell Jun Live Cattle(CME)			85	17	3	20	1271	24
Buy Jun Lean Hogs(CME)	2/25	5/18	80	12	3	15	1220	15
Sell Jun Live Cattle(CME)			85	17	3	20	1687	20
Buy Aug Lean Hogs(CME)	3/03	4/19	80	12	3	15	930	19
Sell Aug Live Cattle(CME)			85	17	3	20	1068	22
Buy Jun Lean Hogs(CME)	3/10	3/21	93	14	1	15	678	56
Sell Jun Live Cattle(CME)			85	17	3	20	555	46
Buy Jun Lean Hogs(CME)	4/05	4/24	80	12	3	15	762	38
Sell Jun Live Cattle(CME)			80	16	4	20	844	42
Buy Dec Live Cattle(CME)	6/06	8/15	80	12	3	15	1309	18
Sell Dec Lean Hogs(CME)			80	16	4	20	1202	17
Buy Dec Live Cattle(CME)	10/03	11/03	93	14	1	15	989	31
Sell Dec Lean Hogs(CME)			90	18	2	20	821	26

Remember one primary function that markets perform is to anticipate the future. Remember also that cattle and hog slaughters are normally at opposite extremes in May/June and that beef and pork demand are at opposite extremes shortly thereafter. Thus, it comes as no surprise that June, July, and August Hogs outperform June and August Cattle from corn harvest, through winter, and on into April/May as both markets work to discount those extremes.

Certain of these spreads have suffered sharp drawdowns along the way. Traders must make allowances for such, given that these two distinct markets respond also to different fundamentals. For example, when the cash cattle market does continue rising into an April peak, bullish enthusiasm and anxiety pull cattle futures higher for longer than normal into a buying climax — often followed by a collapse. Thus, the issue for traders tends more normally to be one of timing than of reaching the ultimate destination.

Figure 6-42: Dec Lean Hogs/Live Cattle Seasonal Pattern

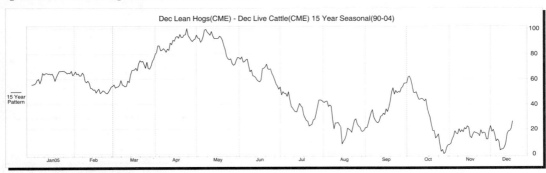

By May, both markets begin realizing those extremes already anticipated. Spreads between them tend to reverse course in order to anticipate future extremes. For example, despite a looming peak in retail demand for pork at the expense of beef, spreads between December contracts begin favoring cattle. The seasonal pattern illustrates and the table's sixth strategy quantifies the more typical initial surge into August, when feedlot inventories will be lowest. This strategy has generated large moves but also encountered serious difficulties.

During October, pork production surges as both hog weights and slaughter numbers increase when corn harvest gets under way but beef consumption rises as temperatures cool. In the cold of February, beef consumption remains high but cattle gain weight slowly so slaughter has yet to increase significantly. Hog slaughter has begun to decline but remains high.

Figure 6-43

Buy Apr Live Cattle(CME) / Sell Apr Lean Hogs(CME)

Enter on approximately 01/30 - Exit on approximately 02/26

CONT YEAR	ENTRY DATE	ENTRY PRICE	EXIT DATE	EXIT PRICE	PROFIT	PROFIT AMOUNT	BEST EQUITY DATE	BEST EQUITY AMOUNT	WORST EQUITY DATE	WORST EQUITY AMOUNT
2005	01/31/05	12.76	02/25/05	11.94	-0.82	-328.00	02/04/05	960.00	02/23/05	-836.00
2004	01/30/04	14.21	02/26/04	15.39	1.18	472.00	02/25/04	784.00	02/06/04	-788.00
2003	01/30/03	23.24	02/26/03	23.46	0.22	88.00	02/04/03	800.00	02/13/03	-172.00
2002	01/30/02	14.56	02/26/02	15.14	0.58	232.00	02/15/02	812.00	02/05/02	-588.00
2001	01/30/01	19.55	02/26/01	18.09	-1.45	-580.00	02/09/01	1140.00	02/20/01	-740.00
2000	01/31/00	11.79	02/25/00	13.66	1.87	748.00	02/15/00	1120.00	02/04/00	-212.00
1999	02/01/99	22.00	02/26/99	25.01	3.02	1208.00	02/26/99	1208.00	02/08/99	-992.00
1998	01/30/98	9.83	02/26/98	16.10	6.26	2504.00	02/26/98	2504.00	02/02/98	-128.00
1997	01/30/97	-9.29	02/26/97	-4.81	4.49	1796.00	02/21/97	2240.00	02/03/97	-48.00
1996	01/30/96	2.69	02/26/96	1.61	-1.08	-432.00	01/31/96	492.00	02/07/96	-1196.00
1995	01/30/95	19.81	02/24/95	20.64	0.84	336.00	02/10/95	1208.00		
1994	01/31/94	6.59	02/25/94	9.56	2.97	1188.00	02/25/94	1188.00	02/03/94	-476.00
1993	02/01/93	18.25	02/26/93	18.71	0.46	184.00	02/08/93	1160.00	02/25/93	-92.00
1992	01/30/92	23.28	02/26/92	23.59	0.30	120.00	02/26/92	120.00	02/07/92	-1264.00
1991	01/30/91	8.28	02/26/91	11.21	2.94	1176.00	02/21/91	2068.00		
1990	01/30/90	13.11	02/26/90	8.07	-5.04	-2016.00	02/06/90	404.00	02/26/90	-2016.00
1989	01/30/89	18.31	02/24/89	19.34	1.03	412.00	02/07/89	844.00	02/01/89	-400.00
1988	02/01/88	8.75	02/26/88	12.68	3.93	1572.00	02/19/88	1972.00		
1987	01/30/87	0.75	02/26/87	5.42	4.68	1872.00	02/23/87	2392.00	02/02/87	-64.00
1986	01/30/86	4.38	02/26/86	9.01	4.64	1856.00	02/26/86	1856.00		

Percentage Correct	80							
Average Profit on Winning Trades				2.09	837.67		Winners	12
Average Loss on Trades				-1.12	-446.67		Losers	3
Average Net Profit Per Trade				1.45	580.80		Total trades	15
Percentage Correct	80							
Average Profit on Winning Trades				2.46	985.25		Winners	16
Average Loss on Trades				-2.10	-839.00		Losers	4
Average Net Profit Per Trade				1.55	620.40		Total trades	20

HYPOTHETICAL PERFORMANCE RESULTS HAVE MANY INHERENT LIMITATIONS, SOME OF WHICH ARE DESCRIBED BELOW. NO REPRESENTATION IS BEING MADE THAT ANY ACCOUNT WILL OR IS LIKELY TO ACHIEVE PROFITS OR LOSSES SIMILAR TO THOSE SHOWN. IN FACT, THERE ARE FREQUENTLY SHARP DIFFERENCES BETWEEN HYPOTHETICAL PERFORMANCE RESULTS AND THE ACTUAL RESULTS SUBSEQUENTLY ACHIEVED BY ANY PARTICULAR TRADING PROGRAM. ONE OF THE LIMITATIONS OF HYPOTHETICAL PERFORMANCE RESULTS IS THAT THEY ARE GENERALLY PREPARED WITH THE BENEFIT OF HINDSIGHT. IN ADDITION, HYPOTHETICAL TRADING DOES NOT INVOLVE FINANCIAL RISK, AND NO HYPOTHETICAL TRADING RECORD CAN COMPLETELY ACCOUNT FOR THE IMPACT OF FINANCIAL RISK IN ACTUAL TRADING. FOR EXAMPLE, THE ABILITY TO WITHSTAND LOSSES OR ADHERE TO A PARTICULAR TRADING PROGRAM IN SPITE OF TRADING LOSSES ARE MATERIAL POINTS WHICH CAN ALSO ADVERSELY AFFECT ACTUAL TRADING RESULTS. THERE ARE NUMEROUS OTHER FACTORS RELATED TO THE MARKETS IN GENERAL OR TO THE IMPLEMENTATION OF ANY SPECIFIC TRADING PROGRAM WHICH CANNOT BE FULLY ACCOUNTED FOR IN THE PREPARATION OF HYPOTHETICAL PERFORMANCE RESULTS AND ALL OF WHICH CAN ADVERSELY AFFECT ACTUAL TRADING RESULTS. RESULTS NOT ADJUSTED FOR COMMISSION AND SLIPPAGE.

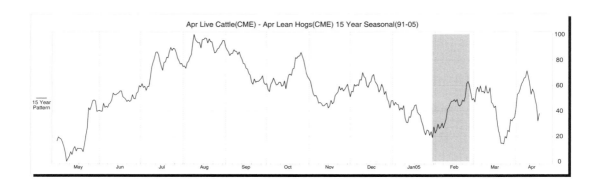

Apr Live Cattle(CME) - Apr Lean Hogs(CME) 15 Year Seasonal(91-05)

Figure 6-44

Buy Jun Lean Hogs(CME) / Sell Jun Live Cattle(CME)

Enter on approximately 02/25 - Exit on approximately 04/19

CONT YEAR	ENTRY DATE	ENTRY PRICE	EXIT DATE	EXIT PRICE	PROFIT	PROFIT AMOUNT	BEST EQUITY DATE	BEST EQUITY AMOUNT	WORST EQUITY DATE	WORST EQUITY AMOUNT
2005	02/25/05	-2.95	04/19/05	-7.73	-4.78	-1912.00	03/01/05	352.00	04/18/05	-1960.00
2004	02/25/04	-7.50	04/19/04	-5.54	1.95	780.00	03/29/04	2788.00	03/04/04	-40.00
2003	02/25/03	-8.83	04/17/03	-11.47	-2.65	-1060.00	03/03/03	960.00	04/10/03	-2116.00
2002	02/25/02	-4.20	04/19/02	-3.89	0.30	120.00	02/28/02	600.00	04/11/02	-2740.00
2001	02/26/01	-6.48	04/19/01	0.50	6.98	2792.00	04/16/01	2880.00	02/27/01	-160.00
2000	02/25/00	-2.87	04/19/00	6.53	9.40	3760.00	04/19/00	3760.00		
1999	02/25/99	-10.70	04/19/99	-7.67	3.02	1208.00	04/19/99	1208.00	03/15/99	-532.00
1998	02/25/98	-9.10	04/17/98	-8.03	1.07	428.00	03/31/98	1300.00	03/10/98	-996.00
1997	02/25/97	14.95	04/18/97	20.84	5.90	2360.00	04/17/97	2492.00	03/11/97	-1552.00
1996	02/26/96	7.75	04/19/96	19.36	11.62	4648.00	04/16/96	4860.00	03/14/96	-140.00
1995	02/27/95	-5.77	04/19/95	-2.70	3.07	1228.00	03/16/95	2316.00		
1994	02/25/94	-0.45	04/19/94	-1.02	-0.57	-228.00	04/18/94	40.00	04/08/94	-1624.00
1993	02/25/93	-5.18	04/19/93	-4.90	0.29	116.00	04/01/93	1996.00	03/01/93	-336.00
1992	02/25/92	-13.08	04/16/92	-8.88	4.20	1680.00	04/13/92	2000.00	03/30/92	-656.00
1991	02/25/91	-2.36	04/19/91	2.04	4.42	1768.00	04/19/91	1768.00		
1990	02/26/90	3.45	04/19/90	9.02	5.57	2228.00	04/19/90	2228.00	03/05/90	-540.00
1989	02/27/89	-10.26	04/19/89	-8.46	1.80	720.00	03/08/89	824.00	04/07/89	-460.00
1988	02/25/88	-5.54	04/19/88	-3.89	1.65	660.00	04/05/88	1956.00	03/03/88	-116.00
1987	02/25/87	0.16	04/16/87	5.12	4.95	1980.00	04/16/87	1980.00	02/27/87	-432.00
1986	02/25/86	-2.18	04/18/86	3.19	5.38	2152.00	04/18/86	2152.00	02/27/86	-172.00

Percentage Correct	80									
Average Profit on Winning Trades					4.35	1740.67		Winners		12
Average Loss on Trades					-2.67	-1066.67		Losers		3
Average Net Profit Per Trade					2.95	1179.20		Total trades		15
Percentage Correct	85									
Average Profit on Winning Trades					4.21	1684.00		Winners		17
Average Loss on Trades					-2.67	-1066.67		Losers		3
Average Net Profit Per Trade					3.18	1271.40		Total trades		20

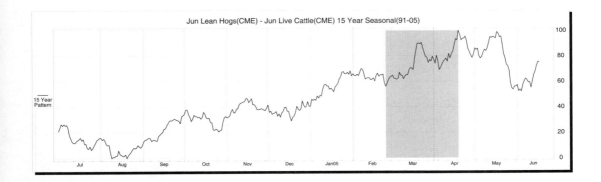

Jun Lean Hogs(CME) - Jun Live Cattle(CME) 15 Year Seasonal(91-05)

Figure 6-45

							BEST	**BEST**	**WORST**	**WORST**

Buy Jun Lean Hogs(CME) / Sell Jun Live Cattle(CME)

Moore Research Center, Inc.

Enter on approximately 02/25 - Exit on approximately 05/18

CONT YEAR	ENTRY DATE	ENTRY PRICE	EXIT DATE	EXIT PRICE	PROFIT	PROFIT AMOUNT	BEST EQUITY DATE	BEST EQUITY AMOUNT	WORST EQUITY DATE	WORST EQUITY AMOUNT
2005	02/25/05	-2.95	05/18/05	-12.11	-9.17	-3668.00	03/01/05	352.00	05/18/05	-3668.00
2004	02/25/04	-7.50	05/18/04	-6.23	1.27	508.00	03/29/04	2788.00	05/06/04	-1660.00
2003	02/25/03	-8.83	05/16/03	-7.17	1.65	660.00	03/03/03	960.00	04/10/03	-2116.00
2002	02/25/02	-4.20	05/17/02	-8.57	-4.38	-1752.00	02/28/02	600.00	04/30/02	-2948.00
2001	02/26/01	-6.48	05/18/01	-4.03	2.45	980.00	04/16/01	2880.00	02/27/01	-160.00
2000	02/25/00	-2.87	05/18/00	2.64	5.52	2208.00	04/24/00	4428.00		
1999	02/25/99	-10.70	05/18/99	-5.25	5.45	2180.00	05/10/99	4180.00	03/15/99	-532.00
1998	02/25/98	-9.10	05/18/98	-3.22	5.88	2352.00	05/18/98	2352.00	03/10/98	-996.00
1997	02/25/97	14.95	05/16/97	15.59	0.65	260.00	04/24/97	2604.00	03/11/97	-1552.00
1996	02/26/96	7.75	05/17/96	30.17	22.43	8972.00	05/17/96	8972.00	03/14/96	-140.00
1995	02/27/95	-5.77	05/18/95	-1.84	3.92	1568.00	03/16/95	2316.00	05/04/95	-328.00
1994	02/25/94	-0.45	05/18/94	0.97	1.43	572.00	05/17/94	700.00	04/08/94	-1624.00
1993	02/25/93	-5.18	05/18/93	-6.05	-0.86	-344.00	04/01/93	1996.00	05/10/93	-1316.00
1992	02/25/92	-13.08	05/18/92	-8.87	4.21	1684.00	05/01/92	2032.00	03/30/92	-656.00
1991	02/25/91	-2.36	05/17/91	2.93	5.31	2124.00	05/07/91	2624.00		
1990	02/26/90	3.45	05/18/90	15.98	12.53	5012.00	05/18/90	5012.00	03/05/90	-540.00
1989	02/27/89	-10.26	05/18/89	-5.43	4.83	1932.00	05/18/89	1932.00	04/07/89	-460.00
1988	02/25/88	-5.54	05/18/88	-1.85	3.68	1472.00	04/05/88	1956.00	03/03/88	-116.00
1987	02/25/87	0.16	05/18/87	7.91	7.74	3096.00	05/15/87	3328.00	02/27/87	-432.00
1986	02/25/86	-2.18	05/16/86	7.60	9.79	3916.00	05/16/86	3916.00	02/27/86	-172.00

Percentage Correct	80				
Average Profit on Winning Trades		5.01	2005.67	Winners	12
Average Loss on Trades		-4.80	-1921.33	Losers	3
Average Net Profit Per Trade		3.05	1220.27	Total trades	15
Percentage Correct	85				
Average Profit on Winning Trades		5.81	2323.29	Winners	17
Average Loss on Trades		-4.80	-1921.33	Losers	3
Average Net Profit Per Trade		4.22	1686.60	Total trades	20

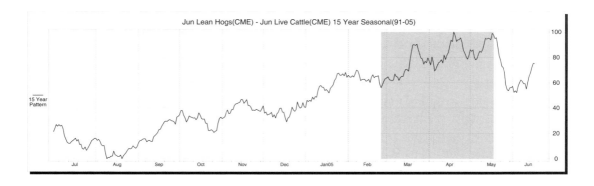

Jun Lean Hogs(CME) - Jun Live Cattle(CME) 15 Year Seasonal(91-05)

15 Year Pattern

Figure 6-46

Buy Aug Lean Hogs(CME) / Sell Aug Live Cattle(CME)

Enter on approximately 03/03 - Exit on approximately 04/19

CONT YEAR	ENTRY DATE	ENTRY PRICE	EXIT DATE	EXIT PRICE	PROFIT	PROFIT AMOUNT	BEST EQUITY DATE	BEST EQUITY AMOUNT	WORST EQUITY DATE	WORST EQUITY AMOUNT
2005	03/03/05	-6.51	04/19/05	-9.05	-2.53	-1012.00	04/04/05	36.00	03/28/05	-1632.00
2004	03/03/04	-14.46	04/19/04	-9.81	4.65	1860.00	04/08/04	3848.00		
2003	03/03/03	-7.02	04/17/03	-7.82	-0.79	-316.00	03/11/03	340.00	04/10/03	-1428.00
2002	03/04/02	-8.92	04/19/02	-7.00	1.93	772.00	04/19/02	772.00	04/11/02	-1796.00
2001	03/05/01	-11.35	04/19/01	-7.18	4.17	1668.00	04/16/01	1760.00	03/20/01	-440.00
2000	03/03/00	-6.51	04/19/00	-0.26	6.25	2500.00	04/18/00	2556.00		
1999	03/03/99	-8.44	04/19/99	-4.85	3.60	1440.00	04/16/99	1452.00		
1998	03/03/98	-11.44	04/17/98	-12.20	-0.75	-300.00	03/31/98	420.00	03/16/98	-1340.00
1997	03/03/97	10.23	04/18/97	18.39	8.17	3268.00	04/18/97	3268.00	03/19/97	-1260.00
1996	03/04/96	5.19	04/19/96	10.24	5.04	2016.00	04/19/96	2016.00	03/15/96	-1244.00
1995	03/03/95	-3.60	04/19/95	-2.29	1.31	524.00	03/20/95	1352.00	03/06/95	-140.00
1994	03/03/94	-3.12	04/19/94	-2.92	0.19	76.00	03/25/94	436.00	04/08/94	-1168.00
1993	03/03/93	-8.56	04/19/93	-6.94	1.61	644.00	03/31/93	2152.00		
1992	03/03/92	-10.67	04/16/92	-9.91	0.76	304.00	03/23/92	748.00	03/30/92	-764.00
1991	03/04/91	-2.70	04/19/91	-1.45	1.25	500.00	03/15/91	980.00	04/10/91	-220.00
1990	03/05/90	-0.64	04/19/90	6.62	7.27	2908.00	04/19/90	2908.00		
1989	03/03/89	-8.50	04/19/89	-5.65	2.85	1140.00	04/18/89	1212.00	03/30/89	-220.00
1988	03/03/88	-6.00	04/19/88	-2.98	3.01	1204.00	04/05/88	2020.00		
1987	03/03/87	-0.62	04/16/87	0.89	1.52	608.00	03/19/87	1040.00	04/03/87	-584.00
1986	03/03/86	-1.14	04/18/86	2.76	3.91	1564.00	04/01/86	1840.00	03/04/86	-32.00

Percentage Correct		80								
Average Profit on Winning Trades					3.24	1297.67		Winners		12
Average Loss on Trades					-1.36	-542.67		Losers		3
Average Net Profit Per Trade					2.32	929.60		Total trades		15
Percentage Correct		85								
Average Profit on Winning Trades					3.38	1352.71		Winners		17
Average Loss on Trades					-1.36	-542.67		Losers		3
Average Net Profit Per Trade					2.67	1068.40		Total trades		20

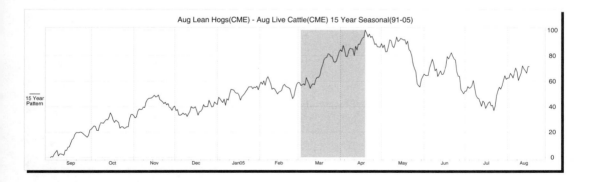

Aug Lean Hogs(CME) - Aug Live Cattle(CME) 15 Year Seasonal(91-05)

15 Year Pattern

Figure 6-47

Buy Jun Lean Hogs(CME) / Sell Jun Live Cattle(CME)

Enter on approximately 03/10 - Exit on approximately 03/21

CONT YEAR	ENTRY DATE	ENTRY PRICE	EXIT DATE	EXIT PRICE	PROFIT	PROFIT AMOUNT	BEST EQUITY DATE	BEST EQUITY AMOUNT	WORST EQUITY DATE	WORST EQUITY AMOUNT
2005	03/10/05	-7.79	03/21/05	-4.26	3.53	1412.00	03/21/05	1412.00		
2004	03/10/04	-7.37	03/19/04	-2.92	4.44	1776.00	03/19/04	1776.00	03/17/04	-92.00
2003	03/10/03	-7.70	03/21/03	-7.61	0.08	32.00	03/12/03	500.00	03/18/03	-32.00
2002	03/11/02	-4.48	03/21/02	-3.71	0.76	304.00	03/13/02	532.00		
2001	03/12/01	-4.57	03/21/01	-3.82	0.74	296.00	03/15/01	1188.00	03/20/01	-212.00
2000	03/10/00	1.78	03/21/00	1.83	0.05	20.00	03/20/00	200.00	03/15/00	-140.00
1999	03/10/99	-10.19	03/19/99	-8.76	1.43	572.00	03/19/99	572.00	03/15/99	-732.00
1998	03/10/98	-11.58	03/20/98	-8.77	2.82	1128.00	03/20/98	1128.00		
1997	03/10/97	12.06	03/21/97	16.38	4.31	1724.00	03/21/97	1724.00	03/11/97	-400.00
1996	03/11/96	9.24	03/21/96	9.61	0.38	152.00	03/21/96	152.00	03/14/96	-736.00
1995	03/10/95	-2.90	03/21/95	-0.65	2.25	900.00	03/16/95	1172.00		
1994	03/10/94	-0.81	03/21/94	-1.14	-0.34	-136.00			03/17/94	-764.00
1993	03/10/93	-3.56	03/19/93	-0.42	3.14	1256.00	03/19/93	1256.00	03/12/93	-408.00
1992	03/10/92	-12.38	03/20/92	-11.23	1.15	460.00	03/18/92	720.00		
1991	03/11/91	1.10	03/21/91	1.76	0.67	268.00	03/21/91	268.00	03/13/91	-284.00
1990	03/12/90	4.23	03/21/90	4.96	0.73	292.00	03/20/90	364.00	03/13/90	-284.00
1989	03/10/89	-9.12	03/21/89	-10.05	-0.92	-368.00	03/14/89	284.00	03/21/89	-368.00
1988	03/10/88	-5.42	03/21/88	-4.45	0.97	388.00	03/17/88	764.00		
1987	03/10/87	1.76	03/20/87	1.61	-0.15	-60.00	03/13/87	600.00	03/20/87	-60.00
1986	03/10/86	-0.42	03/21/86	1.30	1.72	688.00	03/18/86	1300.00		

Percentage Correct	93									
Average Profit on Winning Trades					1.84	735.71		Winners		14
Average Loss on Trades					-0.34	-136.00		Losers		1
Average Net Profit Per Trade					1.69	677.60		Total trades		15
Percentage Correct	85									
Average Profit on Winning Trades					1.72	686.35		Winners		17
Average Loss on Trades					-0.47	-188.00		Losers		3
Average Net Profit Per Trade					1.39	555.20		Total trades		20

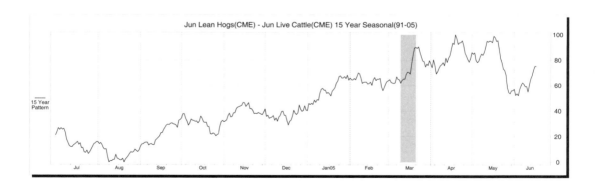

Jun Lean Hogs(CME) - Jun Live Cattle(CME) 15 Year Seasonal(91-05)

Figure 6-48

Buy Jun Lean Hogs(CME) / Sell Jun Live Cattle(CME)

Enter on approximately 04/05 - Exit on approximately 04/24

CONT YEAR	ENTRY DATE	ENTRY PRICE	EXIT DATE	EXIT PRICE	PROFIT	PROFIT AMOUNT	BEST EQUITY DATE	BEST EQUITY AMOUNT	WORST EQUITY DATE	WORST EQUITY AMOUNT
2005	04/05/05	-6.25	04/22/05	-9.81	-3.57	-1428.00	04/11/05	200.00	04/22/05	-1428.00
2004	04/05/04	-3.32	04/23/04	-4.75	-1.42	-568.00	04/08/04	724.00	04/20/04	-1596.00
2003	04/07/03	-12.30	04/24/03	-9.65	2.65	1060.00	04/24/03	1060.00	04/10/03	-728.00
2002	04/05/02	-7.44	04/24/02	-6.42	1.02	408.00	04/19/02	1420.00	04/11/02	-1440.00
2001	04/05/01	-1.07	04/24/01	-0.37	0.70	280.00	04/16/01	720.00	04/06/01	-328.00
2000	04/05/00	3.21	04/24/00	8.20	4.98	1992.00	04/24/00	1992.00		
1999	04/05/99	-11.11	04/23/99	-5.11	6.00	2400.00	04/23/99	2400.00		
1998	04/06/98	-9.46	04/24/98	-7.98	1.49	596.00	04/20/98	1420.00		
1997	04/07/97	18.09	04/24/97	21.45	3.36	1344.00	04/24/97	1344.00	04/09/97	-268.00
1996	04/08/96	15.52	04/24/96	23.15	7.64	3056.00	04/24/96	3056.00		
1995	04/05/95	-5.03	04/24/95	-4.14	0.90	360.00	04/17/95	1336.00		
1994	04/05/94	-3.37	04/22/94	-0.89	2.48	992.00	04/18/94	1212.00	04/08/94	-452.00
1993	04/05/93	-3.96	04/23/93	-6.76	-2.81	-1124.00	04/06/93	472.00	04/23/93	-1124.00
1992	04/06/92	-10.48	04/24/92	-8.50	1.98	792.00	04/13/92	960.00		
1991	04/05/91	-1.12	04/24/91	2.06	3.19	1276.00	04/22/91	1572.00		
1990	04/05/90	5.42	04/24/90	10.47	5.04	2016.00	04/24/90	2016.00	04/06/90	-104.00
1989	04/05/89	-10.73	04/24/89	-9.04	1.69	676.00	04/17/89	968.00	04/07/89	-272.00
1988	04/05/88	-0.64	04/22/88	-4.93	-4.29	-1716.00			04/22/88	-1716.00
1987	04/06/87	0.48	04/24/87	6.70	6.22	2488.00	04/21/87	2556.00		
1986	04/07/86	0.38	04/24/86	5.30	4.93	1972.00	04/23/86	2136.00	04/14/86	-132.00

Percentage Correct		80								
Average Profit on Winning Trades					3.03	1213.00		Winners		12
Average Loss on Trades					-2.60	-1040.00		Losers		3
Average Net Profit Per Trade					1.91	762.40		Total trades		15
Percentage Correct		80								
Average Profit on Winning Trades					3.39	1356.75		Winners		16
Average Loss on Trades					-3.02	-1209.00		Losers		4
Average Net Profit Per Trade					2.11	843.60		Total trades		20

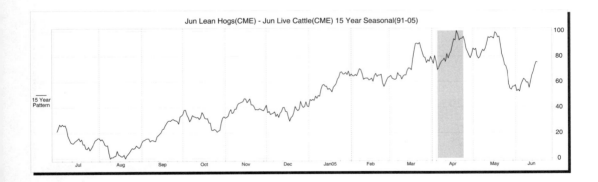

Jun Lean Hogs(CME) - Jun Live Cattle(CME) 15 Year Seasonal(91-05)

Figure 6-49

							BEST EQUITY DATE	BEST EQUITY AMOUNT	WORST EQUITY DATE	WORST EQUITY AMOUNT

Enter on approximately 06/06 - Exit on approximately 08/15

CONT YEAR	ENTRY DATE	ENTRY PRICE	EXIT DATE	EXIT PRICE	PROFIT	PROFIT AMOUNT	BEST EQUITY DATE	BEST EQUITY AMOUNT	WORST EQUITY DATE	WORST EQUITY AMOUNT
2004	06/07/04	30.43	08/13/04	26.39	-4.03	-1612.00			08/03/04	-3072.00
2003	06/06/03	17.52	08/15/03	27.88	10.36	4144.00	08/01/03	4192.00	06/13/03	-240.00
2002	06/06/02	28.55	08/15/02	33.39	4.85	1940.00	08/14/02	2048.00	07/15/02	-372.00
2001	06/06/01	24.54	08/15/01	18.96	-5.58	-2232.00			08/10/01	-2520.00
2000	06/06/00	14.98	08/15/00	19.89	4.92	1968.00	08/15/00	1968.00	06/26/00	-364.00
1999	06/07/99	12.31	08/13/99	23.90	11.58	4632.00	07/20/99	5880.00		
1998	06/08/98	13.59	08/14/98	18.20	4.60	1840.00	08/05/98	2452.00	06/15/98	-132.00
1997	06/06/97	1.90	08/15/97	4.46	2.57	1028.00	08/15/97	1028.00	07/14/97	-1112.00
1996	06/06/96	-7.79	08/15/96	-6.89	0.90	360.00	06/19/96	1356.00	08/12/96	-1112.00
1995	06/06/95	6.25	08/15/95	6.41	0.16	64.00	07/05/95	732.00	06/21/95	-1096.00
1994	06/06/94	8.69	08/15/94	15.72	7.03	2812.00	07/13/94	3224.00	06/07/94	-312.00
1993	06/07/93	16.36	08/13/93	13.70	-2.67	-1068.00	06/28/93	1704.00	07/29/93	-1856.00
1992	06/08/92	12.85	08/14/92	17.54	4.70	1880.00	08/10/92	2388.00		
1991	06/06/91	12.14	08/15/91	16.99	4.84	1936.00	07/25/91	2020.00	06/07/91	-60.00
1990	06/06/90	3.87	08/15/90	8.75	4.87	1948.00	08/09/90	2556.00	07/05/90	-332.00
1989	06/06/89	11.53	08/15/89	17.84	6.30	2520.00	08/10/89	2792.00	06/26/89	-616.00
1988	06/06/88	5.92	08/15/88	15.46	9.54	3816.00	08/12/88	4032.00	06/22/88	-676.00
1987	06/08/87	1.71	08/14/87	2.23	0.52	208.00	06/17/87	816.00	07/22/87	-1208.00
1986	06/06/86	-3.58	08/15/86	-13.61	-10.03	-4012.00			07/16/86	-4652.00
1985	06/06/85	-1.31	08/15/85	3.38	4.69	1876.00	08/09/85	2628.00	06/18/85	-768.00

Percentage Correct	80									
Average Profit on Winning Trades					5.12	2046.00		Winners		12
Average Loss on Trades					-4.09	-1637.33		Losers		3
Average Net Profit Per Trade					3.27	1309.33		Total trades		15
Percentage Correct	80									
Average Profit on Winning Trades					5.15	2060.75		Winners		16
Average Loss on Trades					-5.58	-2231.00		Losers		4
Average Net Profit Per Trade					3.01	1202.40		Total trades		20

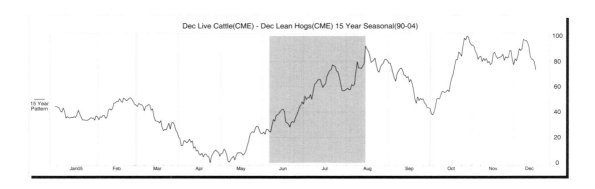

Dec Live Cattle(CME) - Dec Lean Hogs(CME) 15 Year Seasonal(90-04)

Figure 6-50

Buy Dec Live Cattle(CME) / Sell Dec Lean Hogs(CME)

Enter on approximately 10/03 - Exit on approximately 11/03

CONT YEAR	ENTRY DATE	ENTRY PRICE	EXIT DATE	EXIT PRICE	PROFIT	PROFIT AMOUNT	BEST EQUITY DATE	BEST EQUITY AMOUNT	WORST EQUITY DATE	WORST EQUITY AMOUNT
2004	10/04/04	21.51	11/03/04	12.27	-9.25	-3700.00	10/12/04	1160.00	11/03/04	-3700.00
2003	10/03/03	31.99	11/03/03	39.69	7.70	3080.00	11/03/03	3080.00	10/16/03	-760.00
2002	10/03/02	29.38	11/01/02	29.87	0.50	200.00	10/25/02	1176.00		
2001	10/03/01	11.85	11/02/01	14.53	2.68	1072.00	10/25/01	3172.00		
2000	10/03/00	17.71	11/03/00	19.94	2.23	892.00	10/30/00	1572.00	10/12/00	-768.00
1999	10/04/99	22.71	11/03/99	23.89	1.18	472.00	10/11/99	864.00	10/25/99	-1360.00
1998	10/05/98	23.64	11/03/98	29.04	5.40	2160.00	11/03/98	2160.00	10/13/98	-660.00
1997	10/03/97	3.09	11/03/97	5.17	2.07	828.00	10/22/97	1516.00		
1996	10/03/96	-12.46	11/01/96	-8.42	4.05	1620.00	10/24/96	3184.00		
1995	10/03/95	3.92	11/03/95	11.39	7.46	2984.00	11/02/95	3080.00	10/05/95	-220.00
1994	10/03/94	19.78	11/03/94	24.07	4.30	1720.00	10/21/94	2308.00	10/10/94	-72.00
1993	10/04/93	6.98	11/03/93	8.95	1.97	788.00	10/22/93	1024.00	10/12/93	-1416.00
1992	10/05/92	14.20	11/03/92	15.20	1.01	404.00	10/30/92	900.00	10/21/92	-148.00
1991	10/03/91	16.21	11/01/91	17.79	1.58	632.00	10/21/91	1108.00	10/07/91	-104.00
1990	10/03/90	1.62	11/02/90	5.82	4.20	1680.00	10/29/90	2468.00	10/12/90	-132.00
1989	10/03/89	12.61	11/03/89	10.71	-1.90	-760.00	10/04/89	268.00	11/01/89	-1096.00
1988	10/03/88	16.91	11/03/88	17.34	0.43	172.00	10/31/88	660.00	10/18/88	-432.00
1987	10/05/87	3.04	11/03/87	5.21	2.17	868.00	10/16/87	1328.00	10/07/87	-704.00
1986	10/03/86	-11.09	11/03/86	-8.96	2.14	856.00	11/03/86	856.00	10/16/86	-1136.00
1985	10/03/85	2.57	11/01/85	3.71	1.14	456.00	11/01/85	456.00	10/16/85	-600.00

Percentage Correct	93								
Average Profit on Winning Trades				3.31	1323.71		Winners	14	
Average Loss on Trades				-9.25	-3700.00		Losers	1	
Average Net Profit Per Trade				2.47	988.80		Total trades	15	
Percentage Correct	90								
Average Profit on Winning Trades				2.90	1160.22		Winners	18	
Average Loss on Trades				-5.57	-2230.00		Losers	2	
Average Net Profit Per Trade				2.05	821.20		Total trades	20	

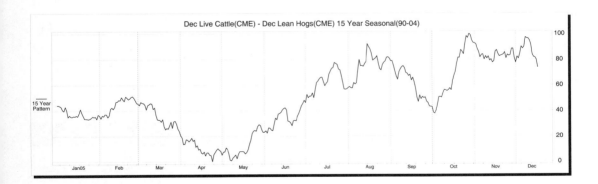

Dec Live Cattle(CME) - Dec Lean Hogs(CME) 15 Year Seasonal(90-04)

Feeder Cattle versus Live Cattle

The costs of feeder cattle and of feed are primary determinants of profitability for cattle feeders. The price relationship between feeders and live cattle, or "fats," helps suggest if, when, and how much profit can be made feeding young cattle to market weight. Thus, feeders versus fats spreads serve not only as trading and hedging vehicles but also as rough analytical tools.

(The industry commonly refers to spreads between feeder cattle and live cattle in terms of their nominal price difference. But their futures contracts differ in size, both in total weight and in the number of animals each represents. The feeder cattle contract calls for 50,000 pounds of animals weighing 650-849 pounds each, normally 60-75 animals. The live cattle contract calls for 40,000 pounds of Choice/Select steers, about 35 animals. In order to properly reflect spread movement in a one-to-one relationship, all strategies herein are calculated as equity spreads rather than nominal price differences.)

Figure 6-51: Aug Feeders/Live Cattle Seasonal Pattern

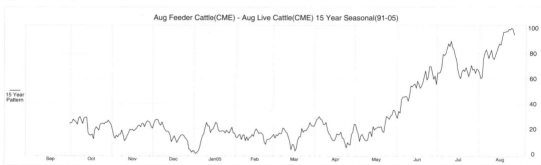

Aug Feeder Cattle(CME) - Aug Live Cattle(CME) 15 Year Seasonal(91-05)

Traders and analysts often use similar delivery months, August/August for example, in their calculations and trading. But the more commercial application is for live cattle marketable 3-5 months after feeders are placed. For example, feeders placed in August can reach market weight in December, those placed in November can be ready as early as February or as late as April. A feedlot operator who intends a future purchase of feeder cattle to feed during corn harvest might hedge this prospective transaction by buying August Feeder Cattle to protect against rising prices and increased costs while simultaneously selling December Live Cattle to protect against declining prices and decreased revenue.

Figure 6-52: Feeders versus Fats Spread Strategies

Moore Research Center, Inc.	Feeders versus Fats Spread Strategies							
Seasonal Strategy	Entry Date	Exit Date	Win Pct	Win Yrs	Loss Years	Total Years	Average Profit	Ave Pft Per Day
Buy Apr Live Cattle(CME)	12/10	3/05	93	14	1	15	865	10
Sell Apr Feeder Cattle(CME)			90	18	2	20	866	10
Buy Apr Live Cattle(CME)	1/10	3/15	87	13	2	15	607	9
Sell Mar Feeder Cattle(CME)			90	18	2	20	722	11
Buy Apr Live Cattle(CME)	1/31	3/04	87	13	2	15	559	17
Sell Apr Feeder Cattle(CME)			90	18	2	20	656	20

Figure 6-52 Feeders versus Fats Strategies continued

▲▲ Moore Research Center, Inc.			*Feeders versus Fats Spread Strategies*					
Seasonal Strategy	Entry Date	Exit Date	Win Pct	Win Yrs	Loss Years	Total Years	Average Profit	Ave Pft Per Day
Buy May Feeder Cattle(CME) Sell Jun Live Cattle(CME)	4/24	5/20	93 90	14 18	1 2	15 20	1013 929	38 34
Buy Aug Feeder Cattle(CME) Sell Aug Live Cattle(CME)	4/24	7/12	87 85	13 17	2 3	15 20	1301 1322	16 17
Buy Aug Feeder Cattle(CME) Sell Dec Live Cattle(CME)	5/16	8/22	87 90	13 18	2 2	15 20	1789 1840	18 19
Buy Aug Feeder Cattle(CME) Sell Dec Live Cattle(CME)	5/21	6/11	100 95	15 19	0 1	15 20	594 478	27 22
Buy Sep Feeder Cattle(CME) Sell Dec Live Cattle(CME)	5/28	7/11	93 85	14 17	1 3	15 20	872 766	19 17
Buy Aug Feeder Cattle(CME) Sell Aug Live Cattle(CME)	6/01	7/09	87 90	13 18	2 2	15 20	925 913	24 23
Buy Nov Feeder Cattle(CME) Sell Apr Live Cattle(CME)	6/19	9/17	80 85	12 17	3 3	15 20	893 1084	10 12
Buy Aug Feeder Cattle(CME) Sell Dec Live Cattle(CME)	6/23	7/11	87 90	13 18	2 2	15 20	434 499	23 26
Buy Aug Feeder Cattle(CME) Sell Dec Live Cattle(CME)	6/23	8/21	87 90	13 18	2 2	15 20	921 1231	15 21
Buy Aug Feeder Cattle(CME) Sell Aug Live Cattle(CME)	7/01	7/11	87 90	13 18	2 2	15 20	335 400	30 36

Figure 6-53: Apr Live/Feeder Cattle Seasonal Pattern

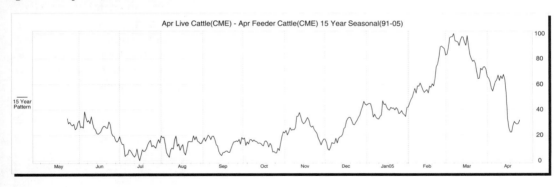

Apr Live Cattle(CME) - Apr Feeder Cattle(CME) 15 Year Seasonal(91-05)

Demand for feeders slows January-March. Feedlots are normally already filled. Those bought 4-5 months prior to the typical May/June peak in slaughter and the low level of beef consumption immediately thereafter are far less likely to be fed profitably. Cash prices for live cattle, however, tend to continue marching higher into March or even April as weight gains remain slow but beef consumption high during winter. Thus, as the first three strategies in the table quantify, feeders have regularly underperformed fats going into March.

Figure 6-54: Aug Feeder/Dec Live Cattle Pattern

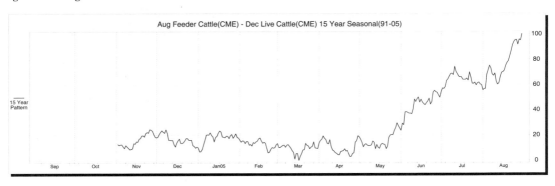

Aug Feeder Cattle(CME) - Dec Live Cattle(CME) 15 Year Seasonal(91-05)

But by April, slaughter begins to rise, normally driving cash cattle prices lower. In contrast, feeder prices tend to be beaten down already. It is when slaughter is peaking and feedlot inventories declining in late April/May that feedlots begin to consider the need to replenish those inventories in time for corn harvest. The first stirrings in these hedging vehicles begin to appear in May Feeders, perhaps as the market attempts to bid some animals away from emerging pasture. It may seem early, but consider that the May Feeders/June Fats spread has tended to suffer but little adversity from late April going into May expiry. Consider further the strategy which encompasses the traditional opening of the outdoor US grilling season in late May when grocers aggressively feature beef. From about May 21 through June 11 in the 15 years 1990-2004, the August Feeders/December Fats spread would never once have suffered a closing drawdown greater than the average move generated.

In fact, these trading and hedging vehicles have performed most consistently while the cash cattle market was suffering most. In its variety of entries, exits, and spread combinations, the table above illustrates how this dynamic permeates the cattle complex from May through August. The corn crop pollinates in July. With feedlot inventories least in August and barring a disaster in the corn crop, demand for feeders then accelerates going into corn harvest whereas beef consumption rises but little until perhaps September.

Figure 6-55: Aug Feeder/Dec Live Cattle Monthly

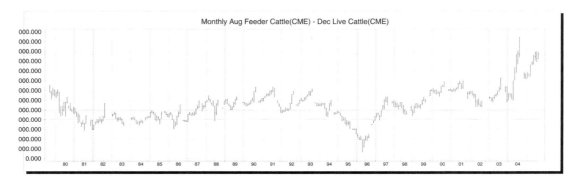

Monthly Aug Feeder Cattle(CME) - Dec Live Cattle(CME)

Figure 6-56

Buy Apr Live Cattle(CME) / Sell Apr Feeder Cattle(CME)

Enter on approximately 12/10 - Exit on approximately 03/05

CONT YEAR	ENTRY DATE	ENTRY PRICE	EXIT DATE	EXIT PRICE		PROFIT AMOUNT	BEST EQUITY DATE	BEST EQUITY AMOUNT	WORST EQUITY DATE	WORST EQUITY AMOUNT
2005	12/10/04	-14287	03/04/05	-15227		-940.00	01/03/05	870.00	03/03/05	-983.00
2004	12/10/03	-11222	03/05/04	-10937		285.00	12/30/03	802.00	02/02/04	-2368.00
2003	12/10/02	-10270	03/05/03	-8005		2265.00	02/27/03	2785.00		
2002	12/10/01	-12647	03/05/02	-10880		1767.00	03/04/02	1830.00	01/10/02	-200.00
2001	12/11/00	-13800	03/05/01	-11390		2410.00	02/12/01	2448.00		
2000	12/10/99	-13972	03/04/00	-13287		685.00	02/10/00	932.00	01/05/00	-370.00
1999	12/10/98	-9940	03/05/99	-9302		638.00	03/05/99	638.00	01/19/99	-810.00
1998	12/10/97	-11847	03/05/98	-11750		97.00	01/05/98	1162.00	02/20/98	-510.00
1997	12/10/96	-7485	03/05/97	-6670		815.00	03/04/97	1043.00	02/03/97	-1040.00
1996	12/11/95	-4017	03/05/96	-3610		407.00	01/04/96	1620.00		
1995	12/12/94	-7402	03/03/95	-5345		2057.00	03/03/95	2057.00	12/16/94	-253.00
1994	12/10/93	-10067	03/04/94	-9980		87.00	01/13/94	530.00	02/22/94	-315.00
1993	12/10/92	-11142	03/05/93	-10095		1047.00	02/24/93	1530.00	12/22/92	-273.00
1992	12/10/91	-8645	03/05/92	-7565		1080.00	02/07/92	1330.00	12/13/91	-282.00
1991	12/10/90	-11677	03/05/91	-11397		280.00	01/18/91	322.00	02/07/91	-545.00
1990	12/11/89	-10652	03/05/90	-9550		1102.00	02/20/90	1265.00	12/22/89	-613.00
1989	12/12/88	-11500	03/03/89	-9890		1610.00	03/03/89	1610.00	01/09/89	-302.00
1988	12/10/87	-11300	03/05/88	-10747		553.00	03/04/88	698.00	02/17/88	-845.00
1987	12/10/86	-7467	03/05/87	-7687		-220.00	01/02/87	185.00	02/03/87	-1000.00
1986	12/10/85	-8540	03/05/86	-7255		1285.00	03/05/86	1285.00	02/06/86	-355.00

Percentage Correct	93								
Average Profit on Winning Trades						994.29		Winners	14
Average Loss on Trades						-940.00		Losers	1
Average Net Profit Per Trade						865.33		Total trades	15
Percentage Correct	90								
Average Profit on Winning Trades						1026.11		Winners	18
Average Loss on Trades						-580.00		Losers	2
Average Net Profit Per Trade						865.50		Total trades	20

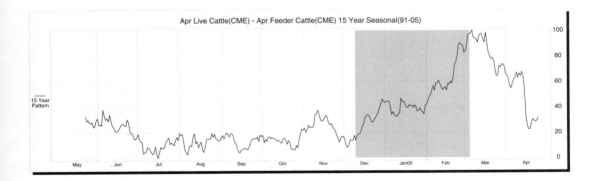

Apr Live Cattle(CME) - Apr Feeder Cattle(CME) 15 Year Seasonal(91-05)

Chapter 6: Meats

257

Figure 6-57

Buy Apr Live Cattle(CME) / Sell Mar Feeder Cattle(CME)

Enter on approximately 01/10 - Exit on approximately 03/15

CONT YEAR	ENTRY DATE	ENTRY PRICE	EXIT DATE	EXIT PRICE		PROFIT AMOUNT	BEST EQUITY DATE	BEST EQUITY AMOUNT	WORST EQUITY DATE	WORST EQUITY AMOUNT
2005	01/10/05	-15087	03/15/05	-17135		-2048.00	02/04/05	720.00	03/15/05	-2048.00
2004	01/12/04	-11877	03/15/04	-12585		-708.00	01/13/04	452.00	02/18/04	-1645.00
2003	01/10/03	-8220	03/14/03	-8110		110.00	02/12/03	1275.00	01/13/03	-97.00
2002	01/10/02	-13257	03/15/02	-11135		2122.00	02/19/02	2580.00		
2001	01/10/01	-13350	03/15/01	-11537		1813.00	03/07/01	2370.00		
2000	01/10/00	-14305	03/15/00	-12667		1638.00	03/15/00	1638.00		
1999	01/11/99	-10275	03/15/99	-9245		1030.00	03/10/99	1440.00	01/15/99	-512.00
1998	01/12/98	-11455	03/13/98	-11415		40.00	02/10/98	228.00	02/20/98	-1012.00
1997	01/10/97	-7662	03/14/97	-6405		1257.00	02/27/97	1530.00	01/29/97	-478.00
1996	01/10/96	-2750	03/15/96	-2592		158.00	01/15/96	243.00	03/06/96	-937.00
1995	01/10/95	-7680	03/15/95	-5962		1718.00	03/03/95	2210.00		
1994	01/10/94	-10187	03/15/94	-10162		25.00	01/13/94	275.00	01/28/94	-723.00
1993	01/11/93	-11765	03/15/93	-9927		1838.00	03/12/93	1850.00	01/12/93	-37.00
1992	01/10/92	-8690	03/13/92	-8675		15.00	02/28/92	415.00	02/13/92	-407.00
1991	01/10/91	-12690	03/15/91	-12600		90.00	01/15/91	648.00	02/07/91	-742.00
1990	01/10/90	-11087	03/15/90	-10380		707.00	03/02/90	1352.00		
1989	01/10/89	-11892	03/15/89	-9342		2550.00	03/15/89	2550.00	02/02/89	-35.00
1988	01/11/88	-12057	03/15/88	-11832		225.00	03/01/88	782.00	02/12/88	-893.00
1987	01/12/87	-8290	03/13/87	-7767		523.00	03/13/87	523.00	02/03/87	-637.00
1986	01/10/86	-8385	03/14/86	-7050		1335.00	03/11/86	1600.00	01/16/86	-370.00

Percentage Correct	87								
Average Profit on Winning Trades						911.85		Winners	13
Average Loss on Trades						-1378.00		Losers	2
Average Net Profit Per Trade						606.53		Total trades	15
Percentage Correct	90								
Average Profit on Winning Trades						955.22		Winners	18
Average Loss on Trades						-1378.00		Losers	2
Average Net Profit Per Trade						721.90		Total trades	20

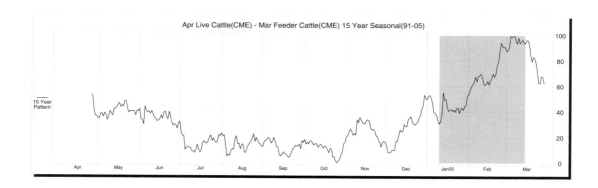

Apr Live Cattle(CME) - Mar Feeder Cattle(CME) 15 Year Seasonal(91-05)

Chapter 6: Meats

Figure 6-58

Buy Apr Live Cattle(CME) / Sell Apr Feeder Cattle(CME)

Enter on approximately 01/31 - Exit on approximately 03/04

CONT YEAR	ENTRY DATE	ENTRY PRICE	EXIT DATE	EXIT PRICE		PROFIT AMOUNT	BEST EQUITY DATE	BEST EQUITY AMOUNT	WORST EQUITY DATE	WORST EQUITY AMOUNT
2005	01/31/05	-14807	03/04/05	-15227		-420.00	02/04/05	590.00	03/03/05	-463.00
2004	02/02/04	-13590	03/04/04	-10857		2733.00	03/04/04	2733.00		
2003	01/31/03	-8337	03/04/03	-8080		257.00	02/27/03	852.00		
2002	01/31/02	-12227	03/04/02	-10817		1410.00	03/04/02	1410.00		
2001	01/31/01	-11847	03/02/01	-11652		195.00	02/12/01	495.00	02/20/01	-510.00
2000	01/31/00	-13965	03/04/00	-13287		678.00	02/10/00	925.00		
1999	02/01/99	-10187	03/04/99	-9535		652.00	03/04/99	652.00	02/16/99	-245.00
1998	02/02/98	-11950	03/04/98	-11720		230.00	02/27/98	523.00	02/20/98	-407.00
1997	01/31/97	-8282	03/04/97	-6442		1840.00	03/04/97	1840.00	02/03/97	-243.00
1996	01/31/96	-2670	03/04/96	-3522		-852.00	02/01/96	45.00	03/04/96	-852.00
1995	01/31/95	-6175	03/03/95	-5345		830.00	03/03/95	830.00	02/02/95	-377.00
1994	01/31/94	-9995	03/04/94	-9980		15.00	02/14/94	195.00	02/22/94	-387.00
1993	02/01/93	-10315	03/04/93	-9950		365.00	02/24/93	703.00	02/09/93	-225.00
1992	01/31/92	-7740	03/04/92	-7475		265.00	02/07/92	425.00	02/13/92	-282.00
1991	01/31/91	-11877	03/04/91	-11687		190.00	03/04/91	190.00	02/07/91	-345.00
1990	01/31/90	-10417	03/02/90	-9535		882.00	02/20/90	1030.00	02/01/90	-3.00
1989	01/31/89	-11432	03/03/89	-9890		1542.00	03/03/89	1542.00	02/02/89	-245.00
1988	02/01/88	-11590	03/04/88	-10602		988.00	03/04/88	988.00	02/17/88	-555.00
1987	02/02/87	-8295	03/04/87	-7742		553.00	03/03/87	648.00	02/03/87	-172.00
1986	01/31/86	-8315	03/04/86	-7557		758.00	03/04/86	758.00	02/06/86	-580.00

Percentage Correct	87								
Average Profit on Winning Trades						743.08		Winners	13
Average Loss on Trades						-636.00		Losers	2
Average Net Profit Per Trade						559.20		Total trades	15
Percentage Correct	90								
Average Profit on Winning Trades						799.06		Winners	18
Average Loss on Trades						-636.00		Losers	2
Average Net Profit Per Trade						655.55		Total trades	20

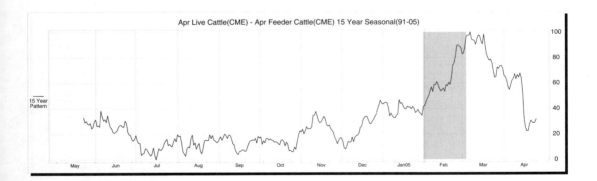

Apr Live Cattle(CME) - Apr Feeder Cattle(CME) 15 Year Seasonal(91-05)

15 Year Pattern

Chapter 6: Meats

259

Figure 6-59

Buy May Feeder Cattle(CME) / Sell Jun Live Cattle(CME)

Enter on approximately 04/24 - Exit on approximately 05/20

CONT YEAR	ENTRY DATE	ENTRY PRICE	EXIT DATE	EXIT PRICE		PROFIT AMOUNT	BEST EQUITY DATE	BEST EQUITY AMOUNT	WORST EQUITY DATE	WORST EQUITY AMOUNT
2005	04/25/05	19477	05/20/05	21487		2010.00	05/19/05	2070.00		
2004	04/26/04	16105	05/20/04	18762		2657.00	05/17/04	3125.00	05/05/04	-60.00
2003	04/24/03	10927	05/20/03	11215		288.00	05/20/03	288.00	05/09/03	-462.00
2002	04/24/02	11510	05/20/02	13427		1917.00	05/20/02	1917.00		
2001	04/24/01	15155	05/18/01	14985		-170.00	05/09/01	442.00	05/18/01	-170.00
2000	04/24/00	14242	05/19/00	14377		135.00	04/28/00	460.00	05/10/00	-450.00
1999	04/26/99	10407	05/20/99	10462		55.00	05/12/99	453.00	05/18/99	-32.00
1998	04/24/98	10465	05/20/98	11337		872.00	05/19/98	1002.00		
1997	04/24/97	10557	05/20/97	12075		1518.00	05/15/97	1818.00		
1996	04/24/96	2055	05/20/96	3802		1747.00	05/16/96	1792.00	04/26/96	-540.00
1995	04/24/95	7640	05/19/95	7982		342.00	05/16/95	630.00		
1994	04/25/94	10867	05/20/94	11577		710.00	05/20/94	710.00	04/28/94	-377.00
1993	04/26/93	12122	05/20/93	12482		360.00	05/14/93	525.00	04/27/93	-247.00
1992	04/24/92	9165	05/20/92	10867		1702.00	05/20/92	1702.00	04/28/92	-38.00
1991	04/24/91	13657	05/20/91	14712		1055.00	05/20/91	1055.00	04/25/91	-80.00
1990	04/24/90	11382	05/18/90	13032		1650.00	05/18/90	1650.00		
1989	04/24/89	9792	05/19/89	10105		313.00	05/18/89	425.00	05/03/89	-455.00
1988	04/25/88	10607	05/20/88	11102		495.00	05/04/88	528.00		
1987	04/24/87	7550	05/20/87	8502		952.00	05/20/87	952.00	05/06/87	-453.00
1986	04/24/86	4820	05/20/86	4792		-28.00	05/12/86	915.00	04/28/86	-215.00

Percentage Correct	93								
Average Profit on Winning Trades				1097.71		Winners	14
Average Loss on Trades				-170.00		Losers	1
Average Net Profit Per Trade				1013.20		Total trades	15

Percentage Correct	90								
Average Profit on Winning Trades				1043.22		Winners	18
Average Loss on Trades				-99.00		Losers	2
Average Net Profit Per Trade				929.00		Total trades	20

HYPOTHETICAL PERFORMANCE RESULTS HAVE MANY INHERENT LIMITATIONS, SOME OF WHICH ARE DESCRIBED BELOW. NO REPRESENTATION IS BEING MADE THAT ANY ACCOUNT WILL OR IS LIKELY TO ACHIEVE PROFITS OR LOSSES SIMILAR TO THOSE SHOWN. IN FACT, THERE ARE FREQUENTLY SHARP DIFFERENCES BETWEEN HYPOTHETICAL PERFORMANCE RESULTS AND THE ACTUAL RESULTS SUBSEQUENTLY ACHIEVED BY ANY PARTICULAR TRADING PROGRAM. ONE OF THE LIMITATIONS OF HYPOTHETICAL PERFORMANCE RESULTS IS THAT THEY ARE GENERALLY PREPARED WITH THE BENEFIT OF HINDSIGHT. IN ADDITION, HYPOTHETICAL TRADING DOES NOT INVOLVE FINANCIAL RISK, AND NO HYPOTHETICAL TRADING RECORD CAN COMPLETELY ACCOUNT FOR THE IMPACT OF FINANCIAL RISK IN ACTUAL TRADING. FOR EXAMPLE, THE ABILITY TO WITHSTAND LOSSES OR ADHERE TO A PARTICULAR TRADING PROGRAM IN SPITE OF TRADING LOSSES ARE MATERIAL POINTS WHICH CAN ALSO ADVERSELY AFFECT ACTUAL TRADING RESULTS. THERE ARE NUMEROUS OTHER FACTORS RELATED TO THE MARKETS IN GENERAL OR TO THE IMPLEMENTATION OF ANY SPECIFIC TRADING PROGRAM WHICH CANNOT BE FULLY ACCOUNTED FOR IN THE PREPARATION OF HYPOTHETICAL PERFORMANCE RESULTS AND ALL OF WHICH CAN ADVERSELY AFFECT ACTUAL TRADING RESULTS. RESULTS NOT ADJUSTED FOR COMMISSION AND SLIPPAGE.

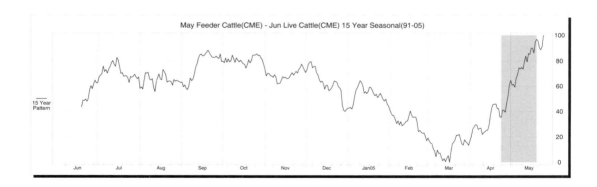

May Feeder Cattle(CME) - Jun Live Cattle(CME) 15 Year Seasonal(91-05)

15 Year Pattern

Jun Jul Aug Sep Oct Nov Dec Jan05 Feb Mar Apr May

Figure 6-60

Buy Aug Feeder Cattle(CME) / Sell Aug Live Cattle(CME)

Enter on approximately 04/24 - Exit on approximately 07/12

CONT YEAR	ENTRY DATE	ENTRY PRICE	EXIT DATE	EXIT PRICE		PROFIT AMOUNT	BEST EQUITY DATE	BEST EQUITY AMOUNT	WORST EQUITY DATE	WORST EQUITY AMOUNT
2004	04/26/04	15912	07/12/04	23307		7395.00	07/12/04	7395.00	05/06/04	-902.00
2003	04/24/03	13990	07/11/03	15227		1237.00	06/30/03	1412.00		
2002	04/24/02	12392	07/12/02	13015		623.00	05/06/02	1353.00	07/01/02	-165.00
2001	04/24/01	15397	07/12/01	15445		48.00	06/21/01	1115.00		
2000	04/24/00	15022	07/12/00	17065		2043.00	07/12/00	2043.00	05/10/00	-687.00
1999	04/26/99	12355	07/12/99	13215		860.00	07/06/99	1172.00	05/07/99	-950.00
1998	04/24/98	11400	07/10/98	10697		-703.00	04/30/98	377.00	06/26/98	-1733.00
1997	04/24/97	12025	07/11/97	14275		2250.00	07/07/97	3017.00	04/30/97	-45.00
1996	04/24/96	2365	07/12/96	3150		785.00	07/05/96	1982.00	04/26/96	-275.00
1995	04/24/95	9387	07/12/95	8360		-1027.00	04/25/95	128.00	06/23/95	-1590.00
1994	04/25/94	11510	07/12/94	11985		475.00	07/05/94	652.00	05/23/94	-1278.00
1993	04/26/93	12982	07/12/93	14317		1335.00	07/12/93	1335.00	04/27/93	-25.00
1992	04/24/92	10097	07/10/92	11307		1210.00	07/09/92	1215.00	05/05/92	-780.00
1991	04/24/91	13567	07/12/91	15405		1838.00	07/11/91	2028.00		
1990	04/24/90	12015	07/12/90	13155		1140.00	07/12/90	1140.00		
1989	04/24/89	11287	07/12/89	12575		1288.00	06/13/89	1560.00	04/28/89	-375.00
1988	04/25/88	11622	07/12/88	11532		-90.00	05/04/88	478.00	06/20/88	-2152.00
1987	04/24/87	9017	07/10/87	11060		2043.00	07/10/87	2043.00	05/28/87	-125.00
1986	04/24/86	6675	07/11/86	9415		2740.00	07/11/86	2740.00	04/28/86	-203.00
1985	04/24/85	8452	07/12/85	9392		940.00	07/11/85	1058.00	05/01/85	-497.00

Percentage Correct	87			
Average Profit on Winning Trades		1633.77	Winners	13
Average Loss on Trades		-865.00	Losers	2
Average Net Profit Per Trade		1300.60	Total trades	15
Percentage Correct	85			
Average Profit on Winning Trades		1661.76	Winners	17
Average Loss on Trades		-606.67	Losers	3
Average Net Profit Per Trade		1321.50	Total trades	20

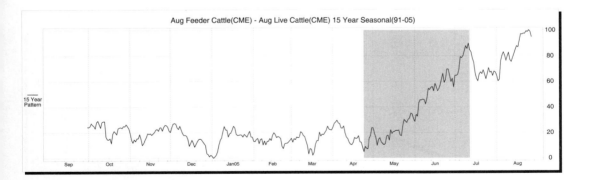

Aug Feeder Cattle(CME) - Aug Live Cattle(CME) 15 Year Seasonal(91-05)

Figure 6-61

Buy Aug Feeder Cattle(CME) / Sell Dec Live Cattle(CME)

Moore Research Center, Inc.

Enter on approximately 05/16 - Exit on approximately 08/22

CONT YEAR	ENTRY DATE	ENTRY PRICE	EXIT DATE	EXIT PRICE		PROFIT AMOUNT	BEST EQUITY DATE	BEST EQUITY AMOUNT	WORST EQUITY DATE	WORST EQUITY AMOUNT
2004	05/17/04	16335	08/20/04	23697		7362.00	08/20/04	7362.00		
2003	05/16/03	13047	08/22/03	16042		2995.00	08/22/03	2995.00	05/22/03	-202.00
2002	05/16/02	11130	08/22/02	11690		560.00	06/18/02	1210.00	08/14/02	-593.00
2001	05/16/01	14525	08/22/01	15110		585.00	06/25/01	1437.00	07/27/01	-245.00
2000	05/16/00	12942	08/21/00	15252		2310.00	08/18/00	2330.00	05/22/00	-25.00
1999	05/17/99	10592	08/20/99	12012		1420.00	07/14/99	2093.00	05/19/99	-40.00
1998	05/18/98	10765	08/21/98	9645		-1120.00	06/10/98	317.00	08/03/98	-1695.00
1997	05/16/97	10030	08/22/97	12302		2272.00	07/18/97	2727.00		
1996	05/16/96	2265	08/21/96	4902		2637.00	08/05/96	2750.00		
1995	05/16/95	7692	08/22/95	6930		-762.00	06/12/95	250.00	06/15/95	-977.00
1994	05/16/94	10017	08/22/94	10997		980.00	08/04/94	2043.00	06/17/94	-1465.00
1993	05/17/93	12992	08/20/93	13792		800.00	08/10/93	1395.00	05/21/93	-160.00
1992	05/18/92	10142	08/21/92	13680		3538.00	08/07/92	3653.00	05/27/92	-82.00
1991	05/16/91	13272	08/22/91	13762		490.00	07/11/91	1523.00	08/12/91	-672.00
1990	05/16/90	11662	08/22/90	14432		2770.00	08/21/90	3085.00	05/17/90	-97.00
1989	05/16/89	10475	08/22/89	12472		1997.00	08/14/89	2302.00	05/31/89	-230.00
1988	05/16/88	11570	08/19/88	11870		300.00	08/16/88	485.00	06/20/88	-3888.00
1987	05/18/87	9087	08/21/87	11937		2850.00	08/20/87	2880.00	05/20/87	-262.00
1986	05/16/86	6887	08/20/86	11075		4188.00	08/20/86	4188.00	05/21/86	-227.00
1985	05/16/85	8650	08/20/85	9285		635.00	08/14/85	1025.00	07/29/85	-1625.00

Percentage Correct	87							
Average Profit on Winning Trades				2209.15		Winners		13
Average Loss on Trades				-941.00		Losers		2
Average Net Profit Per Trade				1789.13		Total trades		15
Percentage Correct	90							
Average Profit on Winning Trades				2149.39		Winners		18
Average Loss on Trades				-941.00		Losers		2
Average Net Profit Per Trade				1840.35		Total trades		20

HYPOTHETICAL PERFORMANCE RESULTS HAVE MANY INHERENT LIMITATIONS, SOME OF WHICH ARE DESCRIBED BELOW. NO REPRESENTATION IS BEING MADE THAT ANY ACCOUNT WILL OR IS LIKELY TO ACHIEVE PROFITS OR LOSSES SIMILAR TO THOSE SHOWN. IN FACT, THERE ARE FREQUENTLY SHARP DIFFERENCES BETWEEN HYPOTHETICAL PERFORMANCE RESULTS AND THE ACTUAL RESULTS SUBSEQUENTLY ACHIEVED BY ANY PARTICULAR TRADING PROGRAM. ONE OF THE LIMITATIONS OF HYPOTHETICAL PERFORMANCE RESULTS IS THAT THEY ARE GENERALLY PREPARED WITH THE BENEFIT OF HINDSIGHT. IN ADDITION, HYPOTHETICAL TRADING DOES NOT INVOLVE FINANCIAL RISK, AND NO HYPOTHETICAL TRADING RECORD CAN COMPLETELY ACCOUNT FOR THE IMPACT OF FINANCIAL RISK IN ACTUAL TRADING. FOR EXAMPLE, THE ABILITY TO WITHSTAND LOSSES OR ADHERE TO A PARTICULAR TRADING PROGRAM IN SPITE OF TRADING LOSSES ARE MATERIAL POINTS WHICH CAN ALSO ADVERSELY AFFECT ACTUAL TRADING RESULTS. THERE ARE NUMEROUS OTHER FACTORS RELATED TO THE MARKETS IN GENERAL OR TO THE IMPLEMENTATION OF ANY SPECIFIC TRADING PROGRAM WHICH CANNOT BE FULLY ACCOUNTED FOR IN THE PREPARATION OF HYPOTHETICAL PERFORMANCE RESULTS AND ALL OF WHICH CAN ADVERSELY AFFECT ACTUAL TRADING RESULTS. RESULTS NOT ADJUSTED FOR COMMISSION AND SLIPPAGE.

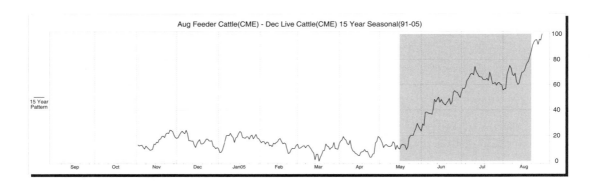

Aug Feeder Cattle(CME) - Dec Live Cattle(CME) 15 Year Seasonal(91-05)

15 Year Pattern

Chapter 6: Meats

Figure 6-62

Buy Aug Feeder Cattle(CME) / Sell Dec Live Cattle(CME)

Enter on approximately 05/21 - Exit on approximately 06/11

CONT YEAR	ENTRY DATE	ENTRY PRICE	EXIT DATE	EXIT PRICE		PROFIT AMOUNT	BEST EQUITY DATE	BEST EQUITY AMOUNT	WORST EQUITY DATE	WORST EQUITY AMOUNT
2005	05/23/05	20282	06/10/05	21085		803.00	06/07/05	1570.00	05/26/05	-5.00
2004	05/21/04	17935	06/10/04	18530		595.00	06/07/04	1140.00	06/01/04	-275.00
2003	05/21/03	12950	06/11/03	13037		87.00	06/02/03	445.00	05/22/03	-105.00
2002	05/21/02	10645	06/11/02	11817		1172.00	06/11/02	1172.00		
2001	05/21/01	15335	06/11/01	15492		157.00	06/08/01	170.00	06/05/01	-18.00
2000	05/22/00	12917	06/09/00	13735		818.00	06/07/00	1048.00		
1999	05/21/99	10890	06/11/99	11835		945.00	06/11/99	945.00	05/27/99	-48.00
1998	05/21/98	10487	06/11/98	10937		450.00	06/10/98	595.00	06/01/98	-197.00
1997	05/21/97	10445	06/11/97	10715		270.00	05/23/97	565.00	06/06/97	-330.00
1996	05/21/96	2867	06/11/96	4097		1230.00	06/04/96	1870.00		
1995	05/22/95	7492	06/09/95	7910		418.00	06/09/95	418.00	05/26/95	-380.00
1994	05/23/94	8752	06/10/94	9162		410.00	06/06/94	450.00	06/01/94	-15.00
1993	05/21/93	12832	06/11/93	13867		1035.00	06/11/93	1035.00		
1992	05/21/92	10212	06/11/92	10487		275.00	06/08/92	355.00	05/27/92	-152.00
1991	05/21/91	13127	06/11/91	13365		238.00	05/31/91	798.00		
1990	05/21/90	11957	06/11/90	12125		168.00	06/06/90	368.00	05/25/90	-320.00
1989	05/22/89	10715	06/09/89	11287		572.00	06/09/89	572.00	05/31/89	-470.00
1988	05/23/88	11235	06/10/88	10205		-1030.00			06/06/88	-1638.00
1987	05/21/87	8960	06/11/87	9295		335.00	06/03/87	502.00		
1986	05/21/86	6660	06/11/86	7267		607.00	05/28/86	947.00		

Percentage Correct	100				593.53			Winners	15
Average Profit on Winning Trades					593.53			Winners	15
Average Loss on Trades								Losers	0
Average Net Profit Per Trade					593.53			Total trades	15

Percentage Correct	95								
Average Profit on Winning Trades					557.11			Winners	19
Average Loss on Trades					-1030.00			Losers	1
Average Net Profit Per Trade					477.75			Total trades	20

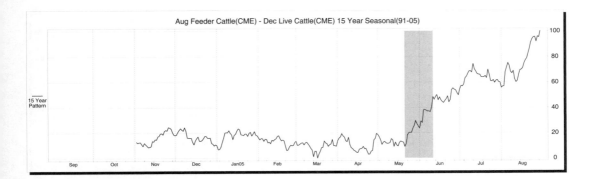

Aug Feeder Cattle(CME) - Dec Live Cattle(CME) 15 Year Seasonal(91-05)

Figure 6-63

Buy Sep Feeder Cattle(CME) / Sell Dec Live Cattle(CME)

Enter on approximately 05/28 - Exit on approximately 07/11

CONT YEAR	ENTRY DATE	ENTRY PRICE	EXIT DATE	EXIT PRICE		PROFIT AMOUNT	BEST EQUITY DATE	BEST EQUITY AMOUNT	WORST EQUITY DATE	WORST EQUITY AMOUNT
2004	05/28/04	17760	07/09/04	20982		3222.00	07/09/04	3222.00	06/01/04	-885.00
2003	05/28/03	13527	07/11/03	14082		555.00	07/07/03	650.00	06/12/03	-285.00
2002	05/28/02	11287	07/11/02	11760		473.00	06/18/02	918.00	05/31/02	-677.00
2001	05/29/01	15105	07/11/01	15132		27.00	06/25/01	557.00	07/05/01	-110.00
2000	05/30/00	13682	07/11/00	15040		1358.00	07/05/00	1425.00	06/02/00	-115.00
1999	05/28/99	11035	07/09/99	12542		1507.00	07/06/99	1687.00	06/03/99	-58.00
1998	05/28/98	10472	07/10/98	9690		-782.00	06/10/98	500.00	06/26/98	-1167.00
1997	05/28/97	10622	07/11/97	12215		1593.00	07/07/97	1633.00	06/09/97	-462.00
1996	05/28/96	3415	07/11/96	3650		235.00	06/04/96	1132.00		
1995	05/30/95	7155	07/11/95	7245		90.00	06/12/95	602.00	06/15/95	-875.00
1994	05/31/94	8982	07/11/94	10195		1213.00	07/11/94	1213.00	06/17/94	-690.00
1993	05/28/93	12497	07/09/93	12577		80.00	06/14/93	935.00	07/06/93	-182.00
1992	05/28/92	9777	07/10/92	11615		1838.00	07/10/92	1838.00	06/01/92	-20.00
1991	05/28/91	13080	07/11/91	14145		1065.00	07/11/91	1065.00	06/24/91	-303.00
1990	05/29/90	11347	07/11/90	11947		600.00	07/09/90	708.00	07/02/90	-115.00
1989	05/30/89	10425	07/11/89	11062		637.00	06/13/89	1207.00		
1988	05/31/88	10772	07/11/88	10062		-710.00			06/20/88	-3040.00
1987	05/28/87	8870	07/10/87	10377		1507.00	07/09/87	1595.00	06/01/87	-5.00
1986	05/28/86	6432	07/11/86	7825		1393.00	07/09/86	1485.00	06/09/86	-385.00
1985	05/28/85	8640	07/11/85	8055		-585.00			07/08/85	-743.00
Percentage Correct	93									
Average Profit on Winning Trades						989.71		Winners		14
Average Loss on Trades						-782.00		Losers		1
Average Net Profit Per Trade						871.60		Total trades		15
Percentage Correct	85									
Average Profit on Winning Trades						1023.12		Winners		17
Average Loss on Trades						-692.33		Losers		3
Average Net Profit Per Trade						765.80		Total trades		20

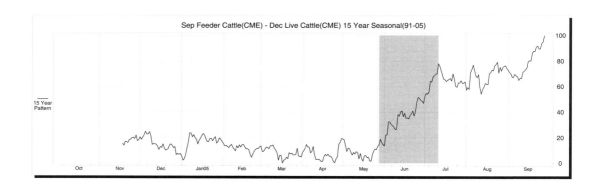

Sep Feeder Cattle(CME) - Dec Live Cattle(CME) 15 Year Seasonal(91-05)

15 Year Pattern

Chapter 6: Meats

Figure 6-64

Buy Aug Feeder Cattle(CME) / Sell Aug Live Cattle(CME)

Enter on approximately 06/01 - Exit on approximately 07/09

CONT YEAR	ENTRY DATE	ENTRY PRICE	EXIT DATE	EXIT PRICE		PROFIT AMOUNT	BEST EQUITY DATE	BEST EQUITY AMOUNT	WORST EQUITY DATE	WORST EQUITY AMOUNT
2005	06/01/05	22480	07/08/05	24245		1765.00	07/08/05	1765.00	06/17/05	-655.00
2004	06/01/04	17180	07/09/04	22555		5375.00	07/09/04	5375.00		
2003	06/02/03	14835	07/09/03	15082		247.00	06/30/03	567.00	06/03/03	-225.00
2002	06/03/02	13077	07/09/02	12622		-455.00	06/18/02	495.00	07/01/02	-850.00
2001	06/01/01	16127	07/09/01	16142		15.00	06/21/01	385.00	06/27/01	-152.00
2000	06/01/00	15557	07/07/00	16700		1143.00	07/06/00	1385.00	06/09/00	-330.00
1999	06/01/99	12775	07/09/99	13432		657.00	07/06/99	752.00	06/30/99	-548.00
1998	06/01/98	10522	07/09/98	10577		55.00	06/10/98	880.00	06/26/98	-855.00
1997	06/02/97	13190	07/09/97	14550		1360.00	07/07/97	1852.00	06/06/97	-695.00
1996	06/03/96	3787	07/09/96	4022		235.00	07/05/96	560.00	06/10/96	-772.00
1995	06/01/95	8447	07/07/95	8032		-415.00	06/13/95	115.00	06/23/95	-650.00
1994	06/01/94	10525	07/08/94	11877		1352.00	07/05/94	1637.00	06/15/94	-80.00
1993	06/01/93	13505	07/09/93	13760		255.00	06/25/93	660.00	07/06/93	-355.00
1992	06/01/92	9652	07/09/92	11312		1660.00	07/09/92	1660.00		
1991	06/03/91	14907	07/09/91	15532		625.00	07/09/91	625.00	06/11/91	-202.00
1990	06/01/90	12737	07/09/90	12975		238.00	06/21/90	353.00	07/03/90	-220.00
1989	06/01/89	11967	07/07/89	12510		543.00	06/13/89	880.00	06/02/89	-25.00
1988	06/01/88	11070	07/08/88	11252		182.00	07/07/88	405.00	06/20/88	-1600.00
1987	06/01/87	9247	07/09/87	10990		1743.00	07/09/87	1743.00	06/15/87	-90.00
1986	06/02/86	7610	07/09/86	9282		1672.00	07/09/86	1672.00	06/09/86	-120.00

Percentage Correct	87									
Average Profit on Winning Trades						1134.15		Winners		13
Average Loss on Trades						-435.00		Losers		2
Average Net Profit Per Trade						924.93		Total trades		15

Percentage Correct	90									
Average Profit on Winning Trades						1062.33		Winners		18
Average Loss on Trades						-435.00		Losers		2
Average Net Profit Per Trade						912.60		Total trades		20

HYPOTHETICAL PERFORMANCE RESULTS HAVE MANY INHERENT LIMITATIONS, SOME OF WHICH ARE DESCRIBED BELOW. NO REPRESENTATION IS BEING MADE THAT ANY ACCOUNT WILL OR IS LIKELY TO ACHIEVE PROFITS OR LOSSES SIMILAR TO THOSE SHOWN. IN FACT, THERE ARE FREQUENTLY SHARP DIFFERENCES BETWEEN HYPOTHETICAL PERFORMANCE RESULTS AND THE ACTUAL RESULTS SUBSEQUENTLY ACHIEVED BY ANY PARTICULAR TRADING PROGRAM. ONE OF THE LIMITATIONS OF HYPOTHETICAL PERFORMANCE RESULTS IS THAT THEY ARE GENERALLY PREPARED WITH THE BENEFIT OF HINDSIGHT. IN ADDITION, HYPOTHETICAL TRADING DOES NOT INVOLVE FINANCIAL RISK, AND NO HYPOTHETICAL TRADING RECORD CAN COMPLETELY ACCOUNT FOR THE IMPACT OF FINANCIAL RISK IN ACTUAL TRADING. FOR EXAMPLE, THE ABILITY TO WITHSTAND LOSSES OR ADHERE TO A PARTICULAR TRADING PROGRAM IN SPITE OF TRADING LOSSES ARE MATERIAL POINTS WHICH CAN ALSO ADVERSELY AFFECT ACTUAL TRADING RESULTS. THERE ARE NUMEROUS OTHER FACTORS RELATED TO THE MARKETS IN GENERAL OR TO THE IMPLEMENTATION OF ANY SPECIFIC TRADING PROGRAM WHICH CANNOT BE FULLY ACCOUNTED FOR IN THE PREPARATION OF HYPOTHETICAL PERFORMANCE RESULTS AND ALL OF WHICH CAN ADVERSELY AFFECT ACTUAL TRADING RESULTS. RESULTS NOT ADJUSTED FOR COMMISSION AND SLIPPAGE.

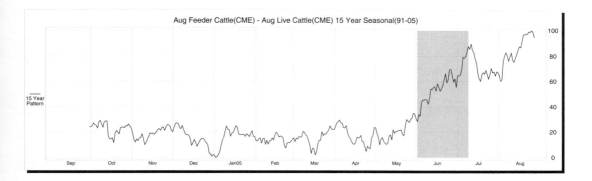

Aug Feeder Cattle(CME) - Aug Live Cattle(CME) 15 Year Seasonal(91-05)

Figure 6-65

Buy Nov Feeder Cattle(CME) / Sell Apr Live Cattle(CME)

Enter on approximately 06/19 - Exit on approximately 09/17

CONT YEAR	ENTRY DATE	ENTRY PRICE	EXIT DATE	EXIT PRICE		PROFIT AMOUNT	BEST EQUITY DATE	BEST EQUITY AMOUNT	WORST EQUITY DATE	WORST EQUITY AMOUNT
2004	06/21/04	18635	09/17/04	20122		1487.00	08/16/04	2515.00	07/15/04	-950.00
2003	06/19/03	12785	09/17/03	16307		3522.00	09/17/03	3522.00		
2002	06/19/02	11392	09/17/02	11510		118.00	09/17/02	118.00	08/14/02	-1522.00
2001	06/19/01	15035	09/17/01	14337		-698.00	06/25/01	170.00	08/10/01	-1400.00
2000	06/19/00	13637	09/15/00	14052		415.00	07/14/00	848.00	09/05/00	-82.00
1999	06/21/99	10992	09/17/99	12470		1478.00	09/17/99	1478.00	06/30/99	-22.00
1998	06/19/98	9155	09/17/98	9545		390.00	09/17/98	390.00	08/03/98	-870.00
1997	06/19/97	10292	09/17/97	10877		585.00	07/21/97	1563.00	09/02/97	-2.00
1996	06/19/96	4330	09/17/96	6112		1782.00	09/17/96	1782.00	07/12/96	-500.00
1995	06/19/95	6402	09/15/95	6125		-277.00	08/07/95	735.00	08/28/95	-515.00
1994	06/20/94	8672	09/16/94	9320		648.00	08/04/94	2765.00	06/22/94	-20.00
1993	06/21/93	12540	09/17/93	12590		50.00	09/07/93	550.00	07/06/93	-555.00
1992	06/19/92	9942	09/17/92	12502		2560.00	08/07/92	2830.00	06/25/92	-10.00
1991	06/19/91	12915	09/17/91	12232		-683.00	07/11/91	905.00	08/08/91	-1313.00
1990	06/19/90	11505	09/17/90	13525		2020.00	09/17/90	2020.00	07/03/90	-743.00
1989	06/19/89	11132	09/15/89	11717		585.00	08/03/89	1168.00	07/05/89	-80.00
1988	06/20/88	8110	09/16/88	11107		2997.00	08/29/88	3622.00	06/23/88	-258.00
1987	06/19/87	9245	09/17/87	11752		2507.00	09/09/87	3357.00		
1986	06/19/86	6915	09/17/86	8665		1750.00	09/05/86	2245.00		
1985	06/19/85	7935	09/17/85	8377		442.00	08/12/85	730.00	07/29/85	-1608.00

Percentage Correct	87									
Average Profit on Winning Trades						603.15		Winners		13
Average Loss on Trades						-662.50		Losers		2
Average Net Profit Per Trade						434.40		Total trades		15
Percentage Correct	85									
Average Profit on Winning Trades						1372.71		Winners		17
Average Loss on Trades						-552.67		Losers		3
Average Net Profit Per Trade						1083.90		Total trades		20

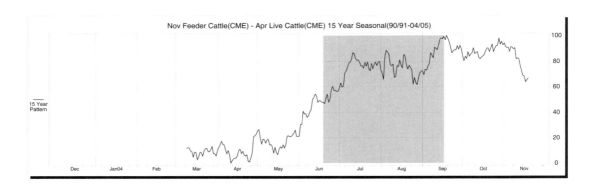

Nov Feeder Cattle(CME) - Apr Live Cattle(CME) 15 Year Seasonal(90/91-04/05)

15 Year Pattern

Figure 6-66

Buy Aug Feeder Cattle(CME) / Sell Dec Live Cattle(CME)

Moore Research Center, Inc.

Enter on approximately 06/23 - Exit on approximately 07/11

CONT YEAR	ENTRY DATE	ENTRY PRICE	EXIT DATE	EXIT PRICE		PROFIT AMOUNT	BEST EQUITY DATE	BEST EQUITY AMOUNT	WORST EQUITY DATE	WORST EQUITY AMOUNT
2004	06/23/04	20817	07/09/04	21547		730.00	07/09/04	730.00	07/01/04	-1425.00
2003	06/23/03	13500	07/11/03	13847		347.00	07/07/03	537.00		
2002	06/24/02	11520	07/11/02	11520		0.00	06/25/02	87.00	07/01/02	-505.00
2001	06/25/01	15962	07/11/01	15142		-820.00			07/05/01	-832.00
2000	06/23/00	14640	07/11/00	15055		415.00	07/05/00	442.00	06/29/00	-235.00
1999	06/23/99	12015	07/09/99	12392		377.00	07/06/99	532.00	06/30/99	-648.00
1998	06/23/98	9485	07/10/98	9725		240.00	07/06/98	695.00	06/26/98	-290.00
1997	06/23/97	11327	07/11/97	12155		828.00	07/07/97	1103.00		
1996	06/24/96	3747	07/11/96	3990		243.00	07/05/96	760.00		
1995	06/23/95	7057	07/11/95	7730		673.00	07/11/95	673.00		
1994	06/23/94	9310	07/11/94	10595		1285.00	07/11/94	1285.00	06/28/94	-113.00
1993	06/23/93	13557	07/09/93	13052		-505.00	06/25/93	280.00	07/06/93	-707.00
1992	06/23/92	11157	07/10/92	12215		1058.00	07/10/92	1058.00	06/25/92	-57.00
1991	06/24/91	13237	07/11/91	14795		1558.00	07/11/91	1558.00		
1990	06/25/90	12335	07/11/90	12422		87.00	07/10/90	112.00	07/02/90	-738.00
1989	06/23/89	11492	07/11/89	11547		55.00	06/26/89	80.00	07/05/89	-462.00
1988	06/23/88	8157	07/11/88	10122		1965.00	07/11/88	1965.00		
1987	06/23/87	10105	07/10/87	10552		447.00	07/09/87	585.00		
1986	06/23/86	8152	07/11/86	9115		963.00	07/09/86	1290.00		
1985	06/24/85	8005	07/11/85	8030		25.00	06/28/85	337.00	07/08/85	-248.00

Percentage Correct	87		
Average Profit on Winning Trades		1138.23	Winners	13
Average Loss on Trades		-491.50	Losers	2
Average Net Profit Per Trade		920.93	Total trades	15

Percentage Correct	90		
Average Profit on Winning Trades		627.56	Winners	18
Average Loss on Trades		-662.50	Losers	2
Average Net Profit Per Trade		498.55	Total trades	20

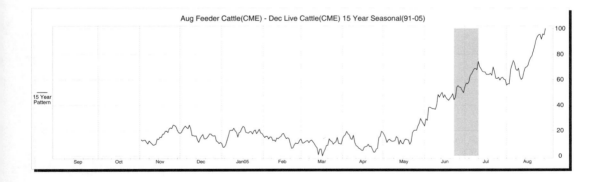

Aug Feeder Cattle(CME) - Dec Live Cattle(CME) 15 Year Seasonal(91-05)

Figure 6-67

Buy Aug Feeder Cattle(CME) / Sell Dec Live Cattle(CME)

Enter on approximately 06/23 - Exit on approximately 08/21

CONT YEAR	ENTRY DATE	ENTRY PRICE	EXIT DATE	EXIT PRICE		PROFIT AMOUNT	BEST EQUITY DATE	BEST EQUITY AMOUNT	WORST EQUITY DATE	WORST EQUITY AMOUNT
2004	06/23/04	20817	08/20/04	23697		2880.00	08/20/04	2880.00	07/01/04	-1425.00
2003	06/23/03	13500	08/21/03	15867		2367.00	08/21/03	2367.00		
2002	06/24/02	11520	08/21/02	11562		42.00	07/12/02	275.00	08/14/02	-983.00
2001	06/25/01	15962	08/21/01	14982		-980.00			07/27/01	-1682.00
2000	06/23/00	14640	08/21/00	15252		612.00	08/18/00	632.00	06/29/00	-235.00
1999	06/23/99	12015	08/20/99	12012		-3.00	07/14/99	670.00	06/30/99	-648.00
1998	06/23/98	9485	08/21/98	9645		160.00	07/06/98	695.00	08/03/98	-415.00
1997	06/23/97	11327	08/21/97	11810		483.00	07/18/97	1430.00	08/12/97	-325.00
1996	06/24/96	3747	08/21/96	4902		1155.00	08/05/96	1268.00	07/12/96	-65.00
1995	06/23/95	7057	08/21/95	7062		5.00	07/11/95	673.00	07/17/95	-180.00
1994	06/23/94	9310	08/19/94	10870		1560.00	08/04/94	2750.00	06/28/94	-113.00
1993	06/23/93	13557	08/20/93	13792		235.00	08/10/93	830.00	07/06/93	-707.00
1992	06/23/92	11157	08/21/92	13680		2523.00	08/07/92	2638.00	06/25/92	-57.00
1991	06/24/91	13237	08/21/91	13600		363.00	07/11/91	1558.00	08/12/91	-637.00
1990	06/25/90	12335	08/21/90	14747		2412.00	08/21/90	2412.00	07/02/90	-738.00
1989	06/23/89	11492	08/21/89	12572		1080.00	08/14/89	1285.00	07/05/89	-462.00
1988	06/23/88	8157	08/19/88	11870		3713.00	08/16/88	3898.00		
1987	06/23/87	10105	08/21/87	11937		1832.00	08/20/87	1862.00		
1986	06/23/86	8152	08/20/86	11075		2923.00	08/20/86	2923.00		
1985	06/24/85	8005	08/20/85	9285		1280.00	08/14/85	1670.00	07/29/85	-980.00

Percentage Correct	87				
Average Profit on Winning Trades			468.54	Winners	13
Average Loss on Trades			-536.00	Losers	2
Average Net Profit Per Trade			334.60	Total trades	15

Percentage Correct	90				
Average Profit on Winning Trades			1423.61	Winners	18
Average Loss on Trades			-491.50	Losers	2
Average Net Profit Per Trade			1232.10	Total trades	20

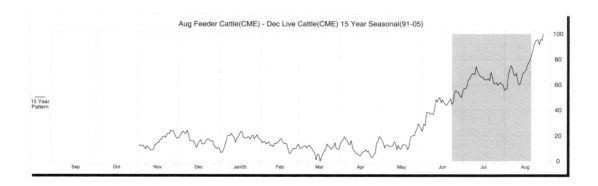

Aug Feeder Cattle(CME) - Dec Live Cattle(CME) 15 Year Seasonal(91-05)

Figure 6-68

Buy Aug Feeder Cattle(CME) / Sell Aug Live Cattle(CME)

Enter on approximately 07/01 - Exit on approximately 07/11

CONT YEAR	ENTRY DATE	ENTRY PRICE	EXIT DATE	EXIT PRICE		PROFIT AMOUNT	BEST EQUITY DATE	BEST EQUITY AMOUNT	WORST EQUITY DATE	WORST EQUITY AMOUNT
2004	07/01/04	20092	07/09/04	22555		2463.00	07/09/04	2463.00	07/02/04	-20.00
2003	07/01/03	15207	07/11/03	15227		20.00	07/11/03	20.00	07/08/03	-182.00
2002	07/01/02	12227	07/11/02	12852		625.00	07/11/02	625.00		
2001	07/02/01	16100	07/11/01	15630		-470.00	07/09/01	42.00	07/11/01	-470.00
2000	07/03/00	16732	07/11/00	17007		275.00	07/11/00	275.00	07/07/00	-32.00
1999	07/01/99	13037	07/09/99	13432		395.00	07/06/99	490.00		
1998	07/01/98	10495	07/10/98	10697		202.00	07/10/98	202.00	07/07/98	-255.00
1997	07/01/97	14877	07/11/97	14275		-602.00	07/07/97	165.00	07/11/97	-602.00
1996	07/01/96	3697	07/11/96	3790		93.00	07/05/96	650.00		
1995	07/03/95	7892	07/11/95	8382		490.00	07/11/95	490.00		
1994	07/01/94	11695	07/11/94	11835		140.00	07/05/94	467.00		
1993	07/01/93	13667	07/09/93	13760		93.00	07/09/93	93.00	07/06/93	-517.00
1992	07/01/92	10802	07/10/92	11307		505.00	07/09/92	510.00		
1991	07/01/91	15230	07/11/91	15595		365.00	07/11/91	365.00	07/02/91	-98.00
1990	07/02/90	12605	07/11/90	13030		425.00	07/11/90	425.00	07/03/90	-88.00
1989	07/03/89	12247	07/11/89	12675		428.00	07/10/89	438.00	07/05/89	-177.00
1988	07/01/88	10995	07/11/88	11402		407.00	07/07/88	480.00		
1987	07/01/87	10322	07/10/87	11060		738.00	07/10/87	738.00	07/06/87	-77.00
1986	07/01/86	8222	07/11/86	9415		1193.00	07/11/86	1193.00		
1985	07/01/85	9295	07/11/85	9510		215.00	07/11/85	215.00	07/08/85	-358.00

Percentage Correct	87								
Average Profit on Winning Trades					468.54		Winners	13	
Average Loss on Trades					-536.00		Losers	2	
Average Net Profit Per Trade					334.60		Total trades	15	
Percentage Correct	90								
Average Profit on Winning Trades					504.00		Winners	18	
Average Loss on Trades					-536.00		Losers	2	
Average Net Profit Per Trade					400.00		Total trades	20	

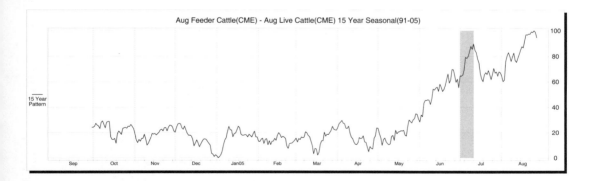

Aug Feeder Cattle(CME) - Aug Live Cattle(CME) 15 Year Seasonal(91-05)

Lean Hogs versus Pork Bellies

These trading and hedging vehicles reflect another relationship between source and product. The driving dynamic is that fresh production of pork is lowest when demand for it is highest. Thus, the industry aggressively accumulates inventory of pork into cold storage while slaughter remains high, and then liquidates that inventory into the peak demand season of summer.

Figure 6-69: Aug Lean Hogs/Pork Bellies Pattern

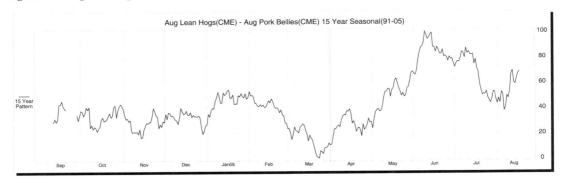

Figure 6-70: Lean Hogs/Pork Bellies Spread Strategies

Moore Research Center, Inc.	Hogs versus Bellies Spread Strategies							
Seasonal Strategy	Entry Date	Exit Date	Win Pct	Win Yrs	Loss Years	Total Years	Average Profit	Ave Pft Per Day
Buy Feb Lean Hogs(CME)	1/06	2/01	80	12	3	15	463	17
Sell Feb Pork Bellies(CME)			80	16	4	20	613	23
Buy May Pork Bellies(CME)	2/25	3/24	87	13	2	15	835	30
Sell Apr Lean Hogs(CME)			85	17	3	20	731	26
Buy Jun Lean Hogs(CME)	5/02	5/19	87	13	2	15	1237	69
Sell Jul Pork Bellies(CME)			80	16	4	20	1078	60
Buy Jul Lean Hogs(CME)	5/02	6/09	100	15	0	15	1399	36
Sell Jul Pork Bellies(CME)			95	18	2	20	1007	26
Buy Oct Lean Hogs(CME)	6/21	7/08	80	12	3	15	557	31
Sell Feb Pork Bellies(CME)			85	17	3	20	704	39
Buy Feb Pork Bellies(CME)	7/08	8/03	87	13	2	15	879	33
Sell Oct Lean Hogs(CME)			80	16	4	20	635	24

A commercial firm that markets product might try to protect a profit margin by buying hog futures to hedge against rising cash prices and thus higher costs while simultaneously selling pork bellies futures to hedge against declining cash prices and thus lower revenue. The seasonal pattern suggests hogs tend modestly to outperform bellies from early November, when storage of deliverable stocks can begin, through peak slaughter and into January. But perhaps as slaughter begins to decline in earnest, the demand for bellies into storage becomes so intense that hogs underperform bellies rather dramatically. By early May, however, with slaughter approaching its seasonal nadir, the market begins to anticipate seasonal movement of pork out of cold storage — inventory liquidation. Deliveries of pork

Figure 6-71

Moore Research Center, Inc.

Buy Feb Lean Hogs(CME) / Sell Feb Pork Bellies(CME)

Enter on approximately 01/06 - Exit on approximately 02/01

CONT YEAR	ENTRY DATE	ENTRY PRICE	EXIT DATE	EXIT PRICE	PROFIT	PROFIT AMOUNT	BEST EQUITY DATE	BEST EQUITY AMOUNT	WORST EQUITY DATE	WORST EQUITY AMOUNT
2004	01/06/04	-31.05	01/30/04	-27.57	3.48	1392.00	01/21/04	1740.00	01/12/04	-440.00
2003	01/06/03	-33.07	01/31/03	-31.64	1.43	572.00	01/24/03	2152.00		
2002	01/07/02	-22.45	02/01/02	-18.62	3.82	1528.00	01/15/02	1648.00	01/08/02	-272.00
2001	01/08/01	-9.90	02/01/01	-11.40	-1.50	-600.00	01/10/01	652.00	01/30/01	-1128.00
2000	01/06/00	-27.12	02/01/00	-33.94	-6.82	-2728.00	01/10/00	752.00	02/01/00	-2728.00
1999	01/06/99	-12.32	02/01/99	-12.32	0.01	4.00	01/25/99	400.00	01/21/99	-1168.00
1998	01/06/98	7.39	01/30/98	4.47	-2.92	-1168.00	01/14/98	972.00	01/30/98	-1168.00
1997	01/06/97	-3.59	01/31/97	-2.94	0.64	256.00	01/17/97	2056.00	01/24/97	-224.00
1996	01/08/96	6.82	02/01/96	8.50	1.67	668.00	01/17/96	1020.00	01/26/96	-252.00
1995	01/06/95	8.67	02/01/95	10.10	1.43	572.00	01/16/95	1528.00		
1994	01/06/94	5.17	02/01/94	9.50	4.34	1736.00	01/25/94	2336.00		
1993	01/06/93	19.81	02/01/93	23.57	3.76	1504.00	01/28/93	1976.00		
1992	01/06/92	17.61	01/31/92	21.95	4.33	1732.00	01/30/92	2080.00		
1991	01/07/91	1.62	02/01/91	4.53	2.92	1168.00	02/01/91	1168.00	01/09/91	-1064.00
1990	01/08/90	14.29	02/01/90	15.06	0.78	312.00	01/30/90	632.00	01/25/90	-1536.00
1989	01/06/89	19.22	02/01/89	19.50	0.27	108.00	01/09/89	392.00	01/18/89	-344.00
1988	01/06/88	6.59	02/01/88	11.35	4.77	1908.00	02/01/88	1908.00	01/08/88	-408.00
1987	01/06/87	-3.51	01/30/87	3.21	6.73	2692.00	01/29/87	3244.00		
1986	01/06/86	-2.71	01/31/86	-1.10	1.61	644.00	01/15/86	708.00	01/23/86	-236.00
1985	01/07/85	-3.87	02/01/85	-3.98	-0.12	-48.00	01/22/85	1616.00	02/01/85	-48.00

Percentage Correct	80									
Average Profit on Winning Trades					2.38	953.67		Winners		12
Average Loss on Trades					-3.75	-1498.67		Losers		3
Average Net Profit Per Trade					1.16	463.20		Total trades		15
Percentage Correct	80									
Average Profit on Winning Trades					2.62	1049.75		Winners		16
Average Loss on Trades					-2.84	-1136.00		Losers		4
Average Net Profit Per Trade					1.53	612.60		Total trades		20

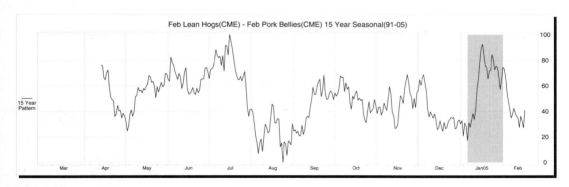

Feb Lean Hogs(CME) - Feb Pork Bellies(CME) 15 Year Seasonal(91-05)

bellies against the July contract are usually the heaviest of the year. Thereafter, the market must more carefully balance supply/demand of bellies into the peak demand of August.

Figure 6-72

Buy May Pork Bellies(CME) / Sell Apr Lean Hogs(CME)

Moore Research Center, Inc.

Enter on approximately 02/25 - Exit on approximately 03/24

CONT YEAR	ENTRY DATE	ENTRY PRICE	EXIT DATE	EXIT PRICE	PROFIT	PROFIT AMOUNT	BEST EQUITY DATE	BEST EQUITY AMOUNT	WORST EQUITY DATE	WORST EQUITY AMOUNT
2004	02/25/04	37.19	03/24/04	38.23	1.03	412.00	03/24/04	412.00	03/15/04	-1948.00
2003	02/25/03	36.01	03/24/03	38.28	2.26	904.00	03/18/03	1520.00	03/05/03	-996.00
2002	02/25/02	20.92	03/22/02	23.64	2.72	1088.00	03/07/02	1600.00	02/26/02	-192.00
2001	02/26/01	15.29	03/23/01	29.12	13.82	5528.00	03/23/01	5528.00	03/02/01	-168.00
2000	02/25/00	31.22	03/24/00	26.12	-5.09	-2036.00	03/02/00	1472.00	03/22/00	-2048.00
1999	02/25/99	8.14	03/24/99	11.75	3.60	1440.00	03/23/99	1532.00	03/02/99	-652.00
1998	02/25/98	-7.32	03/24/98	-5.15	2.17	868.00	03/23/98	928.00	02/27/98	-280.00
1997	02/25/97	3.87	03/24/97	4.56	0.69	276.00	03/03/97	2308.00		
1996	02/26/96	-0.70	03/22/96	1.34	2.04	816.00	03/11/96	1772.00	02/28/96	-808.00
1995	02/27/95	-9.85	03/24/95	-7.37	2.49	996.00	03/20/95	1508.00	03/06/95	-264.00
1994	02/25/94	-9.96	03/24/94	-5.27	4.70	1880.00	03/24/94	1880.00		
1993	02/25/93	-21.25	03/24/93	-15.89	5.35	2140.00	03/22/93	2492.00	03/01/93	-172.00
1992	02/25/92	-18.84	03/24/92	-17.05	1.80	720.00	03/20/92	1000.00	02/26/92	-224.00
1991	02/25/91	-6.55	03/22/91	-4.56	1.98	792.00	03/22/91	792.00	03/15/91	-716.00
1990	02/26/90	-12.48	03/23/90	-20.71	-8.23	-3292.00			03/16/90	-3400.00
1989	02/27/89	-20.59	03/23/89	-19.55	1.04	416.00	03/21/89	616.00	03/03/89	-488.00
1988	02/25/88	-5.51	03/24/88	-5.50	0.01	4.00	03/05/88	968.00	03/15/88	-804.00
1987	02/25/87	3.71	03/24/87	4.11	0.41	164.00	03/20/87	984.00	03/17/87	-504.00
1986	02/25/86	5.35	03/24/86	3.21	-2.15	-860.00			03/11/86	-908.00
1985	02/25/85	5.88	03/22/85	11.78	5.91	2364.00	03/21/85	2556.00		

Percentage Correct	87			
Average Profit on Winning Trades		3.43	1373.85	Winners	13
Average Loss on Trades		-6.66	-2664.00	Losers	2
Average Net Profit Per Trade		2.09	835.47	Total trades	15
Percentage Correct	85			
Average Profit on Winning Trades		3.06	1224.00	Winners	17
Average Loss on Trades		-5.16	-2062.67	Losers	3
Average Net Profit Per Trade		1.83	731.00	Total trades	20

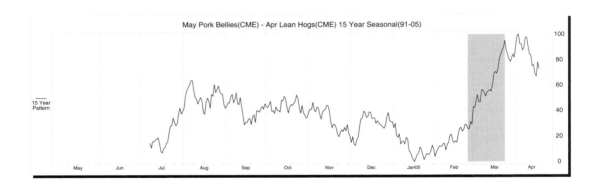

May Pork Bellies(CME) - Apr Lean Hogs(CME) 15 Year Seasonal(91-05)

15 Year Pattern

Figure 6-73

Buy Jun Lean Hogs(CME) / Sell Jul Pork Bellies(CME)

Moore Research Center, Inc.

Enter on approximately 05/02 - Exit on approximately 05/19

CONT YEAR	ENTRY DATE	ENTRY PRICE	EXIT DATE	EXIT PRICE	PROFIT	PROFIT AMOUNT	BEST EQUITY DATE	BEST EQUITY AMOUNT	WORST EQUITY DATE	WORST EQUITY AMOUNT
2004	05/03/04	-37.62	05/19/04	-36.12	1.50	600.00	05/19/04	600.00	05/10/04	-1812.00
2003	05/02/03	-27.90	05/19/03	-25.25	2.65	1060.00	05/19/03	1060.00	05/13/03	-468.00
2002	05/02/02	-15.64	05/17/02	-11.12	4.52	1808.00	05/08/02	2360.00		
2001	05/02/01	-17.25	05/18/01	-10.33	6.92	2768.00	05/16/01	3612.00		
2000	05/02/00	-19.35	05/19/00	-17.92	1.43	572.00	05/10/00	1840.00	05/04/00	-400.00
1999	05/03/99	-0.60	05/19/99	1.61	2.22	888.00	05/17/99	1568.00		
1998	05/04/98	3.42	05/19/98	7.26	3.85	1540.00	05/15/98	2364.00	05/08/98	-288.00
1997	05/02/97	-4.84	05/19/97	-7.54	-2.70	-1080.00	05/13/97	780.00	05/15/97	-1940.00
1996	05/02/96	-8.28	05/17/96	5.32	13.61	5444.00	05/17/96	5444.00		
1995	05/02/95	18.28	05/19/95	21.75	3.47	1388.00	05/19/95	1388.00		
1994	05/02/94	19.60	05/19/94	22.08	2.48	992.00	05/17/94	1288.00		
1993	05/03/93	26.19	05/19/93	27.37	1.17	468.00	05/04/93	656.00	05/14/93	-92.00
1992	05/04/92	30.25	05/19/92	26.19	-4.05	-1620.00			05/19/92	-1620.00
1991	05/02/91	15.71	05/17/91	19.96	4.24	1696.00	05/10/91	2028.00		
1990	05/02/90	16.85	05/18/90	21.92	5.07	2028.00	05/16/90	2644.00	05/03/90	-56.00
1989	05/02/89	32.45	05/19/89	29.97	-2.49	-996.00	05/05/89	180.00	05/12/89	-1440.00
1988	05/02/88	14.40	05/19/88	19.32	4.93	1972.00	05/19/88	1972.00		
1987	05/04/87	-0.50	05/19/87	5.58	6.10	2440.00	05/14/87	2944.00	05/05/87	-108.00
1986	05/02/86	3.00	05/19/86	1.18	-1.81	-724.00			05/14/86	-1244.00
1985	05/02/85	-2.71	05/17/85	-1.92	0.79	316.00	05/13/85	1504.00		

Percentage Correct	87									
Average Profit on Winning Trades					4.09	1634.77		Winners		13
Average Loss on Trades					-3.38	-1350.00		Losers		2
Average Net Profit Per Trade					3.09	1236.80		Total trades		15
Percentage Correct	80									
Average Profit on Winning Trades					4.06	1623.75		Winners		16
Average Loss on Trades					-2.76	-1105.00		Losers		4
Average Net Profit Per Trade					2.69	1078.00		Total trades		20

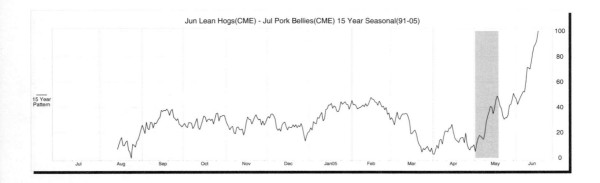

Jun Lean Hogs(CME) - Jul Pork Bellies(CME) 15 Year Seasonal(91-05)

15 Year Pattern

Chapter 6: Meats 273

Figure 6-74

Buy Jul Lean Hogs(CME) / Sell Jul Pork Bellies(CME)

Enter on approximately 05/02 - Exit on approximately 06/09

CONT YEAR	ENTRY DATE	ENTRY PRICE	EXIT DATE	EXIT PRICE	PROFIT	PROFIT AMOUNT	BEST EQUITY DATE	BEST EQUITY AMOUNT	WORST EQUITY DATE	WORST EQUITY AMOUNT
2005	05/02/05	-3.96	06/09/05	-1.75	2.22	888.00	05/31/05	1848.00	05/19/05	-2032.00
2004	05/03/04	-36.92	06/09/04	-33.54	3.37	1348.00	06/08/04	1548.00	05/17/04	-2460.00
2003	05/02/03	-27.00	06/09/03	-23.79	3.20	1280.00	06/09/03	1280.00	05/28/03	-1328.00
2002	05/02/02	-15.05	06/07/02	-6.04	9.00	3600.00	06/07/02	3600.00		
2001	05/02/01	-18.89	06/08/01	-14.00	4.90	1960.00	05/16/01	3300.00		
2000	05/02/00	-21.67	06/09/00	-18.67	2.99	1196.00	05/10/00	2440.00	05/04/00	-84.00
1999	05/03/99	0.87	06/09/99	4.12	3.24	1296.00	06/08/99	1868.00	05/10/99	-200.00
1998	05/04/98	3.40	06/09/98	3.55	0.15	60.00	05/27/98	3088.00	06/08/98	-980.00
1997	05/02/97	-4.04	06/09/97	-3.51	0.53	212.00	05/13/97	680.00	05/22/97	-3220.00
1996	05/02/96	-11.18	06/07/96	-4.43	6.76	2704.00	06/03/96	4352.00		
1995	05/02/95	19.46	06/09/95	23.29	3.83	1532.00	06/05/95	2040.00	05/23/95	-208.00
1994	05/02/94	19.24	06/09/94	22.71	3.48	1392.00	06/09/94	1392.00		
1993	05/03/93	24.08	06/09/93	30.83	6.76	2704.00	06/09/93	2704.00		
1992	05/04/92	27.12	06/09/92	27.33	0.21	84.00	06/01/92	692.00	05/19/92	-1412.00
1991	05/02/91	14.29	06/07/91	16.11	1.82	728.00	05/10/91	2020.00		
1990	05/02/90	15.40	06/08/90	16.46	1.06	424.00	05/16/90	2504.00		
1989	05/02/89	33.64	06/09/89	31.83	-1.82	-728.00	05/03/89	136.00	05/12/89	-1944.00
1988	05/02/88	14.90	06/09/88	16.72	1.81	724.00	05/09/88	1192.00		
1987	05/04/87	-3.98	06/09/87	-0.22	3.76	1504.00	05/22/87	3540.00		
1986	05/02/86	2.92	06/09/86	-4.00	-6.93	-2772.00			06/06/86	-3452.00

Percentage Correct	100						Winners		15
Average Profit on Winning Trades			3.50	1398.93				
Average Loss on Trades						Losers		0
Average Net Profit Per Trade			3.50	1398.93			Total trades		15
Percentage Correct	90						Winners		18
Average Profit on Winning Trades			3.28	1313.11				
Average Loss on Trades			-4.38	-1750.00			Losers		2
Average Net Profit Per Trade			2.52	1006.80			Total trades		20

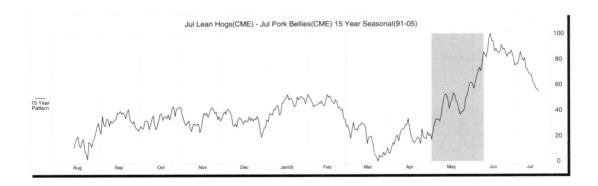

Jul Lean Hogs(CME) - Jul Pork Bellies(CME) 15 Year Seasonal(91-05)

Figure 6-75

Buy Oct Lean Hogs(CME) / Sell Feb Pork Bellies(CME)

Enter on approximately 06/21 - Exit on approximately 07/08

CONT YEAR	ENTRY DATE	ENTRY PRICE	EXIT DATE	EXIT PRICE	PROFIT	PROFIT AMOUNT	BEST EQUITY DATE	BEST EQUITY AMOUNT	WORST EQUITY DATE	WORST EQUITY AMOUNT
2004	06/21/04	-32.53	07/08/04	-31.42	1.10	440.00	07/02/04	1372.00	06/24/04	-48.00
2003	06/23/03	-23.44	07/08/03	-23.57	-0.13	-52.00	06/24/03	340.00	07/01/03	-792.00
2002	06/21/02	-21.50	07/08/02	-20.20	1.30	520.00	07/08/02	520.00	07/01/02	-900.00
2001	06/21/01	-21.62	07/06/01	-19.17	2.44	976.00	07/06/01	976.00	06/26/01	-424.00
2000	06/21/00	-13.85	07/07/00	-13.28	0.57	228.00	06/26/00	548.00	07/06/00	-420.00
1999	06/21/99	-7.48	07/08/99	-12.60	-5.12	-2048.00			07/02/99	-2180.00
1998	06/22/98	-6.03	07/08/98	-1.04	4.98	1992.00	07/08/98	1992.00		
1997	06/23/97	-0.34	07/08/97	3.08	3.43	1372.00	07/07/97	1472.00		
1996	06/21/96	-10.59	07/08/96	-8.48	2.11	844.00	07/08/96	844.00	07/03/96	-8.00
1995	06/21/95	4.88	07/07/95	5.79	0.92	368.00	07/07/95	368.00	07/03/95	-652.00
1994	06/21/94	10.39	07/08/94	13.10	2.71	1084.00	07/08/94	1084.00	06/23/94	-136.00
1993	06/21/93	15.14	07/08/93	13.02	-2.12	-848.00			07/08/93	-848.00
1992	06/22/92	12.42	07/08/92	15.82	3.40	1360.00	07/06/92	1656.00		
1991	06/21/91	10.19	07/08/91	12.21	2.03	812.00	07/02/91	892.00		
1990	06/21/90	12.66	07/06/90	15.91	3.26	1304.00	07/05/90	2116.00		
1989	06/21/89	9.00	07/07/89	9.35	0.35	140.00	06/23/89	160.00	06/28/89	-924.00
1988	06/21/88	-6.69	07/08/88	1.21	7.91	3164.00	07/08/88	3164.00		
1987	06/22/87	0.07	07/08/87	2.23	2.15	860.00	07/02/87	908.00		
1986	06/23/86	-2.80	07/08/86	-1.60	1.21	484.00	07/02/86	1124.00		
1985	06/21/85	-11.10	07/08/85	-8.37	2.72	1088.00	07/02/85	1096.00		

Percentage Correct	80									
Average Profit on Winning Trades					2.35	941.67		Winners		12
Average Loss on Trades					-2.46	-982.67		Losers		3
Average Net Profit Per Trade					1.39	556.80		Total trades		15
Percentage Correct	85									
Average Profit on Winning Trades					2.51	1002.12		Winners		17
Average Loss on Trades					-2.46	-982.67		Losers		3
Average Net Profit Per Trade					1.76	704.40		Total trades		20

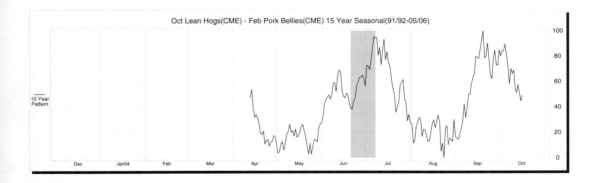

Oct Lean Hogs(CME) - Feb Pork Bellies(CME) 15 Year Seasonal(91/92-05/06)

15 Year Pattern

Chapter 6: Meats

275

Figure 6-76

Moore Research Center, Inc. — Buy Feb Pork Bellies(CME) / Sell Oct Lean Hogs(CME)

Enter on approximately 07/08 - Exit on approximately 08/03

CONT YEAR	ENTRY DATE	ENTRY PRICE	EXIT DATE	EXIT PRICE	PROFIT	PROFIT AMOUNT	BEST EQUITY DATE	BEST EQUITY AMOUNT	WORST EQUITY DATE	WORST EQUITY AMOUNT
2005	07/08/04	31.42	08/03/04	25.42	-6.01	-2404.00			08/02/04	-3192.00
2004	07/08/03	23.57	08/01/03	26.92	3.35	1340.00	07/30/03	2000.00		
2003	07/08/02	20.20	08/02/02	20.95	0.75	300.00	07/26/02	1860.00		
2002	07/09/01	18.13	08/03/01	20.59	2.47	988.00	07/20/01	1028.00	07/13/01	-1772.00
2001	07/10/00	14.60	08/03/00	13.39	-1.20	-480.00	07/12/00	760.00	07/27/00	-1068.00
2000	07/08/99	12.60	08/03/99	13.51	0.92	368.00	08/03/99	368.00	07/15/99	-2492.00
1999	07/08/98	1.04	08/03/98	12.80	11.75	4700.00	08/03/98	4700.00		
1998	07/08/97	-3.08	08/01/97	2.28	5.36	2144.00	08/01/97	2144.00	07/14/97	-488.00
1997	07/08/96	8.48	08/02/96	11.62	3.13	1252.00	08/02/96	1252.00	07/24/96	-1020.00
1996	07/10/95	-7.46	08/03/95	-7.08	0.38	152.00	07/28/95	860.00	07/12/95	-88.00
1995	07/08/94	-13.10	08/03/94	-12.03	1.07	428.00	07/22/94	940.00	07/28/94	-496.00
1994	07/08/93	-13.02	08/03/93	-9.35	3.67	1468.00	08/02/93	1688.00		
1993	07/08/92	-15.82	08/03/92	-12.39	3.43	1372.00	07/30/92	1756.00		
1992	07/08/91	-12.21	08/02/91	-9.50	2.72	1088.00	08/02/91	1088.00	07/22/91	-400.00
1991	07/09/90	-15.46	08/03/90	-14.26	1.19	476.00	08/03/90	476.00	07/23/90	-2024.00
1990	07/10/89	-9.60	08/03/89	-15.99	-6.39	-2556.00	07/12/89	452.00	08/03/89	-2556.00
1989	07/08/88	-1.21	08/03/88	-0.10	1.11	444.00	07/15/88	1240.00	07/11/88	-296.00
1988	07/08/87	-2.23	08/03/87	-0.09	2.13	852.00	07/31/87	1200.00	07/24/87	-788.00
1987	07/08/86	1.60	08/01/86	4.06	2.46	984.00	07/24/86	1804.00		
1986	07/08/85	8.37	08/02/85	7.82	-0.56	-224.00	07/12/85	256.00	07/24/85	-800.00

Percentage Correct	87									
Average Profit on Winning Trades					3.09	1236.62		Winners		13
Average Loss on Trades					-3.61	-1442.00		Losers		2
Average Net Profit Per Trade					2.20	879.47		Total trades		15
Percentage Correct	80									
Average Profit on Winning Trades					2.87	1147.25		Winners		16
Average Loss on Trades					-3.54	-1416.00		Losers		4
Average Net Profit Per Trade					1.59	634.60		Total trades		20

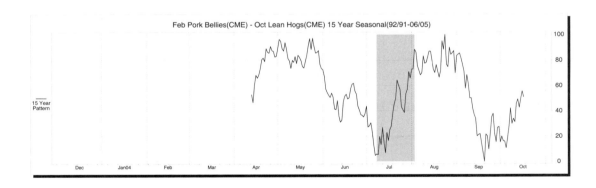

Feb Pork Bellies(CME) - Oct Lean Hogs(CME) 15 Year Seasonal(92/91-06/05)

15 Year Pattern

Chapter 7: Metals

These pure substances are found in the midsection of the Periodic Table of the Elements. All members are crystalline when solid, the natural state for most. Many are characterized by opacity, ductility, conductivity, durability, and a certain degree of luster, giving them as a class a great many industrial applications. Some were discovered in ancient times. As uses for them were found and techniques to refine and work them developed, they characterized certain periods in the advance of civilization, such as the Copper and Iron Ages. Metals especially distinguished for their durability and luster have also been recognized through the ages as stores of value and thus performed as investment vehicles and as media of exchange.

Most metals that are traded on the world's exchanges are grouped together in the Table of the Elements. Nickel, copper, and zinc, for example, have atomic numbers of 28, 29, and 30, respectively. Copper, silver, and gold are in the same (vertical) group in descending order. Palladium and platinum are in the same (vertical) group. Silver has one more proton than palladium; gold one more than platinum.

The London Metal Exchange (LME) began trading in some metals in 1883, and was trading aluminum, copper, lead, nickel, tin, and zinc in 2005. The Bolsa de Mercadorias & Futuros (BM&F) in Brazil has traded gold since 1986. The Amsterdam Exchanges in the Netherlands has listed gold and silver for trading. The Osaka Mercantile Exchange (OME) in Japan has traded aluminum since 1997. The Tokyo Commodity Exchange (TOCOM) has traded gold, silver, and platinum since the early 1980s and palladium and aluminum since the 1990s; its volume of trading in platinum and palladium dwarf that of any other exchange.

US trading in metals is now centered at the New York Mercantile Exchange (NYMEX). Platinum began trading in 1956 and then palladium in 1968. The old Commodity Exchange (COMEX), now a division of NYMEX, launched the silver contract in 1933. The current contract for high-grade copper began trading only in 1988, but copper cathodes traded for decades prior. Gold futures were first traded on December 31, 1974 — the day on which the US ban on ownership of gold by private citizens was lifted.

Intra-market Spreads

Because these metals are both durable and storable, one might expect their futures price structures to be in contango. Under normal conditions of plentiful supply, each progressively deferred delivery month tends to be priced progressively higher to (partially) reflect carrying charges — the cost of storage, insurance, and interest to carry, or hold, the commodity through time. In 2005, that held true for gold, silver, and palladium.

But platinum and copper were in backwardation. When demand outstrips supply and/or production, each progressively deferred delivery month can be priced at progressive discounts to cash because the market wants the commodity sooner rather than later. Thus, the market is unwilling to wait for cheaper prices or to pay for storage. The market for platinum exhibited this feature from 1999 through 2005, and copper did so from 2003 into 2005.

Figure 7-1: December Copper Seasonal Pattern

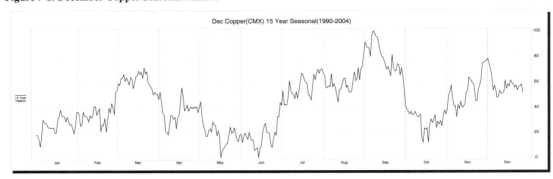

Only in the copper market have any reliable, tradable seasonal spreads between delivery months evolved — and precious few of those. Perhaps because it is so heavily used in construction, copper has tended to exhibit two primary seasonal trends — one during the primary US construction season and another leading up to it. Notice how prices normally rise into March deliveries, an unusual dynamic in futures that suggests strong demand for the physical commodity, perhaps inventory building before construction season begins. The seasonal trend June-August coincides with heaviest usage.

Figure 7-2: May/December Copper Seasonal Pattern

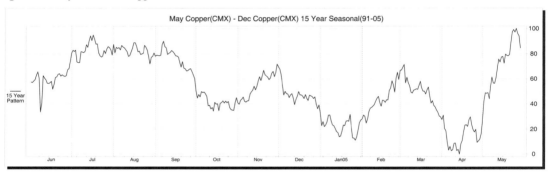

Figure 7-3: Copper Spreads

Moore Research Center, Inc.	Copper							
Seasonal Strategy	Entry Date	Exit Date	Win Pct	Win Yrs	Loss Years	Total Years	Average Profit	Ave Pft Per Day
Buy May Copper(CMX)	2/04	3/16	80	12	3	15	281	7
Sell Dec Copper(CMX)			80	16	4	20	445	11

Nonetheless, spreads have tended to be erratic. The seasonal pattern for May/December suggests several interim trends, but their reliability does not hold up to statistical analysis. One can even conclude that the strategy in the table above is marginal upon examining its details closely. The seasonal move from mid April into late May that looks so powerful? Apparently delivery-driven, for the tradable July/December spread during a similar window would have succeeded in only 10 of the years 1991-2005. The seasonal pattern for May/Dec does suggest, however, a tendency toward strength going into deliveries (early July, September, December, March, and May) and exhaustion thereafter.

Figure 7-4

Buy May Copper(CMX) / Sell Dec Copper(CMX)

Enter on approximately 02/04 - Exit on approximately 03/16

CONT YEAR	ENTRY DATE	ENTRY PRICE	EXIT DATE	EXIT PRICE	PROFIT	PROFIT AMOUNT	BEST EQUITY DATE	BEST EQUITY AMOUNT	WORST EQUITY DATE	WORST EQUITY AMOUNT
2005	02/04/05	9.65	03/16/05	10.40	0.75	187.50	02/18/05	712.50	02/07/05	-100.00
2004	02/04/04	4.34	03/16/04	7.90	3.55	887.50	02/17/04	1125.00	02/05/04	-12.50
2003	02/04/03	-1.04	03/14/03	-1.20	-0.15	-37.50	02/27/03	62.50	02/18/03	-75.00
2002	02/04/02	-1.69	03/15/02	-1.54	0.15	37.50	03/15/02	37.50	02/12/02	-37.50
2001	02/05/01	-0.15	03/16/01	-1.39	-1.25	-312.50	02/07/01	125.00	03/16/01	-312.50
2000	02/04/00	-2.15	03/16/00	-2.04	0.10	25.00	02/07/00	25.00	03/01/00	-137.50
1999	02/04/99	-2.50	03/16/99	-2.49	0.00	0.00	03/05/99	50.00	02/18/99	-25.00
1998	02/04/98	-2.50	03/16/98	-1.00	1.50	375.00	03/12/98	400.00	02/18/98	-100.00
1997	02/04/97	4.45	03/14/97	9.65	5.20	1300.00	03/04/97	1525.00		
1996	02/05/96	6.10	03/15/96	6.90	0.80	200.00	03/13/96	612.50	02/16/96	-400.00
1995	02/06/95	9.20	03/16/95	12.09	2.90	725.00	03/14/95	737.50	03/01/95	-312.50
1994	02/04/94	-0.65	03/16/94	1.45	2.10	525.00	03/16/94	525.00	02/10/94	-62.50
1993	02/04/93	-1.15	03/16/93	-2.20	-1.05	-262.50			03/01/93	-387.50
1992	02/04/92	-0.25	03/16/92	0.90	1.15	287.50	02/28/92	662.50		
1991	02/04/91	2.29	03/15/91	3.39	1.10	275.00	02/28/91	837.50		
1990	02/05/90	3.19	03/16/90	14.45	11.25	2812.50	03/16/90	2812.50		
1989	02/06/89	12.09	03/16/89	17.09	5.00	1250.00	03/03/89	1837.50	02/15/89	-600.00
1988	02/04/88	10.00	03/16/88	11.29	1.30	325.00	02/16/88	1450.00	02/26/88	-1325.00
1987	02/04/87	-1.60	03/16/87	-0.39	1.20	300.00	03/12/87	312.50	02/05/87	-12.50
1986	02/04/86	-1.09	03/14/86	-1.10	-0.00	-0.00	02/05/86	37.50	03/03/86	-87.50

Percentage Correct		80								
Average Profit on Winning Trades					1.61	402.08		Winners		12
Average Loss on Trades					-0.82	-204.17		Losers		3
Average Net Profit Per Trade					1.12	280.83		Total trades		15
Percentage Correct		80								
Average Profit on Winning Trades					2.38	594.53		Winners		16
Average Loss on Trades					-0.61	-153.13		Losers		4
Average Net Profit Per Trade					1.78	445.00		Total trades		20

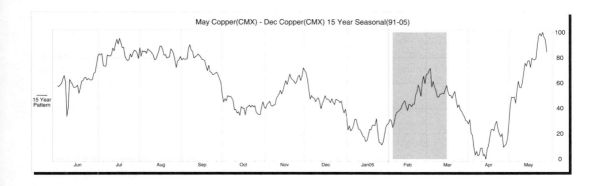

May Copper(CMX) - Dec Copper(CMX) 15 Year Seasonal(91-05)

Inter-market Spreads

Copper is considered an industrial metal, often a leading indicator of economic activity. Although they also have industrial applications, gold, silver, and platinum are precious metals heavily used in jewelry. Through the centuries, gold and silver have been inextricably linked in their investment and monetary capacities. The interplay between gold and platinum, though less well known, has at least in the years 1986-2005 been far more seasonally reliable.

Gold/Silver

Coveted for centuries for its "unique blend of rarity, beauty, and near indestructibility," gold has perhaps the most universal appeal of any metal in the world. "Nations have embraced gold as a store of value and a medium of international exchange; individuals have sought to possess gold as insurance against the day-to-day uncertainties of paper money," says NYMEX. Although it does possess industrial qualities, it is used primarily for jewelry and in monetary investment.

Figure 7-5: Handy & Harmon Gold Seasonal Pattern

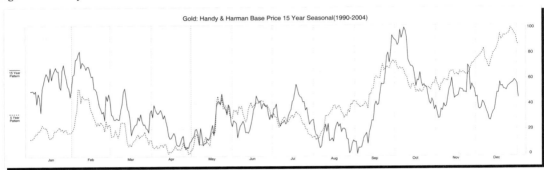

The combination of the 5-year and the 15-year seasonal patterns offers perspective on how patterns can evolve. Gold traded in a secular bear market from its peak in January 1980 to its double bottom in 1999-2001. Despite cyclical rallies along the way, the general trend for two decades was toward progressively lower prices. Thus, a seasonal pattern for any 15-year period, and most 5-year periods, within 1980-2000 would appear as a general downtrend throughout the year. But that changed in 2001. The uptrend into 2005 is now reflected in the 5-year seasonal pattern. The 15-year pattern has flattened as the effects on it of the secular downtrend have been partially neutralized by the recent 5-year uptrend. In other words, secular trends can greatly affect seasonal patterns, illustrated by how this 5-year uptrend has rotated patterns in gold.

With the effects of secular trend reduced, if not wholly removed, certain prominent features on the seasonal landscape appear to affect spreads between gold and both silver and platinum. About 70% of all gold manufactured each year is estimated to go into jewelry. Thus, gold is most heavily consumed during the fourth calendar quarter, when jewelry is most highly prized as gifts for various annual festivities around the globe. Harvest begins in September in India, the world's largest gold consumer, where farmers traditionally convert grain into gold and silver. Thereafter begin the wedding festivals, complete with commensurate golden gifts. Likewise, jewelry is customary during the year-end holidays in Western countries, as it is for celebrating Chinese New Year in February. Thus, gold prices have tended to surge throughout September as demand soars.

Figure 7-6: Handy and Harmon Silver Seasonal Pattern

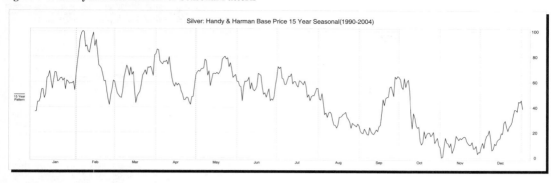

Silver: Handy & Harman Base Price 15 Year Seasonal(1990-2004)

After Chinese New Year is over, demand weakens into mid/late April, coincident with payment of US income taxes — itself coincident with, or even causing, the seasonal peak in US market interest rates, which undercuts demand for non-interest bearing gold. After meandering higher into July, the market tends then to fade into August — when Europe, the global center of the jewelry fabrication industry, is on vacation. Thereafter, demand soars.

Like gold, silver has attracted man's interest for centuries. Ancients used it in coins, ornaments, and jewelry. Silver assumed a key role in the US monetary system from 1792, when Congress based the currency on the silver dollar, until silver coinage was discontinued in 1965. The beginning of the twentieth century saw an even more important economic function emerge, that of an industrial material. Among its other properties, high electrical and thermal conductivity and resistance to corrosion have made silver highly prized in the photographic, electrical, and electronics industries, for example. By the end of the century, perhaps 85% of total world silver consumption went into industrial applications.

Figure 7-7: Dec Gold/Silver Seasonal Pattern

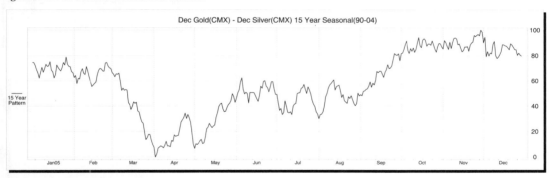

Dec Gold(CMX) - Dec Silver(CMX) 15 Year Seasonal(90-04)

Figure 7-8: Gold/Silver Spread Strategies

Moore Research Center, Inc.	Gold/Silver							
Seasonal Strategy	Entry Date	Exit Date	Win Pct	Win Yrs	Loss Years	Total Years	Average Profit	Ave Pft Per Day
Buy May Silver(CMX)	2/02	2/14	87	13	2	15	699	54
Sell Apr Gold(CMX)			90	18	2	20	636	49
Buy Dec Silver(CMX)	3/03	4/02	80	12	3	15	861	28
Sell Dec Gold(CMX)			80	16	4	20	875	28
Buy Dec Gold(CMX)	8/05	10/18	80	12	3	15	992	13
Sell Dec Silver(CMX)			85	17	3	20	1148	15

Figure 7-9

Buy May Silver(CMX) / Sell Apr Gold(CMX)

Enter on approximately 02/02 - Exit on approximately 02/14

CONT YEAR	ENTRY DATE	ENTRY PRICE	EXIT DATE	EXIT PRICE		PROFIT AMOUNT	BEST EQUITY DATE	BEST EQUITY AMOUNT	WORST EQUITY DATE	WORST EQUITY AMOUNT
2005	02/02/05	-8355	02/14/05	-5825		2530.00	02/14/05	2530.00	02/07/05	-220.00
2004	02/02/04	-9650	02/13/04	-8085		1565.00	02/13/04	1565.00		
2003	02/03/03	-12920	02/14/03	-12495		425.00	02/14/03	425.00	02/05/03	-900.00
2002	02/04/02	-7460	02/14/02	-7310		150.00	02/14/02	150.00	02/07/02	-800.00
2001	02/02/01	-2770	02/14/01	-3310		-540.00			02/14/01	-540.00
2000	02/02/00	-2485	02/14/00	-4640		-2155.00	02/03/00	10.00	02/10/00	-2200.00
1999	02/02/99	-1650	02/12/99	-795		855.00	02/04/99	1370.00		
1998	02/02/98	690	02/13/98	4940		4250.00	02/05/98	5140.00		
1997	02/03/97	-10110	02/14/97	-8160		1950.00	02/14/97	1950.00	02/04/97	-15.00
1996	02/02/96	-12320	02/14/96	-11700		620.00	02/13/96	670.00	02/07/96	-5.00
1995	02/02/95	-14080	02/14/95	-13810		270.00	02/10/95	280.00	02/03/95	-175.00
1994	02/02/94	-11750	02/14/94	-11625		125.00	02/03/94	390.00	02/08/94	-135.00
1993	02/02/93	-14575	02/12/93	-14420		155.00	02/09/93	240.00		
1992	02/03/92	-14835	02/14/92	-14560		275.00	02/06/92	335.00		
1991	02/04/91	-17620	02/14/91	-17610		10.00	02/05/91	265.00	02/12/91	-595.00
1990	02/02/90	-15230	02/14/90	-14995		235.00	02/14/90	235.00	02/06/90	-310.00
1989	02/02/89	-9775	02/14/89	-9145		630.00	02/14/89	630.00		
1988	02/02/88	-12630	02/12/88	-12495		135.00	02/03/88	570.00	02/09/88	-5.00
1987	02/02/87	-12610	02/13/87	-12445		165.00	02/12/87	380.00	02/03/87	-95.00
1986	02/03/86	-4660	02/14/86	-3600		1060.00	02/14/86	1060.00		

Percentage Correct	87							
Average Profit on Winning Trades				1013.85		Winners	13	
Average Loss on Trades				-1347.50		Losers	2	
Average Net Profit Per Trade				699.00		Total trades	15	
Percentage Correct	90							
Average Profit on Winning Trades				855.83		Winners	18	
Average Loss on Trades				-1347.50		Losers	2	
Average Net Profit Per Trade				635.50		Total trades	20	

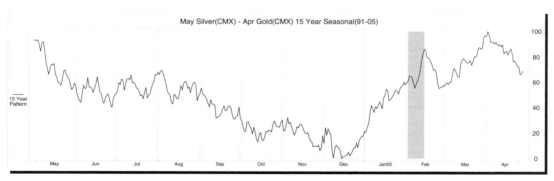

May Silver(CMX) - Apr Gold(CMX) 15 Year Seasonal(91-05)

The arrival of Chinese New Year in early February fixes the peak and imminent decline in seasonal demand for gold. Thus, silver has usually outperformed the yellow metal during the first two weeks of deliveries against February Gold, to which the first strategy in the table attests. (Because gold and silver futures differ in size, spreads between them must be calculated as the difference in their contract equity values, as expressed in US dollars, in order to accurately reflect spread movement.)

Figure 7-10

Buy Dec Silver(CMX) / Sell Dec Gold(CMX)

Enter on approximately 03/03 - Exit on approximately 04/02

CONT YEAR	ENTRY DATE	ENTRY PRICE	EXIT DATE	EXIT PRICE		PROFIT AMOUNT	BEST EQUITY DATE	BEST EQUITY AMOUNT	WORST EQUITY DATE	WORST EQUITY AMOUNT
2005	03/03/05	-7105	04/01/05	-7915		-810.00	03/09/05	585.00	03/28/05	-1285.00
2004	03/03/04	-5690	04/02/04	-1655		4035.00	04/02/04	4035.00		
2003	03/03/03	-11670	04/02/03	-11010		660.00	03/21/03	745.00	03/06/03	-765.00
2002	03/04/02	-6825	04/02/02	-7065		-240.00	03/08/02	210.00	03/22/02	-400.00
2001	03/05/01	-4145	04/02/01	-3955		190.00	03/06/01	235.00	03/12/01	-920.00
2000	03/03/00	-4210	03/31/00	-3145		1065.00	03/28/00	1210.00	03/07/00	-150.00
1999	03/03/99	-3415	04/01/99	-3320		95.00	03/29/99	485.00	03/09/99	-475.00
1998	03/03/98	1195	04/02/98	1535		340.00	04/02/98	340.00	03/17/98	-2005.00
1997	03/03/97	-9785	04/02/97	-10800		-1015.00	03/17/97	985.00	04/02/97	-1015.00
1996	03/04/96	-12620	04/02/96	-11975		645.00	03/26/96	925.00	03/05/96	-90.00
1995	03/03/95	-16160	03/31/95	-12960		3200.00	03/30/95	3415.00		
1994	03/03/94	-11730	03/31/94	-10545		1185.00	03/25/94	1310.00	03/10/94	-260.00
1993	03/03/93	-15205	04/02/93	-14370		835.00	04/02/93	835.00	03/05/93	-5.00
1992	03/03/92	-14760	04/02/92	-13845		915.00	03/20/92	1305.00		
1991	03/04/91	-17945	04/02/91	-16135		1810.00	04/02/91	1810.00		
1990	03/05/90	-15405	04/02/90	-12555		2850.00	03/26/90	3185.00		
1989	03/03/89	-9840	03/31/89	-9645		195.00	03/16/89	1175.00	03/08/89	-290.00
1988	03/03/88	-12065	03/31/88	-11775		290.00	03/04/88	530.00	03/11/88	-1435.00
1987	03/03/87	-13800	04/02/87	-10505		3295.00	04/02/87	3295.00	03/04/87	-240.00
1986	03/03/86	-5955	04/02/86	-7990		-2035.00			04/01/86	-2335.00

Percentage Correct	80								
Average Profit on Winning Trades						1247.92		Winners	12
Average Loss on Trades						-688.33		Losers	3
Average Net Profit Per Trade						860.67		Total trades	15
Percentage Correct	80								
Average Profit on Winning Trades						1350.31		Winners	16
Average Loss on Trades						-1025.00		Losers	4
Average Net Profit Per Trade						875.25		Total trades	20

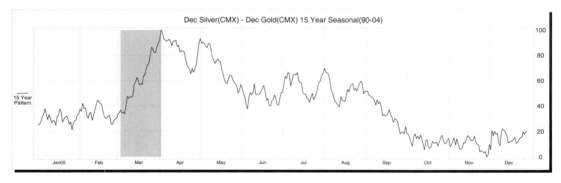

Dec Silver(CMX) - Dec Gold(CMX) 15 Year Seasonal(90-04)

But the true extent of decelerating demand for gold is illustrated by the yawning chasm of the seasonal pattern into which this spread falls during March, climaxed by first deliveries against April Gold. However, as dramatic as the decline appears, and indeed has been in some years, its reliability has hovered around 80% — statistically dependable but perhaps detracting somewhat from any excitement inspired visually. Slight shifts in entry and exit dates confirm the strong dynamic, but one with a more well-defined exit than entry date.

Figure 7-11

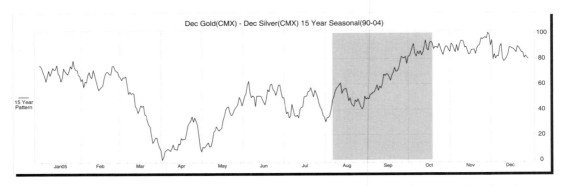

	Moore Research Center, Inc.		*Buy Dec Gold(CMX) / Sell Dec Silver(CMX)*							

Enter on approximately 08/05 - Exit on approximately 10/18

CONT YEAR	ENTRY DATE	ENTRY PRICE	EXIT DATE	EXIT PRICE		PROFIT AMOUNT	BEST EQUITY DATE	BEST EQUITY AMOUNT	WORST EQUITY DATE	WORST EQUITY AMOUNT
2004	08/05/04	5560	10/18/04	6825		1265.00	09/14/04	4040.00		
2003	08/05/03	10350	10/17/03	12520		2170.00	10/07/03	3030.00	08/07/03	-200.00
2002	08/05/02	7650	10/18/02	9530		1880.00	10/09/02	2680.00	08/06/02	-130.00
2001	08/06/01	5810	10/18/01	6665		855.00	09/14/01	1770.00	09/19/01	-305.00
2000	08/07/00	2765	10/18/00	2795		30.00	08/18/00	815.00	10/06/00	-195.00
1999	08/05/99	-1505	10/18/99	4970		6475.00	10/18/99	6475.00		
1998	08/05/98	1980	10/16/98	5420		3440.00	10/09/98	3870.00	08/06/98	-170.00
1997	08/05/97	10570	10/17/97	7830		-2740.00	08/08/97	270.00	10/10/97	-3425.00
1996	08/05/96	13675	10/18/96	13725		50.00	09/20/96	400.00	08/22/96	-925.00
1995	08/07/95	12615	10/18/95	11765		-850.00			08/21/95	-2920.00
1994	08/05/94	12175	10/18/94	12220		45.00	08/15/94	350.00	10/07/94	-1030.00
1993	08/05/93	13910	10/18/93	14835		925.00	09/21/93	1515.00	08/30/93	-970.00
1992	08/05/92	15630	10/16/92	15710		80.00	10/07/92	865.00	08/14/92	-990.00
1991	08/05/91	16235	10/18/91	15640		-595.00	08/08/91	135.00	09/24/91	-2015.00
1990	08/06/90	14245	10/18/90	16100		1855.00	10/11/90	3690.00	09/10/90	-15.00
1989	08/07/89	10940	10/18/89	11440		500.00	10/18/89	500.00	09/22/89	-770.00
1988	08/05/88	9035	10/18/88	9385		350.00	08/30/88	1485.00	10/03/88	-490.00
1987	08/05/87	5040	10/16/87	7830		2790.00	09/18/87	4065.00		
1986	08/05/86	10065	10/17/86	14095		4030.00	10/07/86	5665.00		
1985	08/05/85	1420	10/18/85	1820		400.00	09/26/85	1050.00	10/07/85	-395.00

Percentage Correct	80									
Average Profit on Winning Trades						1589.17		Winners		12
Average Loss on Trades						-1395.00		Losers		3
Average Net Profit Per Trade						992.33		Total trades		15
Percentage Correct	85									
Average Profit on Winning Trades						1596.47		Winners		17
Average Loss on Trades						-1395.00		Losers		3
Average Net Profit Per Trade						1147.75		Total trades		20

One may also note that the strategy (in Figure 7-10) suffered bookend losses 1986-2005, succeeding in 16 of the 18 years between. Such can be the vagaries of seasonal timing and reliability — further suggesting that, in any given year, some attention to detail can benefit real-time users of seasonal research.

The reversal toward gold outperforming silver in the pattern is not as well-defined statistically as it might appear from the chart (in Figure 7-11). For example, comparing prices for dates from early May against those toward month end favors gold generally in 60-73% of recent years. It is from that early August weakness, when European jewelry fabricators go on vacation, through September, when seasonal demand for gold bulges, that gold has most reliably outperformed silver over the last 15 and 20 years.

Gold/Platinum

Clustered tightly in the Periodic Table are six metals that comprise the platinum group — platinum, palladium, iridium, osmium, rhodium, and ruthenium. Platinum and palladium, both listed for futures trading, account for about 90% of the total metal produced from this group of ores. Still, according to NYMEX, "platinum is among the world's scarcest metals," with annual mine production of about "5 million troy ounces a year" versus "82 million" for gold, for example. Known reserves are relatively small, with South Africa accounting for perhaps 80%, Russia 11%, and North America 6%, says NYMEX.

Figure 7-12: Cash Platinum Seasonal Pattern

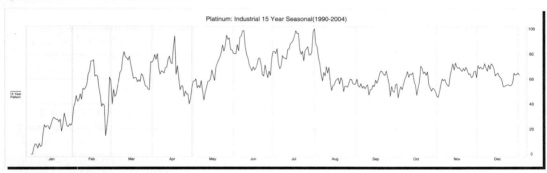

Platinum is used primarily in jewelry, automotive catalysts, chemical and petroleum refining catalysts, and high-tech electronic applications. Because of its low production, concentration of supplies, and industrial value, however, prices can be volatile — also making it attractive to investors.

Figure 7-13: 2 April Platinum/April Gold Pattern

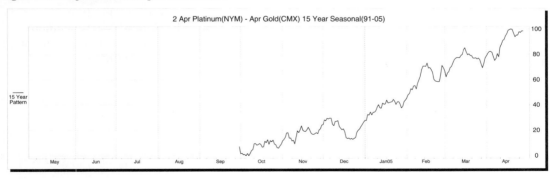

Figure 7-14: Platinum/Gold Spread Strategies

Moore Research Center, Inc.							Platinum/Gold	
Seasonal Strategy	Entry Date	Exit Date	Win Pct	Win Yrs	Loss Years	Total Years	Average Profit	Ave Pft Per Day
Buy Dec Gold(CMX)	9/07	10/02	87	13	2	15	1092	42
Sell 2 Jan Platinum(NYM)			80	16	4	20	1309	50
Buy 2 Apr Platinum(NYM)	12/21	1/17	100	15	0	15	1575	56
Sell Feb Gold(CMX)			90	18	2	20	1357	48
Buy 2 Apr Platinum(NYM)	12/27	2/16	93	14	1	15	2506	48
Sell Apr Gold(CMX)			90	18	2	20	2329	45
Buy 2 Apr Platinum(NYM)	12/30	3/16	93	14	1	15	3085	40
Sell Apr Gold(CMX)			95	19	1	20	3422	44
Buy 2 Apr Platinum(NYM)	1/29	2/16	87	13	2	15	1462	77
Sell Apr Gold(CMX)			85	17	3	20	1394	73
Buy 2 Jul Platinum(NYM)	2/24	4/19	93	14	1	15	2178	40
Sell Jun Gold(CMX)			95	19	1	20	2248	41

As seasonal demand for gold surges into its season of peak consumption during fourth-quarter festivals, holidays, and celebrations, gold has usually outperformed platinum. (Because platinum futures specify 50 ounces and gold 100, the 2:1 relationship affords nominal price comparison.) A closer look at historical detail, however, shows that profitable moves were not uniform, with a few not likely to have covered commission.

But platinum has quite consistently outperformed gold throughout most of the first quarter — and often into deliveries against both April contracts. The countercyclic seasonal patterns for gold and platinum tended to drive dynamic, persistent spread movement. Note the immaculate 15-year record for the first strategy that straddles the new calendar year, for example. With the exception of the last, the other strategies are within that primary seasonal trend. Trading the spread into February, for example, would require rolling out of the February and into the April gold contract so as to avoid delivery complications. The dynamic continues to be tradable into mid March, and holds up well over both 15 and 20 years, when participants would need to begin rolling out of April contracts for both metals. The July Platinum/June Gold position takes advantage of the same dynamic seasonal trend into its mid-April interim climax.

How long this first-quarter seasonal tendency can continue is open to question. As recently as January 1997, gold and platinum prices were equal. By August 2005, platinum was more than twice the price of gold — about $910 and $432, respectively. How significant a portion of that price divergence 1997-2005 occurred in the first calendar quarter?

Figure 7-15

Moore Research Center, Inc.

Buy Dec Gold(CMX) / Sell 2 Jan Platinum(NYM)

Enter on approximately 09/07 - Exit on approximately 10/02

CONT YEAR	ENTRY DATE	ENTRY PRICE	EXIT DATE	EXIT PRICE		PROFIT AMOUNT	BEST EQUITY DATE	BEST EQUITY AMOUNT	WORST EQUITY DATE	WORST EQUITY AMOUNT
2004	09/07/04	-43940	10/01/04	-43920		20.00	09/09/04	2090.00	09/28/04	-2240.00
2003	09/08/03	-32210	10/02/03	-32080		130.00	09/17/03	1940.00		
2002	09/09/02	-22510	10/02/02	-24020		-1510.00	09/11/02	190.00	10/02/02	-1510.00
2001	09/07/01	-16470	10/02/01	-11980		4490.00	10/01/01	4740.00	09/20/01	-2760.00
2000	09/07/00	-32130	10/02/00	-28320		3810.00	09/27/00	4370.00	09/08/00	-500.00
1999	09/07/99	-9690	10/01/99	-8850		840.00	10/01/99	840.00	09/14/99	-2070.00
1998	09/08/98	-7320	10/02/98	-4720		2600.00	10/02/98	2600.00	09/15/98	-340.00
1997	09/08/97	-8290	10/02/97	-9630		-1340.00			09/22/97	-2090.00
1996	09/09/96	-1080	10/02/96	-600		480.00	09/27/96	550.00	09/10/96	-40.00
1995	09/07/95	-4550	10/02/95	-2520		2030.00	10/02/95	2030.00	09/14/95	-580.00
1994	09/07/94	-3110	09/30/94	-2480		630.00	09/27/94	820.00		
1993	09/07/93	-840	10/01/93	-430		410.00	09/21/93	500.00	09/13/93	-130.00
1992	09/08/92	-1380	10/02/92	-1360		20.00	09/18/92	440.00	09/24/92	-390.00
1991	09/09/91	-90	10/02/91	-30		60.00	09/10/91	180.00	09/17/91	-670.00
1990	09/07/90	-9260	10/02/90	-5550		3710.00	09/28/90	6160.00		
1989	09/07/89	-11470	10/02/89	-12840		-1370.00	09/14/89	450.00	10/02/89	-1370.00
1988	09/07/88	-9620	09/30/88	-10330		-710.00	09/21/88	1300.00	09/08/88	-930.00
1987	09/08/87	-13880	10/02/87	-12170		1710.00	09/30/87	2400.00		
1986	09/08/86	-24000	10/02/86	-14520		9480.00	09/30/86	11570.00		
1985	09/09/85	880	10/02/85	1570		690.00	09/18/85	1410.00	09/10/85	-120.00

Percentage Correct	87									
Average Profit on Winning Trades						1479.23		Winners		13
Average Loss on Trades						-1425.00		Losers		2
Average Net Profit Per Trade						1092.00		Total trades		15
Percentage Correct	80									
Average Profit on Winning Trades						1944.37		Winners		16
Average Loss on Trades						-1232.50		Losers		4
Average Net Profit Per Trade						1309.00		Total trades		20

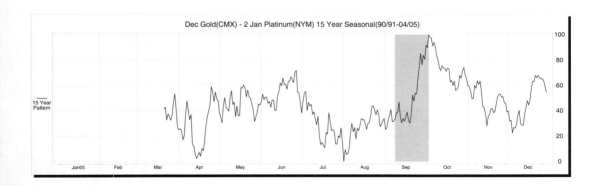

Dec Gold(CMX) - 2 Jan Platinum(NYM) 15 Year Seasonal(90/91-04/05)

15 Year Pattern

Figure 7-16

Buy 2 Apr Platinum(NYM) / Sell Feb Gold(CMX)

Enter on approximately 12/21 - Exit on approximately 01/17

CONT YEAR	ENTRY DATE	ENTRY PRICE	EXIT DATE	EXIT PRICE		PROFIT AMOUNT	BEST EQUITY DATE	BEST EQUITY AMOUNT	WORST EQUITY DATE	WORST EQUITY AMOUNT
2005	12/21/04	39650	01/14/05	43230		3580.00	01/11/05	4460.00	12/23/04	-170.00
2004	12/22/03	37840	01/16/04	44490		6650.00	01/16/04	6650.00		
2003	12/23/02	23680	01/17/03	26220		2540.00	01/17/03	2540.00	12/24/02	-560.00
2002	12/21/01	18550	01/17/02	19820		1270.00	12/31/01	2050.00	12/26/01	-10.00
2001	12/21/00	33120	01/17/01	35970		2850.00	01/10/01	4030.00	12/22/00	-460.00
2000	12/21/99	12230	01/14/00	12550		320.00	12/29/99	1160.00	01/06/00	-1070.00
1999	12/21/98	5730	01/15/99	6610		880.00	01/04/99	2120.00		
1998	12/22/97	5740	01/16/98	8350		2610.00	01/14/98	4820.00	12/23/97	-120.00
1997	12/23/96	620	01/17/97	880		260.00	01/14/97	460.00	12/26/96	-220.00
1996	12/21/95	2030	01/17/96	2110		80.00	01/05/96	540.00	12/28/95	-650.00
1995	12/21/94	3700	01/17/95	3880		180.00	01/12/95	300.00	01/04/95	-660.00
1994	12/21/93	80	01/17/94	430		350.00	01/04/94	630.00	12/27/93	-90.00
1993	12/21/92	2270	01/15/93	2900		630.00	01/07/93	630.00	12/31/92	-320.00
1992	12/23/91	-1790	01/17/92	-1260		530.00	01/17/92	530.00	12/26/91	-330.00
1991	12/21/90	2790	01/17/91	3680		890.00	01/17/91	890.00	01/16/91	-1060.00
1990	12/21/89	9900	01/17/90	9040		-860.00	12/27/89	800.00	01/02/90	-1890.00
1989	12/21/88	11360	01/17/89	11930		570.00	01/09/89	1200.00	12/28/88	-1970.00
1988	12/21/87	2050	01/15/88	1550		-500.00	12/28/87	1090.00	12/30/87	-560.00
1987	12/22/86	8490	01/16/87	12090		3600.00	01/12/87	3890.00	12/31/86	-1560.00
1986	12/23/85	1080	01/17/86	1780		700.00	01/06/86	2170.00		

Percentage Correct	100							
Average Profit on Winning Trades				1574.67		Winners		15
Average Loss on Trades						Losers		0
Average Net Profit Per Trade				1574.67		Total trades		15
Percentage Correct	90							
Average Profit on Winning Trades				1582.78		Winners		18
Average Loss on Trades				-680.00		Losers		2
Average Net Profit Per Trade				1356.50		Total trades		20

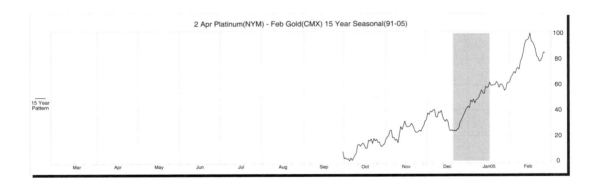

2 Apr Platinum(NYM) - Feb Gold(CMX) 15 Year Seasonal(91-05)

15 Year Pattern

Chapter 7: Metals

Figure 7-17

Buy 2 Apr Platinum(NYM) / Sell Apr Gold(CMX)

Enter on approximately 12/27 - Exit on approximately 02/16

CONT YEAR	ENTRY DATE	ENTRY PRICE	EXIT DATE	EXIT PRICE		PROFIT AMOUNT	BEST EQUITY DATE	BEST EQUITY AMOUNT	WORST EQUITY DATE	WORST EQUITY AMOUNT
2005	12/27/04	42410	02/16/05	42910		500.00	02/01/05	3190.00	01/04/05	-1160.00
2004	12/29/03	38670	02/13/04	43480		4810.00	01/22/04	6430.00		
2003	12/27/02	23810	02/14/03	32280		8470.00	02/14/03	8470.00		
2002	12/27/01	19540	02/15/02	17610		-1930.00	12/31/01	1000.00	02/05/02	-3900.00
2001	12/27/00	33150	02/16/01	34030		880.00	01/10/01	3770.00	02/01/01	-480.00
2000	12/27/99	12710	02/16/00	23740		11030.00	02/16/00	11030.00	01/06/00	-1750.00
1999	12/28/98	6120	02/16/99	7980		1860.00	02/16/99	1860.00	01/28/99	-370.00
1998	12/29/97	6680	02/13/98	8630		1950.00	01/14/98	3750.00		
1997	12/27/96	180	02/14/97	2530		2350.00	02/13/97	2480.00		
1996	12/27/95	1740	02/16/96	1980		240.00	01/05/96	630.00	12/28/95	-560.00
1995	12/27/94	3110	02/16/95	3770		660.00	01/30/95	820.00	01/04/95	-460.00
1994	12/27/93	-200	02/16/94	2000		2200.00	02/16/94	2200.00	01/21/94	-80.00
1993	12/28/92	2410	02/16/93	3760		1350.00	02/11/93	1460.00	12/31/92	-570.00
1992	12/27/91	-2270	02/14/92	840		3110.00	02/13/92	3430.00	01/13/92	-20.00
1991	12/27/90	1800	02/15/91	1910		110.00	01/17/91	1590.00	01/28/91	-1470.00
1990	12/27/89	10190	02/16/90	10460		270.00	02/15/90	480.00	01/02/90	-2680.00
1989	12/27/88	10600	02/16/89	14790		4190.00	02/15/89	4200.00	12/28/88	-1750.00
1988	12/28/87	2530	02/16/88	2000		-530.00			01/29/88	-2590.00
1987	12/29/86	7990	02/13/87	10940		2950.00	01/27/87	4380.00	12/31/86	-1430.00
1986	12/27/85	1240	02/14/86	3350		2110.00	02/14/86	2110.00	02/03/86	-380.00

Percentage Correct	93						
Average Profit on Winning Trades				2822.86		Winners	14
Average Loss on Trades				-1930.00		Losers	1
Average Net Profit Per Trade				2506.00		Total trades	15
Percentage Correct	90						
Average Profit on Winning Trades				2724.44		Winners	18
Average Loss on Trades				-1230.00		Losers	2
Average Net Profit Per Trade				2329.00		Total trades	20

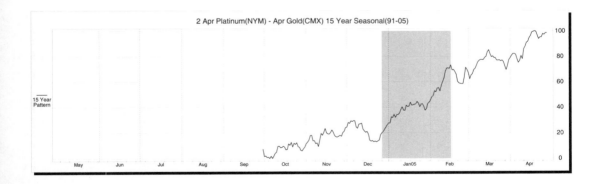

2 Apr Platinum(NYM) - Apr Gold(CMX) 15 Year Seasonal(91-05)

Figure 7-18

			Moore Research Center, Inc.	*Buy 2 Apr Platinum(NYM) / Sell Apr Gold(CMX)*						

Enter on approximately 12/30 - Exit on approximately 03/16

CONT YEAR	ENTRY DATE	ENTRY PRICE	EXIT DATE	EXIT PRICE		PROFIT AMOUNT	BEST EQUITY DATE	BEST EQUITY AMOUNT	WORST EQUITY DATE	WORST EQUITY AMOUNT
2005	12/30/04	41920	03/16/05	44360		2440.00	02/01/05	3680.00	01/04/05	-670.00
2004	12/30/03	38770	03/16/04	49980		11210.00	03/10/04	13560.00		
2003	12/30/02	24660	03/14/03	34700		10040.00	03/12/03	10280.00	12/31/02	-120.00
2002	12/31/01	20540	03/15/02	22330		1790.00	03/11/02	2880.00	02/05/02	-4900.00
2001	01/02/01	33630	03/16/01	32200		-1430.00	01/10/01	3290.00	03/12/01	-2370.00
2000	12/30/99	13050	03/16/00	19470		6420.00	02/16/00	10690.00	01/06/00	-2090.00
1999	12/30/98	7380	03/16/99	8220		840.00	02/23/99	2160.00	01/28/99	-1630.00
1998	12/30/97	6970	03/16/98	10740		3770.00	03/16/98	3770.00		
1997	12/30/96	250	03/14/97	3100		2850.00	02/27/97	3280.00	01/02/97	-10.00
1996	01/02/96	1440	03/15/96	1710		270.00	01/05/96	930.00	02/27/96	-390.00
1995	12/30/94	3280	03/16/95	3610		330.00	01/30/95	650.00	03/02/95	-690.00
1994	12/30/93	370	03/16/94	1780		1410.00	03/11/94	1750.00	01/21/94	-650.00
1993	12/30/92	1910	03/16/93	1940		30.00	02/11/93	1960.00	02/22/93	-970.00
1992	12/30/91	-2010	03/16/92	1660		3670.00	03/16/92	3670.00	01/13/92	-280.00
1991	12/31/90	1430	03/16/91	4060		2630.00	03/11/91	3180.00	01/28/91	-1100.00
1990	01/02/90	7510	03/16/90	10120		2610.00	02/20/90	3570.00		
1989	12/30/88	9820	03/16/89	15420		5600.00	02/17/89	6630.00		
1988	12/30/87	900	03/16/88	5230		4330.00	03/10/88	4460.00	01/29/88	-960.00
1987	12/30/86	6760	03/16/87	11330		4570.00	03/05/87	6000.00	12/31/86	-200.00
1986	12/30/85	1240	03/14/86	6290		5050.00	02/24/86	5490.00	02/03/86	-380.00

Percentage Correct	93						
Average Profit on Winning Trades			3407.14		Winners	14
Average Loss on Trades			-1430.00		Losers	1
Average Net Profit Per Trade			3084.67		Total trades	15
Percentage Correct	95						
Average Profit on Winning Trades			3676.84		Winners	19
Average Loss on Trades			-1430.00		Losers	1
Average Net Profit Per Trade			3421.50		Total trades	20

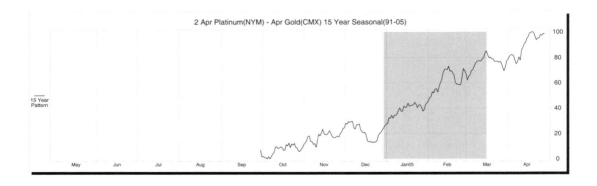

2 Apr Platinum(NYM) - Apr Gold(CMX) 15 Year Seasonal(91-05)

Figure 7-19

Buy 2 Apr Platinum(NYM) / Sell Apr Gold(CMX)

Enter on approximately 01/29 - Exit on approximately 02/16

CONT YEAR	ENTRY DATE	ENTRY PRICE	EXIT DATE	EXIT PRICE		PROFIT AMOUNT	BEST EQUITY DATE	BEST EQUITY AMOUNT	WORST EQUITY DATE	WORST EQUITY AMOUNT
2005	01/31/05	44970	02/16/05	42910		-2060.00	02/01/05	630.00	02/15/05	-2410.00
2004	01/29/04	42190	02/13/04	43480		1290.00	02/13/04	1290.00	02/02/04	-890.00
2003	01/29/03	28010	02/14/03	32280		4270.00	02/14/03	4270.00	01/30/03	-200.00
2002	01/29/02	16860	02/15/02	17610		750.00	02/14/02	1230.00	02/05/02	-1220.00
2001	01/29/01	33320	02/16/01	34030		710.00	02/06/01	740.00	02/01/01	-650.00
2000	01/31/00	16880	02/16/00	23740		6860.00	02/16/00	6860.00	02/04/00	-230.00
1999	01/29/99	5870	02/16/99	7980		2110.00	02/16/99	2110.00		
1998	01/29/98	8280	02/13/98	8630		350.00	02/05/98	1580.00		
1997	01/29/97	560	02/14/97	2530		1970.00	02/13/97	2100.00		
1996	01/29/96	1310	02/16/96	1980		670.00	02/13/96	690.00		
1995	01/30/95	3930	02/16/95	3770		-160.00			02/07/95	-760.00
1994	01/31/94	240	02/16/94	2000		1760.00	02/16/94	1760.00		
1993	01/29/93	3210	02/16/93	3760		550.00	02/11/93	660.00	02/02/93	-240.00
1992	01/29/92	-880	02/14/92	840		1720.00	02/13/92	2040.00		
1991	01/29/91	770	02/15/91	1910		1140.00	02/15/91	1140.00		
1990	01/29/90	9880	02/16/90	10460		580.00	02/15/90	790.00	02/07/90	-990.00
1989	01/30/89	12070	02/16/89	14790		2720.00	02/15/89	2730.00		
1988	01/29/88	-60	02/16/88	2000		2060.00	02/16/88	2060.00		
1987	01/29/87	11770	02/13/87	10940		-830.00	02/09/87	540.00	02/12/87	-930.00
1986	01/29/86	1930	02/14/86	3350		1420.00	02/14/86	1420.00	02/03/86	-1070.00

Percentage Correct	87									
Average Profit on Winning Trades						1857.69		Winners		13
Average Loss on Trades						-1110.00		Losers		2
Average Net Profit Per Trade						1462.00		Total trades		15
Percentage Correct	85									
Average Profit on Winning Trades						1819.41		Winners		17
Average Loss on Trades						-1016.67		Losers		3
Average Net Profit Per Trade						1394.00		Total trades		20

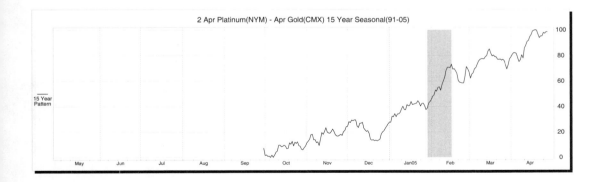

2 Apr Platinum(NYM) - Apr Gold(CMX) 15 Year Seasonal(91-05)

15 Year Pattern

Figure 7-20

Buy 2 Jul Platinum(NYM) / Sell Jun Gold(CMX)

Enter on approximately 02/24 - Exit on approximately 04/19

CONT YEAR	ENTRY DATE	ENTRY PRICE	EXIT DATE	EXIT PRICE		PROFIT AMOUNT	BEST EQUITY DATE	BEST EQUITY AMOUNT	WORST EQUITY DATE	WORST EQUITY AMOUNT
2005	02/24/05	42340	04/19/05	43580		1240.00	03/16/05	1540.00	02/25/05	-700.00
2004	02/24/04	44130	04/19/04	53410		9280.00	04/19/04	9280.00		
2003	02/24/03	29170	04/17/03	29710		540.00	03/18/03	4590.00	04/07/03	-1360.00
2002	02/25/02	17530	04/19/02	24860		7330.00	04/18/02	7610.00	02/26/02	-170.00
2001	02/26/01	32980	04/19/01	34150		1170.00	04/18/01	1520.00	04/02/01	-4860.00
2000	02/24/00	15670	04/19/00	18930		3260.00	04/04/00	6460.00	02/25/00	-1140.00
1999	02/24/99	8720	04/19/99	8050		-670.00	03/26/99	600.00	03/12/99	-1640.00
1998	02/24/98	7690	04/17/98	10020		2330.00	04/14/98	4220.00		
1997	02/24/97	2270	04/18/97	3380		1110.00	02/27/97	1200.00	04/04/97	-960.00
1996	02/26/96	1120	04/19/96	1160		40.00	03/13/96	740.00	04/18/96	-160.00
1995	02/24/95	3430	04/19/95	6030		2600.00	04/05/95	3260.00	03/03/95	-1100.00
1994	02/24/94	1290	04/19/94	1540		250.00	03/31/94	1970.00	02/25/94	-130.00
1993	02/24/93	950	04/19/93	2970		2020.00	04/16/93	2170.00	03/02/93	-180.00
1992	02/24/92	470	04/16/92	580		110.00	04/01/92	1060.00	02/25/92	-430.00
1991	02/25/91	1650	04/19/91	3710		2060.00	03/11/91	3080.00		
1990	02/26/90	9870	04/19/90	10600		730.00	03/26/90	1920.00	04/06/90	-130.00
1989	02/24/89	14060	04/19/89	16090		2030.00	04/14/89	3880.00	04/04/89	-600.00
1988	02/24/88	1190	04/19/88	7530		6340.00	04/04/88	7610.00		
1987	02/24/87	11850	04/16/87	14650		2800.00	04/14/87	3460.00	03/13/87	-730.00
1986	02/24/86	6490	04/18/86	6880		390.00	04/11/86	2540.00	02/27/86	-1570.00

Percentage Correct	93						
Average Profit on Winning Trades			2381.43		Winners	14
Average Loss on Trades			-670.00		Losers	1
Average Net Profit Per Trade			2178.00		Total trades	15
Percentage Correct	95					
Average Profit on Winning Trades			2401.58		Winners	19
Average Loss on Trades			-670.00		Losers	1
Average Net Profit Per Trade			2248.00		Total trades	20

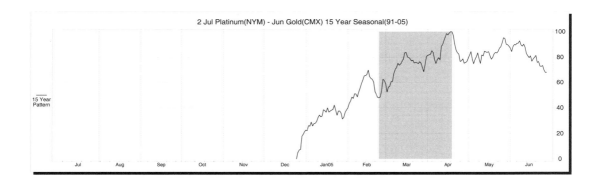

2 Jul Platinum(NYM) - Jun Gold(CMX) 15 Year Seasonal(91-05)

Chapter 8: Softs

Components of the soft agricultural complex are not firmly fixed but broadly include sub-categories of forest, fiber, and food. Lumber serves the timber and home-building industries. Cotton is the world's leading natural textile fiber. Foods include such exotic commodities as coffee and cocoa, grown mostly within 15 degrees latitude of the equator, and also sugar, orange juice, and, in this chapter, rice.

Commodities perhaps most traditionally associated with the softs complex trade at what is now the New York Board of Trade (NYBOT), which in 2004 merged the old Coffee, Sugar, and Cocoa Exchange with the New York Cotton Exchange. The cotton contract for 100 bales (now weighing 50,000 pounds) first traded shortly after the US Civil War, in September 1870. World sugar No. 11 futures for 50 long tons (equivalent to 112,000 pounds) began trading just as the First World War broke out, in 1914. Cocoa, for 10 metric tons (equivalent to 22,046 pounds), was listed in 1925. Coffee futures for about 250 bags (weighing 37,500 pounds) first traded in 1964. After the popularity of frozen concentrated juice caused orange production to increase significantly, the orange juice contract for 15,000 pounds was launched in 1966.

In the early 1970s, before the first financial instruments were developed, lumber futures at the Chicago Mercantile Exchange also served as an informal proxy for trading interest rates. The contract has been revised over the years and currently specifies the 110,000 board-feet which fit on one 73-foot flat car. The rough rice contract, trading with grains at the Chicago Board of Trade, calls for 2,000 hundred-weight (200,000 pounds) and began trading in 1983.

Except for cotton and sugar, spreads play a far less active role in the soft commodities. The lack of volume and open interest in deferred contracts for all these markets, except sugar, not only reflects a lack of commercial spread activity but also deters speculative trade. In certain of them, the only spreads that withstand seasonal scrutiny are delivery-driven.

Cotton

Cotton is produced on every continent in the world except Antarctica. The largest producers are China, the United States, India, Pakistan, and Australia. This natural fiber competes with petroleum-based synthetics in the textile industry. The majority of US cotton is produced in the West and Southwest; but perhaps 40% is produced in the Mississippi Delta and Southeast, regions wherein cotton competes with soybeans for acreage.

Figure 8-1: Cash Cotton Seasonal Pattern

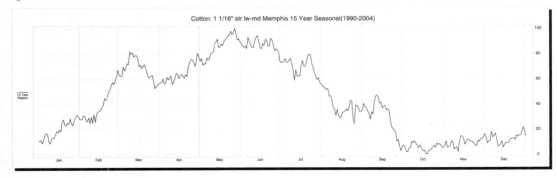

Cotton: 1 1/16" str lw-md Memphis 15 Year Seasonal(1990-2004)

The US cotton crop marketing year runs August-July. Planting begins mid March and runs through May, with harvest mid September through December. Thus, July is the last old-crop contract. Prices tend to rise from the harvest low, often in October, and continue higher as domestic mill consumption rises early in the new year. Planting commences mid March and prices tend to continue higher until the crop is in the ground, at which time new demand begins progressively to focus on new-crop at the expense of old-crop physical supply. The market then tends to decline throughout the growing season and into harvest.

Figure 8-2: Jul/Dec Cotton Seasonal Pattern

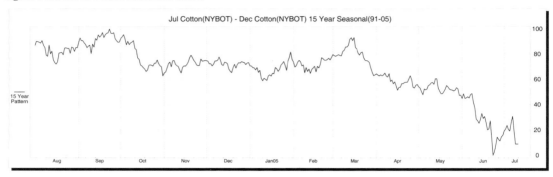

Figure 8-3: Cotton Spread Strategies

Moore Research Center, Inc.	Cotton Spreads							
Seasonal Strategy	Entry Date	Exit Date	Win Pct	Win Yrs	Loss Years	Total Years	Average Profit	Ave Pft Per Day
Buy Dec Cotton(NYBOT)	6/07	6/20	93	14	1	15	677	48
Sell Jul Cotton(NYBOT)			85	17	3	20	592	42
Buy May Cotton(NYBOT)	6/12	8/30	93	14	1	15	755	9
Sell Oct Cotton(NYBOT)			90	18	2	20	642	8
Buy Dec Cotton(NYBOT)	7/05	9/04	87	13	2	15	554	9
Sell Oct Cotton(NYBOT)			85	17	3	20	460	7

July/December (Figure 8-2) is the classic old-crop/new-crop spread, serving as both analytical tool and trading vehicle. Although October is the first official new-crop contract, deliveries against it begin "five business days from the end of the preceding month" — about when harvest itself begins. With usually little or no new-crop cotton available for delivery, it is considered a "bastard month" claimed by neither old- nor new-crop. Thus, December best represents new-crop and attracts both commercial activity and speculative trade.

The seasonal pattern illustrates how demand from typically increasing domestic mill consumption in the new calendar year normally favors old-crop going into March. The bull spread's reliability over 20 years, however, hovers closer to 60% than to 80% or more — better than a tossup but far below any credible threshold of reliability. Likewise, the pattern suggests how the market switches its allegiance to the new-crop December contract after planting begins mid March. But again, reliability suffers. The far more reliable move during June is most likely driven by liquidation of the last long old-crop July contracts prior to First Notice Day. Speculators are forced to sell in order to avoid delivery while commercial consumers look instead to place new long hedges into new-crop December. The frequency of this strategy's recurrence is reinforced by both the modesty and relative infrequency of its drawdowns.

Figure 8-4

Moore Research Center, Inc.	Buy Dec Cotton(NYBOT) / Sell Jul Cotton(NYBOT)

Enter on approximately 06/07 - Exit on approximately 06/20

CONT YEAR	ENTRY DATE	ENTRY PRICE	EXIT DATE	EXIT PRICE	PROFIT	PROFIT AMOUNT	BEST EQUITY DATE	BEST EQUITY AMOUNT	WORST EQUITY DATE	WORST EQUITY AMOUNT
2005	06/07/05	4.01	06/20/05	4.33	0.32	160.00	06/09/05	205.00	06/14/05	-245.00
2004	06/07/04	-0.34	06/18/04	2.45	2.79	1395.00	06/16/04	1470.00	06/14/04	-100.00
2003	06/09/03	2.50	06/20/03	3.09	0.60	300.00	06/13/03	745.00		
2002	06/07/02	4.09	06/20/02	4.39	0.30	150.00	06/19/02	150.00		
2001	06/07/01	4.33	06/20/01	4.85	0.53	265.00	06/20/01	265.00	06/14/01	-85.00
2000	06/07/00	3.53	06/20/00	4.06	0.53	265.00	06/13/00	705.00		
1999	06/07/99	0.13	06/18/99	1.01	0.89	445.00	06/18/99	445.00	06/09/99	-135.00
1998	06/08/98	-0.09	06/19/98	0.92	1.01	505.00	06/17/98	915.00		
1997	06/09/97	2.61	06/20/97	2.98	0.36	180.00	06/19/97	195.00	06/10/97	-90.00
1996	06/07/96	-4.29	06/20/96	1.62	5.91	2955.00	06/20/96	2955.00		
1995	06/07/95	-28.89	06/20/95	-31.50	-2.61	-1305.00			06/16/95	-2305.00
1994	06/07/94	-5.09	06/20/94	-2.53	2.57	1285.00	06/20/94	1285.00		
1993	06/07/93	-1.46	06/18/93	-0.99	0.47	235.00	06/11/93	455.00	06/17/93	-70.00
1992	06/08/92	1.10	06/19/92	1.95	0.84	420.00	06/16/92	665.00		
1991	06/07/91	-13.21	06/20/91	-7.40	5.80	2900.00	06/19/91	3100.00		
1990	06/07/90	-9.71	06/20/90	-6.85	2.85	1425.00	06/20/90	1425.00		
1989	06/07/89	1.26	06/20/89	1.31	0.06	30.00	06/09/89	100.00	06/14/89	-125.00
1988	06/07/88	-4.33	06/20/88	-1.62	2.72	1360.00	06/20/88	1360.00		
1987	06/08/87	-3.29	06/19/87	-5.10	-1.80	-900.00			06/17/87	-1135.00
1986	06/09/86	-33.60	06/20/86	-34.04	-0.45	-225.00	06/11/86	435.00	06/16/86	-295.00

Percentage Correct	93									
Average Profit on Winning Trades					1.64	818.57		Winners		14
Average Loss on Trades					-2.61	-1305.00		Losers		1
Average Net Profit Per Trade					1.35	677.00		Total trades		15
Percentage Correct	85									
Average Profit on Winning Trades					1.68	839.71		Winners		17
Average Loss on Trades					-1.62	-810.00		Losers		3
Average Net Profit Per Trade					1.18	592.25		Total trades		20

HYPOTHETICAL PERFORMANCE RESULTS HAVE MANY INHERENT LIMITATIONS, SOME OF WHICH ARE DESCRIBED BELOW. NO REPRESENTATION IS BEING MADE THAT ANY ACCOUNT WILL OR IS LIKELY TO ACHIEVE PROFITS OR LOSSES SIMILAR TO THOSE SHOWN. IN FACT, THERE ARE FREQUENTLY SHARP DIFFERENCES BETWEEN HYPOTHETICAL PERFORMANCE RESULTS AND THE ACTUAL RESULTS SUBSEQUENTLY ACHIEVED BY ANY PARTICULAR TRADING PROGRAM. ONE OF THE LIMITATIONS OF HYPOTHETICAL PERFORMANCE RESULTS IS THAT THEY ARE GENERALLY PREPARED WITH THE BENEFIT OF HINDSIGHT. IN ADDITION, HYPOTHETICAL TRADING DOES NOT INVOLVE FINANCIAL RISK, AND NO HYPOTHETICAL TRADING RECORD CAN COMPLETELY ACCOUNT FOR THE IMPACT OF FINANCIAL RISK IN ACTUAL TRADING. FOR EXAMPLE, THE ABILITY TO WITHSTAND LOSSES OR ADHERE TO A PARTICULAR TRADING PROGRAM IN SPITE OF TRADING LOSSES ARE MATERIAL POINTS WHICH CAN ALSO ADVERSELY AFFECT ACTUAL TRADING RESULTS. THERE ARE NUMEROUS OTHER FACTORS RELATED TO THE MARKETS IN GENERAL OR TO THE IMPLEMENTATION OF ANY SPECIFIC TRADING PROGRAM WHICH CANNOT BE FULLY ACCOUNTED FOR IN THE PREPARATION OF HYPOTHETICAL PERFORMANCE RESULTS AND ALL OF WHICH CAN ADVERSELY AFFECT ACTUAL TRADING RESULTS. RESULTS NOT ADJUSTED FOR COMMISSION AND SLIPPAGE.

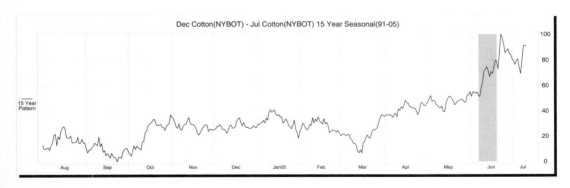

Dec Cotton(NYBOT) - Jul Cotton(NYBOT) 15 Year Seasonal(91-05)

Even though October is illiquid, it can help illustrate how and when commercial interests typically reach forward to price future needs. In fact, once the market is finished with old-crop July, the bastard October contract becomes the "whipping boy" even in spreads against true new-crop December and May, as illustrated and quantified in Figure 8-5 and in Figure 8-6, respectively.

Figure 8-5

Buy May Cotton(NYBOT) / Sell Oct Cotton(NYBOT)

Enter on approximately 06/12 - Exit on approximately 08/30

CONT YEAR	ENTRY DATE	ENTRY PRICE	EXIT DATE	EXIT PRICE	PROFIT	PROFIT AMOUNT	BEST EQUITY DATE	BEST EQUITY AMOUNT	WORST EQUITY DATE	WORST EQUITY AMOUNT
2005	06/14/04	1.39	08/30/04	2.92	1.53	765.00	06/23/04	1600.00		
2004	06/12/03	4.11	08/29/03	4.55	0.43	215.00	07/29/03	455.00	06/17/03	-420.00
2003	06/12/02	5.57	08/30/02	6.64	1.07	535.00	08/27/02	590.00		
2002	06/12/01	3.96	08/30/01	4.05	0.09	45.00	06/19/01	395.00	07/09/01	-580.00
2001	06/12/00	3.22	08/30/00	3.65	0.43	215.00	07/14/00	1030.00	06/20/00	-185.00
2000	06/14/99	0.84	08/30/99	3.23	2.39	1195.00	08/30/99	1195.00		
1999	06/12/98	-1.09	08/28/98	-0.60	0.49	245.00	08/04/98	975.00	07/08/98	-1725.00
1998	06/12/97	2.14	08/29/97	2.25	0.11	55.00	08/26/97	270.00	07/30/97	-240.00
1997	06/12/96	0.93	08/30/96	2.61	1.69	845.00	06/28/96	1215.00		
1996	06/12/95	-5.23	08/30/95	0.70	5.94	2970.00	08/30/95	2970.00	06/26/95	-455.00
1995	06/13/94	0.59	08/30/94	1.04	0.45	225.00	06/29/94	920.00	06/20/94	-290.00
1994	06/14/93	1.33	08/30/93	3.05	1.72	860.00	08/13/93	1160.00	06/21/93	-175.00
1993	06/12/92	1.15	08/28/92	-0.53	-1.70	-850.00	06/17/92	250.00	08/27/92	-1395.00
1992	06/12/91	-3.06	08/30/91	2.25	5.32	2660.00	08/12/91	3635.00	06/17/91	-315.00
1991	06/12/90	-2.79	08/30/90	-0.10	2.68	1340.00	08/17/90	1775.00	07/05/90	-685.00
1990	06/12/89	1.53	08/30/89	2.44	0.92	460.00	08/15/89	525.00	06/15/89	-370.00
1989	06/13/88	-0.76	08/30/88	-1.58	-0.81	-405.00	06/21/88	585.00	08/29/88	-575.00
1988	06/12/87	-0.59	08/28/87	1.15	1.75	875.00	08/25/87	905.00	07/29/87	-375.00
1987	06/12/86	2.08	08/29/86	3.11	1.03	515.00	08/25/86	595.00	06/18/86	-395.00
1986	06/12/85	1.50	08/30/85	1.64	0.15	75.00	08/26/85	380.00	07/24/85	-625.00

Percentage Correct	93									
Average Profit on Winning Trades					1.74	869.29		Winners		14
Average Loss on Trades					-1.70	-850.00		Losers		1
Average Net Profit Per Trade					1.51	754.67		Total trades		15
Percentage Correct	90									
Average Profit on Winning Trades					1.57	783.06		Winners		18
Average Loss on Trades					-1.26	-627.50		Losers		2
Average Net Profit Per Trade					1.28	642.00		Total trades		20

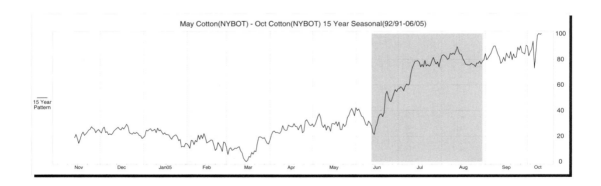

May Cotton(NYBOT) - Oct Cotton(NYBOT) 15 Year Seasonal(92/91-06/05)

15 Year Pattern

Figure 8-6

Buy Dec Cotton(NYBOT) / Sell Oct Cotton(NYBOT)

Enter on approximately 07/05 - Exit on approximately 09/04

CONT YEAR	ENTRY DATE	ENTRY PRICE	EXIT DATE	EXIT PRICE	PROFIT	PROFIT AMOUNT	BEST EQUITY DATE	BEST EQUITY AMOUNT	WORST EQUITY DATE	WORST EQUITY AMOUNT
2004	07/06/04	0.15	09/03/04	0.57	0.42	210.00	08/24/04	440.00	07/16/04	-40.00
2003	07/07/03	1.69	09/04/03	1.85	0.16	80.00	09/03/03	115.00	08/19/03	-280.00
2002	07/08/02	1.67	09/04/02	1.77	0.09	45.00	09/03/02	130.00	08/06/02	-170.00
2001	07/05/01	0.99	09/04/01	1.33	0.35	175.00	07/17/01	370.00	08/23/01	-95.00
2000	07/05/00	2.03	09/01/00	2.07	0.04	20.00	07/14/00	220.00	08/30/00	-75.00
1999	07/06/99	0.32	09/03/99	1.41	1.08	540.00	09/03/99	540.00		
1998	07/06/98	-2.63	09/04/98	0.54	3.18	1590.00	08/21/98	1600.00	07/17/98	-560.00
1997	07/07/97	0.51	09/04/97	0.16	-0.34	-170.00			08/04/97	-365.00
1996	07/08/96	0.57	09/04/96	0.71	0.13	65.00	07/15/96	195.00	07/22/96	-215.00
1995	07/05/95	-5.54	09/01/95	-0.65	4.89	2445.00	09/01/95	2445.00		
1994	07/05/94	0.00	09/02/94	-1.15	-1.16	-580.00	07/12/94	120.00	08/22/94	-870.00
1993	07/06/93	0.67	09/03/93	1.35	0.68	340.00	08/02/93	440.00	07/07/93	-90.00
1992	07/06/92	-1.59	09/04/92	-1.40	0.20	100.00	07/13/92	415.00	08/26/92	-690.00
1991	07/05/91	-2.10	09/04/91	0.45	2.56	1280.00	08/12/91	1630.00		
1990	07/05/90	-5.11	09/04/90	-0.78	4.33	2165.00	09/04/90	2165.00		
1989	07/05/89	0.37	09/01/89	0.92	0.54	270.00	08/08/89	340.00	07/07/89	-50.00
1988	07/05/88	-1.25	09/02/88	-1.50	-0.25	-125.00	08/04/88	145.00	08/19/88	-410.00
1987	07/06/87	-1.07	09/04/87	-0.45	0.61	305.00	08/27/87	445.00	07/30/87	-490.00
1986	07/07/86	0.03	09/04/86	0.78	0.75	375.00	07/30/86	535.00		
1985	07/08/85	0.20	09/04/85	0.32	0.12	60.00	08/26/85	180.00	07/23/85	-225.00

Percentage Correct		87								
Average Profit on Winning Trades					1.39	696.54		Winners		13
Average Loss on Trades					-0.75	-375.00		Losers		2
Average Net Profit Per Trade					1.11	553.67		Total trades		15
Percentage Correct		85								
Average Profit on Winning Trades					1.18	592.06		Winners		17
Average Loss on Trades					-0.58	-291.67		Losers		3
Average Net Profit Per Trade					0.92	459.50		Total trades		20

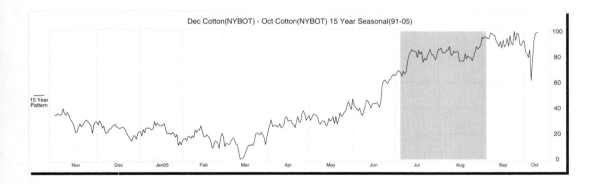

Dec Cotton(NYBOT) - Oct Cotton(NYBOT) 15 Year Seasonal(91-05)

Sugar

Sugar has always been important in international trade because it is considered a luxury item and produced in many countries. The United States is one of the few countries of the world that can raise both sugarcane and sugar beets. Although the sugar refined from each is indistinguishable, the nature and location of each type of plant are quite different.

Sugarcane, a bamboolike grass that grows in tropical and semitropical climes, is harvested fall through spring. Hawaii, Louisiana, and Florida are the primary US producing states, with Brazil, India, and Cuba large international cane producers. Sugar beets are grown in temperate zones, including California, Minnesota, Washington, with northern Europe and Russia among the largest world producers. Beets are planted in early spring and harvested before the first winter freeze.

Because most of the world's sugar is consumed in the same country in which it is grown, perhaps only 20% is available for trade in the free market. This sugar is commonly referred to as world sugar and trades at NYBOT as world sugar #11 (not to be confused with sugar #14, which is subsidized US domestic sugar).

Figure 8-7: October Sugar Seasonal Pattern

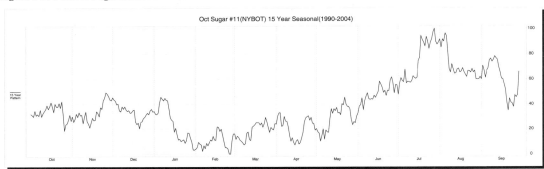

Because both US cane and beet harvest begin in autumn, the crop marketing year for sugar runs September-August. Prices tend to decline into the end of cane harvest in February/March. By the time beet planting gets underway in early spring, prices begin to rise into their seasonal peak in July/August. By then, however, the market begins to anticipate new supply from another Northern Hemisphere harvest.

Figure 8-8: Jul/Oct Sugar Seasonal Pattern

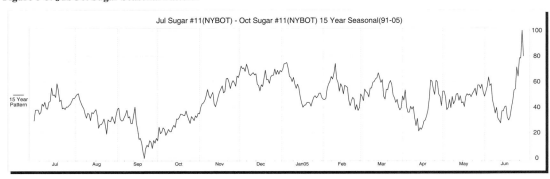

Figure 8-9: Sugar Spread Strategies

![Moore Research Center, Inc. logo]				Sugar Spreads				
Seasonal Strategy	Entry Date	Exit Date	Win Pct	Win Yrs	Loss Years	Total Years	Average Profit	Ave Pft Per Day
Buy May Sugar #11(NYBOT)	2/25	3/11	80	12	3	15	255	17
Sell "Red" May Sugar #11(NYBOT)			80	16	4	20	256	17
Buy Mar Sugar #11(NYBOT)	3/18	4/16	80	12	3	15	276	9
Sell May Sugar #11(NYBOT)			80	16	4	20	273	9

The behavior exhibited by old-crop July against new-crop October (Figure 8-8) suggests why so few spreads in sugar can withstand seasonal scrutiny. Longer-term seasonal trends tend to be replaced by short-term swings. Those swings that have shown a degree of reliabilityactually pivot around the end of cane harvest and the beginning of beet planting. The first of the strategies in the table above is a bull spread between sugar deliverable after one cane harvest and that after the next, between old-crop May and new-crop "Red" May, that most likely reflects a post-harvest recovery from a supply glut. The second strategy, a bear spread between the new-crop March and old-crop May, coincides with planting. A close look at historical detail, however, suggests both hover near the margin of respectability.

Figure 8-10: Monthly May/"Red" May Sugar Spread

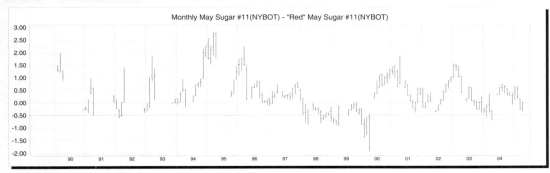

Figure 8-11: Monthly New-crop Mar/Old-crop May Sugar

Figure 8-12

Buy May Sugar #11(NYBOT) / Sell "Red" May Sugar #11(NYBOT)

Enter on approximately 02/25 - Exit on approximately 03/11

CONT YEAR	ENTRY DATE	ENTRY PRICE	EXIT DATE	EXIT PRICE	PROFIT	PROFIT AMOUNT	BEST EQUITY DATE	BEST EQUITY AMOUNT	WORST EQUITY DATE	WORST EQUITY AMOUNT
2005	02/25/05	0.14	03/11/05	0.03	-0.11	-123.20	02/28/05	89.60	03/07/05	-280.00
2004	02/25/04	-0.12	03/11/04	0.29	0.43	481.60	03/11/04	481.60	03/03/04	-112.00
2003	02/25/03	1.26	03/11/03	1.28	0.02	22.40	02/28/03	179.20	03/10/03	-22.40
2002	02/25/02	-0.11	03/11/02	0.17	0.29	324.80	03/11/02	324.80		
2001	02/26/01	1.06	03/09/01	1.13	0.07	78.40	03/05/01	257.60	02/27/01	-100.80
2000	02/25/00	-1.33	03/10/00	-0.98	0.36	403.20	03/10/00	403.20	02/28/00	-44.80
1999	02/25/99	-0.66	03/11/99	-0.79	-0.13	-145.60	02/26/99	22.40	03/04/99	-302.40
1998	02/25/98	-0.41	03/11/98	-0.80	-0.39	-436.80	03/02/98	11.20	03/09/98	-470.40
1997	02/25/97	0.22	03/11/97	0.36	0.15	168.00	03/10/97	201.60	03/04/97	-44.80
1996	02/26/96	1.59	03/11/96	1.97	0.37	414.40	03/11/96	414.40	03/01/96	-134.40
1995	02/27/95	2.12	03/10/95	2.36	0.24	268.80	03/10/95	268.80	02/28/95	-0.00
1994	02/25/94	0.25	03/11/94	0.89	0.65	728.00	03/11/94	728.00		
1993	02/25/93	1.00	03/11/93	1.08	0.07	78.40	03/02/93	123.20	03/09/93	-179.20
1992	02/25/92	-0.58	03/11/92	-0.33	0.25	280.00	03/10/92	291.20		
1991	02/25/91	-0.26	03/11/91	0.87	1.14	1276.80	03/08/91	1366.40		
1990	02/26/90	1.33	03/09/90	1.93	0.60	672.00	03/09/90	672.00	03/01/90	-123.20
1989	02/27/89	0.41	03/10/89	0.56	0.14	156.80	03/09/89	358.40	03/03/89	-224.00
1988	02/25/88	-0.12	03/11/88	-0.15	-0.02	-22.40	03/03/88	100.80	02/26/88	-235.20
1987	02/25/87	-0.83	03/11/87	-0.66	0.17	190.40	03/02/87	392.00		
1986	02/25/86	-1.26	03/11/86	-1.00	0.27	302.40	03/04/86	324.80	02/27/86	-11.20

Percentage Correct	80									
Average Profit on Winning Trades					0.34	377.07		Winners		12
Average Loss on Trades					-0.21	-235.20		Losers		3
Average Net Profit Per Trade					0.23	254.61		Total trades		15
Percentage Correct	80									
Average Profit on Winning Trades					0.33	365.40		Winners		16
Average Loss on Trades					-0.16	-182.00		Losers		4
Average Net Profit Per Trade					0.23	255.92		Total trades		20

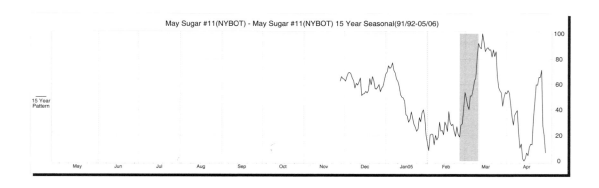

May Sugar #11(NYBOT) - May Sugar #11(NYBOT) 15 Year Seasonal(91/92-05/06)

15 Year Pattern

Figure 8-13

Buy Mar Sugar #11(NYBOT) / Sell May Sugar #11(NYBOT)

Enter on approximately 03/18 - Exit on approximately 04/16

CONT YEAR	ENTRY DATE	ENTRY PRICE	EXIT DATE	EXIT PRICE	PROFIT	PROFIT AMOUNT	BEST EQUITY DATE	BEST EQUITY AMOUNT	WORST EQUITY DATE	WORST EQUITY AMOUNT
2006	03/18/05	0.25	04/15/05	0.33	0.08	89.60	03/28/05	156.80		
2005	03/18/04	-0.18	04/16/04	0.46	0.66	739.20	04/13/04	795.20		
2004	03/18/03	-0.88	04/16/03	-0.50	0.39	436.80	04/15/03	537.60	03/21/03	-134.40
2003	03/18/02	-0.29	04/16/02	-0.25	0.05	56.00	04/04/02	291.20	03/26/02	-44.80
2002	03/19/01	-0.87	04/16/01	-0.88	0.00	0.00	03/30/01	369.60	03/20/01	-22.40
2001	03/20/00	0.85	04/14/00	0.50	-0.34	-380.80			04/10/00	-481.60
2000	03/18/99	0.76	04/16/99	0.79	0.03	33.60	04/13/99	100.80	03/31/99	-56.00
1999	03/18/98	0.46	04/16/98	0.49	0.03	33.60	03/30/98	44.80	03/31/98	-492.80
1998	03/18/97	-0.31	04/16/97	-0.30	0.00	0.00	03/19/97	67.20	04/09/97	-302.40
1997	03/18/96	-2.00	04/16/96	-0.73	1.27	1422.40	04/16/96	1422.40	03/20/96	-156.80
1996	03/20/95	-2.00	04/13/95	-1.68	0.32	358.40	04/13/95	358.40	03/28/95	-716.80
1995	03/18/94	-0.75	04/15/94	-0.14	0.62	694.40	04/12/94	974.40	03/24/94	-67.20
1994	03/18/93	-1.50	04/16/93	-0.31	1.19	1332.80	04/14/93	1556.80	03/22/93	-324.80
1993	03/18/92	0.26	04/16/92	-0.82	-1.09	-1220.80	03/26/92	44.80	04/08/92	-1512.00
1992	03/18/91	-0.69	04/16/91	-0.21	0.49	548.80	04/11/91	571.20		
1991	03/19/90	-1.60	04/16/90	-0.81	0.80	896.00	04/16/90	896.00	03/20/90	-33.60
1990	03/20/89	-0.67	04/14/89	-0.43	0.24	268.80	03/23/89	470.40	04/03/89	-616.00
1989	03/18/88	-0.16	04/15/88	0.08	0.24	268.80	04/14/88	425.60	03/28/88	-67.20
1988	03/18/87	0.62	04/16/87	0.81	0.19	212.80	04/10/87	280.00	03/19/87	-33.60
1987	03/18/86	0.93	04/16/86	0.63	-0.30	-336.00	03/20/86	44.80	04/07/86	-873.60

Percentage Correct	80									
Average Profit on Winning Trades					0.43	478.80		Winners		12
Average Loss on Trades					-0.48	-533.87		Losers		3
Average Net Profit Per Trade					0.25	276.27		Total trades		15
Percentage Correct	80									
Average Profit on Winning Trades					0.41	462.00		Winners		16
Average Loss on Trades					-0.43	-484.40		Losers		4
Average Net Profit Per Trade					0.24	272.72		Total trades		20

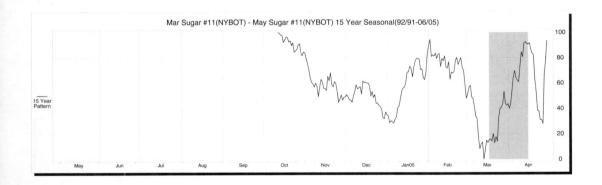

Mar Sugar #11(NYBOT) - May Sugar #11(NYBOT) 15 Year Seasonal(92/91-06/05)

Coffee

Historians think that in the 1600s — even before lattes and espressos! — coffee was already the main nonalcoholic drink of choice in most of Europe and the Americas. It is one of the most internationally traded commodities because production is concentrated in tropical and subtropical climates but consumption is heaviest in the United States, Canada, and Europe. Before World War II, coffee was imported primarily from South and Central America, but several African countries have since become major producers.

Brazil is by far the world's largest producer and exporter, with perhaps 35-40% of the world's market. Because the Brazilian coffee industry's emphasis has been mostly on quantity over quality, however, her coffee is not deliverable against NYBOT futures. Nonetheless, such significant production has enormous influence on world prices. (As an interesting side note, NYBOT coffee is one of the few US contracts with delivery points outside US borders — the Ports of Antwerp and of Bremen/Hamburg.)

Figure 8-14: Cash Coffee Seasonal Pattern

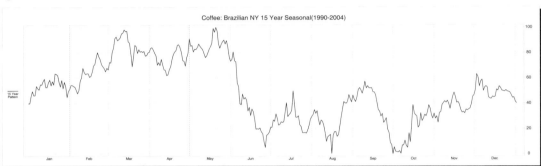

Perhaps because the largest consuming nations are north of the equator, and thus consumption is greatest during the Northern Hemisphere's cooler months of October through March, the crop marketing year is October-September. Thus, December is the first new-crop contract. Note how prices tend to remain high or even rise early in the calendar year when consumption is high. As the cooler temperatures of autumn enter Brazil's coffee-growing regions in May, the market builds a risk premium against the occasional freeze. But Brazil's harvest begins in June and continues through July and August — summer north of the equator when consumption is least. Prices can enjoy a modest post-harvest recovery into September but then tend to fall again into the end of the crop year.

Figure 8-15: New-crop May/Old-crop Sep Coffee Seasonal

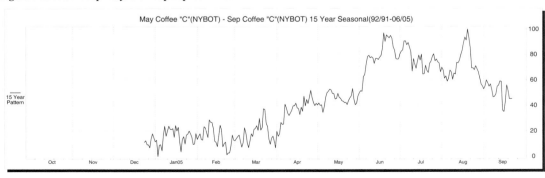

Figure 8-16: Coffee Spread Strategies

Moore Research Center, Inc.							Coffee Spreads	
Seasonal Strategy	Entry Date	Exit Date	Win Pct	Win Yrs	Loss Years	Total Years	Average Profit	Ave Pft Per Day
Buy May Coffee(NYBOT) Sell Sep Coffee(NYBOT)	5/22	6/10	93 95	14 19	1 1	15 20	906 818	45 41
Buy Dec Coffee(NYBOT) Sell Jul Coffee(NYBOT)	5/29	6/20	80 80	12 16	3 4	15 20	1496 1091	65 47
Buy Jul Coffee(NYBOT) Sell Dec Coffee(NYBOT)	8/29	11/21	80 85	12 17	3 3	15 20	654 923	8 11

The seasonal pattern for new-crop May against old-crop September helps illustrate how the market, but especially old-crop, suffers at the May/June confluence of Brazil's new harvest and consumption's decline. The first two strategies in the table above quantify the collapse of old-crop to new-crop at the prospect of new supply amid withdrawn demand. The dynamic is exacerbated in futures by the approach of deliveries against the July contract. Without a concurrent freeze in Brazil, speculators with long positions in nearby, most-active July run — not walk! — for the exits. But also note that the enormous move in 1997 was liquidation after a freeze. Although the May/September strategy has better numbers, liquidity concerns make the December/July spread more tradable.

The last strategy in the table reflects the market's efforts to spread supply throughout the year until next harvest by helping pay for storage. But this strategy also tends to be delivery-driven, with the best part of the move often coming in the final weeks before First Notice Day for new-crop December.

Figure 8-17: Monthly New-crop Dec/Old-crop Jul Coffee

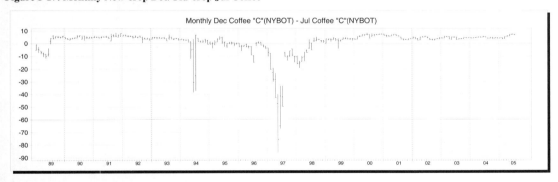

Figure 8-18: Monthly Jul/Dec Coffee (Same Crop Year)

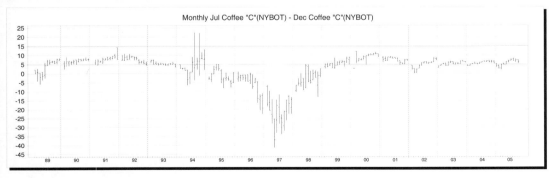

Figure 8-19

Buy May Coffee(NYBOT) / Sell Sep Coffee(NYBOT)

Enter on approximately 05/22 - Exit on approximately 06/10

CONT YEAR	ENTRY DATE	ENTRY PRICE	EXIT DATE	EXIT PRICE	PROFIT	PROFIT AMOUNT	BEST EQUITY DATE	BEST EQUITY AMOUNT	WORST EQUITY DATE	WORST EQUITY AMOUNT
2006	05/23/05	8.19	06/10/05	8.05	-0.15	-56.25	06/01/05	150.00	06/06/05	-75.00
2005	05/24/04	6.79	06/10/04	7.00	0.20	75.00	06/08/04	206.25	05/28/04	-112.50
2004	05/22/03	6.20	06/10/03	7.35	1.15	431.25	05/29/03	525.00		
2003	05/22/02	6.30	06/10/02	6.54	0.25	93.75	06/07/02	150.00	05/29/02	-206.25
2002	05/22/01	10.00	06/08/01	10.10	0.10	37.50	05/31/01	168.75		
2001	05/22/00	8.45	06/09/00	10.90	2.45	918.75	06/05/00	1256.25		
2000	05/24/99	3.50	06/10/99	4.75	1.25	468.75	06/09/99	506.25	06/03/99	-300.00
1999	05/22/98	-11.75	06/10/98	-2.15	9.60	3600.00	06/10/98	3600.00		
1998	05/22/97	-54.29	06/10/97	-39.00	15.30	5737.50	06/10/97	5737.50	05/29/97	-8512.50
1997	05/22/96	-5.59	06/10/96	-4.00	1.60	600.00	06/03/96	1500.00		
1996	05/22/95	4.90	06/09/95	5.34	0.45	168.75	06/07/95	468.75		
1995	05/23/94	-9.40	06/10/94	-6.14	3.25	1218.75	05/26/94	2925.00		
1994	05/24/93	6.40	06/10/93	6.79	0.40	150.00	06/08/93	225.00		
1993	05/22/92	9.70	06/10/92	9.99	0.30	112.50	06/08/92	150.00	05/26/92	-412.50
1992	05/22/91	8.10	06/10/91	8.20	0.10	37.50	06/07/91	150.00	06/05/91	-206.25
1991	05/22/90	6.64	06/08/90	7.00	0.36	135.00	05/31/90	172.50	05/24/90	-146.25
1990	05/22/89	-4.65	06/09/89	-3.98	0.68	255.00	06/07/89	1241.25	05/30/89	-596.25
1989	05/23/88	1.40	06/10/88	2.56	1.16	435.00	06/02/88	453.75	05/31/88	-120.00
1988	05/22/87	3.31	06/10/87	4.53	1.21	453.75	06/09/87	641.25	05/28/87	-318.75
1987	05/22/86	9.06	06/10/86	13.05	3.98	1492.50	05/30/86	3592.50	06/05/86	-198.75

Percentage Correct	93									
Average Profit on Winning Trades					2.60	975.00		Winners		14
Average Loss on Trades					-0.15	-56.25		Losers		1
Average Net Profit Per Trade					2.42	906.25		Total trades		15
Percentage Correct	95									
Average Profit on Winning Trades					2.30	864.28		Winners		19
Average Loss on Trades					-0.15	-56.25		Losers		1
Average Net Profit Per Trade					2.18	818.25		Total trades		20

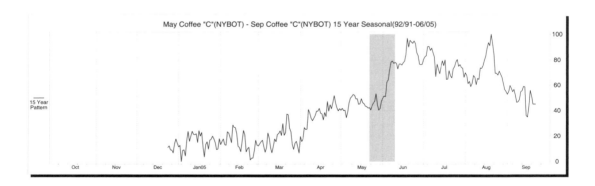

May Coffee "C"(NYBOT) - Sep Coffee "C"(NYBOT) 15 Year Seasonal(92/91-06/05)

Figure 8-20

Buy Dec Coffee(NYBOT) / Sell Jul Coffee(NYBOT)

Enter on approximately 05/29 - Exit on approximately 06/20

CONT YEAR	ENTRY DATE	ENTRY PRICE	EXIT DATE	EXIT PRICE	PROFIT	PROFIT AMOUNT	BEST EQUITY DATE	BEST EQUITY AMOUNT	WORST EQUITY DATE	WORST EQUITY AMOUNT
2005	05/31/05	6.95	06/20/05	7.20	0.25	93.75	06/20/05	93.75	06/06/05	-75.00
2004	06/01/04	4.89	06/18/04	5.59	0.70	262.50	06/18/04	262.50		
2003	05/29/03	5.20	06/20/03	5.15	-0.05	-18.75			06/16/03	-281.25
2002	05/29/02	4.95	06/20/02	5.70	0.75	281.25	06/18/02	393.75		
2001	05/29/01	6.85	06/20/01	7.19	0.35	131.25	06/20/01	131.25	06/15/01	-281.25
2000	05/30/00	6.44	06/20/00	7.50	1.05	393.75	06/13/00	487.50		
1999	06/01/99	2.65	06/18/99	3.64	1.00	375.00	06/17/99	375.00	06/15/99	-2587.50
1998	05/29/98	-7.40	06/19/98	2.59	10.00	3750.00	06/19/98	3750.00		
1997	05/29/97	-86.00	06/20/97	-39.44	46.55	17456.25	06/18/97	19687.50		
1996	05/29/96	-2.54	06/20/96	-7.10	-4.55	-1706.25	05/30/96	131.25	06/18/96	-2081.25
1995	05/30/95	5.50	06/20/95	1.94	-3.55	-1331.25			06/15/95	-1406.25
1994	05/31/94	-5.20	06/20/94	-0.29	4.90	1837.50	06/20/94	1837.50	06/13/94	-1725.00
1993	06/01/93	4.45	06/18/93	4.75	0.30	112.50	06/17/93	187.50	06/03/93	-18.75
1992	05/29/92	4.65	06/19/92	6.29	1.65	618.75	06/19/92	618.75		
1991	05/29/91	5.25	06/20/91	5.75	0.50	187.50	06/19/91	318.75	05/31/91	-56.25
1990	05/29/90	4.84	06/20/90	6.55	1.70	637.50	06/20/90	637.50	06/05/90	-187.50
1989	05/30/89	-10.95	06/20/89	-8.14	2.82	1057.50	06/13/89	2666.25		
1988	05/31/88	2.50	06/20/88	2.68	0.18	67.50	06/15/88	555.00	06/09/88	-296.25
1987	05/29/87	1.79	06/19/87	4.32	2.54	952.50	06/17/87	1312.50		
1986	05/29/86	15.59	06/20/86	6.68	-8.90	-3337.50	05/30/86	195.00	06/18/86	-4815.00

Percentage Correct	80									
Average Profit on Winning Trades					5.67	2125.00		Winners		12
Average Loss on Trades					-2.72	-1018.75		Losers		3
Average Net Profit Per Trade					3.99	1496.25		Total trades		15
Percentage Correct	80									
Average Profit on Winning Trades					4.70	1763.44		Winners		16
Average Loss on Trades					-4.26	-1598.44		Losers		4
Average Net Profit Per Trade					2.91	1091.06		Total trades		20

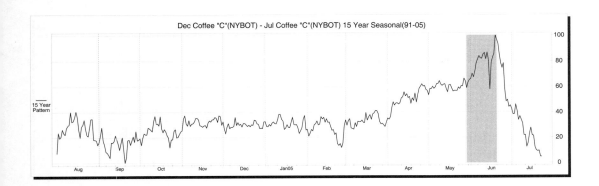

Dec Coffee "C"(NYBOT) - Jul Coffee "C"(NYBOT) 15 Year Seasonal(91-05)

Figure 8-21

Buy Jul Coffee(NYBOT) / Sell Dec Coffee(NYBOT)

Enter on approximately 08/29 - Exit on approximately 11/21

CONT YEAR	ENTRY DATE	ENTRY PRICE	EXIT DATE	EXIT PRICE	PROFIT	PROFIT AMOUNT	BEST EQUITY DATE	BEST EQUITY AMOUNT	WORST EQUITY DATE	WORST EQUITY AMOUNT
2005	08/30/04	6.50	11/19/04	6.90	0.40	150.00	10/04/04	206.25	11/15/04	-300.00
2004	08/29/03	5.60	11/21/03	7.05	1.45	543.75	11/21/03	543.75	09/08/03	-206.25
2003	08/29/02	5.59	11/21/02	8.20	2.60	975.00	11/18/02	1125.00	09/04/02	-93.75
2002	08/29/01	7.00	11/21/01	7.45	0.45	168.75	11/21/01	168.75	09/24/01	-862.50
2001	08/29/00	10.29	11/21/00	11.00	0.70	262.50	11/16/00	543.75	09/12/00	-150.00
2000	08/30/99	6.34	11/19/99	8.54	2.20	825.00	11/18/99	900.00	10/13/99	-1012.50
1999	08/31/98	-4.84	11/20/98	0.50	5.35	2006.25	09/14/98	2550.00	11/03/98	-3037.50
1998	08/29/97	-27.45	11/21/97	-18.90	8.55	3206.25	11/04/97	5775.00	09/04/97	-1668.75
1997	08/29/96	-6.29	11/21/96	-12.09	-5.80	-2175.00	09/19/96	1387.50	11/07/96	-5268.75
1996	08/29/95	-3.19	11/21/95	-5.59	-2.40	-900.00	09/26/95	1368.75	11/14/95	-1668.75
1995	08/29/94	0.09	11/21/94	11.65	11.55	4331.25	10/10/94	8287.50	10/17/94	-450.00
1994	08/30/93	4.84	11/19/93	5.95	1.10	412.50	11/17/93	618.75	09/15/93	-262.50
1993	08/31/92	8.29	11/20/92	6.00	-2.30	-862.50			09/22/92	-1181.25
1992	08/29/91	8.29	11/21/91	9.95	1.65	618.75	11/18/91	975.00	09/24/91	-281.25
1991	08/29/90	7.65	11/21/90	8.29	0.65	243.75	11/09/90	525.00	09/18/90	-300.00
1990	08/29/89	5.03	11/21/89	7.64	2.62	982.50	11/17/89	1233.75		
1989	08/29/88	-1.48	11/21/88	0.00	1.50	562.50	10/12/88	1650.00	09/07/88	-603.75
1988	08/31/87	5.82	11/20/87	6.97	1.14	427.50	11/04/87	828.75	09/21/87	-401.25
1987	08/29/86	-6.36	11/21/86	4.72	11.09	4158.75	11/17/86	5017.50	10/07/86	-4188.75
1986	08/29/85	2.64	11/21/85	9.37	6.74	2527.50	11/21/85	2527.50	10/28/85	-2186.25

Percentage Correct	80					
Average Profit on Winning Trades				3.05	1145.31	Winners	12
Average Loss on Trades				-3.50	-1312.50	Losers	3
Average Net Profit Per Trade				1.74	653.75	Total trades	15
Percentage Correct	85					
Average Profit on Winning Trades				3.51	1317.79	Winners	17
Average Loss on Trades				-3.50	-1312.50	Losers	3
Average Net Profit Per Trade				2.46	923.25	Total trades	20

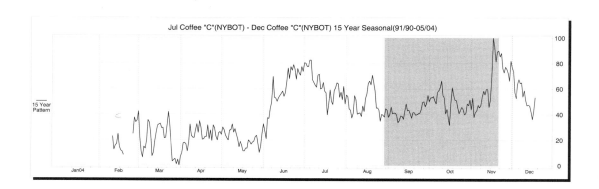

Jul Coffee "C"(NYBOT) - Dec Coffee "C"(NYBOT) 15 Year Seasonal(91/90-05/04)

Cocoa

A tropical plant, cocoa was originally cultivated in Central and South America and introduced to European explorers in the sixteenth century. Not until the twentieth century did Ivory Coast, Ghana, Nigeria, Malaysia, and Papua New Guinea also become major producers. Along with Brazil, the largest consumers are the United States and countries of northern Europe.

Figure 8-22: Cash Cocoa Seasonal Pattern

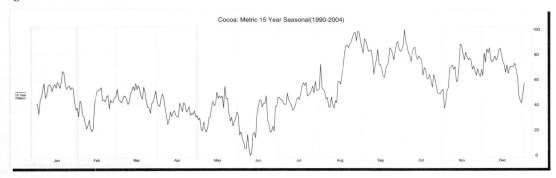

Cocoa beans ripen from October through August and are harvested in two crops. The main crop, which produces about 80% of world production, runs from October through March. The mid-crop accounts for the balance and runs May to August. Thus, the crop marketing year runs October-September, with December the first new-crop contract.

Prices tend to peak between late August and early October, after mid-crop and before the main crop harvest. Once new-crop harvest begins, the cash market tends to remain under pressure into the warmer weather and large supplies of June. But it often then makes its seasonal low and recovers as the end of harvest approaches.

Figure 8-23: New-crop March/Old-crop July Cocoa Pattern

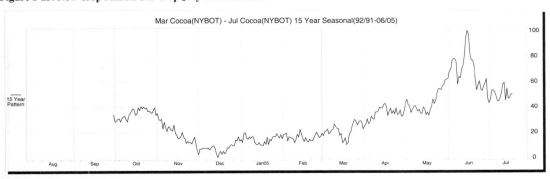

Figure 8-24: Cocoa Spread Strategy

Moore Research Center, Inc.	Cocoa Spread							
Seasonal Strategy	Entry Date	Exit Date	Win Pct	Win Yrs	Loss Years	Total Years	Average Profit	Ave Pft Per Day
Buy Mar Cocoa(NYBOT)	5/19	6/14	93	14	1	15	259	10
Sell Jul Cocoa(NYBOT)			90	18	2	20	276	10

Figure 8-25

Buy Mar Cocoa(NYBOT) / Sell Jul Cocoa(NYBOT)

Enter on approximately 05/19 - Exit on approximately 06/14

CONT YEAR	ENTRY DATE	ENTRY PRICE	EXIT DATE	EXIT PRICE	PROFIT	PROFIT AMOUNT	BEST EQUITY DATE	BEST EQUITY AMOUNT	WORST EQUITY DATE	WORST EQUITY AMOUNT
2006	05/19/05	65.00	06/14/05	67.00	2.00	20.00	06/01/05	140.00		
2005	05/19/04	37.00	06/14/04	51.00	14.00	140.00	06/07/04	140.00	05/28/04	-40.00
2004	05/19/03	-64.00	06/13/03	-9.00	55.00	550.00	05/29/03	690.00		
2003	05/20/02	-128.00	06/14/02	9.00	137.00	1370.00	06/14/02	1370.00		
2002	05/21/01	-23.00	06/14/01	24.00	47.00	470.00	06/04/01	580.00		
2001	05/19/00	95.00	06/14/00	103.00	8.00	80.00	06/14/00	80.00	06/08/00	-50.00
2000	05/19/99	116.00	06/14/99	83.00	-33.00	-330.00	05/20/99	10.00	06/11/99	-360.00
1999	05/19/98	68.00	06/12/98	100.00	32.00	320.00	06/12/98	320.00	05/20/98	-10.00
1998	05/19/97	82.00	06/13/97	108.00	26.00	260.00	06/06/97	310.00		
1997	05/20/96	51.00	06/14/96	59.00	8.00	80.00	06/04/96	120.00	06/07/96	-160.00
1996	05/19/95	92.00	06/14/95	104.00	12.00	120.00	06/06/95	170.00	05/31/95	-40.00
1995	05/19/94	96.00	06/14/94	99.00	3.00	30.00	06/14/94	30.00	05/23/94	-410.00
1994	05/19/93	100.00	06/14/93	117.00	17.00	170.00	06/14/93	170.00		
1993	05/19/92	135.00	06/12/92	155.00	20.00	200.00	06/11/92	210.00		
1992	05/20/91	109.00	06/14/91	150.00	41.00	410.00	06/14/91	410.00	05/31/91	-40.00
1991	05/21/90	58.00	06/14/90	89.00	31.00	310.00	06/14/90	310.00	05/22/90	-50.00
1990	05/19/89	-44.00	06/14/89	73.00	117.00	1170.00	06/02/89	1300.00	05/22/89	-110.00
1989	05/19/88	68.00	06/14/88	84.00	16.00	160.00	06/08/88	320.00		
1988	05/19/87	98.00	06/12/87	87.00	-11.00	-110.00	05/26/87	120.00	06/12/87	-110.00
1987	05/19/86	154.00	06/13/86	164.00	10.00	100.00	06/13/86	100.00	05/23/86	-140.00

Percentage Correct		93								
Average Profit on Winning Trades					30.14	301.43		Winners		14
Average Loss on Trades					-33.00	-330.00		Losers		1
Average Net Profit Per Trade					25.93	259.33		Total trades		15
Percentage Correct		90								
Average Profit on Winning Trades					33.11	331.11		Winners		18
Average Loss on Trades					-22.00	-220.00		Losers		2
Average Net Profit Per Trade					27.60	276.00		Total trades		20

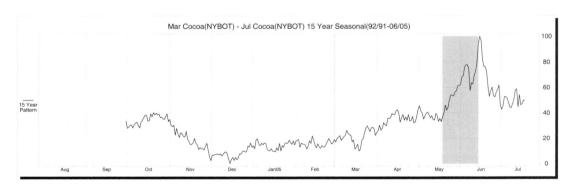

Mar Cocoa(NYBOT) - Jul Cocoa(NYBOT) 15 Year Seasonal(92/91-06/05)

Cocoa spreads tend to exhibit few tradable seasonal trends except for regular liquidation at the approach of deliveries. The typical seasonal low during June in the cash market has tended to coincide with the most prominent of these seasonal moves in futures — driven by liquidation of long July futures to avoid delivery. The average move even in this spread has usually been modest, but so have any drawdowns.

Rough Rice

An annual cereal grain, rice is thought to have been cultivated in China for 5,000 years and has been a food staple for most of the world's population. It grows in climates ranging from temperate to tropical but thrives in sunny, warm, and moist conditions. China and India are the world's largest producers, followed by several other Asian countries, Brazil, and the United States. Arkansas accounts for perhaps a third of US production.

Figure 8-26: November Rough Rice Seasonal Pattern

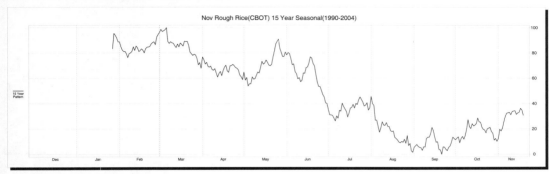

Although the CBOT specifies no crop year for its margin requirements, the USDA considers the marketing year for rice to run August-July. US harvest activity is perhaps most intense in September.

Figure 8-27: Sep/March Rough Rice Seasonal Pattern

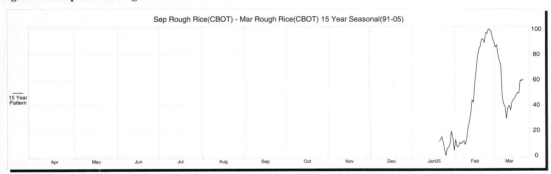

Figure 8-28: Rough Rice Spread Strategy

Moore Research Center, Inc.	Rough Rice Spread							
Seasonal Strategy	Entry Date	Exit Date	Win Pct	Win Yrs	Loss Years	Total Years	Average Profit	Ave Pft Per Day
Buy Sep Rough Rice(CBOT)	1/31	2/25	93	14	1	15	459	18
Sell Mar Rough Rice(CBOT)			95	18	1	19	557	21

The spread that has held up best over the years is this new-crop/old-crop spread that has taken advantage of speculative longs liquidating March contracts to avoid deliveries. Note (in Figure 8-29) how minimal any daily closing drawdowns have been in all but one year.

Figure 8-29

Buy Sep Rough Rice(CBOT) / Sell Mar Rough Rice(CBOT)

Enter on approximately 01/31 - Exit on approximately 02/25

CONT YEAR	ENTRY DATE	ENTRY PRICE	EXIT DATE	EXIT PRICE	PROFIT	PROFIT AMOUNT	BEST EQUITY DATE	BEST EQUITY AMOUNT	WORST EQUITY DATE	WORST EQUITY AMOUNT
2005	01/31/05	0.33	02/25/05	0.49	0.16	320.00	02/23/05	410.00	02/10/05	-220.00
2004	02/02/04	0.00	02/25/04	-0.84	-0.84	-1680.00	02/05/04	80.00	02/24/04	-1700.00
2003	01/31/03	0.95	02/25/03	1.10	0.15	290.00	02/20/03	400.00	02/05/03	-90.00
2002	01/31/02	0.64	02/25/02	0.64	0.01	10.00	02/22/02	50.00	02/12/02	-70.00
2001	01/31/01	0.29	02/23/01	0.33	0.03	60.00	02/01/01	150.00		
2000	01/31/00	0.92	02/25/00	1.35	0.43	860.00	02/22/00	920.00	02/10/00	-120.00
1999	02/01/99	-0.19	02/25/99	-0.15	0.05	90.00	02/25/99	90.00	02/09/99	-200.00
1998	02/02/98	-0.70	02/25/98	-0.59	0.11	210.00	02/11/98	390.00	02/03/98	-40.00
1997	01/31/97	-2.32	02/25/97	-1.81	0.52	1030.00	02/10/97	1390.00		
1996	01/31/96	-0.06	02/23/96	0.22	0.29	580.00	02/08/96	620.00		
1995	01/31/95	0.41	02/24/95	0.51	0.10	200.00	02/17/95	280.00		
1994	01/31/94	-2.40	02/25/94	-0.55	1.85	3700.00	02/25/94	3700.00		
1993	02/01/93	0.56	02/25/93	0.70	0.15	300.00	02/24/93	420.00	02/03/93	-40.00
1992	01/31/92	-0.30	02/25/92	0.01	0.33	660.00	02/25/92	660.00	02/06/92	-460.00
1991	01/31/91	-0.28	02/25/91	-0.16	0.13	260.00	02/20/91	320.00	02/04/91	-160.00
1990	01/31/90	-0.50	02/23/90	0.12	0.63	1260.00	02/22/90	1300.00		
1989	01/31/89	0.30	02/24/89	0.60	0.31	620.00	02/21/89	640.00		
1988	02/01/88	-2.50	02/25/88	-1.71	0.79	1580.00	02/25/88	1580.00		
1987	02/02/87	0.00	02/25/87	0.12	0.12	240.00	02/25/87	240.00	02/06/87	-120.00

Percentage Correct		93								
Average Profit on Winning Trades					0.31	612.14		Winners		14
Average Loss on Trades					-0.84	-1680.00		Losers		1
Average Net Profit Per Trade					0.23	459.33		Total trades		15
Percentage Correct		95								
Average Profit on Winning Trades					0.34	681.67		Winners		18
Average Loss on Trades					-0.84	-1680.00		Losers		1
Average Net Profit Per Trade					0.28	557.37		Total trades		19

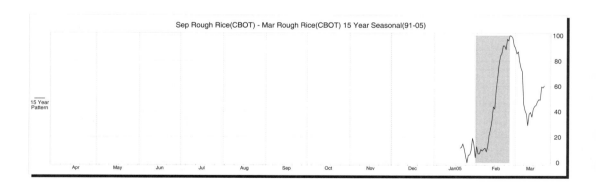

Sep Rough Rice(CBOT) - Mar Rough Rice(CBOT) 15 Year Seasonal(91-05)

Orange Juice

Oranges are grown in several countries, with Brazil and the United States the top producers. The rising popularity of frozen concentrated juice after World War II prompted US orange and juice production both to increase significantly.

Figure 8-30

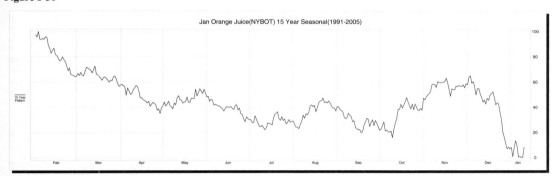

California, Texas, and Arizona are major producers, but Florida is by far the largest. The USDA crop year runs December-November, production in Florida running from January through June with a short break by early March. The only pattern of real significance is the tendency for price to rise into November and then to decline as production progresses. The rise into November anticipates the nadir in old-crop supply going into Florida winter — with its potential for crop-damaging frosts and killer freezes.

Figure 8-31

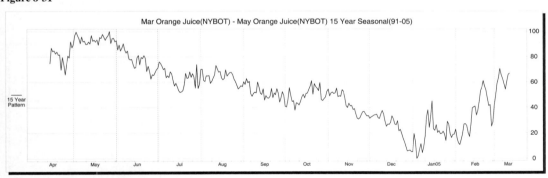

Bear spreads tend to predominate as the market anticipates the beginning of a new production season in January. Thereafter, bull spreads tend to run modestly into each successive delivery period. Despite the seasonal patterns, however, spreads in orange juice have not been able to withstand 20 years of scrutiny with a dependable degree of reliability.

Lumber

Forest products are used in construction, furniture, packaging, and paper products. Among those commonly used in construction is dimensional lumber, especially two-by-fours. Primary US forest regions are the Pacific Northwest, Rocky Mountain, and Southern.

Figure 8-32: Cash Lumber Seasonal Pattern

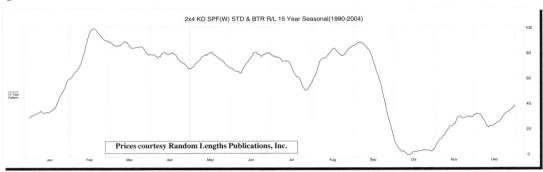

Price patterns in lumber are mostly a function of demand, with the construction season creating a seasonal bulge. Price remains well supported throughout summer. But when the season ends in September, demand collapses. Prices typically plunge into October/November with little retail interest. But the approach of winter in the Pacific Northwest and Rocky Mountains, which slows timber harvest right when inventories are lowest, usually sets the seasonal low. From there, large developers and the wholesale industry begin to price and accumulate inventory for the next season. An old saying by lumber traders goes, "In by Thanksgiving, out by Valentine's Day" — with the process of accumulation continuing into mid February. Once inventories are built, consumption soon takes over. But better weather for harvesting timber helps maintain supply.

Figure 8-33: Mar/Jul Lumber Seasonal Pattern

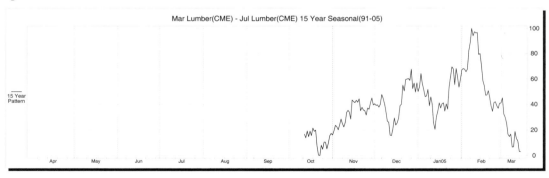

Lumber spreads generally exhibit little in the way of seasonal trends. However, this March/July bull spread reflects the process of accumulation into February. The market also generally prefers bull spreads with July on the long side until June, when better weather increases timber harvest so that fresh supply competes with inventories. Spreads with long September tend to run higher from July into deliveries as the market attempts to ensure supply through late-season projects. The collapse thereafter into September/October is then reflected by pressure on November versus deferred contracts. Except for such short bursts, however, lumber spreads tend to exhibit little in the way of dependable seasonal trends.

Chapter 9: Forex

Late in World Ward II, leaders of the Western world met in Bretton Woods, New Hampshire (USA), and created a new international monetary system meant to cope with economic and financial problems resulting from the Great Depression and the war. The so-called Bretton Woods agreement valued the US dollar against gold and then called on the world's central banks to keep the exchange rates of their own currencies closely fixed to the value of the US dollar.

For years the agreement remained effective and exchange rates stable. But during the 1960s and early 1970s the system began to unravel, eventually to fall apart in August 1971 when US President Nixon attempted to control inflation via several measures, among them devaluing the dollar and suspending its convertibility to gold — "closing the gold window." The other currencies were allowed to float on international foreign exchange markets in an effort to reach a natural equilibrium.

In December 1971, finance ministers of the world's major industrialized nations met at the Smithsonian Institution in Washington, DC, to readjust values and to widen bands within which currencies could trade in an attempt to control their fluctuations. But inflation rose, gold rose, and the dollar continued to fall. The Smithsonian agreement collapsed in 1973, allowing all currencies to float freely and contributing greatly to volatility in their movements.

But in the meantime, the Chicago Mercantile Exchange had introduced the first ever futures contracts for markets other than physical commodities. In 1972, it organized the International Monetary Market (IMM) and in September began trading foreign currency futures — initially the British pound, Canadian dollar, Deutsche mark, Italian lira, Japanese yen, Swiss franc, and Mexican peso. The Australian dollar began trading in 1987. As members of the European Monetary Union prepared for the transition to their single currency, CME launched trading in the euro in 1998.

By 2005, CME listed more than 15 currencies, from the Hungarian forint to the South African rand to the Brazilian real, for trading against the US dollar. Also available for trading on the floor and/or electronically were several cross rates, such as the euroyen and europound. In addition, the New York Board of Trade also listed for trading several major currencies paired against the US dollar and against each other. This chapter, however, will focus on spreads between the major, more liquid forex futures traded at CME.

Members

Currencies included in seasonal spread strategies herein are limited to the Australian dollar, British pound, Canadian dollar, Japanese yen, and Swiss franc. This chapter will touch upon both the US dollar and the eurocurrency, but neither will be included among the historical spread strategies — the US dollar because it is already indexed against a basket of currencies, the eurocurrency because its recent vintage limits historical analysis.

US Dollar: The World's Reserve Currency

No discussion of forex trading would be complete without at least reference to the US dollar, still the world's reserve currency against which all others are measured and in which most internationally traded goods are priced. Despite its own fluctuations, the US dollar remains a store of value held by the billions in the world's central banks.

The FINEX division of the old New York Cotton Exchange, now part of NYBOT, introduced US Dollar Index futures in 1985. As of August 2005, the index was computed as a trade-weighted geometric average of six currencies as follows:

Figure 9-1

Currency	Percentage	Currency	Percentage	Currency	Percentage
Eurocurrency	57.6%	British pound	11.9%	Swedish krona	4.2%
Japanese yen	13.6%	Canadian dollar	9.1%	Swiss franc	3.6%

Figure 9-2: Dollar Index

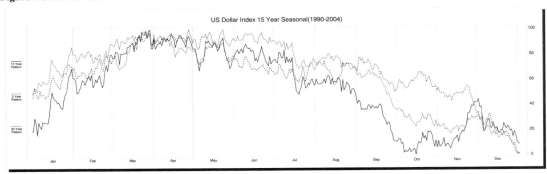

Figure 9-3: 10-Year Treasury Constant Maturity Rate

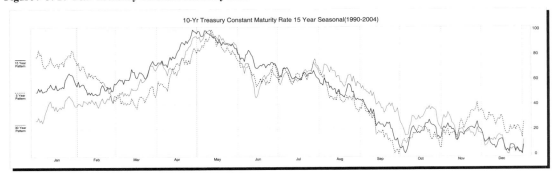

The observant reader will note a close similarity in the seasonal patterns maintained by the US dollar and Treasury yields over the last 30 years (discussed in more detail in the chapter on interest rates). Does perhaps monetary liquidity tighten — placing dollars at a premium — as a massive amount of financial assets are transferred from out of the private and into the public sector in the form of income tax payments due April 15? Does monetary liquidity then loosen through the remainder of the old and into the new US fiscal year beginning October? Would the dollar again strengthen as the new calendar — and tax — year begins?

Eurocurrency: New Kid on the Block

In October 1998, CME launched eurocurrency futures trading in preparation for the twelve members of the European Union to introduce the euro to world money markets on January 1, 1999. After a period of transition, the euro became the common currency of those member countries, replacing by 2002 such long-time national stalwarts as the Deutsche mark,

French franc, and Italian lira. The euro now represents one of the world's three largest economies and, along with the US dollar and the yen, is one of the currencies most widely traded in forex markets and held by central banks.

Figure 9-4: Eurocurrency Seasonal Pattern

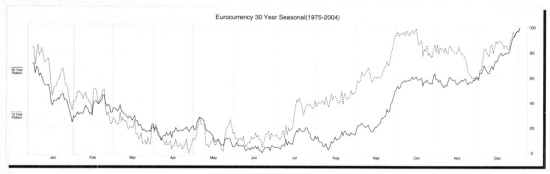

With historical values for currencies it replaced, hypothetical values for the euro can be calculated backward into history. After doing so, one can then construct its hypothetical seasonal pattern. The observant reader will not be surprised at how nearly inverse is its image from the pattern exhibited by the US dollar.

Australian Dollar

The Australian dollar (A$) is often referred to as a commodity currency because the country is so rich in natural resources. Exports of raw materials (coal, gold, alumina, iron ore) and agricultural products (meat, wool, wheat) have historically fueled the economy. Five of the top six export destinations are in Asia, led by Japan and China. Of all the major currency futures, only the A$ is based in the Southern Hemisphere. The fiscal year thus runs July-June. (The CME futures contract specifies 100,000 Australian dollars, with the minimum increment of 0.0001 US$/A$ worth US$10.00.)

Figure 9-5: Australian Dollar Seasonal Pattern

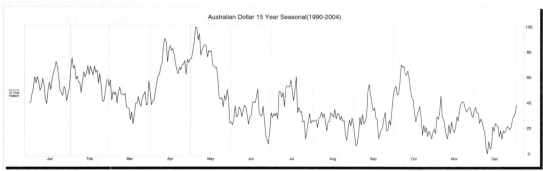

Against the US$, the A$ has tended to weaken into a pronounced low in March as summer in the Southern Hemisphere ends. After recovering into the second calendar and last fiscal quarter, the A$ has then often declined again into August/September.

British Pound

The pound is the currency of a trillion-dollar economy. London is an international trading and financial services center. Though declining relative to services, manufacturing remains a significant part of gross domestic product (GDP) in the birthplace of the Industrial Revolution. With the country's large reserves of coal, natural gas, and petroleum, primary energy production accounts for as much as 10% of GDP. The British fiscal year begins in April. (The CME futures contract specifies 62,500 pounds, with the minimum increment of 0.0001 US$/pound worth US$6.25.)

Figure 9-6: British Pound Seasonal Pattern

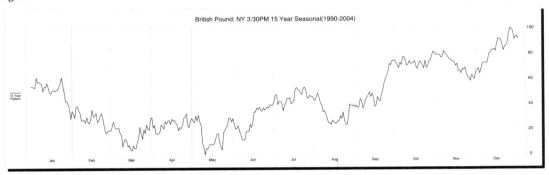

The pound has tended to reach its seasonal low against the US$ either just prior to or shortly after the new British fiscal year begins. It then normally rallies into October and ultimately with a final burst into the end of the calendar year — when it can reverse on a dime.

Canadian Dollar

The Canadian dollar (C$) is also referred to as a commodity currency. Because geography has made their countries such close trading partners, the C$ is perhaps more closely associated with the US$ than any other currency. In the newly trillion-dollar Canadian economy, exports account for roughly a third of GDP, with about 85% going to the United States (from whence come nearly 60% of imports). The high-tech industrial economy is well capitalized with a skilled labor force and great natural resources, the latter including wheat, forest products, minerals, petroleum, and natural gas. The Canadian fiscal year runs April-March. (The CME futures contract specifies 100,000 Canadian dollars, with the minimum increment of 0.0001 US$/C$ worth $10.00.)

Figure 9-7: Canadian Dollar Seasonal Pattern

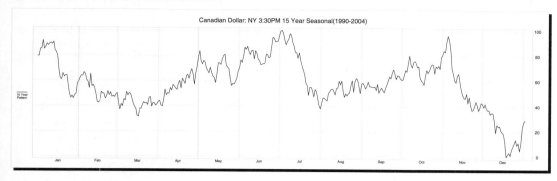

Canadian Dollar: NY 3:30PM 15 Year Seasonal(1990-2004)

Against the US$, the C$ also tends to make a prominent low in March as the old fiscal year draws to a close. It then rises into the beginning of the second fiscal quarter before sagging through the remainder of July. A typically final show of strength into November can then be followed by a decline into December.

Japanese Yen

The yen is the currency of the second most technologically powerful economy in the world and, with China, the United States, and the European Union, among the four largest. Industry is by far the most important sector of an economy driven by exports rather than internal consumption but, with few natural resources, heavily dependent on imports of fuel and raw materials. The Japanese fiscal year runs April-March. (The CME futures contract specifies 12,500,000 yen, with the minimum increment of 0.0001 US cents/yen worth US$12.50.)

Figure 9-8: Japanese Yen Seasonal Pattern

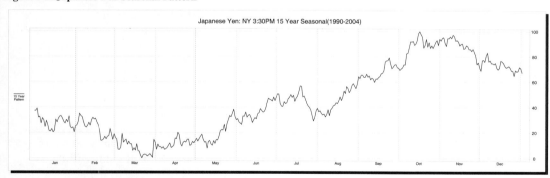

Japanese Yen: NY 3:30PM 15 Year Seasonal(1990-2004)

The pattern above suggests that the two primary seasonal trends in which the yen has moved against the US$ have been less capricious than those of perhaps any other of the major currencies. The yen tends to make its seasonal low at the very end of the Japanese fiscal year and then rise, with but a brief interruption during July, into October. The prominent seasonal high then is, among the major currencies, uniquely characteristic of the yen. Japanese accounting standards consider each half-fiscal year to be nearly as important as the whole. Thus, Japanese multinational corporations have traditionally repatriated funds in order to dress up their balance sheets. Doing so generates domestic demand for yen which draws on international supply, perhaps at the expense of overseas investment. Thus, the yen has exhibited a dynamic tendency to rise throughout August/September and into a final climax in October or early November — leaving the yen exhausted and poised to decline through the end of the fiscal year.

Swiss Franc

The franc is the currency of a small but prosperous economy with a per capita GDP greater than that of the big Western European economies. Long known for its precision instruments, Switzerland also exports machinery and chemicals. That the country continues to play its traditional role as safe haven for international investors is a testament to Swiss political neutrality, banking secrecy laws, and attention to the franc's external value. The Swiss fiscal year runs January-December. (The CME futures contract specifies 125,000 francs, with the minimum increment of 0.0001 US$/franc worth US$12.50.)

Figure 9-9: Swiss Franc Seasonal Pattern

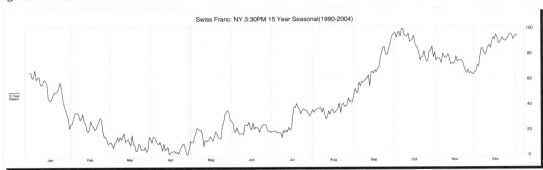

The seasonal pattern of the franc against the US$ looks like nothing so much as a cup-and-handle formation. As the new fiscal year gets underway, the franc begins a smooth, steady decline into a rounding bottom during the second fiscal quarter before rising steadily into the beginning of the new US fiscal year. After a modest decline into late November, the franc then rallies through the last month of the calendar and Swiss fiscal year.

Inter-market Spreads

Because international monetary flows are so affected by macroeconomic trends, forex relationships tend to move in secular trends. Perhaps for this reason do so many analysts and traders minimize or outright dismiss seasonality in currency markets. But even within broader secular trends there remain movements that can perhaps be traced to the seasonal effects of such recurring fundamental causes as fiscal years, tax payments, accounting methods, and agricultural export cycles.

The following page begins a table summarizing a few recurrent movements between major foreign currencies that have held up over the last 15 and even 20 years, throughout which numerous secular forex trends have no doubt variously run, reversed, paused, and finally dissipated. Perhaps seasonal tendencies *can* withstand the test of time. Readers can decide for themselves.

Figure 9-10: Forex Spread Strategies

Moore Research Center, Inc.				Forex Spreads					
Seasonal Strategy	Entry Date	Exit Date	Win Pct	Win Yrs	Loss Years	Total Years	Average Profit	Ave Pft Per Day
Buy Mar Japanese Yen(IMM)	1/06	2/04	87	13	2	15	1717	57
Sell Mar Swiss Franc(IMM)			80	16	4	20	1370	46
Buy Mar Canadian Dollar(IMM)	1/23	3/15	80	12	3	15	1679	32
Sell Mar Swiss Franc(IMM)			80	16	4	20	1512	29
Buy Mar Australian Dollar(IMM)	1/24	2/02	87	13	2	15	1360	136
Sell Mar Swiss Franc(IMM)			84	16	3	19	1240	124
Buy Jun Australian Dollar(IMM)	2/22	4/16	87	13	2	15	1850	34
Sell Jun Swiss Franc(IMM)			89	17	2	19	2054	38
Buy Jun Canadian Dollar(IMM)	2/22	3/26	80	12	3	15	1377	42
Sell Jun Swiss Franc(IMM)			85	17	3	20	1644	50
Buy Mar Australian Dollar(IMM)	2/25	3/04	80	12	3	15	731	91
Sell Mar Swiss Franc(IMM)			84	16	3	19	898	112
Buy Mar Canadian Dollar(IMM)	2/25	3/05	80	12	3	15	595	66
Sell Mar Swiss Franc(IMM)			80	16	4	20	638	71
Buy Mar Australian Dollar(IMM)	2/26	3/06	80	12	3	15	411	46
Sell Mar Japanese Yen(IMM)			84	16	3	19	638	71
Buy Jun Australian Dollar(IMM)	3/18	4/12	87	13	2	15	1396	54
Sell Jun Swiss Franc(IMM)			89	17	2	19	1292	50
Buy Jun British Pound(IMM)	3/19	4/12	100	15	0	15	1313	53
Sell Jun Swiss Franc(IMM)			95	19	1	20	1226	49
Buy Jun Australian Dollar(IMM)	5/02	5/10	87	13	2	15	413	46
Sell Jun Japanese Yen(IMM)			89	17	2	19	482	54
Buy Jun Canadian Dollar(IMM)	5/30	6/04	93	14	1	15	707	118
Sell Jun British Pound(IMM)			80	16	4	20	522	87
Buy Jun Canadian Dollar(IMM)	5/30	6/05	87	13	2	15	1068	153
Sell Jun Japanese Yen(IMM)			80	16	4	20	693	99
Buy Sep British Pound(IMM)	6/08	7/06	87	13	2	15	1259	43
Sell Sep Japanese Yen(IMM)			85	17	3	20	1416	49
Buy Sep British Pound(IMM)	6/11	7/12	87	13	2	15	1370	43
Sell Sep Swiss Franc(IMM)			80	16	4	20	1035	32
Buy Sep Swiss Franc(IMM)	7/14	7/29	87	13	2	15	1524	95
Sell Sep Japanese Yen(IMM)			80	16	4	20	1258	79
Buy Dec Swiss Franc(IMM)	8/17	9/30	80	12	3	15	2568	57
Sell Dec Australian Dollar(IMM)			83	15	3	18	2300	51
Buy Dec British Pound(IMM)	8/18	9/29	80	12	3	15	1571	37
Sell Dec Australian Dollar(IMM)			83	15	3	18	1487	35
Buy Dec Swiss Franc(IMM)	8/31	10/02	87	13	2	15	2016	61
Sell Dec Canadian Dollar(IMM)			80	16	4	20	1619	49
Buy Sep Australian Dollar(IMM)	9/03	9/08	80	12	3	15	250	42
Sell Sep Canadian Dollar(IMM)			83	15	3	18	335	56
Buy Dec Swiss Franc(IMM)	9/12	9/25	87	13	2	15	1043	75
Sell Dec Australian Dollar(IMM)			83	15	3	18	881	63
Buy Dec British Pound(IMM)	9/20	9/29	87	13	2	15	1050	105
Sell Dec Australian Dollar(IMM)			83	15	3	18	985	98

Figure 9-10: Forex Spread Strategies continued

Moore Research Center, Inc.							Forex Spreads	
Seasonal Strategy	Entry Date	Exit Date	Win Pct	Win Yrs	Loss Years	Total Years	Average Profit	Ave Pft Per Day
Buy Dec British Pound(IMM) Sell Dec Canadian Dollar(IMM)	9/20	9/29	87 80	13 16	2 4	15 20	1156 880	116 88
Buy Dec Swiss Franc(IMM) Sell Dec Japanese Yen(IMM)	9/23	10/02	93 80	14 16	1 4	15 20	1401 992	140 88
Buy Dec British Pound(IMM) Sell Dec Swiss Franc(IMM)	10/04	11/13	80 85	12 17	3 3	15 20	1512 1399	37 34
Buy Dec Japanese Yen(IMM) Sell Dec British Pound(IMM)	10/06	10/19	87 80	13 16	2 4	15 20	1690 1312	121 94
Buy Dec British Pound(IMM) Sell Dec Japanese Yen(IMM)	10/17	10/20	93 90	14 18	1 2	15 20	757 692	189 173
Buy Dec British Pound(IMM) Sell Dec Japanese Yen(IMM)	10/17	12/12	87 85	13 17	2 3	15 20	3094 2929	54 51
Buy Dec Australian Dollar(IMM) Sell Dec Japanese Yen(IMM)	11/03	12/02	80 83	12 15	3 3	15 18	1843 1722	61 57
Buy Dec Australian Dollar(IMM) Sell Dec Canadian Dollar(IMM)	11/04	11/15	80 83	12 15	3 3	15 18	448 614	37 51
Buy Dec Australian Dollar(IMM) Sell Dec Japanese Yen(IMM)	11/10	11/28	87 89	13 16	2 2	15 18	1177 1155	62 61
Buy Mar British Pound(IMM) Sell Mar Japanese Yen(IMM)	11/10	1/06	93 90	14 18	1 2	15 20	4178 3468	72 60
Buy Mar Swiss Franc(IMM) Sell Mar Japanese Yen(IMM)	12/07	12/28	80 80	12 16	3 4	15 20	1309 1055	60 48
Buy Mar Canadian Dollar(IMM) Sell Mar Japanese Yen(IMM)	12/28	1/09	87 85	13 17	2 3	15 20	1308 1299	101 100

(*Please Note*: Statistics in the table above are for spreads between CME futures. They are thus analyzed through the prism of the US dollar and may not translate directly to cross-spreads or interbank cash movement. Further, the table is meant only to illustrate a series of seasonal relationships. Attempts to trade all as shown may result in several unintended net positions.)

Figure 9-11

Buy Mar Japanese Yen(IMM) / Sell Mar Swiss Franc(IMM)

Enter on approximately 01/06 - Exit on approximately 02/04

CONT YEAR	ENTRY DATE	ENTRY PRICE	EXIT DATE	EXIT PRICE	PROFIT	PROFIT AMOUNT	BEST EQUITY DATE	BEST EQUITY AMOUNT	WORST EQUITY DATE	WORST EQUITY AMOUNT
2005	01/06/05	10.19	02/04/05	13.59	3.39	4237.50	02/04/05	4237.50		
2004	01/06/04	12.90	02/04/04	14.95	2.05	2562.50	02/02/04	3350.00	01/09/04	-912.50
2003	01/06/03	12.29	02/04/03	9.36	-2.93	-3662.50	01/14/03	412.50	02/04/03	-3662.50
2002	01/07/02	15.96	02/04/02	16.84	0.88	1100.00	02/01/02	1237.50	01/22/02	-1612.50
2001	01/08/01	24.64	02/02/01	26.00	1.36	1700.00	02/02/01	1700.00	01/12/01	-1687.50
2000	01/06/00	31.06	02/04/00	32.35	1.30	1625.00	01/27/00	4150.00	01/11/00	-375.00
1999	01/06/99	17.09	02/04/99	18.46	1.36	1700.00	01/11/99	4925.00	01/14/99	-3012.50
1998	01/06/98	7.50	02/04/98	12.14	4.64	5800.00	02/04/98	5800.00		
1997	01/06/97	12.90	02/04/97	11.73	-1.18	-1475.00	01/21/97	1962.50	02/04/97	-1475.00
1996	01/08/96	9.28	02/02/96	11.79	2.52	3150.00	02/02/96	3150.00	01/12/96	-37.50
1995	01/06/95	22.70	02/03/95	23.14	0.44	550.00	01/13/95	1812.50	01/23/95	-1137.50
1994	01/06/94	21.54	02/04/94	23.70	2.15	2687.50	02/01/94	3012.50	01/12/94	-750.00
1993	01/06/93	12.96	02/04/93	15.06	2.10	2625.00	02/04/93	2625.00	01/22/93	-1825.00
1992	01/06/92	6.95	02/04/92	9.03	2.07	2587.50	01/23/92	4875.00	01/08/92	-750.00
1991	01/07/91	-3.79	02/04/91	-3.34	0.45	562.50	01/30/91	1262.50	01/16/91	-787.50
1990	01/08/90	4.09	02/02/90	1.92	-2.17	-2712.50			02/02/90	-2712.50
1989	01/06/89	14.60	02/03/89	14.74	0.14	175.00	01/10/89	1350.00	01/23/89	-687.50
1988	01/06/88	2.98	02/04/88	5.12	2.14	2675.00	02/03/88	3150.00	01/07/88	-475.00
1987	01/06/87	0.89	02/04/87	0.13	-0.77	-962.50	01/07/87	825.00	01/29/87	-2400.00
1986	01/06/86	0.97	02/04/86	2.95	1.98	2475.00	02/03/86	2512.50	01/09/86	-87.50

Percentage Correct		87								
Average Profit on Winning Trades					1.90	2375.96		Winners		13
Average Loss on Trades					-2.06	-2568.75		Losers		2
Average Net Profit Per Trade					1.37	1716.67		Total trades		15
Percentage Correct		80								
Average Profit on Winning Trades					1.81	2263.28		Winners		16
Average Loss on Trades					-1.76	-2203.12		Losers		4
Average Net Profit Per Trade					1.10	1370.00		Total trades		20

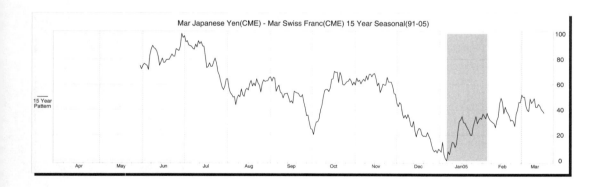

Mar Japanese Yen(CME) - Mar Swiss Franc(CME) 15 Year Seasonal(91-05)

Chapter 9: Forex

321

Figure 9-12

Moore Research Center, Inc.

Buy Mar Canadian Dollar(IMM) / Sell Mar Swiss Franc(IMM)

Enter on approximately 01/23 - Exit on approximately 03/15

CONT YEAR	ENTRY DATE	ENTRY PRICE	EXIT DATE	EXIT PRICE		PROFIT AMOUNT	BEST EQUITY DATE	BEST EQUITY AMOUNT	WORST EQUITY DATE	WORST EQUITY AMOUNT
2005	01/24/05	-24155	03/14/05	-24990		-835.00	02/08/05	1735.00	02/23/05	-2780.00
2004	01/23/04	-25000	03/12/04	-22555		2445.00	03/10/04	3555.00	02/10/04	-1282.50
2003	01/23/03	-26498	03/14/03	-23792		2705.00	03/14/03	2705.00	01/27/03	-527.50
2002	01/23/02	-12370	03/15/02	-12275		95.00	01/31/02	2792.50	03/14/02	-337.50
2001	01/23/01	-10628	03/15/01	-9175		1452.50	02/15/01	2157.50	03/01/01	-597.50
2000	01/24/00	-8888	03/13/00	-6768		2120.00	03/07/00	3180.00	02/22/00	-1040.00
1999	01/25/99	-24723	03/15/99	-19955		4767.50	03/05/99	5412.50		
1998	01/23/98	-18338	03/13/98	-13860		4477.50	03/10/98	5375.00		
1997	01/23/97	-13615	03/14/97	-12588		1027.50	02/19/97	2842.50	01/24/97	-1255.00
1996	01/23/96	-32725	03/14/96	-32118		607.50	02/01/96	2162.50	02/20/96	-1212.50
1995	01/23/95	-28540	03/13/95	-36090		-7550.00	02/07/95	3750.00	03/07/95	-11042.50
1994	01/24/94	-8968	03/14/94	-14100		-5132.50	01/26/94	172.50	03/10/94	-5737.50
1993	01/25/93	-8293	03/15/93	-1890		6402.50	03/05/93	7600.00		
1992	01/23/92	-1183	03/13/92	705		1887.50	03/05/92	3427.50	02/07/92	-3832.50
1991	01/23/91	-13890	03/15/91	-3178		10712.50	03/15/91	10712.50	02/06/91	-1405.00
1990	01/23/90	1760	03/15/90	2265		505.00	03/14/90	1400.00	02/23/90	-3390.00
1989	01/23/89	2970	03/13/89	5093		2122.50	01/31/89	2855.00	02/27/89	-440.00
1988	01/25/88	-14373	03/14/88	-11693		2680.00	03/04/88	5007.50	01/26/88	-457.50
1987	01/23/87	-8623	03/13/87	-4908		3715.00	03/11/87	4282.50	01/28/87	-682.50
1986	01/23/86	10093	03/14/86	6123		-3970.00			03/03/86	-6962.50

Percentage Correct	80			
Average Profit on Winning Trades		3225.00	Winners	12
Average Loss on Trades		-4505.83	Losers	3
Average Net Profit Per Trade		1678.83	Total trades	15
Percentage Correct	80			
Average Profit on Winning Trades		2982.66	Winners	16
Average Loss on Trades		-4371.88	Losers	4
Average Net Profit Per Trade		1511.75	Total trades	20

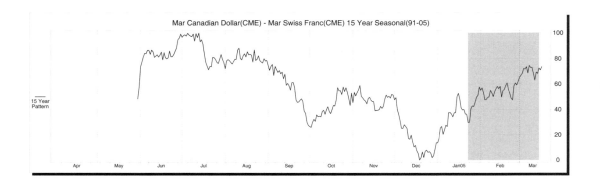

Mar Canadian Dollar(CME) - Mar Swiss Franc(CME) 15 Year Seasonal(91-05)

Figure 9-13

Buy Mar Australian Dollar(IMM) / Sell Mar Swiss Franc(IMM)

Enter on approximately 01/24 - Exit on approximately 02/02

CONT YEAR	ENTRY DATE	ENTRY PRICE	EXIT DATE	EXIT PRICE		PROFIT AMOUNT	BEST EQUITY DATE	BEST EQUITY AMOUNT	WORST EQUITY DATE	WORST EQUITY AMOUNT
2005	01/24/05	-29045	02/02/05	-27473		1572.50	02/02/05	1572.50		
2004	01/26/04	-22975	02/02/04	-23688		-712.50	01/28/04	40.00	02/02/04	-712.50
2003	01/24/03	-33593	01/31/03	-33145		447.50	01/31/03	447.50	01/27/03	-142.50
2002	01/24/02	-22778	02/01/02	-22218		560.00	01/28/02	1012.50		
2001	01/24/01	-21285	02/02/01	-20893		392.50	02/02/01	392.50	01/26/01	-227.50
2000	01/24/00	-12868	02/02/00	-12203		665.00	01/27/00	1375.00	01/28/00	-185.00
1999	01/25/99	-27553	02/02/99	-24940		2612.50	02/01/99	2830.00	01/26/99	-2.50
1998	01/26/98	-19358	02/02/98	-16510		2847.50	01/30/98	2965.00		
1997	01/24/97	-12120	01/31/97	-11950		170.00	01/27/97	1417.50		
1996	01/24/96	-31765	02/02/96	-27660		4105.00	02/02/96	4105.00		
1995	01/24/95	-21795	02/02/95	-21805		-10.00	02/01/95	30.00	01/30/95	-1297.50
1994	01/24/94	-14998	02/02/94	-14650		347.50	01/28/94	960.00		
1993	01/25/93	-19183	02/02/93	-14243		4940.00	02/02/93	4940.00		
1992	01/24/92	-14050	01/31/92	-11945		2105.00	01/31/92	2105.00		
1991	01/24/91	-21983	02/01/91	-21630		352.50	01/30/91	1417.50		
1990	01/24/90	-7630	02/02/90	-6980		650.00	01/31/90	722.50	01/25/90	-1295.00
1989	01/24/89	7200	02/02/89	9250		2050.00	01/31/89	2635.00	01/25/89	-580.00
1988	01/25/88	-21383	02/02/88	-20463		920.00	02/01/88	927.50	01/28/88	-467.50
1987	01/26/87	-16490	02/02/87	-16948		-457.50	01/30/87	605.00	01/28/87	-2225.00

Percentage Correct	87									
Average Profit on Winning Trades						1624.42		Winners		13
Average Loss on Trades						-361.25		Losers		2
Average Net Profit Per Trade						1359.67		Total trades		15
Percentage Correct	84									
Average Profit on Winning Trades						1546.09		Winners		16
Average Loss on Trades						-393.33		Losers		3
Average Net Profit Per Trade						1239.87		Total trades		19

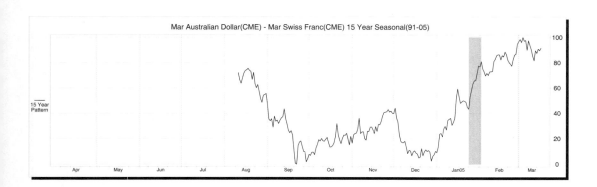

Mar Australian Dollar(CME) - Mar Swiss Franc(CME) 15 Year Seasonal(91-05)

15 Year Pattern

Figure 9-14

Buy Jun Australian Dollar(IMM) / Sell Jun Swiss Franc(IMM)

Enter on approximately 02/22 - Exit on approximately 04/16

CONT YEAR	ENTRY DATE	ENTRY PRICE	EXIT DATE	EXIT PRICE	PROFIT AMOUNT	BEST EQUITY DATE	BEST EQUITY AMOUNT	WORST EQUITY DATE	WORST EQUITY AMOUNT
2005	02/22/05	-29758	04/15/05	-27820	1937.50	04/14/05	3142.50	03/11/05	-840.00
2004	02/23/04	-23645	04/16/04	-22768	877.50	04/06/04	2350.00	03/15/04	-1730.00
2003	02/24/03	-32398	04/16/03	-30420	1977.50	04/15/03	2740.00	03/12/03	-2485.00
2002	02/22/02	-23075	04/16/02	-22078	997.50	03/28/02	1877.50	03/14/02	-515.00
2001	02/22/01	-21915	04/16/01	-21868	47.50	04/16/01	47.50	04/04/01	-3247.50
2000	02/22/00	-16548	04/14/00	-16938	-390.00	03/13/00	2657.50	04/11/00	-530.00
1999	02/22/99	-23240	04/16/99	-19388	3852.50	04/16/99	3852.50	02/26/99	-2247.50
1998	02/23/98	-20633	04/16/98	-18615	2017.50	03/30/98	4285.00	02/24/98	-95.00
1997	02/24/97	-8985	04/16/97	-8340	645.00	03/04/97	2885.00	04/03/97	-1290.00
1996	02/22/96	-31902	04/16/96	-23973	7930.00	04/15/96	8805.00	02/23/96	-372.50
1995	02/22/95	-27498	04/13/95	-35770	-8272.50			04/03/95	-11335.00
1994	02/22/94	-14240	04/15/94	-13605	635.00	02/23/94	650.00	03/31/94	-4467.50
1993	02/22/93	-15013	04/16/93	-12428	2585.00	03/05/93	5082.50	04/01/93	-117.50
1992	02/24/92	-8450	04/16/92	-3938	4512.50	04/16/92	4512.50	02/27/92	-432.50
1991	02/22/91	-18890	04/16/91	-10500	8390.00	03/27/91	10165.00		
1990	02/22/90	-9733	04/16/90	-8115	1617.50	03/14/90	2820.00	02/27/90	-242.50
1989	02/22/89	-695	04/14/89	3590	4285.00	03/31/89	5535.00	02/27/89	-2530.00
1988	02/22/88	-20043	04/15/88	-17430	2612.50	04/13/88	4325.00	02/23/88	-97.50
1987	02/23/87	-16220	04/16/87	-13460	2760.00	04/08/87	3845.00	02/26/87	-267.50

Percentage Correct	87		
Average Profit on Winning Trades	2800.38	Winners	13
Average Loss on Trades	-4331.25	Losers	2
Average Net Profit Per Trade	1849.50	Total trades	15
Percentage Correct	89		
Average Profit on Winning Trades	2804.71	Winners	17
Average Loss on Trades	-4331.25	Losers	2
Average Net Profit Per Trade	2053.55	Total trades	19

HYPOTHETICAL PERFORMANCE RESULTS HAVE MANY INHERENT LIMITATIONS, SOME OF WHICH ARE DESCRIBED BELOW. NO REPRESENTATION IS BEING MADE THAT ANY ACCOUNT WILL OR IS LIKELY TO ACHIEVE PROFITS OR LOSSES SIMILAR TO THOSE SHOWN. IN FACT, THERE ARE FREQUENTLY SHARP DIFFERENCES BETWEEN HYPOTHETICAL PERFORMANCE RESULTS AND THE ACTUAL RESULTS SUBSEQUENTLY ACHIEVED BY ANY PARTICULAR TRADING PROGRAM. ONE OF THE LIMITATIONS OF HYPOTHETICAL PERFORMANCE RESULTS IS THAT THEY ARE GENERALLY PREPARED WITH THE BENEFIT OF HINDSIGHT. IN ADDITION, HYPOTHETICAL TRADING DOES NOT INVOLVE FINANCIAL RISK, AND NO HYPOTHETICAL TRADING RECORD CAN COMPLETELY ACCOUNT FOR THE IMPACT OF FINANCIAL RISK IN ACTUAL TRADING. FOR EXAMPLE, THE ABILITY TO WITHSTAND LOSSES OR ADHERE TO A PARTICULAR TRADING PROGRAM IN SPITE OF TRADING LOSSES ARE MATERIAL POINTS WHICH CAN ALSO ADVERSELY AFFECT ACTUAL TRADING RESULTS. THERE ARE NUMEROUS OTHER FACTORS RELATED TO THE MARKETS IN GENERAL OR TO THE IMPLEMENTATION OF ANY SPECIFIC TRADING PROGRAM WHICH CANNOT BE FULLY ACCOUNTED FOR IN THE PREPARATION OF HYPOTHETICAL PERFORMANCE RESULTS AND ALL OF WHICH CAN ADVERSELY AFFECT ACTUAL TRADING RESULTS. RESULTS NOT ADJUSTED FOR COMMISSION AND SLIPPAGE.

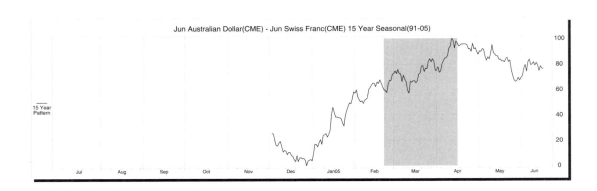

Jun Australian Dollar(CME) - Jun Swiss Franc(CME) 15 Year Seasonal(91-05)

Figure 9-15

Buy Jun Canadian Dollar(IMM) / Sell Jun Swiss Franc(IMM)

Enter on approximately 02/22 - Exit on approximately 03/26

CONT YEAR	ENTRY DATE	ENTRY PRICE	EXIT DATE	EXIT PRICE	PROFIT AMOUNT	BEST EQUITY DATE	BEST EQUITY AMOUNT	WORST EQUITY DATE	WORST EQUITY AMOUNT
2005	02/22/05	-26888	03/24/05	-22483	4405.00	03/24/05	4405.00	02/23/05	-545.00
2004	02/23/04	-25025	03/26/04	-21788	3237.50	03/26/04	3237.50	02/24/04	-1035.00
2003	02/24/03	-25548	03/26/03	-22928	2620.00	03/21/03	2825.00	03/11/03	-1145.00
2002	02/22/02	-11425	03/26/02	-12238	-812.50	03/01/02	932.50	03/14/02	-1395.00
2001	02/22/01	-9205	03/26/01	-8905	300.00	03/26/01	300.00	03/01/01	-2310.00
2000	02/22/00	-10558	03/24/00	-8965	1592.50	03/07/00	4260.00		
1999	02/22/99	-20440	03/26/99	-19110	1330.00	03/26/99	1330.00	02/25/99	-1147.50
1998	02/23/98	-17033	03/26/98	-13825	3207.50	03/25/98	3592.50		
1997	02/24/97	-12815	03/26/97	-12748	67.50	03/04/97	1345.00	03/18/97	-1620.00
1996	02/22/96	-34212	03/26/96	-32108	2105.00	03/08/96	2597.50	02/23/96	-632.50
1995	02/22/95	-29798	03/24/95	-36008	-6210.00	02/23/95	350.00	03/07/95	-10925.00
1994	02/22/94	-11460	03/25/94	-15648	-4187.50	02/23/94	140.00	03/25/94	-4187.50
1993	02/22/93	-4933	03/26/93	-2270	2662.50	03/08/93	4217.50		
1992	02/24/92	540	03/26/92	1815	1275.00	03/05/92	1795.00	03/17/92	-425.00
1991	02/22/91	-10280	03/26/91	-1218	9062.50	03/25/91	9100.00		
1990	02/22/90	-1883	03/26/90	2018	3900.00	03/14/90	4220.00	02/23/90	-472.50
1989	02/22/89	2105	03/23/89	6080	3975.00	03/23/89	3975.00	02/27/89	-850.00
1988	02/22/88	-13043	03/25/88	-10900	2142.50	03/18/88	2835.00	03/11/88	-62.50
1987	02/23/87	-6200	03/26/87	-5935	265.00	03/11/87	1337.50	02/27/87	-1102.50
1986	02/24/86	4610	03/26/86	6550	1940.00	03/25/86	2140.00	03/03/86	-2855.00

Percentage Correct	80								
Average Profit on Winning Trades					2655.42		Winners		12
Average Loss on Trades					-3736.67		Losers		3
Average Net Profit Per Trade					1377.00		Total trades		15
Percentage Correct	85								
Average Profit on Winning Trades					2593.38		Winners		17
Average Loss on Trades					-3736.67		Losers		3
Average Net Profit Per Trade					1643.87		Total trades		20

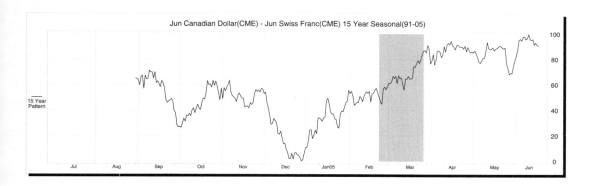

Jun Canadian Dollar(CME) - Jun Swiss Franc(CME) 15 Year Seasonal(91-05)

Figure 9-16

| Moore Research Center, Inc. | Buy Mar Australian Dollar(IMM) / Sell Mar Swiss Franc(IMM) |

Enter on approximately 02/25 - Exit on approximately 03/04

CONT YEAR	ENTRY DATE	ENTRY PRICE	EXIT DATE	EXIT PRICE		PROFIT AMOUNT	BEST EQUITY DATE	BEST EQUITY AMOUNT	WORST EQUITY DATE	WORST EQUITY AMOUNT
2005	02/25/05	-28958	03/04/05	-27978		980.00	03/03/05	1312.50		
2004	02/25/04	-22253	03/04/04	-21663		590.00	03/02/04	1870.00		
2003	02/25/03	-31750	03/04/03	-32220		-470.00	02/26/03	105.00	03/04/03	-470.00
2002	02/25/02	-22378	03/04/02	-21623		755.00	03/01/02	1040.00		
2001	02/26/01	-21918	03/02/01	-22963		-1045.00			03/01/01	-1057.50
2000	02/25/00	-14280	03/04/00	-13960		320.00	03/01/00	832.50	03/02/00	-1167.50
1999	02/25/99	-24485	03/04/99	-22778		1707.50	03/04/99	1707.50	02/26/99	-230.00
1998	02/25/98	-18620	03/04/98	-17128		1492.50	03/02/98	1597.50		
1997	02/25/97	-8050	03/04/97	-5233		2817.50	03/04/97	2817.50		
1996	02/26/96	-30613	03/04/96	-28170		2442.50	03/02/96	2815.00		
1995	02/27/95	-26835	03/03/95	-30455		-3620.00			03/03/95	-3620.00
1994	02/25/94	-15648	03/04/94	-15173		475.00	03/04/94	475.00	03/02/94	-1172.50
1993	02/25/93	-12708	03/04/93	-10843		1865.00	03/01/93	2050.00		
1992	02/25/92	-7770	03/04/92	-6670		1100.00	03/04/92	1100.00	02/27/92	-1287.50
1991	02/25/91	-17620	03/04/91	-16065		1555.00	03/01/91	2562.50		
1990	02/26/90	-7468	03/02/90	-7038		430.00	03/01/90	855.00	02/27/90	-1320.00
1989	02/27/89	-1060	03/03/89	1770		2830.00	03/03/89	2830.00		
1988	02/25/88	-18405	03/04/88	-16705		1700.00	03/04/88	1700.00		
1987	02/25/87	-14108	03/04/87	-12965		1142.50	03/04/87	1142.50	02/26/87	-295.00

Percentage Correct	80									
Average Profit on Winning Trades						1341.67		Winners		12
Average Loss on Trades						-1711.67		Losers		3
Average Net Profit Per Trade						731.00		Total trades		15
Percentage Correct	84									
Average Profit on Winning Trades						1387.66		Winners		16
Average Loss on Trades						-1711.67		Losers		3
Average Net Profit Per Trade						898.29		Total trades		19

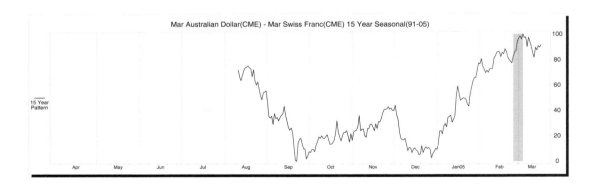

Mar Australian Dollar(CME) - Mar Swiss Franc(CME) 15 Year Seasonal(91-05)

Figure 9-17

Buy Mar Canadian Dollar(IMM) / Sell Mar Swiss Franc(IMM)

Enter on approximately 02/25 - Exit on approximately 03/05

CONT YEAR	ENTRY DATE	ENTRY PRICE	EXIT DATE	EXIT PRICE		PROFIT AMOUNT	BEST EQUITY DATE	BEST EQUITY AMOUNT	WORST EQUITY DATE	WORST EQUITY AMOUNT
2005	02/25/05	-26888	03/04/05	-25738		1150.00	03/03/05	1422.50		
2004	02/25/04	-24413	03/05/04	-22363		2050.00	03/04/04	2750.00		
2003	02/25/03	-25250	03/05/03	-26095		-845.00	02/27/03	122.50	03/05/03	-845.00
2002	02/25/02	-11158	03/05/02	-10825		332.50	03/01/02	730.00	02/28/02	-80.00
2001	02/26/01	-8807	03/05/01	-11098		-2290.00			03/01/01	-2417.50
2000	02/25/00	-6830	03/04/00	-6030		800.00	03/04/00	800.00		
1999	02/25/99	-20785	03/05/99	-19310		1475.00	03/05/99	1475.00		
1998	02/25/98	-14930	03/05/98	-13398		1532.50	03/05/98	1532.50	02/27/98	-317.50
1997	02/25/97	-12110	03/05/97	-11352		757.50	03/04/97	997.50		
1996	02/26/96	-33473	03/05/96	-31415		2057.50	03/02/96	2575.00		
1995	02/27/95	-29215	03/03/95	-33015		-3800.00			03/03/95	-3800.00
1994	02/25/94	-13538	03/04/94	-13063		475.00	03/01/94	572.50	02/28/94	-162.50
1993	02/25/93	-2508	03/05/93	-693		1815.00	03/05/93	1815.00		
1992	02/25/92	1400	03/05/92	2245		845.00	03/05/92	845.00	03/02/92	-1045.00
1991	02/25/91	-9240	03/05/91	-6673		2567.50	03/05/91	2567.50		
1990	02/26/90	-378	03/05/90	380		757.50	03/01/90	1385.00	02/27/90	-340.00
1989	02/27/89	2530	03/03/89	4170		1640.00	03/02/89	2007.50		
1988	02/25/88	-10975	03/05/88	-9710		1265.00	03/04/88	1610.00	02/26/88	-122.50
1987	02/25/87	-6188	03/05/87	-5960		227.50	03/04/87	342.50	02/27/87	-370.00
1986	02/25/86	5050	03/05/86	4998		-52.50	02/26/86	295.00	03/03/86	-1920.00

Percentage Correct	80			
Average Profit on Winning Trades		1321.46	Winners	12
Average Loss on Trades		-2311.67	Losers	3
Average Net Profit Per Trade		594.83	Total trades	15

Percentage Correct	80			
Average Profit on Winning Trades		1234.22	Winners	16
Average Loss on Trades		-1746.88	Losers	4
Average Net Profit Per Trade		638.00	Total trades	20

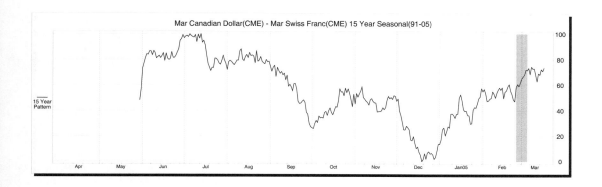

Mar Canadian Dollar(CME) - Mar Swiss Franc(CME) 15 Year Seasonal(91-05)

15 Year Pattern

Figure 9-18

Moore Research Center, Inc. — Buy Mar Australian Dollar(IMM) / Sell Mar Japanese Yen(IMM)

Enter on approximately 02/26 - Exit on approximately 03/06

CONT YEAR	ENTRY DATE	ENTRY PRICE	EXIT DATE	EXIT PRICE		PROFIT AMOUNT	BEST EQUITY DATE	BEST EQUITY AMOUNT	WORST EQUITY DATE	WORST EQUITY AMOUNT
2005	02/28/05	-40573	03/04/05	-40478		95.00	03/04/05	95.00	03/01/05	-802.50
2004	02/26/04	-37088	03/05/04	-35735		1352.50	03/05/04	1352.50	03/03/04	-1552.50
2003	02/26/03	-46133	03/06/03	-45160		972.50	03/03/03	1187.50		
2002	02/26/02	-41645	03/06/02	-43330		-1685.00			03/06/02	-1685.00
2001	02/26/01	-55280	03/06/01	-53463		1817.50	03/02/01	2905.00		
2000	02/28/00	-53303	03/06/00	-56165		-2862.50	03/01/00	1442.50	03/02/00	-3207.50
1999	02/26/99	-43390	03/05/99	-39228		4162.50	03/04/99	4312.50		
1998	02/26/98	-31335	03/06/98	-31025		310.00	03/06/98	310.00	03/02/98	-162.50
1997	02/26/97	-25145	03/06/97	-24595		550.00	03/04/97	1575.00	02/28/97	-1312.50
1996	02/26/96	-44588	03/06/96	-42465		2122.50	03/06/96	2122.50		
1995	02/27/95	-55035	03/06/95	-60955		-5920.00			03/06/95	-5920.00
1994	02/28/94	-48263	03/04/94	-47073		1190.00	03/04/94	1190.00	03/03/94	-1857.50
1993	02/26/93	-36240	03/05/93	-35375		865.00	03/01/93	1395.00	03/03/93	-97.50
1992	02/26/92	-21613	03/06/92	-19250		2362.50	03/05/92	2442.50		
1991	02/26/91	-15768	03/06/91	-14940		827.50	03/01/91	1422.50	02/27/91	-540.00
1990	02/26/90	-7793	03/06/90	-7600		192.50	03/01/90	417.50	02/27/90	-970.00
1989	02/27/89	-19410	03/06/89	-15593		3817.50	03/06/89	3817.50		
1988	02/26/88	-25700	03/05/88	-24493		1207.50	03/03/88	1237.50		
1987	02/26/87	-14528	03/06/87	-13775		752.50	03/04/87	912.50		

Percentage Correct	80									
Average Profit on Winning Trades						1385.63		Winners		12
Average Loss on Trades						-3489.17		Losers		3
Average Net Profit Per Trade						410.67		Total trades		15
Percentage Correct	84									
Average Profit on Winning Trades						1412.34		Winners		16
Average Loss on Trades						-3489.17		Losers		3
Average Net Profit Per Trade						638.42		Total trades		19

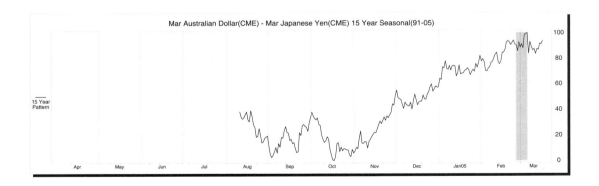

Mar Australian Dollar(CME) - Mar Japanese Yen(CME) 15 Year Seasonal(91-05)

Figure 9-19

Buy Jun Australian Dollar(IMM) / Sell Jun Swiss Franc(IMM)

Enter on approximately 03/18 - Exit on approximately 04/12

CONT YEAR	ENTRY DATE	ENTRY PRICE	EXIT DATE	EXIT PRICE		PROFIT AMOUNT	BEST EQUITY DATE	BEST EQUITY AMOUNT	WORST EQUITY DATE	WORST EQUITY AMOUNT
2005	03/18/05	-28873	04/12/05	-27603		1270.00	04/04/05	1445.00		
2004	03/18/04	-25060	04/12/04	-21570		3490.00	04/06/04	3765.00		
2003	03/18/03	-31665	04/11/03	-29703		1962.50	04/11/03	1962.50	03/31/03	-1015.00
2002	03/18/02	-23238	04/12/02	-21833		1405.00	03/28/02	2040.00	03/19/02	-135.00
2001	03/19/01	-23693	04/12/01	-22508		1185.00	04/12/01	1185.00	04/04/01	-1470.00
2000	03/20/00	-15335	04/12/00	-16645		-1310.00	03/29/00	1387.50	04/11/00	-1742.50
1999	03/18/99	-23593	04/12/99	-21188		2405.00	04/12/99	2405.00		
1998	03/18/98	-18348	04/09/98	-17655		692.50	03/30/98	2000.00		
1997	03/18/97	-8875	04/11/97	-7705		1170.00	04/09/97	2120.00	04/03/97	-1400.00
1996	03/18/96	-28920	04/12/96	-23650		5270.00	04/12/96	5270.00	03/19/96	-40.00
1995	03/20/95	-35973	04/12/95	-34883		1090.00	03/24/95	1605.00	04/03/95	-2860.00
1994	03/18/94	-15633	04/12/94	-14380		1252.50	04/08/94	1575.00	03/31/94	-3075.00
1993	03/18/93	-11258	04/12/93	-14015		-2757.50	03/19/93	85.00	04/01/93	-3872.50
1992	03/18/92	-7145	04/10/92	-6223		922.50	03/26/92	1440.00	04/09/92	-362.50
1991	03/18/91	-12388	04/12/91	-9500		2887.50	03/27/91	3662.50		
1990	03/19/90	-8442	04/12/90	-8438		5.00	04/04/90	1057.50	03/29/90	-892.50
1989	03/20/89	2565	04/12/89	4175		1610.00	03/31/89	2275.00	04/05/89	-647.50
1988	03/18/88	-16848	04/12/88	-16325		522.50	04/11/88	627.50	03/28/88	-3152.50
1987	03/18/87	-14538	04/10/87	-13068		1470.00	04/08/87	2162.50	03/23/87	-627.50

Percentage Correct	87								
Average Profit on Winning Trades				1923.27		Winners	13
Average Loss on Trades				-2033.75		Losers	2
Average Net Profit Per Trade				1395.67		Total trades	15
Percentage Correct	89						
Average Profit on Winning Trades				1682.94		Winners	17
Average Loss on Trades				-2033.75		Losers	2
Average Net Profit Per Trade				1291.71		Total trades	19

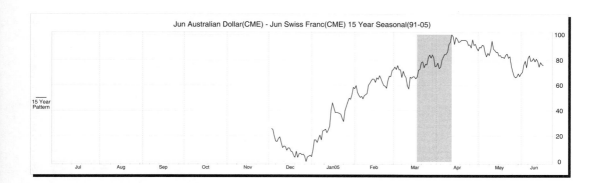

Jun Australian Dollar(CME) - Jun Swiss Franc(CME) 15 Year Seasonal(91-05)

15 Year Pattern

Jul Aug Sep Oct Nov Dec Jan05 Feb Mar Apr May Jun

Chapter 9: Forex

Figure 9-20

Buy Jun British Pound(IMM) / Sell Jun Swiss Franc(IMM)

Enter on approximately 03/19 - Exit on approximately 04/12

CONT YEAR	ENTRY DATE	ENTRY PRICE	EXIT DATE	EXIT PRICE		PROFIT AMOUNT	BEST EQUITY DATE	BEST EQUITY AMOUNT	WORST EQUITY DATE	WORST EQUITY AMOUNT
2005	03/21/05	11394	04/12/05	13088		1693.75	04/12/05	1693.75	03/23/05	-112.50
2004	03/19/04	14988	04/12/04	16719		1731.25	04/06/04	2343.75	03/25/04	-618.75
2003	03/19/03	7200	04/11/03	7887		687.50	04/11/03	687.50	03/31/03	-1475.00
2002	03/19/02	13163	04/12/02	14400		1237.50	03/28/02	1237.50		
2001	03/19/01	15313	04/12/01	16425		1112.50	03/28/01	1737.50	03/20/01	-50.00
2000	03/20/00	21950	04/12/00	22850		900.00	03/29/00	2675.00	04/06/00	-37.50
1999	03/19/99	15788	04/12/99	16000		212.50	03/26/99	462.50	04/06/99	-1875.00
1998	03/19/98	19388	04/09/98	20938		1550.00	04/01/98	2425.00		
1997	03/19/97	12413	04/11/97	15550		3137.50	04/08/97	3637.50		
1996	03/19/96	-10250	04/12/96	-7900		2350.00	04/12/96	2350.00	03/28/96	-475.00
1995	03/20/95	-9575	04/12/95	-9338		237.50	03/30/95	2150.00	04/05/95	-2075.00
1994	03/21/94	5575	04/12/94	5688		112.50	03/23/94	212.50	04/04/94	-1875.00
1993	03/19/93	10250	04/12/93	11225		975.00	04/12/93	975.00	03/30/93	-850.00
1992	03/19/92	23638	04/10/92	26875		3237.50	04/10/92	3237.50		
1991	03/19/91	21963	04/12/91	22487		525.00	04/10/91	600.00	03/25/91	-850.00
1990	03/19/90	16488	04/12/90	17200		712.50	04/04/90	1812.50	03/21/90	-487.50
1989	03/20/89	28288	04/12/89	29550		1262.50	04/10/89	1287.50	04/03/89	-50.00
1988	03/21/88	23438	04/12/88	25219		1781.25	04/08/88	2475.00	03/25/88	-37.50
1987	03/19/87	17519	04/10/87	17088		-431.25	04/08/87	500.00	03/30/87	-1800.00
1986	03/19/86	25538	04/11/86	27031		1493.75	04/07/86	2900.00		

Percentage Correct	100									
Average Profit on Winning Trades						1313.33		Winners		15
Average Loss on Trades								Losers		0
Average Net Profit Per Trade						1313.33		Total trades		15
Percentage Correct	95									
Average Profit on Winning Trades						1313.16		Winners		19
Average Loss on Trades						-431.25		Losers		1
Average Net Profit Per Trade						1225.94		Total trades		20

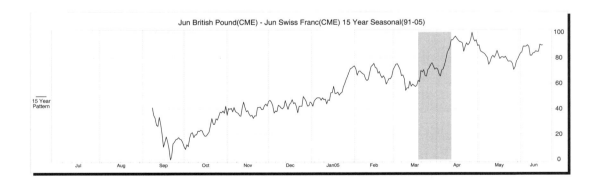

Jun British Pound(CME) - Jun Swiss Franc(CME) 15 Year Seasonal(91-05)

15 Year Pattern

Figure 9-21

Buy Jun Australian Dollar(IMM) / Sell Jun Japanese Yen(IMM)

Enter on approximately 05/02 - Exit on approximately 05/10

CONT YEAR	ENTRY DATE	ENTRY PRICE	EXIT DATE	EXIT PRICE		PROFIT AMOUNT	BEST EQUITY DATE	BEST EQUITY AMOUNT	WORST EQUITY DATE	WORST EQUITY AMOUNT
2005	05/02/05	-41715	05/10/05	-41493		222.50	05/10/05	222.50	05/03/05	-517.50
2004	05/03/04	-41593	05/10/04	-40753		840.00	05/10/04	840.00	05/05/04	-635.00
2003	05/02/03	-42502	05/09/03	-42418		85.00	05/05/03	255.00	05/07/03	-1570.00
2002	05/02/02	-44483	05/10/02	-43793		690.00	05/09/02	1202.50	05/03/02	-340.00
2001	05/02/01	-51175	05/10/01	-50035		1140.00	05/10/01	1140.00	05/08/01	-812.50
2000	05/02/00	-57473	05/10/00	-56813		660.00	05/03/00	1510.00		
1999	05/03/99	-38002	05/10/99	-37583		420.00	05/07/99	1332.50		
1998	05/04/98	-29730	05/08/98	-31035		-1305.00			05/05/98	-1845.00
1997	05/02/97	-21053	05/09/97	-26395		-5342.50			05/09/97	-5342.50
1996	05/02/96	-40893	05/10/96	-39063		1830.00	05/10/96	1830.00		
1995	05/02/95	-77550	05/10/95	-77170		380.00	05/05/95	2342.50	05/09/95	-327.50
1994	05/02/94	-51995	05/10/94	-47185		4810.00	05/10/94	4810.00	05/03/94	-1682.50
1993	05/03/93	-42325	05/10/93	-41790		535.00	05/10/93	535.00	05/04/93	-1357.50
1992	05/04/92	-18405	05/08/92	-18363		42.50	05/08/92	42.50	05/06/92	-762.50
1991	05/02/91	-13048	05/10/91	-11865		1182.50	05/10/91	1182.50		
1990	05/02/90	-4458	05/10/90	-4368		90.00	05/07/90	425.00	05/09/90	-492.50
1989	05/02/89	-15180	05/10/89	-14918		262.50	05/08/89	1262.50		
1988	05/02/88	-24650	05/10/88	-23673		977.50	05/09/88	1040.00		
1987	05/04/87	-20870	05/08/87	-19235		1635.00	05/08/87	1635.00		

Percentage Correct	87				
Average Profit on Winning Trades			987.50	Winners	13
Average Loss on Trades			-3323.75	Losers	2
Average Net Profit Per Trade			412.67	Total trades	15
Percentage Correct	89				
Average Profit on Winning Trades			929.56	Winners	17
Average Loss on Trades			-3323.75	Losers	2
Average Net Profit Per Trade			481.84	Total trades	19

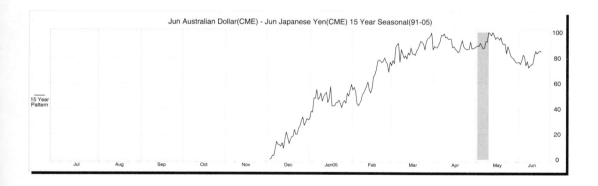

Jun Australian Dollar(CME) - Jun Japanese Yen(CME) 15 Year Seasonal(91-05)

Figure 9-22

Moore Research Center, Inc. *Buy Jun Canadian Dollar(IMM) / Sell Jun British Pound(IMM)*

Enter on approximately 05/30 - Exit on approximately 06/04

CONT YEAR	ENTRY DATE	ENTRY PRICE	EXIT DATE	EXIT PRICE		PROFIT AMOUNT	BEST EQUITY DATE	BEST EQUITY AMOUNT	WORST EQUITY DATE	WORST EQUITY AMOUNT
2005	05/31/05	-33778	06/03/05	-32998		780.00	06/01/05	843.75		
2004	06/01/04	-41799	06/04/04	-40859		940.00	06/04/04	940.00		
2003	05/30/03	-29280	06/04/03	-28403		877.50	06/04/03	877.50	06/02/03	-107.50
2002	05/30/02	-26370	06/04/02	-25825		545.00	05/31/02	895.00		
2001	05/30/01	-24460	06/04/01	-23285		1175.00	06/04/01	1175.00		
2000	05/30/00	-27170	06/02/00	-26435		735.00	06/01/00	910.00		
1999	06/01/99	-33340	06/04/99	-32645		695.00	06/03/99	712.50		
1998	06/01/98	-33865	06/04/98	-33565		300.00	06/02/98	412.50		
1997	05/30/97	-29835	06/04/97	-29195		640.00	06/04/97	640.00		
1996	05/30/96	-22823	06/04/96	-23838		-1015.00			06/03/96	-1207.50
1995	05/30/95	-27298	06/02/95	-26698		600.00	05/31/95	847.50		
1994	05/31/94	-22113	06/03/94	-21553		560.00	06/03/94	560.00	06/01/94	-565.00
1993	06/01/93	-18153	06/04/93	-16000		2152.50	06/04/93	2152.50		
1992	06/01/92	-31110	06/04/92	-30323		787.50	06/03/92	855.00		
1991	05/30/91	-19588	06/04/91	-18748		840.00	06/03/91	1035.00		
1990	05/30/90	-20888	06/04/90	-19468		1420.00	05/31/90	1482.50		
1989	05/30/89	-15145	06/02/89	-17240		-2095.00			06/02/89	-2095.00
1988	05/31/88	-33639	06/03/88	-31318		2321.25	06/03/88	2321.25		
1987	06/01/87	-26861	06/04/87	-27310		-448.75			06/02/87	-1468.75
1986	05/30/86	-19700	06/04/86	-21073		-1372.50			06/03/86	-1745.00

Percentage Correct	93			
Average Profit on Winning Trades	830.54	Winners	14
Average Loss on Trades	-1015.00	Losers	1
Average Net Profit Per Trade	707.50	Total trades	15
Percentage Correct	80			
Average Profit on Winning Trades	960.55	Winners	16
Average Loss on Trades	-1232.81	Losers	4
Average Net Profit Per Trade	521.87	Total trades	20

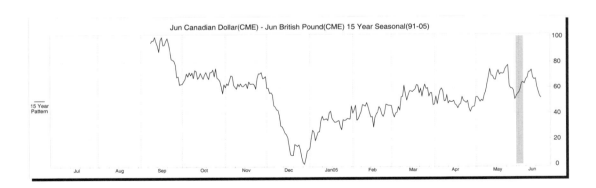

Jun Canadian Dollar(CME) - Jun British Pound(CME) 15 Year Seasonal(91-05)

Figure 9-23

Moore Research Center, Inc. — *Buy Jun Canadian Dollar(IMM) / Sell Jun Japanese Yen(IMM)*

Enter on approximately 05/30 - Exit on approximately 06/05

CONT YEAR	ENTRY DATE	ENTRY PRICE	EXIT DATE	EXIT PRICE		PROFIT AMOUNT	BEST EQUITY DATE	BEST EQUITY AMOUNT	WORST EQUITY DATE	WORST EQUITY AMOUNT
2005	05/31/05	-35578	06/03/05	-35748		-170.00	06/01/05	537.50	06/03/05	-170.00
2004	06/01/04	-40005	06/04/04	-38503		1502.50	06/04/04	1502.50	06/02/04	-172.50
2003	05/30/03	-31768	06/05/03	-31675		92.50	06/05/03	92.50	06/02/03	-782.50
2002	05/30/02	-36408	06/05/02	-35270		1137.50	05/31/02	1182.50		
2001	05/30/01	-39410	06/05/01	-38698		712.50	06/05/01	712.50	05/31/01	-617.50
2000	05/30/00	-51358	06/05/00	-48673		2685.00	06/02/00	3335.00		
1999	06/01/99	-36453	06/04/99	-34333		2120.00	06/04/99	2120.00		
1998	06/01/98	-21053	06/05/98	-20842		210.00	06/05/98	210.00	06/04/98	-650.00
1997	05/30/97	-35085	06/05/97	-35573		-487.50	06/02/97	477.50	06/05/97	-487.50
1996	05/30/96	-43248	06/05/96	-41618		1630.00	06/05/96	1630.00		
1995	05/30/95	-78448	06/05/95	-74938		3510.00	06/01/95	3725.00		
1994	05/31/94	-47113	06/03/94	-46190		922.50	06/03/94	922.50	06/01/94	-402.50
1993	06/01/93	-38140	06/04/93	-37787		352.50	06/04/93	352.50		
1992	06/01/92	-15535	06/05/92	-14793		742.50	06/04/92	1050.00		
1991	05/30/91	-3488	06/05/91	-2435		1052.50	06/05/91	1052.50		
1990	05/30/90	2125	06/05/90	2823		697.50	06/04/90	995.00		
1989	05/30/89	-5045	06/05/89	-4488		557.50	06/05/89	557.50	06/02/89	-1045.00
1988	05/31/88	-18895	06/03/88	-18218		677.50	06/02/88	1105.00		
1987	06/01/87	-11430	06/05/87	-12585		-1155.00			06/02/87	-2562.50
1986	05/30/86	588	06/05/86	-2350		-2937.50			06/05/86	-2937.50

Percentage Correct	87							
Average Profit on Winning Trades				1282.31		Winners	13
Average Loss on Trades				-328.75		Losers	2
Average Net Profit Per Trade				1067.50		Total trades	15
Percentage Correct	80							
Average Profit on Winning Trades				1162.66		Winners	16
Average Loss on Trades				-1187.50		Losers	4
Average Net Profit Per Trade				692.63		Total trades	20

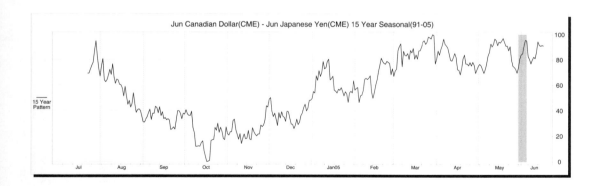

Jun Canadian Dollar(CME) - Jun Japanese Yen(CME) 15 Year Seasonal(91-05)

15 Year Pattern

Figure 9-24

Moore Research Center, Inc.

Buy Sep British Pound(IMM) / Sell Sep Japanese Yen(IMM)

Enter on approximately 06/08 - Exit on approximately 07/06

CONT YEAR	ENTRY DATE	ENTRY PRICE	EXIT DATE	EXIT PRICE		PROFIT AMOUNT	BEST EQUITY DATE	BEST EQUITY AMOUNT	WORST EQUITY DATE	WORST EQUITY AMOUNT
2005	06/08/05	-4075	07/06/05	-2725		1350.00	06/27/05	2675.00	06/09/05	-18.75
2004	06/08/04	-719	07/06/04	-88		631.25	07/06/04	631.25	06/24/04	-2950.00
2003	06/09/03	-3988	07/03/03	-2050		1937.50	06/17/03	2575.00		
2002	06/10/02	-10075	07/05/02	-9600		475.00	06/18/02	1775.00	06/21/02	-275.00
2001	06/08/01	-18363	07/06/01	-11875		6487.50	07/06/01	6487.50		
2000	06/08/00	-25275	07/06/00	-23500		1775.00	07/06/00	1775.00	06/23/00	-1875.00
1999	06/08/99	-6313	07/06/99	-5813		500.00	06/21/99	2537.50	06/17/99	-300.00
1998	06/08/98	11413	07/06/98	11800		387.50	06/25/98	3787.50	06/17/98	-500.00
1997	06/09/97	-10137	07/03/97	-5750		4387.50	07/03/97	4387.50	06/11/97	-1837.50
1996	06/10/96	-20337	07/05/96	-16763		3575.00	07/03/96	3625.00	06/18/96	-650.00
1995	06/08/95	-49863	07/06/95	-48288		1575.00	07/06/95	1575.00	06/27/95	-1325.00
1994	06/08/94	-26875	07/06/94	-30625		-3750.00	06/17/94	587.50	07/01/94	-4512.50
1993	06/08/93	-23238	07/06/93	-21338		1900.00	06/21/93	2950.00	06/25/93	-2825.00
1992	06/08/92	14738	07/06/92	17650		2912.50	07/02/92	3637.50		
1991	06/10/91	15225	07/05/91	9963		-5262.50			07/02/91	-5837.50
1990	06/08/90	21763	07/06/90	27650		5887.50	07/06/90	5887.50		
1989	06/08/89	9100	07/06/89	10313		1212.50	07/06/89	1212.50	06/23/89	-3125.00
1988	06/08/88	12325	07/06/88	12438		112.50	07/05/88	362.50	06/27/88	-2600.00
1987	06/08/87	14094	07/06/87	16731		2637.50	07/06/87	2637.50	06/22/87	-1456.25
1986	06/09/86	18400	07/03/86	17994		-406.25	06/27/86	856.25	06/20/86	-512.50

Percentage Correct	87								
Average Profit on Winning Trades						2145.67		Winners	13
Average Loss on Trades						-4506.25		Losers	2
Average Net Profit Per Trade						1258.75		Total trades	15
Percentage Correct	85								
Average Profit on Winning Trades						2220.22		Winners	17
Average Loss on Trades						-3139.58		Losers	3
Average Net Profit Per Trade						1416.25		Total trades	20

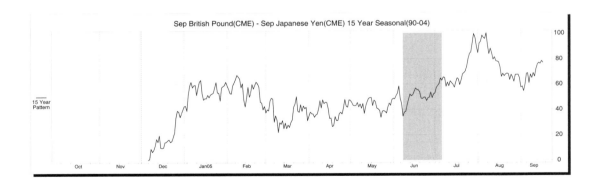

Sep British Pound(CME) - Sep Japanese Yen(CME) 15 Year Seasonal(90-04)

Chapter 9: Forex

Figure 9-25

Buy Sep British Pound(IMM) / Sell Sep Swiss Franc(IMM)

Enter on approximately 06/11 - Exit on approximately 07/12

CONT YEAR	ENTRY DATE	ENTRY PRICE	EXIT DATE	EXIT PRICE		PROFIT AMOUNT	BEST EQUITY DATE	BEST EQUITY AMOUNT	WORST EQUITY DATE	WORST EQUITY AMOUNT
2004	06/14/04	12600	07/12/04	13694		1093.75	06/16/04	1912.50	07/02/04	-475.00
2003	06/11/03	7788	07/11/03	10238		2450.00	07/07/03	3612.50	06/13/03	-412.50
2002	06/11/02	11013	07/12/02	12200		1187.50	07/11/02	1350.00	06/25/02	-762.50
2001	06/11/01	16138	07/12/01	17087		950.00	07/02/01	2462.50	06/12/01	-462.50
2000	06/12/00	17638	07/12/00	18125		487.50	06/22/00	887.50	06/14/00	-1125.00
1999	06/11/99	17713	07/12/99	17763		50.00	07/02/99	675.00	06/25/99	-737.50
1998	06/11/98	16913	07/10/98	19963		3050.00	06/29/98	4262.50		
1997	06/11/97	14125	07/11/97	19538		5412.50	07/03/97	5437.50		
1996	06/11/96	-3700	07/12/96	-2825		875.00	07/05/96	1425.00	06/13/96	-912.50
1995	06/12/95	-9438	07/12/95	-8450		987.50	06/15/95	1375.00	06/27/95	-1350.00
1994	06/13/94	4775	07/12/94	938		-3837.50			07/12/94	-3837.50
1993	06/11/93	8888	07/12/93	10338		1450.00	07/01/93	2837.50	06/23/93	-25.00
1992	06/11/92	27662	07/10/92	27313		-350.00	06/24/92	137.50	07/06/92	-1025.00
1991	06/11/91	20188	07/12/91	21887		1700.00	07/12/91	1700.00	06/17/91	-475.00
1990	06/11/90	17050	07/12/90	22100		5050.00	07/10/90	5887.50		
1989	06/12/89	22237	07/12/89	23150		912.50	07/06/89	1125.00	06/29/89	-1275.00
1988	06/13/88	25525	07/12/88	22825		-2700.00			06/27/88	-3375.00
1987	06/11/87	18463	07/10/87	18838		375.00	07/09/87	581.25	06/23/87	-1681.25
1986	06/11/86	26056	07/11/86	23400		-2656.25			07/11/86	-2656.25
1985	06/11/85	29463	07/12/85	33681		4218.75	07/10/85	5100.00		

Percentage Correct	87								
Average Profit on Winning Trades						1903.37		Winners	13
Average Loss on Trades						-2093.75		Losers	2
Average Net Profit Per Trade						1370.42		Total trades	15
Percentage Correct	80								
Average Profit on Winning Trades						1890.63		Winners	16
Average Loss on Trades						-2385.94		Losers	4
Average Net Profit Per Trade						1035.31		Total trades	20

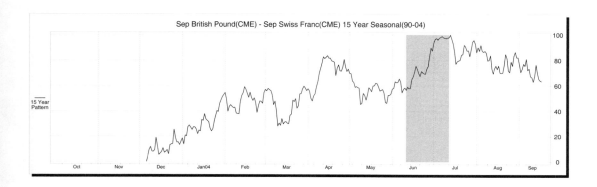

Sep British Pound(CME) - Sep Swiss Franc(CME) 15 Year Seasonal(90-04)

15 Year Pattern

Chapter 9: Forex

335

Figure 9-26

Buy Sep Swiss Franc(IMM) / Sell Sep Japanese Yen(IMM)

Enter on approximately 07/14 - Exit on approximately 07/29

CONT YEAR	ENTRY DATE	ENTRY PRICE	EXIT DATE	EXIT PRICE	PROFIT	PROFIT AMOUNT	BEST EQUITY DATE	BEST EQUITY AMOUNT	WORST EQUITY DATE	WORST EQUITY AMOUNT
2004	07/14/04	-10.37	07/29/04	-11.20	-0.83	-1037.50	07/16/04	12.50	07/23/04	-2075.00
2003	07/14/03	-12.37	07/29/03	-9.45	2.92	3650.00	07/28/03	3712.50	07/15/03	-350.00
2002	07/15/02	-17.62	07/29/02	-16.32	1.31	1637.50	07/26/02	2062.50	07/16/02	-37.50
2001	07/16/01	-23.66	07/27/01	-23.20	0.45	562.50	07/25/01	875.00	07/20/01	-325.00
2000	07/14/00	-32.81	07/28/00	-32.14	0.66	825.00	07/26/00	1662.50	07/19/00	-725.00
1999	07/14/99	-19.64	07/29/99	-19.62	0.02	25.00	07/21/99	325.00	07/19/99	-1687.50
1998	07/14/98	-5.92	07/29/98	-2.98	2.93	3662.50	07/29/98	3662.50		
1997	07/14/97	-20.28	07/29/97	-18.75	1.54	1925.00	07/21/97	2175.00		
1996	07/15/96	-11.05	07/29/96	-9.89	1.17	1462.50	07/16/96	1887.50		
1995	07/14/95	-28.44	07/28/95	-26.87	1.56	1950.00	07/28/95	1950.00		
1994	07/14/94	-25.64	07/29/94	-25.55	0.09	112.50	07/18/94	325.00	07/26/94	-2925.00
1993	07/14/93	-27.14	07/29/93	-28.67	-1.52	-1900.00	07/19/93	1937.50	07/29/93	-1900.00
1992	07/14/92	-5.89	07/29/92	-2.77	3.13	3912.50	07/28/92	4625.00		
1991	07/15/91	-8.48	07/29/91	-7.09	1.39	1737.50	07/24/91	2225.00	07/16/91	-512.50
1990	07/16/90	2.75	07/27/90	6.21	3.47	4337.50	07/27/90	4337.50		
1989	07/14/89	-10.63	07/28/89	-10.19	0.44	550.00	07/25/89	1950.00		
1988	07/14/88	-9.89	07/29/88	-11.13	-1.24	-1550.00	07/15/88	362.50	07/29/88	-1550.00
1987	07/14/87	-1.35	07/29/87	-1.38	-0.02	-25.00	07/22/87	550.00	07/24/87	-437.50
1986	07/14/86	-6.25	07/29/86	-5.15	1.09	1362.50	07/29/86	1362.50	07/17/86	-112.50
1985	07/15/85	-0.21	07/29/85	1.35	1.57	1962.50	07/26/85	2025.00		

Percentage Correct		87								
Average Profit on Winning Trades					1.59	1984.62		Winners		13
Average Loss on Trades					-1.18	-1468.75		Losers		2
Average Net Profit Per Trade					1.22	1524.17		Total trades		15
Percentage Correct		80								
Average Profit on Winning Trades					1.48	1854.69		Winners		16
Average Loss on Trades					-0.90	-1128.13		Losers		4
Average Net Profit Per Trade					1.01	1258.13		Total trades		20

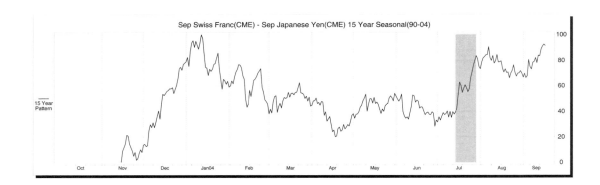

Sep Swiss Franc(CME) - Sep Japanese Yen(CME) 15 Year Seasonal(90-04)

15 Year Pattern

Oct   Nov   Dec   Jan04   Feb   Mar   Apr   May   Jun   Jul   Aug   Sep

Figure 9-27

CONT YEAR	ENTRY DATE	ENTRY PRICE	EXIT DATE	EXIT PRICE		PROFIT AMOUNT	BEST EQUITY DATE	BEST EQUITY AMOUNT	WORST EQUITY DATE	WORST EQUITY AMOUNT

Buy Dec Swiss Franc(IMM) / Sell Dec Australian Dollar(IMM)

Enter on approximately 08/17 - Exit on approximately 09/30

CONT YEAR	ENTRY DATE	ENTRY PRICE	EXIT DATE	EXIT PRICE		PROFIT AMOUNT	BEST EQUITY DATE	BEST EQUITY AMOUNT	WORST EQUITY DATE	WORST EQUITY AMOUNT
2004	08/17/04	30155	09/30/04	28345		-1810.00	09/09/04	902.50	08/27/04	-1910.00
2003	08/18/03	25257	09/30/03	27403		2145.00	09/30/03	2145.00	08/22/03	-1235.00
2002	08/19/02	29765	09/30/02	30968		1202.50	09/05/02	1765.00	09/17/02	-1405.00
2001	08/17/01	22155	09/28/01	28275		6120.00	09/21/01	8777.50	09/05/01	-672.50
2000	08/17/00	14718	09/29/00	18540		3822.50	09/29/00	3822.50	08/21/00	-730.00
1999	08/17/99	18270	09/30/99	18803		532.50	08/20/99	2755.00	09/10/99	-2087.50
1998	08/17/98	24682	09/30/98	31800		7117.50	09/23/98	8140.00	08/18/98	-552.50
1997	08/18/97	9778	09/30/97	14250		4472.50	09/16/97	5565.00	08/20/97	-1502.50
1996	08/19/96	25883	09/30/96	21598		-4285.00	08/27/96	1440.00	09/27/96	-4397.50
1995	08/17/95	30543	09/29/95	33510		2967.50	09/21/95	5805.00	09/13/95	-3615.00
1994	08/17/94	22503	09/30/94	23398		895.00	09/21/94	1980.00	08/31/94	-2692.50
1993	08/17/93	15810	09/30/93	23223		7412.50	09/10/93	9020.00	08/19/93	-62.50
1992	08/17/92	21657	09/30/92	29468		7810.00	09/29/92	8237.50	09/14/92	-705.00
1991	08/19/91	2945	09/30/91	6362		3417.50	09/26/91	3462.50		
1990	08/17/90	17855	09/28/90	14560		-3295.00			09/21/90	-5300.00
1989	08/17/89	688	09/29/89	1038		350.00	09/28/89	372.50	09/22/89	-3155.00
1988	08/17/88	270	09/30/88	2328		2057.50	09/20/88	2935.00	08/23/88	-1745.00
1987	08/17/87	11285	09/30/87	11755		470.00	08/27/87	3517.50	09/23/87	-575.00

Percentage Correct	80			
Average Profit on Winning Trades		3992.92	Winners	12
Average Loss on Trades		-3130.00	Losers	3
Average Net Profit Per Trade		2568.33	Total trades	15
Percentage Correct	83			
Average Profit on Winning Trades		3386.17	Winners	15
Average Loss on Trades		-3130.00	Losers	3
Average Net Profit Per Trade		2300.14	Total trades	18

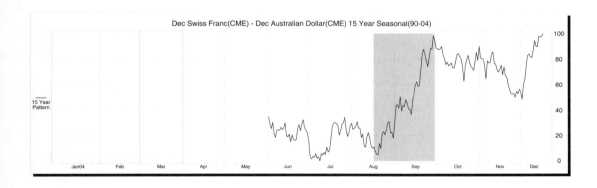

Dec Swiss Franc(CME) - Dec Australian Dollar(CME) 15 Year Seasonal(90-04)

Figure 9-28

Buy Dec British Pound(IMM) / Sell Dec Australian Dollar(IMM)

Enter on approximately 08/18 - Exit on approximately 09/29

CONT YEAR	ENTRY DATE	ENTRY PRICE	EXIT DATE	EXIT PRICE	PROFIT AMOUNT	BEST EQUITY DATE	BEST EQUITY AMOUNT	WORST EQUITY DATE	WORST EQUITY AMOUNT
2004	08/18/04	41981	09/29/04	40678	-1303.75	09/09/04	538.75	09/29/04	-1303.75
2003	08/18/03	33495	09/29/03	36478	2982.50	09/29/03	2982.50	09/16/03	-625.00
2002	08/19/02	41028	09/27/02	43115	2087.50	09/05/02	2652.50	08/27/02	-672.50
2001	08/20/01	36835	09/28/01	42725	5890.00	09/27/01	6385.00	08/24/01	-255.00
2000	08/18/00	34183	09/29/00	38003	3820.00	09/29/00	3820.00	09/11/00	-2150.00
1999	08/18/99	35518	09/29/99	37412	1895.00	08/19/99	2187.50	09/13/99	-705.00
1998	08/18/98	40730	09/29/98	46613	5882.50	08/28/98	7202.50		
1997	08/18/97	26228	09/29/97	28260	2032.50	09/25/97	2537.50	08/21/97	-2320.00
1996	08/19/96	17733	09/27/96	18873	1140.00	09/24/96	1687.50	09/10/96	-340.00
1995	08/18/95	23078	09/29/95	23198	120.00	09/21/95	2045.00	09/13/95	-2725.00
1994	08/18/94	22925	09/29/94	24828	1902.50	09/21/94	2395.00	08/30/94	-1477.50
1993	08/18/93	26823	09/29/93	29670	2847.50	09/10/93	4845.00	08/25/93	-1842.50
1992	08/18/92	46538	09/29/92	39070	-7467.50	09/08/92	5732.50	09/22/92	-13662.50
1991	08/19/91	23020	09/27/91	28588	5567.50	09/10/91	5722.50		
1990	08/20/90	37623	09/28/90	33798	-3825.00	08/23/90	165.00	09/21/90	-6192.50
1989	08/18/89	22490	09/29/89	23875	1385.00	09/29/89	1385.00	09/14/89	-2422.50
1988	08/18/88	25488	09/29/88	26813	1325.00	09/28/88	1925.00	08/23/88	-2225.00
1987	08/18/87	29540	09/29/87	30033	492.50	09/03/87	1911.25	09/21/87	-13.75

Percentage Correct	80			
Average Profit on Winning Trades		3013.96	Winners	12
Average Loss on Trades		-4198.75	Losers	3
Average Net Profit Per Trade		1571.42	Total trades	15

Percentage Correct	83			
Average Profit on Winning Trades		2624.67	Winners	15
Average Loss on Trades		-4198.75	Losers	3
Average Net Profit Per Trade		1487.43	Total trades	18

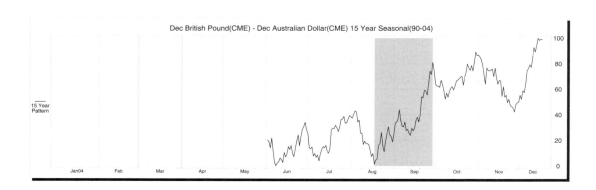

Dec British Pound(CME) - Dec Australian Dollar(CME) 15 Year Seasonal(90-04)

Figure 9-29

| | Moore Research Center, Inc. | Buy Dec Swiss Franc(IMM) / Sell Dec Canadian Dollar(IMM) | | | | | | | | |

Enter on approximately 08/31 - Exit on approximately 10/02

CONT YEAR	ENTRY DATE	ENTRY PRICE	EXIT DATE	EXIT PRICE		PROFIT AMOUNT	BEST EQUITY DATE	BEST EQUITY AMOUNT	WORST EQUITY DATE	WORST EQUITY AMOUNT
2004	08/31/04	22838	10/01/04	21132		-1705.00	09/01/04	240.00	09/27/04	-1957.50
2003	09/02/03	16830	10/02/03	20713		3882.50	10/01/03	4432.50	09/03/03	-437.50
2002	09/03/02	20930	10/02/02	21655		725.00	09/30/02	1087.50	09/17/02	-1240.00
2001	08/31/01	10635	10/02/01	13610		2975.00	09/21/01	4917.50	09/05/01	-1432.50
2000	08/31/00	4283	10/02/00	6138		1855.00	09/29/00	1967.50	09/08/00	-1302.50
1999	08/31/99	16583	10/01/99	17363		780.00	09/02/99	1135.00	09/10/99	-3050.00
1998	08/31/98	24100	10/02/98	28215		4115.00	10/02/98	4115.00	09/02/98	-1320.00
1997	09/02/97	11283	10/02/97	13468		2185.00	09/15/97	3800.00		
1996	09/03/96	31208	10/02/96	26373		-4835.00	09/05/96	177.50	10/02/96	-4835.00
1995	08/31/95	30485	10/02/95	34535		4050.00	09/21/95	6802.50	09/06/95	-1425.00
1994	08/31/94	21000	09/30/94	22798		1797.50	09/09/94	3922.50		
1993	08/31/93	8808	10/01/93	13090		4282.50	09/10/93	4972.50		
1992	08/31/92	15483	10/02/92	21860		6377.50	10/02/92	6377.50	09/14/92	-3640.00
1991	09/03/91	-5398	10/02/91	-2583		2815.00	09/30/91	3310.00	09/05/91	-190.00
1990	08/31/90	9970	10/02/90	10908		937.50	09/17/90	2555.00	09/21/90	-1205.00
1989	08/31/89	-10013	10/02/89	-7348		2665.00	09/29/89	2880.00	09/05/89	-795.00
1988	08/31/88	-263	09/30/88	-2133		-1870.00	09/07/88	1455.00	09/29/88	-2180.00
1987	08/31/87	9115	10/02/87	5865		-3250.00	09/03/87	352.50	10/02/87	-3250.00
1986	09/02/86	5260	10/02/86	5528		267.50	09/19/86	1250.00	09/11/86	-2820.00
1985	09/03/85	-19190	10/02/85	-14860		4330.00	10/01/85	4827.50	09/11/85	-1687.50

Percentage Correct	87							
Average Profit on Winning Trades				2829.04		Winners	13	
Average Loss on Trades				-3270.00		Losers	2	
Average Net Profit Per Trade				2015.83		Total trades	15	
Percentage Correct	80							
Average Profit on Winning Trades				2752.50		Winners	16	
Average Loss on Trades				-2915.00		Losers	4	
Average Net Profit Per Trade				1619.00		Total trades	20	

HYPOTHETICAL PERFORMANCE RESULTS HAVE MANY INHERENT LIMITATIONS, SOME OF WHICH ARE DESCRIBED BELOW. NO REPRESENTATION IS BEING MADE THAT ANY ACCOUNT WILL OR IS LIKELY TO ACHIEVE PROFITS OR LOSSES SIMILAR TO THOSE SHOWN. IN FACT, THERE ARE FREQUENTLY SHARP DIFFERENCES BETWEEN HYPOTHETICAL PERFORMANCE RESULTS AND THE ACTUAL RESULTS SUBSEQUENTLY ACHIEVED BY ANY PARTICULAR TRADING PROGRAM. ONE OF THE LIMITATIONS OF HYPOTHETICAL PERFORMANCE RESULTS IS THAT THEY ARE GENERALLY PREPARED WITH THE BENEFIT OF HINDSIGHT. IN ADDITION, HYPOTHETICAL TRADING DOES NOT INVOLVE FINANCIAL RISK, AND NO HYPOTHETICAL TRADING RECORD CAN COMPLETELY ACCOUNT FOR THE IMPACT OF FINANCIAL RISK IN ACTUAL TRADING. FOR EXAMPLE, THE ABILITY TO WITHSTAND LOSSES OR ADHERE TO A PARTICULAR TRADING PROGRAM IN SPITE OF TRADING LOSSES ARE MATERIAL POINTS WHICH CAN ALSO ADVERSELY AFFECT ACTUAL TRADING RESULTS. THERE ARE NUMEROUS OTHER FACTORS RELATED TO THE MARKETS IN GENERAL OR TO THE IMPLEMENTATION OF ANY SPECIFIC TRADING PROGRAM WHICH CANNOT BE FULLY ACCOUNTED FOR IN THE PREPARATION OF HYPOTHETICAL PERFORMANCE RESULTS AND ALL OF WHICH CAN ADVERSELY AFFECT ACTUAL TRADING RESULTS. RESULTS NOT ADJUSTED FOR COMMISSION AND SLIPPAGE.

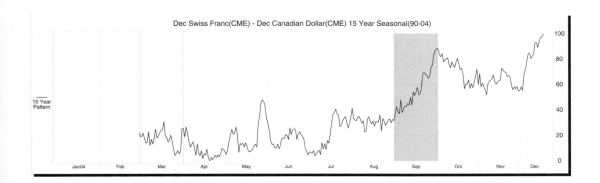

Dec Swiss Franc(CME) - Dec Canadian Dollar(CME) 15 Year Seasonal(90-04)

Figure 9-30

Moore Research Center, Inc. — *Buy Sep Australian Dollar(IMM) / Sell Sep Canadian Dollar(IMM)*

Enter on approximately 09/03 - Exit on approximately 09/08

CONT YEAR	ENTRY DATE	ENTRY PRICE	EXIT DATE	EXIT PRICE	PROFIT	PROFIT AMOUNT	BEST EQUITY DATE	BEST EQUITY AMOUNT	WORST EQUITY DATE	WORST EQUITY AMOUNT
2004	09/03/04	-8.07	09/08/04	-7.92	0.15	150.00	09/08/04	150.00	09/07/04	-270.00
2003	09/03/03	-8.45	09/08/03	-7.90	0.55	550.00	09/08/03	550.00	09/04/03	-300.00
2002	09/03/02	-9.66	09/06/02	-9.40	0.26	260.00	09/04/02	300.00		
2001	09/04/01	-12.17	09/07/01	-11.92	0.25	250.00	09/07/01	250.00	09/05/01	-0.00
2000	09/05/00	-10.87	09/08/00	-12.04	-1.16	-1160.00			09/08/00	-1160.00
1999	09/03/99	-2.35	09/08/99	-2.34	0.01	10.00	09/07/99	250.00		
1998	09/03/98	-6.55	09/08/98	-6.66	-0.11	-110.00			09/04/98	-350.00
1997	09/03/97	0.42	09/08/97	0.57	0.16	160.00	09/04/97	660.00		
1996	09/03/96	6.10	09/06/96	7.21	1.11	1110.00	09/06/96	1110.00	09/04/96	-30.00
1995	09/05/95	0.62	09/08/95	0.66	0.04	40.00	09/07/95	130.00	09/06/95	-250.00
1994	09/06/94	0.95	09/08/94	1.68	0.73	730.00	09/08/94	730.00		
1993	09/03/93	-10.53	09/08/93	-10.01	0.51	510.00	09/08/93	510.00	09/07/93	-120.00
1992	09/03/92	-11.42	09/08/92	-11.54	-0.12	-120.00			09/08/92	-120.00
1991	09/03/91	-9.50	09/06/91	-8.87	0.63	630.00	09/06/91	630.00		
1990	09/04/90	-4.48	09/07/90	-3.75	0.74	740.00	09/07/90	740.00		
1989	09/05/89	-8.98	09/08/89	-7.75	1.23	1230.00	09/08/89	1230.00		
1988	09/06/88	-0.65	09/08/88	-0.21	0.44	440.00	09/08/88	440.00		
1987	09/03/87	-3.85	09/08/87	-3.25	0.61	610.00	09/08/87	610.00		

Percentage Correct		80								
Average Profit on Winning Trades					0.43	428.33		Winners		12
Average Loss on Trades					-0.46	-463.33		Losers		3
Average Net Profit Per Trade					0.25	250.00		Total trades		15
Percentage Correct		83								
Average Profit on Winning Trades					0.49	494.67		Winners		15
Average Loss on Trades					-0.46	-463.33		Losers		3
Average Net Profit Per Trade					0.34	335.00		Total trades		18

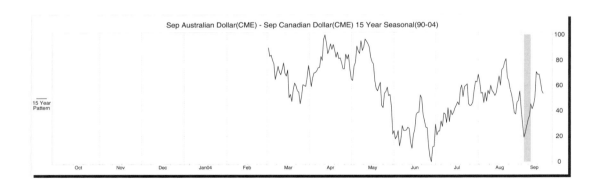

Sep Australian Dollar(CME) - Sep Canadian Dollar(CME) 15 Year Seasonal(90-04)

15 Year Pattern

Figure 9-31

Buy Dec Swiss Franc(IMM) / Sell Dec Australian Dollar(IMM)

Enter on approximately 09/12 - Exit on approximately 09/25

CONT YEAR	ENTRY DATE	ENTRY PRICE	EXIT DATE	EXIT PRICE		PROFIT AMOUNT	BEST EQUITY DATE	BEST EQUITY AMOUNT	WORST EQUITY DATE	WORST EQUITY AMOUNT
2004	09/13/04	30727	09/24/04	28395		-2332.50			09/24/04	-2332.50
2003	09/12/03	25283	09/25/03	25755		472.50	09/25/03	472.50	09/18/03	-980.00
2002	09/12/02	28885	09/25/02	29340		455.00	09/24/02	1102.50	09/17/02	-525.00
2001	09/13/01	24545	09/25/01	29555		5010.00	09/21/01	6387.50		
2000	09/12/00	15425	09/25/00	17443		2017.50	09/22/00	2990.00		
1999	09/13/99	16225	09/24/99	17098		872.50	09/21/99	1532.50		
1998	09/14/98	30550	09/25/98	32030		1480.00	09/23/98	2272.50		
1997	09/12/97	14078	09/25/97	14290		212.50	09/16/97	1265.00	09/22/97	-502.50
1996	09/12/96	22410	09/25/96	22720		310.00	09/24/96	1997.50		
1995	09/12/95	28990	09/25/95	34648		5657.50	09/21/95	7357.50	09/13/95	-2062.50
1994	09/12/94	23388	09/23/94	23415		27.50	09/21/94	1095.00	09/20/94	-235.00
1993	09/13/93	23810	09/24/93	21843		-1967.50	09/15/93	987.50	09/23/93	-2120.00
1992	09/14/92	20953	09/25/92	23783		2830.00	09/25/92	2830.00		
1991	09/12/91	5438	09/25/91	5870		432.50	09/25/91	432.50	09/18/91	-315.00
1990	09/12/90	13045	09/25/90	13215		170.00	09/17/90	2440.00	09/21/90	-490.00
1989	09/12/89	-1698	09/25/89	-1450		247.50	09/20/89	510.00	09/22/89	-770.00
1988	09/12/88	2420	09/23/88	2433		12.50	09/20/88	785.00	09/15/88	-1460.00
1987	09/14/87	11510	09/25/87	11460		-50.00	09/15/87	190.00	09/23/87	-800.00

Percentage Correct	87			
Average Profit on Winning Trades		1534.42	Winners	13
Average Loss on Trades		-2150.00	Losers	2
Average Net Profit Per Trade		1043.17	Total trades	15
Percentage Correct	83			
Average Profit on Winning Trades		1347.17	Winners	15
Average Loss on Trades		-1450.00	Losers	3
Average Net Profit Per Trade		880.97	Total trades	18

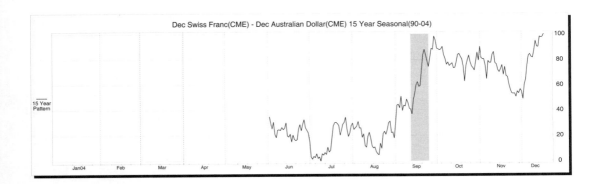

Dec Swiss Franc(CME) - Dec Australian Dollar(CME) 15 Year Seasonal(90-04)

Figure 9-32

Moore Research Center, Inc. — *Buy Dec British Pound(IMM) / Sell Dec Australian Dollar(IMM)*

Enter on approximately 09/20 - Exit on approximately 09/29

CONT YEAR	ENTRY DATE	ENTRY PRICE	EXIT DATE	EXIT PRICE		PROFIT AMOUNT	BEST EQUITY DATE	BEST EQUITY AMOUNT	WORST EQUITY DATE	WORST EQUITY AMOUNT
2004	09/20/04	41375	09/29/04	40678		-697.50	09/21/04	520.00	09/29/04	-697.50
2003	09/22/03	35223	09/29/03	36478		1255.00	09/29/03	1255.00		
2002	09/20/02	42458	09/27/02	43115		657.50	09/27/02	657.50		
2001	09/20/01	42088	09/28/01	42725		637.50	09/27/01	1132.50		
2000	09/20/00	34465	09/29/00	38003		3537.50	09/29/00	3537.50		
1999	09/20/99	37137	09/29/99	37412		275.00	09/27/99	457.50	09/22/99	-560.00
1998	09/21/98	46215	09/29/98	46613		397.50	09/24/98	845.00		
1997	09/22/97	27650	09/29/97	28260		610.00	09/25/97	1115.00		
1996	09/20/96	18173	09/27/96	18873		700.00	09/24/96	1247.50		
1995	09/20/95	21423	09/29/95	23198		1775.00	09/21/95	3700.00		
1994	09/20/94	23940	09/29/94	24828		887.50	09/21/94	1380.00		
1993	09/20/93	30400	09/29/93	29670		-730.00			09/23/93	-2135.00
1992	09/21/92	33270	09/29/92	39070		5800.00	09/29/92	5800.00	09/22/92	-395.00
1991	09/20/91	28008	09/27/91	28588		580.00	09/26/91	612.50	09/24/91	-112.50
1990	09/20/90	33738	09/28/90	33798		60.00	09/27/90	232.50	09/21/90	-2307.50
1989	09/20/89	22025	09/29/89	23875		1850.00	09/29/89	1850.00	09/22/89	-1355.00
1988	09/20/88	27193	09/29/88	26813		-380.00	09/28/88	220.00	09/22/88	-1210.00
1987	09/21/87	29526	09/29/87	30033		506.25	09/25/87	696.25		

Percentage Correct	87			
Average Profit on Winning Trades		1320.96	Winners	13
Average Loss on Trades		-713.75	Losers	2
Average Net Profit Per Trade		1049.67	Total trades	15

Percentage Correct	83			
Average Profit on Winning Trades		1301.92	Winners	15
Average Loss on Trades		-602.50	Losers	3
Average Net Profit Per Trade		984.51	Total trades	18

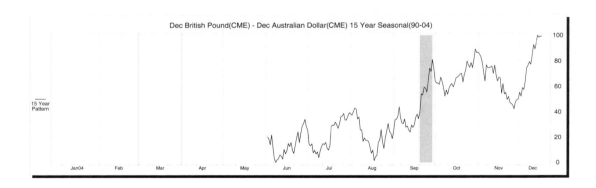

Dec British Pound(CME) - Dec Australian Dollar(CME) 15 Year Seasonal(90-04)

Figure 9-33

Buy Dec British Pound(IMM) / Sell Dec Canadian Dollar(IMM)

Moore Research Center, Inc.

Enter on approximately 09/20 - Exit on approximately 09/29

CONT YEAR	ENTRY DATE	ENTRY PRICE	EXIT DATE	EXIT PRICE		PROFIT AMOUNT	BEST EQUITY DATE	BEST EQUITY AMOUNT	WORST EQUITY DATE	WORST EQUITY AMOUNT
2004	09/20/04	33685	09/29/04	33288		-397.50	09/21/04	460.00	09/29/04	-397.50
2003	09/22/03	28503	09/29/03	29868		1365.00	09/29/03	1365.00		
2002	09/20/02	33318	09/27/02	33825		507.50	09/24/02	857.50		
2001	09/20/01	27658	09/28/01	28395		737.50	09/27/01	842.50	09/21/01	-630.00
2000	09/20/00	20675	09/29/00	25713		5037.50	09/29/00	5037.50		
1999	09/20/99	33557	09/29/99	34392		835.00	09/27/99	1307.50		
1998	09/21/98	39135	09/29/98	39883		747.50	09/28/98	855.00	09/23/98	-82.50
1997	09/22/97	27540	09/29/97	27840		300.00	09/25/97	1245.00		
1996	09/20/96	23743	09/27/96	24103		360.00	09/24/96	627.50		
1995	09/20/95	23303	09/29/95	24198		895.00	09/21/95	2760.00		
1994	09/20/94	23650	09/29/94	24148		497.50	09/27/94	725.00		
1993	09/20/93	19770	09/29/93	18970		-800.00			09/23/93	-1535.00
1992	09/21/92	24530	09/29/92	30960		6430.00	09/29/92	6430.00	09/22/92	-265.00
1991	09/20/91	19468	09/27/91	20178		710.00	09/23/91	765.00	09/26/91	-47.50
1990	09/20/90	29698	09/28/90	29818		120.00	09/27/90	432.50	09/21/90	-2057.50
1989	09/20/89	13985	09/29/89	15705		1720.00	09/26/89	1767.50	09/22/89	-785.00
1988	09/20/88	22593	09/29/88	22683		90.00	09/28/88	800.00	09/22/88	-840.00
1987	09/21/87	26916	09/29/87	25273		-1643.75			09/29/87	-1643.75
1986	09/22/86	18030	09/29/86	17073		-957.50			09/29/86	-957.50
1985	09/20/85	12784	09/27/85	13828		1043.75	09/25/85	3302.50		

Percentage Correct	87				
Average Profit on Winning Trades			1426.35	Winners	13
Average Loss on Trades			-598.75	Losers	2
Average Net Profit Per Trade			1156.33	Total trades	15
Percentage Correct	80				
Average Profit on Winning Trades			1337.27	Winners	16
Average Loss on Trades			-949.69	Losers	4
Average Net Profit Per Trade			879.88	Total trades	20

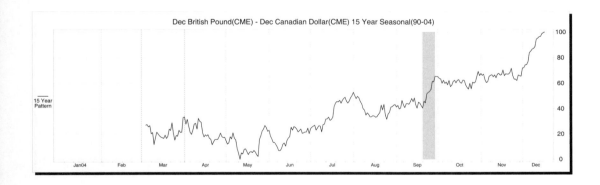

Dec British Pound(CME) - Dec Canadian Dollar(CME) 15 Year Seasonal(90-04)

15 Year Pattern

Figure 9-34

Buy Dec Swiss Franc(IMM) / Sell Dec Japanese Yen(IMM)

Enter on approximately 09/23 - Exit on approximately 10/02

CONT YEAR	ENTRY DATE	ENTRY PRICE	EXIT DATE	EXIT PRICE	PROFIT	PROFIT AMOUNT	BEST EQUITY DATE	BEST EQUITY AMOUNT	WORST EQUITY DATE	WORST EQUITY AMOUNT
2004	09/23/04	-11.11	10/01/04	-10.72	0.40	500.00	09/28/04	787.50	09/24/04	-137.50
2003	09/23/03	-15.51	10/02/03	-14.46	1.05	1312.50	09/30/03	1812.50	09/24/03	-362.50
2002	09/23/02	-14.12	10/02/02	-13.95	0.17	212.50	10/02/02	212.50	09/26/02	-1175.00
2001	09/24/01	-22.96	10/02/01	-21.34	1.61	2012.50	10/02/01	2012.50		
2000	09/25/00	-36.22	10/02/00	-35.04	1.18	1475.00	10/02/00	1475.00		
1999	09/23/99	-31.51	10/01/99	-28.20	3.31	4137.50	09/29/99	5075.00		
1998	09/23/98	-1.90	10/02/98	-0.09	1.81	2262.50	10/02/98	2262.50	09/29/98	-787.50
1997	09/23/97	-14.31	10/02/97	-13.76	0.55	687.50	10/02/97	687.50	09/24/97	-675.00
1996	09/23/96	-10.43	10/02/96	-10.16	0.28	350.00	10/02/96	350.00	09/27/96	-600.00
1995	09/25/95	-13.31	10/02/95	-13.17	0.15	187.50	10/02/95	187.50	09/29/95	-975.00
1994	09/23/94	-24.98	09/30/94	-23.65	1.33	1662.50	09/30/94	1662.50		
1993	09/23/93	-24.88	10/01/93	-24.48	0.40	500.00	09/27/93	725.00	09/24/93	-25.00
1992	09/23/92	-7.52	10/02/92	-2.87	4.64	5800.00	10/02/92	5800.00		
1991	09/23/91	-7.00	10/02/91	-6.96	0.04	50.00	10/01/91	687.50		
1990	09/24/90	4.50	10/02/90	4.39	-0.11	-137.50	09/27/90	737.50	09/25/90	-1462.50
1989	09/25/89	-10.03	10/02/89	-10.57	-0.53	-662.50	09/26/89	400.00	09/29/89	-750.00
1988	09/23/88	-11.12	09/30/88	-11.54	-0.42	-525.00			09/28/88	-562.50
1987	09/23/87	-3.34	10/02/87	-3.04	0.29	362.50	09/29/87	712.50	09/25/87	-175.00
1986	09/23/86	-4.42	10/02/86	-3.32	1.10	1375.00	10/02/86	1375.00	09/26/86	-325.00
1985	09/23/85	1.10	10/02/85	-0.25	-1.37	-1712.50		637.50	09/30/85	-2137.50

Percentage Correct	93			
Average Profit on Winning Trades		1.21	1510.71	Winners	14
Average Loss on Trades		-0.11	-137.50	Losers	1
Average Net Profit Per Trade		1.12	1400.83	Total trades	15
Percentage Correct	80			
Average Profit on Winning Trades		1.14	1430.47	Winners	16
Average Loss on Trades		-0.61	-759.38	Losers	4
Average Net Profit Per Trade		0.79	992.50	Total trades	20

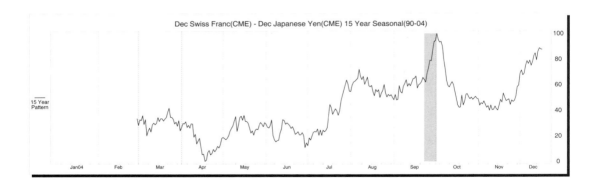

Dec Swiss Franc(CME) - Dec Japanese Yen(CME) 15 Year Seasonal(90-04)

Figure 9-35

Buy Dec British Pound(IMM) / Sell Dec Swiss Franc(IMM)

Enter on approximately 10/04 - Exit on approximately 11/13

CONT YEAR	ENTRY DATE	ENTRY PRICE	EXIT DATE	EXIT PRICE		PROFIT AMOUNT	BEST EQUITY DATE	BEST EQUITY AMOUNT	WORST EQUITY DATE	WORST EQUITY AMOUNT
2004	10/04/04	11781	11/12/04	8988		-2793.75			11/12/04	-2793.75
2003	10/06/03	8956	11/13/03	11663		2706.25	11/06/03	4093.75	10/08/03	-875.00
2002	10/04/02	13538	11/13/02	13013		-525.00	10/17/02	300.00	11/06/02	-1862.50
2001	10/04/01	14863	11/13/01	15200		337.50	11/13/01	337.50	10/19/01	-1600.00
2000	10/04/00	18887	11/13/00	19025		137.50	10/27/00	2537.50	11/09/00	-737.50
1999	10/04/99	18538	11/12/99	20388		1850.00	11/03/99	2387.50	10/15/99	-462.50
1998	10/05/98	11000	11/13/98	13488		2487.50	11/09/98	2837.50	10/07/98	-1375.00
1997	10/06/97	13538	11/13/97	16438		2900.00	10/21/97	4012.50		
1996	10/04/96	-2438	11/13/96	4825		7262.50	11/13/96	7262.50	10/08/96	-662.50
1995	10/04/95	-10388	11/13/95	-12850		-2462.50			10/23/95	-2712.50
1994	10/04/94	1213	11/11/94	2125		912.50	11/09/94	1325.00	10/17/94	-1162.50
1993	10/04/93	6288	11/12/93	9200		2912.50	11/01/93	3012.50	10/13/93	-337.50
1992	10/05/92	5038	11/13/92	8688		3650.00	10/13/92	6300.00		
1991	10/04/91	22875	11/13/91	24450		1575.00	11/13/91	1575.00	10/22/91	-762.50
1990	10/04/90	20438	11/13/90	22163		1725.00	10/05/90	4325.00		
1989	10/04/89	22113	11/13/89	22138		25.00	10/05/89	887.50	10/27/89	-2625.00
1988	10/04/88	25413	11/11/88	26725		1312.50	11/09/88	1537.50		
1987	10/05/87	19100	11/13/87	20131		1031.25	11/05/87	1150.00	10/12/87	-81.25
1986	10/06/86	11544	11/13/86	13681		2137.50	11/06/86	4387.50	10/13/86	-850.00
1985	10/04/85	29394	11/13/85	30188		793.75	10/31/85	1887.50		
Percentage Correct	80									
Average Profit on Winning Trades						2371.35		Winners		12
Average Loss on Trades						-1927.08		Losers		3
Average Net Profit Per Trade						1511.67		Total trades		15
Percentage Correct	85									
Average Profit on Winning Trades						1985.66		Winners		17
Average Loss on Trades						-1927.08		Losers		3
Average Net Profit Per Trade						1398.75		Total trades		20

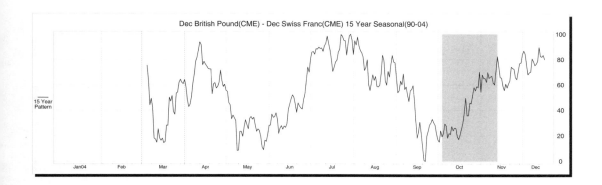

Dec British Pound(CME) - Dec Swiss Franc(CME) 15 Year Seasonal(90-04)

Figure 9-36

Buy Dec Japanese Yen(IMM) / Sell Dec British Pound(IMM)

Moore Research Center, Inc.

Enter on approximately 10/06 - Exit on approximately 10/19

CONT YEAR	ENTRY DATE	ENTRY PRICE	EXIT DATE	EXIT PRICE		PROFIT AMOUNT	BEST EQUITY DATE	BEST EQUITY AMOUNT	WORST EQUITY DATE	WORST EQUITY AMOUNT
2004	10/06/04	2225	10/19/04	3419		1193.75	10/19/04	1193.75	10/07/04	-243.75
2003	10/06/03	9031	10/17/03	10169		1137.50	10/10/03	2668.75		
2002	10/07/02	3600	10/18/02	3600		-0.00	10/09/02	712.50	10/18/02	-0.00
2001	10/09/01	13575	10/19/01	14163		587.50	10/19/01	587.50	10/12/01	-500.00
2000	10/06/00	25888	10/19/00	26175		287.50	10/18/00	1137.50	10/12/00	-275.00
1999	10/06/99	13925	10/19/99	15250		1325.00	10/18/99	1712.50	10/14/99	-462.50
1998	10/06/98	-8263	10/19/98	3925		12187.50	10/19/98	12187.50		
1997	10/06/97	2925	10/17/97	3550		625.00	10/16/97	1375.00	10/07/97	-1062.50
1996	10/07/96	15888	10/18/96	12700		-3187.50			10/18/96	-3187.50
1995	10/06/95	26738	10/19/95	27225		487.50	10/12/95	987.50		
1994	10/06/94	26675	10/19/94	27888		1212.50	10/14/94	1712.50	10/07/94	-900.00
1993	10/06/93	23650	10/19/93	24100		450.00	10/07/93	800.00	10/14/93	-1412.50
1992	10/06/92	-1362	10/19/92	3088		4450.00	10/19/92	4450.00	10/13/92	-2012.50
1991	10/07/91	-10875	10/18/91	-10838		37.50	10/15/91	1487.50		
1990	10/08/90	-26575	10/19/90	-22025		4550.00	10/18/90	4812.50		
1989	10/06/89	-10925	10/19/89	-10412		512.50	10/11/89	2337.50		
1988	10/06/88	-10900	10/19/88	-10038		862.50	10/17/88	1375.00	10/10/88	-425.00
1987	10/06/87	-15950	10/19/87	-16200		-250.00	10/12/87	906.25	10/19/87	-250.00
1986	10/06/86	-7794	10/17/86	-7538		256.25	10/08/86	775.00	10/16/86	-212.50
1985	10/07/85	-29944	10/18/85	-30425		-481.25	10/11/85	718.75	10/18/85	-481.25

Percentage Correct	87									
Average Profit on Winning Trades						2194.71		Winners		13
Average Loss on Trades						-1593.75		Losers		2
Average Net Profit Per Trade						1689.58		Total trades		15
Percentage Correct	80									
Average Profit on Winning Trades						1885.16		Winners		16
Average Loss on Trades						-979.69		Losers		4
Average Net Profit Per Trade						1312.19		Total trades		20

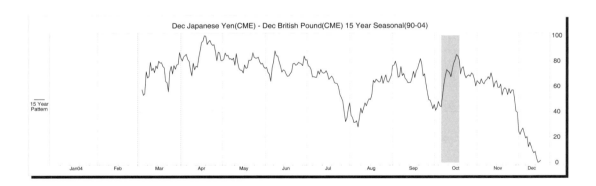

Dec Japanese Yen(CME) - Dec British Pound(CME) 15 Year Seasonal(90-04)

15 Year Pattern

Figure 9-37

Buy Dec British Pound(IMM) / Sell Dec Japanese Yen(IMM)

Enter on approximately 10/17 - Exit on approximately 10/20

CONT YEAR	ENTRY DATE	ENTRY PRICE	EXIT DATE	EXIT PRICE	PROFIT AMOUNT	BEST EQUITY DATE	BEST EQUITY AMOUNT	WORST EQUITY DATE	WORST EQUITY AMOUNT
2004	10/18/04	-2700	10/20/04	-2688	12.50	10/20/04	12.50	10/19/04	-718.75
2003	10/17/03	-10169	10/20/03	-9381	787.50	10/20/03	787.50		
2002	10/17/02	-3738	10/18/02	-3600	137.50	10/18/02	137.50		
2001	10/17/01	-13363	10/19/01	-14163	-800.00			10/19/01	-800.00
2000	10/17/00	-26300	10/20/00	-25138	1162.50	10/20/00	1162.50	10/18/00	-725.00
1999	10/18/99	-15638	10/20/99	-14363	1275.00	10/20/99	1275.00		
1998	10/19/98	-3925	10/20/98	-1550	2375.00	10/20/98	2375.00		
1997	10/17/97	-3550	10/20/97	-2113	1437.50	10/20/97	1437.50		
1996	10/17/96	-13175	10/18/96	-12700	475.00	10/18/96	475.00		
1995	10/17/95	-27663	10/20/95	-27562	100.00	10/19/95	437.50		
1994	10/17/94	-28163	10/20/94	-27375	787.50	10/20/94	787.50		
1993	10/18/93	-23963	10/20/93	-23563	400.00	10/20/93	400.00	10/19/93	-137.50
1992	10/19/92	-3088	10/20/92	-1125	1962.50	10/20/92	1962.50		
1991	10/17/91	9825	10/18/91	10838	1012.50	10/18/91	1012.50		
1990	10/17/90	21787	10/19/90	22025	237.50	10/19/90	237.50	10/18/90	-25.00
1989	10/17/89	9463	10/20/89	10225	762.50	10/19/89	950.00		
1988	10/17/88	9525	10/20/88	10663	1137.50	10/20/88	1137.50		
1987	10/19/87	16200	10/20/87	15906	-293.75			10/20/87	-293.75
1986	10/17/86	7538	10/20/86	7731	193.75	10/20/86	193.75		
1985	10/17/85	29756	10/18/85	30425	668.75	10/18/85	668.75		

Percentage Correct	93			
Average Profit on Winning Trades		868.75	Winners	14
Average Loss on Trades		-800.00	Losers	1
Average Net Profit Per Trade		757.50	Total trades	15

Percentage Correct	90			
Average Profit on Winning Trades		829.17	Winners	18
Average Loss on Trades		-546.88	Losers	2
Average Net Profit Per Trade		691.56	Total trades	20

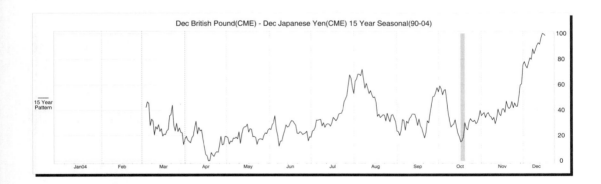

Dec British Pound(CME) - Dec Japanese Yen(CME) 15 Year Seasonal(90-04)

15 Year Pattern

Figure 9-38

Buy Dec British Pound(IMM) / Sell Dec Japanese Yen(IMM)

Enter on approximately 10/17 - Exit on approximately 12/12

CONT YEAR	ENTRY DATE	ENTRY PRICE	EXIT DATE	EXIT PRICE		PROFIT AMOUNT	BEST EQUITY DATE	BEST EQUITY AMOUNT	WORST EQUITY DATE	WORST EQUITY AMOUNT
2004	10/18/04	-2700	12/10/04	906		3606.25	12/10/04	3606.25	11/19/04	-2875.00
2003	10/17/03	-10169	12/12/03	-6856		3312.50	12/10/03	3618.75	11/10/03	-1093.75
2002	10/17/02	-3738	12/12/02	-3025		712.50	12/05/02	1825.00	11/26/02	-2300.00
2001	10/17/01	-13363	12/12/01	-8650		4712.50	12/12/01	4712.50	10/19/01	-800.00
2000	10/17/00	-26300	12/12/00	-21650		4650.00	12/12/00	4650.00	11/08/00	-2050.00
1999	10/18/99	-15638	12/10/99	-20887		-5250.00	10/21/99	1475.00	11/30/99	-7337.50
1998	10/19/98	-3925	12/11/98	-1812		2112.50	11/13/98	5562.50	11/02/98	-1850.00
1997	10/17/97	-3550	12/12/97	7275		10825.00	12/01/97	11712.50		
1996	10/17/96	-13175	12/12/96	-6763		6412.50	12/02/96	8825.00		
1995	10/17/95	-27663	12/12/95	-27163		500.00	11/02/95	5312.50	12/01/95	-487.50
1994	10/17/94	-28163	12/12/94	-27250		912.50	12/08/94	1412.50	11/21/94	-1362.50
1993	10/18/93	-23963	12/10/93	-21150		2812.50	12/10/93	2812.50	11/11/93	-1625.00
1992	10/19/92	-3088	12/11/92	-3513		-425.00	12/07/92	2062.50	11/09/92	-3362.50
1991	10/17/91	9825	12/12/91	16300		6475.00	12/12/91	6475.00		
1990	10/17/90	21787	12/12/90	26825		5037.50	11/29/90	5262.50	10/22/90	-387.50
1989	10/17/89	9463	12/12/89	13662		4200.00	12/12/89	4200.00	10/27/89	-225.00
1988	10/17/88	9525	12/12/88	13275		3750.00	12/07/88	4200.00	10/26/88	-175.00
1987	10/19/87	16200	12/11/87	17419		1218.75	11/30/87	3368.75	10/21/87	-393.75
1986	10/17/86	7538	12/12/86	12538		5000.00	11/10/86	5025.00		
1985	10/17/85	29756	12/12/85	27756		-2000.00	12/02/85	1837.50	11/07/85	-2768.75

Percentage Correct	87									
Average Profit on Winning Trades						4006.25		Winners		13
Average Loss on Trades						-2837.50		Losers		2
Average Net Profit Per Trade						3093.75		Total trades		15
Percentage Correct	85									
Average Profit on Winning Trades						3897.06		Winners		17
Average Loss on Trades						-2558.33		Losers		3
Average Net Profit Per Trade						2928.75		Total trades		20

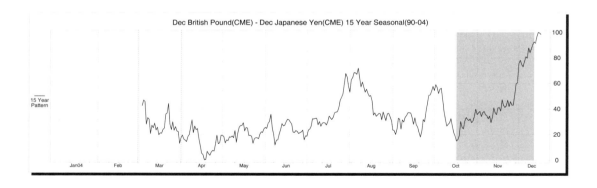

Dec British Pound(CME) - Dec Japanese Yen(CME) 15 Year Seasonal(90-04)

Figure 9-39

Buy Dec Australian Dollar(IMM) / Sell Dec Japanese Yen(IMM)

Enter on approximately 11/03 - Exit on approximately 12/02

CONT YEAR	ENTRY DATE	ENTRY PRICE	EXIT DATE	EXIT PRICE		PROFIT AMOUNT	BEST EQUITY DATE	BEST EQUITY AMOUNT	WORST EQUITY DATE	WORST EQUITY AMOUNT
2004	11/03/04	-42640	12/02/04	-43660		-1020.00	11/10/04	1662.50	11/30/04	-1662.50
2003	11/03/03	-42950	12/02/03	-42133		817.50	12/01/03	1395.00	11/04/03	-1225.00
2002	11/04/02	-46463	12/02/02	-44458		2005.00	12/02/02	2005.00	11/12/02	-2250.00
2001	11/05/01	-52138	11/30/01	-49118		3020.00	11/27/01	3492.50	11/09/01	-787.50
2000	11/03/00	-65195	12/01/00	-58918		6277.50	12/01/00	6277.50		
1999	11/03/99	-55510	12/02/99	-58660		-3150.00	11/19/99	1380.00	11/26/99	-4277.50
1998	11/03/98	-46563	12/02/98	-41555		5007.50	11/27/98	8170.00		
1997	11/03/97	-32255	12/02/97	-29530		2725.00	11/24/97	2825.00	11/04/97	-415.00
1996	11/04/96	-31803	12/02/96	-27403		4400.00	12/02/96	4400.00	11/11/96	-2800.00
1995	11/03/95	-45305	12/01/95	-49913		-4607.50			11/09/95	-6487.50
1994	11/03/94	-54293	12/02/94	-47632		6660.00	12/02/94	6660.00		
1993	11/03/93	-48675	12/02/93	-48318		357.50	11/04/93	532.50	11/12/93	-4025.00
1992	11/03/92	-32533	12/02/92	-32038		495.00	11/06/92	1317.50	11/19/92	-475.00
1991	11/04/91	-18415	12/02/91	-17738		677.50	11/26/91	1532.50	11/25/91	-242.50
1990	11/05/90	-20875	11/30/90	-16895		3980.00	11/29/90	4212.50	11/21/90	-1340.00
1989	11/03/89	-10353	12/01/89	-9513		840.00	11/13/89	1582.50		
1988	11/03/88	-18103	12/02/88	-16293		1810.00	11/29/88	2740.00	11/07/88	-60.00
1987	11/03/87	-24738	12/02/87	-24045		692.50	11/16/87	1675.00	11/05/87	-637.50

Percentage Correct	80				
Average Profit on Winning Trades		3035.21	Winners	12
Average Loss on Trades		-2925.83	Losers	3
Average Net Profit Per Trade		1843.00	Total trades	15

Percentage Correct	83				
Average Profit on Winning Trades		2651.00	Winners	15
Average Loss on Trades		-2925.83	Losers	3
Average Net Profit Per Trade		1721.53	Total trades	18

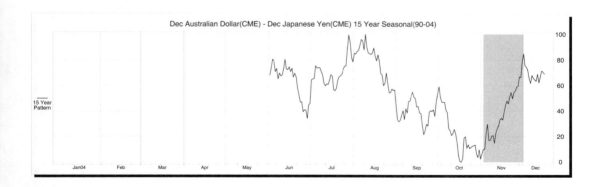

Dec Australian Dollar(CME) - Dec Japanese Yen(CME) 15 Year Seasonal(90-04)

15 Year Pattern

Jan04 Feb Mar Apr May Jun Jul Aug Sep Oct Nov Dec

Figure 9-40

Moore Research Center, Inc. *Buy Dec Australian Dollar(IMM) / Sell Dec Canadian Dollar(IMM)*

Enter on approximately 11/04 - Exit on approximately 11/15

CONT YEAR	ENTRY DATE	ENTRY PRICE	EXIT DATE	EXIT PRICE	PROFIT	PROFIT AMOUNT	BEST EQUITY DATE	BEST EQUITY AMOUNT	WORST EQUITY DATE	WORST EQUITY AMOUNT
2004	11/04/04	-7.30	11/15/04	-6.06	1.23	1230.00	11/15/04	1230.00	11/08/04	-1010.00
2003	11/04/03	-5.06	11/14/03	-4.87	0.20	200.00	11/06/03	850.00	11/12/03	-10.00
2002	11/04/02	-8.23	11/15/02	-6.84	1.40	1400.00	11/15/02	1400.00		
2001	11/05/01	-11.96	11/15/01	-11.22	0.73	730.00	11/13/01	1160.00		
2000	11/06/00	-12.65	11/15/00	-12.33	0.32	320.00	11/09/00	870.00	11/14/00	-210.00
1999	11/04/99	-4.65	11/15/99	-3.68	0.97	970.00	11/15/99	970.00		
1998	11/04/98	-2.82	11/13/98	-0.82	1.99	1990.00	11/12/98	2050.00		
1997	11/04/97	-1.31	11/14/97	-1.24	0.07	70.00	11/05/97	220.00	11/12/97	-520.00
1996	11/04/96	3.54	11/15/96	4.10	0.57	570.00	11/15/96	570.00	11/07/96	-620.00
1995	11/06/95	1.28	11/15/95	-0.49	-1.78	-1780.00	11/07/95	170.00	11/15/95	-1780.00
1994	11/04/94	1.39	11/15/94	2.00	0.61	610.00	11/15/94	610.00		
1993	11/04/93	-9.12	11/15/93	-10.07	-0.96	-960.00			11/12/93	-1200.00
1992	11/04/92	-11.04	11/13/92	-9.73	1.31	1310.00	11/06/92	1570.00		
1991	11/04/91	-10.66	11/15/91	-9.78	0.88	880.00	11/12/91	1110.00	11/05/91	-400.00
1990	11/05/90	-8.01	11/15/90	-8.83	-0.82	-820.00	11/06/90	860.00	11/13/90	-830.00
1989	11/06/89	-7.52	11/15/89	-7.36	0.16	160.00	11/13/89	560.00		
1988	11/04/88	0.98	11/15/88	4.07	3.09	3090.00	11/15/88	3090.00		
1987	11/04/87	-8.40	11/13/87	-7.32	1.08	1080.00	11/06/87	1140.00		

Percentage Correct	80									
Average Profit on Winning Trades					0.86	856.67		Winners		12
Average Loss on Trades					-1.19	-1186.67		Losers		3
Average Net Profit Per Trade					0.45	448.00		Total trades		15
Percentage Correct	83									
Average Profit on Winning Trades					0.97	974.00		Winners		15
Average Loss on Trades					-1.19	-1186.67		Losers		3
Average Net Profit Per Trade					0.61	613.89		Total trades		18

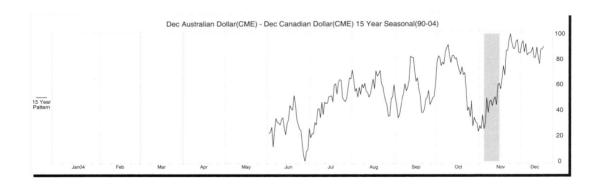

Dec Australian Dollar(CME) - Dec Canadian Dollar(CME) 15 Year Seasonal(90-04)

Figure 9-41

Buy Dec Australian Dollar(IMM) / Sell Dec Japanese Yen(IMM)

Enter on approximately 11/10 - Exit on approximately 11/28

CONT YEAR	ENTRY DATE	ENTRY PRICE	EXIT DATE	EXIT PRICE		PROFIT AMOUNT	BEST EQUITY DATE	BEST EQUITY AMOUNT	WORST EQUITY DATE	WORST EQUITY AMOUNT
2004	11/10/04	-40978	11/26/04	-43078		-2100.00			11/22/04	-2182.50
2003	11/10/03	-44135	11/28/03	-41915		2220.00	11/28/03	2220.00		
2002	11/12/02	-48713	11/27/02	-46735		1977.50	11/22/02	3142.50		
2001	11/13/01	-51138	11/28/01	-49598		1540.00	11/27/01	2492.50	11/14/01	-40.00
2000	11/10/00	-64415	11/28/00	-61598		2817.50	11/24/00	4125.00	11/13/00	-315.00
1999	11/10/99	-55933	11/26/99	-59788		-3855.00	11/19/99	1802.50	11/26/99	-3855.00
1998	11/10/98	-39683	11/27/98	-38393		1290.00	11/27/98	1290.00	11/16/98	-797.50
1997	11/10/97	-31360	11/28/97	-29945		1415.00	11/24/97	1930.00		
1996	11/11/96	-34603	11/27/96	-29460		5142.50	11/27/96	5142.50		
1995	11/10/95	-50903	11/28/95	-48883		2020.00	11/28/95	2020.00		
1994	11/10/94	-52798	11/28/94	-50718		2080.00	11/28/94	2080.00	11/11/94	-432.50
1993	11/10/93	-50450	11/26/93	-48665		1785.00	11/26/93	1785.00	11/12/93	-2250.00
1992	11/10/92	-31810	11/27/92	-31385		425.00	11/12/92	485.00	11/19/92	-1197.50
1991	11/11/91	-17720	11/27/91	-17350		370.00	11/26/91	837.50	11/25/91	-937.50
1990	11/12/90	-19923	11/28/90	-19400		522.50	11/28/90	522.50	11/21/90	-2292.50
1989	11/10/89	-9493	11/28/89	-9113		380.00	11/13/89	722.50	11/22/89	-462.50
1988	11/10/88	-17308	11/28/88	-15438		1870.00	11/28/88	1870.00	11/11/88	-305.00
1987	11/10/87	-25318	11/27/87	-24433		885.00	11/16/87	2255.00		

Percentage Correct	87									
Average Profit on Winning Trades						1815.77		Winners		13
Average Loss on Trades						-2977.50		Losers		2
Average Net Profit Per Trade						1176.67		Total trades		15
Percentage Correct	89									
Average Profit on Winning Trades						1671.25		Winners		16
Average Loss on Trades						-2977.50		Losers		2
Average Net Profit Per Trade						1154.72		Total trades		18

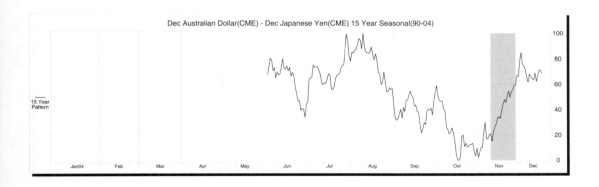

Dec Australian Dollar(CME) - Dec Japanese Yen(CME) 15 Year Seasonal(90-04)

Figure 9-42

Buy Mar British Pound(IMM) / Sell Mar Japanese Yen(IMM)

Enter on approximately 11/10 - Exit on approximately 01/06

CONT YEAR	ENTRY DATE	ENTRY PRICE	EXIT DATE	EXIT PRICE		PROFIT AMOUNT	BEST EQUITY DATE	BEST EQUITY AMOUNT	WORST EQUITY DATE	WORST EQUITY AMOUNT
2005	11/10/04	-3175	01/06/05	-2844		331.25	12/14/04	3793.75	11/19/04	-3881.25
2004	11/10/03	-12413	01/06/04	-4644		7768.75	01/06/04	7768.75		
2003	11/12/02	-6538	01/06/03	-5288		1250.00	12/05/02	3637.50	11/26/02	-487.50
2002	11/13/01	-13950	01/04/02	-5738		8212.50	12/31/01	9125.00	11/20/01	-450.00
2001	11/10/00	-28925	01/05/01	-14363		14562.50	01/05/01	14562.50		
2000	11/10/99	-20100	01/06/00	-16750		3350.00	01/06/00	3350.00	11/30/99	-4650.00
1999	11/10/98	-500	01/06/99	-8375		-7875.00	11/13/98	375.00	01/05/99	-9750.00
1998	11/10/97	3000	01/06/98	6875		3875.00	12/26/97	4550.00		
1997	11/11/96	-11888	01/06/97	-3450		8437.50	12/31/96	10000.00		
1996	11/10/95	-28850	01/05/96	-22975		5875.00	01/05/96	5875.00	12/01/95	-1112.50
1995	11/10/94	-29363	01/06/95	-27350		2012.50	01/04/95	2700.00	11/21/94	-1287.50
1994	11/10/93	-25350	01/06/94	-18938		6412.50	01/05/94	6975.00	11/11/93	-1075.00
1993	11/10/92	-6938	01/06/93	-4025		2912.50	12/07/92	5050.00	12/28/92	-487.50
1992	11/11/91	13062	01/06/92	15038		1975.00	12/24/91	4787.50	11/25/91	-300.00
1991	11/12/90	23275	01/04/91	26850		3575.00	01/02/91	3825.00	11/23/90	-550.00
1990	11/10/89	8800	01/05/90	14200		5400.00	01/05/90	5400.00	11/27/89	-962.50
1989	11/10/88	8900	01/06/89	10738		1837.50	12/07/88	2712.50	11/11/88	-225.00
1988	11/10/87	17156	01/06/88	15306		-1850.00	11/30/87	1343.75	12/31/87	-3450.00
1987	11/10/86	11300	01/06/87	12569		1268.75	12/23/86	1706.25	11/12/86	-2293.75
1986	11/11/85	26931	01/06/86	26969		37.50	12/02/85	3862.50	12/18/85	-931.25

Percentage Correct	93								
Average Profit on Winning Trades				5039.29		Winners	14		
Average Loss on Trades				-7875.00		Losers	1		
Average Net Profit Per Trade				4178.33		Total trades	15		
Percentage Correct	90								
Average Profit on Winning Trades				4394.10		Winners	18		
Average Loss on Trades				-4862.50		Losers	2		
Average Net Profit Per Trade				3468.44		Total trades	20		

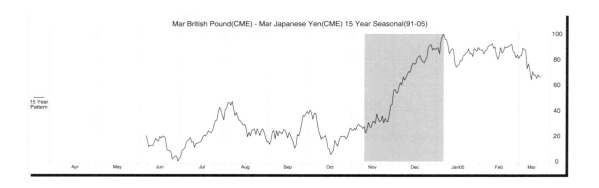

Mar British Pound(CME) - Mar Japanese Yen(CME) 15 Year Seasonal(91-05)

15 Year Pattern

Figure 9-43

Buy Mar Swiss Franc(IMM) / Sell Mar Japanese Yen(IMM)

Moore Research Center, Inc.

Enter on approximately 12/07 - Exit on approximately 12/28

CONT YEAR	ENTRY DATE	ENTRY PRICE	EXIT DATE	EXIT PRICE	PROFIT	PROFIT AMOUNT	BEST EQUITY DATE	BEST EQUITY AMOUNT	WORST EQUITY DATE	WORST EQUITY AMOUNT
2005	12/07/04	-9.73	12/28/04	-9.06	0.67	837.50	12/14/04	1762.50		
2004	12/08/03	-14.25	12/26/03	-13.60	0.65	812.50	12/18/03	1550.00	12/09/03	-100.00
2003	12/09/02	-12.61	12/27/02	-11.65	0.96	1200.00	12/27/02	1200.00	12/13/02	-1637.50
2002	12/07/01	-19.76	12/28/01	-16.84	2.92	3650.00	12/27/01	3887.50		
2001	12/07/00	-32.60	12/28/00	-27.02	5.59	6987.50	12/28/00	6987.50	12/11/00	-300.00
2000	12/07/99	-34.48	12/28/99	-35.64	-1.15	-1437.50	12/08/99	837.50	12/22/99	-1812.50
1999	12/07/98	-11.23	12/28/98	-13.70	-2.47	-3087.50	12/10/98	662.50	12/24/98	-3175.00
1998	12/08/97	-8.37	12/26/97	-7.17	1.21	1512.50	12/15/97	1812.50	12/17/97	-1262.50
1997	12/09/96	-13.39	12/27/96	-12.84	0.54	675.00	12/16/96	1012.50	12/24/96	-225.00
1996	12/07/95	-13.87	12/28/95	-11.21	2.67	3337.50	12/28/95	3337.50	12/11/95	-187.50
1995	12/07/94	-25.39	12/28/94	-24.53	0.86	1075.00	12/28/94	1075.00	12/09/94	-350.00
1994	12/07/93	-25.07	12/28/93	-20.66	4.41	5512.50	12/28/93	5512.50		
1993	12/07/92	-9.57	12/28/92	-12.32	-2.75	-3437.50			12/28/92	-3437.50
1992	12/09/91	-6.31	12/27/91	-5.75	0.56	700.00	12/24/91	2100.00	12/13/91	-425.00
1991	12/07/90	3.24	12/28/90	4.28	1.04	1300.00	12/28/90	1300.00	12/21/90	-1325.00
1990	12/07/89	-6.68	12/28/89	-4.96	1.72	2150.00	12/28/89	2150.00	12/08/89	-225.00
1989	12/07/88	-13.65	12/28/88	-13.61	0.04	50.00	12/15/88	387.50	12/08/88	-87.50
1988	12/07/87	-2.15	12/28/87	-3.34	-1.19	-1487.50	12/08/87	500.00	12/23/87	-1937.50
1987	12/08/86	-2.00	12/26/86	-1.73	0.26	325.00	12/23/86	1700.00	12/09/86	-537.50
1986	12/09/85	-1.38	12/27/85	-1.03	0.34	425.00	12/27/85	425.00	12/18/85	-475.00

Percentage Correct	80				
Average Profit on Winning Trades			1.84	2300.00	Winners	12
Average Loss on Trades			-2.12	-2654.17	Losers	3
Average Net Profit Per Trade			1.05	1309.17	Total trades	15
Percentage Correct	80				
Average Profit on Winning Trades			1.53	1909.38	Winners	16
Average Loss on Trades			-1.89	-2362.50	Losers	4
Average Net Profit Per Trade			0.84	1055.00	Total trades	20

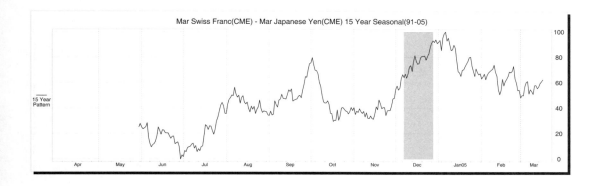

Mar Swiss Franc(CME) - Mar Japanese Yen(CME) 15 Year Seasonal(91-05)

15 Year Pattern

Figure 9-44

Buy Mar Canadian Dollar(IMM) / Sell Mar Japanese Yen(IMM)

Enter on approximately 12/28 - Exit on approximately 01/09

CONT YEAR	ENTRY DATE	ENTRY PRICE	EXIT DATE	EXIT PRICE		PROFIT AMOUNT	BEST EQUITY DATE	BEST EQUITY AMOUNT	WORST EQUITY DATE	WORST EQUITY AMOUNT
2005	12/28/04	-39748	01/07/05	-38493		1255.00	01/04/05	1350.00		
2004	12/29/03	-41110	01/09/04	-39313		1797.50	01/09/04	1797.50		
2003	12/30/02	-42668	01/09/03	-40635		2032.50	01/07/03	2500.00		
2002	12/28/01	-32890	01/09/02	-31953		937.50	01/08/02	1080.00	01/04/02	-292.50
2001	12/28/00	-43955	01/09/01	-41333		2622.50	01/09/01	2622.50	01/03/01	-462.50
2000	12/28/99	-54280	01/07/00	-51160		3120.00	01/06/00	3195.00	01/03/00	-960.00
1999	12/28/98	-44710	01/08/99	-47533		-2822.50			01/08/99	-2822.50
1998	12/29/97	-28038	01/09/98	-25378		2660.00	01/05/98	3937.50		
1997	12/30/96	-35360	01/09/97	-34080		1280.00	01/09/97	1280.00	01/02/97	-935.00
1996	12/28/95	-49613	01/09/96	-46938		2675.00	01/04/96	3495.00		
1995	12/28/94	-55865	01/09/95	-55095		770.00	01/06/95	3105.00		
1994	12/28/93	-37483	01/07/94	-36168		1315.00	01/03/94	2307.50		
1993	12/28/92	-21310	01/08/93	-22200		-890.00			01/05/93	-1017.50
1992	12/30/91	-13415	01/09/92	-12550		865.00	01/09/92	865.00	01/06/92	-555.00
1991	12/28/90	-7027	01/09/91	-5033		1995.00	01/09/91	1995.00	01/03/91	-835.00
1990	12/28/89	-1285	01/09/90	-898		387.50	01/02/90	1187.50	01/04/90	-865.00
1989	12/28/88	-16900	01/09/89	-17085		-185.00	01/06/89	612.50	01/03/89	-1242.50
1988	12/28/87	-25450	01/08/88	-20118		5332.50	01/07/88	5672.50	12/31/87	-1710.00
1987	12/29/86	-6800	01/09/87	-6610		190.00	01/05/87	482.50	12/31/86	-525.00
1986	12/30/85	8863	01/09/86	9513		650.00	01/09/86	650.00	01/02/86	-912.50

Percentage Correct	87								
Average Profit on Winning Trades						1794.23		Winners	13
Average Loss on Trades						-1856.25		Losers	2
Average Net Profit Per Trade						1307.50		Total trades	15
Percentage Correct	85								
Average Profit on Winning Trades						1757.94		Winners	17
Average Loss on Trades						-1299.17		Losers	3
Average Net Profit Per Trade						1299.37		Total trades	20

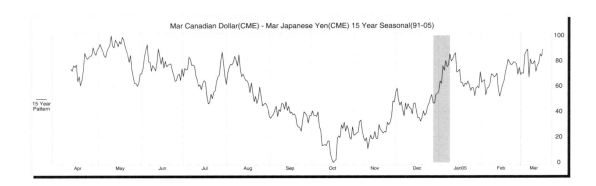

Mar Canadian Dollar(CME) - Mar Japanese Yen(CME) 15 Year Seasonal(91-05)

15 Year Pattern

Chapter 10: Interest Rates

Decades ago, lending rates excited little interest. Except during sporadic financial panics or runs on banks, they tended to be relatively stable. According to FRED, economic data compiled by the Federal Reserve Bank of St. Louis (http://research.stlouisfed.org/fred2/), the prime lending rate charged by US banks as the Roaring Twenties came to a close in 1929 was as high as 6%. By 1934-45, during the depths of the Great Depression, it was 1.5%. In post-war 1947, the prime rate was only 1.75%.

As the US economy grew after World War II, so did the demand for money — and thus did interest rates rise, albeit slowly at first. By the end of 1965, the prime rate had risen again to 5%. But by the late 1960s, US "guns and butter" policies drove government debt levels higher and helped create monetary strains that pushed the prime rate up to 8.5% by mid 1969. By March 1973, rising inflation and a devaluing US dollar precipitated the collapse of the Smithsonian agreement (see Forex chapter), an event which then allowed all currencies to float freely but with greater volatility. By September 1973, the prime rate reached 10%.

Rates then eased modestly for a few years, despite rising inflation and government debt. In January 1976 the innovative CME began trading futures for 13-week Treasury Bills. Shortly thereafter, in August 1977, the CBOT fortuitously began trading 30-Year Treasury Bonds. By October 1978 the prime rate was back to 10%, a level at or above which it was to remain until June 1985. In the interim, the Federal Reserve under Chairman Paul Volcker moved in October 1979 toward a policy of controlling US money supply rather than the level of interest rates. With this historic shift in policy, interest rate levels and prices of US debt instruments became a function of the marketplace.

In late October 1979, the prime rate stood at 15%. By April 1980, it reached 20% and by December of that year its ultimate peak at 21.5%. The effective fed funds rate actually reached its one-day peak in July 1981 at 22.36%. Meanwhile, the new US administration made the conscious decision to borrow rather than tax to finance deficits. Thus, by 1988 government-issued, interest-bearing debt had exploded. Backed by the US government, Treasury debt was considered nearly risk-free but with rates tending to be relatively high. Thereby attracting both domestic and foreign investors, US Treasury securities became global commodities.

Of the various financial instruments listed for futures trading through the years, 30-Year Treasury Bonds remain among the most successful. However, that market has been far surpassed in daily trading volume and open interest by Eurodollars, futures for which the IMM division of CME began trading December 1981 — just a few months after the peak in short-term rates. The benchmark at the long end of the so-called yield curve, absent new Treasury sales of 30-Year bonds, has become 10-Year Treasury Notes, which the CBOT began trading in 1982. The exchange also successfully launched trading in 5-Year T-Notes in 1988 and 2-Year T-Notes in 1990.

The success of those markets created demand for financial futures instruments around the globe, most notably the German Euro-Bund and Euro-Bobl traded on the all-electronic Eurex; Long Gilt, 3-Month Short Sterling, and 3-Month Euribor at the London International Financial Futures and Options Exchange (LIFFE); and 3-Month Australian Treasury Bills and both 3-Year and 10-Year Australian Treasury Bonds traded at the Sydney Futures Exchange. This chapter, however, confines itself to spreads within and among those five most liquid US markets, all of which have significant history.

Intra-market Spreads

Trading in CBOT futures for Treasury bonds and notes is mostly in the lead contract, with relatively little volume in contracts for deferred delivery. Their price structures essentially reflect carrying charges. Because prices move inversely to yield, however, carrying charges in financial instruments — unlike those for storable grains or metals — appear as progressive *discounts* to the lead contract. Nonetheless, deferred CBOT contracts trade but little. The exception — the enormous exception — is in the market for Eurodollars.

Eurodollars

A Eurodollar is any US dollar on deposit in a commercial bank outside the borders of the United States. Its origins lie in the Cold War, when East Bloc countries feared the United States might someday freeze their accounts and confiscate their dollar balances held in New York City banks. To forestall such a possibility, the Soviet government transferred their dollar balances from New York City to London and other financial centers via the Soviet bank in Paris, also known as the *Eurobank*. Hence, the term *Eurodollar* emerged.

In part because of the US dollar's status as the world's reserve currency and in part because of the US trade deficit, enormous sums of US dollars are on deposit around the globe. Thus have Eurodollar deposits become an international capital market funding both private and international public debt. Because they are outside the jurisdiction of the US Federal Reserve, non-US banks do not face the same reserve requirements as do their US counterparts — allowing them both to loan at lower rates and to pay depositors at higher rates.

But Eurodollar deposits are at higher risk because they are not guaranteed by any government. Thus Eurodollar futures have evolved as a benchmark for short-term interest rates tied closely to but always at tradable premium to the rate for 3-month US Treasury bills — commonly considered the safest interest-bearing instrument on the planet.

Figure 10-1: 3-Month T-Bill Yield

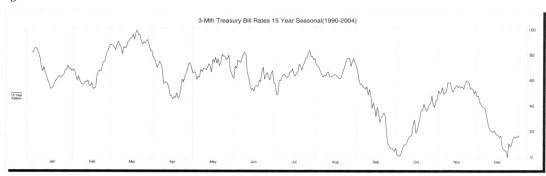

It is generally true that, when demand for money rises, so do market-driven interest rates. Conversely, when demand for money eases, so do rates. The corollary would be that rates tend to rise when monetary liquidity tightens and to fall when liquidity loosens. The pattern for rates on T-Bills shows that rates tend to be highest during March and lowest in early October and/or late December.

Eurodollar futures are indexed to 100, with the price differential representing the interest rate. For example, a price of 94.25 represents market expectations for short-term rates to be 5.75%. Thus, futures prices move inversely to rates. (The contract specifies a Eurodollar Time Deposit for one million US dollars with a three-month maturity. The market always trades 10 years out into the future.)

Figure 10-2: December Eurodollar Seasonal Pattern

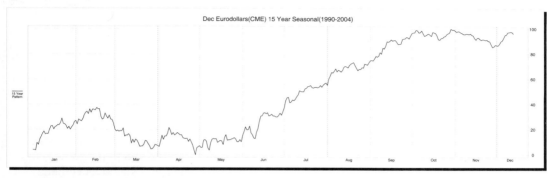

Although the general rise from left to right reflects secular disinflationary trends and thus declining rates, the pattern still implies certain seasonal dynamics. For example, Eurodollar futures prices tend to be lowest March-May. Could that be a function of monetary liquidity tightening into mid April as the private sector is drained by the massive transfer of financial assets into the public sector as US income taxes are paid? Thereafter, prices tend persistently to trend higher into October — the beginning of a new US fiscal year — or even into December — when bonuses are paid, Social Security maximum payments have been reached, and money flows freely during the holidays. In the new year, prices still can rise into February before liquidity begins again to contract into March-May.

Figure 10-3: Deferred Jun/Dec Eurodollar Pattern

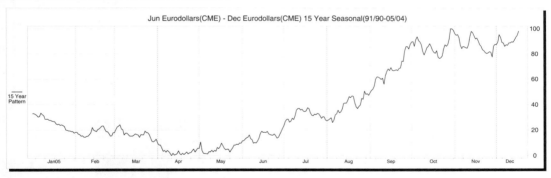

Note the similarity between the pattern of the spread between deferred June and December Eurodollars with that of December. The future, of course, is always more uncertain than the present; and the progressively more distant future is progressively more uncertain. Thus, when rates change, and especially when they trend, deferred contracts of Eurodollars tend to lead — the market extrapolates into the future, with change having a multiplier effect through time. Because big money is first and foremost concerned with long-term survival and advantage, deferred contracts tend to move first, fastest, and farthest in what are called calendar spreads.

Figure 10-4: Eurodollar Calendar Spreads

Moore Research Center, Inc.			Eurodollar Calendar Spreads					
Seasonal Strategy	Entry Date	Exit Date	Win Pct	Win Yrs	Loss Years	Total Years	Average Profit	Ave Pft Per Day
Buy Jun Eurodollars(IMM)	3/01	5/09	80	12	3	15	392	6
Sell "Red" Dec Eurodollars(IMM)			85	17	3	20	469	7
Buy Mar Eurodollars(IMM)	6/05	9/15	93	14	1	15	840	8
Sell Sep Eurodollars(IMM)			90	18	2	20	687	7
Buy Mar Eurodollars(IMM)	6/11	7/18	87	13	2	15	336	9
Sell Sep Eurodollars(IMM)			90	18	2	20	364	10
Buy Jun Eurodollars(IMM)	6/27	9/15	93	14	1	15	918	11
Sell Sep Eurodollars(IMM)			90	18	2	20	716	9
Buy Jun Eurodollars(IMM)	8/06	11/13	93	14	1	15	568	6
Sell Dec Eurodollars(IMM)			95	19	1	20	616	6

The reader will note that "Red" refers to a contract of expiry one year from that of a more nearby. For example, after the December 2004 contract expired and until the December 2005 contract expired, the December 2006 contract was referred to as "Red" December. During that same time, the December 2007 contract was referred to as "Green."

The reader will also note that far more complex Eurodollars spreads are traded and recognized by CME but beyond the scope of this volume — esoteric combinations with such colorful names as Butterfly, Double Butterfly, Condor, and Double Condor.

The statistics in the table confirm the movements depicted in seasonal patterns of calendar spreads, no matter which specific contracts are used. In the table's first strategy, a deferred contract tends to lead a nearby lower into the market's seasonal bottom when monetary liquidity may be tightest. Thereafter, the deferred contracts have usually led the nearby higher — reliably, persistently, and typically with little adversity.

> *Note: Chicago Mercantile Exchange (CME) notes on its Web site (www.cme.com) that, as of this writing, over 80% of volume in the Eurodollar contract is electronic (Globex).*

Figure 10-5

| *Buy Jun Eurodollars(IMM) / Sell "Red" Dec Eurodollars(IMM)*

Enter on approximately 03/01 - Exit on approximately 05/09

CONT YEAR	ENTRY DATE	ENTRY PRICE	EXIT DATE	EXIT PRICE	PROFIT	PROFIT AMOUNT	BEST EQUITY DATE	BEST EQUITY AMOUNT	WORST EQUITY DATE	WORST EQUITY AMOUNT
2005	03/01/05	0.95	05/09/05	0.97	0.02	50.00	03/28/05	750.00	05/05/05	-350.00
2004	03/01/04	1.93	05/07/04	2.77	0.84	2087.50	05/07/04	2087.50	03/24/04	-962.50
2003	03/03/03	1.45	05/09/03	1.01	-0.44	-1100.00	03/21/03	1362.50	05/07/03	-1225.00
2002	03/01/02	2.84	05/09/02	3.03	0.19	475.00	04/17/02	700.00		
2001	03/01/01	0.65	05/09/01	1.32	0.67	1662.50	05/07/01	1712.50		
2000	03/01/00	0.82	05/09/00	0.85	0.03	87.50	05/08/00	162.50	04/05/00	-800.00
1999	03/01/99	0.72	05/07/99	0.83	0.11	262.50	05/07/99	262.50	04/08/99	-362.50
1998	03/02/98	0.27	05/08/98	0.27	0.00	0.00	04/29/98	275.00	04/03/98	-275.00
1997	03/03/97	0.79	05/09/97	0.81	0.02	50.00	04/11/97	800.00	03/10/97	-25.00
1996	03/01/96	0.71	05/09/96	1.25	0.53	1325.00	05/02/96	1500.00	03/04/96	-225.00
1995	03/01/95	0.76	05/09/95	0.28	-0.48	-1200.00	03/06/95	225.00	05/09/95	-1200.00
1994	03/01/94	1.64	05/09/94	2.15	0.52	1300.00	04/04/94	2025.00		
1993	03/01/93	1.87	05/07/93	1.65	-0.21	-525.00	03/15/93	625.00	04/22/93	-750.00
1992	03/02/92	2.71	05/08/92	2.75	0.03	75.00	03/18/92	775.00		
1991	03/01/91	1.53	05/09/91	2.06	0.53	1325.00	05/01/91	1600.00	03/05/91	-100.00
1990	03/01/90	0.62	05/09/90	0.79	0.16	400.00	05/09/90	400.00	03/20/90	-300.00
1989	03/01/89	-0.93	05/09/89	-0.31	0.62	1550.00	04/27/89	1850.00	03/20/89	-500.00
1988	03/01/88	1.34	05/09/88	1.40	0.05	125.00	03/31/88	250.00	03/07/88	-225.00
1987	03/02/87	0.89	05/08/87	1.29	0.40	1000.00	04/22/87	1125.00	03/25/87	-800.00
1986	03/03/86	0.96	05/09/86	1.12	0.17	425.00	05/07/86	425.00	03/31/86	-750.00

Percentage Correct	80							Protective Stop		(509)
Average Profit on Winning Trades					0.29	725.00		Winners		12
Average Loss on Trades					-0.38	-941.67		Losers		3
Average Net Profit Per Trade					0.16	391.67		Total trades		15
Percentage Correct	85									
Average Profit on Winning Trades					0.29	717.65		Winners		17
Average Loss on Trades					-0.38	-941.67		Losers		3
Average Net Profit Per Trade					0.19	468.75		Total trades		20

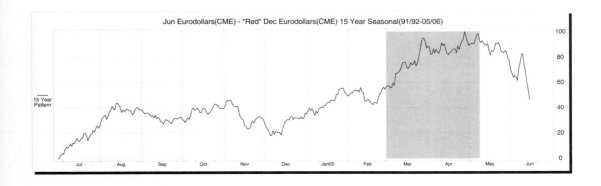

Jun Eurodollars(CME) - "Red" Dec Eurodollars(CME) 15 Year Seasonal(91/92-05/06)

Figure 10-6

Buy Mar Eurodollars(IMM) / Sell Sep Eurodollars(IMM)

Enter on approximately 06/05 - Exit on approximately 09/15

CONT YEAR	ENTRY DATE	ENTRY PRICE	EXIT DATE	EXIT PRICE	PROFIT	PROFIT AMOUNT	BEST EQUITY DATE	BEST EQUITY AMOUNT	WORST EQUITY DATE	WORST EQUITY AMOUNT
2005	06/07/04	-0.95	09/10/04	-0.59	0.36	906.25	09/01/04	1031.25	06/14/04	-187.50
2004	06/05/03	-0.13	09/15/03	-0.13	0.00	12.50	06/10/03	162.50	08/01/03	-725.00
2003	06/05/02	-1.13	09/13/02	-0.04	1.09	2718.75	09/05/02	2981.25	06/07/02	-50.00
2002	06/05/01	-0.56	09/14/01	0.25	0.82	2056.25	09/14/01	2056.25	06/29/01	-300.00
2001	06/05/00	-0.17	09/14/00	0.04	0.22	550.00	09/14/00	550.00	06/23/00	-150.00
2000	06/07/99	-0.42	09/10/99	-0.38	0.05	118.75	07/20/99	437.50	08/10/99	-325.00
1999	06/05/98	-0.06	09/11/98	0.52	0.58	1456.25	09/10/98	1637.50		
1998	06/05/97	-0.33	09/15/97	-0.24	0.09	225.00	07/30/97	512.50	08/08/97	-12.50
1997	06/05/96	-0.54	09/13/96	-0.42	0.13	325.00	08/09/96	650.00	09/05/96	-175.00
1996	06/05/95	0.16	09/15/95	0.29	0.13	325.00	09/14/95	425.00	06/09/95	-600.00
1995	06/06/94	-0.80	09/15/94	-1.01	-0.21	-525.00			09/09/94	-600.00
1994	06/07/93	-0.60	09/13/93	-0.29	0.32	800.00	09/03/93	950.00	06/09/93	-25.00
1993	06/05/92	-0.76	09/14/92	-0.10	0.66	1650.00	09/08/92	1700.00	06/10/92	-25.00
1992	06/05/91	-0.70	09/13/91	-0.26	0.44	1100.00	08/29/91	1300.00	06/10/91	-275.00
1991	06/05/90	-0.15	09/14/90	0.18	0.35	875.00	09/14/90	875.00	08/24/90	-150.00
1990	06/05/89	0.21	09/15/89	0.55	0.35	875.00	07/11/89	1150.00		
1989	06/06/88	-0.52	09/14/88	-0.23	0.30	750.00	09/14/88	750.00	06/17/88	-225.00
1988	06/05/87	-0.54	09/14/87	-1.21	-0.68	-1700.00	06/24/87	200.00	09/08/87	-2050.00
1987	06/05/86	-0.45	09/15/86	-0.15	0.29	725.00	08/26/86	1075.00		
1986	06/05/85	-0.84	09/13/85	-0.64	0.20	500.00	09/13/85	500.00	06/13/85	-325.00

Percentage Correct	93						Protective Stop			(1091)
Average Profit on Winning Trades					0.37	937.05	Winners			14
Average Loss on Trades					-0.21	-525.00	Losers			1
Average Net Profit Per Trade					0.34	839.58	Total trades			15
Percentage Correct	90									
Average Profit on Winning Trades					0.35	887.15	Winners			18
Average Loss on Trades					-0.44	-1112.50	Losers			2
Average Net Profit Per Trade					0.27	687.19	Total trades			20

HYPOTHETICAL PERFORMANCE RESULTS HAVE MANY INHERENT LIMITATIONS, SOME OF WHICH ARE DESCRIBED BELOW. NO REPRESENTATION IS BEING MADE THAT ANY ACCOUNT WILL OR IS LIKELY TO ACHIEVE PROFITS OR LOSSES SIMILAR TO THOSE SHOWN. IN FACT, THERE ARE FREQUENTLY SHARP DIFFERENCES BETWEEN HYPOTHETICAL PERFORMANCE RESULTS AND THE ACTUAL RESULTS SUBSEQUENTLY ACHIEVED BY ANY PARTICULAR TRADING PROGRAM. ONE OF THE LIMITATIONS OF HYPOTHETICAL PERFORMANCE RESULTS IS THAT THEY ARE GENERALLY PREPARED WITH THE BENEFIT OF HINDSIGHT. IN ADDITION, HYPOTHETICAL TRADING DOES NOT INVOLVE FINANCIAL RISK, AND NO HYPOTHETICAL TRADING RECORD CAN COMPLETELY ACCOUNT FOR THE IMPACT OF FINANCIAL RISK IN ACTUAL TRADING. FOR EXAMPLE, THE ABILITY TO WITHSTAND LOSSES OR ADHERE TO A PARTICULAR TRADING PROGRAM IN SPITE OF TRADING LOSSES ARE MATERIAL POINTS WHICH CAN ALSO ADVERSELY AFFECT ACTUAL TRADING RESULTS. THERE ARE NUMEROUS OTHER FACTORS RELATED TO THE MARKETS IN GENERAL OR TO THE IMPLEMENTATION OF ANY SPECIFIC TRADING PROGRAM WHICH CANNOT BE FULLY ACCOUNTED FOR IN THE PREPARATION OF HYPOTHETICAL PERFORMANCE RESULTS AND ALL OF WHICH CAN ADVERSELY AFFECT ACTUAL TRADING RESULTS. RESULTS NOT ADJUSTED FOR COMMISSION AND SLIPPAGE.

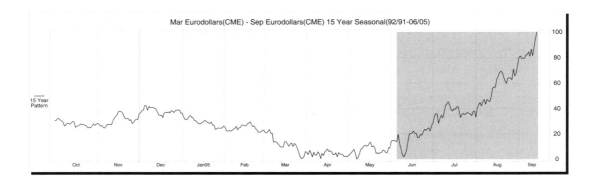

Mar Eurodollars(CME) - Sep Eurodollars(CME) 15 Year Seasonal(92/91-06/05)

15 Year Pattern

Figure 10-7

Buy Mar Eurodollars(IMM) / Sell Sep Eurodollars(IMM)

Enter on approximately 06/11 - Exit on approximately 07/18

CONT YEAR	ENTRY DATE	ENTRY PRICE	EXIT DATE	EXIT PRICE	PROFIT	PROFIT AMOUNT	BEST EQUITY DATE	BEST EQUITY AMOUNT	WORST EQUITY DATE	WORST EQUITY AMOUNT
2006	06/13/05	-0.22	07/18/05	-0.28	-0.05	-125.00	06/24/05	300.00	07/18/05	-125.00
2005	06/14/04	-1.03	07/16/04	-0.77	0.25	637.50	07/09/04	637.50		
2004	06/11/03	-0.10	07/18/03	-0.18	-0.08	-200.00	06/12/03	37.50	06/26/03	-337.50
2003	06/11/02	-1.12	07/18/02	-0.44	0.68	1700.00	07/12/02	1737.50		
2002	06/11/01	-0.52	07/18/01	-0.34	0.18	437.50	07/18/01	437.50	06/29/01	-400.00
2001	06/12/00	-0.21	07/18/00	-0.20	0.01	25.00	07/07/00	250.00	06/23/00	-37.50
2000	06/11/99	-0.48	07/16/99	-0.35	0.13	312.50	06/17/99	337.50		
1999	06/11/98	0.00	07/17/98	0.01	0.02	62.50	07/10/98	175.00	06/17/98	-50.00
1998	06/11/97	-0.31	07/18/97	-0.24	0.08	187.50	07/07/97	300.00		
1997	06/11/96	-0.59	07/18/96	-0.39	0.20	500.00	06/28/96	550.00	07/05/96	-50.00
1996	06/12/95	0.00	07/18/95	0.03	0.04	100.00	07/06/95	425.00		
1995	06/13/94	-0.93	07/18/94	-0.90	0.02	50.00	07/18/94	50.00	07/08/94	-200.00
1994	06/11/93	-0.56	07/16/93	-0.43	0.12	300.00	07/02/93	375.00	06/22/93	-25.00
1993	06/11/92	-0.75	07/17/92	-0.46	0.29	725.00	07/15/92	775.00		
1992	06/11/91	-0.82	07/18/91	-0.68	0.13	325.00	07/12/91	500.00		
1991	06/11/90	-0.18	07/18/90	-0.01	0.16	400.00	07/06/90	425.00		
1990	06/12/89	0.27	07/18/89	0.60	0.34	850.00	07/11/89	1000.00	06/13/89	-50.00
1989	06/13/88	-0.55	07/18/88	-0.42	0.12	300.00	07/15/88	325.00	06/17/88	-175.00
1988	06/11/87	-0.60	07/17/87	-0.54	0.07	175.00	06/24/87	375.00		
1987	06/11/86	-0.37	07/18/86	-0.17	0.21	525.00	07/18/86	525.00	06/16/86	-75.00

Percentage Correct	87							Protective Stop		(437)
Average Profit on Winning Trades					0.16	412.50		Winners		13
Average Loss on Trades					-0.07	-162.50		Losers		2
Average Net Profit Per Trade					0.13	335.83		Total trades		15
Percentage Correct	90									
Average Profit on Winning Trades					0.17	422.92		Winners		18
Average Loss on Trades					-0.07	-162.50		Losers		2
Average Net Profit Per Trade					0.15	364.37		Total trades		20

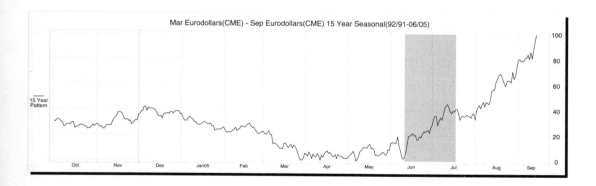

Mar Eurodollars(CME) - Sep Eurodollars(CME) 15 Year Seasonal(92/91-06/05)

Figure 10-8

Buy Jun Eurodollars(IMM) / Sell Sep Eurodollars(IMM)

Enter on approximately 06/27 - Exit on approximately 09/15

CONT YEAR	ENTRY DATE	ENTRY PRICE	EXIT DATE	EXIT PRICE	PROFIT	PROFIT AMOUNT	BEST EQUITY DATE	BEST EQUITY AMOUNT	WORST EQUITY DATE	WORST EQUITY AMOUNT
2005	06/28/04	-1.44	09/10/04	-0.84	0.60	1506.25	09/01/04	1656.25		
2004	06/27/03	-0.40	09/15/03	-0.37	0.04	87.50	07/11/03	225.00	09/02/03	-1175.00
2003	06/27/02	-1.42	09/13/02	-0.28	1.13	2831.25	09/05/02	3143.75	06/28/02	-25.00
2002	06/27/01	-0.92	09/14/01	-0.04	0.88	2193.75	09/14/01	2193.75	06/29/01	-387.50
2001	06/27/00	-0.21	09/14/00	0.03	0.25	625.00	09/13/00	625.00	07/18/00	-112.50
2000	06/28/99	-0.63	09/10/99	-0.58	0.05	118.75	07/20/99	450.00	08/10/99	-587.50
1999	06/29/98	-0.02	09/11/98	0.55	0.58	1443.75	09/10/98	1687.50	07/31/98	-25.00
1998	06/27/97	-0.40	09/15/97	-0.35	0.05	112.50	07/30/97	475.00	08/08/97	-125.00
1997	06/27/96	-0.68	09/13/96	-0.59	0.10	250.00	08/02/96	675.00	07/05/96	-275.00
1996	06/27/95	0.03	09/15/95	0.24	0.21	525.00	09/14/95	625.00	08/17/95	-675.00
1995	06/27/94	-1.26	09/15/94	-1.35	-0.10	-250.00	07/19/94	275.00	09/12/94	-375.00
1994	06/28/93	-0.76	09/13/93	-0.49	0.28	700.00	09/03/93	900.00	07/27/93	-375.00
1993	06/29/92	-0.97	09/14/92	-0.39	0.59	1475.00	09/08/92	1550.00		
1992	06/27/91	-1.09	09/13/91	-0.54	0.55	1375.00	09/09/91	1550.00	07/08/91	-225.00
1991	06/27/90	-0.28	09/14/90	0.01	0.31	775.00	09/14/90	775.00	08/07/90	-300.00
1990	06/27/89	0.23	09/15/89	0.48	0.26	650.00	07/11/89	1150.00	06/29/89	-125.00
1989	06/27/88	-0.75	09/14/88	-0.46	0.29	725.00	08/03/88	750.00	06/28/88	-25.00
1988	06/29/87	-0.68	09/14/87	-1.51	-0.83	-2075.00			09/09/87	-2400.00
1987	06/27/86	-0.59	09/15/86	-0.39	0.21	525.00	08/26/86	1025.00	06/30/86	-25.00
1986	06/27/85	-1.28	09/13/85	-0.98	0.29	725.00	09/13/85	725.00	07/29/85	-200.00

Percentage Correct	93						Protective Stop		(1193)
Average Profit on Winning Trades					0.40	1001.34	Winners		14
Average Loss on Trades					-0.10	-250.00	Losers		1
Average Net Profit Per Trade					0.37	917.92	Total trades		15
Percentage Correct	90								
Average Profit on Winning Trades					0.37	924.65	Winners		18
Average Loss on Trades					-0.47	-1162.50	Losers		2
Average Net Profit Per Trade					0.29	715.94	Total trades		20

HYPOTHETICAL PERFORMANCE RESULTS HAVE MANY INHERENT LIMITATIONS, SOME OF WHICH ARE DESCRIBED BELOW. NO REPRESENTATION IS BEING MADE THAT ANY ACCOUNT WILL OR IS LIKELY TO ACHIEVE PROFITS OR LOSSES SIMILAR TO THOSE SHOWN. IN FACT, THERE ARE FREQUENTLY SHARP DIFFERENCES BETWEEN HYPOTHETICAL PERFORMANCE RESULTS AND THE ACTUAL RESULTS SUBSEQUENTLY ACHIEVED BY ANY PARTICULAR TRADING PROGRAM. ONE OF THE LIMITATIONS OF HYPOTHETICAL PERFORMANCE RESULTS IS THAT THEY ARE GENERALLY PREPARED WITH THE BENEFIT OF HINDSIGHT. IN ADDITION, HYPOTHETICAL TRADING DOES NOT INVOLVE FINANCIAL RISK, AND NO HYPOTHETICAL TRADING RECORD CAN COMPLETELY ACCOUNT FOR THE IMPACT OF FINANCIAL RISK IN ACTUAL TRADING. FOR EXAMPLE, THE ABILITY TO WITHSTAND LOSSES OR ADHERE TO A PARTICULAR TRADING PROGRAM IN SPITE OF TRADING LOSSES ARE MATERIAL POINTS WHICH CAN ALSO ADVERSELY AFFECT ACTUAL TRADING RESULTS. THERE ARE NUMEROUS OTHER FACTORS RELATED TO THE MARKETS IN GENERAL OR TO THE IMPLEMENTATION OF ANY SPECIFIC TRADING PROGRAM WHICH CANNOT BE FULLY ACCOUNTED FOR IN THE PREPARATION OF HYPOTHETICAL PERFORMANCE RESULTS AND ALL OF WHICH CAN ADVERSELY AFFECT ACTUAL TRADING RESULTS. RESULTS NOT ADJUSTED FOR COMMISSION AND SLIPPAGE.

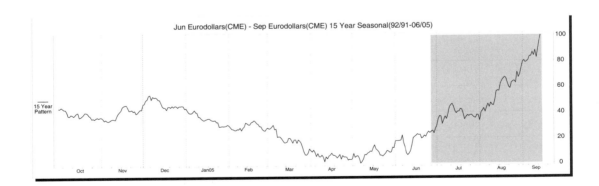

Jun Eurodollars(CME) - Sep Eurodollars(CME) 15 Year Seasonal(92/91-06/05)

Figure 10-9

Buy Jun Eurodollars(IMM) / Sell Dec Eurodollars(IMM)

Enter on approximately 08/06 - Exit on approximately 11/13

CONT YEAR	ENTRY DATE	ENTRY PRICE	EXIT DATE	EXIT PRICE	PROFIT	PROFIT AMOUNT	BEST EQUITY DATE	BEST EQUITY AMOUNT	WORST EQUITY DATE	WORST EQUITY AMOUNT
2005	08/06/04	-0.62	11/12/04	-0.59	0.03	75.00	10/14/04	737.50	08/10/04	-112.50
2004	08/06/03	-0.58	11/13/03	-0.44	0.14	362.50	09/30/03	987.50	09/02/03	-425.00
2003	08/06/02	-0.52	11/13/02	-0.21	0.31	762.50	10/30/02	1000.00	08/16/02	-300.00
2002	08/06/01	-0.48	11/13/01	-0.31	0.17	437.50	11/07/01	737.50	09/21/01	-262.50
2001	08/07/00	0.03	11/13/00	0.34	0.32	793.75	11/13/00	793.75	08/16/00	-25.00
2000	08/06/99	-0.37	11/12/99	-0.09	0.29	712.50	09/28/99	1062.50	08/10/99	-75.00
1999	08/06/98	0.04	11/13/98	0.41	0.37	912.50	10/29/98	1550.00		
1998	08/06/97	-0.18	11/13/97	-0.04	0.14	362.50	11/13/97	362.50	09/10/97	-112.50
1997	08/06/96	-0.25	11/13/96	-0.10	0.15	375.00	11/13/96	375.00	08/30/96	-350.00
1996	08/07/95	-0.15	11/13/95	0.41	0.57	1425.00	11/02/95	1450.00	08/15/95	-100.00
1995	08/08/94	-0.56	11/11/94	-1.00	-0.45	-1125.00			11/11/94	-1125.00
1994	08/06/93	-0.39	11/12/93	-0.32	0.07	175.00	10/15/93	550.00		
1993	08/06/92	-0.42	11/13/92	-0.33	0.10	250.00	08/18/92	350.00	10/20/92	-375.00
1992	08/06/91	-0.50	11/13/91	-0.06	0.44	1100.00	10/01/91	1175.00		
1991	08/06/90	-0.39	11/13/90	0.35	0.76	1900.00	11/12/90	1925.00	08/07/90	-125.00
1990	08/07/89	0.00	11/13/89	0.50	0.50	1250.00	11/13/89	1250.00		
1989	08/08/88	-0.09	11/11/88	0.07	0.18	450.00	11/01/88	550.00	09/21/88	-225.00
1988	08/06/87	-0.57	11/13/87	-0.48	0.10	250.00	10/16/87	650.00	10/26/87	-525.00
1987	08/06/86	-0.30	11/13/86	-0.04	0.26	650.00	11/13/86	650.00	09/08/86	-225.00
1986	08/06/85	-0.83	11/13/85	-0.35	0.48	1200.00	11/12/85	1225.00	08/14/85	-50.00

Percentage Correct	93							Protective Stop		(738)
Average Profit on Winning Trades					0.28	688.84		Winners		14
Average Loss on Trades					-0.45	-1125.00		Losers		1
Average Net Profit Per Trade					0.23	567.92		Total trades		15
Percentage Correct	95									
Average Profit on Winning Trades					0.28	707.57		Winners		19
Average Loss on Trades					-0.45	-1125.00		Losers		1
Average Net Profit Per Trade					0.25	615.94		Total trades		20

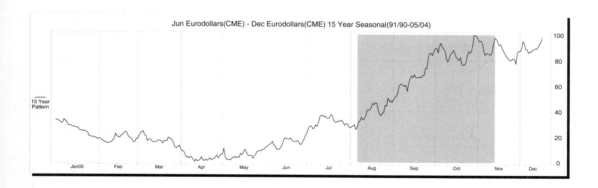

Jun Eurodollars(CME) - Dec Eurodollars(CME) 15 Year Seasonal(91/90-05/04)

Inter-market Spreads

A similar dynamic is at work in the interplay among Treasury instruments of differing maturities. Risk associated with lending and opportunity with borrowing vary with time of obligation. Under normal circumstances, the market compensates investors who commit money at the greater risk of a longer period of time with the greater yield of a higher interest rate. When longer-term rates are higher than shorter-term rates, plotting time-to-maturity on a horizontal axis against yield-to-maturity on a vertical axis forms a graph with an upward slope — referred to as a positive yield curve.

30-Year Treasury Bonds

The long end of the yield curve is fixed by the 30-year T-Bond, a debt instrument of the US government with maturities ranging from 10 to 30 years. For many years, the long bond served as a benchmark for corporate and mortgage debt. As the US budget ran surpluses around the turn of the century, however, the Treasury eliminated new sales of its 30-year bonds. Nonetheless, because of the effects on reinvestment values, long US Treasury bonds are typically the most price sensitive to yield changes of all government-issued debt instruments.

Figure 10-10: 30-Year Treasury Constant Maturity Rate

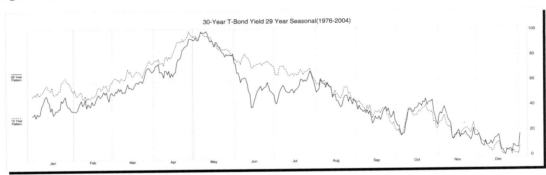

Data from FRED can be used to construct a seasonal pattern for interest rates at the long end of the curve. The most prominent features include the typical peak in market rates in April/May (remember those income tax payments?) and the long, steady decline through at least the end of the US fiscal year, often of the calendar year.

Figure 10-11: December 30-Year T-Bonds Seasonal Pattern

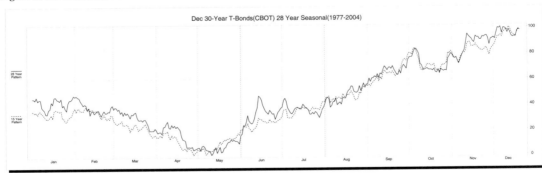

As with Eurodollars, prices for Treasury instruments move inversely with rates. Thus, prices tend to reach a seasonal low in April/May and then to begin a steady journey higher through the remainder of the fiscal, if not always calendar, year.

The CBOT contract for 30-year T-bonds specifies a US Treasury bond with a face value at maturity of $100,000. The bond is to yield 6% and must not be callable for, or else have a maturity of, at least 15 years. Par is on the basis of 100 points, each worth $1,000; the minimum increment is one thirty-second of one point, worth $31.25.

10-Year Treasury Notes

With the end of new Treasury sales of 30-year bonds, the benchmark rate passed on to the 10-year Treasury Note. Treasury bills, bonds, and notes are direct obligations of the US government sold to finance its short- and long-term needs. The Federal Reserve functions as an agent of the Treasury and sells these instruments to a primary market of bank and nonbank securities dealers approved by the New York Federal Reserve Bank. Treasury refunding auctions are held during the second week of the second month of each quarter to sell 10-year and 5-year Treasury notes. Those primary dealers then conduct a secondary market, the function of which is to distribute those instruments to such buyers as commercial banks, savings and loan associations, insurance companies, state and local governments, corporations, pension and trust funds, individuals, and foreign investors.

Figure 10-12: 10-Year Treasury Constant Maturity Rate

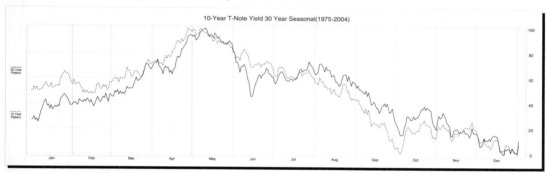

Figure 10-13: December 10-Year T-Notes Seasonal Pattern

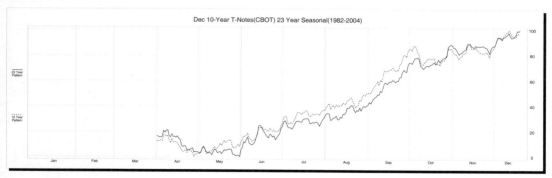

Note the similarity in seasonal patterns to the 30-year T-bond. The seasonal causes and seasonal effects are the same. The observant reader might notice a small difference in the fourth quarter, however. Whereas the 30-year Constant Rate has tended eventually to continue even lower into year end, the 10-year Constant Rate has tended not to do so.

The CBOT contract for 10-year T-notes specifies a US Treasury note with a face value at maturity of $100,000 maturing at least 6 years but not more than 10 years from first delivery day and with a yield of 6%. Notes are priced the same as are bonds, but the minimum increment is one-half of one thirty-second, worth $15.625.

5-Year Treasury Notes

The CBOT contract for 5-year Treasury Notes specifies a US Treasury note of $100,000 face value much the same as the 10-year except that it must have an original maturity of not more than 5 years and 3 months and a remaining maturity of not less than 4 years and 2 months on the first day of delivery.

Figure 10-14: 5-Year Treasury Constant Maturity Rate

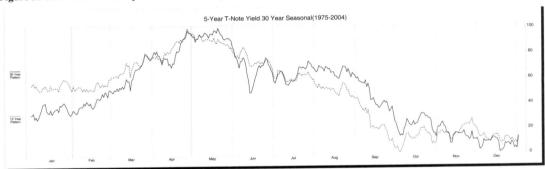

Figure 10-15: December 5-Year T-Notes Seasonal Pattern

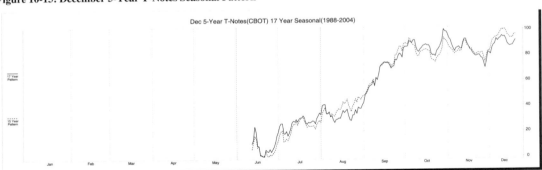

Here again, the seasonal patterns are similar to those for 30-Year bonds and 10-Year notes. Also here again, the observant reader may notice a slight difference in the pattern for rates in the fourth quarter, however, with 5-Year rates slightly higher at year end than in early October.

2-Year Treasury Notes

The CBOT contract for 2-year Treasury Notes differs from those of the 5- and 10-year notes. It is also to yield 6% but specifies a US Treasury note with face value at maturity of $200,000. Just as the 5-year note, it too must have an *original* maturity of not more than 5 years and 3 months; it must have a remaining maturity of not less than 1 year and 9 months from the first day of the delivery month but also not more than 2 years from the last day of the delivery month. It too is priced with par on the basis of 100 points, with each worth $2,000, but the minimum increment is one-quarter of one thirty-second, worth $15.625.

Figure 10-16: 2-Year Treasury Constant Maturity Rate

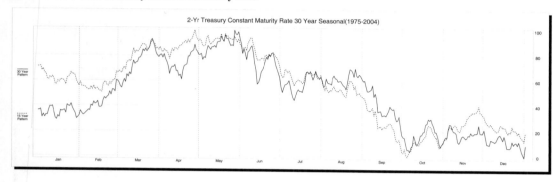

Figure 10-17: December 2-Year T-Notes Seasonal Pattern

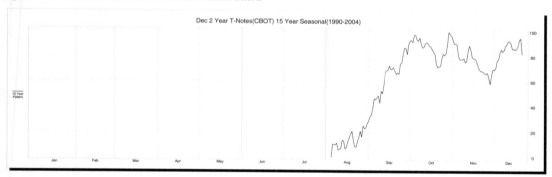

Trading in deferred futures contracts of 2-year T-notes has been so limited through the years that price data is insufficient to construct a seasonal pattern for much more than 5 months prior to expiry, thus presenting a somewhat distorted view of trading patterns throughout the year. Note the pattern for the 2-year Treasury Constant, however, is similar to those for the 30-year T-bond and the 5- and 10-year T-notes, except for the little tail in the fourth quarter.

Yield-Curve Spreads

As discussed earlier, the dynamics of spreads between instruments along the yield curve are similar to those in Eurodollar calendar spreads. Whereas deferred contracts of Eurodollars tend to lead changes in market-driven interest rates, so too instruments at the long end of the yield curve.

NOB Spreads. In fact, one of earliest vehicles for analyzing and trading such trends was the so-called NOB spread. Taking its name from *N*otes *O*ver *B*onds, the NOB was traded as an entity unto itself, its quote calculated by subtracting the price of the bonds from the price of the notes and expressed as the number of thirty-seconds. For example, if notes were priced at 98~12 and bonds at 93~28, the NOB would be quoted as 144. Because the long end of the yield curve tends to lead, traders who thought interest rates were going higher might "go long the NOB" in the expectation that bond prices would decline first, faster, and farther than notes — thereby widening the spread between them. Conversely, traders who thought rates were going lower might "go short the NOB," expecting bonds to rise first, faster, and farther than notes — thereby narrowing the spread.

Figure 10-18: Sep NOB Spread Seasonal Pattern

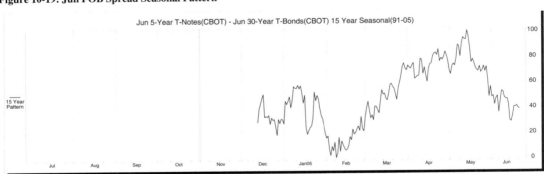

The seasonal pattern for the September NOB illustrates and confirms the tendency for market-driven rates to peak in April/May and to decline thereafter.

FOB Spreads. The FOB takes its name from *F*ive-Year Notes *O*ver *B*onds and trades in much the same way as the NOB. With a wider spread along the yield curve, however, there can be more volatility — much like the kids' game of crack-the-whip.

Figure 10-19: Jun FOB Spread Seasonal Pattern

The FOB (Figure 10-19) also confirms the tendency for rates to rise into April/May.

Others. But the dynamics tend to ripple through all relationships. In movements large and small, the longer end tends to lead. Be careful to notice in the charts below which instrument is on the long side and which on the short. The CBOT recognizes various relationships in various ratios.

Figure 10-20: Mar 30-Year T-Bonds/Mar 2-Year T-Notes

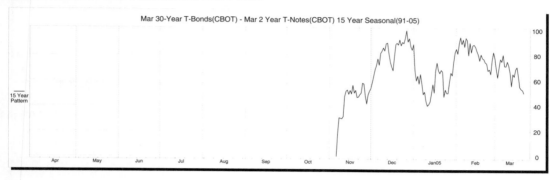

Figure 10-21: Dec 10-Year T-Notes/Dec 5-Year T-Notes

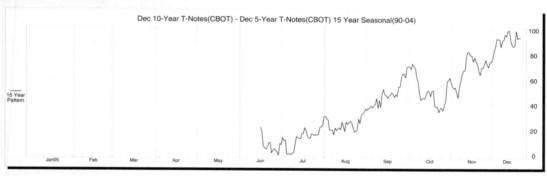

Figure 10-22: Sep 10-Year T-Notes/Sep 2-Year T-Notes

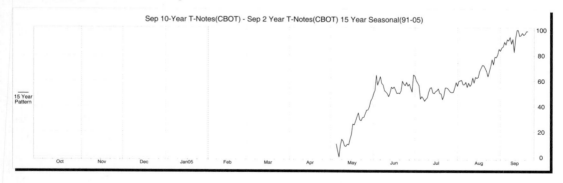

Figure 10-23: Mar 2-Year T-Notes/Mar 5-Year T-Notes

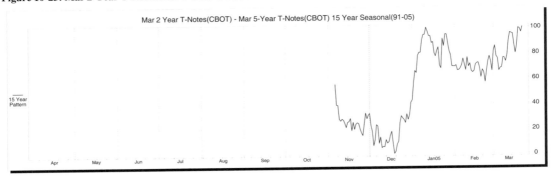

Mar 2 Year T-Notes(CBOT) - Mar 5-Year T-Notes(CBOT) 15 Year Seasonal(91-05)

Seasonal strategies in the table below quantify the more attractive seasonal movements portrayed in the seasonal patterns (all relationships in a ratio of 1:1). Again it is the interplay between instruments of longer and shorter maturity.

Figure 10-24: Yield-Curve Spread Strategies

Moore Research Center, Inc. Seasonal Strategy	Entry Date	Exit Date	Win Pct	Win Yrs	Loss Years	Total Years	Average Profit	Ave Pft Per Day
Buy Sep 30-Year T-Bonds(CBOT) Sell Sep 5-Year T-Notes(CBOT)	5/11	8/02	87 / 88	13 / 15	2 / 2	15 / 17	1036 / 1167	12 / 14
Buy Jun 30-Year T-Bonds(CBOT) Sell Jun 2-Year T-Notes(CBOT)	5/14	5/25	87	13	2	15	600	50
Buy Sep 30-Year T-Bonds(CBOT) Sell Sep 2-Year T-Notes(CBOT)	5/14	6/03	93	13	1	14	1090	52
Buy Sep 10-Year T-Notes(CBOT) Sell Sep 2-Year T-Notes(CBOT)	5/14	6/06	93	13	1	14	617	26
Buy Sep 30-Year T-Bonds(CBOT) Sell Sep 5-Year T-Notes(CBOT)	5/24	6/03	80 / 83	12 / 15	3 / 3	15 / 18	434 / 501	39 / 46
Buy Dec 30-Year T-Bonds(CBOT) Sell Dec 5-Year T-Notes(CBOT)	8/13	11/16	87 / 88	13 / 15	2 / 2	15 / 17	1257 / 1318	13 / 14
Buy Dec 10-Year T-Notes(CBOT) Sell Dec 5-Year T-Notes(CBOT)	8/16	11/13	93 / 94	14 / 16	1 / 1	15 / 17	614 / 624	7 / 7
Buy Dec 10-Year T-Notes(CBOT) Sell Dec 2-Year T-Notes(CBOT)	9/16	10/01	87	13	2	15	415	26
Buy Dec 30-Year T-Bonds(CBOT) Sell Dec 10-Year T-Notes(CBOT)	10/18	11/14	87 / 90	13 / 18	2 / 2	15 / 20	616 / 704	22 / 25
Buy Dec 30-Year T-Bonds(CBOT) Sell Dec 5-Year T-Notes(CBOT)	10/23	10/31	80 / 82	12 / 14	3 / 3	15 / 17	620 / 623	69 / 69
Buy Dec 30-Year T-Bonds(CBOT) Sell Dec 2-Year T-Notes(CBOT)	11/02	11/14	93	14	1	15	681	52
Buy Mar 10-Year T-Notes(CBOT) Sell Mar 5-Year T-Notes(CBOT)	11/06	12/23	87 / 88	13 / 15	2 / 2	15 / 17	478 / 466	10 / 10
Buy Mar 30-Year T-Bonds(CBOT) Sell Mar 5-Year T-Notes(CBOT)	11/06	12/24	87 / 88	13 / 15	2 / 2	15 / 17	1160 / 1160	24 / 24
Buy Mar 30-Year T-Bonds(CBOT) Sell Mar 10-Year T-Notes(CBOT)	11/06	12/27	87 / 85	13 / 17	2 / 3	15 / 20	752 / 756	14 / 15

Figure 10-24: Yield-Curve Spread Strategies continued

Seasonal Strategy	Entry Date	Exit Date	Win Pct	Win Yrs	Loss Years	Total Years	Average Profit	Ave Pft Per Day
Buy Mar 30-Year T-Bonds(CBOT) Sell Mar 5-Year T-Notes(CBOT)	11/27	12/12	87 / 88	13 / 15	2 / 2	15 / 17	660 / 683	41 / 43
Buy Mar 30-Year T-Bonds(CBOT) Sell Mar 2-Year T-Notes(CBOT)	11/27	12/12	87	13	2	15	768	48
Buy Mar 2-Year T-Notes(CBOT) Sell Mar 5-Year T-Notes(CBOT)	12/20	1/26	87	13	2	15	293	8
Buy Mar 2-Year T-Notes(CBOT) Sell Mar 10-Year T-Notes(CBOT)	12/29	1/09	80	12	3	15	399	33
Buy Mar 30-Year T-Bonds(CBOT) Sell Mar 2-Year T-Notes(CBOT)	1/12	1/31	87	13	2	15	858	43
Buy Jun 2-Year T-Notes(CBOT) Sell Jun 30-Year T-Bonds(CBOT)	2/19	4/20	80	12	3	15	896	15
Buy Jun 2-Year T-Notes(CBOT) Sell Jun 30-Year T-Bonds(CBOT)	3/18	3/30	80	12	3	15	499	38

The table header reads: *Moore Research Center, Inc.* — **Yield-Curve Spreads**

Spreads presented herein by no means exhaust all the historically reliable moves in all the combinations. They are representative, and they do tend to be among the best. Thus, readers will again note that the best seasonal strategies tend to come in tight clusters, usually suggesting powerful seasonal dynamics that affect and ripple through the whole complex. The appearance of seemingly duplicate strategies is meant not only to quantify such dynamics but also to reinforce to the reader just how deep and wide can be the seasonal effect.

That there exists such a cluster of seasonal entries in May should come as no surprise. Similarly, one would tend to expect the long end generally to lead the market higher through the end of the year, at which time the tendencies reverse. One may also wish to notice that several seasonal moves have been launched from those quarterly Treasury refunding auctions. Observant traders may have noticed in the past how Treasury instruments tend to weaken into such auctions only to rally out. Barring overriding fundamentals otherwise, dealers tend to wait to see the auction's coverage — the length and depth of bids — before becoming aggressive.

One of the great financial questions early in the twenty-first century has become whether the financial environment is inflationary or nearly deflationary. How spreads between these financial instruments perform can perhaps provide clues. Will they continue to perform as they had during a disinflationary environment? Or will they start behaving differently? Understanding their seasonal tendencies can be the first step in anticipating how to trade these vehicles of normally lower risk in the future.

Figure 10-25

Moore Research Center, Inc. *Buy Sep 30-Year T-Bonds(CBOT) / Sell Sep 5-Year T-Notes(CBOT)*

Enter on approximately 05/11 - Exit on approximately 08/02

CONT YEAR	ENTRY DATE	ENTRY PRICE	EXIT DATE	EXIT PRICE	PROFIT	PROFIT AMOUNT	BEST EQUITY DATE	BEST EQUITY AMOUNT	WORST EQUITY DATE	WORST EQUITY AMOUNT
2005	05/11/05	6~180	08/02/05	7~185	1~005	1015.63	06/27/05	3562.50		
2004	05/11/04	-4~005	08/02/04	-1~075	2~250	2781.25	07/19/04	3359.38	05/13/04	-703.13
2003	05/12/03	1~135	08/01/03	-5~085	-6~220	-6687.50	06/13/03	4312.50	07/31/03	-7125.00
2002	05/13/02	-4~285	08/02/02	-3~260	1~025	1078.13	06/14/02	1578.13	05/17/02	-671.88
2001	05/11/01	-4~150	08/02/01	-1~255	2~215	2671.88	07/24/01	3281.25	05/15/01	-203.13
2000	05/11/00	-2~310	08/02/00	-0~150	2~160	2500.00	07/27/00	2703.13	05/19/00	-609.38
1999	05/11/99	-3~215	08/02/99	-4~135	-0~240	-750.00	05/25/99	734.38	06/24/99	-1328.13
1998	05/11/98	-1~140	07/31/98	0~265	2~085	2265.63	07/06/98	3093.75		
1997	05/12/97	-5~280	08/01/97	-3~180	2~100	2312.50	07/31/97	3218.75	05/27/97	-953.13
1996	05/13/96	-7~115	08/02/96	-5~180	1~255	1796.88	08/01/96	2031.25	06/12/96	-796.88
1995	05/11/95	-6~315	08/02/95	-6~015	0~300	937.50	06/22/95	3296.88		
1994	05/11/94	-10~250	08/02/94	-9~245	1~005	1015.63	06/06/94	1234.38	07/11/94	-968.75
1993	05/11/93	-10~125	08/02/93	-6~210	3~235	3734.38	08/02/93	3734.38	05/13/93	-906.25
1992	05/11/92	-13~160	07/31/92	-12~265	0~215	671.88	07/31/92	671.88	07/17/92	-1640.63
1991	05/13/91	-13~265	08/02/91	-13~200	0~065	203.13	05/21/91	265.63	06/21/91	-1015.63
1990	05/11/90	-13~165	08/02/90	-13~130	0~035	109.38	06/14/90	1265.63	07/24/90	-234.38
1989	05/11/89	-14~280	08/02/89	-10~220	4~060	4187.50	08/02/89	4187.50		

Percentage Correct	87						Protective Stop	(1347)
Average Profit on Winning Trades					1~246	1768.03	Winners	13
Average Loss on Trades					-3~230	-3718.75	Losers	2
Average Net Profit Per Trade					1~012	1036.46	Total trades	15
Percentage Correct	88							
Average Profit on Winning Trades					1~262	1818.75	Winners	15
Average Loss on Trades					-3~230	-3718.75	Losers	2
Average Net Profit Per Trade					1~054	1167.28	Total trades	17

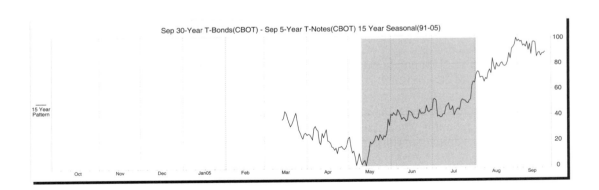

Sep 30-Year T-Bonds(CBOT) - Sep 5-Year T-Notes(CBOT) 15 Year Seasonal(91-05)

15 Year Pattern

Figure 10-26

Buy Jun 30-Year T-Bonds(CBOT) / Sell Jun 2-Year T-Notes(CBOT)

Enter on approximately 05/14 - Exit on approximately 05/25

CONT YEAR	ENTRY DATE	ENTRY PRICE	EXIT DATE	EXIT PRICE		PROFIT AMOUNT	BEST EQUITY DATE	BEST EQUITY AMOUNT	WORST EQUITY DATE	WORST EQUITY AMOUNT
2005	05/16/05	-92391	05/25/05	-91625		765.63	05/24/05	1312.50		
2004	05/14/04	-107375	05/25/04	-106219		1156.25	05/25/04	1156.25		
2003	05/14/03	-97938	05/23/03	-95219		2718.75	05/23/03	2718.75		
2002	05/14/02	-108594	05/24/02	-107844		750.00	05/22/02	875.00	05/17/02	-31.25
2001	05/14/01	-105891	05/25/01	-106094		-203.13	05/21/01	1140.63	05/15/01	-609.38
2000	05/15/00	-102625	05/25/00	-102313		312.50	05/16/00	453.13	05/19/00	-859.38
1999	05/14/99	-104234	05/25/99	-103266		968.75	05/25/99	968.75		
1998	05/14/98	-101266	05/22/98	-100672		593.75	05/20/98	671.88		
1997	05/14/97	-107281	05/23/97	-108156		-875.00			05/22/97	-937.50
1996	05/14/96	-108719	05/24/96	-108250		468.75	05/22/96	515.63	05/16/96	-187.50
1995	05/15/95	-108047	05/25/95	-106703		1343.75	05/25/95	1343.75		
1994	05/16/94	-113078	05/25/94	-113031		46.88	05/17/94	796.88	05/23/94	-546.88
1993	05/14/93	-114828	05/25/93	-114500		328.13	05/24/93	500.00	05/18/93	-390.63
1992	05/14/92	-118984	05/22/92	-118391		593.75	05/21/92	671.88		
1991	05/14/91	-117875	05/24/91	-117844		31.25	05/21/91	890.63		

Percentage Correct		87								
Average Profit on Winning Trades						775.24	Winners			13
Average Loss on Trades						-539.06	Losers			2
Average Net Profit Per Trade						600.00	Total trades			15

HYPOTHETICAL PERFORMANCE RESULTS HAVE MANY INHERENT LIMITATIONS, SOME OF WHICH ARE DESCRIBED BELOW. NO REPRESENTATION IS BEING MADE THAT ANY ACCOUNT WILL OR IS LIKELY TO ACHIEVE PROFITS OR LOSSES SIMILAR TO THOSE SHOWN. IN FACT, THERE ARE FREQUENTLY SHARP DIFFERENCES BETWEEN HYPOTHETICAL PERFORMANCE RESULTS AND THE ACTUAL RESULTS SUBSEQUENTLY ACHIEVED BY ANY PARTICULAR TRADING PROGRAM. ONE OF THE LIMITATIONS OF HYPOTHETICAL PERFORMANCE RESULTS IS THAT THEY ARE GENERALLY PREPARED WITH THE BENEFIT OF HINDSIGHT. IN ADDITION, HYPOTHETICAL TRADING DOES NOT INVOLVE FINANCIAL RISK, AND NO HYPOTHETICAL TRADING RECORD CAN COMPLETELY ACCOUNT FOR THE IMPACT OF FINANCIAL RISK IN ACTUAL TRADING. FOR EXAMPLE, THE ABILITY TO WITHSTAND LOSSES OR ADHERE TO A PARTICULAR TRADING PROGRAM IN SPITE OF TRADING LOSSES ARE MATERIAL POINTS WHICH CAN ALSO ADVERSELY AFFECT ACTUAL TRADING RESULTS. THERE ARE NUMEROUS OTHER FACTORS RELATED TO THE MARKETS IN GENERAL OR TO THE IMPLEMENTATION OF ANY SPECIFIC TRADING PROGRAM WHICH CANNOT BE FULLY ACCOUNTED FOR IN THE PREPARATION OF HYPOTHETICAL PERFORMANCE RESULTS AND ALL OF WHICH CAN ADVERSELY AFFECT ACTUAL TRADING RESULTS. RESULTS NOT ADJUSTED FOR COMMISSION AND SLIPPAGE.

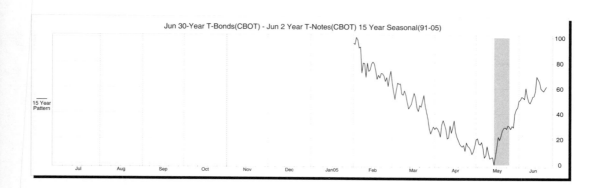

Jun 30-Year T-Bonds(CBOT) - Jun 2 Year T-Notes(CBOT) 15 Year Seasonal(91-05)

Figure 10-27

Buy Sep 30-Year T-Bonds(CBOT) / Sell Sep 2-Year T-Notes(CBOT)

Enter on approximately 05/14 - Exit on approximately 06/03

CONT YEAR	ENTRY DATE	ENTRY PRICE	EXIT DATE	EXIT PRICE		PROFIT AMOUNT	BEST EQUITY DATE	BEST EQUITY AMOUNT	WORST EQUITY DATE	WORST EQUITY AMOUNT
2005	05/16/05	-92188	06/03/05	-90031		2156.25	06/02/05	2875.00		
2004	05/14/04	-107063	06/03/04	-105875		1187.50	05/27/04	1937.50		
2003	05/14/03	-98563	06/03/03	-97266		1296.88	05/23/03	2671.88		
2002	05/14/02	-107938	06/03/02	-107031		906.25	05/30/02	906.25	05/17/02	-125.00
2001	05/14/01	-106078	06/01/01	-104719		1359.38	06/01/01	1359.38	05/15/01	-609.38
2000	05/15/00	-102438	06/02/00	-101078		1359.38	06/01/00	1562.50	05/19/00	-859.38
1999	05/14/99	-104344	06/03/99	-104328		15.63	05/25/99	984.38		
1998	05/14/98	-101484	06/03/98	-100203		1281.25	06/01/98	1359.38		
1997	05/14/97	-107172	06/03/97	-106188		984.38	06/03/97	984.38	05/27/97	-1125.00
1996	05/14/96	-108672	06/03/96	-109047		-375.00	05/22/96	437.50	06/03/96	-375.00
1995	05/15/95	-108094	06/02/95	-106109		1984.38	06/02/95	1984.38		
1994	05/16/94	-112859	06/03/94	-111969		890.63	06/03/94	890.63	05/23/94	-500.00
1993	05/14/93	-115031	06/03/93	-112984		2046.88	06/02/93	2093.75	05/18/93	-343.75
1992	05/14/92	-118453	06/03/92	-118281		171.88	05/21/92	875.00		

Percentage Correct	93							
Average Profit on Winning Trades			1203.13		Winners			13
Average Loss on Trades			-375.00		Losers			1
Average Net Profit Per Trade			1090.40		Total trades			14

HYPOTHETICAL PERFORMANCE RESULTS HAVE MANY INHERENT LIMITATIONS, SOME OF WHICH ARE DESCRIBED BELOW. NO REPRESENTATION IS BEING MADE THAT ANY ACCOUNT WILL OR IS LIKELY TO ACHIEVE PROFITS OR LOSSES SIMILAR TO THOSE SHOWN. IN FACT, THERE ARE FREQUENTLY SHARP DIFFERENCES BETWEEN HYPOTHETICAL PERFORMANCE RESULTS AND THE ACTUAL RESULTS SUBSEQUENTLY ACHIEVED BY ANY PARTICULAR TRADING PROGRAM. ONE OF THE LIMITATIONS OF HYPOTHETICAL PERFORMANCE RESULTS IS THAT THEY ARE GENERALLY PREPARED WITH THE BENEFIT OF HINDSIGHT. IN ADDITION, HYPOTHETICAL TRADING DOES NOT INVOLVE FINANCIAL RISK, AND NO HYPOTHETICAL TRADING RECORD CAN COMPLETELY ACCOUNT FOR THE IMPACT OF FINANCIAL RISK IN ACTUAL TRADING. FOR EXAMPLE, THE ABILITY TO WITHSTAND LOSSES OR ADHERE TO A PARTICULAR TRADING PROGRAM IN SPITE OF TRADING LOSSES ARE MATERIAL POINTS WHICH CAN ALSO ADVERSELY AFFECT ACTUAL TRADING RESULTS. THERE ARE NUMEROUS OTHER FACTORS RELATED TO THE MARKETS IN GENERAL OR TO THE IMPLEMENTATION OF ANY SPECIFIC TRADING PROGRAM WHICH CANNOT BE FULLY ACCOUNTED FOR IN THE PREPARATION OF HYPOTHETICAL PERFORMANCE RESULTS AND ALL OF WHICH CAN ADVERSELY AFFECT ACTUAL TRADING RESULTS. RESULTS NOT ADJUSTED FOR COMMISSION AND SLIPPAGE.

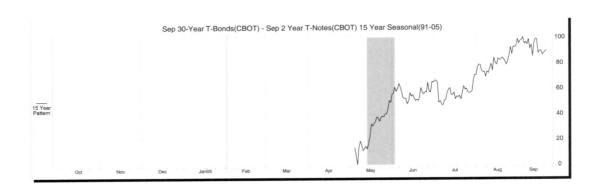

Sep 30-Year T-Bonds(CBOT) - Sep 2 Year T-Notes(CBOT) 15 Year Seasonal(91-05)

Figure 10-28

Moore Research Center, Inc.

Buy Sep 10-Year T-Notes(CBOT) / Sell Sep 2-Year T-Notes(CBOT)

Enter on approximately 05/14 - Exit on approximately 06/06

CONT YEAR	ENTRY DATE	ENTRY PRICE	EXIT DATE	EXIT PRICE		PROFIT AMOUNT	BEST EQUITY DATE	BEST EQUITY AMOUNT	WORST EQUITY DATE	WORST EQUITY AMOUNT
2005	05/16/05	-95391	06/06/05	-94250		1140.63	06/02/05	1312.50		
2004	05/14/04	-102813	06/04/04	-102453		359.38	05/27/04	796.88		
2003	05/14/03	-98797	06/06/03	-98078		718.75	05/23/03	1187.50		
2002	05/14/02	-103828	06/06/02	-102953		875.00	05/31/02	953.13		
2001	05/14/01	-102453	06/06/01	-101578		875.00	06/06/01	875.00	05/15/01	-437.50
2000	05/15/00	-100969	06/06/00	-100047		921.88	06/05/00	1000.00	05/18/00	-390.63
1999	05/14/99	-101266	06/04/99	-101813		-546.88	05/24/99	187.50	06/01/99	-734.38
1998	05/14/98	-100641	06/05/98	-100125		515.63	06/05/98	515.63		
1997	05/14/97	-102922	06/06/97	-102625		296.88	06/03/97	1078.13	05/27/97	-406.25
1996	05/14/96	-103453	06/06/96	-103375		78.13	05/22/96	156.25	05/29/96	-171.88
1995	05/15/95	-102750	06/06/95	-102078		671.88	06/06/95	671.88		
1994	05/16/94	-105953	06/06/94	-104922		1031.25	06/06/94	1031.25	05/23/94	-93.75
1993	05/14/93	-106656	06/04/93	-105406		1250.00	06/04/93	1250.00	05/18/93	-312.50
1992	05/14/92	-109547	06/05/92	-109094		453.13	05/21/92	687.50		

Percentage Correct	93									
Average Profit on Winning Trades						706.73	Winners			13
Average Loss on Trades						-546.88	Losers			1
Average Net Profit Per Trade						617.19	Total trades			14

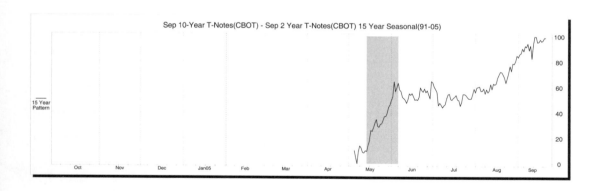

Sep 10-Year T-Notes(CBOT) - Sep 2 Year T-Notes(CBOT) 15 Year Seasonal(91-05)

Figure 10-29

Moore Research Center, Inc. — *Buy Sep 30-Year T-Bonds(CBOT) / Sell Sep 5-Year T-Notes(CBOT)*

Enter on approximately 05/24 - Exit on approximately 06/03

CONT YEAR	ENTRY DATE	ENTRY PRICE	EXIT DATE	EXIT PRICE	PROFIT	PROFIT AMOUNT	BEST EQUITY DATE	BEST EQUITY AMOUNT	WORST EQUITY DATE	WORST EQUITY AMOUNT
2005	05/24/05	8~030	06/03/05	8~290	0~260	812.50	06/02/05	1359.38	05/25/05	-359.38
2004	05/24/04	-3~190	06/03/04	-3~165	0~025	78.13	05/27/04	875.00	06/02/04	-15.63
2003	05/27/03	3~090	06/03/03	3~155	0~065	203.13	05/29/03	312.50	06/02/03	-375.00
2002	05/24/02	-4~310	06/03/02	-4~230	0~080	250.00	05/30/02	343.75	05/28/02	-62.50
2001	05/24/01	-3~140	06/01/01	-2~220	0~240	750.00	06/01/01	750.00	05/25/01	-843.75
2000	05/24/00	-3~095	06/02/00	-1~200	1~215	1671.88	06/01/00	1765.63		
1999	05/24/99	-3~005	06/03/99	-3~195	-0~190	-593.75	05/25/99	78.13	06/03/99	-593.75
1998	05/26/98	-0~010	06/03/98	0~070	0~080	250.00	06/01/98	312.50		
1997	05/27/97	-6~265	06/03/97	-5~185	1~080	1250.00	06/03/97	1250.00		
1996	05/24/96	-6~220	06/03/96	-7~140	-0~240	-750.00			06/03/96	-750.00
1995	05/24/95	-5~200	06/02/95	-4~210	0~310	968.75	06/02/95	968.75	05/26/95	-93.75
1994	05/24/94	-10~115	06/03/94	-9~220	0~215	671.88	06/03/94	671.88	05/31/94	-296.88
1993	05/24/93	-10~205	06/03/93	-9~235	0~290	906.25	06/01/93	1000.00	05/25/93	-93.75
1992	05/26/92	-13~220	06/03/92	-13~270	-0~050	-156.25	05/29/92	203.13	06/03/92	-156.25
1991	05/24/91	-14~045	06/03/91	-13~300	0~065	203.13	05/30/91	546.88		
1990	05/24/90	-13~075	06/01/90	-12~150	0~245	765.63	06/01/90	765.63	05/25/90	-359.38
1989	05/24/89	-12~295	06/02/89	-12~200	0~095	296.88	06/02/89	296.88	05/25/89	-15.63
1988	05/24/88	-18~175	06/03/88	-17~035	1~140	1437.50	06/03/88	1437.50		

Percentage Correct	80			Protective Stop	(565)
Average Profit on Winning Trades		0~214	667.97	Winners	12
Average Loss on Trades		-0~160	-500.00	Losers	3
Average Net Profit Per Trade		0~139	434.38	Total trades	15
Percentage Correct	83				
Average Profit on Winning Trades		0~224	701.04	Winners	15
Average Loss on Trades		-0~160	-500.00	Losers	3
Average Net Profit Per Trade		0~160	500.87	Total trades	18

HYPOTHETICAL PERFORMANCE RESULTS HAVE MANY INHERENT LIMITATIONS, SOME OF WHICH ARE DESCRIBED BELOW. NO REPRESENTATION IS BEING MADE THAT ANY ACCOUNT WILL OR IS LIKELY TO ACHIEVE PROFITS OR LOSSES SIMILAR TO THOSE SHOWN. IN FACT, THERE ARE FREQUENTLY SHARP DIFFERENCES BETWEEN HYPOTHETICAL PERFORMANCE RESULTS AND THE ACTUAL RESULTS SUBSEQUENTLY ACHIEVED BY ANY PARTICULAR TRADING PROGRAM. ONE OF THE LIMITATIONS OF HYPOTHETICAL PERFORMANCE RESULTS IS THAT THEY ARE GENERALLY PREPARED WITH THE BENEFIT OF HINDSIGHT. IN ADDITION, HYPOTHETICAL TRADING DOES NOT INVOLVE FINANCIAL RISK, AND NO HYPOTHETICAL TRADING RECORD CAN COMPLETELY ACCOUNT FOR THE IMPACT OF FINANCIAL RISK IN ACTUAL TRADING. FOR EXAMPLE, THE ABILITY TO WITHSTAND LOSSES OR ADHERE TO A PARTICULAR TRADING PROGRAM IN SPITE OF TRADING LOSSES ARE MATERIAL POINTS WHICH CAN ALSO ADVERSELY AFFECT ACTUAL TRADING RESULTS. THERE ARE NUMEROUS OTHER FACTORS RELATED TO THE MARKETS IN GENERAL OR TO THE IMPLEMENTATION OF ANY SPECIFIC TRADING PROGRAM WHICH CANNOT BE FULLY ACCOUNTED FOR IN THE PREPARATION OF HYPOTHETICAL PERFORMANCE RESULTS AND ALL OF WHICH CAN ADVERSELY AFFECT ACTUAL TRADING RESULTS. RESULTS NOT ADJUSTED FOR COMMISSION AND SLIPPAGE.

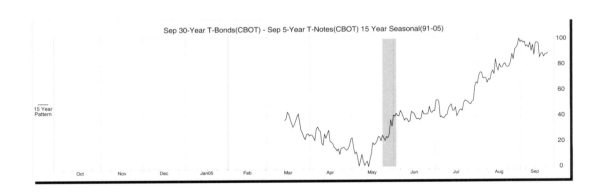

Sep 30-Year T-Bonds(CBOT) - Sep 5-Year T-Notes(CBOT) 15 Year Seasonal(91-05)

Figure 10-30

Buy Dec 30-Year T-Bonds(CBOT) / Sell Dec 5-Year T-Notes(CBOT)

Moore Research Center, Inc.

Enter on approximately 08/13 - Exit on approximately 11/16

CONT YEAR	ENTRY DATE	ENTRY PRICE	EXIT DATE	EXIT PRICE	PROFIT	PROFIT AMOUNT	BEST EQUITY DATE	BEST EQUITY AMOUNT	WORST EQUITY DATE	WORST EQUITY AMOUNT
2004	08/13/04	-0~005	11/16/04	2~060	2~065	2203.13	10/25/04	2781.25	08/24/04	-656.25
2003	08/13/03	-6~290	11/14/03	-2~040	4~250	4781.25	09/30/03	5593.75		
2002	08/13/02	-2~090	11/15/02	-1~180	0~230	718.75	09/24/02	3015.63	10/23/02	-1562.50
2001	08/13/01	-2~005	11/16/01	-1~290	0~035	109.38	11/07/01	3203.13	09/20/01	-3250.00
2000	08/14/00	0~090	11/16/00	-0~080	-0~170	-531.25	08/24/00	312.50	10/03/00	-2828.13
1999	08/13/99	-4~195	11/16/99	-4~175	0~020	62.50	08/26/99	703.13	10/19/99	-2031.25
1998	08/13/98	0~280	11/16/98	1~115	0~155	484.38	10/05/98	3984.38	11/06/98	-671.88
1997	08/13/97	-4~240	11/14/97	-1~115	3~125	3390.63	11/14/97	3390.63	08/22/97	-281.25
1996	08/13/96	-6~020	11/15/96	-4~020	2~000	2000.00	11/14/96	2218.75	09/10/96	-1765.63
1995	08/14/95	-7~015	11/16/95	-2~190	4~145	4453.13	11/08/95	4781.25		
1994	08/15/94	-10~205	11/16/94	-12~105	-1~220	-1687.50	08/16/94	718.75	11/11/94	-2390.63
1993	08/13/93	-6~275	11/16/93	-6~060	0~215	671.88	10/15/93	3156.25	08/19/93	-312.50
1992	08/13/92	-12~290	11/16/92	-12~235	0~055	171.88	11/16/92	171.88	10/13/92	-2015.63
1991	08/13/91	-13~200	11/15/91	-13~110	0~090	281.25	09/27/91	1218.75	10/22/91	-765.63
1990	08/13/90	-15~285	11/16/90	-14~045	1~240	1750.00	11/16/90	1750.00	09/24/90	-1406.25
1989	08/14/89	-11~175	11/16/89	-10~125	1~050	1156.25	11/02/89	1562.50	09/25/89	-406.25
1988	08/15/88	-18~100	11/16/88	-15~295	2~125	2390.63	10/31/88	3500.00		

Percentage Correct	87						Protective Stop		(1634)
Average Profit on Winning Trades					1~199	1621.39	Winners		13
Average Loss on Trades					-1~035	-1109.38	Losers		2
Average Net Profit Per Trade					1~082	1257.29	Total trades		15
Percentage Correct	88								
Average Profit on Winning Trades					1~205	1641.67	Winners		15
Average Loss on Trades					-1~035	-1109.38	Losers		2
Average Net Profit Per Trade					1~102	1318.01	Total trades		17

HYPOTHETICAL PERFORMANCE RESULTS HAVE MANY INHERENT LIMITATIONS, SOME OF WHICH ARE DESCRIBED BELOW. NO REPRESENTATION IS BEING MADE THAT ANY ACCOUNT WILL OR IS LIKELY TO ACHIEVE PROFITS OR LOSSES SIMILAR TO THOSE SHOWN. IN FACT, THERE ARE FREQUENTLY SHARP DIFFERENCES BETWEEN HYPOTHETICAL PERFORMANCE RESULTS AND THE ACTUAL RESULTS SUBSEQUENTLY ACHIEVED BY ANY PARTICULAR TRADING PROGRAM. ONE OF THE LIMITATIONS OF HYPOTHETICAL PERFORMANCE RESULTS IS THAT THEY ARE GENERALLY PREPARED WITH THE BENEFIT OF HINDSIGHT. IN ADDITION, HYPOTHETICAL TRADING DOES NOT INVOLVE FINANCIAL RISK, AND NO HYPOTHETICAL TRADING RECORD CAN COMPLETELY ACCOUNT FOR THE IMPACT OF FINANCIAL RISK IN ACTUAL TRADING. FOR EXAMPLE, THE ABILITY TO WITHSTAND LOSSES OR ADHERE TO A PARTICULAR TRADING PROGRAM IN SPITE OF TRADING LOSSES ARE MATERIAL POINTS WHICH CAN ALSO ADVERSELY AFFECT ACTUAL TRADING RESULTS. THERE ARE NUMEROUS OTHER FACTORS RELATED TO THE MARKETS IN GENERAL OR TO THE IMPLEMENTATION OF ANY SPECIFIC TRADING PROGRAM WHICH CANNOT BE FULLY ACCOUNTED FOR IN THE PREPARATION OF HYPOTHETICAL PERFORMANCE RESULTS AND ALL OF WHICH CAN ADVERSELY AFFECT ACTUAL TRADING RESULTS. RESULTS NOT ADJUSTED FOR COMMISSION AND SLIPPAGE.

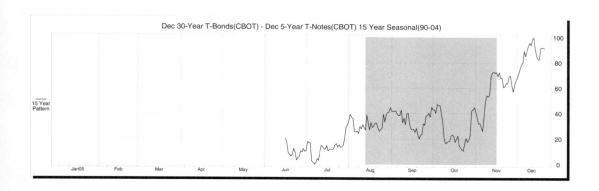

Dec 30-Year T-Bonds(CBOT) - Dec 5-Year T-Notes(CBOT) 15 Year Seasonal(90-04)

Figure 10-31

Moore Research Center, Inc.

Buy Dec 10-Year T-Notes(CBOT) / Sell Dec 5-Year T-Notes(CBOT)

Enter on approximately 08/16 - Exit on approximately 11/13

CONT YEAR	ENTRY DATE	ENTRY PRICE	EXIT DATE	EXIT PRICE	PROFIT	PROFIT AMOUNT	BEST EQUITY DATE	BEST EQUITY AMOUNT	WORST EQUITY DATE	WORST EQUITY AMOUNT
2004	08/16/04	1~100	11/12/04	2~000	0~220	687.50	09/22/04	1015.63	08/23/04	-62.50
2003	08/18/03	-0~285	11/13/03	0~230	1~195	1609.38	09/30/03	2046.88		
2002	08/16/02	0~055	11/13/02	1~180	1~125	1390.63	10/09/02	1640.63		
2001	08/16/01	0~110	11/13/01	1~065	0~275	859.38	11/01/01	1390.63	09/20/01	-781.25
2000	08/16/00	-0~010	11/13/00	0~040	0~050	156.25	10/23/00	500.00	09/18/00	-718.75
1999	08/16/99	-1~280	11/12/99	-1~100	0~180	562.50	11/12/99	562.50	10/26/99	-390.63
1998	08/17/98	0~130	11/13/98	1~160	1~030	1093.75	10/05/98	2484.38		
1997	08/18/97	-1~020	11/13/97	-0~070	0~270	843.75	11/13/97	843.75	08/25/97	-312.50
1996	08/16/96	-1~250	11/13/96	-0~220	1~030	1093.75	11/12/96	1093.75	09/05/96	-296.88
1995	08/16/95	-1~160	11/13/95	-0~120	1~040	1125.00	10/13/95	1328.13	08/18/95	-109.38
1994	08/16/94	-2~295	11/11/94	-4~100	-1~125	-1390.63	08/17/94	78.13	11/07/94	-1390.63
1993	08/16/93	-1~195	11/12/93	-1~185	0~010	31.25	10/15/93	968.75	11/05/93	-218.75
1992	08/17/92	-3~250	11/13/92	-3~230	0~020	62.50	09/10/92	171.88	11/06/92	-781.25
1991	08/16/91	-4~225	11/13/91	-4~145	0~080	250.00	09/27/91	765.63	10/23/91	-312.50
1990	08/16/90	-6~000	11/13/90	-5~055	0~265	828.13	11/13/90	828.13	09/24/90	-546.88
1989	08/16/89	-3~215	11/13/89	-3~115	0~100	312.50	11/07/89	453.13	09/25/89	-500.00
1988	08/16/88	-6~280	11/11/88	-5~250	1~030	1093.75	10/31/88	1656.25	08/17/88	-156.25

Percentage Correct	93			Protective Stop	(798)
Average Profit on Winning Trades		0~242	756.70	Winners	14
Average Loss on Trades		-1~125	-1390.63	Losers	1
Average Net Profit Per Trade		0~196	613.54	Total trades	15
Percentage Correct	94				
Average Profit on Winning Trades		0~240	750.00	Winners	16
Average Loss on Trades		-1~125	-1390.63	Losers	1
Average Net Profit Per Trade		0~200	624.08	Total trades	17

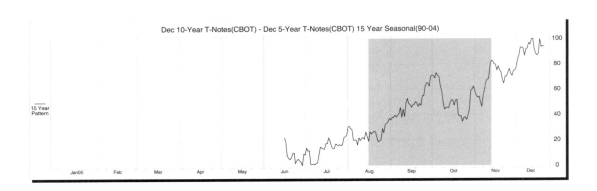

Dec 10-Year T-Notes(CBOT) - Dec 5-Year T-Notes(CBOT) 15 Year Seasonal(90-04)

15 Year Pattern

Chapter 10: Interest Rates

Figure 10-32

Buy Dec 10-Year T-Notes(CBOT) / Sell Dec 2-Year T-Notes(CBOT)

Enter on approximately 09/16 - Exit on approximately 10/01

CONT YEAR	ENTRY DATE	ENTRY PRICE	EXIT DATE	EXIT PRICE		PROFIT AMOUNT	BEST EQUITY DATE	BEST EQUITY AMOUNT	WORST EQUITY DATE	WORST EQUITY AMOUNT
2004	09/16/04	-98766	10/01/04	-99031		-265.63	09/27/04	859.38	10/01/04	-265.63
2003	09/16/03	-102922	10/01/03	-101063		1859.38	09/30/03	1953.13		
2002	09/16/02	-99484	10/01/02	-99406		78.13	09/24/02	921.88		
2001	09/17/01	-101594	10/01/01	-101328		265.63	10/01/01	265.63	09/20/01	-906.25
2000	09/18/00	-100438	09/29/00	-99781		656.25	09/29/00	656.25		
1999	09/16/99	-102250	10/01/99	-102484		-234.38	09/24/99	453.13	10/01/99	-234.38
1998	09/16/98	-98250	10/01/98	-96813		1437.50	10/01/98	1437.50		
1997	09/16/97	-101766	10/01/97	-101609		156.25	09/22/97	234.38	09/25/97	-15.63
1996	09/16/96	-103344	10/01/96	-103141		203.13	09/26/96	218.75	09/19/96	-187.50
1995	09/18/95	-102172	09/29/95	-101828		343.75	09/29/95	343.75	09/22/95	-125.00
1994	09/16/94	-106375	09/30/94	-106266		109.38	09/19/94	156.25	09/27/94	-140.63
1993	09/16/93	-103516	10/01/93	-103219		296.88	10/01/93	296.88	09/21/93	-375.00
1992	09/16/92	-108688	10/01/92	-108344		343.75	10/01/92	343.75	09/23/92	-796.88
1991	09/16/91	-107641	10/01/91	-107375		265.63	10/01/91	265.63	09/26/91	-140.63
1990	09/17/90	-109047	10/01/90	-108344		703.13	10/01/90	703.13	09/24/90	-234.38

Percentage Correct	87			
Average Profit on Winning Trades		516.83	Winners	13
Average Loss on Trades		-250.00	Losers	2
Average Net Profit Per Trade		414.58	Total trades	15

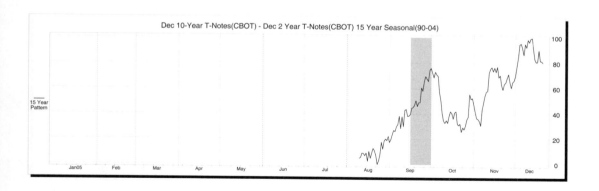

Dec 10-Year T-Notes(CBOT) - Dec 2 Year T-Notes(CBOT) 15 Year Seasonal(90-04)

15 Year Pattern

Figure 10-33

Moore Research Center, Inc. — *Buy Dec 30-Year T-Bonds(CBOT) / Sell Dec 10-Year T-Notes(CBOT)*

Enter on approximately 10/18 - Exit on approximately 11/14

CONT YEAR	ENTRY DATE	ENTRY PRICE	EXIT DATE	EXIT PRICE	PROFIT	PROFIT AMOUNT	BEST EQUITY DATE	BEST EQUITY AMOUNT	WORST EQUITY DATE	WORST EQUITY AMOUNT
2004	10/18/04	-0~045	11/12/04	-0~005	0~040	125.00	10/21/04	593.75	11/10/04	-343.75
2003	10/20/03	-4~075	11/14/03	-3~000	1~075	1234.38	11/14/03	1234.38		
2002	10/18/02	-4~000	11/14/02	-2~235	1~085	1265.63	11/08/02	1921.88	10/23/02	-500.00
2001	10/18/01	-2~175	11/14/01	-1~015	1~160	1500.00	11/07/01	2031.25	10/19/01	-109.38
2000	10/18/00	-1~070	11/14/00	-1~020	0~050	156.25	10/30/00	625.00	11/10/00	-250.00
1999	10/18/99	-4~110	11/12/99	-3~065	1~045	1140.63	11/12/99	1140.63	10/19/99	-140.63
1998	10/19/98	-0~130	11/13/98	0~050	0~180	562.50	11/13/98	562.50	10/22/98	-750.00
1997	10/20/97	-2~150	11/14/97	-1~060	1~090	1281.25	11/14/97	1281.25		
1996	10/18/96	-4~180	11/14/96	-3~070	1~110	1343.75	11/14/96	1343.75	10/24/96	-250.00
1995	10/18/95	-2~090	11/14/95	-2~130	-0~040	-125.00	11/08/95	250.00	10/26/95	-437.50
1994	10/18/94	-8~180	11/14/94	-8~130	0~050	156.25	10/31/94	406.25	11/11/94	-156.25
1993	10/18/93	-3~110	11/12/93	-4~170	-1~060	-1187.50	10/19/93	93.75	11/04/93	-1875.00
1992	10/19/92	-10~080	11/13/92	-9~160	0~240	750.00	11/13/92	750.00		
1991	10/18/91	-9~030	11/14/91	-8~260	0~090	281.25	11/12/91	468.75	10/22/91	-343.75
1990	10/18/90	-9~310	11/14/90	-9~070	0~240	750.00	11/14/90	750.00		
1989	10/18/89	-7~090	11/14/89	-6~310	0~100	312.50	11/01/89	656.25		
1988	10/18/88	-10~050	11/14/88	-10~000	0~050	156.25	11/03/88	593.75	10/26/88	-281.25
1987	10/19/87	-12~130	11/13/87	-10~020	2~110	2343.75	11/05/87	2656.25	10/20/87	-156.25
1986	10/20/86	-12~000	11/14/86	-10~140	1~180	1562.50	11/04/86	1750.00		
1985	10/18/85	-13~180	11/14/85	-13~030	0~150	468.75	11/12/85	625.00	10/25/85	-31.25

Percentage Correct	87						Protective Stop		(800)
Average Profit on Winning Trades				0~260	811.30		Winners		13
Average Loss on Trades				-0~210	-656.25		Losers		2
Average Net Profit Per Trade				0~197	615.63		Total trades		15
Percentage Correct	90								
Average Profit on Winning Trades				0~274	855.03		Winners		18
Average Loss on Trades				-0~210	-656.25		Losers		2
Average Net Profit Per Trade				0~225	703.91		Total trades		20

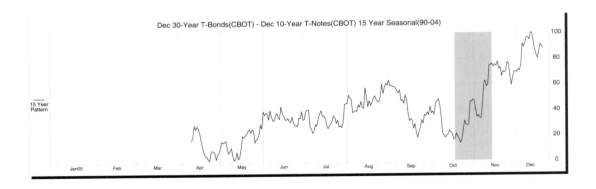

Dec 30-Year T-Bonds(CBOT) - Dec 10-Year T-Notes(CBOT) 15 Year Seasonal(90-04)

Figure 10-34

Buy Dec 30-Year T-Bonds(CBOT) / Sell Dec 5-Year T-Notes(CBOT)

Enter on approximately 10/23 - Exit on approximately 10/31

CONT YEAR	ENTRY DATE	ENTRY PRICE	EXIT DATE	EXIT PRICE	PROFIT	PROFIT AMOUNT	BEST EQUITY DATE	BEST EQUITY AMOUNT	WORST EQUITY DATE	WORST EQUITY AMOUNT
2004	10/25/04	2~245	10/29/04	2~150	-0~095	-296.88			10/27/04	-765.63
2003	10/23/03	-3~235	10/31/03	-3~030	0~205	640.63	10/24/03	734.38		
2002	10/23/02	-3~270	10/31/02	-3~025	0~245	765.63	10/29/02	937.50		
2001	10/23/01	-2~005	10/31/01	0~185	2~190	2593.75	10/31/01	2593.75		
2000	10/23/00	-0~055	10/31/00	-0~270	-0~215	-671.88			10/31/00	-671.88
1999	10/25/99	-6~160	10/29/99	-5~075	1~085	1265.63	10/29/99	1265.63	10/26/99	-93.75
1998	10/23/98	0~070	10/30/98	1~095	1~025	1078.13	10/27/98	1312.50		
1997	10/23/97	-2~205	10/31/97	-1~195	1~010	1031.25	10/31/97	1031.25		
1996	10/23/96	-6~020	10/31/96	-5~020	1~000	1000.00	10/31/96	1000.00	10/24/96	-218.75
1995	10/23/95	-2~250	10/31/95	-2~225	0~025	78.13	10/24/95	390.63	10/26/95	-468.75
1994	10/24/94	-12~215	10/31/94	-12~020	0~195	609.38	10/31/94	609.38	10/26/94	-78.13
1993	10/25/93	-5~160	10/29/93	-5~105	0~055	171.88	10/28/93	265.63	10/27/93	-93.75
1992	10/23/92	-14~150	10/30/92	-14~050	0~100	312.50	10/30/92	312.50	10/28/92	-62.50
1991	10/23/91	-14~085	10/31/91	-13~160	0~245	765.63	10/30/91	968.75		
1990	10/23/90	-15~190	10/31/90	-15~205	-0~015	-46.88	10/25/90	156.25	10/29/90	-343.75
1989	10/23/89	-10~130	10/31/89	-10~080	0~050	156.25	10/31/89	156.25	10/27/89	-265.63
1988	10/24/88	-15~305	10/31/88	-14~260	1~045	1140.63	10/31/88	1140.63	10/25/88	-78.13

Percentage Correct	80						Protective Stop	(806)		
Average Profit on Winning Trades					0~275	859.38	Winners	12		
Average Loss on Trades					-0~108	-338.54	Losers	3		
Average Net Profit Per Trade					0~198	619.79	Total trades	15		
Percentage Correct	82									
Average Profit on Winning Trades					0~265	829.24	Winners	14		
Average Loss on Trades					-0~108	-338.54	Losers	3		
Average Net Profit Per Trade					0~199	623.16	Total trades	17		

HYPOTHETICAL PERFORMANCE RESULTS HAVE MANY INHERENT LIMITATIONS, SOME OF WHICH ARE DESCRIBED BELOW. NO REPRESENTATION IS BEING MADE THAT ANY ACCOUNT WILL OR IS LIKELY TO ACHIEVE PROFITS OR LOSSES SIMILAR TO THOSE SHOWN. IN FACT, THERE ARE FREQUENTLY SHARP DIFFERENCES BETWEEN HYPOTHETICAL PERFORMANCE RESULTS AND THE ACTUAL RESULTS SUBSEQUENTLY ACHIEVED BY ANY PARTICULAR TRADING PROGRAM. ONE OF THE LIMITATIONS OF HYPOTHETICAL PERFORMANCE RESULTS IS THAT THEY ARE GENERALLY PREPARED WITH THE BENEFIT OF HINDSIGHT. IN ADDITION, HYPOTHETICAL TRADING DOES NOT INVOLVE FINANCIAL RISK, AND NO HYPOTHETICAL TRADING RECORD CAN COMPLETELY ACCOUNT FOR THE IMPACT OF FINANCIAL RISK IN ACTUAL TRADING. FOR EXAMPLE, THE ABILITY TO WITHSTAND LOSSES OR ADHERE TO A PARTICULAR TRADING PROGRAM IN SPITE OF TRADING LOSSES ARE MATERIAL POINTS WHICH CAN ALSO ADVERSELY AFFECT ACTUAL TRADING RESULTS. THERE ARE NUMEROUS OTHER FACTORS RELATED TO THE MARKETS IN GENERAL OR TO THE IMPLEMENTATION OF ANY SPECIFIC TRADING PROGRAM WHICH CANNOT BE FULLY ACCOUNTED FOR IN THE PREPARATION OF HYPOTHETICAL PERFORMANCE RESULTS AND ALL OF WHICH CAN ADVERSELY AFFECT ACTUAL TRADING RESULTS. RESULTS NOT ADJUSTED FOR COMMISSION AND SLIPPAGE.

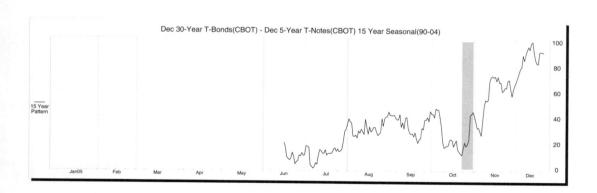

Dec 30-Year T-Bonds(CBOT) - Dec 5-Year T-Notes(CBOT) 15 Year Seasonal(90-04)

Figure 10-35

Moore Research Center, Inc. — *Buy Dec 30-Year T-Bonds(CBOT) / Sell Dec 2-Year T-Notes(CBOT)*

Enter on approximately 11/02 - Exit on approximately 11/14

CONT YEAR	ENTRY DATE	ENTRY PRICE	EXIT DATE	EXIT PRICE		PROFIT AMOUNT	BEST EQUITY DATE	BEST EQUITY AMOUNT	WORST EQUITY DATE	WORST EQUITY AMOUNT
2004	11/02/04	-98391	11/12/04	-98375		15.63	11/04/04	421.88	11/10/04	-750.00
2003	11/03/03	-106047	11/14/03	-104375		1671.88	11/14/03	1671.88	11/10/03	-625.00
2002	11/04/02	-105063	11/14/02	-103125		1937.50	11/08/02	3500.00	11/05/02	-93.75
2001	11/02/01	-102703	11/14/01	-102688		15.63	11/07/01	1625.00		
2000	11/02/00	-100422	11/14/00	-100281		140.63	11/14/00	140.63	11/06/00	-750.00
1999	11/02/99	-105688	11/12/99	-104797		890.63	11/12/99	890.63	11/03/99	-62.50
1998	11/02/98	-99016	11/13/98	-98141		875.00	11/13/98	875.00	11/06/98	-531.25
1997	11/03/97	-102797	11/14/97	-102188		609.38	11/14/97	609.38	11/04/97	-234.38
1996	11/04/96	-106563	11/14/96	-105156		1406.25	11/14/96	1406.25		
1995	11/02/95	-103453	11/14/95	-103953		-500.00	11/08/95	109.38	11/10/95	-625.00
1994	11/02/94	-115453	11/14/94	-115188		265.63	11/14/94	265.63	11/11/94	-421.88
1993	11/02/93	-108875	11/12/93	-108781		93.75	11/12/93	93.75	11/05/93	-859.38
1992	11/02/92	-118953	11/13/92	-118188		765.63	11/13/92	765.63	11/06/92	-828.13
1991	11/04/91	-118031	11/14/91	-117156		875.00	11/12/91	1296.88	11/06/91	-421.88
1990	11/02/90	-117984	11/14/90	-116828		1156.25	11/14/90	1156.25	11/08/90	-328.13

Percentage Correct	93			
Average Profit on Winning Trades		765.63	Winners	14
Average Loss on Trades		-500.00	Losers	1
Average Net Profit Per Trade		681.25	Total trades	15

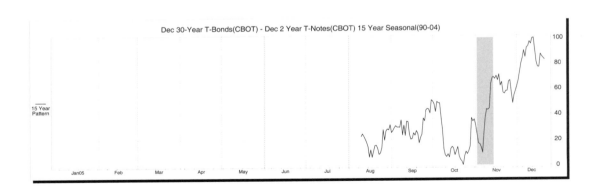

Dec 30-Year T-Bonds(CBOT) - Dec 2 Year T-Notes(CBOT) 15 Year Seasonal(90-04)

Figure 10-36

Moore Research Center, Inc. — Buy Mar 10-Year T-Notes(CBOT) / Sell Mar 5-Year T-Notes(CBOT)

Enter on approximately 11/06 - Exit on approximately 12/23

CONT YEAR	ENTRY DATE	ENTRY PRICE	EXIT DATE	EXIT PRICE	PROFIT	PROFIT AMOUNT	BEST EQUITY DATE	BEST EQUITY AMOUNT	WORST EQUITY DATE	WORST EQUITY AMOUNT
2005	11/08/04	2~030	12/23/04	2~100	0~070	218.75	12/15/04	718.75	12/02/04	-312.50
2004	11/06/03	0~030	12/23/03	0~235	0~205	640.63	12/18/03	1015.63	11/07/03	-62.50
2003	11/06/02	0~255	12/23/02	1~120	0~185	578.13	11/13/02	875.00	11/27/02	-187.50
2002	11/06/01	1~160	12/21/01	-0~205	-2~045	-2140.63	11/07/01	187.50	12/17/01	-2734.38
2001	11/06/00	-0~075	12/22/00	1~210	1~285	1890.63	12/22/00	1890.63		
2000	11/08/99	-1~065	12/23/99	-2~030	-0~285	-890.63	11/12/99	203.13	12/23/99	-890.63
1999	11/06/98	0~255	12/23/98	1~205	0~270	843.75	12/10/98	1265.63		
1998	11/06/97	-0~140	12/23/97	0~010	0~150	468.75	12/22/97	484.38	11/07/97	-31.25
1997	11/06/96	-0~250	12/23/96	-0~240	0~010	31.25	11/29/96	500.00	12/18/96	-250.00
1996	11/06/95	-0~085	12/22/95	0~080	0~165	515.63	12/04/95	687.50	11/15/95	-187.50
1995	11/07/94	-4~125	12/23/94	-3~025	1~100	1312.50	12/06/94	1390.63		
1994	11/08/93	-1~230	12/23/93	-1~170	0~060	187.50	12/09/93	328.13	11/22/93	-281.25
1993	11/06/92	-4~230	12/23/92	-3~040	1~190	1593.75	12/22/92	1671.88		
1992	11/06/91	-4~275	12/23/91	-3~240	1~035	1109.38	12/23/91	1109.38	11/25/91	-171.88
1991	11/06/90	-5~210	12/21/90	-4~270	0~260	812.50	12/12/90	1359.38	11/08/90	-203.13
1990	11/06/89	-3~155	12/22/89	-3~120	0~035	109.38	11/07/89	468.75	11/20/89	-93.75
1989	11/07/88	-5~235	12/23/88	-5~030	0~205	640.63	12/23/88	640.63	11/11/88	-140.63

Percentage Correct	87						Protective Stop			(622)
Average Profit on Winning Trades					0~251	784.86	Winners			13
Average Loss on Trades					-1~165	-1515.63	Losers			2
Average Net Profit Per Trade					0~153	478.13	Total trades			15
Percentage Correct	88									
Average Profit on Winning Trades					0~234	730.21	Winners			15
Average Loss on Trades					-1~165	-1515.63	Losers			2
Average Net Profit Per Trade					0~149	465.99	Total trades			17

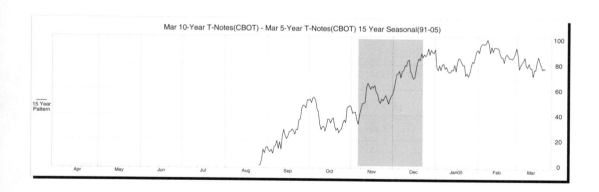

Mar 10-Year T-Notes(CBOT) - Mar 5-Year T-Notes(CBOT) 15 Year Seasonal(91-05)

Figure 10-37

Moore Research Center, Inc. *Buy Mar 30-Year T-Bonds(CBOT) / Sell Mar 5-Year T-Notes(CBOT)*

Enter on approximately 11/06 - Exit on approximately 12/24

CONT YEAR	ENTRY DATE	ENTRY PRICE	EXIT DATE	EXIT PRICE	PROFIT	PROFIT AMOUNT	BEST EQUITY DATE	BEST EQUITY AMOUNT	WORST EQUITY DATE	WORST EQUITY AMOUNT
2005	11/08/04	1~145	12/23/04	2~195	1~050	1156.25	12/15/04	2453.13	12/02/04	-531.25
2004	11/06/03	-3~280	12/24/03	-1~140	2~140	2437.50	12/18/03	2953.13	11/10/03	-125.00
2003	11/06/02	-3~025	12/24/02	-0~315	2~030	2093.75	11/08/02	2546.88		
2002	11/06/01	0~155	12/24/01	-4~125	-4~280	-4875.00	11/07/01	765.63	12/17/01	-6093.75
2001	11/06/00	-1~200	12/22/00	1~215	3~095	3296.88	12/14/00	3312.50		
2000	11/08/99	-4~290	12/23/99	-7~085	-2~115	-2359.38	11/15/99	625.00	12/21/99	-2375.00
1999	11/06/98	-0~125	12/24/98	1~040	1~165	1515.63	12/09/98	3390.63		
1998	11/06/97	-1~290	12/24/97	0~030	2~000	2000.00	12/22/97	2046.88		
1997	11/06/96	-4~260	12/24/96	-4~150	0~110	343.75	12/03/96	1343.75	12/18/96	-406.25
1996	11/06/95	-2~245	12/22/95	-1~190	1~055	1171.88	12/11/95	1578.13	11/10/95	-437.50
1995	11/07/94	-12~275	12/23/94	-9~105	3~170	3531.25	12/23/94	3531.25	11/11/94	-125.00
1994	11/08/93	-7~000	12/23/93	-6~100	0~220	687.50	12/09/93	1015.63	11/22/93	-750.00
1993	11/06/92	-14~190	12/24/92	-11~120	3~070	3218.75	12/23/92	3281.25		
1992	11/06/91	-14~085	12/24/91	-12~180	1~225	1703.13	12/23/91	1703.13	11/22/91	-375.00
1991	11/06/90	-15~070	12/24/90	-13~235	1~155	1484.38	12/12/90	2671.88	11/08/90	-578.13
1990	11/06/89	-10~125	12/22/89	-10~100	0~025	78.13	11/07/89	625.00	11/17/89	-515.63
1989	11/07/88	-15~295	12/23/88	-13~220	2~075	2234.38	12/23/88	2234.38	11/17/88	-421.88

Percentage Correct	87							Protective Stop		(1509)
Average Profit on Winning Trades					1~287	1895.43		Winners		13
Average Loss on Trades					-3~198	-3617.19		Losers		2
Average Net Profit Per Trade					1~051	1160.42		Total trades		15
Percentage Correct	88									
Average Profit on Winning Trades					1~255	1796.88		Winners		15
Average Loss on Trades					-3~198	-3617.19		Losers		2
Average Net Profit Per Trade					1~051	1159.93		Total trades		17

HYPOTHETICAL PERFORMANCE RESULTS HAVE MANY INHERENT LIMITATIONS, SOME OF WHICH ARE DESCRIBED BELOW. NO REPRESENTATION IS BEING MADE THAT ANY ACCOUNT WILL OR IS LIKELY TO ACHIEVE PROFITS OR LOSSES SIMILAR TO THOSE SHOWN. IN FACT, THERE ARE FREQUENTLY SHARP DIFFERENCES BETWEEN HYPOTHETICAL PERFORMANCE RESULTS AND THE ACTUAL RESULTS SUBSEQUENTLY ACHIEVED BY ANY PARTICULAR TRADING PROGRAM. ONE OF THE LIMITATIONS OF HYPOTHETICAL PERFORMANCE RESULTS IS THAT THEY ARE GENERALLY PREPARED WITH THE BENEFIT OF HINDSIGHT. IN ADDITION, HYPOTHETICAL TRADING DOES NOT INVOLVE FINANCIAL RISK, AND NO HYPOTHETICAL TRADING RECORD CAN COMPLETELY ACCOUNT FOR THE IMPACT OF FINANCIAL RISK IN ACTUAL TRADING. FOR EXAMPLE, THE ABILITY TO WITHSTAND LOSSES OR ADHERE TO A PARTICULAR TRADING PROGRAM IN SPITE OF TRADING LOSSES ARE MATERIAL POINTS WHICH CAN ALSO ADVERSELY AFFECT ACTUAL TRADING RESULTS. THERE ARE NUMEROUS OTHER FACTORS RELATED TO THE MARKETS IN GENERAL OR TO THE IMPLEMENTATION OF ANY SPECIFIC TRADING PROGRAM WHICH CANNOT BE FULLY ACCOUNTED FOR IN THE PREPARATION OF HYPOTHETICAL PERFORMANCE RESULTS AND ALL OF WHICH CAN ADVERSELY AFFECT ACTUAL TRADING RESULTS. RESULTS NOT ADJUSTED FOR COMMISSION AND SLIPPAGE.

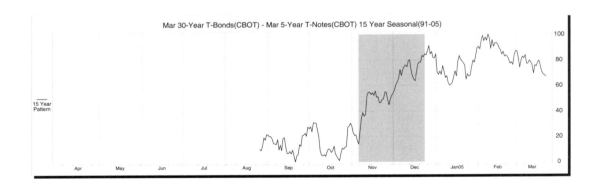

Mar 30-Year T-Bonds(CBOT) - Mar 5-Year T-Notes(CBOT) 15 Year Seasonal(91-05)

15 Year Pattern

Figure 10-38

Moore Research Center, Inc. — Buy Mar 30-Year T-Bonds(CBOT) / Sell Mar 10-Year T-Notes(CBOT)

Enter on approximately 11/06 - Exit on approximately 12/27

CONT YEAR	ENTRY DATE	ENTRY PRICE	EXIT DATE	EXIT PRICE	PROFIT	PROFIT AMOUNT	BEST EQUITY DATE	BEST EQUITY AMOUNT	WORST EQUITY DATE	WORST EQUITY AMOUNT
2005	11/08/04	-0~205	12/27/04	-0~065	0~140	437.50	12/15/04	1734.38	12/02/04	-218.75
2004	11/06/03	-3~310	12/26/03	-2~030	1~280	1875.00	12/18/03	1937.50	11/10/03	-78.13
2003	11/06/02	-3~280	12/27/02	-2~060	1~220	1687.50	11/19/02	1859.38		
2002	11/06/01	-1~005	12/27/01	-3~195	-2~190	-2593.75	11/07/01	578.13	12/07/01	-3468.75
2001	11/06/00	-1~125	12/27/00	-0~015	1~110	1343.75	12/14/00	1593.75	11/10/00	-171.88
2000	11/08/99	-3~225	12/27/99	-4~305	-1~080	-1250.00	11/15/99	484.38	12/21/99	-1546.88
1999	11/06/98	-1~060	12/24/98	-0~160	0~220	687.50	11/30/98	2281.25		
1998	11/06/97	-1~150	12/26/97	0~020	1~170	1531.25	12/22/97	1562.50		
1997	11/06/96	-4~010	12/27/96	-3~160	0~170	531.25	12/03/96	875.00	12/18/96	-156.25
1996	11/06/95	-2~160	12/27/95	-1~170	0~310	968.75	12/08/95	1000.00	11/21/95	-343.75
1995	11/07/94	-8~150	12/27/94	-6~030	2~120	2375.00	12/27/94	2375.00	11/11/94	-125.00
1994	11/08/93	-5~090	12/27/93	-4~260	0~150	468.75	12/06/93	812.50	11/19/93	-531.25
1993	11/06/92	-9~280	12/24/92	-8~040	1~240	1750.00	12/24/92	1750.00		
1992	11/06/91	-9~130	12/27/91	-9~020	0~110	343.75	11/12/91	812.50	12/04/91	-500.00
1991	11/06/90	-9~180	12/27/90	-8~140	1~040	1125.00	12/12/90	1312.50	11/08/90	-375.00
1990	11/06/89	-6~290	12/27/89	-7~030	-0~060	-187.50	11/07/89	156.25	11/17/89	-437.50
1989	11/07/88	-10~060	12/27/88	-8~180	1~200	1625.00	12/27/88	1625.00	11/17/88	-312.50
1988	11/06/87	-10~030	12/24/87	-10~000	0~030	93.75	11/23/87	218.75	12/11/87	-1406.25
1987	11/06/86	-10~300	12/26/86	-9~270	1~030	1093.75	12/04/86	1406.25	11/07/86	-406.25
1986	11/06/85	-13~120	12/27/85	-12~050	1~070	1218.75	12/26/85	1281.25		

Percentage Correct	87							Protective Stop		(978)
Average Profit on Winning Trades					1~052	1163.46		Winners		13
Average Loss on Trades					-1~295	-1921.88		Losers		2
Average Net Profit Per Trade					0~241	752.08		Total trades		15
Percentage Correct	85									
Average Profit on Winning Trades					1~041	1126.84		Winners		17
Average Loss on Trades					-1~110	-1343.75		Losers		3
Average Net Profit Per Trade					0~242	756.25		Total trades		20

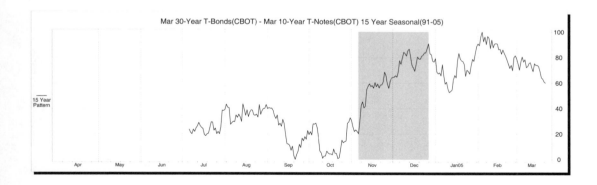

Mar 30-Year T-Bonds(CBOT) - Mar 10-Year T-Notes(CBOT) 15 Year Seasonal(91-05)

15 Year Pattern

Figure 10-39

Buy Mar 30-Year T-Bonds(CBOT) / Sell Mar 5-Year T-Notes(CBOT)

Enter on approximately 11/27 - Exit on approximately 12/12

CONT YEAR	ENTRY DATE	ENTRY PRICE	EXIT DATE	EXIT PRICE	PROFIT	PROFIT AMOUNT	BEST EQUITY DATE	BEST EQUITY AMOUNT	WORST EQUITY DATE	WORST EQUITY AMOUNT
2005	11/29/04	1~245	12/10/04	2~275	1~030	1093.75	12/08/04	1437.50	12/02/04	-843.75
2004	11/28/03	-2~170	12/12/03	-2~150	0~020	62.50	12/05/03	718.75	12/03/03	-468.75
2003	11/27/02	-2~225	12/12/02	-0~265	1~280	1875.00	12/12/02	1875.00		
2002	11/27/01	-3~015	12/12/01	-4~165	-1~150	-1468.75	12/04/01	828.13	12/07/01	-2390.63
2001	11/27/00	0~030	12/12/00	1~010	0~300	937.50	12/07/00	1078.13	12/04/00	-46.88
2000	11/29/99	-6~045	12/10/99	-4~295	1~070	1218.75	12/10/99	1218.75	12/02/99	-93.75
1999	11/27/98	2~045	12/11/98	2~120	0~075	234.38	12/09/98	859.38		
1998	11/28/97	-0~275	12/12/97	-0~080	0~195	609.38	12/12/97	609.38	12/09/97	-500.00
1997	11/27/96	-4~010	12/12/96	-5~015	-1~005	-1015.63	12/03/96	562.50	12/12/96	-1015.63
1996	11/27/95	-2~210	12/12/95	-1~090	1~120	1375.00	12/11/95	1468.75	11/28/95	-78.13
1995	11/28/94	-11~005	12/12/94	-10~020	0~305	953.13	12/09/94	1218.75	11/29/94	-109.38
1994	11/29/93	-6~310	12/10/93	-6~140	0~170	531.25	12/09/93	984.38	11/30/93	-296.88
1993	11/27/92	-12~255	12/11/92	-11~240	1~015	1046.88	12/11/92	1046.88	11/30/92	-31.25
1992	11/27/91	-14~205	12/12/91	-13~280	0~245	765.63	12/06/91	781.25		
1991	11/27/90	-14~075	12/12/90	-12~175	1~220	1687.50	12/12/90	1687.50	11/29/90	-93.75
1990	11/27/89	-10~235	12/12/89	-10~215	0~020	62.50	12/04/89	203.13	11/29/89	-15.63
1989	11/28/88	-15~240	12/12/88	-14~035	1~205	1640.63	12/12/88	1640.63		

Percentage Correct		87						Protective Stop		(859)
Average Profit on Winning Trades					0~305	953.13		Winners		13
Average Loss on Trades					-1~078	-1242.19		Losers		2
Average Net Profit Per Trade					0~211	660.42		Total trades		15
Percentage Correct		88								
Average Profit on Winning Trades					0~301	939.58		Winners		15
Average Loss on Trades					-1~078	-1242.19		Losers		2
Average Net Profit Per Trade					0~219	682.90		Total trades		17

HYPOTHETICAL PERFORMANCE RESULTS HAVE MANY INHERENT LIMITATIONS, SOME OF WHICH ARE DESCRIBED BELOW. NO REPRESENTATION IS BEING MADE THAT ANY ACCOUNT WILL OR IS LIKELY TO ACHIEVE PROFITS OR LOSSES SIMILAR TO THOSE SHOWN. IN FACT, THERE ARE FREQUENTLY SHARP DIFFERENCES BETWEEN HYPOTHETICAL PERFORMANCE RESULTS AND THE ACTUAL RESULTS SUBSEQUENTLY ACHIEVED BY ANY PARTICULAR TRADING PROGRAM. ONE OF THE LIMITATIONS OF HYPOTHETICAL PERFORMANCE RESULTS IS THAT THEY ARE GENERALLY PREPARED WITH THE BENEFIT OF HINDSIGHT. IN ADDITION, HYPOTHETICAL TRADING DOES NOT INVOLVE FINANCIAL RISK, AND NO HYPOTHETICAL TRADING RECORD CAN COMPLETELY ACCOUNT FOR THE IMPACT OF FINANCIAL RISK IN ACTUAL TRADING. FOR EXAMPLE, THE ABILITY TO WITHSTAND LOSSES OR ADHERE TO A PARTICULAR TRADING PROGRAM IN SPITE OF TRADING LOSSES ARE MATERIAL POINTS WHICH CAN ALSO ADVERSELY AFFECT ACTUAL TRADING RESULTS. THERE ARE NUMEROUS OTHER FACTORS RELATED TO THE MARKETS IN GENERAL OR TO THE IMPLEMENTATION OF ANY SPECIFIC TRADING PROGRAM WHICH CANNOT BE FULLY ACCOUNTED FOR IN THE PREPARATION OF HYPOTHETICAL PERFORMANCE RESULTS AND ALL OF WHICH CAN ADVERSELY AFFECT ACTUAL TRADING RESULTS. RESULTS NOT ADJUSTED FOR COMMISSION AND SLIPPAGE.

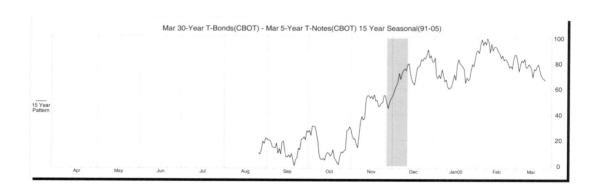

Mar 30-Year T-Bonds(CBOT) - Mar 5-Year T-Notes(CBOT) 15 Year Seasonal(91-05)

Figure 10-40

Moore Research Center, Inc. — Buy Mar 30-Year T-Bonds(CBOT) / Sell Mar 2-Year T-Notes(CBOT)

Enter on approximately 11/27 - Exit on approximately 12/12

CONT YEAR	ENTRY DATE	ENTRY PRICE	EXIT DATE	EXIT PRICE		PROFIT AMOUNT	BEST EQUITY DATE	BEST EQUITY AMOUNT	WORST EQUITY DATE	WORST EQUITY AMOUNT
2005	11/29/04	-98719	12/10/04	-97234		1484.38	12/08/04	1796.88	12/02/04	-1015.63
2004	11/28/03	-104906	12/12/03	-104844		62.50	12/05/03	843.75	12/03/03	-578.13
2003	11/27/02	-105031	12/12/02	-103000		2031.25	12/11/02	2093.75		
2002	11/27/01	-105844	12/12/01	-107563		-1718.75	12/04/01	1078.13	12/07/01	-2828.13
2001	11/27/00	-99531	12/12/00	-98672		859.38	12/07/00	906.25	12/04/00	-187.50
2000	11/29/99	-106594	12/10/99	-105234		1359.38	12/10/99	1359.38	12/02/99	-140.63
1999	11/27/98	-97578	12/11/98	-97203		375.00	12/09/98	1062.50		
1998	11/28/97	-101344	12/12/97	-100891		453.13	12/12/97	453.13	12/09/97	-687.50
1997	11/27/96	-105188	12/12/96	-106500		-1312.50	12/03/96	656.25	12/12/96	-1312.50
1996	11/27/95	-103734	12/12/95	-102125		1609.38	12/04/95	1734.38	11/28/95	-125.00
1995	11/28/94	-112672	12/12/94	-110953		1718.75	12/09/94	1968.75	11/29/94	-125.00
1994	11/29/93	-109703	12/10/93	-109016		687.50	12/09/93	1171.88	11/30/93	-343.75
1993	11/27/92	-117313	12/11/92	-116000		1312.50	12/11/92	1312.50		
1992	11/27/91	-118922	12/12/91	-118203		718.75	12/06/91	906.25		
1991	11/27/90	-116578	12/12/90	-114703		1875.00	12/12/90	1875.00	11/29/90	-78.13

Percentage Correct	87							
Average Profit on Winning Trades						1118.99	Winners	13
Average Loss on Trades						-1515.63	Losers	2
Average Net Profit Per Trade						767.71	Total trades	15

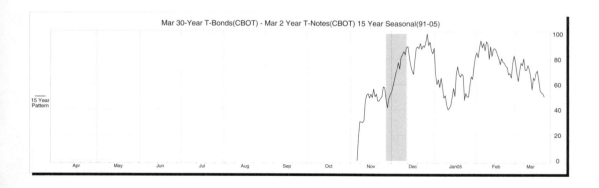

Mar 30-Year T-Bonds(CBOT) - Mar 2 Year T-Notes(CBOT) 15 Year Seasonal(91-05)

15 Year Pattern

Figure 10-41

Buy Mar 2-Year T-Notes(CBOT) / Sell Mar 5-Year T-Notes(CBOT)

Enter on approximately 12/20 - Exit on approximately 01/26

CONT YEAR	ENTRY DATE	ENTRY PRICE	EXIT DATE	EXIT PRICE		PROFIT AMOUNT	BEST EQUITY DATE	BEST EQUITY AMOUNT	WORST EQUITY DATE	WORST EQUITY AMOUNT
2005	12/20/04	99922	01/26/05	99906		-15.63	12/28/04	234.38	01/24/05	-109.38
2004	12/22/03	102234	01/26/04	102297		62.50	01/02/04	390.63	01/15/04	-375.00
2003	12/20/02	102031	01/24/03	102313		281.25	01/10/03	812.50	12/30/02	-250.00
2002	12/20/01	103078	01/25/02	103422		343.75	01/11/02	468.75		
2001	12/20/00	99594	01/26/01	100469		875.00	01/24/01	1015.63		
2000	12/20/99	100391	01/26/00	100672		281.25	01/21/00	359.38		
1999	12/21/98	99609	01/26/99	99766		156.25	01/11/99	421.88		
1998	12/22/97	100406	01/26/98	100609		203.13	01/23/98	234.38	01/05/98	-125.00
1997	12/20/96	101344	01/24/97	101578		234.38	01/07/97	250.00		
1996	12/20/95	100891	01/26/96	101156		265.63	01/25/96	359.38	01/22/96	-1109.38
1995	12/20/94	100906	01/26/95	101734		828.13	01/26/95	828.13	12/27/94	-140.63
1994	12/20/93	102813	01/26/94	102609		-203.13	01/03/94	31.25	12/28/93	-328.13
1993	12/21/92	104391	01/26/93	104578		187.50	12/31/92	546.88		
1992	12/20/91	104469	01/24/92	104766		296.88	01/17/92	640.63	12/27/91	-93.75
1991	12/20/90	102219	01/25/91	102813		593.75	01/09/91	1015.63		

Percentage Correct	87									
Average Profit on Winning Trades						354.57		Winners		13
Average Loss on Trades						-109.38		Losers		2
Average Net Profit Per Trade						292.71		Total trades		15

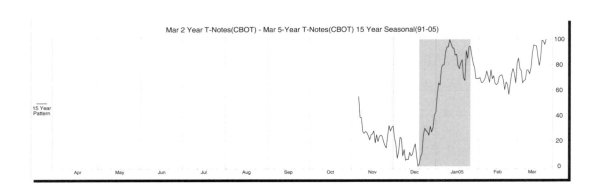

Mar 2 Year T-Notes(CBOT) - Mar 5-Year T-Notes(CBOT) 15 Year Seasonal(91-05)

15 Year Pattern

Chapter 10: Interest Rates

Figure 10-42

Buy Mar 2-Year T-Notes(CBOT) / Sell Mar 10-Year T-Notes(CBOT)

Enter on approximately 12/29 - Exit on approximately 01/09

CONT YEAR	ENTRY DATE	ENTRY PRICE	EXIT DATE	EXIT PRICE		PROFIT AMOUNT	BEST EQUITY DATE	BEST EQUITY AMOUNT	WORST EQUITY DATE	WORST EQUITY AMOUNT
2005	12/29/04	98047	01/07/05	97719		-328.13			01/03/05	-421.88
2004	12/29/03	101656	01/09/04	100953		-703.13	01/05/04	718.75	01/09/04	-703.13
2003	12/30/02	99922	01/09/03	101656		1734.38	01/09/03	1734.38		
2002	12/31/01	103828	01/09/02	103969		140.63	01/02/02	265.63	01/07/02	-46.88
2001	12/29/00	98266	01/09/01	98750		484.38	01/03/01	734.38	01/02/01	-328.13
2000	12/29/99	102656	01/07/00	102859		203.13	01/05/00	625.00	12/30/99	-46.88
1999	12/29/98	97906	01/08/99	98688		781.25	01/08/99	781.25		
1998	12/29/97	100531	01/09/98	100188		-343.75	12/30/97	187.50	01/05/98	-515.63
1997	12/30/96	102063	01/09/97	102656		593.75	01/07/97	796.88		
1996	12/29/95	100391	01/09/96	100797		406.25	01/09/96	406.25	01/03/96	-62.50
1995	12/29/94	103813	01/09/95	104469		656.25	01/09/95	656.25		
1994	12/29/93	104078	01/07/94	104188		109.38	01/03/94	687.50		
1993	12/29/92	107938	01/08/93	108578		640.63	01/08/93	640.63	01/04/93	-31.25
1992	12/30/91	107609	01/09/92	108250		640.63	01/08/92	750.00	12/31/91	-140.63
1991	12/31/90	107578	01/09/91	108547		968.75	01/09/91	968.75	01/03/91	-484.38

Percentage Correct	80				
Average Profit on Winning Trades		613.28		Winners	12
Average Loss on Trades		-458.33		Losers	3
Average Net Profit Per Trade		398.96		Total trades	15

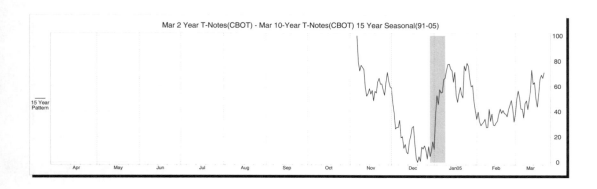

Mar 2 Year T-Notes(CBOT) - Mar 10-Year T-Notes(CBOT) 15 Year Seasonal(91-05)

Figure 10-43

Buy Mar 30-Year T-Bonds(CBOT) / Sell Mar 2-Year T-Notes(CBOT)

Enter on approximately 01/12 - Exit on approximately 01/31

CONT YEAR	ENTRY DATE	ENTRY PRICE	EXIT DATE	EXIT PRICE		PROFIT AMOUNT	BEST EQUITY DATE	BEST EQUITY AMOUNT	WORST EQUITY DATE	WORST EQUITY AMOUNT
2005	01/12/05	-96094	01/31/05	-94219		1875.00	01/31/05	1875.00		
2004	01/12/04	-103563	01/30/04	-103156		406.25	01/22/04	1484.38	01/28/04	-406.25
2003	01/13/03	-104969	01/31/03	-102875		2093.75	01/24/03	2093.75		
2002	01/14/02	-107125	01/31/02	-106531		593.75	01/22/02	750.00	01/23/02	-265.63
2001	01/12/01	-100875	01/31/01	-100438		437.50	01/18/01	1234.38	01/29/01	-796.88
2000	01/12/00	-108391	01/31/00	-105031		3359.38	01/28/00	3875.00	01/18/00	-187.50
1999	01/12/99	-99844	01/29/99	-98031		1812.50	01/29/99	1812.50		
1998	01/12/98	-99656	01/30/98	-100328		-671.88	01/13/98	15.63	01/23/98	-2093.75
1997	01/13/97	-107500	01/31/97	-107344		156.25	01/14/97	515.63	01/27/97	-515.63
1996	01/12/96	-103828	01/31/96	-103000		828.13	01/22/96	2328.13		
1995	01/12/95	-111375	01/31/95	-110891		484.38	01/18/95	703.13	01/23/95	-296.88
1994	01/12/94	-108578	01/31/94	-108516		62.50	01/28/94	156.25	01/17/94	-1109.38
1993	01/12/93	-117922	01/29/93	-116391		1531.25	01/25/93	1828.13		
1992	01/13/92	-116375	01/31/92	-118000		-1625.00			01/30/92	-1828.13
1991	01/14/91	-117672	01/31/91	-116141		1531.25	01/17/91	2125.00		

Percentage Correct	87		Protective Stop	(1116)
Average Profit on Winning Trades		1167.07	Winners	13
Average Loss on Trades		-1148.44	Losers	2
Average Net Profit Per Trade		858.33	Total trades	15

HYPOTHETICAL PERFORMANCE RESULTS HAVE MANY INHERENT LIMITATIONS, SOME OF WHICH ARE DESCRIBED BELOW. NO REPRESENTATION IS BEING MADE THAT ANY ACCOUNT WILL OR IS LIKELY TO ACHIEVE PROFITS OR LOSSES SIMILAR TO THOSE SHOWN. IN FACT, THERE ARE FREQUENTLY SHARP DIFFERENCES BETWEEN HYPOTHETICAL PERFORMANCE RESULTS AND THE ACTUAL RESULTS SUBSEQUENTLY ACHIEVED BY ANY PARTICULAR TRADING PROGRAM. ONE OF THE LIMITATIONS OF HYPOTHETICAL PERFORMANCE RESULTS IS THAT THEY ARE GENERALLY PREPARED WITH THE BENEFIT OF HINDSIGHT. IN ADDITION, HYPOTHETICAL TRADING DOES NOT INVOLVE FINANCIAL RISK, AND NO HYPOTHETICAL TRADING RECORD CAN COMPLETELY ACCOUNT FOR THE IMPACT OF FINANCIAL RISK IN ACTUAL TRADING. FOR EXAMPLE, THE ABILITY TO WITHSTAND LOSSES OR ADHERE TO A PARTICULAR TRADING PROGRAM IN SPITE OF TRADING LOSSES ARE MATERIAL POINTS WHICH CAN ALSO ADVERSELY AFFECT ACTUAL TRADING RESULTS. THERE ARE NUMEROUS OTHER FACTORS RELATED TO THE MARKETS IN GENERAL OR TO THE IMPLEMENTATION OF ANY SPECIFIC TRADING PROGRAM WHICH CANNOT BE FULLY ACCOUNTED FOR IN THE PREPARATION OF HYPOTHETICAL PERFORMANCE RESULTS AND ALL OF WHICH CAN ADVERSELY AFFECT ACTUAL TRADING RESULTS. RESULTS NOT ADJUSTED FOR COMMISSION AND SLIPPAGE.

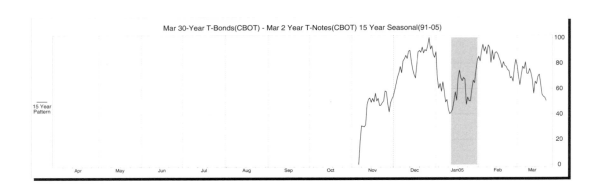

Mar 30-Year T-Bonds(CBOT) - Mar 2 Year T-Notes(CBOT) 15 Year Seasonal(91-05)

Figure 10-44

Buy Jun 2-Year T-Notes(CBOT) / Sell Jun 30-Year T-Bonds(CBOT)

Enter on approximately 02/19 - Exit on approximately 04/20

CONT YEAR	ENTRY DATE	ENTRY PRICE	EXIT DATE	EXIT PRICE		PROFIT AMOUNT	BEST EQUITY DATE	BEST EQUITY AMOUNT	WORST EQUITY DATE	WORST EQUITY AMOUNT
2005	02/22/05	95031	04/20/05	93813		-1218.75	03/22/05	1968.75	04/19/05	-1265.63
2004	02/19/04	102656	04/20/04	105500		2843.75	04/20/04	2843.75	03/17/04	-3250.00
2003	02/19/03	102563	04/17/03	102625		62.50	03/21/03	1937.50	03/12/03	-2515.63
2002	02/19/02	106063	04/19/02	107844		1781.25	03/14/02	2687.50	02/22/02	-625.00
2001	02/20/01	100688	04/20/01	105203		4515.63	04/20/01	4515.63	03/20/01	-1421.88
2000	02/22/00	102000	04/20/00	100500		-1500.00	02/28/00	1453.13	04/07/00	-2843.75
1999	02/19/99	100969	04/20/99	101594		625.00	04/01/99	2140.63	02/22/99	-156.25
1998	02/19/98	100719	04/20/98	100875		156.25	03/05/98	1578.13	04/03/98	-765.63
1997	02/19/97	106047	04/18/97	108328		2281.25	04/11/97	2921.88		
1996	02/20/96	106469	04/19/96	108406		1937.50	04/05/96	2656.25	03/04/96	-406.25
1995	02/21/95	110781	04/20/95	110797		15.63	03/07/95	765.63	03/14/95	-781.25
1994	02/22/94	110297	04/20/94	113219		2921.88	04/04/94	4015.63		
1993	02/19/93	115734	04/20/93	113844		-1890.63	04/02/93	500.00	03/09/93	-2578.13
1992	02/19/92	118688	04/20/92	118828		140.63	04/20/92	140.63	03/24/92	-1656.25
1991	02/19/91	115406	04/19/91	116172		765.63	03/19/91	2015.63		

Percentage Correct		80								
Average Profit on Winning Trades						1503.91		Winners		12
Average Loss on Trades						-1536.46		Losers		3
Average Net Profit Per Trade						895.83		Total trades		15

HYPOTHETICAL PERFORMANCE RESULTS HAVE MANY INHERENT LIMITATIONS, SOME OF WHICH ARE DESCRIBED BELOW. NO REPRESENTATION IS BEING MADE THAT ANY ACCOUNT WILL OR IS LIKELY TO ACHIEVE PROFITS OR LOSSES SIMILAR TO THOSE SHOWN. IN FACT, THERE ARE FREQUENTLY SHARP DIFFERENCES BETWEEN HYPOTHETICAL PERFORMANCE RESULTS AND THE ACTUAL RESULTS SUBSEQUENTLY ACHIEVED BY ANY PARTICULAR TRADING PROGRAM. ONE OF THE LIMITATIONS OF HYPOTHETICAL PERFORMANCE RESULTS IS THAT THEY ARE GENERALLY PREPARED WITH THE BENEFIT OF HINDSIGHT. IN ADDITION, HYPOTHETICAL TRADING DOES NOT INVOLVE FINANCIAL RISK, AND NO HYPOTHETICAL TRADING RECORD CAN COMPLETELY ACCOUNT FOR THE IMPACT OF FINANCIAL RISK IN ACTUAL TRADING. FOR EXAMPLE, THE ABILITY TO WITHSTAND LOSSES OR ADHERE TO A PARTICULAR TRADING PROGRAM IN SPITE OF TRADING LOSSES ARE MATERIAL POINTS WHICH CAN ALSO ADVERSELY AFFECT ACTUAL TRADING RESULTS. THERE ARE NUMEROUS OTHER FACTORS RELATED TO THE MARKETS IN GENERAL OR TO THE IMPLEMENTATION OF ANY SPECIFIC TRADING PROGRAM WHICH CANNOT BE FULLY ACCOUNTED FOR IN THE PREPARATION OF HYPOTHETICAL PERFORMANCE RESULTS AND ALL OF WHICH CAN ADVERSELY AFFECT ACTUAL TRADING RESULTS. RESULTS NOT ADJUSTED FOR COMMISSION AND SLIPPAGE.

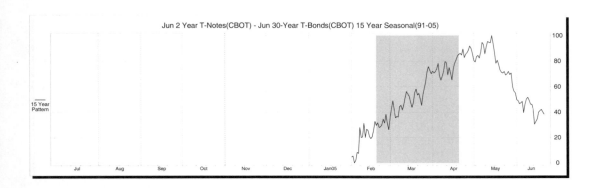

Jun 2 Year T-Notes(CBOT) - Jun 30-Year T-Bonds(CBOT) 15 Year Seasonal(91-05)

15 Year Pattern

Figure 10-45

Moore Research Center, Inc. — *Buy Jun 2-Year T-Notes(CBOT) / Sell Jun 30-Year T-Bonds(CBOT)*

Enter on approximately 03/18 - Exit on approximately 03/30

CONT YEAR	ENTRY DATE	ENTRY PRICE	EXIT DATE	EXIT PRICE		PROFIT AMOUNT	BEST EQUITY DATE	BEST EQUITY AMOUNT	WORST EQUITY DATE	WORST EQUITY AMOUNT
2005	03/18/05	96375	03/30/05	95906		-468.75	03/22/05	625.00	03/30/05	-468.75
2004	03/18/04	99938	03/30/04	101563		1625.00	03/30/04	1625.00	03/23/04	-375.00
2003	03/18/03	102406	03/28/03	103625		1218.75	03/21/03	2093.75		
2002	03/18/02	107531	03/28/02	108422		890.63	03/28/02	890.63		
2001	03/19/01	99594	03/30/01	101703		2109.38	03/29/01	2421.88	03/20/01	-328.13
2000	03/20/00	101453	03/30/00	100734		-718.75			03/30/00	-718.75
1999	03/18/99	101625	03/30/99	102266		640.63	03/29/99	1234.38		
1998	03/18/98	101000	03/30/98	101203		203.13	03/30/98	203.13	03/24/98	-343.75
1997	03/18/97	108281	03/27/97	108500		218.75	03/27/97	218.75	03/24/97	-500.00
1996	03/18/96	107531	03/29/96	107672		140.63	03/28/96	343.75	03/21/96	-1093.75
1995	03/20/95	110500	03/30/95	110531		31.25	03/23/95	515.63	03/27/95	-359.38
1994	03/18/94	111484	03/30/94	112984		1500.00	03/30/94	1500.00	03/22/94	-531.25
1993	03/18/93	114438	03/30/93	115219		781.25	03/26/93	812.50	03/23/93	-234.38
1992	03/18/92	117328	03/30/92	117438		109.38	03/20/92	312.50	03/24/92	-296.88
1991	03/18/91	117250	03/28/91	116453		-796.88	03/19/91	171.88	03/28/91	-796.88

Percentage Correct	80		Protective Stop	(649)
Average Profit on Winning Trades		789.06	Winners	12
Average Loss on Trades		-661.46	Losers	3
Average Net Profit Per Trade		498.96	Total trades	15

HYPOTHETICAL PERFORMANCE RESULTS HAVE MANY INHERENT LIMITATIONS, SOME OF WHICH ARE DESCRIBED BELOW. NO REPRESENTATION IS BEING MADE THAT ANY ACCOUNT WILL OR IS LIKELY TO ACHIEVE PROFITS OR LOSSES SIMILAR TO THOSE SHOWN. IN FACT, THERE ARE FREQUENTLY SHARP DIFFERENCES BETWEEN HYPOTHETICAL PERFORMANCE RESULTS AND THE ACTUAL RESULTS SUBSEQUENTLY ACHIEVED BY ANY PARTICULAR TRADING PROGRAM. ONE OF THE LIMITATIONS OF HYPOTHETICAL PERFORMANCE RESULTS IS THAT THEY ARE GENERALLY PREPARED WITH THE BENEFIT OF HINDSIGHT. IN ADDITION, HYPOTHETICAL TRADING DOES NOT INVOLVE FINANCIAL RISK, AND NO HYPOTHETICAL TRADING RECORD CAN COMPLETELY ACCOUNT FOR THE IMPACT OF FINANCIAL RISK IN ACTUAL TRADING. FOR EXAMPLE, THE ABILITY TO WITHSTAND LOSSES OR ADHERE TO A PARTICULAR TRADING PROGRAM IN SPITE OF TRADING LOSSES ARE MATERIAL POINTS WHICH CAN ALSO ADVERSELY AFFECT ACTUAL TRADING RESULTS. THERE ARE NUMEROUS OTHER FACTORS RELATED TO THE MARKETS IN GENERAL OR TO THE IMPLEMENTATION OF ANY SPECIFIC TRADING PROGRAM WHICH CANNOT BE FULLY ACCOUNTED FOR IN THE PREPARATION OF HYPOTHETICAL PERFORMANCE RESULTS AND ALL OF WHICH CAN ADVERSELY AFFECT ACTUAL TRADING RESULTS. RESULTS NOT ADJUSTED FOR COMMISSION AND SLIPPAGE.

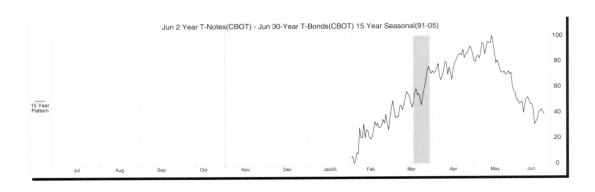

Jun 2 Year T-Notes(CBOT) - Jun 30-Year T-Bonds(CBOT) 15 Year Seasonal(91-05)

Chapter 11: Chronology

Placed at the end of each volume in MRCI's series of annually reproduced special historical reports is a chronological summary of all strategies presented in that issue. Such a review is meant to provide convenient reference to seasonal movements throughout the year, saving readers from any need to search hundreds of pages of text, tables, and charts. Instead, one can easily find what market has exhibited what seasonality when. This publication, perhaps more than any other, begs the following complete list of every seasonal spread strategy published herein with the page number on which can be found its table of supporting historical detail. Again, these are emphatically *not* recommendations but rather statistics — which confirm the past but cannot predict the future. Neither is the following meant to be construed as a trading system. Perhaps it can, however, help the reader better understand how markets have tended to behave and thus anticipate similar recurrences in the future.

Those who cannot remember the past are condemned to repeat it.
Santayana, *The Life of Reason*

Moore Research Center, Inc.	Chronological Summary								
Seasonal Strategy	Entry Date	Exit Date	Win Pct	Win Yrs	Loss Years	Total Years	Average Profit	Ave Pft Per Day	Page
Buy 2 May Corn(CBOT) Sell 3 May Oats(CBOT)	1/03	2/14	87 85	13 17	2 3	15 20	979 1086	23 25	128
Buy Jul Corn(CBOT) Sell 2 Jul Oats(CBOT)	1/03	2/19	87 90	13 18	2 2	15 20	613 735	13 15	129
Buy May Corn(CBOT) Sell 2 May Oats(CBOT)	1/05	4/11	80 85	12 17	3 3	15 20	615 1096	6 11	130
Buy Feb Lean Hogs(CME) Sell Feb Pork Bellies(CME)	1/06	2/01	80 80	12 16	3 4	15 20	463 613	17 23	271
Buy Mar Japanese Yen(IMM) Sell Mar Swiss Franc(IMM)	1/06	2/04	87 80	13 16	2 4	15 20	1717 1370	57 46	321
Buy Dec Wheat(CBOT) Sell May Wheat(CBOT)	1/07	2/28	93 90	14 18	1 2	15 20	344 367	6 7	107
Buy 2 Mar Corn(CBOT) Sell 3 Mar Oats(CBOT)	1/08	1/25	87 85	13 17	2 3	15 20	737 782	41 43	131
Buy Jul Wheat(CBOT) Sell Mar Wheat(CBOT)	1/09	2/08	93 90	14 18	1 2	15 20	406 418	13 13	108
Buy Apr Crude Oil(NYM) Sell Apr Heating Oil #2(NYM)	1/09	2/16	80 80	12 16	3 4	15 20	366 401	9 10	71

Seasonal Strategy	Entry Date	Exit Date	Win Pct	Win Yrs	Loss Years	Total Years	Average Profit	Ave Pft Per Day	Page
Buy Mar Corn(CBOT)	1/10	1/25	93	14	1	15	432	27	132
Sell 2 Mar Oats(CBOT)			85	17	3	20	429	27	
Buy Apr Live Cattle(CME)	1/10	3/15	87	13	2	15	607	9	258
Sell Mar Feeder Cattle(CME)			90	18	2	20	722	11	
Buy Mar Wheat(MGE)	1/11	2/22	87	13	2	15	563	13	111
Sell Mar Wheat(CBOT)			85	17	3	20	436	10	
Buy Mar Wheat(KCBT)	1/11	2/22	87	13	2	15	493	11	112
Sell Mar Wheat(CBOT)			80	16	4	20	401	9	
Buy Mar 30-Year T-Bonds(CBOT)	1/12	1/31	87	13	2	15	858	43	390
Sell Mar 2-Year T-Notes(CBOT)									
Buy Jul Heating Oil #2(NYM)	1/15	2/20	87	13	2	15	454	12	25
Sell Mar Heating Oil #2(NYM)			85	17	3	20	610	16	
Buy Mar Canadian Dollar(IMM)	1/23	3/15	80	12	3	15	1679	32	322
Sell Mar Swiss Franc(IMM)			80	16	4	20	1512	29	
Buy Mar Australian Dollar(IMM)	1/24	2/02	87	13	2	15	1360	136	323
Sell Mar Swiss Franc(IMM)			84	16	3	19	1240	124	
Buy Jul Wheat(MGE)	1/27	2/08	93	14	1	15	460	35	194
Sell Jul Soybeans(CBOT)			95	19	1	20	468	36	
Buy 2 Apr Platinum(NYM)	1/29	2/16	87	13	2	15	1462	77	291
Sell Apr Gold(CMX)			85	17	3	20	1394	73	
Buy Apr Live Cattle(CME)	1/30	2/26	80	12	3	15	581	21	246
Sell Apr Lean Hogs(CME)			80	16	4	20	620	42	
Buy Sep Rough Rice(CBOT)	1/31	2/25	93	14	1	15	459	18	310
Sell Mar Rough Rice(CBOT)			95	18	1	19	557	21	
Buy Apr Live Cattle(CME)	1/31	3/04	87	13	2	15	559	17	259
Sell Apr Feeder Cattle(CME)			90	18	2	20	656	20	
Buy May Silver(CMX)	2/02	2/14	87	13	2	15	699	54	282
Sell Apr Gold(CMX)			90	18	2	20	636	49	
Buy May Copper(CMX)	2/04	3/16	80	12	3	15	281	7	279
Sell Dec Copper(CMX)			80	16	4	20	445	11	
Buy Jun Unleaded Reg.(NYM)	2/08	3/29	93	14	1	15	782	16	58
Sell Jun Heating Oil #2(NYM)			90	18	2	20	668	13	
Buy Jul Soybeans(CBOT)	2/09	5/01	80	12	3	15	563	7	163
Sell Jul Soybean Meal(CBOT)			80	16	4	20	524	6	
Buy May Corn(CBOT)	2/10	2/19	87	13	2	15	333	33	119
Sell May Wheat(CBOT)			85	17	3	20	319	32	
Buy Sep Soybeans(CBOT)	2/11	5/01	80	12	3	15	1146	14	181
Sell Sep Corn(CBOT)			85	17	3	20	1232	15	

Seasonal Strategy	Entry Date	Exit Date	Win Pct	Win Yrs	Loss Years	Total Years	Average Profit	Ave Pft Per Day	Page
Buy Sep Soybeans(CBOT) Sell 2 Sep Corn(CBOT)	2/11	5/01	93 95	14 19	1 1	15 20	1165 1149	15 14	182
Buy Jun Unleaded Reg.(NYM) Sell Jun Crude Oil(NYM)	2/13	3/30	93 95	14 19	1 1	15 20	884 918	19 20	77
Buy May Soybeans(CBOT) Sell May Wheat(KCBT)	2/14	3/22	87 80	13 16	2 4	15 20	1422 1230	38 33	195
Buy Jul Lean Hogs(CME) Sell Dec Lean Hogs(CME)	2/15	5/11	93 95	14 19	1 1	15 20	942 1003	11 12	238
Buy Jun Lean Hogs(CME) Sell Oct Lean Hogs(CME)	2/17	3/10	87 90	13 18	2 2	15 20	482 468	22 21	239
Buy Jun 2-Year T-Notes(CBOT) Sell Jun 30-Year T-Bonds(CBOT)	2/19	4/20	80	12	3	15	896	15	391
Buy Jun Australian Dollar(IMM) Sell Jun Swiss Franc(IMM)	2/22	4/16	87 89	13 17	2 2	15 19	1850 2054	34 38	324
Buy Jun Canadian Dollar(IMM) Sell Jun Swiss Franc(IMM)	2/22	3/26	80 85	12 17	3 3	15 20	1377 1644	42 50	325
Buy Jul Soybeans(CBOT) Sell Jul Wheat(KCBT)	2/23	3/21	80 80	12 16	3 4	15 20	1029 918	38 34	196
Buy Jul Unleaded Reg.(NYM) Sell Jul Heating Oil #2(NYM)	2/23	5/04	87 80	13 16	2 4	15 20	926 1115	13 16	55
Buy Jul Soybeans(CBOT) Sell Jul Wheat(CBOT)	2/24	3/21	80 85	12 17	3 3	15 20	919 883	35 34	197
Buy Jul Unleaded Reg.(NYM) Sell Jul Heating Oil #2(NYM)	2/24	3/29	100 100	15 20	0 0	15 20	620 670	18 20	59
Buy 2 Jul Platinum(NYM) Sell Jun Gold(CMX)	2/24	4/19	93 95	14 19	1 1	15 20	2178 2248	40 41	292
Buy Jul Unleaded Reg.(NYM) Sell Jul Crude Oil(NYM)	2/24	4/27	93 90	14 18	1 2	15 20	983 1133	16 18	76
Buy Jul Soybeans(CBOT) Sell Jul Corn(CBOT)	2/24	5/01	87 85	13 17	2 3	15 20	1291 1208	19 18	183
Buy Mar Australian Dollar(IMM) Sell Mar Swiss Franc(IMM)	2/25	3/04	80 84	12 16	3 3	15 19	731 898	91 112	326
Buy Mar Canadian Dollar(IMM) Sell Mar Swiss Franc(IMM)	2/25	3/05	80 80	12 16	3 4	15 20	595 638	66 71	327
Buy May Sugar #11(NYBOT) Sell "Red" May Sugar #11(NYBOT)	2/25	3/11	80 80	12 16	3 4	15 20	255 256	17 17	300
Buy May Pork Bellies(CME) Sell Apr Lean Hogs(CME)	2/25	3/24	87 85	13 17	2 3	15 20	835 731	30 26	272

Moore Research Center, Inc.

Seasonal Strategy	Entry Date	Exit Date	Win Pct	Win Yrs	Loss Years	Total Years	Average Profit	Ave Pft Per Day	Page
Buy Jun Lean Hogs(CME)	2/25	4/19	80	12	3	15	1179	22	247
Sell Jun Live Cattle(CME)			85	17	3	20	1271	24	
Buy Jun Lean Hogs(CME)	2/25	5/18	80	12	3	15	1220	15	248
Sell Jun Live Cattle(CME)			85	17	3	20	1687	20	
Buy Jun Unleaded Reg.(NYM)	2/25	5/26	87	13	2	15	1445	16	60
Sell Jun Heating Oil #2(NYM)			80	16	4	20	1579	17	
Buy Mar Australian Dollar(IMM)	2/26	3/06	80	12	3	15	411	46	328
Sell Mar Japanese Yen(IMM)			84	16	3	19	638	71	
Buy Jul Soybeans(CBOT)	2/28	4/27	87	13	2	15	836	14	184
Sell 2 Jul Corn(CBOT)			80	16	4	20	709	12	
Buy Jul Unleaded Reg.(NYM)	2/28	5/09	80	12	3	15	735	10	28
Sell Nov Unleaded Reg.(NYM)			84	16	3	19	736	10	
Buy Jun Eurodollars(IMM)	3/01	5/09	80	12	3	15	392	6	359
Sell "Red" Dec Eurodollars(IMM)			85	17	3	20	469	7	
Buy May Soybeans(CBOT)	3/02	3/23	87	13	2	15	781	35	198
Sell May Wheat(KCBT)			80	16	4	20	613	28	
Buy Jun Unleaded Reg.(NYM)	3/03	3/30	80	12	3	15	734	26	78
Sell Jun Crude Oil(NYM)			85	17	3	20	777	28	
Buy Dec Silver(CMX)	3/03	4/02	80	12	3	15	861	28	283
Sell Dec Gold(CMX)			80	16	4	20	875	28	
Buy Jul Natural Gas(NYM)	3/03	4/12	81	13	3	16	547	13	40
Sell Dec Natural Gas(NYM)									
Buy Aug Lean Hogs(CME)	3/03	4/19	80	12	3	15	930	19	249
Sell Aug Live Cattle(CME)			85	17	3	20	1068	22	
Buy May Soybeans(CBOT)	3/08	3/27	87	13	2	15	464	23	145
Sell Nov Soybeans(CBOT)			85	17	3	20	361	18	
Buy Jul Soybeans(CBOT)	3/08	6/09	80	12	3	15	458	5	146
Sell Nov Soybeans(CBOT)			80	16	4	20	428	5	
Buy Jun Lean Hogs(CME)	3/10	3/21	93	14	1	15	678	56	250
Sell Jun Live Cattle(CME)			85	17	3	20	555	46	
Buy Sep Oats(CBOT)	3/12	4/18	80	12	3	15	154	4	94
Sell May Oats(CBOT)			80	16	4	20	166	4	
Buy Jun Unleaded Reg.(NYM)	3/12	5/09	80	12	3	15	542	9	29
Sell Oct Unleaded Reg.(NYM)			80	16	4	20	765	13	
Buy Jun 2-Year T-Notes(CBOT)	3/18	3/30	80	12	3	15	499	38	392
Sell Jun 30-Year T-Bonds(CBOT)									
Buy Jun Australian Dollar(IMM)	3/18	4/12	87	13	2	15	1396	54	329
Sell Jun Swiss Franc(IMM)			89	17	2	19	1292	50	

Chronological Summary

Seasonal Strategy	Entry Date	Exit Date	Win Pct	Win Yrs	Loss Years	Total Years	Average Profit	Ave Pft Per Day	Page
Buy Mar Sugar #11(NYBOT) Sell May Sugar #11(NYBOT)	3/18	4/16	80 80	12 16	3 4	15 20	276 273	9 9	301
Buy Jun British Pound(IMM) Sell Jun Swiss Franc(IMM)	3/19	4/12	100 95	15 19	0 1	15 20	1313 1226	53 49	330
Buy Apr Feeder Cattle(CME) Sell May Feeder Cattle(CME)	3/23	4/18	93 95	14 19	1 1	15 20	370 429	14 16	226
Buy Jul Soybean Meal(CBOT) Sell Sep Soybean Meal(CBOT)	3/26	6/26	93 95	14 19	1 1	15 20	419 443	5 5	151
Buy Aug Lean Hogs(CME) Sell Dec Lean Hogs(CME)	4/03	7/26	93 90	14 18	1 2	15 20	1045 1185	9 10	240
Buy Aug Soybean Meal(CBOT) Sell Mar Soybean Meal(CBOT)	4/04	7/11	100 100	15 20	0 0	15 20	619 667	6 7	153
Buy Jun Lean Hogs(CME) Sell Jun Live Cattle(CME)	4/05	4/24	80 80	12 16	3 4	15 20	762 844	38 42	251
Buy 3 Dec Oats(CBOT) Sell 2 Dec Corn(CBOT)	4/06	4/24	87 90	13 18	2 2	15 20	976 866	51 46	133
Buy Aug Lean Hogs(CME) Sell Oct Lean Hogs(CME)	4/06	5/23	87 90	13 18	2 2	15 20	336 439	7 9	241
Buy Dec Live Cattle(CME) Sell Jun Live Cattle(CME)	4/10	5/20	87 85	13 17	2 3	15 20	478 408	12 10	217
Buy May Unleaded Reg.(NYM) Sell Sep Unleaded Reg.(NYM)	4/12	4/27	93 90	14 18	1 2	15 20	652 18	41 51	30
Buy Jun Unleaded Reg.(NYM) Sell Jun Heating Oil #2(NYM)	4/12	4/27	93 85	14 17	1 3	15 20	515 592	32 37	61
Buy Jul Soybeans(CBOT) Sell Jul Corn(CBOT)	4/15	5/03	87 85	13 17	2 3	15 20	709 683	37 36	185
Buy Sep Natural Gas(NYM) Sell Jun Natural Gas(NYM)	4/18	4/30	94	15	1	16	306	24	42
Buy Dec Natural Gas(NYM) Sell Jun Natural Gas(NYM)	4/22	5/22	81	13	3	16	809	26	43
Buy Jul Soybean Meal(CBOT) Sell Dec Soybean Meal(CBOT)	4/23	6/26	93 95	14 19	1 1	15 20	381 502	6 8	154
Buy May Feeder Cattle(CME) Sell Jun Live Cattle(CME)	4/24	5/20	93 90	14 18	1 2	15 20	1013 929	38 34	260
Buy Aug Feeder Cattle(CME) Sell Aug Live Cattle(CME)	4/24	7/12	87 85	13 17	2 3	15 20	1301 1322	16 17	261
Buy Aug Soybean Meal(CBOT) Sell Aug Soybean Oil(CBOT)	4/24	7/14	93 95	14 19	1 1	15 20	971 1128	12 14	172

Seasonal Strategy	Entry Date	Exit Date	Win Pct	Win Yrs	Loss Years	Total Years	Average Profit	Ave Pft Per Day	Page
Buy Jul Soybeans(CBOT)	4/27	5/10	87	13	2	15	475	34	164
Sell Jul Soybean Oil(CBOT)			90	18	2	20	503	36	
Buy May Oats(CBOT)	4/29	5/11	100	15	0	15	189	15	95
Sell Jul Oats(CBOT)			100	20	0	20	174	13	
Buy Jul Soybean Meal(CBOT)	4/29	6/24	87	13	2	15	814	14	173
Sell Jul Soybean Oil(CBOT)			90	18	2	20	1084	19	
Buy Jun Australian Dollar(IMM)	5/02	5/10	87	13	2	15	413	46	331
Sell Jun Japanese Yen(IMM)			89	17	2	19	482	54	
Buy Jun Lean Hogs(CME)	5/02	5/19	87	13	2	15	1237	69	273
Sell Jul Pork Bellies(CME)			80	16	4	20	1078	60	
Buy Jul Lean Hogs(CME)	5/02	6/09	100	15	0	15	1399	36	274
Sell Jul Pork Bellies(CME)			95	18	2	20	1007	26	
Buy Dec Soybean Oil(CBOT)	5/04	7/26	100	15	0	15	264	3	158
Sell Aug Soybean Oil(CBOT)			100	20	0	20	243	3	
Buy Dec Corn(CBOT)	5/08	8/07	93	14	1	15	272	3	89
Sell Sep Corn(CBOT)			90	18	2	20	263	3	
Buy Sep 30-Year T-Bonds(CBOT)	5/11	8/02	87	13	2	15	1036	12	372
Sell Sep 5-Year T-Notes(CBOT)			88	15	2	17	1167	14	
Buy Jul Corn(CBOT)	5/12	6/01	87	13	2	15	405	19	120
Sell Jul Wheat(MGE)			85	17	3	20	466	22	
Buy Sep Corn(CBOT)	5/12	6/17	87	13	2	15	408	11	121
Sell Sep Wheat(CBOT)			85	17	3	20	517	14	
Buy Jun 30-Year T-Bonds(CBOT)	5/14	5/25	87	13	2	15	600	50	373
Sell Jun 2-Year T-Notes(CBOT)									
Buy Sep 30-Year T-Bonds(CBOT)	5/14	6/03	93	13	1	14	1090	52	374
Sell Sep 2-Year T-Notes(CBOT)									
Buy Sep 10-Year T-Notes(CBOT)	5/14	6/06	93	13	1	14	617	26	375
Sell Sep 2-Year T-Notes(CBOT)									
Buy Dec Natural Gas(NYM)	5/14	6/28	93	14	1	15	1190	26	44
Sell Jul Natural Gas(NYM)									
Buy Jan Soybean Oil(CBOT)	5/16	8/17	93	14	1	15	277	3	159
Sell Sep Soybean Oil(CBOT)			95	19	1	20	301	3	
Buy Aug Feeder Cattle(CME)	5/16	8/22	87	13	2	15	1789	18	262
Sell Dec Live Cattle(CME)			90	18	2	20	1840	19	
Buy Mar Cocoa(NYBOT)	5/19	6/14	93	14	1	15	259	10	308
Sell Jul Cocoa(NYBOT)			90	18	2	20	276	10	
Buy Aug Feeder Cattle(CME)	5/21	6/11	100	15	0	15	594	27	263
Sell Dec Live Cattle(CME)			95	19	1	20	478	22	

Chronological Summary

Seasonal Strategy	Entry Date	Exit Date	Win Pct	Win Yrs	Loss Years	Total Years	Average Profit	Ave Pft Per Day	Page
Buy Dec Corn(CBOT)	5/21	6/29	87	13	2	15	173	4	90
Sell Jul Corn(CBOT)			85	17	3	20	166	4	
Buy May Coffee(NYBOT)	5/22	6/10	93	14	1	15	906	45	304
Sell Sep Coffee(NYBOT)			95	19	1	20	818	41	
Buy Aug Soybean Meal(CBOT)	5/23	7/11	93	14	1	15	623	12	155
Sell Mar Soybean Meal(CBOT)			95	19	1	20	646	13	
Buy Jan Natural Gas(NYM)	5/23	7/21	93	14	1	15	1299	22	41
Sell Sep Natural Gas(NYM)									
Buy Sep 30-Year T-Bonds(CBOT)	5/24	6/03	80	12	3	15	434	39	376
Sell Sep 5-Year T-Notes(CBOT)			83	15	3	18	501	46	
Buy Dec Unleaded Reg.(NYM)	5/24	6/28	93	14	1	15	974	27	31
Sell Aug Unleaded Reg.(NYM)			89	17	2	19	856	24	
Buy Aug Soybeans(CBOT)	5/26	7/10	93	14	1	15	485	11	147
Sell Mar Soybeans(CBOT)			95	19	1	20	541	12	
Buy Jul Heating Oil #2(NYM)	5/28	6/21	93	14	1	15	1323	53	62
Sell Jul Unleaded Reg.(NYM)			89	17	2	19	1201	48	
Buy Sep Feeder Cattle(CME)	5/28	7/11	93	14	1	15	872	19	264
Sell Dec Live Cattle(CME)			85	17	3	20	766	17	
Buy Dec Coffee(NYBOT)	5/29	6/20	80	12	3	15	1496	65	305
Sell Jul Coffee(NYBOT)			80	16	4	20	1091	47	
Buy Aug Crude Oil(NYM)	5/29	6/29	93	14	1	15	751	23	79
Sell Aug Unleaded Reg.(NYM)			89	17	2	19	732	23	
Buy Jun Canadian Dollar(IMM)	5/30	6/04	93	14	1	15	707	118	332
Sell Jun British Pound(IMM)			80	16	4	20	522	87	
Buy Jun Canadian Dollar(IMM)	5/30	6/05	87	13	2	15	1068	153	333
Sell Jun Japanese Yen(IMM)			80	16	4	20	693	99	
Buy Aug Feeder Cattle(CME)	6/01	7/09	87	13	2	15	925	24	265
Sell Aug Live Cattle(CME)			90	18	2	20	913	23	
Buy Sep Wheat(MGE)	6/02	7/03	93	14	1	15	258	8	113
Sell Sep Wheat(KCBT)			90	18	2	20	306	10	
Buy Aug Feeder Cattle(CME)	6/03	8/22	87	13	2	15	560	7	227
Sell Oct Feeder Cattle(CME)			85	17	3	20	617	8	
Buy Jul Soybeans(CBOT)	6/05	6/21	87	13	2	15	723	43	199
Sell Jul Wheat(CBOT)			85	17	3	20	1056	62	
Buy Mar Eurodollars(IMM)	6/05	9/15	93	14	1	15	840	8	360
Sell Sep Eurodollars(IMM)			90	18	2	20	687	7	
Buy Feb Natural Gas(NYM)	6/06	7/22	100	15	0	15	823	18	45
Sell Nov Natural Gas(NYM)									

Seasonal Strategy	Entry Date	Exit Date	Win Pct	Win Yrs	Loss Years	Total Years	Average Profit	Ave Pft Per Day	Page
Buy Dec Live Cattle(CME)	6/06	8/15	80	12	3	15	1309	18	252
Sell Dec Lean Hogs(CME)			80	16	4	20	1202	17	
Buy Jan Soybean Oil(CBOT)	6/06	8/25	93	14	1	15	172	2	160
Sell Sep Soybean Oil(CBOT)			95	19	1	20	225	3	
Buy Dec Cotton(NYBOT)	6/07	6/20	93	14	1	15	677	48	295
Sell Jul Cotton(NYBOT)			85	17	3	20	592	42	
Buy Sep British Pound(IMM)	6/08	7/06	87	13	2	15	1259	43	334
Sell Sep Japanese Yen(IMM)			85	17	3	20	1416	49	
Buy Oct Soybean Meal(CBOT)	6/08	9/06	80	12	3	15	470	5	174
Sell Oct Soybean Oil(CBOT)			85	17	3	20	778	9	
Buy Sep British Pound(IMM)	6/11	7/12	87	13	2	15	1370	43	335
Sell Sep Swiss Franc(IMM)			80	16	4	20	1035	32	
Buy Mar Eurodollars(IMM)	6/11	7/18	87	13	2	15	336	9	361
Sell Sep Eurodollars(IMM)			90	18	2	20	364	10	
Buy May Cotton(NYBOT)	6/12	8/30	93	14	1	15	755	9	296
Sell Oct Cotton(NYBOT)			90	18	2	20	642	8	
Buy Jul Oats(CBOT)	6/13	7/13	93	14	1	15	438	14	96
Sell Dec Oats(CBOT)			80	16	4	20	323	10	
Buy Nov Feeder Cattle(CME)	6/18	9/10	80	12	3	15	487	6	228
Sell Mar Feeder Cattle(CME)			85	17	3	20	518	6	
Buy Dec Natural Gas(NYM)	6/19	7/22	93	14	1	15	949	28	46
Sell Sep Natural Gas(NYM)									
Buy Nov Feeder Cattle(CME)	6/19	9/17	80	12	3	15	893	10	266
Sell Apr Live Cattle(CME)			85	17	3	20	1084	12	
Buy Oct Lean Hogs(CME)	6/21	7/08	80	12	3	15	557	31	275
Sell Feb Pork Bellies(CME)			85	17	3	20	704	39	
Buy Dec Soybean Meal(CBOT)	6/21	8/07	80	12	3	15	587	12	165
Sell Nov Soybeans(CBOT)			85	17	3	20	790	16	
Buy 3 Sep Oats(CBOT)	6/22	7/31	100	15	0	15	1513	38	134
Sell 2 Sep Corn(CBOT)			85	17	3	20	1262	32	
Buy Oct Live Cattle(CME)	6/22	9/12	80	12	3	15	705	8	218
Sell Apr Live Cattle(CME)			80	16	4	20	767	9	
Buy Oct Live Cattle(CME)	6/22	8/05	80	12	3	15	419	9	219
Sell Apr Live Cattle(CME)			80	16	4	20	524	12	
Buy Aug Feeder Cattle(CME)	6/23	7/11	87	13	2	15	434	23	267
Sell Dec Live Cattle(CME)			90	18	2	20	499	26	
Buy Sep Soybean Meal(CBOT)	6/23	7/28	80	12	3	15	564	16	166
Sell Sep Soybeans(CBOT)			85	17	3	20	890	25	

Seasonal Strategy	Entry Date	Exit Date	Win Pct	Win Yrs	Loss Years	Total Years	Average Profit	Ave Pft Per Day	Page
Buy Aug Feeder Cattle(CME)	6/23	8/21	87	13	2	15	921	15	268
Sell Dec Live Cattle(CME)			90	18	2	20	1231	21	
Buy Sep Oats(CBOT)	6/24	7/25	93	14	1	15	758	24	135
Sell Sep Corn(CBOT)			90	18	2	20	533	17	
Buy May Corn(CBOT)	6/25	9/27	100	15	0	15	171	2	87
Sell Dec Corn(CBOT)			100	20	0	20	188	2	
Buy Jul Corn(CBOT)	6/25	8/07	80	12	3	15	261	6	91
Sell Sep Corn(CBOT)			80	16	4	20	321	7	
Buy Jun Eurodollars(IMM)	6/27	9/15	93	14	1	15	918	11	362
Sell Sep Eurodollars(IMM)			90	18	2	20	716	9	
Buy Dec Wheat(CBOT)	6/30	7/23	87	13	2	15	534	22	122
Sell Dec Corn(CBOT)			85	17	3	20	548	23	
Buy Aug Feeder Cattle(CME)	7/01	7/11	87	13	2	15	335	30	269
Sell Aug Live Cattle(CME)			90	18	2	20	400	36	
Buy Dec Soybean Meal(CBOT)	7/01	9/14	80	12	3	15	281	4	175
Sell Dec Soybean Oil(CBOT)			85	17	3	20	703	9	
Buy Dec Cotton(NYBOT)	7/05	9/04	87	13	2	15	554	9	297
Sell Oct Cotton(NYBOT)			85	17	3	20	460	7	
Buy Sep Wheat(CBOT)	7/07	7/22	87	13	2	15	685	43	123
Sell Sep Corn(CBOT)			85	17	3	20	654	41	
Buy Sep Wheat(KCBT)	7/07	8/27	80	12	3	15	654	13	124
Sell Sep Corn(CBOT)			85	17	3	20	797	14	
Buy Feb Pork Bellies(CME)	7/08	8/03	87	13	2	15	879	33	276
Sell Oct Lean Hogs(CME)			80	16	4	20	635	24	
Buy Nov Crude Oil(NYM)	7/08	10/14	87	13	2	15	909	9	17
Sell Apr Crude Oil(NYM)			90	18	2	20	856	9	
Buy May Wheat(CBOT)	7/12	8/20	93	14	1	15	227	6	98
Sell Sep Wheat(CBOT)			90	18	2	20	312	8	
Buy Dec Wheat(CBOT)	7/12	7/28	93	14	1	15	792	47	200
Sell Nov Soybeans(CBOT)			85	17	3	20	894	53	
Buy Dec Wheat(MGE)	7/13	7/21	87	13	2	15	783	87	201
Sell Nov Soybeans(CBOT)			80	16	4	20	723	80	
Buy Sep Wheat(CBOT)	7/13	7/28	93	14	1	15	1029	64	202
Sell Sep Soybeans(CBOT)			85	17	3	20	1120	70	
Buy Sep Corn(CBOT)	7/13	7/31	93	14	1	15	654	34	186
Sell Sep Soybeans(CBOT)			85	17	3	20	751	40	
Buy Mar Wheat(KCBT)	7/13	8/08	80	12	3	15	978	36	203
Sell Mar Soybeans(CBOT)			85	17	3	20	1087	40	

Seasonal Strategy	Entry Date	Exit Date	Win Pct	Win Yrs	Loss Years	Total Years	Average Profit	Ave Pft Per Day	Page
Buy Sep Wheat(KCBT)	7/14	7/21	87	13	2	15	834	104	204
Sell Sep Soybeans(CBOT)			80	16	4	20	927	116	
Buy Sep Swiss Franc(IMM)	7/14	7/29	87	13	2	15	1524	95	336
Sell Sep Japanese Yen(IMM)			80	16	4	20	1258	79	
Buy Aug Lean Hogs(CME)	7/14	8/07	93	14	1	15	489	20	242
Sell Oct Lean Hogs(CME)			95	19	1	20	621	25	
Buy Oct Crude Oil(NYM)	7/14	9/17	80	12	3	15	739	11	18
Sell Apr Crude Oil(NYM)			85	17	3	20	704	11	
Buy Dec Soybean Meal(CBOT)	7/15	7/29	87	13	2	15	294	20	167
Sell Nov Soybeans(CBOT)			90	18	2	20	577	38	
Buy Dec Wheat(KCBT)	7/15	9/30	87	13	2	15	1072	14	125
Sell Dec Corn(CBOT)			90	18	2	20	1028	13	
Buy Jul Soybeans(CBOT)	7/15	10/03	73	11	4	15	290	4	139
Sell Nov Soybeans(CBOT)			80	16	4	20	451	6	
Buy Sep Soybean Oil(CBOT)	7/16	8/07	87	13	2	15	690	30	168
Sell Sep Soybeans(CBOT)			90	18	2	20	726	32	
Buy Jul Soybeans(CBOT)	7/16	9/28	80	12	3	15	258	3	140
Sell Nov Soybeans(CBOT)			75	15	5	20	448	6	
Buy May Soybeans(CBOT)	7/17	7/31	80	12	3	15	319	21	148
Sell Sep Soybeans(CBOT)			80	16	4	20	427	28	
Buy Dec Wheat(KCBT)	7/17	8/14	100	15	0	15	269	9	114
Sell Dec Wheat(MGE)			100	20	0	20	263	9	
Buy Dec Wheat(CBOT)	7/19	8/06	93	14	1	15	329	17	115
Sell Dec Wheat(MGE)			95	19	1	20	304	16	
Buy Nov Unleaded Reg.(NYM)	7/23	9/11	80	12	3	15	541	11	32
Sell Feb Unleaded Reg.(NYM)			80	16	4	20	558	11	
Buy Dec Live Cattle(CME)	7/23	10/15	80	12	3	15	477	6	220
Sell Jun Live Cattle(CME)			85	17	3	20	635	7	
Buy Dec Unleaded Reg.(NYM)	7/23	10/28	80	12	3	15	405	4	33
Sell Feb Unleaded Reg.(NYM)			80	16	4	20	468	5	
Buy Oct Unleaded Reg.(NYM)	7/24	8/21	93	14	1	15	885	31	34
Sell Feb Unleaded Reg.(NYM)			95	19	1	20	734	25	
Buy Dec Heating Oil #2(NYM)	7/24	8/21	80	12	3	15	542	19	69
Sell Dec Crude Oil(NYM)			80	16	4	20	445	15	
Buy Dec Heating Oil #2(NYM)	7/31	10/12	80	12	3	15	1109	15	22
Sell May Heating Oil #2(NYM)			80	16	4	20	997	13	
Buy Dec Crude Oil(NYM)	8/05	10/12	87	13	2	15	904	13	19
Sell Jun Crude Oil(NYM)			90	18	2	20	837	12	

Seasonal Strategy	Entry Date	Exit Date	Win Pct	Win Yrs	Loss Years	Total Years	Average Profit	Ave Pft Per Day	Page
Buy Dec Gold(CMX)	8/05	10/18	80	12	3	15	992	13	284
Sell Dec Silver(CMX)			85	17	3	20	1148	15	
Buy Jun Eurodollars(IMM)	8/06	11/13	93	14	1	15	568	6	363
Sell Dec Eurodollars(IMM)			95	19	1	20	616	6	
Buy Jan Heating Oil #2(NYM)	8/07	9/12	87	13	2	15	632	17	56
Sell Jan Unleaded Reg.(NYM)			85	17	3	20	551	15	
Buy Dec Soybean Meal(CBOT)	8/07	10/13	80	12	3	15	921	14	176
Sell Dec Soybean Oil(CBOT)			80	16	4	20	1057	16	
Buy Nov Heating Oil #2(NYM)	8/08	9/16	80	12	3	15	558	14	23
Sell Apr Heating Oil #2(NYM)			80	16	4	20	506	13	
Buy Nov Heating Oil #2(NYM)	8/09	9/09	87	13	2	15	547	17	72
Sell Nov Crude Oil(NYM)			85	17	3	20	527	16	
Buy Mar Soybeans(CBOT)	8/12	9/04	87	13	2	15	550	23	169
Sell Mar Soybean Oil(CBOT)			90	18	2	20	599	25	
Buy Nov Soybeans(CBOT)	8/13	9/12	80	12	3	15	1012	33	187
Sell Dec Corn(CBOT)			80	16	4	20	867	28	
Buy Dec 30-Year T-Bonds(CBOT)	8/13	11/16	87	13	2	15	1257	13	377
Sell Dec 5-Year T-Notes(CBOT)			88	15	2	17	1318	14	
Buy "Red" Dec Corn(CBOT)	8/16	9/20	93	14	1	15	350	10	92
Sell Dec Corn(CBOT)			90	18	2	20	293	8	
Buy Dec 10-Year T-Notes(CBOT)	8/16	11/13	93	14	1	15	614	7	378
Sell Dec 5-Year T-Notes(CBOT)			94	16	1	17	624	7	
Buy Dec Swiss Franc(IMM)	8/17	9/30	80	12	3	15	2568	57	337
Sell Dec Australian Dollar(IMM)			83	15	3	18	2300	51	
Buy Jan Feeder Cattle(CME)	8/17	11/10	93	14	1	15	325	4	229
Sell Mar Feeder Cattle(CME)			95	19	1	20	288	3	
Buy Mar Soybeans(CBOT)	8/18	9/05	87	13	2	15	717	38	188
Sell 2 Mar Corn(CBOT)			90	18	2	20	646	34	
Buy Dec British Pound(IMM)	8/18	9/29	80	12	3	15	1571	37	338
Sell Dec Australian Dollar(IMM)			83	15	3	18	1487	35	
Buy Nov Natural Gas(NYM)	8/29	9/14	100	15	0	15	549	32	47
Sell Oct Natural Gas(NYM)									
Buy Dec Live Cattle(CME)	8/29	11/12	80	12	3	15	692	9	221
Sell Jun Live Cattle(CME)			80	16	4	20	774	10	
Buy Jul Coffee(NYBOT)	8/29	11/21	80	12	3	15	654	8	306
Sell Dec Coffee(NYBOT)			85	17	3	20	923	11	
Buy Dec Swiss Franc(IMM)	8/31	10/02	87	13	2	15	2016	61	339
Sell Dec Canadian Dollar(IMM)			80	16	4	20	1619	49	

Seasonal Strategy	Entry Date	Exit Date	Win Pct	Win Yrs	Loss Years	Total Years	Average Profit	Ave Pft Per Day	Page
Buy Sep Australian Dollar(IMM)	9/03	9/08	80	12	3	15	250	42	340
Sell Sep Canadian Dollar(IMM)			83	15	3	18	335	56	
Buy Dec Wheat(KCBT)	9/05	11/26	87	13	2	15	533	6	116
Sell Dec Wheat(CBOT)			80	16	4	20	309	4	
Buy Dec Gold(CMX)	9/07	10/02	87	13	2	15	1092	42	287
Sell 2 Jan Platinum(NYM)			80	16	4	20	1309	50	
Buy Dec Wheat(MGE)	9/11	10/01	93	14	1	15	974	46	205
Sell Nov Soybeans(CBOT)			85	17	3	20	876	42	
Buy "Red" Nov Soybeans(CBOT)	9/11	10/20	80	12	3	15	351	9	143
Sell Nov Soybeans(CBOT)			80	16	4	20	464	12	
Buy Dec Wheat(KCBT)	9/11	10/21	87	13	2	15	979	24	206
Sell Nov Soybeans(CBOT)			85	17	3	20	1094	27	
Buy Dec Swiss Franc(IMM)	9/12	9/25	87	13	2	15	1043	75	341
Sell Dec Australian Dollar(IMM)			83	15	3	18	881	63	
Buy Mar Wheat(KCBT)	9/16	10/01	87	13	2	15	782	49	207
Sell Mar Soybeans(CBOT)			80	16	4	20	673	42	
Buy Dec 10-Year T-Notes(CBOT)	9/16	10/01	87	13	2	15	415	26	379
Sell Dec 2-Year T-Notes(CBOT)									
Buy Dec Corn(CBOT)	9/16	10/04	93	14	1	15	574	30	189
Sell Nov Soybeans(CBOT)			90	18	2	20	541	28	
Buy Dec Wheat(CBOT)	9/16	10/22	80	12	3	15	618	17	208
Sell Nov Soybeans(CBOT)			85	17	3	20	854	23	
Buy Dec Wheat(MGE)	9/18	10/01	87	13	2	15	853	61	209
Sell Nov Soybeans(CBOT)			80	16	4	20	678	48	
Buy Dec British Pound(IMM)	9/20	9/29	87	13	2	15	1050	105	342
Sell Dec Australian Dollar(IMM)			83	15	3	18	985	98	
Buy Dec British Pound(IMM)	9/20	9/29	87	13	2	15	1156	116	343
Sell Dec Canadian Dollar(IMM)			80	16	4	20	880	88	
Buy Dec Wheat(CBOT)	9/21	10/01	87	13	2	15	638	58	210
Sell Nov Soybeans(CBOT)			85	17	3	20	632	57	
Buy Dec Wheat(CBOT)	9/23	10/22	87	13	2	15	312	10	101
Sell Jul Wheat(CBOT)			80	16	4	20	301	10	
Buy Dec Swiss Franc(IMM)	9/23	10/02	93	14	1	15	1401	140	344
Sell Dec Japanese Yen(IMM)			80	16	4	20	992	88	
Buy Jan Soybean Meal(CBOT)	9/27	10/05	80	12	3	15	346	38	170
Sell Jan Soybeans(CBOT)			85	17	3	20	329	37	
Buy Dec Soybean Meal(CBOT)	10/02	11/02	87	13	2	15	322	10	150
Sell Jul Soybean Meal(CBOT)			90	18	2	20	322	10	

Seasonal Strategy	Entry Date	Exit Date	Win Pct	Win Yrs	Loss Years	Total Years	Average Profit	Ave Pft Per Day	Page
Buy Dec Live Cattle(CME) Sell Dec Lean Hogs(CME)	10/03	11/03	93 90	14 18	1 2	15 20	989 821	31 26	253
Buy Dec British Pound(IMM) Sell Dec Swiss Franc(IMM)	10/04	11/13	80 85	12 17	3 3	15 20	1512 1399	37 34	345
Buy Feb Live Cattle(CME) Sell Aug Live Cattle(CME)	10/05	11/07	80 80	12 16	3 4	15 20	441 422	13 12	222
Buy Dec Japanese Yen(IMM) Sell Dec British Pound(IMM)	10/06	10/19	87 80	13 16	2 4	15 20	1690 1312	121 94	346
Buy Dec Unleaded Reg.(NYM) Sell Dec Heating Oil #2(NYM)	10/06	11/05	87 85	13 17	2 3	15 20	1075 883	35 28	63
Buy Dec Unleaded Reg.(NYM) Sell Dec Crude Oil(NYM)	10/07	10/24	80 80	12 16	3 4	15 20	454 490	25 27	80
Buy Nov Natural Gas(NYM) Sell Dec Natural Gas(NYM)	10/11	10/26	93	14	1	15	788	49	48
Buy Jan Unleaded Reg.(NYM) Sell Jan Heating Oil #2(NYM)	10/12	10/31	87 80	13 16	2 4	15 20	401 319	20 16	64
Buy Feb Lean Hogs(CME) Sell Dec Lean Hogs(CME)	10/15	11/07	87 85	13 17	2 3	15 20	583 456	24 19	233
Buy Dec British Pound(IMM) Sell Dec Japanese Yen(IMM)	10/17	10/20	93 90	14 18	1 2	15 20	757 692	189 173	347
Buy Dec British Pound(IMM) Sell Dec Japanese Yen(IMM)	10/17	12/12	87 85	13 17	2 3	15 20	3094 2929	54 51	348
Buy Dec 30-Year T-Bonds(CBOT) Sell Dec 10-Year T-Notes(CBOT)	10/18	11/14	87 90	13 18	2 2	15 20	616 704	22 25	380
Buy Dec 30-Year T-Bonds(CBOT) Sell Dec 5-Year T-Notes(CBOT)	10/23	10/31	80 82	12 14	3 3	15 17	620 623	69 69	381
Buy Mar Soybeans(CBOT) Sell 2 Mar Corn(CBOT)	10/31	12/09	93 90	14 18	1 2	15 20	638 618	16 15	190
Buy Dec 30-Year T-Bonds(CBOT) Sell Dec 2-Year T-Notes(CBOT)	11/02	11/14	93	14	1	15	681	52	382
Buy Dec Australian Dollar(IMM) Sell Dec Japanese Yen(IMM)	11/03	12/02	80 83	12 15	3 3	15 18	1843 1722	61 57	349
Buy Dec Australian Dollar(IMM) Sell Dec Canadian Dollar(IMM)	11/04	11/15	80 83	12 15	3 3	15 18	448 614	37 51	350
Buy Mar 10-Year T-Notes(CBOT) Sell Mar 5-Year T-Notes(CBOT)	11/06	12/23	87 88	13 15	2 2	15 17	478 466	10 10	383
Buy Mar 30-Year T-Bonds(CBOT) Sell Mar 5-Year T-Notes(CBOT)	11/06	12/24	87 88	13 15	2 2	15 17	1160 1160	24 24	384

Seasonal Strategy	Entry Date	Exit Date	Win Pct	Win Yrs	Loss Years	Total Years	Average Profit	Ave Pft Per Day	Page
Buy Mar 30-Year T-Bonds(CBOT)	11/06	12/27	87	13	2	15	752	14	385
Sell Mar 10-Year T-Notes(CBOT)			85	17	3	20	756	15	
Buy Jun Lean Hogs(CME)	11/07	1/10	100	15	0	15	979	15	234
Sell Feb Lean Hogs(CME)			100	20	0	20	871	13	
Buy Dec Australian Dollar(IMM)	11/10	11/28	87	13	2	15	1177	62	351
Sell Dec Japanese Yen(IMM)			89	16	2	18	1155	61	
Buy Mar British Pound(IMM)	11/10	1/06	93	14	1	15	4178	72	352
Sell Mar Japanese Yen(IMM)			90	18	2	20	3468	60	
Buy Jul Wheat(CBOT)	11/17	2/16	100	15	0	15	649	7	102
Sell Mar Wheat(CBOT)			95	19	1	20	533	6	
Buy Mar Natural Gas(NYM)	11/22	11/30	93	14	1	15	628	70	49
Sell Jan Natural Gas(NYM)									
Buy Mar 30-Year T-Bonds(CBOT)	11/27	12/12	87	13	2	15	660	41	386
Sell Mar 5-Year T-Notes(CBOT)			88	15	2	17	683	43	
Buy Mar 30-Year T-Bonds(CBOT)	11/27	12/12	87	13	2	15	768	48	387
Sell Mar 2-Year T-Notes(CBOT)									
Buy Apr Natural Gas(NYM)	11/29	12/15	87	13	2	15	493	29	50
Sell May Natural Gas(NYM)									
Buy May Unleaded Reg.(NYM)	12/03	1/27	93	14	1	15	571	10	81
Sell May Crude Oil(NYM)			95	19	1	20	605	11	
Buy May Unleaded Reg.(NYM)	12/05	2/03	93	14	1	15	830	14	65
Sell May Heating Oil #2(NYM)			95	19	1	20	899	15	
Buy Apr Lean Hogs(CME)	12/06	1/08	100	15	0	15	603	18	235
Sell Feb Lean Hogs(CME)			95	19	1	20	549	16	
Buy Mar Swiss Franc(IMM)	12/07	12/28	80	12	3	15	1309	60	353
Sell Mar Japanese Yen(IMM)			80	16	4	20	1055	48	
Buy Jun Lean Hogs(CME)	12/07	3/09	93	14	1	15	608	7	236
Sell Apr Lean Hogs(CME)			95	19	1	20	601	6	
Buy Jan Unleaded Reg.(NYM)	12/10	12/16	93	14	1	15	565	81	35
Sell May Unleaded Reg.(NYM)			90	18	2	20	475	68	
Buy Jan Unleaded Reg.(NYM)	12/10	12/28	87	13	2	15	679	36	36
Sell May Unleaded Reg.(NYM)			85	17	3	20	646	34	
Buy Nov Soybeans(CBOT)	12/10	2/04	80	12	3	15	178	3	144
Sell May Soybeans(CBOT)			80	16	4	20	369	6	
Buy Apr Live Cattle(CME)	12/10	3/05	93	14	1	15	865	10	257
Sell Apr Feeder Cattle(CME)			90	18	2	20	866	10	
Buy Feb Unleaded Reg.(NYM)	12/11	1/06	93	14	1	15	760	28	37
Sell Jun Unleaded Reg.(NYM)			95	19	1	20	721	27	

Seasonal Strategy	Entry Date	Exit Date	Win Pct	Win Yrs	Loss Years	Total Years	Average Profit	Ave Pft Per Day	Page
Buy Mar Crude Oil(NYM) Sell Sep Crude Oil(NYM)	12/11	1/16	80 85	12 17	3 3	15 20	859 872	23 24	20
Buy Apr Unleaded Reg.(NYM) Sell Apr Crude Oil(NYM)	12/11	1/16	80 85	12 17	3 3	15 20	423 515	11 14	82
Buy Apr Unleaded Reg.(NYM) Sell Apr Heating Oil #2(NYM)	12/11	1/31	93 95	14 19	1 1	15 20	944 980	18 19	66
Buy Mar Unleaded Reg.(NYM) Sell Mar Crude Oil(NYM)	12/11	2/03	93 90	14 18	1 2	15 20	851 745	15 14	83
Buy Feb Crude Oil(NYM) Sell Feb Heating Oil #2(NYM)	12/12	1/15	87 85	13 17	2 3	15 20	715 822	20 23	73
Buy Jul Wheat(CBOT) Sell May Wheat(CBOT)	12/17	2/28	93 85	14 17	1 3	15 20	412 374	6 5	103
Buy Mar Unleaded Reg.(NYM) Sell Mar Heating Oil #2(NYM)	12/19	2/03	87 90	13 18	2 2	15 20	1365 1428	29 30	57
Buy Mar 2-Year T-Notes(CBOT) Sell Mar 5-Year T-Notes(CBOT)	12/20	1/26	87	13	2	15	293	8	388
Buy Jul Wheat(KCBT) Sell Mar Wheat(KCBT)	12/20	2/08	87 85	13 17	2 3	15 20	405 381	8 7	104
Buy Jun Natural Gas(NYM) Sell Mar Natural Gas(NYM)	12/20	2/16	93	14	1	15	4095	69	51
Buy 2 Apr Platinum(NYM) Sell Feb Gold(CMX)	12/21	1/17	100 90	15 18	0 2	15 20	1575 1357	56 48	288
Buy Jun Natural Gas(NYM) Sell Feb Natural Gas(NYM)	12/21	1/23	93	14	1	15	3933	116	52
Buy Mar Crude Oil(NYM) Sell Mar Heating Oil #2(NYM)	12/21	1/31	80 80	12 16	3 4	15 20	598 722	14 17	74
Buy Apr Crude Oil(NYM) Sell Apr Heating Oil #2(NYM)	12/21	2/19	87 85	13 17	2 3	15 20	585 579	10 9	70
Buy May Natural Gas(NYM) Sell Apr Natural Gas(NYM)	12/21	3/12	93	14	1	15	1185	14	53
Buy Jul Wheat(CBOT) Sell Mar Wheat(CBOT)	12/22	2/12	100 95	15 19	0 1	15 20	600 557	11 11	105
Buy Jul Wheat(KCBT) Sell May Wheat(KCBT)	12/23	2/28	93 90	14 18	1 2	15 20	311 298	5 4	106
Buy 2 Mar Corn(CBOT) Sell Mar Soybeans(CBOT)	12/24	2/09	87 85	13 17	2 3	15 20	593 601	12 13	180
Buy Jul Wheat(CBOT) Sell Jul Soybeans(CBOT)	12/26	2/03	87 85	13 17	2 3	15 20	739 803	18 20	211

Seasonal Strategy	Entry Date	Exit Date	Win Pct	Win Yrs	Loss Years	Total Years	Average Profit	Ave Pft Per Day	Page
Chronological Summary									
Buy Jul Wheat(KCBT)	12/26	2/08	80	12	3	15	743	17	212
Sell Jul Soybeans(CBOT)			85	17	3	20	874	19	
Buy 2 Apr Platinum(NYM)	12/27	2/16	93	14	1	15	2506	48	289
Sell Apr Gold(CMX)			90	18	2	20	2329	45	
Buy Apr Live Cattle(CME)	12/27	3/05	87	13	2	15	585	8	223
Sell Aug Live Cattle(CME)			90	18	2	20	631	9	
Buy Mar Canadian Dollar(IMM)	12/28	1/09	87	13	2	15	1308	101	354
Sell Mar Japanese Yen(IMM)			85	17	3	20	1299	100	
Buy Mar 2-Year T-Notes(CBOT)	12/29	1/09	80	12	3	15	399	33	389
Sell Mar 10-Year T-Notes(CBOT)									
Buy 2 Apr Platinum(NYM)	12/30	3/16	93	14	1	15	3085	40	290
Sell Apr Gold(CMX)			95	19	1	20	3422	44	
Buy Jul Lean Hogs(CME)	12/31	3/13	93	14	1	15	852	12	237
Sell Dec Lean Hogs(CME)			95	19	1	20	843	12	

For **Moore Research Center, Inc.** products and information:

Web site: http://www.mrci.com
E-mail: sales@mrci.com

Toll-Free: (800) 927-7259
or (541) 484-7256
Fax: (541) 484-0243

Note: These trade strategies have worked with historical consistency. No representation is being made that they will work this year or in the future. Please check current market fundamentals and technical conditions before considering these trades. This information is not a recommendation to buy or sell at this time, but merely a historical presentation of trade strategies. Past results are not necessarily indicative of future results. No representation is being made that an account will or is likely to achieve profits or incur losses similar to those shown.